INTERNATIONAL DIVISION OF LABOUR AND REGIONAL DEVELOPMENT

INTERNATIONAL DIVISION OF LABOUR AND REGIONAL DEVELOPMENT

R. P. MISRA
Editor

CONCEPT PUBLISHING COMPANY, NEW DELHI-110059

ISBN 81-7022-247-8

First Published 1989

Rameshwar Prasad **Misra** (*b.* 1930 -   )

Published by
Ashok Kumar Mittal
Concept Publishing Company
A/15-16, Commercial Block, Mohan Garden
NEW DELHI-110059 (India)

Lasertypeset by
Microtech Advance Printing Systems Pvt. Ltd.
H-13, Bali Nagar
NEW DELHI-110015

Printed at
B.D. Offest Works
B-218, Naraina Ind. Area
NEW DELHI-110028

Preface

The International Geographical Union (IGU) Commission on International Division of Labour and Regional Development (C-11) was established in 1984. The Commission aims at analysing the sub-national implications of the division of the world into two major blocks of countries, *i.e.* those which are industrialized and possess advanced technologies and those which are now trying to industrialize and do not possess advanced technologies. In each of the two blocks, not all the countries have reached the same stage of development. But each is marked by a certain degree of dynamism the effects of which are felt not only within their own boundaries but also outside.

Thus the new technologies, which constitute the hallmark of the countries of the North, have repercussions on the product mix of the developing countries of the South. Countries and sub-national regions once on the way to recovery and redevelopment have now fallen in the debt trap. Products which had easy access to the markets once are outpriced in their own markets. Regions which were depressed once have recovered. And many others which were advanced have become backward. The more rapid the technological and socio-economic changes, the greater the regional instabilities.

The commission studies the rise and fall of national and regional economies; assesses the regional impacts of structural changes; analyses the responses of different regions to common threats; creates scenarios and evolves strategies that could be adopted to ward off the ill effects and hasten readjustments. The experiences differ from region to region and country to country. There are countries like Japan whose phenomenal success in the economic field and technological achievements have not given rise to any substantial and long-term regional adjustment problems. Then there are countries in the early stages of development which are unable to cope with the problems generated by a variety of structural changes taking place in the global economy. Shifts in trade, productivity and competitiveness have made many regions unstable.

Among its various activities the Commission has an extensive publication programme. This volume is a part of this activity. It has emerged from 21 contributions made by various ordinary and corresponding members to the main concerns of the Commission. Many of the papers have already been published in international journals. They cover a wide spectrum of themes and thrusts but they all converge on the impact of economic restructuring at the global level on national and sub-national economies.

I am confident that the volume will make a distinct contribution to the theory and practice of regional development.

New Delhi
March 1, 1988

R. P. MISRA, Chairman,
IGU Commission on
International Division of Labour
and Regional Development

Contents

List of Figures

List of Contributors

Abiodun, Josephine Olu
Professor, Department of Geography, University of Ife, Ile-Ife Nigeria.

Castells, Manuel
Department of City and Regional Planning, University of California, Berkeley, USA.

Celant, Attilio
Department of Regional Analysis, University of Rome, Rome, Italy.

Chatterjee, Lata
Department of Urban Affairs and City Planning, Boston University, Boston, USA.

De[illegible], P.B.
Institute of Economic Growth, Delhi, India.

F[illegible]el, Folker
Starnberg Institute for the Study of Global Structures, Developments and Crises, Federal Republic of Germany

Gana, Jerry
Department of Geography, Ahmadu Bello University, Zaria, Nigeria.

Hafkamp, Wim
Department of Economics, University of Amsterdam, Netherlands.

Heinrichs, Jurgen
Starnberg Institute for the Study of Global Structures, Developments and Crises, Federal Republic of Germany.

Helmsing, Bert
Institute of Social Studies, The Hague, Netherlands.

Hoensch, Fritz
Institute for Geography and Geoecology, Liepzig German Democratic Republic.

Holst, Mathias
University of Trier, Trier, FRG.

Jang, Yeong-Hee
Department of Urban Affairs and City Planning, Boston University, Boston, USA.

Knodgen, Gabriele
Federal Environmental Agency, Berlin.

Kreye, Otto
Starnberg Institute for the Study of Global Structures, Developments and Crises, Federal Republic of Germany.

Lakshmanan, T.R.
Centre for Energy and Environment, Boston University, Boston, USA.

Madhavan, M.C.
c/o Indian Council for Scientific and Industrial Research, New Delhi, India.

Mazrui, Ali
Director, African Institute of Development, Dakar, Senegal.

Miyakawa, Yasuo, Department of Geography, Aichi Educational University, Kariyashi, Japan.

Miranda, Mariana
Department of Geography, Federal University of Rio-de-Janeiro, Rio-de-Janeiro, Brazil.

Misra, R.P.
Department of Geograpny, Delhi School of Economics, University of Delhi, Delhi, India.

Nijkamp, Peter
Department of Economics, Free University, Amsterdam, Netherlands.

Qutub, Ishaq Y.
Professor, Department of Sociology, University of Kuwait, Kuwait.

Singh, Vijai P.
University Centre for Social and Urban Research, University of Pittsburgh, Pittsburgh, USA.

Thomas, Morgan D.
Department of Geography, University of Washington, Seattle, USA.

ONE

Introduction

R.P. MISRA

The contemporary world is passing through an structural crisis during which a transition must be made from a set of socio-economic and institutional arrangements shaped by a reliance on the 1950s and 1960s mass production technologies based on cheap petroleum, to another based on a new constellation of flexible technologies dependent on low-cost electronics. The emerging socio-economic-technical system, in which international trade and cross-country technical diffusion play an increasingly important role, is being characterized by new patterns of investment propelling and propelled by new communication infrastructural networks, by new patterns of business organization, by novel institution formation, by fresh social-spatial structures and by evolving new labour processes.

This broad ranging transition in a global political economy has important implications for national and regional development patterns and policies. First, in a highly competitive global economy with rapid rates of technology transfer across national boundaries, each country becomes a 'region' in the world economy focussing growth prospects and thereby blurring the distinctions between national and regional policy. The post-Second World War notion of regional policy drawn from a distributive view of national product on spatial equity grounds becomes less persuassive at a time when each nation is engaged in the serious game of acquiring an increasing or non-decreasing share of the global product. This may further accentuate spatial inequalities in development.

Second, on a closer inspection it turns out that the dynamism of a country's economy in the new dispensation of technology stems from a few regions within national territories. Some of the formerly dominant regions may register serious relative erosion as the mass production of the past could not cope with new technological imperatives.

The industrial nations of the North have been the major beneficiaries of recent global technological changes but the spread effects are being widely felt. Emergence of Japan, South Korea, Hong Kong, Singapore, Brazil, India and China as industrial powers of some consequence is indicative of this change. With these spread effects, the national economies are getting more internationalized. So it is no longer possible to protect economically inefficient and less competitive industries, even though they may employ a large labour force.

One of the major implications of the internationalization of national economies is the decline of old industrial regions in West Europe and North America. Physical decay due to low tax base, massive unemployment, population decline and fiscal problems have made them less attractive for new ventures. The old industries which once were the prime engines of growth became irrelevant.

New countries of growth based on new technologies and organizational structures are emerging. But the older regions in the recent past have tried to build up new initiatives to recapture the old ethos and pre-eminence.

The mature industrial regions of North America and Western Europe derived their power from textiles, steel, coal and heavy industrial equipment manufacturing. They attracted labour force not only from within the country but also internationally. The great advantage these regions had of early start and closeness to the source of raw materials and markets was taken away by new technological breakthroughs and discovery of new sources of raw materials and energy. The competition mounted by newly industrializing countries of the East particularly Japan, Korea, Taiwan posed new challenges to their dominant positions. Coal-based industry found it difficult to compete with oil-based industry. Long-range policies to counter these secular trends were absent. Only short-term palliatives like modernization or cut-back in production were used to postpone the immediate problem. By 1980s, the whole old-time industrial structure of once fast growing regions came tumbling down. Most of the steel plants were closed down leading to severe unemployment, decline in population resulting from out-migration, and erosion of the tax base.

In the newly industrializing countries, regional obsolescence was not so noticeable, but a similar process on a milder scale was clearly seen in, for example, Bombay and Calcutta regions in India – one known for textiles and the other for coal and steel.

Since mid-1980s new initiatives have come from a combination of forces to face the challenges posed by global restructuring at the regional level. The federal, the provincial and local governments have joined hands with universities or have even established new institutions to study the root causes of the decline, and to suggest policies and strategies to get over the problems. New opportunities are being sought to secure comparative advantage both nationally and internationally.

In recognition of the seriousness of the regional problems emerging from global changes and of the need to generate literature on the experiences of various countries of the world to get over the problems. The International Geographical Union constituted a Commission charged with the responsibility to examine these issues and promote research on International Division of Labour and Regional Development.

The papers included in this volume were discussed by the Commission from time to time. It was found that quite a number of them deserved to be publicized more widely. Such of the papers have been included in this volume. A short preview of the papers is also given.

A SHORT PREVIEW OF THE PAPERS

In his paper on "Burden of Underdevelopment" Mazrui refers to three pathologies of African development: pathology of technical backwardness; pathology of maldistribution; and pathology of fragmented economy. The first points to the paradox of a least developed continent endowed with richest resources; the second to the maldistribution of resources and income in favour of white minority; and the third to the utter poverty in the midst of plenty. Africa was the white man's burden and continent whose resources were meant to enrich the West European whites, until "suddenly somebody noticed in Bombay that the emperor's new clothes of modern technology were not the clothes at all – the British Raj was naked".

The Second World War cut down the white man to size, exposed Africans to world beyond and brought a series of social and economic changes favourable to the emancipation of the continent and its people from the clutches of European power, it also incorporated its economy in the world capitalist system in the name of overseas development. African economy underwent structural changes of far-reaching consequences. Africa became more dependent on Europe; export orientation led to expansion of area under cash crops (at the cost of food crops) and the emphasis shifted from rural to urban centres – all these leading to spatial disparities in development within the country. Much of the new investment went to white dominated countries.

Mazrui pleads for an alternative development or modernization style which is responsive to the highest level of knowledge; encourages innovations and enlarges social empathies. This style calls for seven strategies: 1. indigenization; 2. domestication; 3. diversification; 4. horizontal interpenetration (cooperation among developing countries); 5. vertical counterpenetration; 6. domestic austerity; and 7. encouraging extravagance in the North to dissipate their resources.

Frobel, Folker et al. (Ch. 3) start from where Mazrui stopped. "The capitalist world system is in the grip of a crisis; its symptoms and its consequences are clearly visible. . . . Two closely linked processes have contributed to the crisis; first, the gradual erosion of the United States global hegemony and second, internal contradictions within the industrialized countries". They contend that the post-war quarter century witnessed the success of world capitalism. As the crisis of the system deepens, their increasing effort to incorporate the developing countries in the system through new channels like World Bank, International Monetary Fund (IMF), military aid, multinational corporations, consultancy, etc. Production structures have become overwhelmingly oriented to the world market; these are paralleled by consumption structures heavily dependent on imports.

They conclude that "never before in the history of capitalist mode of production has the contrast between the enormous unmet needs of the vast bulk of humanity, living in poverty, and an enormous unused productive capacity been so glaring as in the periphery (Third World) today. And never before has the capitalist mode of production been shown to be so irrational as in the current crisis".

Frobel advises the developing world to follow the socialist path and gives the example of China, without realizing that State capitalism too must pass through the same crisis as private capitalism sooner or later requiring openness (glasnost) and restructuring (perestroika).

The effects of changes in division of labour among countries on division of labour on sub-national territories is the main concern of chapter 4 contributed by Bert Helmsing. Using Colombian data, the paper says that the first three decades of this century – the process of regional economic integration started as domestic industrialization and external trade expanded. But the process was slow. Only a small part of the territory and population was affected by it. The colonial division of labour among national territories continued.

Some clear changes in the inter-regional division of labour became visible by mid-fifties resulting from physical integration of the country, opening new lands and existing agriculture to external influences and formation of national oligopolies and markets for manufactured products. It was only after 1971 that the sectoral growth processes became increasingly regionally selective. The author concludes that the relationship between international and inter-regional division of labour appears, at least in the case of Colombia, tenuous. Helmsing has, however, failed to appreciate the fact that the opening of the new areas was necessary before regional change in the division of labour could take place.

Manuel Castells explores the connection between high technology, economic restructuring and urban-regional process and in consequence new spatial division of labour internationally, inter-regionally and within the large metropolitan areas (ch. 5). The need to understand the main trends of the process of economic restructuring and the specificity of the process of production identified under the term high technology is emphasized in the paper.

High technology is treated as a process (not as industry), a particular way to produce characterized by the key role of *information*. This technology is tending to replace labour massively not only in the USA but in other parts of the world also. The spatial implications of this restructuring of the labour process is increasing international and inter-regional division of labour between skilled production and routine assembly operations. The largest metropolitan areas are experiencing growth of corporate services, high-tech manufacturing, decline of traditional activities and development of new downgraded, yet booming, economic sectors. Dualistic structures of production are being re-enforced and re-created.

The Welfare State is in crisis. There is increasing militarization of the economy. Expenditure on social services and welfare is being cut all over the world. The warfare state is reshaping the urban and regional structures and a new territorial division of labour based on polarized growth and selective development reflecting itself in international dependency, inter-regional cleavages, intra-metropolitan dualism and simultaneous growth and decay of cities and regions, has set in motion.

The next two chapters (Ch. 6 and 7) focus on environmental issues. Comparing the expenditures on environmental protection, between developed and developing countries, Knodgen concludes that the latter "are still inclined towards the position that strict environmental regulations may hinder capital imports and consequently, stunt economic growth". Research on relocation to developing countries of environmentally polluting industries shows that "environmental costs are seldom a reason to relocate production" except in cases of firms which are experiencing static or reduced demand as a result of product obsolescence or hazards related to product use.

Hafkamp and Nijkamp have analysed the relationships between the economy of a nation and environmental quality by broadening the scope of the Triple Layer Model (TLM) – economic sub-model, labour market sub-model and pollution sub-model. An interactive multi-decision maker optimization procedure has been suggested to bring about a compromise between conflicting groups.

Discussion on the Role of Information Technology in the evolution of the service sector (Ch. 8) opens with the remarks that services have replaced production of goods as the dominant mode of economic activity in the industrialized affluent economies. The typical picture of a modern economy is not one of factories engaged in the fabrication of goods but that of a society engaged in the production and consumption of services – a society of dining, of travelling, of learning, of medical visits and healing, of business and legal consultancies, of transmission and reception of various messages and leisure activities.

After surveying the major characteristics of the service sector, the paper focusses on the central attribute of the service activity, i.e. consumers of the service are the intrinsic participants in the production process. To produce a service, a consumer and the producer must interact for the delivery of the service to be complete. Thus the context within which the knowledge technologies of service production are brought to bear on the problems of the consumer is essentially a process of transaction between producer and consumer. The latter also is utilized in the production of service output.

Morgan D. Thomas (Ch. 9) covers a similar field but from a different perspective, i.e. role of innovation in the process of economic development and the way the process of innovation shapes the competitive environment of firms and industries. The paper presents a particular way of viewing the competitive behaviour of 'new technology-based' firms and industries; provides a perspective on key elements in the development process of an industry-technology life-cycle; and finally focusses attention on selected relationships between innovation and competition.

Migration of skilled manpower from developing countries is the main concern of Chapter 10. Unlike in the earlier period when developing country migrants were recruited for plantation development in colonial territories, the growth in the size of developing country migrants in the post-Second World War period was brought about by the opening up of employment opportunities in developed countries, increased access to higher education facilities in developed countries, improved communication among countries and increased skilled employment opportunities in some developing countries.

The 'brain drain' has undermined the ability of some, if not all, the developing countries to reach the critical mass needed for scientific and technological breakthroughs and has adversely affected the implementation of development programmes while contributing immensely to the growth of economies of receiving countries. The paper outlines the United Nations programme to counter the ill-effects of this phenomenon.

Education plays a major role in rural transformation in developing countries. Budgetary allocations for education have therefore been increasing for the last three decades. The misfit between the attributes of inherited education system and the realities of rapidly changing societies has however belied to a considerable extend the hopes of rapid positive change in rural economy, society, and polity. Lakshmanan and Misra (Ch. 11) suggest a model of rural development system which can be used for educational planning. They advocate a functional view of education (instead of structural or institutional) which answers questions like: how does general education relate to vocational education and how do schools prepare students for future occupations and what types of learning are possible in and out of school?

Three different groups can be identified with three different learning needs: (1) persons engaged in primary activities (farming and related activities), (2) off-farm production (industry, commerce, repairs, etc.), and (3) service (rural planner, experts, etc.). The secondary education must cater to the needs of all the three. Unfortunately, at present, secondary level is an upgraded version of the primary level general education. And higher education is unmindful of the needs of rural development.

Miyakawa's paper on regional disequilibrium and supranational organizations (Ch. 12) suggests a direct regional impact of what international organizations and firms do. Taking the example of Japan he says that a supranational organization (general headquarters) changed fundamentally Japan's industrial structure and system, after the Second World War. Its influence on regional development especially in agricultural and coal-producing areas was phenomenal. IMF, World Bank, General Agreement on Tariffs and Trade (GATT), etc., also exerted influence on rehabilitation of Japanese economy particularly on the development of Tokaido Megalopoles.

Urban expansion causes restructuring of rural economy through agricultural diversification, new employment opportunities, etc. within the city escalation of land prices, is experienced all over the world. Various corrective measures have been adopted by national governments. Although only partially successful the land readjustment in urban development followed in Japan and South Korea holds good potential as policy instrument. The paper on Development and Impact of Land Prices in South Korea (Ch. 13) examines the land readjustment method and its influence on land prices in South Korea.

The influence international division of labour has on the backward areas in advanced countries like Italy and strategies for readjustment to ward off its ill-effects constitute the main theme of

Chapter 14 contributed by Attilio Celant. The thesis of the paper is that the transformation cost has become far less important in location economic activities. The internationalization of economic systems clearly favours stronger countries but it also favours economies which can control cost of production through high-tech inputs.

The backward regions in advanced countries have new opportunities to catch up but they suffer from certain inelasticities that do not allow a growth process to begin. The cost of labour and capital is almost the same as in developed regions. Secondly, the social patterns are static and crystallized. Economic action alone does not change the situation. Imitating mechanisms which produce territoriality and introduce the society into dynamic phenomena such as cultural growth and a greater tendency to acquire new technologies are of crucial importance.

Because of varying stages of development and differences in organization and product mix, researchers have noted regional imbalances in business cycle sensitiveness of multiplant enterprises. Chapter 15 by Mathias Holst presents a research report on this aspect. The paper concludes that "by introducing the phenomenon of functional division of labour within multiplant enterprises a certain progress in explaining regional imbalances in the business cycle sensitiveness is to be achieved. The theory concerning the spatial and functional division of labour on the one hand illustrates that an influence of multiplant enterprises on regional development and with that on business cycle fluctuations via external control is evident. On the other, the presented empirical study of the manufacturing industry in the Federal Republic of Germany was able to demonstrate sufficiently the effects of the external control...."

The impact of multinational establishments on regional development is further explored by Abiodun with reference to Nigeria in Chapter 16. She has marshalled enough data from three States of the country to prove that the multinational corporations are important channels for the diffusion of innovations needed in the development process. To benefit optimally from the advantages that the corporations could transmit to the population and the economy as a whole, their activities should remain complementary to those of rural population and the government should carefully oversee them lest they adversely affect the growth of indigenous capabilities.

Using the Centre-peripnery concept, Gana (Ch. 17) analyses the political economy of industrial change in Nigeria and asserts that "the current strategy places too much emphasis on the creation of industrial growth poles with the power to create a matrix of growth impulses and a calculus of linkages within the economy. The hope is that such development impulses would trickle down and transform the vast rural economy as well. This Growth Pole Strategy has clearly failed. It is, therefore, necessary to effect a radical integration of industrial growtb with a sound strategy of rural development".

The post-Second World War international division of labour had its most serious implications for Cuban Economy (Ch. 18). Cuba is a mono-crop economy based on sugarcane. The capital and market were traditionally located in the USA. As such the Cuban economy was at the mercy of the international capital. The revolution of 1959 changed the situation drastically. One of the major innovations brought into the system is Agro-industrial complexes (CAI) connecting centres of material – technical equipment for the production and processing of sugarcane and sugar, actual production of care and sugar, chemical and food industries based on derivatives, fuel, cellulose and fodder industries for the utilization of side products, storage and transport as well as housing and public construction, social and cultural provision and qualification, and basic and applied research.

Despite these efforts, the spatial structure of the Cuban sugar economy, because of the historical process of division of labour, is characterized by a high rate of concentration and specialization, by an effective regional-administrative intergration of the social division of labour between cane growing and processing and by typical regime of landuse with a characteristic social and technical infrastructure and a close connection with ports as well.

The role of planned colonization in the expansion of frontier in Amazonia (Ch. 19), presents another case of the impact of international capital and division of labour on income and asset distribution in developing countries. This paper brings to attention the inherent contradictions in pursuing an unbridled capitalist path of development. The international capital forces governments in many developing countries rich in natural resources to abandon or compromise the goals of redistributive justice and environmental quality.

Ishaq Y. Qutub examines the problems of urbanization in Arab countries with a case study of Kuwait emerging from international migration and involvement of multinationals in construction projects (Ch. 20). "The work camps of Asian contracting corporations, which operate on self-sufficiency basis – food, personnel and equipment – tend to form new communities, alien to the urban structure and to the national authenticity. These turn-key contracts contribute little to the improvement of local skills and technical know-how."

Regional Structural Change in International Perspective (Ch. 21) gives the progress report of a project on the above theme carried out by the University Centre for Social and Urban Research, University of Pittsburgh. The focus of the report is a mature industrial region in and around Pittsburgh which has to restructure itself under the impact of the decline of coal and steel industries, which constituted its economic base. "Complacency on the part of industries in the old industrial regions in the USA delayed the introduction of new technology and the substitution of capital for labour to improve quality of product and reduce cost of production."

"The recession of 1980 brought a new era for public-private and university partnership. The partners themselves enhanced their own interests by cooperating in regional economic development initiatives. A strong regional economy provides a strong tax base and helps retain highly trained manpower. It also directly and indirectly generates resources for the benefit of educational and non-profit institutions. Even though, the economies of old industrial regions are becoming more and more service oriented, some of them have begun to modernize certain components of their old manufacturing industries. The use of modern technology and mechanization along with a skilled labour force make such an initiative promising."

The last chapter reviews the situation of Third World Peasantry in the process of global socio-economic and technological changes (Ch. 22) as presented in two volumes of Third World Peasantry: A Continuing Saga of Deprivation. "Here is a formidable fare that should help readers to realize the plight of the peasant form of farming which only a few decades ago dominated these predominantly agricultural economies. The editors, Prof. P.B. Desai, have done a commendable job in bringing together so much material on the impact of varied approaches to development, particularly agricultural development, on the patterns of living and livelihood of those who, by force of circumstances, continue to cling to their peasant ways".

To sum up, the volume brings to focus the structural changes still in offing and the responses of various nations and regions to these changes. When read in relation to each other, these papers present a coherent status report on the challenges and opportunities of technological change in both developed and devoloping countries.

TWO

The Burden of Underdevelopment

ALI MAZRUI

Until the 1970s, the terms "poor countries" and "underdeveloped countries" were virtually interchangeable. Clearly countries like South Yemen or Tanzania were both poor and underdeveloped.

But the emergence of oil power has shattered this easy equation. Virtually all Third World countries are still technically underdeveloped, but only some of them are now poor. South Yemen and Tanzania are still good illustrations of the old equation. They are both poor and underdeveloped. But in the 1970s it had become difficult to think of Saudi Arabia as a poor country. On the contrary, this is one of the best endowed countries in the world in oil-wealth and dollar reserves – while being at the same time one of the least developed.

What is true of Saudi Arabia as a country is substantially true of Africa as a continent. In terms of resources, Africa is one of the best endowed regions of the world, but it is still the least developed of the inhabited continents. The is *the pathology of technical backwardness.*

A related paradox is that, per head of each group's population, the richest inhabitants of Africa are non-Africans. The poorest in per capita terms are indigenous Africans themselves. That is one reason why the highest standards of living are among the white people in Southern Africa.

Of course, there are rich Blacks as well as rich whites in the continent. But again, we find that there are more white millionaires per head of the white population of the continent than there are black millionaires in relation to numbers of blacks around. This is *the pathology of maldistribution.*

The third interrelated paradox is that while the continent as a whole is, as indicated, rich in resources, it is so fragmented that it includes the majority of the poorest nations of the world. The paradox here is of a rich continent which contains many poverty-stricken societies. This is *the pathology of a fragmented economy*.

Let us look at these paradoxes in greater detail.

Estimates of Africa's resources are on the whole tentative. Not enough prospecting for resources under the ground has taken place, but it is already fair to say that Africa has 96 per cent of the non-Communist world's diamonds, 60 per cent of its gold, 42 per cent of its cobalt, 34 per cent of its bauxite and 28 per cent of its uranium.

Africa's iron reserves are probably twice those of the United States, and its reserves of chrome are the most important by far outside the Soviet Union.

In the 1970s the United States had imported 98 per cent of its manganese from abroad, nearly half of which was from Africa.

The West's interest in Africa's oil has also significantly increased, partly in proportion to the political uncertainties surrounding the Middle Eastern suppliers. Had Nigeria joined the Arab oil embargo of the United States in 1973, the consequences for America would have been severe. In 1974–the year following the embargo–the United States' balance-of-payment deficit with Nigeria was already $3 billion. It rose to $5 billion two years later. For the time being America's dependence on Nigerian oil continues to be critical.

Then there is Africa's agricultural potential. The Republic of Sudan, Africa's largest country in square miles, may indeed develop into a major bread-basket for parts of Africa and the Middle East before the end of the century. More effective irrigation would facilitate full exploitation of the impressive fertility of this part of the continent.

Then there are Africa's water resources, with some of the greatest rivers of the world. Potentialities for building dams and generating hydroelectric power have only just begun to be exploited.

Solar energy for domestic and public purposes is still in its infancy. But it should be remembered that Africa is the most exposed of all continents to the sun. The Equator cuts Africa right in the middle. And Africa is the only continent which is cut by both the Tropic of Cancer and the Tropic of Capricorn. Tapping solar energy in Africa, once the technique becomes sophisticated, could be an additional impressive source of power and energy.

With regard to uranium, Africa's resources may be significantly greater than at present estimated. One country that became a uranium-producing State fairly recently is Niger, formerly a French colony.

Against this background of mineral, agricultural and other resources in Africa there is also the disconcerting fact that Africa has some of the least developed countries in the world. The overwhelming majority of the countries that the United Nations regards as the "poorest" in the world are in fact in Africa. They range from Upper Volta to Rwanda and Burundi and from Somalia to Tanzania.

The continent itself seems to be well endowed with resources, but a disproportionate number of people in the population of the continent are undernourished and underprivileged. A situation where a continent is well endowed but the people are poor is a situation of anomalous underdevelopment.

A substantial part of the explanation lies in the nature of Africa's economic interaction with the Western world across time. Trade is the oldest of the different areas of economic interaction, foreign investment being relatively recent. Trade between Europe and Africa goes back to the slave trade and the traffic in firearms and later in primary commodities.

Agricultural potentialities of Africa were realized quite early, though these potentialities continue to be underutilized. As a writer put it back in 1879, Africa contained:

> . . . . millions of square miles of rich and fertile lands, some of which are open and parklike in their appearance; and others covered with extensive forests of valuable timber, where the sound of the woodman's axe has never yet been heard, and which only require the culture of the husbandman to make them produce an ample return for labour. (Flint, p. 486.)

But the fertile land was accompanied in some cases by a harsh climate for the European and sometimes even for the local inhabitants. The mosquito and the tse-tse fly took their toll.

It was not until the last quarter of the 19th century that an entirely new potential source of wealth began to be taken seriously. As a Western historian has put it:

> By 1875 the discovery of diamonds in South Africa had provided a striking indication of the entirely unexpected riches to be found in Africa, and given new meaning to the wise remark made by Samuel Parchas more than two hundred years earlier : And yet may Africa have a Prerogative in Rarities, and some seeming Incredibilities be true. (Flint, p. 487)

But in fact much of British investment for more than half a century went to South Africa. Up to 1936 South Africa received nearly half of Africa's total capital inflow from outside. In the rest of Africa there was in the initial phases a relatively heavy proportion of infrastructural investment. The period of perhaps greatest railway building activity was from 1890 to 1914. Some of the railway lines which were built had no immediate prospects, but were truly a kind of investment in the future. The railway line from Mombasa in Kenya to the lakes in the interior of East Africa was built between 1896 and 1901. At the time it was widely regarded as a lunatic venture, a white elephant in a dark continent with a gloomy future. But in fact the railway line came to serve Kenya and Uganda exceptionally well.

There was considerable talk in Western circles at the time about a possible Cape-to-Cairo railway line. Unfortunately that trans-continental dream never materialized.

In subsequent years there was also investment in Africa's sources of power and energy. Africa may have nearly 30 per cent of the world's potential for hydroelectric power. Some moves towards tapping these immense resources were made, especially after the Second World War. The Owen Falls dam in Uganda across the Nile generates power for Uganda itself and for about a third of Kenya's needs. The Volta River project in Ghana was later linked to aluminium smelting, and could be part of the basis of further development in Ghana when some of the other economic problems of the country are transcended.

The Second World War was an important divide in Africa's developmental experience. There is widespread consensus that the war definitely contributed towards Africa's *political* liberation. It did this partly by undermining western Europe's capacity to hold on to empires. Britain was exhausted and substantially impoverished by the time the war ended. France had been humiliated in defeat at the hands of the Germans.

Related to this exhaustion and impoverishment of western Europe following its own fratricidal war was the destruction of the myth of European invincibility in the eyes of the colonized people. Suddenly somebody noticed in Bombay that the emperor's new clothes of modern technology were not clothes at all – the British Raj was naked ! And when the Indians started pointing fingers and exposing the nakedness of their Emperor, other subject peoples elsewhere heard it too. That is one reason why the precedent set by India in challenging British rule became an important inspiration to many African nationalists.

White Man Cut Down to Size

At a more individual level the war also cut the white man down to size in African eyes. The colonial situation until then cried out loud for two processes of humanization. The colonized Africans had their humanity reduced partly because they were regarded as part devils and part monkeys. They certainly had their adulthood reduced when they were often equated with children. As I was growing up in Mombasa in the 1940's, the film censors declared some films as being "not suitable for Africans and children under 16". And since the population of Mombasa was in part racially mixed, and many Arabs looked like Africans, there were two kinds of identification tests at the door of the Regal Cinema in Mombasa. An African who wanted desperately to see the particular film could try and convince the ticket clerk that he was really an Arab. Secondly, the fifteen-year-old who was desperate to see the film had to convince the clerk that he was really 16. This equation of Africanity with childhood began to be undermined as a result of war experiences and the role of African soldiers in combat as brave and determined adults.

On the other hand, Europeans had been portrayed as superadult and virtually superhuman. The war in turn humanized white men in the eyes of their African colleagues as they fought together in the Horn of Africa, in North Africa, in places like Malaya and elsewhere. To witness a white man scared to death under fire was itself a revelation to many Africans, who had previously seen white men only in their arrogant commanding postures as a colonial elite.

So, while the image of the African was humanized by being pulled up from equation with devils, monkeys and children, the image of the white man was humanized by being pulled down from equation with supermen, angels, and the gods themselves.

The third effect of the war was to broaden the general, social and political horizons not only of ex-servicemen who had served in the war, but of many Africans who had remained behind. The idea of listening to the radio for *overseas* news concerning the war gathered momentum during the war. Individual Africans in a township were, in terms of conversations among themselves, identified as being either pro-British or pro-German. My father, for his sins, was pro-British and I remember long debates he used to have with his friends in a relaxed mood debating the significance of the latest news item about the war abroad, and whether it was good news or bad news for the different fans of the British on one side and the Germans on the other. I was a child then listening with rapture to this kind of exchange. It was clear that the grown-ups regarded the contending forces in Europe partly as soccer teams writ large, and the Africans were placing their bets on the two European powers at war with each other. We should remember that East Africa had once known both German rule in Tanganyika, Rwanda and Burundi, and British rule in Uganda and Kenya. The two colonial and former colonial powers at war with each other were on one side ominous masters, and on the other frivolous soccer teams in deadly rivalry with each other.

But the very tendency of my father and his friends to debate the progress of the war almost as if it were the progress of a football match increased their interest in world affairs and broadened their vision of human possibilities. For millions of Africans all over the continent the Second World War was an important internationalizing experience. By the end of it many Africans were ready to agitate for freedom and independence.

The Second World War was also liberating for Africa because at the end of it the pinnacle of world power was no longer in western Europe but had divided itself between Washington and Moscow. The two superpowers both had a tradition of anti-imperialism in at least some sense, though both superpowers are also guilty of other forms of imperialism. What is clear is that the rise of the Soviet Union and the pre-eminence of the United States after the Second World War created two pressures on European powers to make concessions to African nationalists struggling for independence. The West's fear of the Soviet Union sometimes retarded the process of liberation, but in the end facilitated that process, convincing Westerners that it was a good idea to give independence to moderate Africans while there was still time and avert the threat of radicalizing Africans still further and driving them into the hands of the Soviet Union.

But although the Second World War was indeed politically liberating in the sense we have mentioned for Africans, that same war was an important stage in the incorporation of Africa into the world capitalist system. Partly in pursuit of war needs, African agriculture was modified to produce urgently needed supplies and food for Europe at war. In some parts of Africa there was a major depression later when the war demand for African-produced goods declined, but the structure of African agriculture had by then already entered a new phase of export bias. The trend towards slanting African agriculture in this direction continued unabated.

Some of the post-war schemes for African development initiated by the colonial powers were indeed failures. One of the most spectacular of the failures was the groundnut scheme in Tanganyika, flamboyantly conceived in terms of large-scale groundnut development, and deemed to be an appropriate strategy of interdependence between Africa and Europe. The scheme was designed to help supply Europe with certain food oils while generating development in Africa. As it turned out, the scheme was ill-conceived, badly located and disastrously implemented by the British authorities in East Africa.

But on balance the principle of developing African agriculture to serve European needs was quite well entrenched. The war had helped to consolidate it.

Another way in which the war created the foundations of further economic dependency lay in the manner in which it helped to transform colonial policy from the morality of maintaining law and order in Africa (*Pax Britannica*) to a new imperial morality of increasing development in the colonies and pursuing the welfare of the colonized people. Britain established the Colonial Development and Welfare Fund as part of the machinery of this new imperial vision. It was not enough to stop Africans fighting each other. It was not enough to control cattle raids between different communities and tribes. It was not enough making an example of political agitators in order to maintain the mystique of *Pax Britannica*. It was not enough to use the slogan of law and order. Imperial power was a kind of trust, a mandate to serve the subject peoples.

The vision itself was of course much older than the Second World War. It was even explicit in Rudyard Kipling's notorious poem, "The White Man's Burden", first published in *The Times* on February 4, 1899.

"Take up the White Man's burden–
Send forth the best ye breed–
Go bind your sons to exile
To serve your captive's need.
To wait in heavy harness,
On flattered folk and wild–
Your new caught, sullen peoples,
Half-devil and half-child.

Take up the White Man's burden–
The savage wars of peace–
Fill full the mouth of Famine
And bid the sickness cease;

Take up the White Man's burden–
No tawdry rule of kings,
But toil of serf and sweeper–
The tale of common things.
The ports ye shall not enter,
The roads ye shall not tread,
Go make them with your living,
And mark them with your dead."

The developmental imperative of service was certainly very explicit in this poem. But on balance it was not in fact until the Second World War that development as a major imperative of colonial policy became a genuine exertion. New projects for rural development were more systematically implemented, and new trends in educational policy were soon discernible. Virtually all the major universities in black Africa were established after the Second World War, many of them soon after the war in response to the new developmental imperative in colonial policy.

But these thrusts of development were themselves a further aggravation of Africa's incorporation into Western capitalism. The Colonial Development and Welfare Fund contributed in its own way towards deepening both Africa's economic dependency on the West and Africa's cultural imitation of the West.

Important biases in the direction of development included, firstly, the export bias we have just mentioned. Cash crops for export were given priority as against food for local people. One-quarter to one-third of the total cultivated area in some of the more fertile colonies was devoted to the production of such export commodities as cocoa in Ghana, coffee in Uganda, groundnuts in Senegal and the Gambia, pyrethrum in Tanganyika and tea in Kenya.

Another distortion which occurred in the development process was the urban bias. Much of the economic change internally subordinated the needs of the countryside to the needs of the towns. One consequence was the volume of migration from rural areas to urban centres. The crisis of habitability continued to beset the lot of the country folk. Young men struggled for a while, then downed their tools, and hit the high road towards the uncertain fortunes of the capital city.

A third bias within each country was the subregional distortion. Some parts of the country were just much more developed than others. This burden of uneven development had its own stresses and strains. By being more developed than its neighbours the Buganda subregion of Uganda, for example, acquired not only extra leverage, but also the passionate jealousies and distrust of other parts of the country. With less than one-fifth of the population of Uganda, Buganda held sway and exercised undue leverage over the political and economic destiny of the country as a whole. Uganda is now very difficult to govern with the help of Buganda, and very difficult to govern without their help. The chronic instability of Uganda is partly the result of ethnic confrontations and partly the outcome of uneven development among the different subregions and groups in the country.

The fourth distortion in the history of development in Africa was the distortion which occurred in parts of the continent settled and, at least for a while, controlled by white settlers. In 1938, out of a total of £ 1,222 million capital invested in Africa no less than £ 555 million was invested in South Africa from outside. A further £ 102 million was invested in Rhodesia. These countries under white settler control acquired in addition considerable economic muscle in their own parts of the continent, with leverage over their neighbours. Rhodesia exercised economic influence over Zambia, Malawi, Botswana and Mozambique.

Kenya, while it was still a colonial territory, exercised considerable economic influence on the neighbouring countries of Tanganyika, Uganda and Zanzibar. South Africa itself is now basically a giant in the southern African subcontinent with considerable potential for buying friends or neutralizing enemies.

The fifth bias in Africa's development takes us back to capitalism. For in this case we are indeed dealing with the capitalist bias in Africa's recent economic history--absorption into international structures of trade and capital flows, belief in the efficacy of market forces, faith in the profit motive and private enterprise, distrust of State initiatives in the economy, and optimism about the developmental value of foreign investments.

It is partly the nature of these five biases in the history of economic change in the continent that has condemned the continent to the paradox of retardation –a continent well endowed in mineral wealth and agricultural potential which is at the same time a continent of the countries which the United Nations has calculated to be the poorest in the world.

Can Africa Modernize Without Westernizing?

The question which arises is what is to be done to help Africa to transcend this predicament of retardation? Can Africa modernize without Westernizing?

My own definition of modernization is change in the direction which is compatible with the present stage of human knowledge, and which does justice to the human person as an innovative and social being.

If a society does not want to take into account present-day levels of knowledge, science and scholarship, that society is pre-modern.

If a society suppresses innovativeness, and insists on doing things according only to tradition, that society is pre-modern.

If a society interprets the concept of man as a social being too narrowly, limiting social loyalties to clans and tribes or even just to nations, turns its back on the outer world of fellow human beings, that society is still pre-modern.

If modernity is defined according to these three basic principles of responsiveness to highest levels of knowledge, encouragement of innovation, and enlargement of social sympathies, there are clearly different roads to modernity.

For the Third World the best way of modernizing without Westernizing is, on the one side, to adopt those three principles of modernity that I have mentioned and, on the other, to pursue strategies of decolonization and of reducing dependency. It is a dual effort–to modernize and decolonize at the same time. In a sense, it is an effort–to decolonize modernity.

Given those three principles of the modern approach, how do we marry them to strategies of decolonization and liberation?

I myself would recommend seven strategies of liberation. The first is to some extent already underway. This is the strategy of indigenization of personnel, as programmes for the Africanization of administration, management, clerical manpower and the like got underway. This use of indigenous human resources is certainly an important aspect. In the Southern African situation the increased use of indigenous personnel in different areas of economic activity will in turn prove to be the Achilles heel of the racially-based economic system, undermining its very foundations. But elsewhere in Africa, there is a danger that the indigenization of personnel is merely window-dressing; substituting black faces in the front for white faces, but maintaining a system of dependency and distortion all the same.

In spite of these reservations there is no escaping the necessity of increased utilization of indigenous human resources as part of this first strategy of liberation.

Also fundamental to the strategy of indigenization is the need to develop further indigenous resources as against relying on imports where this option is open. Greater utilization of hydroelectric power, for example, would sometimes reduce dependence on imported coal or oil.

Greater utilization of indigenous technology and know-how must also be mentioned. The struggle for simpler forms of technology is part of the process of reducing reliance on outsiders for sophisticated know-how. In recent times there has even been increased interest in traditional African medicine with special reference to some of the herbs which were used in therapy. Experience was the medical school of pre-colonial African doctors and medicine men. Some of these herbs, under modern chemical analysis, have yielded important information on their own medicinal values.

In terms of the African economy as a whole, there is also the slow process of attempting to indigenize control and decision-making in major industries and firms. Nigeria has been moving in that direction in the 1970's. The Ivory Coast, on the other hand, continues to rely disproportionately on French personnel and advisers for areas of economic activity which in many other parts of Africa have long been under indigenous control.

My second strategy for transcending dependency is the strategy of domestication. This is different from indigenization. Domestication involves making a resource which is foreign, more relevant and more appropriate for the African situation. For example, the African university today is basically a foreign institution transmitting foreign culture and technique, consolidating foreign academic traditions, and even preparing the way for foreign ideologies among students and future teachers. Domesticating the African university would involve making it more relevant to local needs, and more responsive to branches of knowledge and understanding available elsewhere on the local scene. The teaching of African history instead of British imperial history at Makerere University was a modest venture in the domestication of the department of history.

Parliament in Nairobi is in conception a foreign institution. It has all the paraphernalia of Parliament at Westminster without the sanctity of tradition and stamp of authenticity. Budget day is very much like budget day at Westminster, with the black briefcase of Kenya's equivalent of the Chancellor of the Exchequer. The Speaker wears regalia reminiscent of the Speaker of the House of Commons. And for more than a decade after independence the language of discussion in Kenya's National Assembly was exclusively English.

But when the late President Kenyatta ordered that deliberations in the Kenyan Parliament were, from 1974, to be in Kiswahili, this was a major stage in the domestication of the parliamentary institution in Kenya. Anomalies have remained. The language of debate is indeed Kiswahili, but the laws come before Parliament couched in the English language. The official language of the constitution when it is being interpreted in the law courts is English but the basic language of national politics is Kiswahili. Domesticating the political system, borrowed from a liberal democratic tradition from outside, has necessitated its own Swahilization.

Domesticating the economy itself involves a reduction of its export-orientation, and an enhancement of the focus on domestic food needs and other local requirements.

Sometimes emphasizing labour-intensive technology instead of capital-intensive is itself a form of domesticating the techniques of production, distribution, communication and exchange. Labour-intensive technology is a form of democratizing modernity, involving more and more people in the process of modern production, and utilizing a major resource of even the poorest of the African countries–the human resource.

My third strategy for transcending dependency is the strategy of diversification. I start from the premise that there are occasions when freedom begins with the multiplication of one's masters. If one is owned and controlled by only one power, freedom is often particularly restrictive. But if an African society cultivates the skills to have more than one hegemonic power competing for it, this has possibilities of liberation. To be dependent on two giants, especially when the giants have rivalries between them, is sometimes an opportunity to play one against the other–and maximize one's own options.

African societies must, therefore, diversify and sometimes multiply their trading partners. This at times may require that they also diversify what they produce, avoiding predicaments of excessive dependence on one or two commodities.

Thirdly, there is the need to diversify one's investors. French-speaking countries tend to be excessively preoccupied with facilitating French investment. To that extent their freedom of manoeuvre is more restricted than among those English-speaking countries that have already moved beyond their original metropole and cultivated new potential Western risk-takers to invest in their societies.

Fourthly, there is the need to diversify one's aid donors. Many of these aid donors insist on bilateral aid between the giver and the receiver, but new aid institutions have grown up, such as the Arab

Bank for African Development. Indeed, the emergence of oil-rich members of the Organization of Petroleum Exporting Countries has introduced a qualitative stage in the diversification of potential aid donors for African countries. In relation to gross national product (GNP), the OPEC countries give a higher percentage of aid than do Western countries. But there is clearly no room for complacency, especially since OPEC is also responsible for new and sometimes crippling oil prices. Nevertheless, the rise of OPEC to new levels of power has been one of the most important and healthiest developments of the 1970s, as we shall later elaborate.

There are other areas of diversification which Africans need to explore, including exposing themselves to a wider range of foreign cultural influences than they have done so far. To be exposed only to the Western cultural impact creates a deeper condition of dependency than to be exposed to a variety of influences from Canada to India, from Germany to China, from Japan to the Soviet Union.

Ideologically, Africa also needs to diversify its options. Closed ideological systems perpetrate mental and intellectual dependency. African societies should be open enough to let contending ideological forces compete for leverage. Thus Western individualism, Marxist class concepts, Gandhian ideas of compromise, and indigenous values underpinning African cultures themselves can be let loose on the free market of ideas.

My fourth strategy for transcending dependency is a strategy which I call, in my own jargon, horizontal interpenetration. By this I mean the capacity of developing countries themselves to interpenetrate each other in trade, investment, aid and other forms of contact. Until now the bulk of the trade of the world goes on between the rich industrialized countries of the Northern Hemisphere themselves (north-north trade). Second in importance is the economic interaction between the Northern Hemisphere and the developing countries of the Third World (north-south trade and the like). Only thirdly in importance is trade and investment and aid among developing countries themselves (south-south economic interaction).

What is required is greater cooperation, contact and interaction among African countries themselves and between African countries and countries of Asia and Latin America. Cases of horizontal interpenetration include Egypt's and India's export of manpower to other developing countries, the Arab world's aid to African and Asian countries and Cuba's military assistance to Angola, Ethiopia and other African countries. All these are cases where the resources of one Third World country are made available for specific purposes to serve the needs of another Third World country. The acceleration of this trend is an important aspect of the whole struggle against dependency.

My fifth strategy for transcending these economic handicaps is the strategy of what I call vertical counterpenetration into the citadels of power. Under this strategy the aim is to increase the share of the Third World in the economies of the developed industrial nations themselves, and therefore enhance Third World leverage over those economies. The beginnings of counter-penetration lie in the psychological discovery that the resources of Third World societies are not necessarily merely a basis of dependency on the Western world, but could be converted into power over the Western world. For decades oil in the Middle East was one additional reason why the oil producers were controlled by others. And then a number of countries formed a producers cartel called the Organization of Petroleum Exporting Countries–and before very long a resource which had caused its possessors to be subjugated became a weapon of the possessors capable of being wielded against the imperial powers that had once dominated them.

Of course oil is an exceptional case in terms of its potential for use against the industrial nations. But my generalization is still correct–that the spirit of counterpenetration by the Third World into the Northern Hemisphere must begin with a re-evaluation by Third World societies on how best to utilize their own resources to maximize international leverage. At least as important is the need for Third World countries, including members of OPEC, to maintain a sense of solidarity against the industrial nations.

I am not myself upset when members of OPEC invest or buy shares in Krupp industries in Germany, or Kuwait seeks a portion of the Benz Bonanza, or Saudi princes invest in real estate in London or California, or when Nigerian funds are carefully placed in Western banks. All these are cases of counterpenetration.

If Nigeria had not effectively discovered that its oil could be a weapon to use in fostering enlightened Western policies for southern Africa, and if Nigeria had not thus counterpenetrated Western economies, the impact of Lagos on Western policy-making would have been reduced accordingly.

The Nuclear Holocaust

I, therefore, do not agree with those Third World scholars and analysts who feel the Third World actually disengage from the international capitalist system. It is too late to disengage. The northern industrialized countries hold the planet Earth hostage. The industrialized countries could gradually destroy the world through pollution and other forms of ecological damage. Or the industrialized nations could impoverish the world by an indiscriminate and reckless depletion of resources. But the most ominous of all dangers is that the industrialized countries could destroy the world in a nuclear holocaust.

Given that the industrialized nations are now in a position to hold the whole planet Earth hostage either to satisfy their industrialized luxuries, or in a catastrophic war among themselves, Third World countries simply cannot afford to pull out of the system. They must remain part of the system, but seek the kind of terms which would enable them to exercise greater influence over the Northern Hemisphere.

That is why it would be singularly irresponsible if we stopped the process which is now already increasing the influence of the Third World on the economic strategies of the Northern Hemisphere. The gains which OPEC has enabled the Third World to make must not be thrown away in a mood of militant abdication and withdrawal.

My sixth strategy is that of domestic austerity in the Third World. There ought to be greater circumspection with regard to consumption patterns, greater restraint in the importation of luxury goods.

There must also be a narrowing of the gap between the elites and the masses, a strategy of income distribution and, where appropriate, land reform.

But the austerity need not go to the extent of hampering the satisfaction of basic human needs. Efforts should be made to make possible minimum nutrition levels, minimum health care, minimum educational opportunities for children and the like. But ultimately the push in each developing country should be in the direction of discipline, restraint, and austerity. It is often easier said than done, but experiments are already underway in places like Tanzania, Somalia, Mozambique and Guinea-Bissau.

The seventh strategy for transcending dependency is the transitional strategy of encouraging northern extravagance for the time being. In the immediate future it would be disastrous for the Third World if the United States and its allies succeeded in drastically cutting down the consumption of oil. An America self-sufficient in oil is an America invulnerable to external pressures. Indeed, the federal government in the United States has been urging Americans to be economical in oil partly on the argument that this would make the United States secure from external pressures.

And yet the United States itself exerts a variety of external pressures on other societies. True interdependence in the world requires mutual vulnerability to each other's pressures. If the northern industrialized countries can play havoc with the economies of Third World societies just by drinking less coffee than they have done the previous year, or using less copper this decade than in the last, it is imperative that the Southern Hemisphere should also discover ways of exerting counter-pressures on the industrialized nations. Successful economies in petroleum consumption by the developed States must be prevented at all costs.

The British philosopher, Bertrand Russell, used to say that civilization was born out of the pursuit of luxury. What Russell might have added is that civilization declined sometimes out of the pursuit of excessive luxury. The current extravagance in consumption of oil in the United States, and even the exceptionally high standard of living in Western Europe as a whole, might have reached the stage of excessive luxury. The decline of Western civilization might well be at hand. It is in the interest of humanity that such a decline should take place, allowing the different segments of the human race to enjoy a more equitable share not only of the resources of the planet but also of the capacity to control the march of human history.

I am not of course recommending the total collapse of Western civilization. That too would be disastrous for the human race, for it is a civilization that has enhanced man's control over nature, enriched man's own creativity and inventiveness, and deepened man's understanding of the ultimate and the spiritual.

The West took the technology of production all the way from the spinning wheel to computerized manufacture. The West took the technology of destruction all the way from the bow and arrow to the neutron bomb. And the West took the technology of communication all the way from smoke signals to electronic and satellite media.

But these achievements had their costs and their distortions. The technology of production, symbolized by the civilian factory, became a declaration of war on nature. The northern industrialized countries engaged in reckless depletion of resources and damage to the environment, from pollution of rivers, lakes and the sea to threats to the ozone layer.

If the technology of production declared war on nature, the West's technology of destruction was inevitably a declaration of war on man. The arms race and the competition of northern industrialized countries attained new heights of sophisticated destructiveness. The search for new forms of annihilation continues to keep Soviet and Western scientists constantly in a state of exhilarated competition for the ultimate secrets of a future holocaust.

The technology of communication, ranging from electronic media to publishing, became at times a declaration of war on ultimate values. Human aggression and an enjoyment of violence have been sustained and nourished by the abuse of television and film.

Restraints on avarice and acquisitiveness have been undermined by the very ethos of capitalism as communicated and over-communicated through its own instruments of dissemination.

The natural human weakness of lust has at times been recklessly exploited by the West's technology of communication, with negative consequences for the sacred drive of sexuality.

The West's technology of communication has at times undermined in Africa the imperative of moral riciprocity among people. Western culture has eroded some of the principles of collective responsibility in village life and tribal mores.

And finally, the West's technology of communication has often distorted the balance of information and cognition between different societies. This is what the information gap is all about – what Nigerians know about Zambians is often derived from Western news agencies and media. My information about what is happening in India currently is disproportionately from the British Broadcasting

Corporation and *The New York Times.* The Third World feels constantly under northern scrutiny, spied upon, observed, analysed, sometimes manipulated by the barrage of northern media. There is very little counterpenetration by Third World media into the centres of news and gossip within the Northern Hemisphere.

Given then that the Western world and the Soviet bloc permitted the technology of production to become a declaration of war on nature and the environment, the technology of destruction to become a declaration of war on man, and the technology of communication to be a declaration of war on ultimate values, a partial decline of civilizations of the Northern Hemisphere is a necessary precondition for creating a genuinely new international order. After all, the old territorial colonization was possible because the West controlled the means of destruction. As the English poet, Hilaire Belloc, put it:

> "Whatever happens, we have got
> The Maxim gun, and they have not!"

The newer forms of economic imperialism are perpetrated by those who control the means of production, sometimes acting through the medium of transnational corporations with their tentacles in different parts of the world.

As for cultural imperialism, this is best perpetrated by those who control the means of communication, from *Time* magazine to cowboy films, from the BBC to visiting professors at African universities.

As we indicated, Africa and the rest of the Third World cannot withdraw from the system without abdicating their responsibility for the planet as a whole. The Third World as a whole must, therefore, say to the Northern Hemisphere: "Let us re-negotiate the terms of our co-existence on this shared planet. Let us sign a global treaty to help establish greater economic and social justice not only between men but also between societies." Thanks to the West's inventiveness, the clock of technology has indeed gone past the hour. It has ominous chimes of destruction. What is more, it is an alarm clock – still ringing. "Ladies and Gentlemen, it is time to wake up." In the new dawn the poor and the meek of Africa may not inherit the Earth but, hopefully, they will finally inherit their own continent.

[illegible]

[illegible] ... as indicated by the damage [illegible] ... [illegible] ... on [illegible] ...

[illegible] ... Whatever happens, we have got

The Maxim gun, and they have not.

The [illegible] ...

[illegible] ... [illegible] ... [illegible] ...

THREE

The Effects of International Developments on Domestic Economies and Social Development in Developing Countries

FOLKER FROBEL, JURGEN HEINRICHS & OTTO KREYE

The Current Crisis of the Capitalist World-System

The capitalist world-system is in the grip of a crisis; its symptoms and its consequences are clearly visible. But a proper understanding of the current international developments and their effects requires an inquiry into the origins of the crisis.[1]

Although the crisis has its familiar economic, political and ecological aspects in the Western industrialized countries, it is in fact a crisis of the world capitalist system as a whole, including much of the Third World too. The socialist countries have not been spared, the extent to which they are affected depending on how far they have become integrated into the capitalist world system.

Two closely linked processes have contributed to the crisis; first, the gradual erosion of the United States global hegemony, and second, internal contradictions within the industrialized countries.

At the end of the Second World War, the dominance of the United States seemed assured. It provided the context within which free international in fact transnational-mobility of capital could be guaranteed, evidenced most clearly in the progressive global spread of States corporations, later followed by western European and Japanese firms. The growing economic and political strength of western Europe and Japan gradually eroded the dominance of the United States, which was further weakened by political changes in the periphery. In addition, transnational corporations achieved a level of economic and political power to a large degree independent of their home governments. This power was sufficiently strong in some cases to override the authority of many States of even powerful supra-national institutions.

The model of capital accumulation that came into being in the period after the Second World War has been analysed by Michael Aglietta, Giovanni Arrighi, Robert Boyer, André Gunder Frank, David Gordon, André Granou, Eric Hobsbawm, Stephen Hymer, Ernest Mandel, James O'Connor, Christian Palloix, Thomas Weisskopf and others.[2] The hegemony enabled the USA to impose a new model of accumulation, in which the tendencies towards international and internal conflict inherent in the pre-war system were to be counteracted by two major departures from the preceding model: firstly, an extensive – including international – freedom for corporate activity, and secondly, the systematic extension of the market for mass consumer goods in the industrialized countries. By inducing a high rate of capitalist growth against the background of these new preconditions, it was hoped that a course could be steered between the Scylla of realization crises (the fatal "flaw" in the previous system) and the Charybdis of valorization crises. Such a strategy would simultaneously facilitate the political integration of the workers' movement(s), which, despite its exhaustion and decimation through war and crisis, still represented a serious oppositional factor in view of the collapse in the credibility of the capitalist economic and social system following the events of the previous three decades.

Relations between developed market-economy countries and developing countries were fostered by a policy of closer international, in fact transnational, links: for example, the dissolution of the old colonial systems of preferences and their replacement by a free trade policy. In the circumstances following the Second World War, this policy implied a great overseas expansion of the United States capital into the industrialized and developing countries.

Despite the various forms and degrees of resistance encountered in the immediate post-war years, the USA succeeded in exerting political and economic pressure to install the new model of accumulation in western Europe, and to a more limited extent in Japan. Once established the model was able to generate precisely those features which rendered its continued functioning an increasingly attractive proposition to the organized working class, and which further enabled it to determine capitalist development in the Western industrialized countries and the world-economy as a whole over the subsequent two and a half decades; that is, high rates of growth, expanding mass incomes, a trend towards full employment and the expansion of the social welfare system.

The very success of the model led to shortages of labour, despite large-scale labour migration into the industrialized countries. As a consequence, profit margins were squeezed and the dominance of capital was threatened. The corporate response took two forms. The first was the method of economizing on labour power by cutting back investment and introducing labour-saving technologies. The second was the method of relocating plants in cheaper and/or more profitable alternative sites, specifically in developing countries.

The combination of these two methods had the effect that the period of labour shortage in the industrial countries was followed by large-scale unemployment, a fall in real wages and measures for curbing the size of the Welfare State. The consequential decline in mass purchasing power reinforced the tendency towards the under-utilization of capacities and growing unemployment; opportunities for profitable productive investment declined.

After functioning successfully for 25 years, the post-war capitalist economy has now run into serious difficulties, and there is little prospect of an improvement in the situation. The doctrines of conservative economics, which dominate policy in most of the large industrialized countries, assume that capital accumulation can be revived simply by further cheapening labour as a factor of production, despite continuing mass unemployment; and diminishing mass purchasing power.

The transnational corporations have an obvious interest in maintaining the present world market system. In this they are supported by institutions, such as the World Bank and in particular International Monetary Fund (IMF), which are forcing more and more countries, especially in the Third World, to adopt measures that are inconsistent with the interests of the bulk of their populations and that are intended to intensify integration into the capitalist world system.

How the crisis will end is still unclear. Those conservative forces seeking to preserve the essentials of the existing system, in fact to use the crisis as a means of saving it, undeniably have the upper hand at present. Eric Hobsbawm has observed on this point "capitalism lived with (slumps), capitalism lived through them, capitalism survived them."[3] Nevertheless, as the crisis persists, and as the failure of conservative policy becomes evident, new political forces will perhaps come to the fore and work for the establishment of an entirely different social system.

Against this background, we now consider the effects of the crisis on the Third World.

The Crisis and the Periphery

The experience of the early 1980s has shown more than ever before that the developing countries of Asia, Africa and Latin America which are integrated into the capitalist world market have little prospect of benefiting from an independent and self-reliant path of development. Owing to the social and political crisis of the capitalist world system, it would be a fallacy to think that underdevelopment can be overcome within the present system.

Social and economic conditions for the majority of the population in many if not most nations of the capitalist periphery steadily worsened in the course of the immediate post-war decades. In the last few years their situation has become parlous. A number of countries are now on the brink of default.

The economic crisis is not reflected directly in altered, or reversed, growth rates for industrial and agricultural production, and foreign trade – in fact these have not fallen as dramatically in the developing countries as in some industrialized countries – but rather in unbalanced sectoral and regional growth, increasing dependency, and their social effects. The evidence includes:

- Stagnation and drop in industrial, agricultural and service output intended for consumption by the population, in particular foodstuffs. Simultaneously, an increase in capital-intensive agricultural, industrial and service output for mostly foreign markets–controlled by transnational corporations–including the production of food. The consequence is an accentuation of the disequilibria between domestically oriented and world market-oriented production to the detriment of output for domestic consumption.
- Indebtedness of the developing countries to the public and private international financial institutions, and a consequential dependency amounting to subordination to the international

financial system. Indebtedness has now reached such heights– $ 810 billion at the end of 1983[4] – that debt service now absorbs a large share of the economic surplus of these countries.

- Further encroachments on and destruction of the rural subsistence economy, that is, that part of the economy in which the bulk of the rural population of the developing countries produces what it needs for subsistence or has been able to do so uptil now. The rapidly advancing destruction of this sector by capital-intensive export-agriculture explains the emigration of large numbers of the rural population.[5]
- Extensive damage to the environment in the countries of the periphery, often exceeding the environmental damage in the industrialized countries.

Most of these indicators relate to manifestations of under-development which look more like a continuation of the trends and processes known only too well in the developing countries, rather than anything startlingly new. But the fact that they have come virtually to dominate social and economic development, at the expense of an independent or alternative development in individual countries, regions and branches, puts them in a new light. In addition, almost all the countries and regions of the periphery which once appeared to demonstrate the possibility of capitalist prosperity even in the periphery – at least in the individual cases of what are variously described as threshold countries, semi-periphery, economic miracle countries, newly industrializing countries are now compelled to abandon any idea of a nationally determined economic policy.

The main cause of this state of affairs is not difficult to spot: compared with the two post-war decades of boom in the capitalist centres, the crisis-ridden 1970s offered far fewer obstacles to the integration of the peripheral countries into the world market, and in particular to the opening up of countries for investment-seeking international capital.

The levers which enabled this accelerated opening-up and integration to take place, and continue to do so, are both numerous and diverse, ranging from management contracts to military pressure. Amongst the most important of these levers are private foreign investment, export and import credits, technology transfer, weapons transfer, development advice and consultancy, the Green Revolution, infrastructural investments and petro-dollar recycling.

The actors were, and are, primarily transnational corporations in co-operation with the World Bank and IMF, and in collaboration with the respective national bourgeoisies. The fields of investment were, and are, high-price domestic markets and production for export. Production structures have become overwhelmingly oriented to the world market; these are paralleled by consumption structures heavily dependent on imports.

The world market orientation of developing countries has also made them more vulnerable to fluctuations in world demand. The crisis-induced drastic fall in world demand is also impinging on those areas of production and services that operate within the ambit of transnational capital. Increases in exports of manufactured goods are heavily concentrated in a few developing countries. The drop in demand and the collapse in commodity prices have brought about a corresponding fall in the developing countries' export earnings. The situation is aggravated by the general absence of any effective State control and the widespread practice of transfer pricing.

Never before in the history of the capitalist mode of production has the contrast between the enormous unmet needs of the vast bulk of humanity, living in poverty, and an enormous unused productive capacity – unused because its use is not profitable – been so glaring as in the periphery today. And never before has the capitalist mode of production been shown to be so irrational as in the current crisis.

The Political Crisis

The economic crisis and the threat of economic bankruptcy of entire States find a counterpart in the political crisis of both the bourgeois-democratic State – where it has survived – and the bourgeois military State. A series of coups, putschs and external interventions have more or less ousted bourgeois-democratic State forms and other reform-oriented regimes in the Third World.

The political crisis of the *bourgeois-democratic* State in the periphery is scarcely surprising. The replacement of bourgeois-democratic forms by *bourgeois-military* State forms seems to have acquired a certain inevitability. The existing structures of the capitalist world system and the imperatives of capital accumulation prevent the bourgeois State of the periphery from fulfilling the promise of development, conceived as an improvement in living standards. The strategy of the bourgeoisies of the periphery, who chose integration into the world market to maintain their own rule, can prevent neither growing social inequality and impoverishment nor economic bankruptcy. Social peace under such circumstances means simply the repression of labour and peasant movements and of any other movements for reform. The continued rule of the bourgeoisie depends in the final analysis on the support of the military.

But nor will the *bourgeois-military* State solve the economic crisis. On the contrary, unproductive military expenditure imposes a growing burden on national income, and secondly, economic concessions have to be granted to foreign capital in return for external military support. The bourgeois-military State of the periphery–as it has evolved in recent years and decades–is characterized by certain indicators of political crisis, viz.:

- The continuing and expanding diversion of resources to military purposes,[6] particularly in the Middle East.
- The maintenance and intensification of a state of emergency over a number of years, the suspension of freedoms, the maintenance of bans on trade unions and political parties for many years, the use of torture as a routine political instrument.
- Progressive surrender of national, political and economic sovereignty in return for external political, military and economic support. This includes the support, establishment of foreign military bases on national territory, the abandonment of protectionist economic policies, and the creation of enclaves for foreign capital in which the operation of nation labour legislation is suspended (free zones, etc.)
- Exacerbation of class antagonisms to such a degree that even the bourgeois and petit bourgeois middle classes, frequently willing aides and auxiliaries of the bourgeois-military State, are deprived of political power and threatened in their economic existence.
- Loss of political, economic, social and military control over entire areas, provinces, regions, with the growth of separatist and secessionist movements.

In its efforts to regain control over the conflicts generated by the economic and political crisis, the bourgeois-military State of the periphery seeks salvation through collaboration with imperialism. The price to be paid for this "assistance" is virtually the eclipse of the

State in the economy. In handing over control of economic activity to transnational corporations, their economies become effectively fully subordinated to the dictates and vagaries of the valorization of capital.

The current intensification of the economic and political crisis in certain countries exemplifies how the ruling bourgeois-military class of the periphery has very rapidly created its own crisis by stepping up the exploitation of the working population by both internal and external forces.[7]

Although Hobsbawm's observation that crisis is the constant accompaniment of capital applies both to the capitalism of the centre and to that of the periphery, nevertheless, the undisguised and growing inability of the peripheral bourgeoisies to guarantee even a minimum of economic, political and social stability creates conditions in which resistance to bourgeois-military rule can become so widespread that peasant and proletarian movements and certain strata of the middle classes may form alliances to oppose the prevailing system.

The Intensification of the Crisis

The period since 1945 has been the integration of most countries of the periphery into the world capitalist market. There are, however, exceptions. Power relations in a small group of countries have changed sufficiently for them to be able to resist successfully further integration, withdraw from it, or, at least, bring the scale and nature of their integration into the world market gradually under national control. This group comprises, among others, certain socialist developing countries.

The advance of socialist developing countries shows that it is feasible to create, within the time-span of a generation if not less, the foundations of an agricultural and industrial economy capable of satisfying the basic needs of the mass of the population. This presupposes a fundamental change in the relations of production and distribution, and in the nature of the country's incorporation into the international division of labour.[8] No doubt, it is the intensification of the conflict over fundamental change in the relations of production and distribution and in the incorporation of the developing countries into the capitalist international division of labour, which gives a special character to the class struggles of the present.

We would venture the thesis that all political movements seeking fundamental change as the prerequisite for overcoming under-development would always attempt to follow the path of change through parliamentary and non-violent means if such a path held out any likelihood of success. Historical experience suggests, however, that almost any attempt to change the structures of the capitalist world system by parliamentary democratic means meets resistance.[9]

Historical experience also shows that any change in power structures, as constituted in the relations of production and distribution in the capitalist world system, is only possible through the growth and application of power. For the exploited classes the most potent source of power lies in their political will to overcome exploitation. As development in the post-war period illustrated, this political will can be a force for changing power relations if the resolution to do so grips a majority of the people of a social class, a nation, a region or a group of States. Success naturally requires more; both the prevailing conditions for the accumulation on a worldscale, and the balance of power between the superpowers have to be conducive too.

Conversely, it was the lack of political will for change in the Western industrialized countries which allowed these countries – including their socialist and social-democratic parties and trade union organizations to become the conservative bastion of the global capitalist system during the two or three post-war decades. As Samir Amin once observed: "Nothing is happening in the North."[10] Whether this will remain the case in the present period of deepening crisis is a matter for speculation. Given its position as the power-house of world capitalism, it is necessary, if not sufficient, that far-reaching changes have to be made in the North before fundamental changes can occur in the capitalist world system.

The critical factor in turning the potential political will of the exploited classes into an effective transforming force is their capacity and preparedness for forming an alliance. The stars on the Chinese national flag still symbolize the alliance of peasants, proletariat and bourgeoisie which Mao Tse-tung regarded as a crucial prerequisite for the success of the Chinese war of liberation in the 1930s. Mao regarded this alliance as possible since all these classes suffered, albeit in differing degrees.[11] Though of a different character, the alliance of peasants, urban proletariat, middle class, and rural and urban marginalized groups was important in certain developing countries in that it facilitated revolutionary changes in national and international power structures.

In many countries and regions of the Third World, the economic crisis of the capitalist world system is not only giving renewed impetus to new alliances between and within the urban and rural proletariat, these alliances are also extending to the middle classes. Where this happens it is possible that the crisis may engender political forces strong enough to make further changes in international power structures, and push ahead with the delinking of the countries of the periphery from their present, all too unequal, incorporation into the international division of labour. It remains to be seen whether this possibility will crystallize in political action.

The present time of crisis is, of course, also a period in which conservative politics in the Western industrialized countries aim not only at entrenching the status quo of international relations of production and distribution, but also at changing the capitalist world system so that both obstacles to the valorization of capital and more importantly – the relative independence of a number of countries in the periphery are removed.

The United States has placed itself in the vanguard of the conservative politics of restoration – with the added intention of returning the USA to its former position of undisputed hegemonial power in the capitalist world system. Official American doctrine envisages a policy along the following lines:

- Firstly, retention of existing political and economic structures throughout the world in so far as they facilitate the unlimited pursuit and maintenance of American political, economic, and military interests.
- Secondly, regaining lost spheres of influence in the Third World and recapturing American control of those regions in which limits are currently placed on the maintenance of American political, economic and military interests.
- Thirdly, the prevention of any development in the Third World which could imply a change in global power relations to the detriment of the United States.

The revitalization of the military is given first priority in the implementation of this policy. What the inner dynamics of the capitalist mode of production cannot achieve, namely stable economic and political structures, and what political control cannot successfully execute, namely, the prevention of anti-capitalist movements in the periphery, is to be carried out using military means.

The International Monetary Fund (IMF) has had a leading role in advocating conservative policies for some considerable time. IMF exerts its influence on the countries of the periphery through its ability to grant or withhold vital stand-by credits, thus negating any pretensions to truly independent policies or development.

The reason why the mere control over credit enables IMF to render such effective support to conservative policies for controlling the periphery is not difficult to find. It lies in the consequences of the accelerated integration of many countries of the periphery into the world market in the post-war period. The exploitation of the periphery, on the one hand, and even more so, the unbalanced sectoral and regional export-oriented and import-dependent economic structures of the periphery, on the other, have forced increasing numbers of countries to tread the humiliating path to IMF and apply for stand-by credits. If a country's economy is on the verge of breakdown, if vital goods cannot be imported, if economic bankruptcy is threatening, credit-seeking countries have little choice but to accept IMF's terms and conditions, which correspond to the main criteria of conservative economic policy.[12]

In recent years more than 100 countries have been forced to approach IMF for stand-by credits. The conditions which IMF attaches to the granting of credits, requiring in essence the application of liberal-conservative policies in the credit-seeking countries, hardly vary from one country to another, and pay scant regard to specific national economic circumstances. Under the guise of stabilization programmes, IMF regularly demands the abandonment of any national economic policy, and in particular any self-reliant policy for agriculture, industry, trade, finance, or social welfare geared to the needs of the population. In place of such policies IMF requires the establishment of economic and social conditions which impose few if any limitations on the operations of transnational corporations. Almost without exception the conditions call for:

- The liberalization of external trade and payments, and in particular the removal of import controls, foreign exchange controls and other protectionist instruments;
- The removal of restrictions on the activities of foreign capital, such as discrimination against foreign capital, in particular branches and sectors, and limitations on the transfer of profits;
- The devaluation of national currencies (frequently, the payment of individual branches of loans already granted is made dependent on additional devaluations;
- The reduction of State subsidies for food, health and transportation which shelter the low-income groups;
- Change in budgetary policy intended to reduce direct and indirect taxes on companies and to increase direct or indirect subsidies for companies (e.g. provision of investment finance, infrastructure and industrial inputs);
- A reorientation of national economic policy and development towards increased promotion of production for export, with the concomitant neglect of areas producing for domestic demand and consumption, and an eventual increased dependency on imports;
- State intervention in the determination of wages and other incomes, whereby–notwithstanding the free market principles otherwise propagated by IMF–the State is assigned the role of guaranteeing low wage levels.

In reality, IMF's policy of "conditionality", or the withholding of a loan, portrayed as a policy of financial stabilization, ignores the prerequisites for stable trade and payments;[13] it is in fact a policy designed to perpetuate the integration of the developing countries in the capitalist world market.

The insistence on the uninhibited transfer of profits has a destabilizing effect on trade and payments, since it renders a considerable portion of foreign currency earnings unavailable for meeting payment obligations. The insistence on devaluation, allegedly to boost exports and limit imports, in combination with the liberalization of trade and payments, exercises a destabilizing effect since, with declining demand on world markets, it can only lead to a fall in export earning and an increase in the price of vital imports. The insistence on cutting State subsidies which benefit the poorest sections of the population has a directly destabilizing effect. "Its inevitable result is to turn the population against the government and to dismember social alliances supporting regimes embarking on a course of internal reforms and economic independence, often resulting in the demise of the government and the installation of authoritarian regimes."[14]

The policies of IMF have so far fallen short of their goal of stabilization. IMF is now itself on the brink of a liquidity crisis and now finds itself confronted with a series of debtors teetering on the verge of default.

The implementation of IMF's policy aimed at maintaining the existing structures of capitalism does not relieve the poverty of the Third World. Sooner or later the costs of maintaining a minimum of political stability in the face of the disruptions wrought by the crisis will exceed the gains which this stability is intended to guarantee. Even some conservative voices are now being raised about the course of the present crisis. Kissinger–one of the architects of conservative global politics–seems to have started doubting the wisdom of a policy "forcing developing countries to reduce their standard of living drastically over a long period (which) is likely to weaken precisely those moderate governments that are the most likely to accept Western Advice.[15]

Against Pessimism

The struggles for or against the imperatives of global capital are certain to intensify in the coming years. It is equally certain that at present the champions of conservative economics are on the offensive given the proved incapacity of reformist social-democratic policies to manage the crisis. But there should also be no doubt that the political, economic, social and ecological effects of these policies will strengthen the resistance to the imperatives of capital accumulation on a world scale, not only in the countries of the periphery, but in the Western industrialized countries and the socialist countries.

As far as this latter group is concerned, it should not be overlooked that conservative policies, especially the revival of the military, serve to reinforce the populations' rejection of the capitalist system and its corollaries.

In a few years' time the conservative policies, currently followed in the majority of Western industrialized countries, will be found incapable of dealing with any of their pressing economic, ecological and social problems (as they have already been found wanting in the periphery). Resistance to world capitalism will grow in the Western industrialized countries with the support of many heterogeneous movements.

There is hope, therefore, that resistance to further and greater exploitation and plunder in the countries of the periphery, to the imperatives of capital accumulation on a world scale, will find allies amongst a growing number of people in the Western industrialized countries, and – in defiance of anti-social offensive in the socialist countries too.

There seems to be a certain pessimism, according to which the possibility of a transformation of the capitalist world system into a truly humanized system is not viewed as possible since even non-capitalist countries seem incapable of disentangling themselves from the imperatives of accumulation in a largely capitalist world. This pessimism feeds off the fact that countries whose declared development perspectives are non-capitalist, in fact socialist relations of production and distribution have only made small advances along their intended paths. However, such pessimism and resignation is not justified.

Delinking from the world market system and a transformation of the system itself do not take place through individual regions and countries suddenly replacing capitalism by socialism.

Delinking from the system, and the transformation of the system itself, are a process which cannot be governed by a single strategy. The heterogeneous anti-capitalist movements worldwide will have to shape their own strategies in the light of the existing conditions.

NOTES

1. For a more elaborated discussion of the causes of the crisis, see Folker Frobel, Jurgen Heinrichs, Otto Kreye, "Wage aus der Wirtschaftskrise?", in *Physik, Philosophie und Politik*, Festschrift fur Carl Friedrich von Weizsacker, ed. by Klaus Michael Meyer-Abich (Munchen; Hanser, 1982), pp. 145-167; forthcoming English version: "Dead end; Western economic responses to the global economic crisis", In *Development as Social Transformation* (United Nations University publication).
2. Michel Aglietta, *Regulation et crises du Capitalisme* (Paris; Calamann-Levy, 1976); Giovanni Arrighi, "Towards a theory of capitalist crisis". *New Left Review,* No. 111, September-October 1978; Robert Boyer, "La crise actuelle :une mise en perspective historique" Critiques de 1 *economie politique*, Nouvelle série, 7-8, April-September 1979; Andre Gunder Frank,

Reflections on the World Economic Crisis, in Frank, *Reflections on the World Economic Crisis* (New York; Monthly review Press, 1981); David Gordon, 'Stages of accumulation and long economic cycles', in *Processes of the World system,* ed. by Terence K. Hopkins and Immanuel Wallerstein (Beverly Hills, London L Sage; 1980); Andre Granou, "La nouvelle crise du capitalisme", *Les Temps Modernes,* No. 328, 1973; Eric J. Hobsbawm, "The crisis of capitalism in historical perspective", *Socialist Revolution,* No. 30, 1976; Stephen Hymer, "International politics and international economics: A radical approach", in Hymer, *The Multinational Corporation: A Radical Approach* (Cambridge : Cambridge University Press, 1979), pp. 256-272; Ernest Mandel, *Late Capitalism* (London; NLB, 1975); James O'Connor, "Accumulation Crisis", 1978 (mimeo); Christian Palloix, *Travail and Production* (Paris; Maspero, 1978); Thomas Weisskopf, "The current economic crisis in historical perspective", *Social Review,* No. 57, 1981, pp. 9-53.

3. Eric Hobsbawm, op. cit., p. 78.
4. World Bank estimate (Neue Zurcher Zeitung, February 11, 1983).
5. For a recent study on this subject, see Ernest Feder, *Perverse Development* (Quezon City; Foundation for Nationalist Studies, 1983).
6. The growth of military spending of developing countries over the period 1972-1981 was about twice as high as that of their gross domestic product. See *Trade and Development Report,* 1982. (UNCTAD/TDR/-2/Rev.1), United Nations publication, Sales No. E. 82. II d. 12, paras. 536-550.
7. The bourgeois-military class still ruling in a certain country once justified the liquidation of a bourgeois-democratic government on the ground that it would install an exemplary model of stable social and political development for the periphery, as prescribed by economic, neo-classical economics.
8. For a contribution to this debate, see Samir Amin, "Crisis, nationalism, and socialism", in Samir Amin, Giovanni Arrighi, Andre Gunder Frank, and Immanuel Wallerstein, *Dynamics of Global Crisis* (New York and London, Monthly Review Press, 1982), p. 218; see also Samir Amin, "After the new international economic order: the future of international economic relations", *Trade and Development,* No. 4, 1982 United Nations publication, Sales No. E. 83. II. D.1.
9. See Herbert Marcuse, *Counterrevolution and Revolt* (Boston; Beacon Press, 1972); "The Western world has reached a new stage of development; now, the defense of the capitalist system requires the organization of counterrevolution at home and abroad. . . . The counterrevolution is largely preventive and, in the Western World, altogether preventive," pp.1-2.
10. cf. Samir Amin, "La vocation Africaine et Asiatique du Marxisme" Project "Strategies for the future of Africa", Dakar, 1983 (mimeo).
11. Mao Tse-tung, "On the tactics in the struggle against Japanese imperialism" (27 December 1935), *Selected Works,* vol. 1 (Peking, Foreign Languages Press, 1968) pp. 153-178).
12. We cannot broach the question here whether this explanation, which certainly applies in cases like Brazil, fully accounts for cases like Zaire. Owing to Brazil's high level of integration into the world capitalist market economy, it dare not risk being unable to import the inputs indispensable for its economy, in particular petroleum and food for its huge urban masses, who lack access to direct subsistence. By contrast, a country like Zaire with a relatively low degree of capitalist market integration could (as Tanzania

has done) risk being unable to pay for its imports, since its population could still, if necessary, resort to national sources of food and other vital materials.

13. Sally A. Shelton, Vice-President of International Business Government Counsellors and from 1979 to 1981 U.S. Ambassador in the Caribbean, puts it this way in an article contributed (together with Richard Nuccio) to the *New York Times;* "This year's crisis will develop because, not in spite of, the conclusion of IMF agreements by the major debtor countries; because, not in spite of, the renegotiation of their debt." (*International Herald Tribune*, January 28-29, 1984.

14. "The Terra Nova Statement on the International Monetary System and the Third World". (A working group to consider the nature of the international monetary system and its impact on Third World countries was convened at Terra Nova Hotel, Kingston, Jamaica, October 5-7, 1979. The meeting was sponsored by the Dag Hammarskjold Foundation, the Institute for Policy Studies, the International Foundation for Development Alternatives (IFDA), the Latin American Institute for Transnational Studies (ILET) and the Third World Forum, and organized with the collaboration of the National Planning Agency of Jamaica)

15. Henry A. Kissinger, "Saving the world economy", *Newsweek*, January 24. 1983.

FOUR

Economic Structure, Trade and Regions

BERT HELMSING

Introduction

The effects of the changes in the international division of labour (between countries) on the interregional division of labour within each of the participating countries are by no means well understood.

In regional studies literature two main views are held on this issue. The first one considers each largely a separate issue, treating different dimensions of development, at different levels of analysis. Regions were seen as open economies, but mostly its contacts with the "rest of the world" were not differentiated with regard to their domestic or international origin. With the increasing attention to the multinational enterprise a point of overlap and contact was created, namely, the locational analysis of the MNC's and its regional consequences (of Storper, 1981 and Hayter and Watts, 1983).

The second view has particularly gained acceptance with the rise of dependency-cum-imperialism approaches to regional development. Realizing the danger of gross generalization, this view holds that the international division of labour takes predominance over the interregional structure of a country. A top-down sequential conditioning takes place: international centre periphery structures shape (inter) regional centre periphery relationships. Quite true, there are considerable differences between, for instance, Myrdal (1957), Frank (1968), Slater (1975) or Massey (1978), and one is much more specific than the other on this issue. But on the whole it is argued that a Third World country finds itself in an (historically developed) unequal trade relation with centre countries, and that its internal (interregional) structure is not only historically shaped by that trade relation, but also that the continued (postcolonial) international trade dependency causes a worsening of the (inter) regional problem. A macrocephalous urbanization process (metropolitanization or development of primacy) is seen as one of the results of the international insertion (of Quijano and Castells in Schteingart 1973). Similarly, as interregional economic relations remain structured along "international colonialist" lines, regional inequalities are exacerbated.

Although some mechanisms through which international effects are mediated downwards are identified (MNC's and state policies), many conclusions are based on a sort of parallel argumentation (e.g. c-p relations of one level that are "reproduced" at another level). This has a certain common sense appeal. After all, regions are more open economies than nations and, therefore, are bound to be more susceptible to external influences. Perhaps matters are not so clear-cut however. Historically, and prior to processes of national integration by industry, quite some Latin American countries had one or some individual regional economies that had strong international ties, stronger than those with other regions with which it formed a national unit. It is reasonable to argue that this fact influenced the regional shape of the national integration process and the interregional division of labour that evolved with and which was a product of it. However, international factors are not the only ones involved. In some cases and instances they do play a key role, in others clearly not or at a very reduced level, along with other factors.

In this paper and on the basis of a review of the Colombian national and the regional development processes we will discuss the relation between the two divisions of labour. In doing so we will hold the view that as the national integration proceeds, the interregional division of labour more and more complements the international trade participation of the regions. That is to say, national integration processes draw regional economies increasingly into market and trade relations. This may either be international or interregional trade, such depending on a number of factors. Since it is unlikely that both the interregional and international trade account of a region can remain negative in the long run, a trade deficit on one account has to be compensated by a trade surplus on the other account. For example, a region may be a large net international exporter and because of it, at the same time, a large net interregional importer. Similarly a region (e.g. the capital region) may be a large international net importer, and at the same time dominate interregional trade.

In the following three sections we will discuss the major features of the Colombian development process focussing on agriculture, industry and international trade, describing functional and spatial processes. In the first one the early industrialization process (1900-1950) is briefly analysed against a background of some historical facts. The second section deals with the period in which major transformations took place in agriculture and in which industry largely completes its import substitution process. The third section describes the changes that took place in the 1967-1980 period in which the relation with the international economy was altered under the new economic policy of export promotion.

A comparison of the regional changes as they took place under different national and international conditions of each period allows us to appraise in Section 5 the relation between the international and the interregional division of labour.

Early Industrialization and Agricultural Change

One of the early development problems of Colombia was that it lacked a strong international sector. The country failed for a long time to develop a viable export base and because of this the country lacked also the resources to build and maintain a strong central State. There were a number of shortlived attempts to replace gold production which already before Independence had entered into decline. None of those (tobacco, quina and some textile products) succeeded. Taking into account its geographical features, there was in fact little that united the various regions.

In passing it is perhaps useful to mention that the country is carved up by three spurs of the Andes Mountains, which run north-south and around the various valleys regions have developed. The eastern highlands are the most populated part of the country (Cundinamarca, Boyaca and Santander). In the north the Andes gives way to the Atlantic Coast region, of which some parts because of their role in the natural transport system have a long development history. Finally there are several vast natural regions with very low population densities, such as the Llanos Orientales, the Amazon region and the Pacific Coast.

These geographical features constitute formidable barriers to communication and movement. For instance, by the end of the 19th century it was cheaper to transport a commodity from Liverpool to

Medellin, than from Medellin to Bogota (Ospina Vasquez, 1951 and McGreevey, 1975). The weak export base and the absence of a dominant national elite, able to displace the old landed groups, led three decades after Independence to the adoption of a federal structure which enabled a minimization of conflict among the variously structured regional oligarchies. In fact only by the end of the 19th century the "Regeneration" culminated in the reinstitutionalization of a unitary political-administrative structure (1986), but with considerable powers vested in the departments (Ruiz, 1982). Departments had a large resource base, controlled key functions such as police, education, immigration, land settlement, roads and railways, etc. (Tirado Mejia, 1981). This change towards a unitary system coincided, not surprisingly perhaps, with the development of coffee as a new export sector from 1870 onwards.

Traditional regional power was gradually circumscribed as new departments were created and functions transferred to or displaced by the central government. The "War of a Thousand Days" (1899-1902) was the last of a regionally inspired civil war, which resulted in the creation of five new departments (Narino, Caldas, Atlantico, Huila and Norte Santander). The growth of the coffee exports contributed to the strengthening of the central government. The growing revenues derived from these enabled the expansion of central government institutions and activities, either directly financed or on the basis of now accesible foreign loans.

In the first decade of the present century coffee came to constitute around one-third of total Colombian exports. Partly due to the changing world market in coffee in favour of the fast growing post-First World War US economy, coffee exports rose rapidly to 70 per cent of total exports in the 1920's. This share went down during the Great Depression only to recover after the Second World War, rising to more than 75 per cent in the 1950's.

Without doubt it was the growth of coffee production and exports that in various ways enabled industrialization to take place (Urrutia, 1979). First of all, the structure of coffee production was much less concentrated than in other agricultural sectors, generating a more favourable distribution of (monetary income), and thus constituted an important source of demand for manufactured products. Secondly, the growing coffee exports generated the foreign exchange necessary to finance the imports of industrial machinery and raw materials. To this, one may add as a third point, that the coffee exports stimulated the creation of the much needed transport infrastructure, which enabled the physical entry and movement of industrial equipment. During the 1920's great advances were made in the expansion of the various railway networks of the country (Mcgreevey, 1975). Finally, the emergence of the industrial bourgeoisie is related, though not exclusively, with coffee production and trade (Brew, 1977).

In addition to coffee, several other factors should be kept in mind which contributed to the establishment and consolidation (as from 1930) of the manufacturing sector. First of all the temporal interruption of foreign competition particularly during the First and Second World Wars, and during the depression when protective measures, made necessary because of the reduced capacity to import, created a similar effect. A further factor of importance has been the import of foreign loans and capital, particularly during the 1920's with which the public works in transports were partly financed. Foreign (US) private capital concentrated mostly in oil extraction (Escorcia, 1978).

The main branches of manufacturing concerned basic consumer goods, such as food, beverages, textiles and clothing. The development of the sector as a whole was based entirely on internal final demand and continued to rely on import of intermediate and capital goods.

Industrialization was not a widespread phenomenon, but developed largely in the Antioquia-Caldas coffee region (Medellin and to some extent Pereira and Manizales), in the eastern coffee region, Cundinamarca (Bogota), and some port cities, like Barranquilla. Notwithstanding it constituted a powerful stimulus to the integration of local and regional markets. This is also evidenced by the tendency of oligopoly formation, first on a regional and later on a national basis. In the production of textiles, beer, tobacco, and some food products like chocolates such processes occurred in the 1930's and 1940's. Periods of reduction of competitive imports, marked great spurts in oligopoly formation by means of absorption of competing firms, followed by periods of incorporation of new technical progress leading to larger plant size, which in its turn led to a further consolidation of these market structures (Helmsing, 1979).

In Table 4.1 annexed it can be seen that the two most industrial regions accounted for 50 per cent of total manufacturing net output. The growth of industries, trade and the state fomented urbanization. Not only is the growth of urban population higher than the rural one, but particularly the departmental capital grew at above average rates. Within this group the largest ones (Bogota, Medellin, Cali) and towns located in coffee producing area grew fastest.

TABLE 4.1: **Manufacturing Net Output and Employment, 1945-1980 by region**

	Net output					Employment				
	1945	1958	1967	1975	1980	1945	1958	1967	1975	1980
Antioquia	25.3	24.8	23.7	21.1	22.6	26	24	25	24	25
Atlantica	13.1	9.0	8.3	7.7	6.2	11	10	9	8	8
Bolivar	3.3	2.7	3.7	4.9	6.2	4	2	2	2	2
Boyaca	2.2	2.2	2.5	2.6	2.6	3	3	2	2	2
V. Caldas	6.0	5.2	4.6	4.9	4.9	6	5	5	5	6
Cauca	1.1	0.7	0.7	0.9	0.6	1	1	1	1	1
Cordoba	a	0.1	0.2	0.1	0.1	a	0	0	0	0
Cundinamarca	25.3	27.1	25.8	30.3	28.0	20	30	30	33	33
Huila	0.3	0.4	0.3	0.3	0.3	1	0	0	0	0
Magdalena	0.9	0.6	1.0	0.6	0.6	1	1	1	1	1
Meta	b	0.1	0.4	0.3	0.3	b	0	0	0	0
Narino	0.6	0.6	0.6	0.4	0.4	1	1	1	1	0
Nor. Santander	1.1	0.9	0.9	0.8	1.0	2	1	1	1	1
Santander	5.3	5.3	5.5	5.2	7.8	7	5	4	4	4
Tolima	2.7	1.5	1.1	1.0	1.1	3	1	1	1	1
Valle	12.6	18.5	20.3	18.5	17.1	13	16	17	16	16
Total	100.0	100.0	100.0	100.0	100.0	100	100	100	100	100

a = included in Bolivar
b = not available

Source: Census of Manufacturing Production, Bogota, various years taken from: Helmsing (1983 b)

With regard to agriculture, it is important to recall some fundamental historical aspects. The agrarian structure is dominated by the latifundium-minifundium complex. Large haciendas are found in the fertile valleys, high plains and lowlands, whereas peasant holdings are situated alongside on less fertile land and on the mountain slopes. Agriculture was most developed in the more temperate Andean regions. Some subtropical regions were just recently colonized (Antioqueno Colonization) but tropical agriculture was virtually undeveloped. Very extensive livestock production, if anything at all, prevailed in regions such as the Coasta Atlantica and the Llanos Orientales.

The developments of coffee production had relatively little direct effect on domestic agriculture. Its labour requirements made that it could be easily incorporated into peasant household production in the newly settled lands of Antioquia and Caldas. In Cundinamarca where most production was organized on large haciendas, it did put, however, pressure on traditional tenancy relations. The major impacts on agriculture came from the public works, the industrial expansion and the urban growth. The demands for labour contributed to uproot traditional forms of tenure that had tied labour to the land. Secondly, there were local regional impacts in terms of demands for urban food and industrial raw materials. These effects were mostly felt in the Andean regions in the interior (Cundinamarca, Tolima and Valle). Peasant organization during the thirties produced some positive change during the Liberal governments (improvements in land tenure laws and some land redistribution).

The regional pattern of the development of agricultural production was relatively clear. Market production expanded most around the big cities and in a pattern consistent with the industrialization process. Cundinamarca and to a lesser extent Antioquia concentrated most of the agricultural production, but maintained diversified production areas (Bejarano, 1979).

With regard to the regional distribution of Colombia's international exports it is found, not surprisingly, that by the end of the period (1950) Caldas and Antioquia were the major contributors, each with respectively 37 and 21 per cent of total Colombian exports (see Table 4.2). Being the third coffee producing region Cundinamarca ranks third with 12 per cent. Other regions contribute with secondary exports products, such as Magdalena (banana), Santander (tobacco). Consistent with the pattern of industrialization and urbanization the four most developed departments concentrate 83 per cent of the international imports, but within this group there is a manifest differentiation in the sense that Cundinamarca alone accounts for almost one-third (31%) of total imports. The relatively more prominent role of port or port related towns such as Barranquilla and Call is in all probability due to the fact that here we find more specialized import trade firms.

TABLE 4.2: **Origin of International Exports and Destination of International Imports Distribution by Region, 1950-1980**

	Exports					Imports				
	1950	1958	1967	1975	1980	1950	1958	1967	1975	1980
Antioquia	21	22	28	22	27	19	13	11	13	14
Atlantica	1	1	4	4	4	18	14	11	6	6
Bolivar	1	3	5	9	5	4	4	4	1	2
Boyaca	0	0	1	0	2	0	1	4	0	0
Caldas	37	45	35	29	37	5	3	3	2	2
Cauca	1	2	2	1	2	0	0	0	0	0
Cordoba	0	0	1	0	0	0	0	0	0	0
Cundinamarca	12	5	7	13	10	31	46	49	60	61
Choco	0	0	0	0	0	0	0	0	0	0
Guajira	0	0	0	0	0	0	0	0	0	0
Huila	0	0	0	0	0	0	0	0	0	0
Magdalena	3	4	4	5	3	1	1	1	0	1
Meta	0	0	0	0	0	0	0	0	0	0
Narino	0	1	1	1	0	1	0	1	0	0
Nor. Santander	8	9	3	1	0	2	0	0	0	0
Santander	7	4	2	1	0	2	3	3	1	3
Tolima	4	2	1	1	1	1	0	0	1	0
Valle	5	2	6	12	9	15	14	12	14	11
Total	100	100	100	100	100	100	100	100	100	100

Source: Anuario de Comercio Exterior, DANE, Bogota (various years).

If we look at the net interregional foreign exchange flow we find that Caldas contributes 64 per cent and the two Santanderes another 22 per cent. The largest net user is Candinamarca (38%), followed immediately by Atlantico (33%), and at a lower level Valle (19%). It is interesting to observe that Antioquia, much in line with its "independent" reputation, generated within its own department the foreign exchange it requires to finance its international imports. Finally it is important to mention that a number of regions had no or hardly any direct international trade participation. Here we not only refer to aparted frontier regions such as Choco and Meta, but also old established but subsistence regions like Narino, Huila, Boyaca and Cauca. From this brief account it can be concluded that this first period has been a very dynamic one, various processes of change in part reinforced each other : the production and export of coffee created demand and the reduction of competitive imports due to external factors stimulated a domestic supply response in manufacturing. Furthermore, coffee production made possible an accumulation of capital which under the prevailing conditions could best be profitably invested in the domestic industry; the infrastructure made possible by and necessary for the mobilization of the coffee exports, unified and extended some regional markets for industrial production. The infrastructural works employed rural labour, stimulated rural-urban migration and contributed to the formation of urban labour markets. The migration fuelled the process of urbanization which in its turn amplified the demand not only for industrial products but also for agriculture. Given the technological conditions of agriculture, these new opportunities could best be met through raising local regional peasant production. The development of Colombia as an industrializing, agricultural mono exporting nation contributed to shape the interregional division of labour, particularly in as far as the Andean interior is concerned. Immediately it should be added that many regional economies were as yet little affected, particularly the Atlantic Coast and the southern part of the country. Not to mention the fact that large parts of the territory were not even settled at that time.

Impact Substitution and the Evolving Interregional Division of Labour

The change from the one to the other period was marked by a spectacular investment boom following immediately the Second World War and the beginning of years of rural conflict, known as "La Violencia".

The first greatly expanded domestic manufacturing capacity and together with balance of payment problems as a result of (temporary) decline in coffee export earnings, induced governments to adopt import substitution policies. The recurrent and in many respects systematic government protectionist intervention marks an important difference with the previous period. Although it should be added immediately that the policy was dominated by b.o.p. considerations rather than a conscious and deliberate industrial development objectives (Montes y Candelo, 1981).

For the period as a whole (1950-1967) manufacturing industry grew at an average real rate of 8.1 per cent. The greatest contribution came from the intermediate product sector namely, 3.7 per cent, while the consumer goods sector contributed 2.7 per cent, and the capital goods sector only 1.7 per cent (Montes y Candelo, *ibid*). This is the stage in the import substitution process which the country had already achieved. The importance of import substitution as a source of growth is well illustrated in the following Table 4.3.

TABLE 4.3: **Percentage Change in Manufacturing Production by Subsectors, 1951-1968**

	Change in domestic demand	Change in exports	Import substitution	Total
Consumer goods	93.5	3.6	3.1	100.0
Intermediate goods	71.8	−0.5	28.7	100.0
Capital goods	53.3	0.6	46.1	100.0
Total manufacturing	84.2	1.1	14.7	100.0

Source: Montes y Candelo (1981), *op cit.* Table 6

Although sectorwise the pattern of manufacturing growth conformed the import substitution model, it should be stressed that on the whole changes in domestic demand (final and intermediate) were far more important than the external sector, either on the import or on the export side. In fact the increase in import duties on consumer goods hardly produced any growth effect at all, and consequently must be seen in the context of domestic price rises.

To analyse the regional pattern of changes a shift and share analysis has been conducted over the period 1945-1958 and 1958-1967. Limitations of space prevent us to elaborate on the details. These can be found elsewhere. (Helmsing, 1983 and Helmsing, forthcoming) The major conclusions are presented here. The regional pattern of output change in the 1945-1958 period reveals some very clear changes. Whereas industry in Antioquia, the "oldest" industrial area, grew slightly below the national average, Cali (Valle) becomes firmly established as the third industrial centre of the country. The extraordinary growth of output in Cali can to a large extent be explained by the expansion of the Buena Venture harbour at the Pacific coast which made Cali an attractive alternative transhipment point to Barranquilla in the North. Output growth in the latter department (Atlantico) consequently fell behind. This trend continued up to the present day. A second important region is found in the agro-processing, particularly sugar refining. Valle together with the capital city region Cundinamarca contained almost the entire positive shift. Peripheral regions such as Narino, Norte Santander, Tolima and Magdalena have not only a relatively unfavourable industrial structure, but these performed also worse than elsewhere (neg. shares). The same also applies to regions that do not have a clear peripheral status such as Bolivar and Viejo Caldas.

The fact that the period is one of protection from foreign imports, one could interpret the relative interregional changes as in a zero sum context. That is to say there is a direct relation between the high growth of the central industrial regions and the relatively poor industrial growth performance in the periphery.

In the second part of the period the slow growth of domestic demand manifested itself in a relative stagnation of consumer goods industries, something which explained the relative standstill of the "early" industrial regions, such as Cundinamarca and Antioquia. In contrast, Valle continued to grow fast; thanks to the growth of foreign dominated intermediate goods production. A parallel differentiation is found within the periphery, where some regions experience fast growth on the basis of a particular branch of intermediate production (e.g. Santander, Bolivar and Boyaca), while other regions continued to stay behind.

Perhaps two conclusions stand out: (a) the far greater source of growth was domestic demand, rather than the external sector (import substitution or export growth). Changes in the domestic conditions of demand (e.g. migration) and the evolving oligopolistic market structure must, therefore, be seen as the principal factors explaining the regional pattern of change (b). For those sectors where the external sector constituted a more important role, the regional pattern of change is not of a centre-periphery nature, but differentiation took place within both.

In order to explain the developments in agriculture a number of factors need to be taken into account. I have already mentioned the "Violencia" which in certain regions had devastating effects. It contributed to uproot the traditional tenure relations and distribution of ownership. Many peasant small holders/tenants left their holdings, often never to return (Oquist, 1978). The rural exodus from the areas of violence which may have involved more than two million people–mostly ended up in the towns but also led to settlement of new land mostly in tropical regions (e.g. Caqueta, Putumayo, Meta, Medio Magdalena).

Another major factor has been new technology that came available after the Second World War, which made large-scale entrepreneurial production feasible (Kalmanovitz, 1976). Supply condition shifted in favour of the landlords. Thirdly there was a considerable increase in demand for agricultural products. During the intercensal period 1951-1964 urban growth was as high as 5.7 per cent per annum. The proportion of population living in towns rose from 39 per cent in 1951 to 53 per cent in 1964. Also the growth of industry stimulated the demand for agricultural output. The latter did not result automatically. It is known that textile firms continued to import cotton. Only after the domestic market was shielded from foreign competition, could the *agricultural import substitution process* start (cotton, soya, sorghum, and African palm oil).

During the fifties the government agricultural support system was built up, i.e agricultural extension, some marketing facilities and credit. The growth of the public sector for the greater part took place at the national level, and implied a de facto centralization process.

Finally one should recognize the role of producer association as vehicles for the rapid diffusion of technological know how and as the channels for procurement of inputs and marketing of output (cotton, rice, coffee, banana). These associations often emerged in a response to monopolistic trade and industrial firms.

Table 4.4 annexed summarizes some of the main aggregate features of agricultural development. The so-called commercial crops, which refer to those that are predominantly used as inputs for industry, have been the most dynamic elements in the transformation of Colombian agriculture. Their share in the value of crop production almost doubled from 10 to 19 per cent and continued to grow thereafter but at a lower pace. The fact that on the whole neither land not labour productivities changed very rapidly, indicates that a geographical widening of the base of transformation occurred. Only in the sixties and early seventies a strong deepening took place.

The production of basic foodstuffs such as maize, cassave, plantain, and potato–with the noteable exception of rice at the end of the period–remained within the realm of peasant production. Given the

TABLE 4.4: **Annual Growth Rates Agricultural Production, Land and Employment Colombia, 1951-1973**

	production		employment		crop acreage	
	51/64	64/73	51/64	64/73	51/64	64/73
Commercial crops	8.3	3.8	8.5	-4.1	7.4	2.1
Mixed crops	1.7	-0.7	1.1	-8.0	0.8	-0.4
Traditional crops	2.6	0.7	2.2	-4.2	0.8	2.1
Plantation	2.1	0.4	1.6	-4.8	2.3	0.6
Minor crops	3.0	5.0	1.6	-1.2	2.3	10.6
Agriculture	3.0	1.2	2.0	-5.0	2.0	2.0
Livestock	4.0	4.1	1.2	-3.8	2.0	1.5
Total	3.3	2.9	1.7	-3.7	1.0	1.2

Based on: DNP, 1977, *op cit*, p. 158

fact that productivity increases were very low, the only way to explain increased supply is through the continuation of market incorporation of peasant agriculture and the expansion of the latter through land settlement. In the sixties the development of the agro-industrial complex took a great leap forward. It had two major features. Firstly, the growth in production resulted in exportable surpluses (cotton, rice and sugar). Secondly, the new technologies that enabled the large increases in productivities–HYV's and related inputs, raised the capital requirements of production and this threatened to marginalize the participation of the small holder farmers. The number of small holdings as well as agricultural wage employment, which had gone up in the fifties, went down in the sixties.

At the moment that industrial growth slackened and the employment absorption capacity of industry was severely reduced, capitalist agriculture started to expel rural labour and peasant agriculture was threatened to be marginalized. Two policy solutions were put forward to solve the "social" problem. One was to keep the peasants in the countryside. Recognizing the social function of landownership, land reform would be the principal instrument. The second was an urban solution via a programme of (labour-intensive) urban housing construction. Both solutions were experimented with by successive governments. Though there were outspoken differences with regard to the "social" issue, there were remarkable similarities on how to tackle the economic problems. Instead of seeking to stimulate domestic demand–eventually by means of some redistributive measures–a re-orientation towards external demand was aimed for. To this end a number of major reforms were introduced in 1968.

What were the regional aspects of the emerging structure of agricultural production? As already implied above there was a considerable expansion of the agricultural frontier. First, in terms of a transformation of the estates to capitalist production. Particularly in the interior and later in the Atlantic Coast. Secondly, in terms of peasant land settlement, which occurred on a fairly large scale in the south and south-east of the country, but extended basically to tropical areas all over the country (Helmsing, 1982). On the basis of regional land use data available for the principal sixteen crops it was found that agricultural production expanded most notably in the Atlantic Coast. Here expansion occurred in commercial crops like cotton, sorghum and rice. In addition, Antioquia extends its local regional agricultural frontier considerably. With regard to the commercial crops it can be concluded that some already specialized production areas switch to other (more profitable) crops and new specialized production regions emerge (sorghum, barley), in part replacing existing ones (barley, rice and cotton). With regard to the mixed and traditional crops, changes in the interregional distribution of production are much more limited. Either there are no specialized production areas at all (maize and plantain), and when they are there (mostly for climatic reasons only) these tend to account for a growing proportion of production (potato, beans, and tobacco).

With regard to the changes in the regional participation in international trade the following major conclusions can be drawn. Whereas exports in the 1950s were completely dominated by coffee, which originated for the greater part in two regions (Caldas and Antioquia), in the sixties a considerable diversification started to develop (cotton, rice and sugar), which extended regional participation (Atlantico, Bolivar and Valle). The most remarkable changes are found, however, on the import side. There is a persistent tendency for Cundinamarca, the capital city region, to monopolize international import trade. Its share went up from 31 per cent in 1950 to 49 per cent in 1967. All other regions (except Boyaca and Santander) see their direct participation decline. Unfortunately we do not have detailed information on the sectoral composition at the regional level. However, it appears that this change cannot be explained adequately by the urbanization, regional, agricultural and industrialization processes alone. As to the pattern of international net foreign exchange flows, based on the analysis of the trade balances of each region, it can be concluded that while the number of net contributors increased with a less polarized distribution, the opposite occurred with the net receivers. Consequently interregional trade must be dominated increasingly by the capital region as this constitutes a way to cover its growing deficit.

Perhaps a major conclusion of the analysis of sectoral and spatial change in the period is that the evolving interregional division of labour does not arise so much from externally induced factors, but from physical and economic integration of the country (growth of Cali vs decline of Barranquilla and formation of national oligopolies), and the considerable extension of the land frontier and the development of national market organization of industrialized agriculture. If any externally conditioned process is of importance it is the import substitution process but not with regard to industry but concerning agriculture.

International Restructuring and Regional Differentiation

In 1968 a number of reforms were carried out which aimed at exports as a new source of accumulation and growth, and to the end a structural adjustment of the economy was an imperative. The exchange rate regime was changed so as to avoid large b.o.p. problems by means of frequent small devaluations (crawling peg). Fiscal incentives for exports were increased drastically first only for manufactured products but later (1970) also for agricultural ones. New export promotion institutions and funds were created, including free trade zone in the main cities. Finally, the Andean Pact gave an additional export stimulus (Bejarano, 1978). Later governments extended this policy in neo-liberal fashion by considerably lowering the nominal tariffs on manufactured imports. It should be added, however, that the latter policies were also inspired by other events, in particular the coffee price bonanza of 1975-76.

Together with the economic reorientation, an institutional reform also took place, which expanded considerably the role of national, semi-autonomous public agencies. Some figures on the distribution of expenditures by level of government are quite revealing in this respect. In 1950-52 the share of central government and agencies in total public expenditure was 63 per cent. In 1969-71 this share had risen to 79 per cent (DNP, 1977) and in 1980 it had become 85 per cent (Controlaria General de la Republica, 1983).

The effects of the new policy on the growth of manufacturing industry can be seen in Table 4.5.

It is clear that in both sub-periods export has become a much more important source of growth. For the sector as a whole exports contributed 9 to 10 per cent respectively to the average real rate of growth.

TABLE 4.5: **Decomposition of Growth in Manufacturing by Sector, 1967-1974 and 1974-1980**

	1967-1974				1974-1980			
	total change	domestic change	export change	import subst	total change	domestic change	export change	import subst.
Light cons gds	5.35	4.92	0.61	-0.18	5.18	4.64	0.67	-0.12
Cons dur gds	9.52	6.42	0.65	2.46	7.95	8.98	1.02	-2.05
Intermed. gds	10.92	10.30	0.92	-0.28	5.47	5.57	0.27	-0.04
Capital gds	10.00	6.79	0.35	2.96	6.03	8.67	0.64	-3.04
Total	8.52	7.48	0.74	0.30	5.63	5.90	0.54	-0.82

Source: R. Chica Avella, 1983, table 2, pp. 83-84

However it should be added immediately that domestic demand had become less important. On the contrary it even increased somewhat. The problem is that trade liberalization had a negative effect, particularly in the second sub-period. Without going in too much detail suffice it to say here that the rhythm of capital accumulation went down in the second part of the seventies not only due to the world recession but also due to restrictive policies of the government to curb the inflationary effects of the coffee, and illegal drug trade booms had a similar impact (Piedrahita, 1980). The latter ones are the main cause that the world recession started really to be felt in Colombia only in the eighties.

The change in economic policy attracted a considerable increase in the volume of foreign investment. By 1974 firms with (major and minor) foreign participation were estimated to contribute no less than 45 per cent of total manufacturing exports (Arango, 1976). In this respect there is a clear link between the changing participation of Colombia in this international division of labour and the role this played for the foreign firms active in the country.

If we look at the pattern of regional change for the period as a whole it can be concluded that within the industrial core a "re-concentration" occurred favouring the capital city region, Cundinamarca. The Cali region in particular lagged behind. And it is notable that Atlantico in the north (Barranquilla) did not benefit clearly from the export drive. In spite of its free trade zone it continued to stay behind. Also the trend of "differentiation within the periphery" continued very clearly during this period. Bolivar and Santander experienced an above average growth, which is almost entirely due to their insertion as producer of intermediate resource based output (chemicals, oil and oil derivates).

The effect of foreign investment on the regional industrial division of labour is not simply one of accentuation of trends. In fact 80 per cent of foreign investment up to 1974 is estimated to be concentrated in the three principal regions. In this context it is striking to observe that foreign investment became much more important to Antioquia and Valle than to Cundinamarca. The effect was hence opposite to the overall tendency towards concentration and centralization.

For agriculture, the new policy orientation aided and strengthened an already emerging tendency. The new policy measures offered new incentives for the expansion of capitalist agriculture.

Now that both manufacturing industry and capitalist agriculture were leaving the confines of the domestic market, price intervention lost rationale. Price control systems were either altered or eliminated altogether and the international prices came to rule more directly the domestic market. For the period as a whole the pattern of growth was influenced by three different processes. Firstly, with regard to the non-traditional agricultural exports the initial expansion (to 12 per cent of total exports in 1975) was followed by the progressive collapse of international market prices and the skyrocketing of prices of chemical inputs. Secondly, the traditional export of coffee was greatly affected by the price boom in 1975 and the subsequent production increase following a frost calamity in Brazil. The share of coffee in total exports, which had gone down to 43 per cent in 1974, subsequently rose again to 59 per cent in 1980 (Parra Escobar, 1982). The complex problem the government had to face was to absorb the vast increase in the purchasing power caused by the booms and to avoid an inflationary process and revaluation of the peso which would undermine the recently developed export diversification. Exchange controls were adopted and the trade liberalization after 1975 was in part a response to mitigate domestic inflation and upward valuation of the currency. However, the policy failed partly because of a decline in non-traditional exports as a result of the world recession. The other reason refers to the third major ongoing process in agriculture. That is to say the stagnation of peasant agriculture. Several factors need to be considered here. First of all Colombia had passed in the late sixties the structural transformation point after which its rural population started to decline in absolute numbers (Johnston and Kilby, 1975). The shares of rural and urban population in 1973 were the reverse of 1951. Rural population was only 36 per cent (DNP, 1977). Secondly, and related with it was the fact that the continued land settlement in the outlying tropical regions did not compensate any more the rural exodus in the Andean zone and the older established tropical regions. Thirdly, the agricultural policy had for decades neglected peasant *production*. There was no adequate extension or research, neither credit nor marketing, to raise peasant agricultural productivities. Since the extension of the agro-industrial complex had not been fast enough to incorporate traditional and mixed crops into the realm of large-scale capitalist agriculture–though certainly inroads were made, e.g. in rice, cassava and potato–peasant agriculture came to constitute a real economic problem. In 1976 an integrated rural development programme was initiated, which still is being carried out.

The changes in the regional division of labour in agriculture in this period are not so easily to establish. On the whole it appears that live-stock production intensified and was partly displaced in a Von Thuenen like manner to outlying regions (Llanos, Amazonas). With regard to industrial crops specialization continued and was accompanied by important shifts from one region to another (rice, sorghum and barley). Production became entirely organized at the national level. With regard to the mixed and traditional crops no such tendencies could be clearly observed except for cassava and to an extent maize. If the concentration patterns at the level of each region are examined it is found that in the core regions levels of specialization acutely declined. The agro-regions in the north and interior show marked tendencies towards specialization in a few crops. In the peripheral regions such as Cauca, Norte Santander, Narino and Boyaca, specialization levels are not only lower but these remain stable or decline. The regional peasant economics that continue to predominate in these regions maintain diversified crop patterns.

With respect to the regional participation in international trade, the following major trends could be observed. Consistent with the changes in the relative importance of coffee exports, Caldas' contribution first declined to an all-time low of 26 per cent in 1974, and to rise again to somewhat below 40 per cent. A similar pattern of change is found for Antioquia–the only core region with a positive international trade balance–although not only coffee but also manufactured exports play a role here. In an opposite manner Cundinamarca, Bolivar and Valle first increased their participation, thanks to non-traditional exports and which later declined. For the remainder, most peripheral regions no major change was observed. In Table 4.6 annexed the importance of international exports is measured for each region. Not only is there a very large absolute variation among regions, but there is also considerable change over

TABLE 4.6: **International Exports in Relation to Gross Product by Region, Colombia, 1960 and 1975**

	1960	1975		1960	1975
Antioquia	17.4	16.8	Hulia	0.6	0.0
Atlantico	3.8	6.5	Magdalena	18.4	25.3
Bolivar	5.8	17.1	Meta	0.0	0.0
Boyaca	1.5	0.7	Narina	7.3	3.8
V. Caldas	71.6	52.5	Norte Santander	44.6	3.5
Cordoba	2.0	1.5	Santander	10.7	1.2
Cundinamarca	2.7	5.1	Tolima	7.6	1.5
Choco	3.7	4.2	Valle	1.8	10.5
Guajira	0.0	1.6	Colombia	17.5	14.0

Source: Annuario and Comercio Exterior, Dane, Bogota (various years) Cuentas Regionales de Colombia, Innandes, Bogota.

the period which does not conform a c–p pattern. The tendency already observed since 1950 of a concentration of international import trade continues almost unimpededly. By 1971 Cundinamarca concentrated 62 per cent and throughout the seventies it maintained this. With this the region became the only major interregional net receiver of foreign exchange.

Some Final Observations and Conclusions

During the first three decades of the present century the country began a process of integration of the various regional economies aided by the development of external trade and of domestic industrialization. Up to the beginning of the fifties only a relatively small part of the territory and population was affected by it. Several regional economies were not yet drawn into a market based interregional division of labour, while the first stage of the industrial import substitution was already almost completed and with it the basis of the regional industrial structure.

In the second period some clear changes could be observed in the interregional division of labour and these do not so much arise from externally induced processes of specialization, as from physical integration of the country, a considerable incorporation of new land and existing agricultural regions and the formation of *national* oligopolies and markets for manufactured products. If any externally conditioned factor played an important role it was an *agricultural* import substitution process. In the third period considered here sectoral growth processes became increasingly regionally selective. This seems to be the key feature of the changes in the interregional division of labour. Neither core nor periphery advances stay behind in a uniform fashion. Differentiation takes place within each and there is reason to doubt that the observed changes in the country's participation in the international division of labour are the prime cause. The centralization in government and in business, both foreign and Colombian, and in agriculture and industry (and other sectors) contributed to increase the leakage and transfer of benefits and resources to core regions, so that macro analytically impact multipliers of export growth in peripheral regions decline (Helmsing, 1983).

Although it is difficult to come up with conclusive evidence it must be concluded in the case of Colombia that the effects of the changing participation in the international division of labour are much less evident than expected. Considerable changes took place in the interregional economic structure. Most of these changes can, however, be attributed to other factors than the changing international participation, such as physical integration, land settlement and agricultural transformation and the centralization of government and enterprise.

REFERENCES

Arango, J.A. (1976). Inversion extranjera en la industria manufacturera Colombiana. *Boletin Mensual de Estadistica* nrs 302 and 303 Bogota: DANE

Bejarano, J.A. (1978). Industrialization y politica economica. In *Colombia Hoy*, eds M. Arrubla, J. a. Bejarano. J.G. Cobo Borda, J. Jaramillo Uribe, S. Kalmanovitz, J.O. Melo, A. Tirado Mejia, pp 221-271. Bogota: Siglo Veintiuno Editores.

Bejarano, J.A. (1979). *El regimen agrario de la economia exportadora a la economia industrial*. Bogota: editorial La Carreta.

Brew, R. (1977). *El desarrollo economico de Antioquia desde la Independencia hasta 1920*. Bogota: Banco de la Republica.

Castells. M (1973). La urbanizacion dependiente en America Latina. In *Urbanizacion y dependencia en America Latina*, ed. M. Schteingart Buenos Aires: editorial SIAP.

Chica Avella, R. (1983). El desarrollo industrial Colombiano, 1958-1980. *Desarrollo y Sociedad* nrs 12: 19-125.

Controlaria General de la Republica (1983). *Estadistica Fiscal del Estado*, 1977-1981, Bogota: Controlaria General de la Republica.

Departmento Nacional de Planeacion (1977). La Economia Colombiana 1950-1975 *Revista de Planeacion y Desarrollo* 3, 9: 7-278.

Escorcia, J. (1978). *Historia economica y social de Colombia*. Bogota: editorial Presencia.

Hayter, R and Watts, H.D. (1983). The geography of the enterprise: a reappraisal: *Progress in Human Geography* 7, 2: 157-182.

Helmsing, B. (1983). Agricultural production in the periphery: settlement schemes reconsidered. *Development and Change* 13,3:401-419.

Helmsing, B. (1983a). Agricultura, industria y desarrollo de regiones. *Revista Interamericana de Planificacion* 17, 66:91-117.

Helmsing, B. (1983b). Industrialization and regional division of labour: analysis of patterns of change in Colombia. Working Paper no. 19. The Hague: Institute of Social Studies.

Helmsing, B. (Forthcoming) Dependency or differentiation? Regions and industrialization in Colombia. *Tijdschrift voor Economische en Sociale Geografie*.

Johnston, B.F. and Kilby, P. (1975). *Agricultural and Structural Transformation*. London: Oxford University Press.

Massey, D. (1979). In what sense a regional problem? *Regional Studies* 13: 233-244.

Mcgreevey, W.P. (1975). *Historia economica de Colombia*, 1845-1930. Bogota: Editorial Tercer Mundo.

Montes, G. and Candelo, R. (1981). El crecimiento industrial y la generacion de empleo en Colombia: entre la substitucion de importaciones y la promocion de exportaciones. *Revista de Planeacion y Desarrollo*, 13, 1/2: 87-132.

Myrdal, G. (1957). *Economic theory and underdeveloped regions.* London: Duckworth.

Ospina Vasquez, L. (1974). *Industria y proteccion en Colombia*. Medellin: Editorial Oveja Negra (first published 1955).

Oquist, P. (1978). *Violencia, conflicto y politica en Colombia*. Bogota: Banco Popular.

Parra Escobar, E. (1982). La economia Colombiana: 1971-1981. *Controversia* n r. 100. p. 97.

Quijano. A. (1973). Dependencia, cambio social y urbanizacion en America Latina. In Schteingart, M. op cit.

Ruiz Llano, J. (1982). *Administrative reform in Colombia: the limits of decentralization.* The Hague: Institute of Social Studies, M.A. thesis.

Slater, D. (1975). Colonialism and the spatial structure of underdevelopment—outlines of an alternative approach with special reference to Tanzania. *Progress in Planning* 4: 137-162.

Storper, M. (1981). Toward a structural theory of industrial location in *Industrial Location and Regional Systems*, eds J. Rees, G. Hewings, H. Stafford. New York: Bergin Publisher Inc. Tirado Mejia. A. 1981. Algunas caracteristicas regionales de Colombia. Paper presented in National Seminar on Decentralization, Bogota, Sept. 1982 Universidad de los Andes—Cider and FESCOL.

Urrutia, M. (1979). *Cincuenta anos de desarrollo Economico Colombiano*. Bogota: Editorial La Carreta.

FIVE

Technological Change, Economic Restructuring and the New Spatial Division of Labour

MANUEL CASTELLS

Cities and regions, worldwide, are undergoing a fundamental change under the combined impact of two intertwined processes: the current technological revolution, particularly in the fields of micro-electronics and communications, and the restructuring of capitalism (and of the international economy) to supersede the world crisis of the 1970's. This paper explores the connection between high technology, economic restructuring and the urban-regional process, resulting in a new spatial division of labour internationally, interregionally and within the large metropolitan areas.

The current process of technological change is characterized, as everybody knows, by the fact that it represents a new form of production, based on information and knowledge as the major sources of productivity. Yet, its development is taking place within the existing modes of production (capitalism and statism) whose logic it tends to reinforce. Furthermore, high technological activities are largely determined by their role in the process of economic restructuring taking place in all capitalist countries and, therefore, in the international economy, as such economy is basically shaped by the logic of advanced capitalism.

Thus, to understand the structural sources of the new spatial division of labour, we have to recall the main trends of the process of economic restructuring as well as the specificity of the process of production generally identified under the term "high technology".

The high technology refers to something else than to a new technique of production. It is a *new form of production* (based on information) and, therefore, of social organization. But its development is taking place within the context of the fundamental restructuring of our economic system. It is irrelevant to ask which comes first. Both processes, the restructuring of capitalism and the informational mode of development, are historically linked. They go together, reinforcing each other. Today, we are not in the crisis any more (though we might be soon in another recession). We are rather in the phase of implementation of economic policies aimed at reorganizing the very bases of the model of accumulation *within the realm of capitalism.*[1] Though "Reaganomics" have generally been associated with the main premises of this new model, we would not like to reduce the debate to a simple critique of the policy of a given U.S. Administration. In fact, the Reagan Administration has considerably departed from some key postulates of Reaganomics, such as the reduction of the government deficit. To understand in-depth the process of change we are undergoing, we have to look at the essential, lasting elements of the new economic model that is being put forward both in the USA and in Europe (regardless of the political tendency, since similar policies are implemented both by the Thatcher *and by Mitterrand since* 1983), and are also largely imposed on many Third World countries by the means of the requirements of the International Monetary Fund to refinance overdue debt payments:

(a) The first, the most fundamental attempt, is to redefine the relationship between capital and the labour in the production process, increasing productivity and dramatically reducing labour costs, breaking down, if necessary, the social contract reached between business and organized labour in almost all capitalist countries in the aftermath of the 1930's Great Depression and after widespread social mobilization by workers. So, when things come to the worst, capitalism returns to its most straightforward logic to raise profits: to extract more value from labour by increasing both relative and absolute surplus value, that is, trimming employment, containing wages and benefits, and increasing productivity through work speed-up, rationalization and automation.

(b) Secondly, the fight against inflation is led through budgetary restrictions that disregard the social contract also in the sphere of collective consumption, while at the same time the military budget is increased, both to provide markets for the industry and to ensure the new tools of world power. And again, this is true at the same time for the USA and for France. It represents what, following the hypothesis I formulated years ago, we call the transition from the Welfare State to the Warfare State.

(c) The third major trend, and the most global one, is the growing internationalization of the capitalist economy with a total interdependency of the different national economies and new, international division of labour, with the emergence of competitive economies in the Asian Pacific rim. The interpenetration of the national economies happens at the level of capital, labour, markets, and of the production process, in an economic space of increasingly variable geometry. Corporations, governments and individuals (through migration) all have incorporated themselves into the new dynamics of the international economy. Countries and nations have ceased to be the economic units of our historical reality.

It is our hypothesis that high technology is playing a major role in these processes of fundamental realignment. So, in the following pages we will briefly try to examine the relationship between high technology, the labour process, the transformation of the public sector and the internationalization of the economy. We will also focus, for each one of the three major processes under analysis, on the urban and regional consequences of the role played by high technology in the overall process.

Our analysis will rely mainly on information on the USA, but we will refer, in a more casual way, to other societies, and we will emphasize the impact of each process on the spatial dimension of the international economy.

High Technology, Labour and the Urban Process

What we refer to as "high technology" is not an industry, an activity or a device; it is *a process, a particular way to produce* characterized by the key role that *information* plays in the production process. In this sense, "high technology" (understood as information-based production) is penetrating everywhere, and most rapidly in those activities where capital finds strong resistance from labour. Thus, it eliminates labour massively.[2] At the same time, because it requires a great input of skills, of knowledge, of managerial capabilities, it greatly expands the sphere of highly skilled, professional labour, yet falling short of matching quantitatively the jobs it suppresses.[3] Furthermore, the development of information-based production is not limited to manufacturing: it actually requires a concomitant expansion of so-called "producer services", so that the distinction between goods-producing and service producing industries is increasingly blurred.[4] The productivity generated by high technology and the income it induces in the highly paid professional sectors create the basis (both in terms of investment and demand) for a wide range of service activities and consumer-oriented downgraded manufacturing, fed by labour displaced from other sectors or other countries. Both processes reinforce each other and require each other. So, polarization of the labour force is a fundamental and necessary process of the informational mode of development.[5] Yet, this polarization does not amount to a new process of class formation, because the two poles are not in direct relationship of production. Both are elements of the same system of polarized growth and re-skilling-de-skilling of labour. But the class relationships have been obscured in the process. To the cleavage between ownership and management introduced in the capitalist pole, we now have to add the cleavage between machines and manual workers, and between information-processing and actual material production spreading all over the labour process. It does not follow that we are in a classless society, but that the relationship between production relations and people's experience is much more abstract, and can be found only at the level of the whole dynamics of the system, which has less and less meaning at the level of social political practice, that emerge around different, more cultural categories and strategic forms of behaviour.

In spite of some uncertainty of existing information, several trends seem to appear quite distinctively in terms of the impact of high technology on the labour process:

(a) By spurring automation in factories and offices, high technology directly suppresses a substantial number of working hours. The fact that this translates into the suppression of jobs is a matter of the social organization of our economy, not of the technology,

(b) By putting pressure on the existing jobs, technological change curbs labour and makes it less resilient to capital's strategies,

(c) While hightech activities generate new economic growth, and thus jobs, the new jobs in hightech industries fall largely behind the number of jobs their impact eliminates,

(d) The occupational structure of hightech industry is characterized by a bipolar distribution of skills, rank and income. Such an occupational structure is amplified by the social characteristics of labour with white male at the top, women and minorities at the bottom,

(e) By contributing to a more dynamic economy, hightech does create jobs indirectly. But these jobs tend to be in a growing service sector (basically in business services and in personal services, much less in public services) whose occupational structure tends to follow also the bimodal polarized pattern of hightech, if anything even more pronounced. So, the new jobs created are less skilled, less paid, more insecure and, above all, less unionized than those destroyed,

(f) Consumer durables manufacturing that survives automation is dramatically downgraded in the same terms that the low end of the service sector, more and more using immigrant labour (sometimes undocumented in the USA), women and minorities.

It does not follow that micro-electronics or biotechnology is part of a capitalist conspiracy to exploit workers. But it is clear that technological change takes place in certain historical conditions and that its use is shaped by these conditions. What in our epoch amounts to be a major instrument in the undermining of the bargaining power achieved by labour through hard social struggles, *vis-a-vis* capital.

Since this analysis refers mainly to the USA, it seems useful to consider the variation of the effects of high technology on labour in other context that, for the sake of simplicity, we will reduce to three situations:

(a) In Western Europe, the strength of the labour movement and of socialist parties (in Italy of the Communist Party) represents an obstacle to the over-exploitation of labour. This is, in our opinion, the main reason for the tremendous difference in job creation between the USA and Europe.

During the 1970's, while the U.S. economy generated 20 million new jobs (most of them in services), Western Europe lost two million jobs. This trend is likely to accelerate with the introduction of new technology. The more labour resists, the more there will be an incentive for automation, particularly in the heavily unionized manufacturing sectors.[6] New jobs are being created, but many of them, for instance in Italy or in Spain, are being provided by the informal economy, to save labour costs by cutting social benefits.[7] Thus, the real debate will increasingly be the sharing of working-time, and the social and political pressures on capital to force the social redistribution of some of the productivity gains of the technological revolution,

(b) In the newly industrialized countries (such as Korea or Brazil), it seems that the tendency is towards a simultaneous increase in the exploitation of labour and in productivity through advanced technology, to increase their competitiveness in the international economy. While this process will still be largely under the financial control of international capital (through the mechanisms of lending and of the interest rates dictated by the U.S. economy) the overall process is likely to improve the relative position of NICs as manufacturing centres,

(c) For most of the developing world, including large sectors of the NICs the new technologies will increase the surplus population, putting political pressure on the public sector to absorb labour in government-sponsored jobs, and fuelling even more a sprawling urban informal economy, as well as the process of migration to the new global or regional work centres.

Now, if we turn to *the spatial consequences of the restructuring of the labour process,* we can summarize the trends in three major features:

(i) There is an increasing the international and interregional division of labour between skilled production and routine assembly operations, particularly in high technology industries,[8] but not only for them.[9] What the new technologies allow is precisely the disjunction between different operations across spatial distance, with communications being able to restore the necessary links between different production units.[10] There follows a considerable acceleration of the process of uneven development and the disequilibrium of the spatial structure.[11] The polarization of hightech-dominated production leads to sharp regional cleavages and to the formation of "ghettoized" areas of selective economic activity (of the San Jose's Silicon Valley or Boston's Route 128 type), increasingly distinct or remote non-metropolitan locations of low-skilled jobs.[12] And this not only for electronics but for most manufacturing and service activities that can be disassociated in space according to the specific characteristics of their labour force;[13]

(ii) The largest metropolitan areas are going through three combined, but distinct processes, *within the same space*: growth of corporate services and high-tech manufacturing, decline of traditional activities (both in services and manufacturing), and development of the new downgraded, *yet booming*, economic sectors.[14] This process of *polarized growth* creates very distinct spheres, yet it has to relate these spheres within the same functional unit. We observe, therefore, the rise of dualized metropolises that segregate internally their activities, social groups, and cultures, while reconnecting them in terms of their structural interdependency.[15] These metropolises are real magnets at the world level, attracting people, capital, minds, information, materials and energy, while keeping separate the channels of functioning of all these elements in the actual fabric of the metropolis. We are not in a situation of crisis and decline, but in a process of interactive growth between elements that ignore each other, while in fact being part of the same system. We are witnessing the rise of urban schizophrenia. Or, in other words, the separation between cities and society within the same space;

(iii) The spatial dynamics of cities and regions of a specific country will depend upon their place within the hierarchy of functions and processes in the international division of labour. For instance, the higher the country in the hierarchy of financial capital, the more advanced corporate services will play a role in its metropolises, and vice versa.[16] The larger the traditional manufacturing sector in a given city, the more its decline or rise will depend upon the vulnerability of labour to capital.[17] The larger the public sector in a given economy, the more the dynamics of regions and cities will be relatively autonomous of international flows of capital and commodities. Thus, to some extent, the relationship between labour, capital and cities is itself determined by the global dynamics of capital and by the specific form this dynamics takes within the socio-political context of each country.

High Technology and the Spatial Form of the Warfare State

The most far-reaching element of the current economic restructuring is the transformation of the role the State has held in the economy for the last 50 years.[18] Not that it is withdrawing from economic interventionism, quite the opposite. But the form and the context of government intervention are deeply changing, shifting their focus from accumulation and redistribution to selective accumulation and military reinforcement. It would be a mistake to consider this trend solely a product of the Reagan Administration, though its policy represents a qualitative step in this direction.[19] But, the last two years of the Carter Administration already showed a significant reversal of the redistribution role of the State, actually echoing policy orientations developed by the Nixon-Ford years. And in Western Europe similar orientations toward retrenchment of social expenditures and to the imposition of strict limits on collective consumption are apparent in Thatcher's England, in Mitterrand's France, in Kohl's Germany or in Craxi's Italy.[20]

The Welfare State is in crisis,[21] not because of excessive social transfers, but because an increasingly older demographic structure, combined with increased costs of health care and higher unemployment underlines the conflict between private appropriation and collective redistribution of the economic surplus. Thus, when the State was riding the crest of economic growth with socially accepted inflation during the 1960's, it could provide both for social welfare and for capital investment, including the military and aerospace expenditures. In the case of the USA, the Great Society's programmes, the Vietnam War, and the "Man in the Moon" were financed at the same time. But the price of doing it without excessive taxation was precisely increasing government borrowing (particularly at the State and the local levels), and money supply, triggering an inflationary trend that went out of control, once energy and food prices skyrocketed. In other words, to buy social peace and pursue social redistribution without altering its support of capital investment and business profits, the government (all governments) financed their expenditures with inflationary measures. When, to curb inflation, they had to choose between different chapters in the Budget, they went on trimming social expenditures, precisely at the moment when the economic crisis created most hardship for more people in all countries. The retrenchment of the Welfare State has been particularly pronounced in the sphere of human and community services.[22] The partial dismantlement of the Welfare State in the USA and the impact of this trend on urban programmes and services have been documented by Norman J. Glickman, in one of the most synthetic studies on the matter.[23] He shows a dramatic and rapid reduction from 1979 onwards, from 12.4 per cent of federal outlays to 9.1 per cent in 1982 and a projected 7.5 per cent in 1984.

In a parallel movement, the emphasis of federal spending has been shifted to defence spending. Arms demand, and thus arms production, has soared on a world level. While countries such as France, Israel, Italy, West Germany, England and Brazil (not to mention the USSR) are active exporters in the weaponry business, the USA is the leading producer and active exporter in absolute numbers. According to the Boston Study Group, U.S. production accounted in 1970 for about 20 per cent of total arms transfers in the world, and the figure in 1982 was 45 per cent.[24] The movement is accelerating; in 1974, foreign sales of U.S. weapons amounted to $ 10 billion; in 1982, to $ 21 billion, and in 1983, the projection was $ 31 billion.[25] Concerning its own military spending, the U.S. Government is engaged in a massive build-up, particularly since 1981: actual spending rose from $ 156 billion in 1981 to $ 205 billion in 1983. But the real acceleration is yet to come: the Reagan proposal for 1985 was $ 264.4 billion, for 1989, if re-elected, an astounding $ 398.8 billion. To complete the picture of military spending we should also include a proportion of the budget of other administrations (such as for NASA, an estimated 25 per cent), Department of Energy (Nuclear-related Research), CIA-covert operations, and National Guard's expenses (supported by individual States).

The tendency is very clear in the world in general and in the USA in particular: fiscal austerity for social expenditures, and tremendous expansion of military expenditures.[26] We are witnessing an increasing militarization of the economy as Martin Carnoy and myself have argued elsewhere.[27] Why is this so? Certainly, any trend related to the State has primarily political roots.[28] Increasing competition between the superpowers, struggles of liberation in the Third World, manipulation of national antagonisms both by governments and by foreign agents, fights of influence over countries between the West and the East and a rampant Cold War are all elements of an increasingly tense and dangerous world. The response, particularly in the USA after the defeat of Vietnam, has been to raise the stakes, using the technological superiority of the West to try to alter the balance of power, with the ultimate illusion of winning an advantageous edge that will enable the USA to impose its conditions around the world. The Soviet Union followed the same logic, having committed itself to a military build-up even greater than the one by the USA in proportion to its GNP, and the process has spiralled. The National State in general, and the American State in particular, are getting ready for war of all kinds, from an all-out war to a limited commando operation, passing through "limited local nuclear wars" or large-scale battles with conventional weapons and, of course, military support and training for subrogated armies.

The current economic restructuring is fundamentally shaped and conditioned by this political-historical trend. It is not the other way around. It is not because of the economic crisis the governments engage in military spending. This is too much a mechanistic view of how governments operate. What is true is that the economic crisis has increased international tensions, creating a favourable environment for the military build-up. But the defence policy itself has deeper historical and political roots that we cannot analyse here, in this already too broad paper. What matters for our subject is that the State, while disengaging from its commitment to Welfare (having politically subdued, at least for now, social resistance to austerity politics), has engaged itself in war-preparation activities. And the economy, whose dependency from military expenditures was *decreasing* during the 1960's and first half of the 1970's, is now being restructured around a core of highly profitable industries directly related to military production. *And here is where high technology enters into the picture.*

Many of the technological breakthroughs of the past 40 years, particularly in the field of electronics, have been induced or supported by military demand or the space programme.[29] The emphasis on performance, the low elasticity of price, and the abundant funding, characteristic of the military, were key elements that helped the scientific research and the technological developments more than a short-term commercial demand, necessarily concerned with market profitability.[30] In this sense, the State continues to be the Prince for scientists and researchers, provided they accept the lack of control over the use of their inventions.

Nevertheless, during the mid-1970's, consumer products and new machinery were becoming increasingly important applications of the high technology, especially in electronics. But the new surge in defence spending has reversed the trend in the USA, actually leaving the lead in consumer electronics to Japan. In the USA the gigantic military build-up of the past 10 years is spurring development of the high-tech industries, which in turn rely on the defence market to produce for other purposes a modified version of their products. Thus, the process seems to be operating in the way shown in the below diagram.

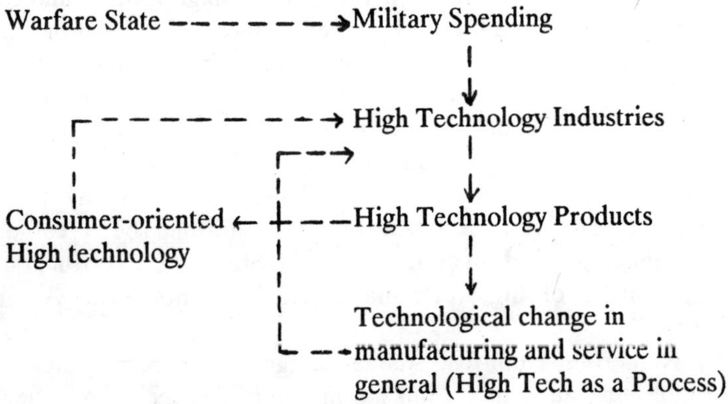

So, we do not pretend that all high-tech is military-related production. But the source of most high-tech industries is, and this has a necessary impact on the type of high-tech industries, on their products, on the employment and, as we will see, on the urban and regional consequences of high-tech-induced economic development.

But it should be clear that the *growing militarization of the U.S. economy is not a result of high technology.* In fact, the Japanese experience shows that high-tech can expand very rapidly in consumer-oriented, or even in social-service oriented products. And many current developments in the USA also follow this pattern (from computer-stimulated walking systems for quadraplegics to factory robots). But the bulk and the core of high-tech manufacturing, and therefore of the characteristics of the technologies being researched, are connected to the military market.

Ann Markusen is currently pioneering research in this field. Based on her own study and on another empirical study by David Henry, she shows that: "heavily defence-dependent manufacturing sectors are dominated by those in the high-tech category and that a substantial proportion of high-tech industries are important military suppliers".[31] As she points out, the effect of the Reagan Administration defence build-up is particularly visible in the growth of defence output in all but one of the 36 four-digit sectors studied. A striking figure is the 141 per cent defence output growth in electronic computing equipment. In her study, Markusen calculated that these 36 sectors of military-related high-tech production accounted, in 1977, for 47 per cent of all high-tech manufacturing employment. Given the rapid increase since 1977, the proportion is likely to be higher now and, if we consider the projections, it will be even more so in the near future. Also the regression analysis by Glassmeier, Hall and Markusen[32] showed that defence spending per capita across a set of 226 metropolitan areas was the most significant variable explaining high-tech dependence in the economy of a given metropolitan area, a result that is confirmed by a completely independent study carried out by Steven Pinkerton on the distribution of high-tech manufacturing among the American States.[33]

Numerous empirical studies all go in the same direction of establishing an intimate linkage between high-tech production and military procurement. For instance, a study found that in 1970, defence spending accounted for 48 per cent of all aeronautical engineers, 23 per cent of physicists, 21 per cent of electrical engineers, 19 per cent of all mathematicians and 16 per cent of industrial engineers.[34] And another study reported that 59 per cent of the aeronautical engineers, 38 per cent of the physicists, 22 per cent of the electrical engineers, 20 per cent of the technical engineers, and 20 per cent of the metallurgical engineers were employed by the Defence Department or by defence-related industries.[35] Thus, the expansion of high technology production in the USA is, in general, a direct consequence of the militarization of the economy, although its impact on the economy, on the society and on spatial forms goes far beyond the original matrix.

This evolution from the Welfare State to the Warfare State is reshaping the urban and regional structure of the USA. Norman Glickman has attempted to measure this impact by calculating the rates of growth and decline of federal outlays for selected programmes, between 1981-1984, for different cities and regions, typologized by a number of key variables.[36] He shows that all welfare-related programmes decline substantially, while Defence spending increases sharply, particularly in the chapter "procurement". But even more interesting is the fact that inter-city and inter-regional variations of both social and defence expenditures follow almost systematically opposite patterns. Defence spending increase is more pronounced than average in high-income, non-declining low unemployment and "low-hardship" areas; in medium and small, rather than large cities; and overwhelmingly concentrated in suburbs, though this last result (interestingly enough) is exclusively due to the high suburban concentration of *defence procurement.* In terms of regions, while concentration ratios for social expenditures vary across the country, depending upon programmes, defence expenditures are heavily concentrated in the West, South Central, South Atlantic, Mountain and particularly in the Pacific regions. A study by Glassmeier, Hall and Markusen also reports similar trends with high-tech defence-related activities being the most spatially concentrated of all high-tech sectors, and showing a preference for the Southwest and the West, for medium-size cities and for suburban locations when they are adjacent to large metropolitan areas.[37] Why is this so? Markusen proposes a number of reasons: large extensions of underdeveloped land are required, both for building of huge material structures and for the requirements of testing equipment; clear weather all the year around for easy testing of aircraft and missiles; skilled labour, isolated from the metropolitan environment, and if possible from unions, located in self-contained residential communities close to the production facility, is also a fundamental condition of military-related production; but the main reason seems to be historical and cultural:

the existence of huge military bases (for instance linked to the war in the Pacific) and the anti-urban, anti-"big city world" feeling of the military, particularly significant if we consider the sizeable cross-over between the Army and management positions in the military industry. Also, Western and Southwestern States have consistently lobbied to attract military-related production facilities. Ann Markusen poses the question of the spatial form of the military-industrial complex. Could it be–we ask–the endless Southwestern desert or the infinite Pacific Ocean, ridden by the last cowboys, the nuclear cowboys, in their winged, propelled horses, coming back in the evening to their small, clean town, to pray in the community church together with their family, which also has remained nuclear and indestructible?

Whatever the reasons, it is clear that the military connection of most high-tech activities, induced by the State, has had an enormous impact on the spatial dynamics of the USA, shifting investment, jobs and people toward new lands in the outskirts of the metropolitan areas, and in the south and western regions where new activities and new social environments could be recreated, far away from the constraints of a State that was the depository of the social contract agreed upon by classes after decades of struggle. The new urban and regional landscape segregates social universes besides classes or races, adding a new cleavage to the already existing forms of segregation. It is the cleavage between the emerging production system, determined by the Warfare State and generator of a new culture[38] (still unnamed), and the declining system of production and social organization, in which the State had become too deeply penetrated by interest groups and historic compromises to be an adequate tool for the commanding height of the economic and political elites. The restructuring of the State actually precedes, and determines, the restructuring of the economy, itself relying on a high technology-led process of production, that fundamentally reshapes the spatial forms. The Welfare State was born in the furnaces of life of the large inner cities. The Warfare State expands over an abstract space of distance and silence.

The New International Economy, Technological Change and Spatial Structure

The growing internationalization of the economy is a fundamental element of the economic restructuring under way in the capitalist system. Though it has been a crucial feature of the expansionary period of 1945-73, the crisis of 1974-75 and the subsequent policies of both corporations and governments have increased the interdependency of the national economies, trying to overcome the crisis by winning a competitive edge over other economic units by investing, producing or selling in the most advantageous locations at each particular moment.

The process of internationalization concerns certainly the exchange of commodities, but international trade is by no means the most important, let alone the newest, aspect of the new world economy. The process of internationalization concerns, as well, capital flows, migration of labour, the production process, and the organization of management of economic units.[39] The combined result of this process is a complete reorganization of national economies and of their spatial structure, and this is even more so for less developed and newly industrialized countries.

Which are the main features of such a process? First of all, the organizational logic of multinational corporations gives support to the tendency toward a space of flows attempting to supersede the space of places.[40] Nevertheless, at the same time, the global reach of the corporation needs a network of advanced services, a material infrastructure, a series of communications facilities, and even a social milieu, that have come to be associated with the high-ranking downtowns in the largest metropolitan areas of the world.[41] So, we find both a tendency toward the delocalization of the logic of the economic process and toward the concentration of decision-making units in a few commanding heights of the international economy.

Secondly, much of high technology manufacturing epitomizes the new spatial division of labour, with the locationally distinct hierarchy between research and design, and assembly-line operations therefore spearheading the new space of global production. Furthermore, high technology makes possible, and actually accelerates the internationalization of the production process[42] at three levels:

(a) Because the value of the products in "high-tech" is increasingly linked to their informational component, the light weight of many of these components, together with transportation technology, make easier the spatial division of labour:

(b) The process of automation and the increasing precision of machine tools (particularly numerical machines and robotization of the assembly process) make possible a large-scale standardization of the components of most manufacturing activities, and their recombination wherever the location appears to be more convenient;

(c) The growing importance of skilled professional labour and the decreasing importance of unskilled labour in high-tech reorganized manufacturing reinforce the trend toward the decision to locate high-level operations in a few limited areas of the world, while having a very broad choice of locations for routine operations, including fully automated plants closer to the company's basis. The application of high technology to all manufacturing definitely segments the production process, thus favouring its internationalization.

In the third place, we should remember that high technology is, above all, *a new process of production and management*. Therefore, the more the economy becomes open, internationalized and competitive, the more the appropriation of high tech, and its implementation in the factories, offices and communication systems of a company or of a country become crucial in winning a competitive edge. In this sense, the internationalization of the economy tremendously reinforces the growth and the importance of high technology activities. Furthermore, because of this importance, investment in high-tech production, of the conquest of markets for high-tech products (in growing demand) become key elements in the strategy to dominate the international economy. The competition between Japanese and American companies in electronics, or the global battle over telecommunications systems illustrate at which point high-tech sectors have become the decisive *economic elements* (and not just the technological ones) in the new worldwide competition for wealth, information and power.

Fourthly, given the strategic role of the high-tech sectors in the international economy, their development creates a new structure of international *dependency* (and not just interdependency) between countries, companies, regions, cities and social groups. Without access to the know-how, whichever the speed in the diffusion of innovation, countries or economic units will always be under the structurally prevailing logic of the dominant poles of the system (even if they succeed in being better off in absolute terms), *as far as they continue to play by the current rules of the international economy.*

Which leads us to our last, and fundamental point. Because of the political, indeed historical implication, of the repositioning in a world economy, *increasingly internationalized and structured by high technology,* national governments (or even local and regional governments) cannot be limited to their traditional roles. As Zysman and Cohen have indicated in their comprehensive study of recent trends in the international economy,[43] the *developmental States* (which-ever the type: Japan, France or Brazil) have forcefully entered the arena of economic restructuring with international competition as their main concern. It follows that multinational corporations are not alone in the "game" any more and that the National States try to recover the initiative they have lost to the private sector, by using their resources and influence *both as national political actors* and *as international economic actors.* It follows that national industrial policies, geared toward the new connection between high-tech and the world economy, become the core of economic restructuring, and therefore of urban and regional reorganization.

We thus now turn to summarize the trends we have been able to observe in the spatial restructuring under the conditions of the new international economy:

(1) The internationalization of the economy actually reinforces the spatial polarization between sectors in different regions and as their metropolitan areas.[44] For instance, in the USA, since manufacturing exports are decreasing and the manufacturing imports are on the rise, the old-line industries are increasingly hurt by international competition. Furthermore, outflow of capital investment (for instance in the automobile) and shift of capital toward the promising new high-tech sectors will augment intersectoral differentiation, and therefore the distance between spatial areas we have been able to associate with each economic sector.

(2) Yet, this general tendency has to be qualified on two grounds in the case of the USA:

   (i) Given the importance of agricultural exports, and the foreseeable jump in agricultural productivity through biotechnology, the new international economy favours the farming States, particularly in the Midwest, but only as far as they are part of the agro-business international complex.[45]

(ii) Direct foreign investment is likely to counteract some of the de-industrializing processes of regions and cities.[46] Yet, it will do so at the expense of lowering labour costs, therefore likely bypassing strong union cities and interventionist local governments.[47]

(3) The concentration of economic power on a world level in a few hundreds of major corporations is spanning growth of advanced corporate services and headquarters in a few major metropolises, consolidating the formation of what Friedman and Wolf have called *the world city.*[48] We would just like to add that an internal hierarchy exists between world cities, and that what should be emphasized is the crucial role of communications for the formation of world cities, and vice versa, the cumulative structuring of communication networks around the communication hubs that world cities come to represent.

(4) The new process of international migration concentrates a new labour force, and therefore the informal economy, precisely in these *world cities*, whose "underground" component has also to be underlined as a part of the same system. The urban informal economy is part of the same process of restructuring represented by the internationalization of the economy.[49]

(5) Finally, perhaps the most striking effect of the new international economy on cities and regions is the loss of their autonomy *vis-a-vis* the worldwide economic actors that control their activities in terms of a global logic largely ignored and uncontrolled by local and regional societies. A rapidly changing economic space determined by economic units whose size and transnationality place them above social pressures and political controls is a *tendency* that, favoured by the internationalization process *and* by high-tech, wishes to impose the abstraction of a space of strategic decisions over the experience of place-based activities, cultures and politics. Yet, the reactions of developmental States in the international economy creates a new dynamics, equally abstract in its horizon, but more directly rooted in political pressures and

social values.[50] High technology and the process of internationalization give rise to the space of managerial flows, but the historical dynamics of the decision-making process in the world economy restore the space of historically conditioned meaning. It is in middle of this dialectics that cities and regions live, die, struggle, change. And with them people.[51]

Conclusion

The process of techno-economic restructuring that is altering the basic structure of our societies is simultaneously reshaping their spatial structure, as we have tentatively shown in this paper. At a higher level of abstraction we can summarize the main spatial trends characteristic of the new division of labour as follows :

(i) The internationalization of the economy, allowed and stimulated by the new communication technologies, creates a *space of variable geometry* which changes constantly under the impulse of strategies of multinational corporations and developmental states. Specific cities and regions increasingly lose control over their own destiny, and their historical and social meaning tends to be dissociated from their economic performance and from their functional role.

(ii) The new technologies allow for the emergence of a *space of flow substituting for a space of places*, that is, communications and decisions over information and symbols (money, for instance) tend to prevail over the expression of social processes and cultural significance related to a given locality. The logic of largescale organizations fits perfectly into a spatial form that abstracts itself from historical specificity to endlessly accommodate itself to new information and instructions received according to the position of each locate in a network of exchanges.

(iii) The new model of capitalist growth, supported by the Warfare State and by the informational mode of development, induces *a new territorial division of labour, based on polarized growth and selective development*, that reflects itself in international dependency, inter-regional cleavages, inter-metropolitan dualism and *simultaneous* life and death of cities and regions.

Nevertheless, societies are not only the expression of economic and technological processes. They are conflicting historical realities resulting from the debates between social actors (classes, genders, ethnic groups, regional and national identities, institutional apparatuses). In fact, most of the techno-economic processes of restructuring we have analysed here are the result of political decisions and organizational strategies. Thus, the spatial forms emerging from such a process are only tendencies that will be confronted by alternative projects from class-based demands, social movements and political programmes. The new spatial structure will result from the interaction between the two processes, namely, the techno-economic restructuring and the new social movements. Yet, unless these social movements and the political actors place themselves within the new historical realm resulting from the technological revolution and the restructuring of capitalism, it is unlikely that they will be able to reverse the current tendencies. And these tendencies go beyond the simple redefinition of the territorial division of labour : they point toward the dissolution of the space of experience into the logic of the space of power.

NOTES

1. See : Manuel Castells, *The Economic Crisis and American Society,* Princeton: Princeton University Press, 1980; Martin Carnoy, Derek Shearer and Russell Rumberger, *A New Social Contract,* New York : Harper and Row, 1983; Samuel Bowles, David Gordon, Thomas Weisskopf, *Beyond the Wasteland,* New York : Doubleday 1983; and, the most updated analysis of the perspectives on the economic restructuring : Barry Bluestone and Bennett Harrison, *The Economic State of the Union in 1984. Uneven Recovery, Uncertain Future,* Washington D.C. : Paper Delivered at a Meeting of Progressive Economists, January 1984; Martin Carnoy and Manuel Castells, "After the Crisis?", *World Policy Journal,* May 1984.
2. Ann R. Markusen, *High Tech Jobs, Markets and Economic Development Prospects,* Berkelly : Institute of Urban and Regional Development, Working paper, April 1983; William Serrin, "High Tech Is No Jobs Panacea, Experts Say", *The New York Times,* Sept. 18, 1983; and Special Supplement "High Technology Jobs Outlook for the 1983's", *The New York Times,* March 25, 1984.
3. Patrick Walker, *The Distribution of Skill and the Division of Labour : 1950-1978,* Amherst : University of Massachussets, Dept. of Economics, Ph.D. Dissertation, May 1983, reported by Bluestone and Harrison, op. cit., 1984; Barbara Baran, *The Transformation of the Office Industry : Impacts on*

the Workforce, Berkeley : University of California, Department of City Planning, Master Thesis, 1982.

4. Thomas Stanback, *Understanding the Service Economy,* Baltimore : The Johns Hopkins University Press, 1979.
5. Bluestone and Harrison, op. cit., 1984; Lester C. Thurow, "The Disappearance of Middle Class", *The New York Times,* Feb. 5,1984.
6. See, for instance : Warren Getler, "Climbing Labour Costs Lift German Robot Use", *International Herald Tribune,* July 12, 1984.
7. See Special Issue of the Journal *Inchiesta* (Bologna), Fall 1983, "L'Economia Informale".
8. Jeff Henderson and Allen Scott, *The American Semiconductors Industry and The New International Division of Labour,* Hongkong : University of Kong Hong, Centre for Urban Studies and Planning, Working Paper, 1984; Michael Storper, *The Spatial Division of Labour : Technology, the Labour Process and the Location of Industries,* Berkeley : University of California, Department of Geography, Ph.D. Dissertation, 1982.
9. Larry Sawers and William Tabb (editors), *Sunbelt/Snowbelt. Urban Development and Regional Restructuring,* New York : Oxford University Press, 1984.
10. Lionel Nicol, *Information Technology, Information Networks and On-Line Information Services,* Berkeley : University of California, IURD, Working Paper, 1983.
11. Bernard L. Weinstein and Robert E. Firestine, *Regional Growth and Decline in the U.S.,* New York : Praeger, 1978; and John Mollenkopf, *The Contested City,* Princeton : Princeton University Press, 1983.
12. Anna Lee Saxenian, *Silicon Chips and Spatial Structure* : The *Industrial Basis of Urbanization in Santa Clara County, California,* Berkeley : University of California, Department of City Planning, Master Thesis, 1980.
13. Amy Glasmeier, Peter Hall and Markusen, *Recent Evidence on High Technology Industries' Spatial Tendencies,* Berkeley : IURD, Working Paper, October 1983.
14. The excellent analysis by Edward Soja, Rebecca Morales and Goetz Wolff, "Urban Restructuring : An Analysis of Social and Spatial Change in Los Angeles", in *Economic Geography,* Vol. 59, No. 2, April 1983, pp. 195-230.
15. Saskia Sassen-Koob, "The New Labour Demand in Global Cities", in Michael P. Smith (editor), *Cities in Transformation,* Beverly Hills : Sage Publications, 1984, pp. 139-172.
16. Thomas M. Stanback et al, *Services : The New Economy,* New Jersey : Rowman and Allanheld, 1981.
17. Barry Bluestone and Bennett Harrison, *The Deindustrialization of America,* New York : Basic Books, 1982.
18. Colin Crouch (editor), *State and Economy in Contemporary Capitalism,* London : Croom Helm, 1979; Carnoy, Shearer and Rumberger, op. cit., 1983.
19. John L. Palmer and Isabel Sawhill (editors), *The Reagan Experiment,* Washington D.C. : The Urban Institute Press, 1982.
20. Special Issue of *Problemi della Transizione* (Bologna), January 1984.
21. OECD, *The Welfare State in Crisis,* Paris : OECD, 1981.
22. Larry Hirschorn et al, *Cutting Back : Retrenchment and Redevelopment in Human and Community Services,* San Francisco : Jossey Bass, 1983.
23 Norman, J. Glickman, *Economic Policy and the Cities : In Search of Reagan's Real Urban Policy,* Paper Presented at the North American Meeting of the Regional Science Association, Chicago 11-13 Nov. 1983.

24. Boston Study Group, reported by Markusen, op. cit., 1984.
25. Michael Klare "Opening the Floodgates : Arms Diplomacy of the Reagan Administration" in Ronald Dellums (editor), *Defense Sense : The Search for a Rational Military Policy,* Cambridge, Mass. : Ballinger, 1983.
26. Lloyd Dumas (editor), *The Political Economy of Arms Reduction,* Boulder : Westview Press, 1982; Jacques Gansler, *The Defense Industry,* Cambridge, Mass. : MIT Press, 1980.
27. Martin Carnoy and Manuel Castells, op. cit., 1984.
28. Martin Carnoy, *The State and Political Theory,* Princeton : Princeton University Press, 1984.
29. See the findings of a recent research report : Richard C. Carlson, Theodore R. Lyman, *US Government Programmes and their Influence on Silicon Valley,* Report prepared for the Ministry of Industry and Research, Government of France, Menlo Park, California : SRI International, May, 1984.
30. See one of the best sources on the topic of technology and spatial restructuring : Servet Mutlu, *Inter-regional and International Mobility of Industrial Capital,* Berkeley : University of California, Department of City Planning, Ph.D. Dissertation, 1979.
31. Ann Markusen, *Defense Spending and the Geography of High Tech Industries,* Berkeley : IURD, Working Paper, May 1984, p. 27.
32. Glasmeier, Hall and Markusen, op. cit., 1983.
33. Steven J. Pinkerton, *High Technology Growth and Regional Structure,* Los Angeles : School of Urban and Regional Planning, University of Southern California, Seminar Paper, May 1984.
34. Richard Dempsey and Douglas Schurde, "Occupational Impact of Defense Expenditures", *Monthly Labour Review,* December 1971, pp. 12-15.
35. Max A. Rutziek, "Skills and Location of Defense-Related Workers", *Monthly Labour Review,* 93, Feb. 1970, pp. 11-16.
36. Norman J. Glickman, op. cit., 1983.
37. Glasmeier, Hall and Markusen, op. cit., 1983.
38. Anna Lee Saxenian, *Silicon Valley and Route* 128 : *Regional Prototypes or Historic Exceptious?,* Research Paper, MIT : Program in Science Technology, and Society, 1984.
39. Frobel et al, op. cit., 1980; and Alejandro Portes and John Walton, *Class, Labour and the International System,* New York : Academic Press, 1981.
40. For a development of this hypothesis on the emergence of a space of flows, see : Manuel Castells, "Crisis, Planning and the Quality of Life" in *Society and Space,* 1983, 1.
41. Robert Cohen, *The Corporation and the City,* New York, Columbia University's Conservation of Human Resources Project 1978.
42. Ken Trachte and Robert Ross, *The Crisis of Detroit and the Emergence of Global Capitalism,* Paper delivered at the 78th Annual Meeting of the American Sociological Association, Detroit, Sept. 3, 1983.
43. John Zysman and Stephen S. Cohen, *The Mercantilist Challenge to the Liberal International Trade Order,* Washington D.C.; Joint Economic Committee, US Congress, Nov. 1982.
44. Norman J. Glickman, *International Trade, Capital Mobility and Economic Growth : Some Implications for American Cities and Regions in the* 1980's, a Report to the President's Commission for a National Agenda for the 1980's, Washington D.C.: June 3-4, 1980.
45. Ibid.
46. *Business Week,* June 4, 1984, pp. 103-104.
47. Erica Schoenberger, *The Regional Impact of Foreign Investment in US*

Manufacturing, Berkeley : Department of City Planning, University of California, Ph.D. Dissertation, forthcoming.

48. John Friedmann and Goetz Wolff, *World City Formation,* Los Angeles : UCLA, Comparative Urbanization Studies, Feb., 1982.
49. *Proceedings of the International Seminar on the Urban Informal Economy at Core and Periphery,* held at the Johns Hopkins University, Department of Sociology, June 8-10, 1984.
50. Manuel Castells, *Multinational Capital, National States and Local Communities,* Berkeley : IURD, Working Paper, Nov., 1980.
51. For a development of this theme, see : Manuel Castells, *The City and the Grassroots,* London : Edward Arnold, 1983.

SIX

Does Environmental Regulation Cause Industrial Flight?

GABRIELE KNODGEN

During a meeting held in July 1975, the West German Government decided that the total costs generated by environmental protection policy in Germany should not exceed those of other comparable, highly industrialized countries (Umwelt, 1975). This political aim reflects the concern of West German industry and the trade unions that German environmental policy may be highly detrimental to the international competitiveness of German industry as a whole (BDI, 1979, p. 40).

A comparison of investments for environmental protection in the Federal Republic of Germany, Japan and the United States, from 1971 to 1978 (Table 6.1), shows that German environmental policy was successful in this respect. Although international comparison of statistics on environmental investment costs is problematic because of widely differing statistical recording (OECD, 1974, pp. 21), the data are however sufficiently accurate to indicate that there are significant differences in the costs of environmental protection from country to country. For example, the Japanese share of total investments spent for environmental protection is much higher than the corresponding share in West Germany. Likewise, American industry as a whole, invested a high percentage of total investments in environmental protection. The results also differ among industrial sectors, but there is no sector in our comparison where German industry invested more than the two other countries.

Although German industry invests less for environmental protection than other highly industrialized countries, German investments are still relatively high in comparison to some developing countries. Developing countries are still inclined towards the position that strict

TABLE 6.1: International Comparison of Industrial Investments for Environmental Protection 1971-1978

Country	Industrial sector	Environmental Protection Investments (in Percentage of Total Investments)								
		Manufacturing industry	Iron and steel	Non-ferrous metals	Mineral oil-processing	Chemical industry	Pulp and paper	Machine manufacturing	Electrical engineering	Textile industry
Federal Republic of Germany[a]		5.2	10.4[e]	8.0	20.6	11.0	9.9	1.4	1.8	1.5
Japan[b]		14.0[d]	15.9	11.8	21.6	17.0[f]	17.8	5.8	—	9.4
United States of America[c]		7.7	14.7	19.0	9.8	9.7	15.6	2.1	4.3	3.6

a = Production and product-related environmental investments for clean air, water protection, waste treatment, noise reduction.
b = Only production-related environmental investment.
c = Only production-related environmental investment; 1971-72, only for clean air and water protection; 1973-1978, including waste treatment.
d = Manufacturing industry without pharmaceutical, shipbuilding or food-processing industry.
e = Iron industry, including drawing, rolling and casting.
f = Chemical and petrochemical industry without pharmaceutical industry.

Sources: Surveys and Calculations of the IfO-Institute, Munich; Japan Ministrv of International Trade and Industry; McGraw-Hill Surveys: U.S. Department of Commerce.

environmental regulation may hinder capital imports and, consequently, stunt economic growth. Many developing countries hope that they can solve their specific environmental problems–e.g. undernourishment, disease, epidemics, inadequate housing, poor sanitation, insufficient irrigation and soil erosion–by augmenting their share of world industrial production (Lima Declaration of 1975).

But can developing countries really improve their welfare if they try to attract industries by neglecting environmental protection? Can they augment income and employment, and consequently get a better supply in consumer goods in exchange for environmental damages? And is it really the case that the international differences in environmental protection costs have a strong impact on industrial siting? Do firms actually relocate to developing countries for environmental reasons? To answer these questions, it is first necessary to study those environmental policies which may provide incentives for a firm's decision to relocate. Production costs for individual firms are only directly affected by environmental policies based on the "polluter-pays"-principle.[1] Environmental policy can regulate both products and production processes. As firms cannot escape that regulation governing negative environmental impacts of products by relocating their production units, we can thus restrict our analysis to those regulations governing production processes.

Environmental regulations governing production processes increase the costs of production relative to other countries. This is contrary to what can be expected in foreign countries with less stringent regulations. As a result, firms can either (a) substitute environmentally intensive forms of production with what are now relatively cheaper, less harmful forms of production and exchange the products on the world market; or (b) they can relocate the production units. Whether industries choose to relocate their production units to developing countries, or whether they adjust to rising production costs by switching to different products or using alternative methods of production depends on the relative mobility of capital in comparison with the mobility of products or the flexibility to adjust production processes. The higher the cost of transport and costs for changing method of production are, in comparison with the costs for setting up or expanding production facilities, and the more the exchange of goods is hindered by tariffs or non-tariff trade barriers, the greater is the probability that factors of production, and not the products, will move.

Terms of Trade Effects

If the adjustment to changing relative costs for environmental protection can be achieved by changing international trade patterns, developing countries would improve their international competitiveness, but worsen their terms of trade (Grubel, 1976). Higher costs for environmental protection in industrialised countries induce rising prices and as a result, developing countries have to pay more for their imports in real terms from these countries. The greater is the volume of imports and the lesser the substitutes for exports of developing countries are affected by rising prices, the more important will be this effect on the terms of trade. The effect on the terms of trade cannot be neglected, as the developing countries usually are unable to switch their production immediately and without additional costs in the production of those goods that have risen in price. Thus industrialised countries can partly shift social costs of production to the developing countries.

Developing countries can react to this shift of costs by regulating the environmental pollution or by setting tariffs or trade barriers. But such a "revenge" can only be successful if they have an impact on world market prices. Therefore, they can only threaten with measures concerning products that have a significant share in the world market and that cannot be substituted easily. However, the latest experience shows that even those countries that are well endowed with natural resources have limited threat-potential. Therefore, we can expect an even more restricted or no threat-potential at all from the least developed countries.

Employment Effects

One important aim of developing countries is to augment their share in world industrial production. If they really would attract capital which is flowing out from an industrial country, in order to escape high production costs caused by environmental regulation, they may achieve this aim, but risk employment losses. If, through their disregard for environmental damages, developing countries in fact induce increased relocation of environment intensive industries, then production in these countries will at the same time specialize towards capital and human capital intensive industries.[2] If, as is generally desired, more efficient technologies are imported along with capital, there is danger that in some cases a reduction in employment may result in developing countries (Johnson, 1970, p. 46). If the technologies transferred with the capital are also made available to domestic industries, production in environmentally intensive industries will become more profitable for these producers as well, and not only for those who came from the outside. This will draw capital away from relatively labour intensive production. The greater expansion of capital-intensive production at the expense of labour-intensive production may then reduce the total demand for labour, which thus reduces labour income and/or employment. This effect, if it occurs, is reinforced because it is precisely small industries that cannot make a production shift and which are thus driven out of the market by those few who survive the transition through capital expenditures.

Trade Barriers as a Cause for Capital Movements

The developing countries may judge that differing costs for environmental regulation are not a sufficient incentive for relocation of production and may therefore try to further stimulate capital movements by protecting their markets by tariffs or non-tariff trade barriers. Market access becomes more difficult for foreign suppliers. They can only avoid trade barriers by setting up their own production facilities within the market. If the industrialized country regulates the production of a product that is imported from a developing country, the developing country can enforce to relocate the production to the site, where production becomes relatively cheaper, by raising a tariff on imports of the product.

Empirical surveys (Wells, 1973; Mason, 1973; White, 1976; Morley and Smith, 1977) indicate that the enforcement of direct foreign investment by protectionistic measures or other investment incentives have mainly negative consequences for the developing countries. The protection against competition for multinational companies allows them to produce in a profitable way without being forced to employ more domestic labour. If these firms would maximise profits one would expect that they would hire from the labour force that is prepared to work for low wages.

One possible explanation for the relatively capital intensive production could be the fact that appropriate labour intensive production technologies are not yet developed. It may be more profitable to install well known technologies in an environment where they are less suitable than to bear research and development costs for new technologies. These costs may be higher than efficiency losses as a result of less appropriate technologies (Johnson, 1970, p. 41). But the empirical surveys show that capital intensity of production is increasing with the market protectionism. Such a correlation cannot be explained by high costs for the development of new production technologies. As an explanation for these behaviours, especially for large firms, various organizational theories like "organizational slack", "managerial discretion", "X-inefficiency" or "satisfying behaviour" can more likely be quoted (Baumol, 1959; Williamson, 1967; Cyert and March, 1963; Leibenstein, 1976). More capital intensive production technologies are also linked with non-monetary returns: "Capital-intensive technologies involve large quantities of shiny new equipment, which convey the aura of being up-to-date and yield high prestige. They may bring out the engineering instincts in entrepreneurs. They require less administrative efforts on the part of entrepreneurs, particularly with those to be supervised" (White, 1976, 580).

More competitive markets are likely to force the companies to minimize costs and therefore they have to produce with and even develop labour intensive production technologies. As a result a developing country for which industrialization is not an end in itself and which does not only want the enrichment of a few privileged people, will achieve more labour intensive technologies in the competitive markets with free trade. Without this incentive for additional capital imports given by the tariffs, industrial growth may be weaker but environmental degradation could be avoided that could very likely not be compensated by positive income effects.

Empirical Results

Whether industries do relocate their production facilities from developed to developing countries, or whether they adjust to rising production costs by switching to different products or using alternative methods of production, has been subject to a research project carried out by the International Institute for Environment and Society, Science Centre Berlin (IIES) in cooperation with Conservation Foundation (CF), Washington, D.C.[3]

Research Findings of the U.S. Study

In the United States as in the Federal Republic of Germany, many observers expressed concern that the costs and logistics of complying with environmental regulations might be emerging as a significant factor in the competitiveness and location of industries involved in world trade. Policy-makers, labour unions, business leaders, environmentalists, as well as academics expected that one response to the competitive problems would before American firms, particularly multi-national corporations with experience operating overseas, to shift more productive facilities to countries where regulatory difficulties could be minimized (Leonard, 1982, 2). Thus, since 1979, the Conservation Foundation has monitored key U.S. industries to assess whether, in fact, there is any indication that large numbers of U.S.-based industries have been pushed abroad by environmental regulations and whether the U.S. industrial base has thereby been negatively affected. In addition, the Conservation Foundation has conducted case study research in several rapidly industrializing countries that are among the favourite locations for new factories built by U.S. multinational corporations.

Leonard (1982) draws three overall conclusions from the research:-

(i) environmental regulations have not caused a significant exodus of U.S. industries;
(ii) a few industries do appear to have been pushed abroad;
(iii) most newly constructed plants owned by U.S. companies in rapidly industrializing countries over comply with local environmental and workplace health standards.

The investigation of overseas investment and foreign trade patterns by U.S. manufacturing industries from 1970 to 1981 shows that the overall overseas investment patterns of U.S. industries have not changed significantly according to the change of production costs caused by environmental regulations. The two groups of manufacturing industries that appeared most likely to be pushed abroad by increased pollution-control costs and regulatory restrictions–chemicals and metals–have not expanded their overseas production faster than those of all manufacturing industries. Instead of a rising import as an expected result of a substitution of local production, overall exports by the chemicals and metals industries grew much faster than imports.

However, primary metals industries show a trend towards faster than average expansion and higher percentages of investment in, and imports from, less developed countries can be detected. But there is not enough evidence that environmental costs or regulations are a cause for this exception. One other possible explanation can be the tendency of developing countries not only to export natural resources, but also refined products.

Although there may be individual exceptions, in general, regulatory costs have not overridden more traditional factors like market considerations, transportation and labour costs, or political stability that determine how most firms select overseas locations for production. It appears that most individual industries–even within those industries with a slightly higher tendency to relocate for environmental reasons–have responded to environmental regulations with technological innovations, changes in production processes or raw materials, more efficient process controls, and other adaptations that have proved more economical and less drastic than the flight from these regulations.

The small number of industries that appear to have been influenced by environmental factors to relocate, appear to be either producing highly toxic, dangerous or carcinogetic products that have been severely curtailed in new plant construction and in some cases, disrupted or they are industries where environmental factors have combined with other changing locational incentives. For some basic mineral processing industries, as well as, for a small number of producers of organic chemical intermediates factors as material availability or the international product cycle, speed the international dispersion.

Although individual firms may have fled the U.S. in search of pollution havens outside the advanced industrial countries – that have no macro impacts on U.S. statistics–there is stronger evidence given by case study research in important rapidly industrializing countries (Ireland, Spain and Mexico) that most firms that have invested in recent years appear to have taken anti-pollution measures beyond those required by laws in these particular countries. As plants are generally very similar to those built in the U.S., it is obvious that technologies transferred by the firms take advantage of advances already made at home. Another explanation for that, is the fact that firms expect their plants to last from 20 to 40 years and cannot expect that environmental regulation will not be significantly stricter during the lifetime of the plant. The research findings show that the U.S. companies even had a positive impact in combating industrial-related pollution problems in the industrializing countries by introducing new pollution control technologies, training technicians in pollution control, transferring technical data, and sometimes, building joint waste treatment facilities with local governments.

Already now, firms can face serious economic and political problems in rapidly industrializing countries if they operate abroad by ignoring environmental and public health considerations. The Conservation Foundation research discovered examples of U.S. firms being closed, fined, or slapped with new restrictions in all three countries as a result of their failure to take action to protect the environment and workers' health.

Research Findings of the FRG Study

The International Institute for Environment and Society designed a questionnaire to determine the weight of environmental factors in investment decisions of German industries (Knodgen, 1982). The sample was chosen from the set of those firms known to have made significant investments in developing countries since the inception of stricter environmental laws in West Germany, namely, since the early 1970's. One hundred and fifty companies participated in the study. In most cases, only investments made since 1974 were investigated because time lags between investment decisions and actual investments make it likely that investments made prior to 1974 were not decided upon after the implementation of the stricter governmental environmental policies referred to above. Also, information concerning investment decisions concluded before this period are not very reliable since the details involved are often forgotten or distorted. No investments made before 1972 are included in this study.

The survey results show that costs of environmental protection play a relatively minor role in the investment decisions (see Table 6.2). There are only a few cases where environmental regulations have been a decisive factor in industrial decision-making, and in these cases, environmental regulations constituted only one among a number of other factors which were considered to be at least of equal importance (see Table 6.3). For those firms whose production

TABLE 6.2: **Motives for Investment in the Developing Country (in the percentage of the total sample -- 149 firms)**

	Investment Motive	Very Important 1	2	3	4	Totally Unimportant 5	Arithmetic Mean	Mode
1.	Maintenance of market share; opening of new markets	68	14	3	3	13	1.8	1
2.	Low transport costs, advantageous transport facility	11	24	21	20	25	3.2	5
3.	Availability of skilled labour	11	24	25	22	18	3.1	3
4.	Low labour costs	31	24	22	14	9	2.5	1
5.	Securing of raw materials	9	13	11	20	48	3.9	5
6.	Energy supply	5	7	17	26	45	4.0	5
7.	Avoidance of trade barriers	44	21	11	6	18	2.3	1
8.	Currency fluctuations	8	18	22	19	34	3.5	5
9.	Expected social obligations of firms such as codetermination schemes, stock sharing and tax reform	3	20	11	22	44	4.0	5
10.	Strict environmental regulations in the FRG	2	3	7	20	69	4.5	5
11.	Especially lax environmental regulations in the host country	1	4	5	21	69	4.5	5
12.	Incentives for investment by private and governmental agencies in the host country	4	16	18	18	44	3.5	5
13.	Promotion of investment by private and governmental agencies in the FRG	8	21	18	21	32	3.8	5
14.	Political stability in the host country	11	37	24	11	17	2.9	2
15.	Well-developed local infrastructure	10	33	28	14	15	2.9	2

processes generate severe environmental problems in the FRG, there are two additional factors which are, on the average as restrictive : natural resources and energy supply (see Table 6.4). An analysis of variance among investment motives reveals another relation (see Table 6.5). Companies which rate environmental protection as a "very important" or "important" motive for investment, also rate two other motives even higher. On the average, "political stability in the host country" and "expected social obligations such as codetermination schemes, stock sharing and tax reforms" are rated even more important. This result indicates that environmental regulations do not induce firms to relocate because of increases in production costs; rather they more or less provide and indication of the overall political situation. That is, demands for increased environmental protection are seen only as an additional threat to industries which view themselves as already endangered.

TABLE 6.3: **Motives for Investment in the Developing Country (in the percentage of the firms which rated "environment" either in the FRG or the developing country with 1 or 2-13 firms)**

	Investment Motive	Very Important 1	2	3	4	Totally Unimportant 5	Arithmetic Mean	Mode
1.	Market	62	15	8	8	8	1.9	1
2.	Transport	15	23	39	8	15	2.9	3
3.	Skilled labour	8	23	46	8	15	3.0	3
4.	Labour costs	54	23	15	8	0	1.8	1
5.	Raw materials	15	23	15	31	15	3.1	4
6.	Energy supply	15	15	39	15	15	3.0	3
7.	Trade barriers	46	15	23	8	8	2.2	1
8.	Currency fluctuations	23	15	46	0	15	2.7	3
9.	Social obligations	23	46	15	8	8	2.3	2
10.	Environmental regulations in the FRG	23	39	31	0	1	2.3	2
11.	Environmental regulations in the host country	15	46	8	31	0	2.5	2
12.	Investment incentives in the host country	8	39	15	15	23	3.1	2
13.	Investment promotion in the FRG	8	23	23	23	23	3.3	2
14.	Political stability	31	46	15	0	8	2.1	2
15.	Infrastructure	31	15	39	8	8	2.5	3

TABLE 6.4: **Rating of Investment Motives in Percentage of the Groups. "Environmental Protection is Important for Production in the FRG"**

Investment Motive		Very Important 1	2	Totally Unimportant 3	4	5	Significance r	Level
Market env.-intensive	yes:	68,1	16,5	2,2	2,2	11,0	0,06	0,22
	no:	67,2	10,3	3,4	3,4	15,5		
Transport env.-intensive	yes:	12,1	25,3	20,9	19,8	22,0	0,08	0,17
	no:	10,3	20,7	20,7	19,0	29,3		
Skilled Labour env.-intensive	yes:	11,0	23,1	30,8	22,0	13,2	0,07	0,19
	no:	12,1	25,9	15,5	20,7	25,9		
Labour Costs env.-intensive	yes:	23,1	25,3	26,4	17,6	7,7	-0,13	0,05
	no:	43,1	20,7	15,5	8,6	12,1		
Raw Materials env.-intensive	yes:	8,8	17,6	9,9	22,0	41,8	0,14	0,04
	no:	8,6	5,2	12,1	15,5	58,6		
Energy Supply env.-intensive	yes:	5,5	7,7	22,0	26,4	38,5	0,14	0,04
	no:	5,2	5,2	10,3	24,1	55,2		
Trade Barriers env.-intensive	yes:	45,1	22,0	8,8	5,5	18,7	0,02	0,42
	no:	43,1	19,0	13,8	6,9	17,2		
Currency Fluctuations env.-intensive	yes:	8,8	17,6	23,1	18,7	31,9	0,04	0,31
	no:	6,9	19,9	19,0	19,0	36,2		
Social Obligations env.-intensive	yes:	5,5	18,7	7,7	20,9	47,3	-0,02	0,41
	no:	0,0	20,7	17,2	22,4	39,7		
Env. reg. in the FRG env.-intensive	yes:	2,2	5,5	6,6	23,1	62,6	0,15	0,04
	no:	1,7	0,0	6,9	13,8	77,6		
Env. reg. in the host country env.-intensive	yes:	2,2	5,5	3,3	24,2	64,8	0,10	0,11
	no:	0,0	1,7	8,6	15,5	74,1		
Invest. incent. in host country env.-intensive	yes:	7,7	22,0	14,3	23,1	33,0	-0,03	0,35
	no:	8,6	19,0	24,1	17,2	31,0		
Invest. promo. in the FRG env.-intensive	yes:	1,1	12,2	17,8	22,2	46,7	-0,20	0,01
	no:	8,6	22,4	19,0	10,3	39,7		
Political stability env.-intensive	yes:	14,3	30,8	27,5	9,9	17,6	0,00	0,49
	no:	6,9	46,6	17,2	12,1	17,2		
Infrastructure env.-intensive	yes:	11,1	30,0	28,9	15,6	14,4	-0,02	0,42
	no:	8,6	37,9	25,9	12,1	15,5		

TABLE 6.5: **Investment Motives and Importance of Environmental Motives (Analysis of Variance between the Groups)**

	Environmental Regulations in the FRG			Environmental Regulations in the host country		
	r	F	Significance Level	r	F	Significance Level
Market	-0.02	0.42	0.80	-0.08	0.83	0.51
Transport	0.19	1.79	0.13	0.09	1.02	0.40
Skilled Labour	0.02	1.23	0.30	0.05	0.30	0.88
Labour Costs	0.14	1.78	0.14	0.21	1.78	0.14
Raw Materials	0.28	3.55	**0.01**	0.21	2.05	0.09
Energy Supply	0.30	3.88	**0.005**	0.32	4.47	**0.002**
Trade Barriers	0.05	0.44	0.78	0.02	0.90	0.47
Currency Fluctuations	0.26	3.28	**0.01**	0.17	1.32	0.26
Social Obligations	0.43	8.98	**0.000**	0.40	7.61	**0.000**
Investment Incentives in the host country	0.04	0.96	0.43	0.15	1.56	0.19
Investment Promotion in the FRG	0.19	2.70	**0.03**	0.23	2.71	**0.03**
Political Stability	0.25	3.51	**0.01**	0.26	3.71	**0.01**
Infrastructure	0.14	1.08	0.37	0.06	0.54	0.71

In particular, our research examined whether it is possible to identify and specify differences according to country, industrial sector or firm size. The results show that:-

- those firms which verified that environmental protection played a role in their investment decision have no particular preference for specific countries. It seems that there are no pronounced pollution havens for German industry;
- those firms which rate strict environmental regulation in the FRG as "very important" or "important" (see Table 6.6) belong, without exception, to the basic industries (particularly, non-ferrous metals and the chemical industry);
- environmental protection is equally important for big and small firms (see Table 6.7). Big enterprises invest in developing countries to open new markets or to maintain their market share. For smaller companies, production costs are relatively more important. But, the higher importance attached to cost factors is only applicable to those costs other than environmental ones.

TABLE 6.6: **Motives for Investment and Primary Industrial Sectors**

Investment Motive		Arithmetic Mean	F	Significance Level
Market		1.8	4.7	**0.00**
	B	1.5		
	I	1.6		
	C	2.6		
	F	1.0		
Transport		3.2	1.4	0.24
	B	2.9		
	I	3.4		
	C	3.2		
	F	3.0		
Skilled Labour		3.1	1.4	0.26
	B	3.0		
	I	3.3		
	C	2.8		
	F	2.0		
Labour Costs		2.5	2.6	**0.05**
	B	2.8		
	I	2.5		
	C	2.0		
	F	3.0		
Raw Materials		3.9	4.2	**0.01**
	B	3.5		
	I	4.3		
	C	3.5		
	F	3.0		
Energy Supply		4.0	1.9	0.14
	B	3.7		
	I	4.2		
	C	3.9		
	F	4.0		
Trade Barriers		2.3	2.0	0.12
	B	2.2		
	I	2.1		
	C	2.9		
	F	1.0		
Currency Fluctuations		3.5	2.9	**0.04**
	B	3.4		
	I	3.3		
	C	4.1		
	F	5.0		
Social Obligations		3.8	0.4	0.75
	B	3.9		
	I	3.9		
	C	3.7		
	F	3.0		

(Contd.)

Table 6.6 (Contd.)

Environment Regulations in the FRG		4.5	7.7	0.00
	B	4.0		
	I	4.8		
	C	4.5		
	F	5.0		
Environment Regulations in the host country		4.5	3.5	0.02
	B	4.2		
	I	4.7		
	C	4.5		
	F	5.0		
Investment Incentives in the host country		2.5	0.5	0.66
	B	3.6		
	I	3.4		
	C	3.5		
	F	2.0		
Investment Promotion in the FRG		3.8	0.2	0.86
	B	4.0		
	I	3.8		
	C	3.7		
	F	4.0		
Political Stability		2.9	0.8	0.48
	B	2.6		
	I	3.0		
	C	4.8		
	F	3.0		
Infrastructure		2.9	0.82	0.48
	B	2.7		
	I	3.0		
	C	3.0		
	F	3.0		

Note: Number of firms in sample by industrial sector.
B=47 I=69 C=30 F=1 Total No. = 147.

(B=Basic Industry; I=Investment Goods; C=Consumer Goods; F=Food Processing).

One plausible explanation for the minor influence of environmental protection on investments in developing countries is the selection of particular production technologies in the developing countries:-

- many firms no longer use old, polluting technologies. With the development of new technologies, firms cannot only reduce their emissions, but they also experience improved productivity.
- the application of emission-intensive technologies is in many cases economically disadvantageous. The reduction of emissions often implies conserving raw materials.
- most firms neither develop nor implement new technologies which incorporate the relatively inexpensive production factor "environment" more intensively in the developing countries. Firms simply do not expect that the cost advantage can be maintained throughout the whole period of investment.
- as most of the firms anticipate a reduction in the cost differential, they prefer to install less environmentally intensive technologies to avoid, in most cases, very expensive retooling costs for the future.

TABLE 6.7: **Investment Motives and Size of Firms (Variance Analysis)**

	Number of Employees		Sales	
	r	Significance Level	r	Significance Level
Market	-0.24	0.001	-0.22	0.004
Transport	0.03	0.38	-0.01	0.43
Skilled Labour	0.10	0.11	0.07	0.19
Labour Costs	0.19	**0.01**	0.26	**0.001**
Raw Marterials	0.07	0.19	0.02	0.40
Energy Supply	-0.10	0.11	-0.03	0.35
Trade Barriers	-0.17	**0.02**	-0.16	**0.02**
Currency Fluctuations	-0.06	0.24	-0.05	0.26
Social Obligations	0.13	**0.05**	0.17	**0.02**
Environmental Regulations in the FRG	-0.01	0.45	0.01	0.43
Environmental Regulations in the host country	0.03	0.36	0.05	0.26
Investment Incentives in the host country	-0.10	0.10	-0.06	0.22
Investment Promotion in the FRG	0.11	0.10	0.11	0.09
Political Stability	-0.15	**0.03**	-0.21	**0.005**
Infrastructure	-0.08	0.15	-0.12	0.07

The decisive factor for future relocation based on environmental considerations is thus the expectation concerning cost differentials induced in the FRG relative to other countries. On one hand, in the most important developing countries, firms anticipate stricter environmental regulations; on the the other hand, they expect a reduction in the increase of environmental costs, particularly environmental investments in the FRG. The majority of firms expect stricter environmental regulations in developing countries; opinions differ only with regard to time for and degree of adjustments (see Table 6.8). Expectations of decreasing costs for environmental protection in the FRG (see Table 6.9) are relatively exceptional, but only one-third of the firms investigated expect that costs will increase greatly. Rising costs for environmental protection are primarily due to an increase in operating costs. Rising costs for operation may indicate that a firm has taken the decision to adjust to increased demands for environmental protection by investing in the FRG rather than by relocating to a developing country.

TABLE 6.8: **Anticipated Changes in Environmental Protection in Developing Countries**

Environmental protection will increase and reach the level of that in the industrial countries in the long term.	36.5%
A more critical view will be taken; environmental protection will increase.	15.5%
Environmental protection will increase slowly and gradually.	12.8%
Environmental protection will increase, but not as much as in the FRG.	14.9%
Environmental protection will increase.	10.1%
Environmental protection will not (inevitably) increase in more industrialized areas, countries and densely populated areas.	11.5%

Note: (148 firms; multiple indications possible) (Changes indicated by more than 10% of the firms).

TABLE 6.9: **Anticipated Development of Outlays for Environmental Protection Within the Enterprise**

	For all of West German Industry	Investments	Operating Costs	Total
Decrease Greatly	2	3	1	1
Decrease Somewhat	3	2	1	1
No Change	8	40	20	22
Increase Somewhat	47	56	81	79
Increase Greatly	90	48	45	46
Number of Firms	150	149	148	149

Future relocations for environmental reasons are correspondingly low. Relocating to a developing country – excluding relocation within the FRG – is the least important reaction of firms, considered as an adjustment, to expected changes in environmental policy (see Table 6.10). Among the thirty firms in our sample which do not totally exclude future relocation for environmental reasons, our results indicate that twenty-six of these have not as yet made any plans, three are thinking it over generally, while only one firm has actually made concrete plans. Consequently, we can expect that "industrial flight" to developing countries is not likely to occur, at least so long as environmental protection policy develops in accordance with the firms' range of expectations.

TABLE 6.10: **Reactions of Firms in the Next Five Years to Increasing Cost of Environmental Protection (in percentages).**

	Very High Significance 1	2	3	4	No Significance 5
Change in production process (148)	7	14	18	12	51
Change in production programme (148)	4	5	10	16	65
Additional environmental protection investments (146)	14	19	22	14	32
Reduction in production (146)	5	8	8	10	69
Relocation within the FRG (146)	2	4	4	10	80
Relocation to (other) industrial countries (147)	2	6	5	7	80
Relocation to developing countries (148)	2	4	7	7	80

Firms will usually react by making additional environmental investments or by improving production processes. Changes in the composition of products or reductions in the scale of production are less important. As a result, we can expect that there will be no major indirect exports of environmentally intensive production. Stricter environmental regulations are not an important incentive for German firms to export pollution, basically by specializing in "clean" production at home, while leaving "dirty" production to the developing countries and importing the products from there. Should changes in the international division of labour occur, they would not necessarily be due to modifications in environmental protection policy in the more industrialized countries. One possible alternative explanation is that developing countries want to reduce exports of raw materials in favour for processed goods and products. Such development policies can generate an increase in pollution in developing countries, since initial stages of production and especially basic industrial production are relatively environmentally intensive.

A comparison of future reactions to the expected environmental protection policies with motives for past investments reveals interesting relations which confirm previous results (see Table 6.11). Firms which indicate that labour costs are high, and those who feel threatened by political obligations, consider relatively more seriously future relocation for environmental reasons to developing countries than do environmentally intensive producers. The firms which want to reduce production because of rising environmental costs are those firms which rated "political stability" as a consideration for past investments significantly higher than the average firm. On all sides, political conditions are held to be responsible for industrial difficulties. This result confirms the contention that environmental policy rarely constitutes a motive for investment because it induces rises in the production costs. More important is that the environmental policy generally seems to signify for firms an indicator for the political situation and not for rising costs.

The more market-oriented firms will mainly improve their production process. They will invest in environmental protection and may take special precautions in selecting an appropriate site for their production units within the FRG–for example, by relocating out of municipal or urban centres. These firms will not relocate outside the FRG for environmental reasons.

The empirical survey can, finally, explain why the "industrial flight" argument still plays such an important role in political discussion. Firms use the argument of potential relocation as a "threat" in their negotiations with authorities, even when relocating is not a feasible alternative. Such threats are designed to encourage authorities to modify or reduce the environmental protection requirements at the firm's home-base location.

Conclusions

The empirical research on industrial relocation to developing countries conducted in the U.S. and the FRG come to very similar results though using different research methods. Both studies show that environmental costs are very seldom a reason to relocate

TABLE 6.11: **Relations between Expected Reactions to Changes in Environmental Protection Policy over the next five years and Investment Motives (correlation coefficient and significance level)**

Future Reactions Investment motive	Changes in production process	Changes in production programme	Additional environ. protec. invest.	Reduction in production	Relocation with in the FRG	Relocation to (other) industr. countries	Relocation to develop. countries
Market	0.19	0.09	0.13	0.03	0.13	-0.04	-0.06
	(0.01)	(0.14)	(0.07)	(0.36)	(0.06)	(0.29)	(0.23)
Tansport	0.03	0.04	0.05	0.00	0.05	-0.05	-0.01
	(0.34)	(0.30)	(0.27)	(0.49)	(0.29)	(0.26)	(0.44)
Skilled Labour	0.07	0.12	-0.03	0.11	0.08	0.08	0.07
	(0.22)	(0.08)	(0.35)	(0.10)	(0.17)	(0.16)	(0.18)
Labour Costs	-0.01	0.08	-0.09	0.13	0.06	0.15	0.16
	(0.45)	(0.17)	(0.13)	(0.06)	(0.22)	(0.04)	(0.02)
Raw Mateials	0.10	0.16	0.19	0.15	0.20	0.16	0.09
	(0.12)	(0.03)	(0.01)	(0.04)	(0.01)	(0.03)	(0.14)
Energy Supply	0.20	0.08	0.17	0.08	0.15	0.13	0.02
	(0.01)	(0.18)	(0.02)	(0.16)	(0.04)	(0.06)	(0.38)
Trade Barriers	0.06	0.07	0.10	-0.03	0.10	-0.08	-0.05
	(0.24)	(0.20)	(0.12)	(0.38)	(0.11)	(0.18)	(0.26)
Currency Fluctations	0.11	-0.06	0.19	0.07	0.06	-0.04	-0.03
	(0.08)	(0.23)	(0.01)	(0.20)	(0.22)	(0.32)	(0.38)
Social Obligations	0.04	0.04	0.02	0.19	0.16	0.07	0.12
	(0.30)	(0.34)	(0.41)	(0.01)	(0.03)	(0.21)	(0.07)
Env. reg. in the FRG	0.22	0.15	0.28	0.33	0.20	0.31	0.38
	(0.00)	(0.03)	(0.00)	(0.00)	(0.01)	(0.00)	(0.00)

(Contd.)

Table 6.11 (Contd.)

Future Reactions Investment motive	Changes in production process	Changes in production programme	Additional environ. protec. invest.	Reduction in production	Relocation with in the FRG	Relocation to (other) industr. countries	Relocation to develop. countries
Env. reg. in the host country	0.18 (0.01)	0.11 (0.10)	0.23 (0.00)	0.31 (0.00)	0.20 (0.01)	0.38 (0.00)	0.41 (0.00)
Invest. Incent. in host country	-0.01 (0.47)	-0.02 (0.40)	-0.09 (0.15)	0.00 (0.49)	0.27 (0.00)	-0.01 (0.45)	-0.01 (0.48)
Invest. promo. in the FRG	-0.04 (0.33)	-0.23 (0.00)	0.00 (0.48)	0.09 (0.14)	0.02 (0.39)	0.02 (0.41)	0.06 (0.25)
Political Stability	-0.02 (0.39)	0.03 (0.35)	0.04 (0.30)	0.24 (0.00)	-0.07 (0.21)	0.00 (0.48)	0.07 (0.19)
Infrastructure	0.07 (0.20)	0.04 (0.31)	0.03 (0.35)	0.02 (0.39)	0.14 (0.05)	-0.08 (0.16)	-0.10 (0.10)

Note: Figures in parentheses denote percentage.

production. Even in these cases, where environmental regulations do have an influence on siting decisions; they are usually only one factor among others. There is no reason to believe that the major long-term trend in international industrial location is being significantly intensified by environmental regulations in industrialized countries like the U.S. or the FRG.

The two studies do not come to the result that environmental regulations have not burdened the companies, nor do the findings mean that environmental regulations are not important in the industrial location process. They only show that environmental cost differentials could not offset larger trends shaping aggregate international industrial siting patterns.

The American and German studies indicate that the few exceptions from these patterns are often firms that are experiencing static or reduced demand as a result of product obsolescence or hazards related to product use and therefore, find few incentives to make new investments in modernizing plants, developing new technologies, or installing expensive pollution control equipment. We cannot see any reason why the developing countries should try to attract this kind of industries. The empirical research confirms that developing countries, consciously maintaining low environmental standards in the hopes of attracting new industries, have chosen an economically unwise strategy. They risk to get industries producing products that are obsolete, extremely hazardous, or subject to consumer standards without getting in exchange for improvement on their employment.

For the industrialized countries, the research findings mean that a relaxation of regulatory standards would not have the desired effect of restoring or even improving the long-term competitiveness. On the contrary, the result could be the loss of an incentive for technological progress and manufacturing process changes which speed up the modernization of the industrial structure and create a new industrial sector, the pollution-control industry with improving chances in export markets.

As firms operating abroad only can expect short-term benefits from cost savings made by failing to take environmental protection measures–that may be offset by the need to make expensive technological adjustments at a later date–and as the pollution control industry has a vested interest in enlarging export markets, industrialized countries even have a strong interest in seeing that environmental regulations are enacted and enforced in countries where they operate production facilities. The survey results indicate that in some cases, the multinational companies already have tried to convince local government to set stricter environmental standards to improve their comparative advantage in the competition with national or transnational firms that have not yet developed environmental protection technologies.

As the results show rather convincingly that environmental costs are very seldom (among other factors) a reason to relocate production, it seems, then, more important to examine the factor "political situation" with regard to avoidable problems in industrial siting within the industrialised countries. General improvements can be expected by improving the flexibility and economic efficiency of environmental policy instruments rather than by lowering standards for environmental protection.

NOTES

1. State investments for environmental protection can only have indirect impacts on international competitiveness according to the particular method of investment financing. Higher taxes or higher rates of interest as a result of increased state credits can generate capital exports. The overall impact of such an environmental policy on the national economy will usually be stronger as there is no incentive for the firms to mitigate the negative environmental effects of their production processes.
2. The proportion of environment investment in the processing industry for the year 1971-77 correlates, with high significance (r=0,92), with the capital intensity calculated from the input-output table of industries in the FRG. The correlation with human capital intensity and with energy intensity, respectively, is also highly significant (Knödgen, 1979, p. 413).
3. The project was partially financed by the German Marshall Fund of the United States.

REFERENCES

Baumol, W.J. (1959). *Business Behavior, Value and Growth*, New York: Macmillan Co.

B D I (Bundesverband der Deutschen Industrie e. V.) (Ed. 1979). *Umweltschutz and industrielle Entwicklung in der Bundesrepublik Deutschland*, Köln.

Cyert, R.M. and J.G. March (1963). *A Behavioral Theory of the Firm*, Englewood Cliffs, N.J.: Prentice Hall.

Grubel, H.G. (1976). Some Effects of Environmental Controls on International Trade: The Heckscher-Ohlin-Model, in: I. Walter (Ed.) *Studies in International Environmental Economics*, New York: John Wiley & Sons, pp. 9-27.

Johnson, H.G. (1970). "The Efficiency and Welfare Implications of the International Corporation", in: Ch. P. Kindleberger (Ed.): *The International Corporation*, Cambridge, Mass. und London: MIT Press.

Knödgen, G. (1979). Environmental and Industrial Siting: Preliminary Results of an Empirical Survey of Investment by West German Industry in Developing Countries, in: *Zeitschrift Für Umweltpolitik*, 2, pp. 407-434.

Knödgen, G. (1982). *Umweltschutz and industrielle Standortentscheidung*, Frankfurt/M., New York: Campus Verlag.

Leibenstein, H. (1976). *Beyond Economic Man: A New Foundation for Microeconomics*, Cambridge, Mass.: Harvard University Press.

Leonard, H.J. (1982). *Siting New Industry: An International Perspective*. A Summary of the International Findings of the Conservation Foundation's Industrial Siting Project, Washington, D.C.: The Conservation Foundation.

Lima Declaration and Plan of Action on Industrial Development and Cooperation (March 1975): Second General Conference of the United Nations Industrial Development Organization (UNIDO), Lima, Peru, pp. 12-26.

Mason, R. H. (1973). "Some Observations on the Choice of Technology by Multinational Firms in Developing Countries" in: *The Review of Economics and Statistics* 55, pp. 349-355.

Morley, S.A. and G.W. Smith (1977). "Limited Search and the Technology Choices of Multinational Firms in Brazil", in: *Quarterly Journal of Economics* 91, pp. 263-287.

OECD (1974). *Economic Implications of Pollution Control - A General Assessment*, Paris; OECD.

Umwelt (1975). No. 42, July 25, p. 12.

Wells, L.T. (1973). "Economic Man and Engineering Man: Choice of Technology in a Low Wage Country", in: *Public Policy 21*, pp. 319-342.

White, L.J. (1976). "Appropriate Technology, X-Inefficiency, and a Competitive Environment: Some Evidence from Pakistan", in: *Quarterly Journal of Economics* 110, pp. 575-589.

Williamson, O. (1967). *The Economics of Discretionary Behavior: Managerial Objectives in a Theory of the Firm*, Englewood Cliffs: Prentice-Hall.

SEVEN

Towards an Integrated National-Regional Environmental-Economic Model

WIM HAFKAMP & PETER NIJKAMP

Economic-environmental model-building has become increasingly complicated over the last decade. Systems-theoretic concepts, optimal control models and multidisciplinary analyses have become necessary tools for environmental-economic analyses. There is a strong tendency toward integrated policy analyses in which economic, environmental, energy and regional aspects are brought together in one coherent framework (Lakshmanan and Nijkamp, 1980). This tendency toward integrated modelling is mainly caused by the fact that the post-war economic growth paradigm inter-twined with technological, scientific and educational progress and rising population numbers, has neglected the social and ecological dimensions of this process and hence has lead to a serious threat for the man-made and natural environment. This development does not only take place in the developed countries, but also in the Third World countries, especially in those areas where a rapid industrial expansion is not accompanied by sufficient resources for environmental protection. Integrated planning and policy models are essentially necessary means to restore the balance in favour of invironmental dimensions (cf. also Guldman and Schefer, 1980).

These remarks can be illustrated as follows. Air pollution was once – centuries ago – a fairly local problem. Since the beginning of the so-called Industrial Revolution (in the middle of the nineteenth century) areas with a high concentration of manufacturing industries have been suffering from air pollution. This was mainly caused by burning coal for traction (steam engines) and for other heating processes. On a world scale, however, the annual amounts of coal (and other fossil fuels) which are used in our technological processes have continued to rise due to the economic progress, which required a wide variety of new products. The pollution effects have demonstrated a similar pattern. They are no longer a "now and then" problem on a very local scale. Permanent emissions of large amounts of air pollutants (e.g. sulphur oxides, nitrogen oxides, particles etc.) cause a chain of environmental effects leading to damages both to human health and to the natural environment. Part of the emissions end up within the area of origin; in that case, it has an effect on human health, value of dwellings, quality of agricultural products and the natural environment. Another part of the pollutants leaves the area of origin and hence has an influence on environmental conditions in adjacent areas (Nijkamp, 1977). Remaining parts of the air pollutants return to the earth in so-called acid rains. For instance, in Europe acid rains containing air pollutants from Great-Britain, Germany and Poland form a major environmental problem in Scandinavia.

The problem of dispersion of air pollutants will be dealt within greater detail in later section of this paper. It is clear that, in many countries, problems of air quality – and environmental quality in general have become increasingly urgent. In this contribution we shall analyse the relationships between the economy of a nation and environmental quality. We do so by presenting the second stage of the so-called Triple-Layer-Model (TLM). A complete description of the structure of TLM is given elsewhere (Hafkamp and Nijkamp, 1981). Here, only a brief summary of TLM will be given.

A Triple-Layer-Model: Summary

The Triple-Layer-Model consists of three submodels:

An Economic Submodel

Which is a National-Regional economic model of the Dutch economy. It is the result of coupling the Secmon-Model to a multiregional input-output model of five Dutch regions. The Secmon-model has been developed by Driehuis (Driehuis, 1978). It is primarily developed as a simulation model of the Dutch economy which analyses long-term effects of a great variety of economic policies. Main goal variables included in this model are inflation, unemployment, economic growth and current accounts. Main policy instruments are taxes and public expenditure, monetary instruments, exchange rate, wage-and-price control and labour market policy.

A Labour Market Submodel

Which describes employment (supply and demand) in the regions and sectors. The demand for labour is analysed through the production structure; gross production, capacity and capacity use in capital-intensive sectors, as well as import substitution are important elements here. The supply of labour is analysed through wages, prices and growth of income. Also demographic data play an important role.

A Pollution Submodel

Which contains a description of emission and diffusion of air pollutants. Introduction of anti-pollution technology also takes place in this model. A major part of air pollution is caused by combustion of fossil fuels. Therefore, it is important to take into account the availability of several types of energy.

The model we present here is a theoretical multiregional model of an economy where economic, socio-political and environmental aspects of a society are of main importance. Public decision-making and planning in a spatial system will be analysed in a way analogous to allocation mechanisms in formalized economics with public goods and external effects (a.o. Ruys, 1975). We shall explicitly deal with (groups of) individuals belonging to a certain region of the spatial system and to a certain interest group (e.g. environmentalists, labour unions).

A general view of the model is given in section 3. The actual model, in terms of definitions, relationships, etc., is given in section 4, while section 5 contains suggestions for public decision-making. Some extensions of the model and links to the operational version of the model are given in section 6. The operational version itself of TLM is extensively presented in Hafkamp and Nijkamp. 1981.

The Conceptual Model

The model focuses on two kinds of relationships:

a. relationships between people and their natural and economic environment.
b. relationship between (groups of) individual people.

Consequently, pollution and conflicting interests in abating pollution take a central place. The assumption is made that in a spatial system consisting of a set of regions, the population is subdivided into three more or less homogeneous groups;

(i) environmentalists,
(ii) employment protectors,
(iii) growth idealists.

In each of the regions production and consumption of (private) goods takes place. As a result, the by-products, viz. the pollutants, (air pollution, noise, etc.) are dumped as waste into the (natural) environment of this spatial system. This pollution may cross the regional borders. Therefore, pollution affects the welfare positions of individuals in any other region because of diffusion effects and spatial spillovers. The resulting environmental decay and environmental concern lead to the emergence of a first interest group; the *environmentalists.*

A social aspect of production of goods and services is employment. The employment situation throughout the whole spatial system concerns any individual: not only somebody's own employment counts – a job means satisfaction, social status, perspectives, etc., and for many people income without work is frustrating – but also the employment situation of others – it is difficult for many employed people to share their income with unemployed people. The concern about unemployment and the distributional aspects of the labour market leads to a second interest group; *employment protectors.*

A last group can be associated with the traditional economic objective of income maximization (at a micro level and at a macro level). This objective presupposes a maximization of production and hence leads to the third interest group; *growth idealists.*

The above mentioned three groups constitute the basis for social, economic and environmental conflicts: although everyone needs income and employment and a livable environment, it is clear that in a society groups (or forces) are present which focus primarily on one of these three needs while neglecting the other aspects or considering them only as side conditions. This problem will be formalized in the next section.

Definitions and Concepts

The following frame of reference is assumed for the environmental analysis presented below. The spatial system consists of a set of regions:

$$R = \{1, 2, \ldots\ldots R\} \tag{1}$$

A set of individuals is associated with each of these regions:

$$I_r = \{1_r, 2_r, \ldots\ldots I_r\}\, r \in \overline{R} \tag{2}$$

Feasible 'states' of the spatial system in terms of regional income, environmental quality are described by :

$$S = \{s = (s_1, s_2, \ldots\ldots s_R) \in R^{3\times R} \\ \mid s_r = (y_r, 1_r, z_r) \in R^3\} \tag{3}$$

s is an R-tuple of vectors describing the state of the entire spatial system.

s_r is a vector describing the state of the system for region r.

Y_r denotes regional income.

1_r denotes regional employment.

Z_r denotes regional environmental quality.

S is a closed, compact and convex set. Various policy mixes (combinations of regional economic policy, environmental policy and labour market policy) are supposed to enable a central government to control the spatial system so as to reach in principle any situation which is reflected by an element of S. We shall not give a detailed model here to describe this process, as we are primarily dealing with problem of public decision-making in terms of outcomes.

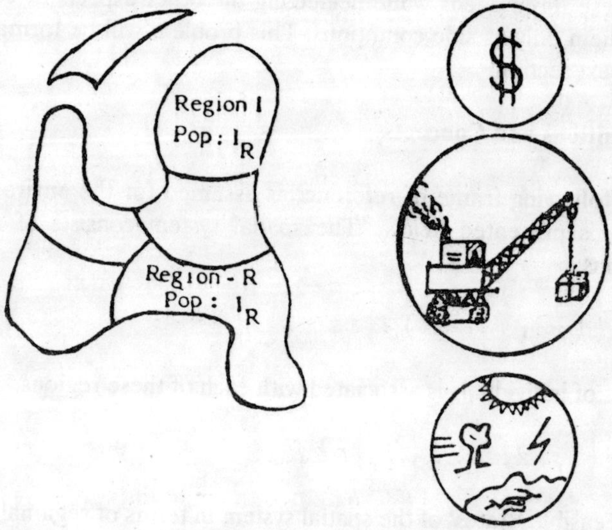

FIG. 7.1 : Regions, individuals and objectives in a spatial system

Individuals in region r are assumed to have an identical 'consumption set', X_r, denoted by:

$$X_r = \{x_r \mid x_r = (y_r, l_r, z_r) \in R^3 +\} \quad r \in \overline{R} \tag{4}$$

Although the assumption is made that all individuals in a region have the same consumption set, they have, of course, different preferences. As mentioned already, we distinguish three interest groups. There are various ways of incorporating this in individual welfare functions. Some of these are given below under the heading Procedures for Public Decision-Making. Here we presuppose the existence of individual, twice differentiable, concave welfare functions:

$$W_{ir}(x_r) \quad r \in \overline{R}, i_r \in \overline{I}_r \tag{5}$$

Implying that individual welfare in region r is determined by income, employment and environmental quality in region r only.

Next, a choice set C is defined which serves as the basis for individuals to decide which objective should first be raised as the most urgent one:

$$C = \left\{ c_{i_r} \in R^3 \mid C_{i_r} + (a_1, a_2, a_3) \wedge a_j, \sum_{j=1}^{3} a_j \in \{0, 1\}, j = 1, 2, 3 \right\}$$

which means that during each stage of the choice process only one objective can be increased in value (in other words, a_j is a zero–one variable). The spatial system composed of individuals can now shortly be characterized by:

$$EE = \{R, I_r, S, (X_r, w_{ip}, C)\} \tag{7}$$

The spatial system EE can–from the point of view of individuals–be regarded as an economy with external effects only. The set of Pareto-optimal states in the system can now be defined as follows:

$$PO = \{ s \in S \mid \exists r \in R, \exists i_r \in \bar{I}_r; w_{i_r}(S_r') > w_{i_r}(S_r) \Rightarrow s' \notin S \vee$$

$$\exists r \in \bar{R}, E j_r \in \bar{I}_r; w_{j_r}(S_r') \leq w_{j_r}(S_r)\} \tag{8}$$

A state of the system is called Pareto-optimal, if an improvement of any individual welfare position is only possible (i.e. within S) through affecting at least one other's individual welfare position. It should be noted that here an efficiency criterion is defined rather than an equilibrium criterion. The set of Pareto-optima is also known as the set of efficient or non-dominated solutions.

The existence of interest groups which want to maximize regional income, employment and environmental quality makes it impossible to identify one single overall best solution. Consequently, formally a multi-decision maker, multi-objective problem has to be solved. This presents us with two questions:

(i) which state of the system is a compromise for the conflicting interests among groups?

(ii) how can this be attained?

These, and assorted questions are dealt below.

Procedures for Public Decision-Making

This section deals with problems at a crossroads mathematical programming and mathematical economics. In the field of mathematical programming, much work has already been done to formulate optimization procedure for problems with multiple objectives (Keeney and Raiffa, 1976; Cohon, 1979; Rietveld, 1981 and Nijkamp and Spronk, 1981).

These procedures have not been specifically designed for economic decision-making. A criterion according to which they are often distinguished is the information available on the decision-maker's preferences. (Hwang and Masud, 1979). Three cases are distinguished:

1. Full information (on the decision-maker's preferences)
2. Limited information
3. No information

In the field of mathematical economics, much work has been done on production and pricing of public goods and on social choice theory. The main problem here is to formulate adequate allocation mechanisms and procedures for socio-political decision-making. The existence of utility functions or preference ordering is usually presupposed (Ruys, 1975). Here, much attention is paid to the multi-person-aspect of decision-making. This leads to an important role of game-theory in the formulation of economic models (Nijkamp, 1979).

In this section, we shall try to combine the advantages of both approaches. We will apply Zeleny's method of displaced ideals (Zeleny, 1974) in combination with a simple voting procedure (majority rule). Zeleny's method is used because it requires only a limited, but clear communication process between analysis and decision-makers in the search process of an optimal compromise solution; it also asks the decision-makers to make the simplest possible choice – which objective is most urgently to be improved in the next optimization stage of the communication process.

Though this method is quite clear and simple in the case of a single decision-maker, it does not specify a decision rule for selecting a "most urgent" objective if there are many decision-makers involved. This lack can be overcome by using procedure. The preference relationships, defined in the previous section should be interpreted as "tacit preferences"; preferences which decision-makers themselves are not explicitly and entirely aware of.

Clearly, if all individuals would have a set of known welfare functions as specified in section 4 an interactive compromise procedure would be superfluous in selecting an optimal (compromise) state for system EE, since in that case a straightforward traditional optimization problem would arise. We make the assumption, however, that individuals are not explicitly aware of welfare functions describing their preferences. We also assume that they are unable to give precise information on their preference by specifying weights (trade-offs) attached to the various objectives (income. emnloyment and environmental quality).

Without these assumptions, it would be fairly easy for central government to ootimise simply a social welfare function of the type:

$$w(s)=\sum_{r=1}^{R}\sum_{i_r=1_r}^{I_r} w i_r s_r) \qquad (9)$$

or to optimize a weighted sum of the objectives, using information on trade-offs, given by the individuals.

The steps of the interactive compromise procedure are contained in Fig. 7.2. The selection itself of an unsatisfactory value of an objective has received only little attention in the literature. Usually it is assumed that, in a case of a number of decision-makers, an (unspecified) bargaining procedure takes place. In this paper, we suggest a procedure for selecting the most unsatisfactory value of an objective. We do so by first letting individuals choose a "most unsatisfactory" level of an objective (by means of voting) and by next assuming a central authority that counts the votes concerning the most unsatisfactory objective and, next, adjusts the constraint set accordingly. For the spatial system the procedure then takes the following form:

Initiate

The vector optimization problem to be solved is:

$$\begin{aligned} &\max s=\left(S_1, S_2, \ldots S_R\right) \\ &s.t.\ s \in S \\ &s_r > s^0_{\ ir}=0 \end{aligned} \qquad (10)$$

where s^o_r denotes the lower bounds on regional objectives during this phase (i.e. iteration no. 0). This procedure means that first the regional objective profiles s_r are taken into account. This implies a decentralization policy to the regions, so that they are supposed to make decisions regarding the values of the three objectives in each region. The reverse procedure would lead to a centralized policy in which the aggregate values of the three objectives are first set at the national level, while later an allocation of the values of these objectives over all regions takes place.

Separate Optimization of Objectives

All $3 \chi R$ objectives are optimised subsequently, leading to outcome contained in Table 7.1. This is done by solving the following $3 \chi R$ maximization problems:

$$\begin{aligned} &\max Y_r \\ &\max I_r \qquad r \in \bar{R} \\ &\max Z_r \\ &\text{s.t. } s \in S_t \quad t=0, 1, 2, \ldots \\ &\quad s_r > s_{Lr} \end{aligned} \qquad (11)$$

where t represents the iteration stage.

TABLE 7.1 : **Results of separate optimization of objectives in iteration no. t.**

State/Optimization	$y_1\ l_1\ z_1$	$y_2\ l_2\ z_2$	...	...	$y_R\ l_R\ z_R$
y_1	$y_1^{max,t}$				
l_1	$l_1^{max,t}$				
z_1	$z_1^{max,t}$				
y_2					
l_2					
z_2					
.					
.					
y_R					$y_R^{max,t}$
l_R					$l_R^{max,t}$
z_R					$z_R^{max,t}$

Maximization of y_r, l_r, z_r leads to $s^t y_r$, $s^t l_r$, $s^t z_r$, respectively. Table 7.1 is a pay-off table, which reflects the conflicts both between objectives and between regions. For instance, the first column of this table indicates the consequences of a separate optimization of income in region 1 for all other objectives in all other regions. Thus, each row contains both the maximum and the minimum value of the objective concerned. Formally this means:

$$y_r^{\max}, \,^{t}\!= \max y_r,\; l_r^{\max}, \,^{t}\!= \max l_r,\; z_r^{\max}, \,^{t}\!= \max z_r \quad r \in \bar{R}$$

$$s^{t}_{y_r},\; l^{st}_r,\; s^{t}_{z_r}$$

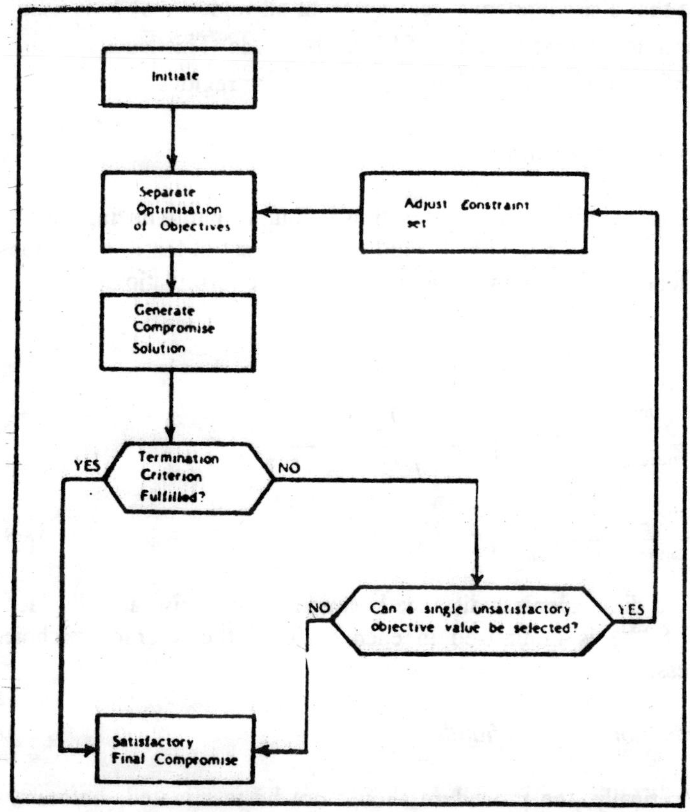

FIG. 7.2: Flow diagram for an interactive multi-decision maker optimization procedure

	y	s_1	w_1	Dl_1
AB	z	s_2	w_2	Dl_2
	s	s_3	w_3	Dl_3
			w_4	
			w_5	

Resulting in the state vector $s^{max,t} = (s^{max,t},...s^{max,t})$. The minima for the objectives are found in an analogous way.
$y_r^{min,t}$, $l_r^{min,t}$ and $z_r^{min,t}$ are associated with state vector $s^{min,t} = (s^{min,t}$ $s_R^{min,t})$. The values of $s^{max,t}$ are called the ideal solutions. It should be noted that a simultaneous realization of all values in $s^{max,t}$ is usually impossible, so that a trade-off has to be made. This leads of course to conflicts both among objectives and among regions.

Generate Compromise

The compromise in the tth iteration is found by minimizing the discrepancy between the ideal solution and the set of feasible solutions. This leads to the following minimum distance formulation:

$$\min d(s, s^{max,t}) = \sum_{r=1}^{R}$$

$$[\left| \frac{y_r^{max,t} - y_r}{y_r^{max,t} - y_r^{min,t}} \right|^2 + \left| \frac{l_r^{max,t} - l_r}{l_r^{max,t} - l_r^{min,t}} \right|^2$$

$$+ \left| \frac{z_r^{max,t} - z_r}{z_r^{max,t} - z_r^{min,t}} \right|^2]^{1/2} \qquad (12)$$

Thus, a dimensionless distance between compromise and displaced ideal $S^{max,t}$) is minimized in each stage of the interactive choice process.

Termination Criterion fulfilled

Theoretically, the procedure should not be terminated, before the distance, calculated under 3, equals zero. In that case, only one feasible solution is left for the maximization problem. Practically, however, the procedure is normally stopped when the abovementioned distance d(s, $s^{max,t}$) between the ideal solution and the set of efficient solutions becomes very small (e.g. less than 0.10).

Select Unsatisfactory Objective Value

This procedure is more complicated and can be treated as follows:
a. Individuals in all regions of the system determine which objective

value is most unsatisfactory. This can be done by means of a voting procedure for each individual. In formal mathematical terms, this voting procedure can be described as follows: Each individual vote vector V^t_{ir} is characterized by elements zero and one, indicating whether or not a certain objective has an unsatisfactory value:

$$V^t_{i_r}(S^t_r) \in C, \text{ such that } [\forall v^t_{i_r} \in C, v^t_{i_r} \neq v^t_{i_r} \Rightarrow \text{grad } w_{i_r}(s^t_r).$$

$$v^t_{i_r} > \text{grad } w_{i_r}(S^t_r).v^t_{i_r} = (0,0,0)] \quad (13)$$

The latter condition states that an individual chooses one objective which has the highest (marginal) increase in individual welfare. Otherwise he will vote for a neutral position.

b. The central authority counts the individual votes; this results in a vote vector v^t_r for each region and a vote vector v^t for the entire system:

$$v^t_r = \sum_{i_r=1_r}^{I_r} v^t_{i_r}, \text{ where } v^t = (v^t_1, v^t_2, \ldots v^t_R). \quad (14)$$

Next the central authority determines the share u^t_r of votes per region for the objectives:

$$u^t_r = \frac{v^t_r}{I_r}, \text{ where } u^t = (u^t_1, u^t_2, \ldots u^t_R). \quad (15)$$

In this way, the objective in each region within the system, which received the highest percentage of votes in that region, is now selected. This leads to an "adjustment vector" (composed of zero's and ones) for the selection of objectives of a certain category in a certain region which have to be increased in

$\mathbf{a}^t_r = (a^t_{1r}, a^t_{2r}, a^t_{3r})$ such that :

$$a^t_{jr} = \begin{cases} 1 \text{ if } u^t_{jr} = \max\limits_{k \in R} u^t_{jk} & 1\ \{1, 2, 3,\} \\ 0 \text{ else} \end{cases} \quad (16)$$

and $a^t = (\mathbf{a}^t_1, \mathbf{a}^t_2, \ldots \mathbf{a}^t_R)$.

It should be noted here that this aggregation procedure for individual preferences is different from Arrow's problem, as in this case only a zero-one decision has to be made instead of a ranking of priorities which might lead to transitivity problems in the aggregation stage.

Adjust Constraint Set

The constraint set is now adjusted to the choice made under 5 by calculating lower bounds on objectives for the next iteration (t+1):

$$S_L^{t+1} = \left(S_1^{t+1}, S_2^{t+1}, \ldots\ldots S_R^{t+1} \right),$$

$$\text{where } S_r^{t+1} = \left(y_r^{t+1}, l_r^{t+1}, z_r^{t+1} \right)$$

such that:

$$y_r^{t+1} = y_{Lr}^t + a_{1r}^t \left(y_r^t - y_{Lr}^t \right)$$

$$l_r^{t+1} = l_{Ir}^t + a_{2r}^t \left(l_r^t - l_{Lr}^t \right) \qquad (17)$$

$$z_r^{t+1} = z_{Lr}^t + a_{3r}^t \left(z_r^t - z_{Lr}^t \right)$$

Satisfactory Final Compromise

A final compromise solution reached at the Tth iteration will be denoted by:

$$S^c = \left(S_1^c, S_2^c, \ldots\ldots S_R^c \right). \qquad (18)$$

This procedure leaves us with the question whether or not the final compromise reached in the procedure is equal to the "optimum state" that would be reached by optimizing a social welfare function of the type:

$$W(S) = r = 1\, i_r = 1\, i_{rr} . W_{ir}\left(S_r \right), \text{ where } i0 \text{ and } r$$

$$= 1\, i_r = 1\, ir = 1. \qquad (19)$$

i_r are weights, attached to the individual welfare functions.

The maximum of (18) is defined as:

$$W(S^o) = \max w(S) \quad \text{s.t. } s\ S \tag{20}$$

Now, the question can be dealt with by investigating the following possibilities:

1. Do both approaches lead to the same optimal state of the system? i.e. $s^c = s^o$
2. Do both approaches lead to the same level of social welfare? i.e. $w(s^c) = w(s^o)$.
3. Do both approaches lead to the same level of individual welfare? i.e.

$$W_{i_r}(S_r^c) = w_{i_r}(S_r^o), \forall r R, \forall i_r l_r.$$

It can be demonstrated that a situation with a single decision-maker leads to an affirmative answer to the abovementioned questions. This can be clarified by using a simple example with only a single decision-maker and two objectives. (Fig. 7.2): This figure shows that the final compromise solution of the interactive optimization procedure is indeed equal to the solution found by optimizing the welfare function w(z, y).

The three abovementioned questions cannot be answered positively for the regional system EE with multiple decision groups. If, for example, individual preferences are exclusively oriented to one issue and the related interest groups are relatively stable in size, then the voting procedure will have the same outcome (decision vector a^t) through all iterations. In that case, one interest group dominates the others, so that a final compromise is achieved that corresponds to one column of the pay-off matrix. This choice is, in general, not compatible with a social welfare solution.

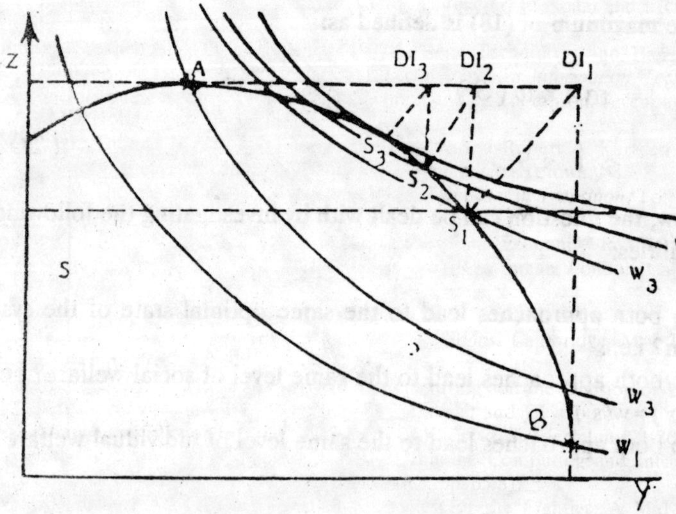

FIG 7.3 : Interactive compromise procedure for a case of a single decision-maker with two objectives

legend: y : Objective (viz. income)
z : objective (viz. environmental quality)
S : the set of feasible states
w_i : some iso-welfare curves
Dl_t : displaced ideal at t^{th} iteration
s^t : compromise solution at t^{th} iteration
AB : all efficient solutions are on arc AB

In the first iteration a first displaced ideal is calculated by optimizing z and y within the set of feasible states, leading to A and B respectively and from thereon to Dl_1. Minimizing the distance to S leads to the first compromise s^1. Now, suppose the decisionmaker's welfare function is such that at state s^1 the marginal welfare of a change in z exceeds the marginal welfare of a change in y. He will then decide to ask that during the next iteration the level for z in s^1 is taken as a lower bound on z. In iteration 2 the displaced ideal will move to Dl_2 where the actions are repeated. In this figure the third compromise is a final compromise to the decision-maker. In s^3 the marginal welfare of variable z is apparently equal to the marginal welfare of variable y.

Conclusions

The model presented in this contribution and the decision-making procedure are merely very stylized pictures of a complex reality. We did not extensively deal with the problem of how a specific state in the system is actually reached, once it is chosen as a final compromise. Instead, explicit attention was paid to theoretic aspects of alternative procedures for public decision-making in a spatial economic-environmental system.

The interactive compromise procedure leaves it entirely up to individual preferences which policy actions are taken. It is accordance with the process aspects of real world planning problems. It also can be adapted to strongly differing institutional and political contexts. Although the use of such a procedure does not presuppose information about individual trade-offs, it creates the possibilities of assessing *ex post* the implicit trade-ffs of the actual choices. In this respect, the abovementioned interactive choice strategies are not *prescriptive* in nature, but can merely be regarded as valuable tools for ·onalizing the decision-making process in a complex system.

REFERENCES

Cohon, J.L., (1978). *Multiobjective Programming and Planning,* Academic Press, New York.

Driehuis, W., (1978). *Een Sectoral Model t.b. v. de Analyse van de Nederlandse Economie op Lenge Termijn* (SECMON) (Amsterdam).

Hafkamp, W., and Nijkamp, P., (1981). *Towards an Integrated National Regional Environmental Economic Model,* Research Memorandum (University of Amsterdam).

Hwang, C., and Masud, A., (1979). *Multiple Objective Decision-Making Methods and Applications,* Springer, Berlin.

Keeney, R. and Raiffa, H., (1976). *Decisions with Multiple Objectives,* Wiley, New York.

Lakshmanan, T.R., and Nijkamp, P., (1980). *Economic-Environmental — Energy Interactions,* Martinus Nijhoff, Boston.

Nijkamp, P., (1977). *Theory and Application of Environmental Economics,* North-Holland, Amsterdam.

Nijkamp, P., (1979). *Multidimensional Spatial Data and Decision Analysis,* Wiley, New York.

Nijkamp, P. and Spronk, J., (1981). *Multicriteria Analysis: Operational Methods,* Gower, Farnborough.

Rietveld, P., (1980). *Multiple Objective Decision Methods and Regional Planning,* North-Holland, Amsterdam.

Ruys, P., (1974). *Public Goods and Decentralisation,* Tilburg University Press.

Guldman, J. and Shefer, D., (1980). *Industrial Location and Air Quality Control,*

Wiley, New York.
Zeleny, M., (1976). *The Theory of Displaced Ideal, Multiple Criteria Decision Making*, Ed. M. Zeleny, Berlin.

EIGHT

The Evolution of the Service Sector: Role of Information Technologies

T. R. LAKSHMANAN

I. INTRODUCTION

Services have replaced production of goods as the dominant mode of economic activity in the industrialized affluent economies. The "typical" picture of a modern economy is not one of factories engaged in the fabrication of goods but that of a society engaged in the production and consumption of services – a society of dining, of travelling, of learning, of medical visits and healing, of business and legal consultancies, of transmission and reception of various messages and of leisure activities.

While the nature and dimensions of the changeover to an economy of service activities (that currently account for the greater portion of the national product in advanced societies) is beginning to be noticed, the vitality and dynamism of the service sector has received little if any attention in the literature (barring a few exceptions such as Fuchs, 1968; Gershuny, 1978; Stanbeck, et al 1981). This neglcct of the service sector reflects a long-term bias against services among economic analysts of various stripes from Adam Smith, through Marx, Veblen to Baumol (1967) and Walker (1985). Adam Smith viewed services as unproductive. Marx adopts a similar position when he relegates into the "superstructure" all activities which are remote from material production. Also, he suggests:

> Services are consumed the moment they are produced. . . (services) do not exist as a utility different from the process, a use-thing which does not function as an article of commerce, does not circulate as a commodity after it has been produced. (cited by Burger, 1970, p. 74)

Further, there have been arguments that services are not subject to scale economies, that in many cases substitution of capital for labour is not possible and worst of all suffer from the "cost disease" (Baumol, 1967).

Such points of view have discouraged serious analyses of service production as well as the development of statistical concepts and measurement so that the available picture of the service sector is somewhat sketchy and fragmented. The result has been a general neglect of the vitality and dynamism of the service sector.

To understand this dynamism, it may be useful to view the role of services in contemporary economies from two perspectives. The first is to view services as complementary to goods production (either as independent activities or as integral parts of the process of goods production). As the manufacturing sector increases its productivity by extending its markets (e.g. foreign or new product markets) and increasing the division of labour, there is great stimulus to the demand for services which can reduce the relevant transaction and adjustment costs. Specialized dynamic producer services develop in response to the incidence of transaction costs that represent the costs of bringing supply and demand sides of the market together (e.g. costs of uncertainty, of risk, of asymmetrical distribution of information, and of coordination and control).[1] To address the adjustment costs that are incurred in increasing the supply of resources that have long gestation periods (e.g. highly skilled labour, sophisticated capital goods, organizational resources), a variety of educational, engineering consultancy, management and strategic planning services emerge. At least 50 per cent of the final value of the manufactured products exported by 36 industrialized or newly industrializing countries are drawn from such services (Nusbaumer, 1987).

Some services can also be viewed as autonomous activities carried out to respond to a specific demand that may or may not be complementary to the demand for goods. Such services include a variety of largely non-profit human capital services (e.g. education, health, welfare, etc.) and some public services such as consumer protection, environmental protection, equal opportunity, etc.

A fundamental characteristic of most services is the participation and modification of the consumer in the service production. Consequently, the efficiency and quality of the service delivery depends to a great degree on the quality of all agents – producer and consumer–participating in the production. To facilitate such joint production, the content of work is transmitted among the production agents as information on the purposes and modalities of the service rendered. Such information in general (acquired or accumulated) together with the information flows among various economic actors and institutions performs for the services the same role that raw materials perform for goods production. The economy is an organization for linking, on the one hand, individuals by interaction through technical processes of production and distribution and, on the other, by communication networks of information flow necessary for coordination and control among the individuals. Gradually over time, there has been a qualitative change, in which the cerebral labour (of design, coordination and control) has become more significant than manual or physical labour as a key factor of production.

This systematic exploitation of intelligence and knowledge in the production of services is a major reason for the growing importance of information and the emergence of "information societies". Thus the historical process of progressive expansion of goods production to wider global markets, which creates the demand for better links between various segments of the market in the form of service activities, has led in turn to increasing demand for information and the information-rich societies. Such societies engage in the accumulation and conservation of data, in the development of knowledge (structured information) via a variety of research, applied studies and software. They also develop the capability to process and transmit the information and to incorporate the relevant knowledge in capital goods, software and organizations. In this process, the production of services becomes more efficient and of higher quality. Over time, the development in information technologies may promote changes in the labour process and organization of service delivery, a development which, in turn, will likely increase the productivity of services further.

The objective of this paper is to explore such a role that information technologies may play in the dynamic transformation underway in the service sector. The paper opens in Section II with a survey of the major characteristics of the service sector. It focuses on the central attribute of the service activity, namely, that consumers of the service are intrinsic participants in the production process. To produce a service, the consumer and the producer must interact for the delivery of the service to be complete. Thus the context within which the knowledge technologies of service production are brought to bear on the problems of the consumer is essentially a process of transaction between the producer and consumer. This transactional process involves not only the exchange of information between the producer and consumer, but also the utilization of the consumer in the production of service output.

Service activities differ from one another in the nature of their producer-consumer interface, specifically in the levels and types of information exchanged and degree and type of participation of the consumer in service production. Indeed, we present a classification of service sector activities based on the nature of this producer-consumer interface, which affects the context and scope of the technology of service production. Since each category of service activity differs from the other in the quality and quantity of information flow, the type of knowledge technologies available and the environment of service production, the classification can provide clues to the likely future technological behaviour of these sectors. In particular, how can the development in information technologies (IT) be exploited to improve the efficiency and quality of information generation and use in service activities, thereby improving the productivity of service activities?

To address this issue of the role of IT in increasing the efficiency and quality of services, we survey briefly, in Section III the relevant developments in information technologies (IT) and activities. To explore the potential for the diffusion of IT in the service sector, it is necessary to understand the relationship between the nature of information technologies, the different levels of content and form of information and knowledge and the nature of the work organization in the service sector that would affect the speed of diffusion of technical change.

Anderson and Johansson (1984) distinguish between the levels of content, instrumentality and generality in different types of information communicated among economic agents, using categories such as data, knowledge, competence and creativity. We adopt their categories and elaborate in Section IV on the potentials offered by IT to increase information, knowledge, competence and creativity. At the same time, we identify the types of changes likely to take place progressively in the technology of service production. For example, the first class of changes may pertain to more efficient ways of carrying out older production tasks as in the use of peripheral activities such as automated personnel, billing and financial systems. A second level of change pertains to the change in the core technologies of service production through the use of IT. In the long run, the next level of change involves the exploitation of the network attributes of distributed information systems in the development of new services. This would involve not only debundling and reorganizing existing services (as a form of cost competition) but also the development of entirely new service products (dynamic competition). However, a prerequisite for the latter development is often a set of complementary institutional innovations (Lakshmanan, 1987). Such innovations could be in the social organization of the particular service or in the labour process of the sector.[2] We attempt briefly in this section to link the types of knowledge available through IT and the phases of changes in the technology and organization of service production in the form of a sequence model of service sector evolution.

Section V illustrates these ideas regarding the role that information technologies play in the transformation of a few service sectors initially, but in more detail in the health care sector. In that sector, we highlight the interplay of innovations in IT, in other medical technology and the innovations in the social organization of medical care (e.g. the emergence of perspective payment systems) to produce new configurations of health care in the USA.

II. TECHNOLOGIES IN THE SERVICE SECTOR

A Capsule Profile of the Service Sector

The structural shift toward services in the industrialized countries has been widely documented (Inman, 1985; Summers, 1985; Daniels,

1985; Stanbeck, et al 1981). Whether measured by output of labour shares, services are an important part of total economic activity. Employment in service industries and white-collar occupations has greatly outpaced the growth of employment in goods production in the U.S. (Stanbeck, et al 1981; Levenson, 1985).

Two hypotheses have been put forward for the relative growth of service employment in the economy (Fuchs, 1968; Gershuny, 1978). First, since services have an income elasticity of demand higher than 1, as real incomes per capita climb, real services per capita grow faster than the proportional rise in income. Thus services account for an increasing proportion of income and national employment as well. Second, automation and increasing division of labour rise with economic growth, services once produced in the household or the firm can be contracted out more efficiently to specialists outside the organizations (often with higher service quality and/or lower average costs). Thus services such as housekeeping, day care, food production, data processing, financial services, legal and advertising services are provided in new establishments that are statistically measured as service activity.

The major growth segments of the service sector are:

1. *Human Capital Services:* Largely non-profit services: e.g. education and health –reflecting the greater need for investments in human capital and in increasingly sophisticated, internalized arena of production of goods and services.
2. *Producer Services:* These result from increasing division of labour, the growth in size and importance of large corporations; to the rising importance of planning, developmental and complex managerial functions; to the growth of markets; and to changes in the organizational and institutional arrangements of the private sector, and
3. *The Producer-Service-like Functions in the Public Sector:* These functions reflect the need to protect consumer interests and worker rights, to further equal opportunity; to regulate markets as necessary, to promote national economic interest in a rapidly expanding international system of production, service delivery and exchange (Stanbeck, et al 1981).

The significant growth of these classes of services does not represent a major movement to freestanding services purchased on the market as much as a joint provision of goods and services. Rising real income and increasing diversity of consumer demand have led to greater product differentiation that is responded to by joint provision of goods and services. The consumption of services turns out to be strongly complementary to consumption of goods (Gershuny, 1978; Hirschorm, 1981; Stanbeck, et al 1981).

Service Sector Technologies

The enormous diversity of activities encompassed in the service sector has often led to loose definitions and ascription of attributes to the sector that are both misleading and analytically unhelpful.

Typical of such characteristics attributed to the sector as a whole are its low rates of productivity growth, its labour intensity, low capital intensity and its major role in the slowdown in productivity in the overall economy in the last 15 years.[3] Since these characterizations are not accurate, we engage in a definitional digression.

The first attribute of service activities is that they involve a change in (or for) the consumers or the goods they possess. Three types of such changes in the asset structure of the consumer during service production can be noted (Garn, et al 1976). In one type there is a change in the tangible asset structure of the consumer and provider of services (e.g. retail services, repair and maintenance services for durable goods, economic development activities). In a second type of service activities, there are changes in the human capital of the consumers (e.g. education and training; counseling and health care services). The third type of activities include primary brokerage activities (e.g. referral programmes and real estate sales) where the output appears as change in the personal assets of clients who are providers and clients who are consumers of the service. However, a few services involve change neither in the consumers nor in their goods. For example, rental services allow persons to make use of goods without acquiring them – a change in accessibility created for the consumer. Thus the change process involved is *in* or *for* the consumer and confers on him or her time, place and form utility (Riddle, 1985).

The second general attribute of service activity is that consumers are intrinsic participants in the production process. This distinguishes the production of goods from that of services. In goods production, resources–labour, capital, energy and materials– are combined. (Fig. 8.1).

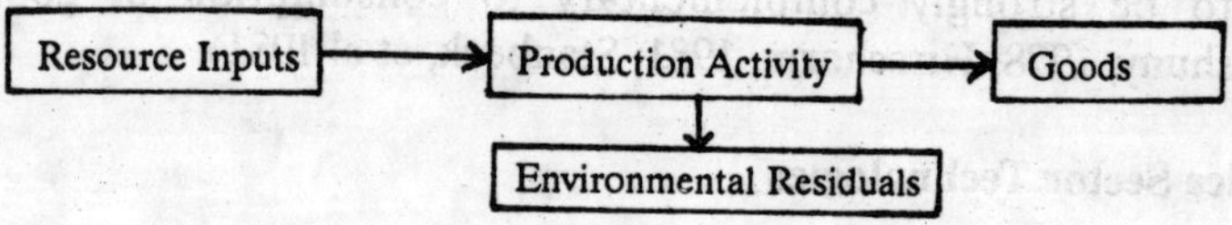

FIG. 8.1 : Production of Goods

A production unit is subject to a variety of opportunities and constraints on its actions. However, the transaction between the producer and consumer will not directly affect the level of output. The asset positions of the seller and buyer are altered during sales but the output is not affected by the attitude or behaviour of the seller or buyer. This enables the analyst to view goods producing units as self-contained units for analysis of efficiency.

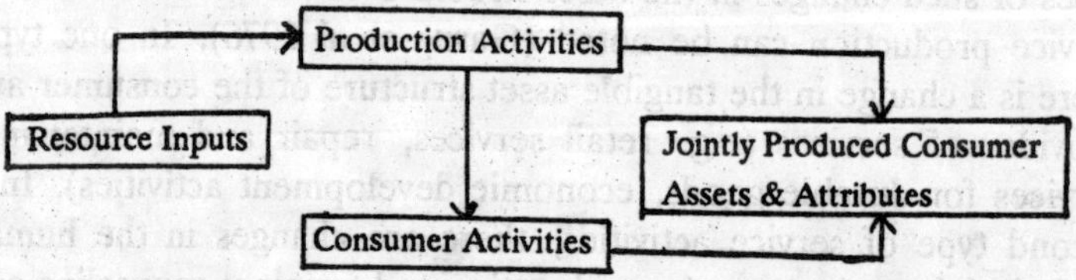

FIG. 8.2: The Production of Service Output (After Garn et al 1976)

This is not the case with production of services (Fig. 8.2), where the consumer of services is part of the process of service production. The final output is jointly produced. Becker (1965) conceptualized the market goods as intermediate goods that individuals combine with their time and skills to produce final products or commodities (e.g. meals, entertainments recreation, etc) they consume. Becker's notions have been extended by social indicator researchers (Garn et al 1976) so as to view consumers as producers in the realm of service production. For example, the provision for quality health services requires the participation of the patient in the form of producing accurate medical histories, cooperating in the treatment, etc. In other words, the efficiency of the service production cannot be solely attributed to the activities of the producer. The consumer's actions bear upon the efficiency and effectiveness of the services.

There are other differences in the technology of manufacturing and service operations. First, a major characteristic of manufacturing technologies is concerned with materials processing and often with the provision and sequencing of workflow activities and the Fordist mode of labour organization (Mills and Moburg, 1980; Blackburn, Coombs and Green, 1985). In contrast, service technologies are "knowledge technologies" that are defined as; "a set of ideas that express the goals of work, its functional importance and the rationale for the methods employed" (Thompson, 1967; Dubin, 1968). Unlike goods production, where raw material inputs pass through a linear conversion process into a final output, technologies may be applied in the service sector outside the conversion process (Mills and Moburg, 1980). The ambience surrounding queues, waiting rooms, post-operative care facilities and the restaurant lounges may greatly contribute to the technologies used in the health services produced and consumed. The transactional nature of the interaction and several information exchange sub-processes lead to a reciprocal rather than a linear sequence. Since the distinction between inputs, outputs and conversions are muddled in the service process, the work process has a greater degree of reciprocity and feedback and is clearly non-Fordist.

Further, given the non-material nature of some service outputs, their utility depends upon the manner of provision and often service workers may assist the consumer in socially constructing perceptions of the value of service outputs (Butler, 1980).

Further, as noted earlier, service technologies depend on the consumer not only to provide the information that constitutes the raw material to be worked on, but also to participate in the service production.

We briefly characterize the nature of service provider–consumer interface along two dimensions. First, in terms of the four *functions* the service client can perform (Normann, 1984):

(i) *Specification* of the service: e.g. by participation in the diagnosis of the problems by providing health data, specifying items in a menu of services that are desired as in a restaurant, etc.

(ii) *Self Service:* where the consumer is used as primary input without interaction with the producer (e.g. retailing, automatic banking, etc.). The idea is to reduce the labour costs of service.

(iii) *Coproduction:* where the client carries out part of the production (e.g. client's staff doing data collection and some analysis for market analysis; residents participating in housing services delivery; the student contribution to education, etc).

(iv) *Development* of the services in a professional organization (e.g. in advertising auditing, consulting).

A second way to characterize the producer-client interface is via the labour-capital dimension (Fig. 8.3). While service producers position themselves in one of the four cells initially, they may change their technologies over time. Thus a producer engaged in traditional labour-intensive conventional training (Cell 1) may shift over time into computer aided training which involves the client using producer's specialized capital (Cell 2).

Client / Producer	Labour	Capital
Labour	Conventional Training Welfare Agency	Car Repair; Computer Software
Capital	Computer-aided training; Automatic bank teller	Automatic Carwash

FIG. 8.3 : Different Types of Producer-Client Interfacing

A Technology-Based Classification of Services

Given these patterns of producer-consumer interface and our interest in service technologies, we proceed to a classification of service activities that highlights the differences among the activities in the type, generality and instrumentality of information exchanged at this interface during service production. Such a classification will throw light on the relative potential of information technologies and their diffusion in various sectors. We present now such a classification that may be appropriate for analysing technical change. It builds on the ideas of Mills and Moburg (1980) and Baumol (1985) and is based on the nature and intensity of producer-consumer contact and the types of skills and knowledge brought to the service by the clients. The kinds of encounters between producers and clients will depend upon the degree of environmental uncertainty (reflecting the complexity of the information exchanged).

We adopt Mills and Moburg (1980) to our purposes and we recognize four classes of services:

(i) Quasi-industrial Services (QI)
(ii) Routine Interactive Services (RI)
(iii) Task Interactive Services (TI)
(iv) Personal Interactive Services (PI)

Quasi-industrial Services (QI)

The term Quasi-industrial Services refers to a class of services whose technologies are closest of that of goods production. They are complementary to goods production and include the greater part of the Browning and Singlemann (1975) category of distributive services. Examples would be transportation, communications and wholesale activities. Such organizations operate in stable environments and the information resources exchanged at the producer-consumer interface are direct and simple. Since the consumer's demands are known and the consumer can monitor the activity of the producer, the latter can develop technologies that are amenable to economies of scale and considerable capital/labour substitution. New physical technologies for materials assembly, and digital communication and intelligence information technologies for automated warehousing operations are broadly applicable and hence the appellation Quasi-industrial for these services.

Routine Interactive Services (RI)

In these activities, the direct interaction between the service employee and the consumer is limited and the information transmitted is relatively limited. However, that information input is vital to the production function since the customer knows what he or she wants. An example of this is the interaction between a bank teller and a customer. Examples of such activities are retail outlets, fast food restaurants, banks, etc.

These activities occur in environments with low uncertainty. The customer needs and production technologies are well known. The service provider is less involved with production and more in dispensing them. Specifying in advance responses to consumer demands, there is a tendency to standardize activities and set up large-scale operations, thereby increasing productivity. The consumer may be incorporated in the self-service mode and the information exchanged is simple in nature. This group includes services using self-service, e.g. retail and personal services amenable to "industrialization" (Levitt, 1976) e.g. fast food restaurants. Customer involvement is minimal and is often completely removed in some predictable environments by employing appropriate equipment (ATM's in banks).

Task Interactive Services (TI)

The term task interactive pertains to the technologies in task accomplishment that are paramount in these activities. Examples are legal firms, engineering and architectural firms and marketing and advertising organizations. The focus is on the encounter between the provider of the service and the consumer and the tasks or skills needed to provide the services (Mills, 1986). The firms in this sector possess a body of knowledge that is relevant to the problem to be solved.

Moderate to high degree of uncertainty characterizes the environment of these activities. The technologies to solve these task-oriented problems are known, but large amounts of information and effort are expended before the customer's needs are known. The consumer is aware of his problem but looks for the expertise of the provider. Further, the uncertainty exists because of the uniqueness of the client's needs and the contingencies in specific situations, which may prevent the imposition of precise standards on service performance. Since TI service environments are inherently uncertain, the producer-consumer interface tends to be concentrated and periodic. If a client requires litigation, the lawyer would work out the feasibility of the solution, though the outcome may be beyond his control. Thus there may be much uncertainty in such services.

Personal Interactive Services (PI)

The environment on these services are both dynamic and complex. The consumers are unaware or imprecise about their problems or solutions. Thus the service producer and consumer jointly strive to diagnose the problem. The body of knowledge that exists is such that the cause-effect relationship between what the service producer does and the outcome of the action is not sound. It is in this category that "professionals" and professional organizations originally developed. Examples of such services are health care, psychological consulting, welfare agencies, etc.

These activities operate in dynamic and complex environments. The complexity derives from the environmental uncertainty since consumers are often imprecise or unaware of their problems (e.g. health provision, welfare services, etc.). The health professional will utilize considerable knowledge technology in diagnosing the problem. The consumer participates in this diagnosis by providing information. Each service episode may refer to an entirely different set of problems so that the diagnostic process is continuous. Further, the knowledge technology used to address a problem may have limited predictive power. For example, a welfare worker's efforts at assisting a client to be self-sufficient may not work. Thus there is much scope for creativity.

The characteristics of services as outlined here pose special problems for the market provision of services. As Holmstrom (1985) suggests, the quality of services provision is difficult to assess. Whereas the service provider may know product quality, the buyer often does not. A doctor will clearly know much more about the probabilities of success of a medical procedure than his or her patient. So does a lawyer understand more often basic merits of a case than his or her client. This "asymmetry" of information between sellers and buyers of service poses severe problems for market provision (Holmstrom, 1985). Two kinds of problems arise: "adverse selection" and "moral hazard".

Adverse selection occurs when the consumer is unable to observe and monitor the activities of the service producer. The patient may be unable to determine whether the procedures and tests the doctor implemented are appropriate. There is potential for adverse selection when the service is oversupplied.

Moral hazard occurs when the quantity and quality of the service rendered is difficult to verify. In the case of unsatisfactory outcomes or "failures" the recipient of the service cannot distinguish perfectly between incompetence and bad luck and this has bad incentive effects on the service provider. Such problems of monitoring and assessing the performance of such service providers can often create a variety of new services – informative advertising and certifications, warranties and contingent contracts, seller reputation, etc. More generally there are two mechanisms for addressing the quality problem resulting from adverse selections and moral hazard; monitoring and bonding activities: in the private sector, the importance of reputation of the service sector becomes important.

The magnitude and dimensions of these four service sector classes, computed from the U.S. Census public use data for 1983, show that the smallest category of services is the quasi-industrial (QI) at about 7 million workers. It had also the highest average wage ($14,050), reflecting its high capital intensity sectors and the rapid penetration of information technologies. The numerically largest group is the routine interactive (RI) services involving highly routinized operations with minimal exchange of information and knowledge (25 million). The average wage is the lowest at $ 5,366, reflecting the highest proportion of part-time employment of any category. The next numerous group is the personal interactive (PI) at 24.2 million. The wages are second highest reflecting the greater premium for the professional groups here. The task interactive group (TI) is half the size of the PI group and has an average wage of $ 8,000. This aggregate analysis conceals perhaps more than it reveals. A separate analysis of these patterns by cross-tabulating these four service sectors with five major occupational categories (that reflect generalized levels of training rather than the census classes) is underway and may throw light on the categories of skills among workers and the corresponding wages.

III. INFORMATION ACTIVITIES AND TECHNOLOGIES

The Emergence of the Information Sector

The symbiotic relationship between the growth of new information technologies and the transformation of services is often commented on (Kimbel, 1987; Faulhaber et al, 1986; Nusbaumer, 1987; Lakshmanan, 1988). As noted earlier, the growth of services reflects partly the increasing global nature of business (resulting from dramatic drops in unit transportation and communication costs). With expanding markets and increasing division of labour, there is a greater need for coordination, for integration and binding together the increasingly differentiated, specialized parts and functions of the global market system. The greater the number of participants and the finer the division of labour, the more complex the technological process and the greater the range of goods and services an economic system generates, the more "economic intelligence" or "technological and scientific information" the economic process requires. The economic system becomes more information intensive.

Such changes in the information environment accompanying broad structural changes have been noted for over two decades. Fritz Machlup's (1962) pioneering analysis of the "knowledge industries" (as including education, research, publishing and broadcasting) suggested that over 31 per cent of the U.S. labour force in 1962 was working in such occupations. Bell (1973), using a narrower definition of knowledge workers as only information producers, estimated the core of a knowledge society as 12.2 per cent the U.S. employment in 1963. The concept of "information sector" as the segment of the workforce that primarily produces, processes, or distributes information goods and services was elaborated by Marc Porat (1975). Porat's broad definition includes not only Machlup's knowledge workers, but also all who use information as a productive input irrespective of industrial sectors where their jobs belong. Figure 8.4 drawn from Katz (1986) relates some of the different definitions of information workers.

The long-term trend of information workforce (Fig. 8.4) shows a steady growth in the USA and other developed countries (OECD 1986). Increases in the total factor productivity in the information handling of tasks induced by new technologies (e.g. computers, data and text processing systems) have raised employment so far (Kimbel, 1987). One must note that many of the information occupations have appeared for the first time in the last few decades and there should be a distinction between the expansion of the information sector from economic growth and the increase in demand for information occupations resulting from increasing division of labour and specialization (Lamberton, 1982). One must also note that the growth of information is dominant in the service sector but not limited to it. The increasing complexity of the external environment of goods production has created greater demand for information occupations as well.

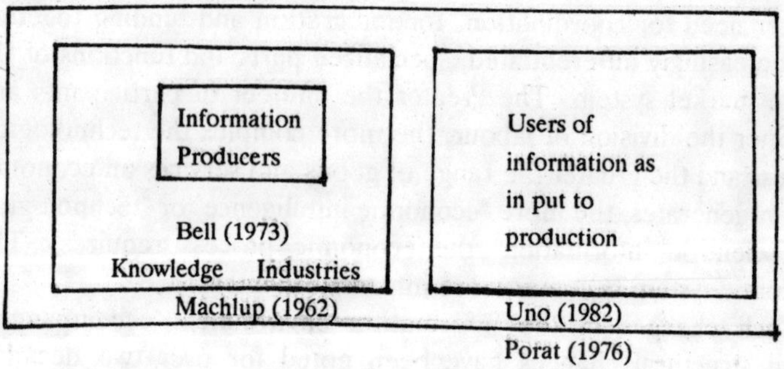

FIG. 8.4: Different Definitions of Information Activities

Evolution of Information Technologies

What is the contribution that information makes that provides a stimulus to such phenomenal growth of information activities? How is all the information provided by this burgeoning sector used in the economy?

Part of the answer lies in the relationship of information processing technologies to the ensemble of already existing technologies. Jacques Ellul (1980) has suggested that the growth of IT has created a technological system out of independent autonomous technical specializations and ensembles. At the middle of the century, technology had included all areas of human activity, but different technical specializations tended to be independent, autonomous and unintelligible to outsiders. For example, urban water and sewage treatment, power, telephone networks or different modes of transport were the realm of specialists with conflict-prone encounters with other groups (Cerezuelle, 1986). The solution was to develop institutional arrangements that would mediate the diversity (e.g. the rapid growth of bureaucracy). More recently IT has made possible for each technological process to be planned not only with an eye on the specific task at hand but also from the point of view of disseminating information about it, and with an understanding of the condition of technology in the larger environmental context. Thus the various technologies have unified into a system through the use of information transmitted from one sector to the other (Ellul, 1980).

It is through reciprocal and integrated information that a flexible, informal, technological intersection of various technical subsystems takes place. Over time, the need for coherence leads to a relentless drive toward a global, economic, organizational and trans-technical integration. Each undertaking has to adjust to an ever-growing range of factors in a global environment of innovations, resources, markets, etc. That is why information must be organized and programmed to include different kinds and levels of data.

To perform this integrative function, the information or knowledge sector has two components: the information and communication infrastructure and the flows and content of information over that infrastructure. The communication infrastructure is technical in nature including telegraph, telephon radio, television, etc. It provides the highway along which information travels. Recent developments in telecommunication and data processing technologies have reduced structural differences between those two technologies, permitting the interconnection of computers to the telecommunications network and the development of a wide variety of "intelligent" products, production processes and service activities that involve collection, processing, receiving, transmitting and acting upon information. Further, the application of these systems has led to a wide variety of IT products, of more "intelligent" products (which incorporate greater information processing capability) and new generations of electronics-based equipment and related systems such as robots, computer controlled machine tools and text and word processors.

The IT sector is not limited to the traditional transmission of basic voice and message communications, but in view of convergence of market and technology structure, now provides a variety of voice, text, data and video transmission services: electronic mail, wide area telephone services (WATS), voice message services, teleconferencing, computerized data transmission, videotex and data base access software-defined "virtual" networks, environmental control, etc.

A major new development is the linking of computers and terminals into flexible configurations called networks. Networking lets computer systems and terminals share resources and exchange information files and programmes. Before some form of networking, business services, for example, had to be produced at or near the point of consumption, namely, the point of manufacture. With networking, that allows receipt and delivery of information instantaneously, the business services can be separated geographically, since the cost of communications has also dropped rapidly.[4]

All of this has led to the development of new services that link users and producers of information. Individuals at highly dispersed locations can put in and take out information into the networks. A worldwide British construction company can use the network to allocate its resources in the most efficient manner-utilize Indian engineers, Jordanese workers, Swedish building materials, British managers, Japanese finance and American insurance in a major building project in the Middle East. Networks are at the heart of the contemporary methods of business operation.

Networks can operate at three levels (Feketuty and Hauser, 1986):

(i) *Private Networks*.

that link units inside a large organization, to improve information service, lower price and generate new business potential as in many multinational corporations.

(ii) *Limited Participation Networks*

that facilitate sharing of information within an industry (e.g. SITA in air travel and SWIFT in banking).

(iii) *Public Networks*

currently, these are mainly available as only data networks that can be accessed to at a price.

IV. TYPES OF KNOWLEDGE AND PATTERNS OF TECHNOLOGY DIFFUSION

We suggest here that emerging information technologies (IT) have the potential to provide types of knowledge that vary in generality, power and instrumentality. These types of knowledge make *possible* the transformation of service sector tasks in ways that will provide not only greater production efficiency and new service products, but also be the basis for a future general expansion.

Before we proceed to tackling this broad topic in this brief paper, we draw attention first to the larger context of IT, in terms of other technologies and social and institutional conditions that will ultimately determine the application and diffusion of various technologies.

A Digression About Context

Since technology is the "how" and "what" of production, the diffusion of any major technical development is very much a socio-economic and political matter. The "evolutionary" theorists of technical change focus on analysis of cumulative processes that affect the pattern and spread and diffusion of innovations in the larger economy (Usher, 1954; Rosenberg, 1976; David, 1975; Nelson and Winter, 1982).

If a technical innovation is to be widely diffused, several contributory factors must operate. First, there is a period of critical "secondary inventions" and design modifications that improve the quality and efficiency and thus the adoption chances. Second, there is a role of development of human skills and capital goods capacity upon which the use of the new technique depends in order to be effectively exploited. In the earlier stages, IBM and other high technology firms have had to develop not only the sophisticated machinery and the trained labour they need to produce and sell but also to educate the consumers. At a later stage of development of the technology, adjustment costs such as human skill development are borne in the larger society.

Third, the diffusion of an innovation is facilitated by complementary productive technologies. The growing productivity of an economy is thus the complex outcome of a large number of interlocking, mutually reinforcing technologies, the individual components of which are not that significant. Thus an interrelated clustering of innovations will simulate rapid diffusion (Rosenberg, 1976). Nelson and Winter (1982) develop the concept of technological trajectories or direction of advance common to a wide range of technologies.

Fourth, a variety of complementary and mutually supporting social innovations are critical to the diffusion of technologies in the broader society (Lakshmanan, 1987). Such innovations include new institutions, management approaches, reorganization of the labour process, the development of supporting physical infrastructures, devices to promote mobility in factor and geographic space and finally newer ways of life.

This view of cumulative causation has been elaborated in structural terms by the French regulation school (e.g. Aglietta, 1979). This school points to a structural whole of economic, social, institutional and ideological arrangements that can be labelled an "accumulation regime" characterized by a specific mode of economic organization and social regulation. The development of capitalism is viewed as characterized by succession of such regimes.[5]

The key question from these perspectives is that the introduction of IT is in a socio-technical system, so that interest is in the way societies reproduce and adapt themselves, using and reshaping IT. For instance, the spread of IT depends crucially on infrastructure just as automobiles depend upon highways and service stations; or VCR's depend upon video programming and a network of video rental outlets. Infrastructure for IT services would comprise:

- Electronic networks (similar to a road system)
- Maintenance and support organizations
- Organizations for training and computer literacy
- Legal infrastructure in terms of security safeguards, privacy rights, etc.

Thus the growth and spread of major technologies has to be viewed in specific socio-economic technical systems that represent particular clusters of process and product technology, infrastructure, social organizations and ways of life. These components of such systems adapt and evolve in response to introduction of IT or other major techniques – either in a cumulative evolutionary manner or in periodic radical steps (Elster, 1983; Rosenberg, 1976; Freeman, 1987). It is the interaction between new physical technologies and the social institutional responses that determines the modifications of knowledge technologies and organizations and thus the speed of diffusion of technologies. There is a scope here for a variety of alternative political and social "evolutions" as IT gets introduced. However, each of such a potential trajectory will exhibit widespread use of the information technology (Perez, 1985).

IT and Types of knowledge

The growth of an economic sector such as the service sector is a process of knowledge accumulation, the progressive development of embodied knowledge, a development of behaviours that incorporate an understanding of the environmental context that is good enough for survival and growth. This implies that we must have knowledge of the external world in order to construct knowledge technologies, since the latter are essential to the pursuit of knowledge towards further evolution.

Technologies purposely applied to the pursuit of knowledge are part of a larger class technology in general (Levinson, 1986). How does technology information oriented or otherwise contribute to this growth of knowledge? Technologies not only embody knowledge in their material structures, but are deliberately designed to help generate and disseminate other knowledge by the way they operate. Such cognitive evolution takes on a special form when technology is directed to the acquisition of knowledge. Levinson (1986) recognizes the contributions of four kinds of information technology:

(i) *Perception Extenders*
(e.g. telescopes, microscopes and similar technologies that extend external experience and thus the generation of knowledge in areas inaccessible to naked senses).

(ii) *Cognitive Processing Enhancers*
(e.g. computers that enhance the operation of our internal cognitive faculties, promoting the creation of new

knowledge from huge quantities of experience that might have otherwise overwhelmed unaided human capacities).

(iii) *Information Disseminators by High Levels of Abstraction*
(e.g. written, spoken or computer languages that facilitate the communication, criticism and dissemination of abstract information).

(iv) *Information Dissemination by High Levels of Realism*
(Image and sound producing equipment that provide representations of high degree of correspondence to sense perceived reality).

While these different kinds of IT make possible knowledge that covers all the necessary cognitive bases (external, internal, abstract and sensory), what kinds of knowledge are relevant to levels of dynamic changes in production, thereby influencing economic evolution?

Anderson and Johansson (1984) make an important contribution in this regard by recognizing four types of knowledge and production. These types, in increasing order of complexity, are:

1. *Information* (or data):
elemental units with a limited structure that can be aggregated, disaggregated and transmitted.
2. *Knowledge:*
Structurally ordered information.
3. *Competence:*
which is knowledge embodied within our hardware (machinery, instruments, etc.) software and orgware (institutions, organizations, etc.) and,
4. *Creativity:*
which is the concept of the highest order, implying a capacity to order and reorder information with the aid of a knowledge system.
We adopt this classification and elaborate on its potential for our purposes.

Knowledge is of two types: the first is the facts of the domain–the widely shared knowledge obtained from books and journals. The second is the heuristic knowledge, which is obtained from experience, good practice and good judgement in the field, getting a feel for the problem, learning when to go by the book and when to skip the rules. In this manner, a repertory of rules of thumb are "heuristics", that combined with the domain of knowledge produces experts.

Another perspective on knowledge would distinguish between generality, power and instrumentality. Generality can be viewed as the "number" of the aspect of a solution. It indicates the *scope* of a solution or the class of problems that can be handled by that solution (Malvey, 1985). Power is the "size" quality of the problem, the degree of fit or explanation achieved by a solution. Only for the situation of a near-perfect knowledge can we have both general and powerful solutions – mostly narrow, technical problems. At the other end are broad problems where the "solutions" have low power and low generality.

The ideas in technological knowledge become embodied in "things". These "things" could be hardware, software, or an organization. The embodiment of knowledge in the form of competence serves two purposes:

1. The embodiment of knowledge is designed to generate and disseminate other knowledge by means of their operation. For instance, a telescope not only incorporates theories of optics, and techniques of lens making, but improves our knowledge of the universe when it is pointed at the stars. Computers similarly embody not only great engineering and gadgetry, but also greatly speed up the sorting and classification of numerical information. The result is that the computer reduces the numerosity of the universe, the sheer expanse and myriads of detail to humanly graspable dimensions–allowing us to expand our cognitive faculties. Since competence gives this "double assist" to human cognition, it may be viewed as an artifact of cognition whose purpose is further cognition. (Levinson, 1986)
2. A second purpose is the distinction between machinery and commodity (Bergmann, 1986) that is crucial to the speed of diffusion of technology–for example, a technological device such as a digital watch. While the machinery undergoes revolutionary changes that remove it from the comprehension of the common person, the commodity develops continuously making fewer and

fewer demands on the user's competence or care (hence "user friendly"). This tendency is quite general and can be observed for most IT items that surround us.

Referring to creativity, Anderson and Johansson note that "We assume that the creative process is synergistic and this implies that information, knowledge and competence are brought into an intensive interaction with each other in order to shape new knowledge, i.e. new products, new processes and even new scientific fields." They continue by saying that "the social dimension of knowledge and competence communication seems to be extremely strong and gives a very large relative efficiency of face-to-face communication".

Types of Knowledge and Patterns of Technology Diffusion

What changes in the organization of production of services are consistent with these kinds of knowledge explosions generated by IT, so that higher levels of productivity can be realized? Put another way, what changes in the organization of service production and delivery would appear to be strategically necessary (and can be directed if recognized early enough) if the opportunities for profitable investment in the new technology-based services are to be realized?

We do not attempt to develop future socio-technological trajectories to respond to these questions. Instead, we identify the kinds of successive phases of diffusion of technologies that may be indicated by the different types of knowledge made available by IT.

1. The first phase of technology diffusion occurs with the widespread use of data to rationalize *peripheral activities* in the organization. In this phase, the focus is on doing older tasks more cheaply and with better quality, taking advantage of the enormous growth of cheap computing power. It is a case of a high power, general capability to manipulate data that is being used in financial, personnel data systems. In the early stages, with large computers, this was a centralized function. With the development of minicomputers, this capacity to manipulate and process data was extended to various departments; with the development of microcomputers and greater cost reductions, the potential for distributed processing has become available.

2. Since distributed intelligence in organizational terms means distributed decision making, the second phase of IT extending to and modifying part of the *Core Technology* of service production is possible, if relevant knowledge and competence in the system are harnessed for the task.

The first part of this phase is focused on reorganization based on cost competition. Specific types of change are:

(a) *Economics of Scale*: The idea is to link various units of autonomous services with the aim of reaping potential economies of scale through IT.

(b) *Substitution* of relatively abundant or less costly productive factors for relatively scarcer and expensive ones.
This involves *debundling* older activities into components which can be recombined so that cheaper labour can be used or different forms of output can be provided.

(c) Increased division of labour and specialization of functions.

3. Development of new service products and task reorganization.

V. TECHNOLOGY DIFFUSION IN THE HEALTH CARE SECTOR

Illustrations in the Health Care Sector

Phases in Diffusion	Characteristics	Illustrations
1. Modification of Peripheral Activities	Manipulation of data; New ways of doing old jobs. Minimal use of knowledge systems and competence. oximately 2-3% of overall hospital costs.	Data processing expenditures $ 1.6 billion (1983); 64% in financial records. Patient care only 21.8% Appr-
2. Some changes in the core technologies' use of knowledge and competence in the form of expert systems	(a) Economics of Scale	(a) Consolidation of small independent providers into larger units
	(b) Substitution of factors	(b) Less trained paramecidals for doctors; Capital for labour through robots for physical work;

		ambulatory care for inpatient care.
	(c) Specialization and division of labour. All these being helped by DRG (prospective pricing system) a financial innovation.	(c) Patient care monitoring by IT; Use of special diagnostic expert systems to complement physician work, eg. MYCIN
3. Major changes in the core technologies.	Debundling older activities and reorganizing.	Many of the craft aspects of health care modified; Career ladders changed for many workers. Newer labour process.

NOTES

1. This elementary function of communication is the foundation of the economic worth of services. Specific forms of this function include various types of transportation, or intermediation such as traders, suppliers, customs agents, insurers, bankers, advertisers, etc. In addition, there are a group of service activities contributing indirectly to goods fabrication: design and consulting services, accounting, administrative, rental services, etc.
2. We pursue in separate paper (Lakshmanan 1988) the nature of labour process reorganization in the context of 'distributed intelligence' technologies in the information intensive service sector that become input adaptable, market adaptable flexible systems.
3. An analysis of 145 industry groups in terms of capital stock per work hour shows that the service industry groups formed nearly one-half of the 30 groups in the top 2 deciles and the bottom 3 deciles of industry ranking by capital intensity did not contain any service industries (Kutscher and Mar 1983). Further the range of productivity growth noted in the service sector is not significanly different from the range among goods producing sectors (Kutscher and Mark 1983). The growth of services cannot possibly be the cause of the recent slowdown in productivity in the larger economy (Fuchs 1985).
4. A typical international telex message cost $ 3/minute in 1970. Fifteen years later, it has dropped to a few cents per minute. In the near future, computer transmission is expected at 1.5 megabits per second.
5. Examples of such changes with accompanying sshifts in the space economy are the heavy industry at the turn of the century, the mass production of consumer durables betwen the 1920's and the 1960s.

REFERENCES

Aglietta, M., (1979). *A Theory of Capitalistic Regilation* London, N.L.B., Publishers.

Andersson, Ake and B. Johansson, "Knowledge Intensity and Product Cycles in Metropolitan Region," International Institute for Applied Systems Analysis (IIASA), Working Paper, Lexenburg, Austria, 1984, 44 pages.

Barras, Richard, "Towards a Theory of Innovation in Services," *Research Policy*, 5, 4: pp. 161-173.

Baumol, William, (1967). "The Macroeconomics of Unbalanced Growth," *American Economic Review*, 57, 415-26.

Baumol, William, (1985). "Productivity Policy and the Service Sector" in *Managing the Service Economy: Prospects and Problems* (ed) R.P. Inman, London. Cambridge University Press. 301-317.

Berg, Sanford, V., (1973). "Determinants of Technological Change in the Service Industries," *Technological Forecasting and Social Change*, 5, pp. 407-426.

Blackburn, Phillip R. Coombs and K. Green, (1985). *Technology, Economic Growth and the Labour Process*. New York, St. Martin's Press.

Browning, H.C. and J. Singlemann, (1975). *The Emergence of a Service Society*, Springfield, VA, National Technical Information Service.

Burger, A., (1970). *Economic Problems of Consumers' Services* Budapest, Akedemai Kiado.

Butler, R.J. (1980). "User Satisfaction with a Service", *Journal of Management Studies* 17, pp. 1-18.

Cerezuelle, David (1986). "Information Technology and Technology System," in *Philosophy and Technology II* (eds) C. Mitcham and A. Husning. Boston, D. Reidel Publishing Co., pp. 217-225.

Chase, Richard B. and David Tansik, (1983). "The Customer Contact Model for Organizational Design" *Management Science* 29, 1037-50.

Chatterjee, Lata, (1986). "Coproduction and Low Income Strategies"; paper presented at the International Housing Research Conference, Gavle, Sweden, June 10-13. Boston University Centre for Energy and Environmental Studies Research Paper No. 4.

Coile, Russell C. Jr., (1986). *The New Hospital*, Rockville, MD, Aspen Publishers.

Daniels, P.W., (1985). *Service Industries: A Geographic Appraisal*, London, Methuen.

David, P. (1970). *Technical Choice, Innovation and Economic Growth*, Cambridge, MA, Cambridge University Press. *

Davis, Lance E. and Douglass C. North, (1971). *Institutional Change and American Economics Growth*, Cambridge, U.K., Cambridge University Press.

Dubin, R. (1968). *Human Relations and Administration* Englewood Cliffs, NJ, Prentice Hall.

Ellul, Jacques, (1980). *The Technological System* (trans) Joachim Neugroschel. New York, Continuum.

Elster, Jon, (1985). *Explaining Technical Change*, Cambridge, U.K., Cambridge University Press.

Faulhaber, G., E. Noam and R. Talsey (eds) (1986). *Services in Transition*. Cambridge, MA, Ballinger.

Fecketekufy, G. and K. Hauser, (1986). "The Impact of Information Technology on Trade in Services," in *Services in Transition* (eds) G. Faulhaber, E. Noam and R. Talsey. Cambridge, MA Ballinger, pp. 81-97.

Field, Alexander J., (1981). "The Problem with Neoclassical Institutional Economics: A critique with special reference to the North-Thomas Model of Pre-1500 Europe," *Exploration in Economic History*, 18, 74-98.

Fitzsimmons, James a. and R.S. Sullivan, (1982). *Service Operations Management, New York, McGraw-Hill.*

Freeman, Christopher, (1987). "The Case for Technological Determinism," in *Information Technology: Social Issues* (eds) R. Finnegan, G. Salaman and K. Thompson. London, Hodder and Stoughton,. pp. 3-18.

Fuchs, Victor, (1968). *The Services Economy*, New York: National Bureau of National Research and Columbia University Press.

Garn, Harvey A., (1973). "Public Services on the Assembly Line," *Evaluation*, Vol. 1, No. 2.

Garn, Harvey A., (1975). "Programme Evaluation and Policy Analysis of Community Development Corporations," in *The Social Economy of Cities*, Vol. 9, Urban Affairs Annual Previews: Sage Publications, Inc.

Garn, Harvey A., M.J. Flex, M. Springer and J.B. Taylor, (1976). *Models for Indicator Development*, Washington, D.C.: Urban Institute (Paper 1206-17).

Gershuny, J.I., (1978). *After Industrial Society: The Emerging Self Service Economy*, MacMillan, London.

Gershuny, J.I. and R.E. Pahl, (1979). "Towards an Alternative Society," Paper read at Social Science Research Council Workshop on Unemployment and Employment, London, September 28.

Gillispie, A.E. and M.E. Hepworth, (1986). "Telecommunications and Regional Development in the Information Society," New Castle Studies of the Information Economy. Working Paper No. 1, University of New Castle upon Tyne, October.

Gramlich, Edward M., "Government Services," in *Managing the Service Economy* (ed) Robert Inman, London, Cambridge University Press, 273-289.

Hirsch, Fred, (1976). *Social Limits of Growth*, Cambridge, MA, Harvard University Press.

Hirschman, A., (1958). *The Strategy of Economic Development*, New Haven, Yale University Press.

Hirshorn, L., (1985). "Information Technology and the New Service Game," in *High Technology, Space and Society*, (ed.) Manual Castels, Beverly Hills, Sage Publications, 172-90.

Holmstrom, Bengt, (1985). "The Provision of Services on a Market Economy," in *Managing the Service Economy: Prospects and Problems* (ed) Robert P. Inman, London, Cambridge University Press, 183-213.

Ikegami, N. and Seth B. Goldsmith, (1985). "Quality Circles: The Myth and Reality of Hospital Management," *H C M Review*, Summer 10 (3) pp. 45-53.

Kimball, Dieter, (1987). "Information Technology Today and Tomorrow," *Telecommunications Policy* December, pp. 377-389.

Kikuchi, Massao and Yujiro Hayami, (1980). "Inducements to Institutional Innovation in Agrarian Community," *Economic Development and Cultural Change*, October 21-36.

Kraemer, Kenneth L. and J.L. King, (1983). "Information Technology and Local Government in the Next Decade," in *The Impact of New Technologies on Information Systems in Public Administration*, (ed) H. Krause, New York, North Holland Press, pp. 177-198.

Kutscher, R.E. and Jerome A. Mark, (1983). "The Service Producing Sector: Some Common Perception Reviewed," *Monthly Labour Review*, April 21-24.

Lakshmanan, T.R. and Lata Chatterjee, (1986). "Technical Change and Metropolitan Evolution," *Regional Science and Urban Economics*, February, pp. 7-30.

Lakshmanan, T.R., (1987). "Technological and Institutional Innovations in the Service Sector" Paper presented at the symposium on Research and Development, Industrial Change and Economic Policy (RICE), University of Karlstad, Sweden June, 21-26.

Lakshmanan, T.R., (1988). "Infrastructure and Economic Transformation" in *Advances in Spatial Theory and Dynamics* (eds) Ake Andersson, P. Nijkamp, D Batten and B. Johansson, New York, North Holland, 1988.

Lakshmanan, T.R.. (1988). "Structural Trends in the Service Sector and the Emerging Labour Process", Paper prepared for presentation at the Boston University Urban Studies Dinner Group

Leff, Nathaniel H., (1984). "Externalities, Information Costs, and Social Benefit — Cost Analysis for Economic Development: An Example from Telecommunications," *Economic Development and Cultural Change* Vol. 32, #.2, 255-275.

Levenson, Irving, (1985). "Services in the U.S. Economy," in *Managing the Service Economy: Prospects and Problems*, (ed) Robert P. Inman, London, Cambridge University Press, pp. 80-102.

Levinson, Paul, (1986). "Information Technologies and Evolution", in *Philosophy and Technology II* (eds) C. Mitcham and A. Huning, Boston, D. Reidel Publishing Co., pp. 29-47.

Levitt, Theodore, (1976). "The Industrialization of Service," *Harvard Business Review*, September.

Linder, Steffan, (1970). *The Harried Leisure Class*, New York: Columbia University Press.

Malvey, Man, (1981). *Simple Systems, Complex Environments*, Beverly Hills, CA, Sage Publications.

Miles, Ian, J. Bessant, K. Curry and H. Rush, (1987). "IT Futures in Households and Communications," in *Information Technology: Social Issues* (eds) R. Finnegan, G. Salaman and K. Thompson, Sevenoaks Kent, U.K., Hudder and Stoughton, pp., 225-244.

Mills, Peter K. and Newton Marguiles, (1980). "Toward a Core Typology of Service Organizations," *Academy of Management Review*, 5:2, pp. 255-265.

Mills, Peter K. and D.J. Moburg, (1982). "Perspective on the Technology of Service Operations," *Academy of Management Review*, 7:3 pp. 467-78.

Mills, Peter, K., (1986). *Managing Service Industries: Organizational Practices in a Post Industrial Economy*, Cambridge, MA, Ballinger.

Nelson, Richard R., (1986). "Institutions Supporting Technical Advance in Industry," *American Economic Review*, 76:2, pp. 186-89.

Nelson, Richard R. and Sidney G. Winter, (1982). *An Evolutionary Theory of Economic Change*, Cambridge, MA, Harvard University Press.

North, Douglass C. and R.P. Thomas, (1970). "An Economic Theory of the Growth of the Western World," *The Economic History Review*, 23:1, 1-17.

North Douglass C., (1981). *Structure and Chance in Economic History*, New York, W.W. Norton, Co.

North Douglass C. and John J. Wallis, (1982). "American Governmental Expenditures: A Historical Perspective," *American Economic Review*, May, 336-40.

Normann, Richard, (1984). *Service Management*, New York, John Wiley & Sons.

Nusbaumer, Jacques, (1987). *The Service Economy: Lever to Growth*, Boston, Kluwer.

OECD, (1986). *Trends in the Information Economy*, IICP Series Paper II, Paris.

Olson, Mancur, (1982). *Rise and Decline of Nations*, New Haven, CT, Yale University Press.

Perez, Carlota, (1985). "Microeconomics Long Waves and World Structural Change: New Perspectives for Developing Countries," *World Development*, 13, 3, pp. 441-463.

Petit, Pascal, (1986). *Slow Growth and the Service Economy*, New York, St. Martin's Press.

Porat, Marc V., (1982). "Information, Communication and Division of Labour," in *Communications, Economics, and Development* (ed) M. Jusswale and D.M. Lamberton, London, Pergamon, pp. 75-81.

Reinhardt, Uwe R., (1981). "Proposed Changes in the Organization of Health Care Delivery: An Overview and Critique," in *Health Services Research, Planning and Change*, (ed) John B. McKinlay, Cambridge, MA MIT Press, pp. 267-320.

Riddle, Dorothy I., (1986). *Service-Led Growth*, New York, Praeger.

Roehrich, Robert L., (1984). "The Relationship Between Technological and Business Innovation," *The Journal of Business Strategy*, 5:2, Fall, pp. 60-73.

Scheffer, Richard M., (1986). "Information Technology and the U.S. Health Care Industry," in *Services in Transition* (ed) G. Faulhaber, E. Noam and I.R. Tasley, Cambridge, MA, Ballinger, pp. 7-20.

Smith, Stephen and David Wield, (1987). "New Technology and Bank Work: Banking on IT as an Organizational Technology," in *Information Technology: Social Issues*, (eds) R. Finnegan G. Salamon and K. Thompson, Sevenoaks Kent, U.K., Hodder and Stoughton., pp. 98- 113.

Stanbeck, Thomas M. Jr., P.J. Bearse, T.J. Noyelle and Robert A. Karased, (1981). *Services: The New Economy*, Allanheld, Osmun, & Co., Totowa, NJ.

Stanbeck, Thomas M. and T.J. Noyelle, (1982). *The Cities in Transition*, Totowa, NJ, Allanheld, Osmun, & Co.

Summers, Robert, (1985). "Service in the International Economy," in *Managing the Service Economy: Prospects and Problems*, (ed) R.K. Inman, London, Cambridge University Press, pp. 27-48.

Thompson, J.D. (1967). *Organizations in Action*, New York, McGraw Hill.

Usher, A.P., (1954). *A History of Mechanical Inventions*, Cambridge, MA, Harvard University Press.

Varaiya, Pravin, (1987). Productivity in Manufacturing and the Division of Labour," paper presented at the Symposium on Research and Development, Industrial Change and Economic Policy, University of Karlstad, Sweden, June 21-26.

Vitalari, N.P. and A. Venkatesh, (1987). "Inhome Computing and Information Services," *Telecommunications Policy*, March, pp. 65-81.

Vracio, Robert A., (1985). "Hospital Strategies for the Eighties: A Mid-Decade Look," *H C M Review*, Fall, 10 (4), pp. 9-19.

Williamson, Oliver, (1980). "Transaction Cost Economics: The Governance of Contractual Relations," *Journal of Law and Economics*, March.

NINE

Economic Development and the Process of Innovation: A Competitive Firm and Industry Framework

MORGAN D. THOMAS

During the last decade and a half there has been a significant increase in interest in the role technical innovation plays in the growth of economies, industries and firms. Theorizing with respect to this role has been greatly stimulated by the rediscovery of innovation as the key explanatory element in Schumpeter's seminal theory of economic development in a capitalist economy (Schumpeter, 1934, 1939, 1950).

The critical economic development implications of the relationship between innovation and behavioural competition at firm and industry levels are enunciated in Schumpeter's theory. Contemporary studies are providing major contributions to the clarification and further development of some important aspects of this relationship (Rosenberg, 1982; Rosenbloom, 1981; Nelson and Winter, 1982; Porter, 1980; Abernathy, 1978; Abernathy, Clark and Kantrow, 1983). These new studies are beginning to ask questions about innovation's role in shaping the competitive environment (Abernathy and Clark, 1985). Furthermore, in recent years key members of innovative firms are increasingly grappling with the problem of incorporating innovation into the development of long-term firm strategy. Based on his comprehensive review of the literature on innovation, Rosenbloom (1981) concludes that we need to integrate more effectively, in a conceptual framework, our understanding of the process of innovation. Such a framework should provide useful guidance for the development of technology policy by competitive firms and governments.

This paper represents a response to a widespread recognition that there are very important reasons why we need a better understanding of both the role of innovation in the process of economic development and of the way the process of innovation shapes the competitive environment of firms and industries. In the sections of the paper which follow several heuristic frameworks are articulated: the first presents a way of viewing the competitive behaviour of "new technology based" firms and industries; the second provides a perspective on key elements in the development process of an industry technology life-cycle; and the third focuses attention on selected relationships between innovation and competition. The concluding section provides a brief assessment of the frameworks and a few observations concerning contemporary relationships between conceptual research and practice.

A Theoretical Framework

Context

At this time there is merit in addressing the question: How should we proceed to explore specific ways and means of improving our understanding of the relationships between technical innovation and economic development at the level of the firm and industry? A response to this question is presented, in this section, in the form of a heuristic framework designed to guide this exploration. Within this framework a number of conceptualizations are articulated, first, to provide an overall theoretical context for the paper and, second, to give a specific direction to a subsequent response to the question: "Why" and "How" does technical innovation shape the competitive environments of "new" technology based firms and industries?

Evolutionary Theory of Economic Development

Dissatisfaction with the guidance provided by orthodox macroeconomic growth theory has led eventually to the discovery by many scholars of a more satisfactory, realistic and stimulating body of literature which is now increasingly referred to as evolutionary theory of economic development and change. Technical change and innovation play key roles in this body of theory. Evolutionary theorists tend to recognize explicitly the strong connection between the nature and direction of their theorizing and Schumpeter's seminal ideas concerning long-term economic development and innovation (Schumpeter, 1934, 1939, 1950).

Nelson and Winter (1982) provide probably the most rigorous, thought provoking statement of this theory. The essence of evolutionary theory is its concern with the dynamic processes by which firm behaviour patterns and market outcomes are jointly determined over time. Search and selection are interacting processes that carried on simultaneously within firms. Information obtained from the decision environment not only influences the nature of firm decisions it also is used to give direction to the search within the selection or decision environment of the firm. Over time, firms evolve as a result of the joint interactive process between search and selection. Thus the condition of the firms' industry in each time period has an influence on its condition in the following period. This evolutionary process, however, is not deterministic because search outcomes by firms are partly stochastic. In other words, what the industry condition in a specific time period really "determines" is the probability distribution of its condition in the next time period (Nelson and Winter, 1982).

Of particular interest with respect to the central purpose of this paper are the role profits play in the evolutionary process of economic development theory at the level of the firm. Profits from successful innovation are regarded as disequilibrium phenomena. They are mainly generated as a result of the lead that innovation initially provides innovator firms over competitors. *Ex ante* the commercial success of innovation is very hard to predict in any detail, because of the uncertainly of outcome conditions that are integrally related to the process of innovation. Even though firms in an industry may be subject to the same broad economic influences, differences in the outcomes of their individual search and selection processes result in different decisions being made. *Ex post* some decision makers are proven right and others wrong. We may infer then that there is a coexistence of efficient and inefficient firms at all points of time. Evolutionary theory stresses these essential aspects of Schumpeterian competition, namely the diversity of firm characteristics and experience and the cumulative interaction of that diversity with industry structure (Nelson and Winter, 1982). A number of these aspects are discussed more fully in subsequent sections of this paper.

Behavioural Competition: Selected Conceptualizations

A great deal of the theorizing at the microeconomic level concerning the role of innovations and technical change in the process of economic development has been based on the seminal contributions on the subject by Schumpeter (1934, 1939, 1950). One of his key ideas was the notion of behavioural competition. He argued that it was not price competition but the competition founded on the entrepreneurial behaviour of the entrepreneur, who carried out innovation, that was responsible for the process of "creative destruction". Firms which continued to innovate successfully grew and drove non-innovating firms out of their industry. Commercially successful major radical innovations eventually destroyed even well established monopolies but, in so doing, Schumpeter believed that the vigorous new industries created offered the promise of a more prosperous future.

Schumpeter, in essence, forcefully and plausibly argued that innovations, manifested in the development of new technical possibilities by innovator firms, were a most potent source of competitive advantage, at both the level of the firm and industry. Consequently, innovations may be viewed as a vital means of generating various kinds of scaler, structural and locational changes in firms and industries. How do we now utilize Schumpeter's conceptualization of the process of "creative destruction" to achieve a better understanding of the competitive behaviour of innovative firms? In other words, how do these firms use technical innovations to enhance their competitive position within their respective industries? Conceptually we may assume that firms in the same industry produce products that are close substitutes for each other. We may also assume competition between firms in an industry continually works to drive down the rate of return on invested capital toward the competitive floor rate of return where "normal" profits are earned. A firm whose long run rate of return is customarily less than the competitive floor rate of return would be expected to go out of business. High, long run, rates of return in an industry would be expected to stimulate an inflow of investments by new entrants and existing firms (Porter, 1980, 1983). Technical innovation as a competitive variable may then be viewed as a powerful force which has the potential of increasing significantly the competitive position of the innovator firm within its industry. The firm may be able to do this by altering the industry's competitive structure.

Industry Competitive Structure

In any industry, if we view competition broadly, there are five fundamental competitive forces at work. The collective strength of these forces determines the ability of firms to earn rates of return on investment in excess of the opportunity cost of capital. The five forces are the threat of entry, substitution, bargaining power of suppliers, bargaining power of sustomers and rivalry among incumbent competitors. Underlying each of these five forces are sets of economic, technical and situational determinants which define the rules of competition in the industry (Porter, 1983).

Firm Competitive Strategy

"Every firm competing in an industry has a competitive strategy, whether explicit or implicit" (Porter, 1980, xiii). Firm competitive strategies differ in a wide variety of ways. In a given industry strategic dimensions such as the following capture some of the firm's options:

> *Specialization*: the degree to which it focuses its efforts in terms of the width of its line, the targeted customer segments, and the geographic markets served;. . . .
> *Product Quality*: its level of product quality, in terms of raw materials, specifications, adherence to tolerances, features and so on;. . . .
> *Technological Leadership*: the degree to which it seeks technological leadership versus following or imitation. . . a firm could be a technological leader but deliberately not produce the highest quality product in the market; quality and technological leadership do not necessarily go together,. . . (Porter, 1980, 127-28).

One may view the objective of a firm's competitive strategy to be the creation for itself of a defensible position against the competitive forces it believes it will encounter, over its planning period. These underlying competitive forces are both generated within its industry as well as by potential new entrant firms currently associated with other industries. One approach a firm may adopt to accomplish its strategy objective is to find the least vulnerable industry position with respect to the competitive forces. For example, a particular market segment may provide a safe niche against the threat of substitute products.

The other approach to strategy formulation is to develop a strategy that is meant to change industry competitive structure in ways that would enhance the firm's competitive advantage (Nelson and Winter, 1982; Porter, 1983). Clearly technical innovation can and does play a most potent role in the use of this approach in the formulation of competitive strategies by innovative science and technology based firms.

Schumpeter (1934, 1939, 1950) stressed the importance of this competitive role by innovations. More recently Porter (1983, 3, 4), drawing on his own extensive studies and those carried out by other researchers, concluded that:

> What makes technology unique as a strategic variable is its considerable power to change the competitive rules of the game. . ., Where a firm's technological innovations are appropriable, these impacts of technological change on structure are the fundamental motivations underlying the firm's choice of technological strategies.

These technological strategy choices may be made on the basis of evaluations and assessments of the probably impact of the firm's innovative activities on changing industry wide entry barriers, buyer and supplier power, substitution threats and rivalry forces. Sound competitive strategy by the firm "can lead to two broad types of competitive advantage: lower cost or differentiation (uniqueness)" (Porter, 1983, 4). The firm when developing a technology strategy is, however, dealing with technical, economic and other kinds of phenomena that have well-known varying uncertainty characteristics over the life cycles of its products.

Organizational Behaviour of the New Technology Based Firm

At this time it is pertinent to ask: How does a new technology based firm, as an organization, behave in response to the changes in its business environment brought about by such factors as those associated with technical innovation and competitive structure of its industry? For the purposes of this discussion it is useful to differentiate between routine and non-routine behaviour by "fallible" firm decision-makers. The fallibility of these decision-makers is frequently manifested for example when a new business situation facing the firm is assessed as requiring "routine" instead of "non-routine responses"; or when incorrect information and methods are used in making a decision which affects the future of this type of firm.

Regular and predictable behaviour by the firm may be viewed as "routine" behaviour. When firms encounter new problems or situations with which they have had no experience and about which they have no information they face conditions of complete uncertainty. Such a situation would be encountered by a firm faced with a decision as to whether or not it should undertake the process of transforming a primary invention into a commercially successful radical product innovation. Responses to various kinds of problems encountered by firms will be developed under varying degrees of uncertainty, in terms of the nature of the responses and their implementation. Problems which firms believe are not appropriate to deal with in a regular and predictable fashion may be viewed as requiring non-routine responses. In this paper we are concerned with processes that are hard to predict, such as, innovation and economic development. We are, therefore, primarily concerned with non-routine behaviour in firms engaged in the process of technical change in an industry with a dynamic competitive structure (Thomas, 1985, 1986a).

There is now a considerable body of literature developed by researchers who use managerialist, behaviouralist, and organizational heterodox approaches in studying the behaviour of business firms (Marris, 1964; Williamson, 1970, 1975, 1981, 1985; Simon, 1959, 1965; Cyert and March, 1963; Penrose, 1959; Chandler, 1962, 1977). Of the conceptual frameworks that provide guidance and assistance when attempting to explain the behaviour of firms, the framework articulated by Nelson and Winter (1982) seems to have the greatest flexibility and scope for dealing with firms in innovative industries. Their framework is also compatible with Schumpeter's concept of behavioural competition and an integral key component in the conceptual foundation for an evolutionary theory for economic change and development.

Briefly, the crucial elements in Nelson and Winter's framework are the three concepts *organizational routine, search,* and *selection* or *decision environment*. Organizational "routine" represents the set of routines and procedures that, at any time, firms have developed to provide ways of doing things and also determining what to do. When dealing with non-routine business problems, under conditions of uncertainty, established organizational routines are an inadequate source of guidance to firm when determining what to do. Firms, in such situations, tend to adapt their routines and procedures to take into account, as best they can, the nature and business implications for the firm of the perceived conditions of uncertainty related to the problem. In so doing firms frequently risk their future survival on attempts to adapt their organizational routines.

Organizational "search" denotes all those firms activities associated with the evaluation of current routines and the processes whereby "routines" are modified or replaced. The firm's organizational "selection environment" is the whole collection of considerations which affects its viability and need to change. The "selection environment" is defined by conditions both inside and outside the firm's industry (Nelson and Winter, 1982).

The Innovation Process at Firm and Industry Levels

Theorizing about long-term economic development takes place within a broad and comprehensive contextual framework composed of dynamic social, institutional, ideological, technological, economic and other structural elements. Each individual element, in turn, tends to have many dynamic dimensions and each element has its own changing spatio-temporal set of attributes (Thomas, 1986b).

Evolutionary economic development theory, among other things, must explain the process within a capitalist economy that ensures a long-term rise in its capacity to supply increasingly diverse economic goods to its population. Of particular interest in this paper, concerning this process of continuing transformation, is the role that advancing technology plays in facilitating a long-term rise in an economy's capacity to supply increasingly diverse economic goods to its population. These advancements in technology are manifested in the dynamic innovative activities and characteristics of industries and firms.

Innovation, in the form of advancing technology, is clearly regarded as a major explanatory factor in the process of evolutionary economic development at the level of the firm, industry and economy. It is, however, a complex concept with many meanings. To fulfil the purposes of this paper there is considerable merit in providing, at this time, working definitions of not only innovation and technological change but also definitions for a number of related concepts. Attention is primarily focused on the technological and economic aspects of these concepts.

Definitions

We will begin by defining *technology* as consisting of society's pool of knowledge concerning the industrial, mechanical and practical arts. "It is made up of knowledge concerning physical and social phenomena, knowledge regarding the application of basic principles to practical work, and knowledge of the rules of thumb of practitioners and craftsmen" (Mansfield, *et al* 1982). Recently Dosi (1984; 83) stressed that "theoretical" as well as the "practical" pieces of knowledge which together make up the set or pool of knowledge which we define as technology. These pieces of knowledge in the set may also be viewed as including "know-how, methods, procedures, experience of successes and failures and also, of course, physical devices and equipment."

Commercial products and processes represent various combinations of pieces of knowledge in a specific technology set. The first commercial production of a "new combination" of existing pieces of knowledge in a specific technology set represents *incremental technical innovation*. Whereas, the first commercial production of a "new combination" of pieces of knowledge in new technology set represents a *"radical" technical innovation* and the beginning of the life-cycle for a specific product. It is the carrying out of further successful innovation activities on the radical product and the process related to it that results in incremental innovation. The *technical innovation life-cycle*, however, may be viewed as having a pre-commercial and a commercial phase. All technical innovations represent discontinuous technical events and are, therefore, a source of disequilibrium in the economy.

Conceptually, the pre-commercial phase for a specific radical product begins: when an invention or set of inventions establish the level of *technical feasibility* which induces a firm to decide to explore the technical possibilities of producing eventually a radical product (or process). This action represents the making of a non-routine decision by the firm. If the R & D activities which follow establish an acceptable level of *economic feasibility* for the embryonic radical product then the firm tends of make another non-routine decision to produce commercially, for the first time, the radical product innovation. The commercial production of the radical innovation signals a discontinuous change in the path of technical progress and a future for the innovation that is fraught with both technical and commercial uncertainties (Clark, 1983).

Implicit in the above discussion there is a crucial connection between technical innovation and technical change. Technical innovation is viewed as the creation of new technical knowledge and a widely held definition for technical change is the creation and development of new technical possibilities. The application of new technical possibilities is another frequently used but narrower concept of technical change. It is, however, usually incorporated as an integral part of the broader notion that technical change is the "development of new technical possibilities" (Heertje, 1977, 3). The broader concept of technical change is sometimes still referred to as technological change. Nevertheless in the contemporary literature on the subject it is the prevailing practice to refer to the broad and narrow definitions as technical change (Elster, 1983). This practice is followed in this paper.

Invention-Innovation Relationship

Before presenting a conceptualization of the innovation process the relationship between invention and innovation needs further discussion. Let us regard an invention as a novel idea, "an original way of utilizing physical and chemical phenomena, or a combination of technical operations already known into a new process" (Heertje, 1977, 69). An invention frequently represents a substantial cumulative synthesis of old knowledge with new acts of insight (Usher, 1971, 50). Relatively few inventions, however, reach the stage of commercial application or in other words become innovations.

Many scholars establish and emphasize a clear distinction between an invention and its commercial application (Schumpeter 1934, Mueser, 1985). This distinction is more readily made when the inventor is other than the innovator and there is no apparent connection between them. Contemporary scholars, however, stress the inventive activities that are increasingly associated with the R & D expenditures and activities of innovative firms.

When inventions are viewed as a continuous stream of improvements and innovation, there is greater compatibility with the deterministic notion that inventions are systematically developed and are the inherent product of prevailing technical, economic and social conditions. Consequently, the distinction between invention and innovation becomes then rather blurred. Whereas, the distinction between invention and innovation is clearer when inventions are viewed as more or less incidental results of the creative mentalities of inventors (Heertje, 1977).

Usher (1971) provides a useful perspective on the invention – innovation relationship and I propose to adapt and use this viewpoint in subsequent discussions of the complex innovation process within innovative industries and firms. Based on the general principles of Gestalt analysis, Usher (1971, 48) identifies three distinct steps in the process of primary invention, which are:

(i) the perception of an unsatisfactory pattern;
(ii) the setting of the stage to react to pattern;
(iii) the primary act of insight or the primary invention.

The fourth step involves the "critical revision and development" of the primary invention. When this course of action culminates in the commercial application of the critically revised and further developed primary invention, Usher (1971) refers to the resulting commercial product as a secondary invention. Whereas, in this paper it is called a radical product innovation.

Usher further identifies a fifth step which leads to tertiary invention or incremental innovation as it is referred to by contemporary researchers (*Ibid*). A tertiary invention (or incremental innovation) improves a given product or process but does not extend the invention's field of use. Thus, tertiary inventions according to Usher (1971, 54) "may increase the efficiency of the secondary invention (radical innovation) or add to its convenience and safe operation;

but remains subordinate in importance." Usher's conception of the process of invention and innovation underscores the uncertainty associated with an act of insight as well as the lengthy period usually involved for the cumulative synthesis of individual inventions to occur, particularly in the case of major inventions and innovations.

Creation of New Technical Opportunities

We will now explore the process whereby new technical opportunities are created within firms and their industries. For this purpose, a contextual setting is provided by the previously enunciated evolutionary economic development theory and firm-industry competitive structure frameworks. We will begin this task by exploring crucial, technical and economic relationships between the process of innovation and technical change in firms over time. Subsequently we will explore relationships between selected changes in innovative firms and the process of technical change.

Innovation

The process of creating and developing new technical possibilities has attracted considerable theoretical and empirical study over the last quarter century. Nevertheless, we are far from having a full understanding of the nature and the economic, technical, spatial, social and other dimensions of this complex process. In this presentation I intend to restrict discussion to a few tentative ideas and perspectives concerning the technical and economic dimensions of the process of technical innovation in firms primarily found in the so-called "high technology industries." As compared to other firms, these "innovative" or "new" technology based firms spend more on research and development (R & D) relative to their sales, and employ a higher proportion of technology and science-oriented workers. In other words, they manifest a relatively strong emphasis on activities related to the process of technical innovation.

The conceptualizations presented in this paper represent very simple abstractions of the extremely complex processes we seek to understand. They also represent a "partitioning" of the individual process system under discussion. These are time-honoured methods of dealing with complex systems which are made up of a large number of parts that interact in a non-simple way. Simon (1982) has observed that in such systems the whole is more than the sum of the parts. Because of the given properties of the parts, and the laws of their interaction, it is not a trivial matter to infer the properties of the whole.

Empirically we have studied the processes of radical and incremental innovation in relatively few firms and in only a very small number of industries. There is great debate concerning the appropriateness of the methodologies used and the validity of the results of the studies carried out on the process of innovation and technical change. The importance of the subject denies us the right to abandon our theorizing, model building and empirical studies for the clinical appeal of *a priori* speculation. It seems certain that: our conceptualizations of innovation, technical change and economic development processes; and our theories which explain their relationships and various implications, will require refinement, modification and greater accuracy. These limitations and problems must be kept in mind when we articulate and use conceptualizations of innovation, technical change and economic development processes.

Technological Paradigm or Industry Technology Life-Cycle

I will now articulate one way of conceptualizing the processes of radical and incremental innovation from a technical perspective. There are, of course, other ways of conceptualizing this phenomenon. I propose to view the innovation life-cycle of a radical product (process) within the context of a *technological paradigm*. In a broad impressionistic analogy with the Kuhnian definition of a scientific paradigm, a technological paradigm may be thought of as:

> a model and a pattern of solution of *selected* technological problems, based on *selected* principles derived from natural sciences and on *selected* material technologies (Dosi, 1984, 83).

In this definition of a technological paradigm there is no suggestion that there exists only a uni-direction deterministic sequence of "science-technology-production." Solution sequences for selected technological problems may originate from production or technology as well as from science. The nature and influence of the complex relationships among science, technology and production represent topics subject to considerable contemporary debate (Rosenberg, 1976; Freeman, 1979; Price, 1984 and Walsh, 1974).

Dosi (1984, 88) suggests that:

> the emergence of new technological paradigms is contextual to the explicit emergence of economically defined "needs". In other words, the supply side determines the "universe" of possible modalities through which generic "needs" or productive requirements (which as such do not have any direct economic significance) are satisfied.

The technology of a specific technological paradigm may, for example, be related to generic "needs" or "tasks" such as transporting people and commodities; providing electrical power; and switching and amplifying electrical signals. For example, the latter generic "need" is, among others, related to the semi-conductor set of technologies. Despite empirical support for the notion of the technological paradigm and its utility by such eminent researchers on the innovation process as Rosenberg (1976), Nelson and Winter (1977), Abernathy and Utterback (1978); Sahal (1982) and Dosi (1984) further development and testing of the concept are necessary. At present we find these major researchers using very similar concepts to Dosi's technological paradigm but they are known by different names such as: "technological imperatives" (Rosenberg); and "technological regime" (Nelson and Winter, 1977).

A change in paradigm seems to induce strongly or require the industrially relevant firms to start immediately in the technical problem-solving activity within the new paradigm. Know-how transferability from one paradigm to another or even within a paradigm from one trajectory pathway to another is not smooth and it is costly to bring about successfully.

The emergence of technological paradigms tends to depend on a new synthesis of a great many proven established ideas or, in other words, inventions. This creative symbiosis, however, materializes infrequently but when it does, the consequences tend to be striking. In effect they represent a technical break with the past in an otherwise evolutionary system of technical progress. The birth of a new technological paradigm or a new industry technology life cycle represents the creation of new technical possibilities. As these possibilities are developed and applied commercially they achieve the defined status of either radical or incremental product-process innovations.

Another characteristic that serves to identify the creation of a technological paradigm is the associated creation and presence of a significant technique with greater adaptability to its task environment. We may view this technique, if it is applied commercially, as the first radical innovation created within the context of that specific technological paradigm. *Subsequently other radical innovations tend to be created.* (This aspect is discussed further later in this paper.) Further advances and technical progress in each new technique usually take place during the pre-commercial and commercial phases of its innovation life cycle. These creative technical advances which indicate technical progress in a technique may be viewed as incremental innovations. Some of these are process innovations and others are product innovations.

It seems that positive and the negative *heuristics* exist within specific dynamic sets of technologies associated with particular technological paradigms. These heuristics embody strong prescriptions on the directions of technical change which should be pursued or neglected. The use of heuristics, however, does not guarantee either desirable or unique outcomes. Product innovation, it seems, involves a great deal of trial and error and emphasis on scaling and learning processes by the innovative firm as it attempts to cope with the state of *technological uncertainty* associated with innovation. An element that is common to a wide range of technologies is the increasing mechanization of operations that have been done by hand (Nelson and Winter, 1977).

Selected technical problems associated with specific material technologies are usually discussed in relation to a set or cluster of technologies such as bio-technical, organic chemistry, and semi-conductor technologies. Normal technological progress within a specific paradigm, for example, the semi-conductor technological paradigm, may be defined by its *technological trajectory.* In other words, the pattern of "normal" problem-solving activity within a technological paradigm, characterized by incremental innovation, defines the paradigm's aggregate *technological trajectory*. This trajectory may be specified by a semilogarithmic form of the technometric function devised by Sahal (1984) for the U.S. computer industry.

Economic variables as well as technical variables define the various dimensions of the technological trajectory's pattern of "normal" problem-solving activity. The trajectory may be thought of as:

> the movement of multi-dimensional trade-offs among technological variables that the paradigm defines as relevant. Progress can be defined as the improvement of these trade-offs. One could imagine the trajectory as a "cylinder" in the multi-dimensional space (Dosi, 1984, 85).

Individual firms tend to have their own pathway within this "cylinder" or aggregate trajectory (Thomas, 1986b). These firms attempt to profit as long as possible by keeping confidential or protecting their economic control over firm specific and plant and product system-specific technology; as well as their organizational and economic expertise.

De-Maturity and the Industry Technology Life-Cycle

Under certain conditions, a major change may be effected in an industry's technological trajectory (Clark, 1983, 112-115). This "de-maturity" or rejuvenation may occur in a particularly robust technological paradigm. Firms stimulated by intense and growing foreign competition, or because of other reasons, begin to conduct exploratory research and discover, on the outer edge of the industry's technological trajectory, new productive directions in which industry technology may develop. Once the change is made in the trajectory sources of "normal" problem-solving activity they tend to generate a new burst of incremental innovation. The pattern is reminiscent of the early development phase for the particular technology and industry. Subsequently renewed "normal" technological progress resumes (Dosi, 1984). Clark (1983), for example, suggests that the process of "de-maturity" in the American automobile industry began in the early 1970's. There are also indications that the early 1980's witnessed the beginning of a "de-maturity" phase in the American machine tools industry (Friar and Horwitch, 1986).

Decline in the Industry Technology Life-Cycle

Older technologies are largely overthrown by newer technologies through revolutionary design. In the recent past this was the case when a specific cluster of technologies, for example, reciprocating engines in commercial aircraft, vacuum tubes and mechanical calculators were overthrown by radical innovations such as jet engines, solid state electronics and electronic computers (Abernathy and Clark, 1985). The overthrow of these older technologies renders much technical and human capital obsolete. Resultant adverse human and economic costs, however, are not always offset by the substitution of the new technologies.

Innovation and Competition: Selected Relationship

Life-Cycles

More than half a century ago Kuznets (1930, 254) perceptively noted:

> As we observe various industries within a given national economy, we see that the lead in development shifts from one branch to another. . . . Within one country we can observe a succession of different branches of activity in the vanguard of the country's economic development and within each industry we can notice a conspicuous slackening in the rate of increase.

These insights with respect to the process of structural change are relevant with respect to subnational economies as well.

During the last quarter century there has been considerable interest in the use of product life-cycle and industry technology life-cycles in examining and explaining industry development paths. Much of the work on product life-cycles originated in early studies by Kuznets (1930), Burns (1934) and more recent studies by Vernon (1966, 1979) and Hirsch (1967). The form and duration of the industry technology cycle is based on the notion suggested by Nelson (1962) that there is a relationship between the total number of patents and the age of the industry. Over long periods of time this relationship tends to follow an S curve. Magee (1977) refined Nelson's notion and introduced and described the stages of the industry technology life-cycle which he wished to differentiate from the product cycle. Despite its suggestive promise of emphasis on the more comprehensive and complex industry technology cycle Magee's concept was disappointing because it was so similar to the "simple" product life-cycle.

Explaining well the process of industrial development remains, and probably will remain, a worthy challenge into the foreseeable future. Nevertheless, despite the seemingly unsurmountable difficulties associated with responding successfully to the challenge, some useful insights concerning the process of industrial development may still be revealed by integrating a number of conceptualizations articulated earlier in this paper. This synthesis focuses attention on a number of significant aspects of the relationship between innovation and competition.

A New Industry

Conceptually the birth of a "new industry" begins with the first commercial production of a radical product innovation by an innovator firm. This first radical innovation may also be viewed as the first innovation produced within the new technological paradigm. The first radical product establishes both the first product life-cycle in a specific product industry and the commercial birth of a new technological paradigm's *industry technology life-cycle*. Unfortunately this conceptual classification scheme of product and industry technology life-cycles may not, however, coincide with products and industries in the U.S. Standard Industrial Classification Manual!

The new technological paradigm and the new radical product may be also viewed as ushering in a "revolutionary" design. Design here means a revolutionary "adaptation of means to some preconceived end" (Layton, 1972). The commercial launch of the ne' product is quickly followed by the production of similar products b firms whose technologies belong to the same technology paradigm as the innovator firm. Imitator firms which use legal and illegal means, with various degrees of commercial success, for obtaining the "revolutionary" design or some other similar design(s), are also part of the growing matrix of competitive firms in the early development phase of this "new industry".

Product and Organizational Product

For many reasons it is desirable that we have the means of defining the characteristics of specific radical and other products as they move along their individual product life-cycles. Many firms have a number of products, at a particular time, that are at different points along their *organizational product life-cycles*. Firms may also have products that represent different *organizational product "generation" life-cycles*.

Saviotti and Metcalfe (1984; 14) recently made significant progress towards dealing with this definitial problem at the conceptual level. In their framework:

> a product is considered a combination of three sets of characteristics, one describing the technical features of the product, one describing the services performed by the product, and one describing the methods of its production. These sets of characteristics are related by patterns of mapping.

Every product embodies a particular technology and is produced in a firm by means of a process. This product is simultaneously both the output of the firm that produces it and an input of the firm or other users that purchase it. The product is purchased for the services it provides. We can visualize in these integral dimensions of the product dynamic sets of technological and economic interrelationships and interdependences. These are important elements in the "selection" or "decision" environment of the firm. Changes and upward movement in all three sets of characteristics represent incremental innovations and "normal" technological progress within the technological paradigm.

Characteristic Technology Cycles

At the level of the industry Sahal (1981) identifies what he calls *characteristic technology cycles*. This kind of subordinate cycles seems to be identified with key elements in the design for a major product in a specific industry technological paradigm or industry technology life-cycle. He found, for example, that the growth in the tractive performance of locomotives during the period 1904-1967 was characterized by two technology cycles of approximately 26 years duration. The first cycle, namely, the "superheater cycle" exemplified the gradual application of the multiple expansion principle in the locomotive engine and this application dominated much of the innovative activity during the period 1908-1934. The "diesel cycle" which followed in the period 1937-1963, exemplified the gradual application of the diesel engine and electric transmission in rail transportation, accounting for the dominant share of innovative activities in that industry.

Sahal (1984) also presents persuasive evidence for the existence, in the period 1951-1979, of four *technology cycles* within the technology life-cycle for the computer industry. These subordinate technology cycles are evidenced by the so-called "component generations" of approximately 8-12 years duration as distinguished from product life-cycles of approximately 3-4 years duration. Each new generation, on average, effected a 10-fold increase in speed, a 20-fold increase in memory capacity, and a 10-fold increase in reliability, while reducing the component cost 10-fold and the system cost 2.5-fold (Hodges, 1977). The four cycles are identified as the "vacuum tube cycle" 1951-1958; "transistor cycle" 1959-1963; "small-scale integrated circuit cycle" 1964-1969; and "large-scale integrated circuit cycle" 1969-1979 (Sahal, 1984, 160).

In a most intriguing analysis of process and product innovations in the computer industry Sahal (1984) notes the emergence of what he calls a *butterfly pattern of innovative activity*. Three noteworthy features of this pattern are identified. First, initially process innovations contribute more than product innovations to technical progress. Second, over time product innovations gain in importance and process innovations gradually decline in importance. This finding is just the opposite of the product life-cycle prescription found by Hirsch (1965). Third, there appears to be a *conservation effect in technical change processes*. This finding is supported by evidence which suggests that the loss in relative importance of process innovations, in the study period, is almost exactly compensated for by the gain in the relative importance of product innovations. Estimates based on technometric functions, used in determining whether newly developed computers are ahead or behind time, suggest that the computer industry in the United States may well be losing some of its technical vigour (Sahal, 1984).

This kind of research provides the kind of information that should be useful in the development of technology strategy in the industry. The author is well aware of the tentative nature of his findings and that there appear to be very different sequences of interaction between product and process innovation in certain other industries. It should also be noted that Sahal's data on the sequence of interaction between product and process innovation in the U.S. computer industry end in 1972 when the industry's technical vigour was high. If Sahal is correct that the computer industry is currently losing some of its innovative capability then as the industry moves towards the mature phase of its technology life-cycle, process innovations may well increase in importance relative to product innovations.

Innovations and the Industry Technology Life-Cycle

Sahal and other scholars have demonstrated important relationships between process and product innovations and competitiveness at firm and industry levels. In a most stimulating paper Abernathy and Clark (1985) recently developed a framework for analysing the competitive implications of various types of innovations. Their framework is based on the concept of transilience – the capacity of an innovation to influence the established systems of production and marketing. Their analyses, based on the technical history of the U.S. auto industry, show that their categories of innovation are closely linked to different managerial environments and to different patterns of evolution.

Because there is no single acceptable classification scheme for innovations it is sometimes difficult to equate types of innovation in one schema to types of innovation in another schema. It appears that Abernathy and Clark (1985; 7) identify two types of radical innovations. The first is the *revolutionary innovation* that:

- disrupts and renders established technical and production competence obsolete, yet is applied to exiting markets and customers;

the second is the *architectural innovation* which:
- lays down the architecture of the industry, the broad framework within which competition will occur and develop.

Both types of innovation disrupt existing linkages and create new linkages within and between industries. The creation of obsolesence in fixed and human capital is, however, a characteristic associated with radical innovations that give birth to new industries. These are the kind that Schumpeter referred to as sources of "creative destruction" in the capitalist economy. The architectural type of radical innovations are more clearly identified with the creation of design concepts that have a great bearing as to how long proprietary designs continue to provide a competitive edge for individual firms within an industry. Collectively this type of innovation has a great bearing on the competitive viability of the industry specific technology. In my schema Abernathy and Clark's "revolutionary" innovation is a radical innovation whereas their "architectural" innovation is a major incremental innovation. Intuitively, I believe that major architectural innovations probably initiated Sahal's four so called "characteristic technology cycles" in the U.S. computer industry technology life-cycles. These cycles were described earlier in this paper.

The two additional types of innovations that complete the transilience framework are the "niche creating" and "regular" innovations. "Niche creating" product innovations conserve and strengthen established designs and through the use of existing technology open up new markets. An example of this type of innovation is the Sony Walkman which created a niche in personal audio products through the mating of established technologies used in making light weight earphones and portable radios and cassette players.

"Regular" process innovations also build on established technologies and their applications are in existing markets. This type of innovation serves to entrench existing skills and resources. Cumulatively "regular" innovations bring about dramatic improvements in performance, cost reduction and productivity, often through increased mechanization and by taking advantage of scale economies (Abernathy and Clark, 1985).

Perceived Potential and Limits of Technology

Within the technology cycle framework we may also discuss a set of dimensions which are related to both Sahal's technology cycles and Abernathy and Clark's typology of innovations. These dimensions, as articulated in Foster (1985), provide information concerning the nature of the relationship between technical performance and research effort over the life of the technology cycle. This kind of information is relevant when discussing innovation, competition and technology strategy at firm and industry levels.

The radical or revolutionary innovation launches the commercial phase of the technology life-cycle for a particular technology. This technology has theoretical and practical limits. The R & D mission of firms in the technology industry is to advance towards these limits.

The current "state of the art" determines how much advancement is possible. The difference between what is possible and the technical limit may be called the *technical potential*. When a firm's technical potential is high, as it seems to be in contemporary "high-tech" industries, then technology is likely to be an important element in its business strategy. By the same token, if its technical potential is low, then other business functions are likely to loom larger for the firm.

Early in the commercial life of a particular technology R & D programmes in firms within the technology industry build knowledge bases, draw and test lines of engineering, identify problems and discard unworkable approaches. Progress initially, towards the technical limits of the technology, tends to be slow. Subsequently the pace increases and typically the maximum rate of progress is reached when approximately half the potential has been achieved. Thereafter, the technology begins to be constrained as technical limits are reached and there is a slowing down in the rate of performance improvement. In other words, diminishing rates of return accrue to R & D inputs. This pattern of relationship between research effort and technical performance over the technology cycle is referred to as the *S-curve phenomenon* because it tends to have a log normal form.

R & D productivity may be defined as the improvement in the performance of the product or process divided by the incremental effort required. Thus the relationship between technical progress and R & D investment determines R & D productivity at various stages of development along the S-curve. For competitive firms the end objective is not R & D productivity but the rate of profit earned from the R & D investment, i.e. the *R & D return*. Another useful variable is the *R & D yield* which represents the profit derived from a particular technical advance (innovation). R & D yield, however, is a function of the competitive structure of the technology industry: supply/demand conditions, firm strategies, substitute products, relative power of suppliers and buyers, and other external influences.

Within firms, controlling and improving R & D productivity is primarily the responsibility of the R & D department. Whereas, R & D yield is the result of competitor strategies and market conditions and these matters are traditionally the responsibility of "business units" within the firms. Both dimensions should be analysed independently but ultimately they need to be coupled if they are to be used successfully by firms in providing guidance in the development of their technology strategies (Foster, 1985).

Strategy Alternatives

This is an opportune time to explore briefly, tentatively and suggestively, a number of relationships which have been identified between competitive firms and technology based strategies in young and in mature technology industries that have emerged in the United States during the last thirty years (Abernathy and Utterback, 1978; Utterback and Abernathy, 1975; Bollinger, *et al* 1983; Cooper, 1973; Friar and Horwitch, 1985; Rothwell, 1984; Macdonald, 1985). Before discussing these relationships, however, there is merit in focusing attention briefly on selected dimensions related to the evaluation of the new technology industries that emerged during this recent period in United States industrial history. Industry origins and the patterns of change in internal and external selection environments of firms over industry technology life-cycles represent a number of the dimensions that are examined.

Industry Origin

If we examine the origins of these new technology industries we observe a number of similarities and differences. This is also the case when we compare the origin of specific industries in the United States with their counterparts in other countries. We find, for example, that the commercial origin of the semi-conductor industry in the United States was dominated by small entrepreneurial firms. Whereas in the United Kingdom, Western Germany and Japan this industry in each case was launched by a few large firms. Our understanding of the processes which underlie the birth of contemporary high industries and firms is unfortunately incomplete. This is especially the case with respect to roles "spinoffs" and incubator firms play in the birth of new high-tech firms (Senker, 1985; Beesley and Hamilton, 1984).

Be that as it may, there seems to be a growing consensus that innovation by small "new" technology based entrepreneurial firms is exceptionally important in the birth of new industries (Freeman *et al* 1982) and they could well serve as important vehicles for the regeneration of economic development in regional and national economies (Rothwell, 1982; Steed, 1982). Considerable interest in the critical role of these small entrepreneurial firms in the early growth of high-tech industries in the United States was stimulated in the latter half of the 1970s by the entrepreneurially launched personal compute industry. The true spark for this industry came from an entrepreneurial small-firm environment that was made up of hobbyists, publicists and promoters, technological champions, and entrepreneurs (Friar and Horwitch, 1985).

The relationship between firm size and innovation is a topic that has been intensely debated over the last decade and a half. On the one side are those who stress the behavioural and organizational strengths of small firms in this innovation process. On the other side are those who argue that large size and monopoly power are perquisites for economic progress via technical change (Rothwell, 1984). Unfortunately the debators have not been aware of the need to conduct their debate on a sector by sector basis. In addition neither side has given due consideration to the high probability that the relative contributions of large and small firms to the innovation process, in a particular industry, might well depend on the age of that industry. Recent studies also suggest that we can expect the relationship between firm size and innovation to vary between the different phases of not only the industry technology life-cycle but also the different phases of the Kondratiev type "long waves" (Freeman, 1986; Freeman, *et al* 1982, 1986; Kaplinsky 1981; Clark, *et al* 1984; Thomas, 1986b, c). In addition, the type of innovation typically produced by small and large sized firms, at different stages in the industry cycle may also vary, i.e., product or process innovations (Rothwell, 1984).

During the 1980's, however, there has been a growing emphasis in the literature on the dynamic complementary roles of small and large firms in technical innovation activities. To some extent this trend represents the explicit recognition of an important relationship between innovation and firm strategy which has been identified in studies of a number of narrowly defined new technology based industries (Rothwell, 1984; Macdonald, 1985; Friar and Horwitch, 1986; Kaplinsky, 1983; Hamilton, 1985; Doz, *et al* 1986).

In this period the marked growth in the development and use of technology as a strategic competitive factor has also served to focus more sharply the interest of academics as well as key decision-makers in firms on the dynamic complementarities of small and large firms over the industry technology life-cycle (Hamilton, 1986; Friar and Horwitch, 1985). Since the rejuvenated "bio-technology industry" came into being with successful cloning of the first gene in

1973 its emerging phase has exemplified this close dynamic relationship between small and large firms. There has also been considerable diversity in the form and nature of these relationships. At present bio-technology represents a set of techniques with potential application and strategic impact in a number of established industries, some of which will doubtless experience major restructuring in the next few decades. The question as a whether or not a new "bio-technology industry" will emerge cannot be answered at this time (Hamilton, 1985).

Selection Environment and Strategy

In essence firms and their environment are relatively unstructured at start-up in an emerging industry and a contemporary example is provided by the new set of vendors for artificial intelligence models. The production characteristics in an emerging industry are characterized as: uncoordinated and vague; loose and unsettled relationships between process elements; high rate of change; process is composed of unstandardized and manual operations and it is fluid and adaptable; production capacity is flexible; product innovation generates simple process innovation; and the introduction of a new technology composed of elements diffused from other industries (Kaplinsky, 1983). The sector characteristics at start-up in an emerging industry are characterized by: a diversity of unstandardized products; performance requirements are ambiguous; rate of product change is rapid; demand not known, or uncertain; product market ill-defined; new technologies adapt to emergent needs in the market; and the product, administrative and production process development are in an uncoordinated state (Macdonald, 1985).

Hesitant demand growth, relatively small number of early starters, and the industry-wide rather than firm-specific effect of marketing effort tends to limit rivalry within the emerging industry. Technical specifications rather than price provide the bases for competition among firms. Entry is relatively easy for new arrivals which do not have to recover any special expenses beyond financing the most recent business intelligence on the new industry! Where capital costs are relatively high, however, entry is more difficult, e.g. in bio-technology.

During the dynamic early growth phase of the emerging industry technology cycle, when entry barriers are relatively low, the new entrepreneurial firms are joined by firms from other industries. These usually larger firms possess superior production or marketing expertize that has applicability in a growing industry. Initially the small and "larger" firms remain more or less distinct. Even so there develops fairly quickly a vital interplay between the two types of firms. People, technology, technique and relevant managerial knowledge percolate through the system. Nevertheless, for various reasons many of the small entrepreneurial firms do not survive this early industry development phase. Even relatively large start-up firms in the personal computer industry were unable to create sustainable businesses. For example MITS, IMSAI and Processor Technology, which accounted for 50 per cent share of the U.S. market in 1976, failed in 1977 (Frair and Horwitch, 1986).

The growth phase in the industry technology life-cycle is usually characterized by the trend to concentration. In some industries, however, where firms produce small batches or individualized products to customers' specification, the firms may remain small. For example, in 1972, 83 per cent of firms in the British scientific instruments industry had less than 100 employees (Rothwell, 1984). Firms in the industry concentrate as products and processes become standardized. They become fewer in number and larger in size and they tend to extend their range of applications programmes to provide comprehensive cover to the broadening limits of the industry market (Kaplinsky, 1983). During this expansionary phase aggregate industry growth rates can be very high necessitating raising substantial financial resources. The U.S. computer aided design (CAD) industry growth rate was approximately 80 per cent per annum during this phase from 1974 to 1980 (Kaplinsky, 1983). The industry environment at this time tends to be conducive to the emergence of "predators" amongst established industry firms. In other words, larger multiregional or multinational firms from outside the industry as a speculative investment take over, or take a substantial share of, these established industry firms.

A number of the post-Second World War industry technology life-cycles have now reached maturity, for example, the CAD and semiconductor industries. In this phase of constrained market development in the CAD industry we observe two divergent trends –

a continued tendency to concentration and an opposing tendency for the entry of new small firms selling microprocessor driven, limited capability dedicated systems (Kaplinsky, 1983).

Technology Strategy

Contemporary literature in the field of strategic management provides ample evidence of the recognition of technology as a top-level strategic concern in "new" technology based industries. This is especially the case within the large firms in these industries. Technology strategy is also of increasing interest to key decision-makers in the more commercially progressive and successful new entrepreneurial firms in emerging industries such as bio-technology (Friar and Horwitch, 1985).

In nascent industries with ambivalent or even amorphous structure some three broad strategy options have been identified by Macdonald (1985) as being used implicitly if not explicitly by new entrepreneurial firms. Some start-up firms dedicate organizational effort to serving a market in which the demand is too small for a late or larger entry to have a significant advantage. In other words, these high technology firms develop small volume niches as protection. They will as a result, however, remain technically static as they age as organizations and eventually become "low-tech" firms.

Another group of start-up firms seems to exercise the option of exiting from the industry as more powerful firms enter. These firms exploit risk as a shelter and a barrier to competition. Such firms must be technologically versatile and well managed. Entry and exit behaviour to be successful also demands sensitivity to industry signals.

Firms that take the third strategy option tend to aspire to both pushing the new technology to its extreme practical limit and to becoming a large successful firm. Key decision-makers in these firms need a great deal of luck and skill in conjecture because they need to make the right moves before their competitors. These decision-makers must gain experience rapidly in lessening expectations and risking more in order to accelerate events in the lives of their firms. Firms attempt gradually to establish a series of barriers, abandoning some like windows along the industry life-cycle and maintaining others that eventually converge on the structure of the growing industry or on that of a strategic group within the industry (Macdonald, 1985). Strategies pursued reflect increasing commitment to more focused programmes over time (Hamilton, 1985).

In his study of the CAD industry in the United States Kaplinsky (1983) found that the key to the discussion of firm size and technical change lies in the barriers raised against new entrants. The incentives to new entrants into the industry are substantial because investment in the CAD sector is a relatively profitable activity. Nevertheless, the industry continues to be dominated by a small number of firms which suggests that existing barriers to entry must be effective. Kaplinsky found the primary barrier to entry in the CAD industry to be technology.

The scale of software inputs necessary to offer a competitive package of applications programmes was the major source of protection for existing producers against new entrants into the industry. The CAD sector, in comparison to the U.S. manufacturing industry in general, still invests a very large proportion of sales in R & D. Most CAD suppliers employ more than 100 software writers each year and the number continues to increase. A number of firms were able to detail their vast stocks of software. The critical protective factors for existing firms, however, were that the software development occurred in a relatively specialized industry in the context of a general shortage of software writers, and that the necessary software development is sequential in nature. It is also evident that existing firms in the CAD industry have developed effective ways of protecting their proprietary information. The ruling by the U.S. Supreme Court in 1981 that *firmware*, i.e. software incorporated in the hardware, can be patented has contributed to this protection (Kaplinsky, 1983).

The vital importance of technical innovation to the development of technology based firms and industries is well understood. There is also a growing realization that it is increasingly crucial to establish strategic linkages between firms and to develop varied structures for encouraging innovation. Since the mid 1970s there has been considerable experimentation in the use of external-oriented strategic practices for acquiring new technology. Firms use such methods as: licensing; contracting the development of new technology; joint ventures or acquire a share or all of another firm for monitoring or buying technology. This trend reflected greater cooperation among competitors and a possible lessening of the use of technology *per se* as a purely competitive tool.

There is growing evidence, however, that this trend has peaked and now there is a renewed focus on internal methods of creating new technology, i.e. firms tend increasingly to reply on their own R & D staff at divisional and corporate levels and/or rely on the establishment of internal ventures or entrepreneurial units to innovate. This incipient trend suggests that the pursuit of external methods for obtaining new technology generated an unacceptably high level of complexity for firms. It seems that there is also a growing perceived need by firms to regain total proprietary control over all activities directed towards technical innovation (Friar and Horwitch, 1986).

The question concerning the relative effectiveness of external and internal oriented strategic practices for acquiring new technology will probably be one of increasing interest to firms whose technology has begun to be constrained by its practical limits and whose rate of economic performance consequently begins to slow down. Such firms, if they focus their R & D activities on improving the performance of current technology, may well face commercial disaster in the not too distant future as they vainly attempt to make a transition to a more profitable new technology.

In the mid-1950s when the transistor replaced the vacuum tube, the ten leading producers of vacuum tube components were caught without any new technology alternatives. Only four of these ten producers belatedly attempted to secure an entry into the new solid-state technology field. All four failed and not one of these large and powerful vacuum tube producing firms is a force in today's $ 10 billion semiconductor industry (Foster, 1986). At present the leverage in computer development is shifting from hardware to software. There are indications that major changes will accompany the transition if it continues to gain momentum. The question is already being asked as to who will be most likely to survive such fundamental changes – the large hardware manufacturers, like IBM, Siemens and Fuijitsu, where manufacturing is an entrenched and powerful corporate function, or the smaller companies that now dominate the software industry? (Foster, 1986). For top management technological transitions represent extremely disruptive challenges. Evidently these discontinuities are now facing contemporary "new" technology based firms in a growing number of industries. Technological transition, it seems, is emerging as a complex multifaceted research problem of great practical importance and academic interest.

Concluding Section

This paper represents a conceptual contribution to the literature which attempts to improve our understanding of the role of innovation in the process of economic development. The contribution was presented in the form of three heuristic frameworks.

In the first framework evolutionary economic development theory provided the foundation for conceptualizing competitive behaviour and strategies in technology based firms and industries. Theoretical notions developed by Schumpeter, Nelson, Winter and Porter were found to be especially useful in the articulation of this first heuristic framework. The framework identified key elements in the dynamic process within which firm behaviour patterns and market outcomes are generated over time. Attention was focused especially on the diversity of firm characteristics, experience and capabilities and on how this diversity interacted over time with industry structure.

Firms face uncertainties of outcome when they make decisions which are related to the process of innovation. Nelson and Winter's framework composed of the three concepts – "organizational routine", "search" and "selection environment" is especially useful in conceptualizing the nature and implications of the process involved in making non-routine decisions. For example firm decisions which are related to innovation, and changes in investment and location.

The second heuristic conceptual framework focused attention on the uncertainties of technological outcome related to the process of innovation. Innovation was shown to be a very complex concept with many meanings. The conceptualization of the innovation process was carried out within both the innovation life-cycle, and the industry technology life-cycle or technology paradigm frameworks. The evolutionary nature of innovation and technical change and the uncertainties, discontinuities and continuities associated with the technical dimensions of these processes were revealed, and their importance underscored, by the use of these life-cycle frameworks. These exploratory conceptualizations also indicated that our understanding of the process of innovation is still relatively minimal.

Work carried out for this paper suggests that future conceptualization of innovation would benefit greatly from greater agreement with respect to the definition and classification of key concepts used in the conceptualization of the process of technical innovation. Unfortunately we still do not possess an acceptable metric for deciding clearly and accurately how "radical" or how economically or technologically important a particular innovation may be. It would also be most helpful if we were able to agree as to how we should measure the "breadth" and "robustness" of the various technologies associated with products, component generations, characteristic technology and industry technology life-cycles.

The third and last heuristic conceptual framework focused attention on selected dimensions of the uncertainties of both economic and technological outcomes related to the process of innovation in contemporary "high-tech" firms and industries. In effect, this set of conceptualizations represented both a synthesis and the further development of key elements from the first two heuristic frameworks.

This third heuristic framework provided a number of insights concerning certain selected relationships between innovation and competition at firm and industry levels. The examination of these relationships was carried out within the context of product and industry technology life-cycle frameworks. Again these life-cycle frameworks were shown to be most useful, in this case, in identifying important technological and economic dimensions of the role innovation plays in the development patterns of "new" technology based firms and industries. The perspectives provided by the third heuristic framework were especially illuminating in the examination of technology strategy as a subject or major concern to too level management in technology based industries. This is also a subject that is attracting increasing attention from a growing number of researchers in a variety of academic disciplines.

This paper identified an important and challenging research agenda which is connected to the role innovation plays in the process of economic development at the level of the firm and industry in a competitive framework. It also provided a number of suggestions how some of these research problems may be usefully addressed.

REFERENCES

Abernathy, W.J. (1978). *The Productivity Dilemma*. Johns Hopkins, Baltimore.

Abernathy, W.J. and K.B. Clark (1985). Innovation: mapping the winds of creative destruction. *Research Policy, 14*, 3-22.

Abernathy, W.J.; K.B. Clark and A.M. Kantrow (1983). *Industrial Renaissance: Producing a Competitive Future for America*. Basic Books, New York.

Abernathy, W.J. and J.M. Utterback (1978). Patterns of industrial innovation, *Technology Review, 80*, 40-47.

Beesley, M.E. and R.T. Hamilton (1984). Small firms' seedbed role and the concept of turbulence, *The Journal of Industrial Economics, 33*, 217-231.

Bollinger, L.; K. Hope and J.M. Utterback (1983). *Research Policy, 12*, 1-14.

Burns, A.F. (1934). *Production Trends in the United States since 1870*. National Bureau of Economic Research, New York.

Chandler, A. (1962). *Strategy and Structure*. MIT Press, Cambridge, Mass.

Chandler, A. (1977). *The Visible Hand: The Managerial Revolution in American Business*. Harvard University Press, Cambridge, Mass.

Clark, J., C. Freeman and L. Soete (1984). Long waves, inventions, and innovations. In C. Freeman (ed.) *Long Waves in the World Economy*. Frances Pinter, London.

Clark, K.B. (1983). Competition, technical diversity, and radical innovation, *Research on Technological Innovation Management and Policy, 1*, 103-149.

Cooper, A.C. (1973). Technical entrepreneurship: What do we know? *R & D Management, 3*, 59-64.

Cyert, R.M. and J.G. March (1963). *A Behavioural Theory of the Firm*, Prentice-Hall, Englewood Cliffs, N.J.

Dosi, G. (1984). Technological paradigms and technological trajectories. The determinants and directions of technical change and the transformation of the economy. In C. Freeman (ed.) *Long Waves in the World Economy*. Frances Pinter, London.

Doz, Y. (1986). Technological Innovation and Interdependence: A challenge for the large, complex firm. *Technology in Society, 7*, 105-125.

Elster, J. (1983). *Explaining Technical Change*, Cambridge University Press, Cambridge.

Foster, R.N. (1986). Timing Technological Transitions. *Technology in Society, 7*, 127-141.

Freeman, C. (1979). The determinants of innovation. *Futures, 11*, 205-215.

Freeman, C., J. Clark and L. Soete (1982). *Unemployment and Technical Innovation*, Greenwood Press, Wesport, Connecticut.

Friar, J. and M. Horwitch (1986). The Emergence of Technology Strategy: A new dimension of strategic management. *Technology in Society, 7*, 143-178.

Hamilton, W.F. (1986). Corporate strategies for managing emerging technologies. *Technology in Society, 1*, 197-212.

Heertje, A. (1977). *Economics and Technical Change*, Weidenfeld and Nicolson, London.

Hirsch, S. (1967). *Location of Industry and International Competitiveness*. The Clarendon Press, Oxford.

Hirsch, S. (1972). The United States electronics industry in international trade. In L.T. Wells (ed.) *The Product Life Cycle and International Trade*. Division of Research, Graduate School of Business Administration, Harvard University, Boston.

Hodges, D.A. (1977). Microelectronic memories. *Scientific American*, September, 130-145.

Kaplinsky, R. (1983). Firm size and technical change in a dynamic context. *The Journal of Industrial Economics, 32*, 39-58.

Kuznets, S.S. (1930). *Secular Movements in Production and Prices*. Houghton Mifflin, New York.

Layton, E. (1972). Technology as knowledge. *Technology and Culture, 15*, 31-41.

Marris, R. (1964). *The Economic Theory of "Managerial" Capitalism*. Macmillan, New York.

Macdonald, R.J. (1985). Strategic alternatives in emerging industries. *J. Prod. Innov. Manag., 3*, 158-169.

Magee, S.P. (1977). Multinational corporations, the industry technology cycle and development. *Journal of World Trade Law, 11*, 297-321.

Mansfield, E., A. Romeo, M. Schwartz, D. Teece, S. Wagner, and P. Brach (1982). *Technology Transfer, Productivity, and Economic Policy*. Norton and Co., New York.

Mueser, R. (1985). Identifying technical innovations. *IEEE Transactions on Engineering Management*, EM-32, November, 158-176.

Nelson, R.R. (1962). Introduction. In National Bureau of Economic Research, *The Rate and Direction of Inventive Activity: Economic and Social Factors*. Princeton University Press, Princeton.

Nelson, R.R., and S.G. Winter (1977). In search of a useful theory of innovation. *Research Policy, 5*, 36-76.

Nelson, R.R., and S.G. Winter (1982). *An Evolutionary Theory of Economic Change*. The Belknap Press of Harvard University Press, Cambridge, Mass.

Penrose, E.T. (1959). *The Theory of the Growth of the Firm*, Wiley, New York.

Porter, M.E. (1980). *Competitive Strategy: Techniques for Analysing Industries and Competitors*. The Free Press, New York.

Porter M.E. (1983). The technological dimension of competitive strategy. *Research on Technological Innovation, Management and Policy, 1*, 1-33.

Price, D. (1984). The science/technology relationship, the craft of experimental science and policy for the improvement of high technology innovation. *Research Policy, 13*, 3-20.

Rosenberg, N. (1974). Science, invention and economic growth. *Economic Journal, 84*, 90-108.

Rosenberg, N. (1976). *Perspectives on Technology*, Cambridge University Press, Cambridge.

Rosenberg, N. (1982). *Inside the Black Box: Technology and Economics*. Cambridge University Press, Cambridge.

Rosenbloom, R.S. (1981). Technological innovation in firms and industries: An assessment of the State of the art. In P. Kelly and M. Kranzberg *et al.* (eds) *Technological Innovation: A Critical Review of Current Knowledge*. San Francisco Press, San Francisco.

Rothwell, R. (1982). The role of technology in industrial change: implications for regional policy. *Regional Studies, 16*, 361-369.

Rothwell, R. (1984). The role of small firms in the emergence of new technologies, *Omega, 12*, 19-29.

Sahal, D. (1984). The innovation dynamics and technology cycles in the computer industry. *Omega, 12*, 153-163.

Saviotti, P.P. and J.S. Metcalfe (1984). A theoretical approach to the construction of technological output indicators. *Research Policy, 13*, 141-151.

Schumpeter, J.A. (1934). *The Theory of Economic Development*. Harvard University Press, Cambridge.

Schumpeter, J.A. (1939). *Business Cycles*. McGraw-Hill, New York.

Schumpeter, J.A. (1950). *Capitalism, Socialism and Democracy*. Harper and Row, New York.

Senker, J. (1985). Small high technology firms: Some regional implications. *Technovation, 3*, 243-262.

Simon, H.A. (1959). Theories of decision making in economics. *American Economic Review, 49*, 253-283.

Simon, H.A. (1965). *Administrative Behavior*. Free Press, New York.

Simon, H.A. (1982). *The Sciences of the Artificial*. The MIT Press, Cambridge.

Steed, G.P.F. (1982). *Threshold Firms*. Canadian Government Printing Centre, Hull, Quebec.

Thomas, M.D. (1985). Regional economic development and the role of innovation and technological change. In A.R. Thwaites and R.P. Oakey (eds.) *The Regional Economic Impact of Technological Change*. Frances Pinter, London.

Thomas, M.D. (1986a). Growth and structural change: The role of technical innovations. In A. Amin and J. Goddard (eds.) *Technological Change, Industrial Restructuring and Regional Development*. George Allen and Unwin, London.

Thomas, M.D. (1986b). The innovation factor in the process of microeconomic industrial change: Conceptual explorations. In E. Wever and G.A. van der Knaap (eds.) *New Technology and Industrial Change*. Croom Helm, Beckenham.

Thomas, M.D. (1986c). Schumpeterian perspectives on entrepreneurship in economic development: A commentary. Forthcoming in *Geoforum*.

Usher, A.P. (1971). Technical change and capital formation. In N. Rosenberg (ed.) *The Economics of Technological Change*. Penguin Books, Baltimore.

Utterback, J.M. and W.J. Abernathy (1975). A dynamic model of process and product innovation. *Omega, 3*, 639-656.

Vernon, R. (1966). International investment and international trade in the product cycle. *Quarterly Journal of Economics, 80*, 190-207.

Vernon, R. (1979). The product cycle in a new international environment. *Oxford Bulletin of Economics and Statistics, 41*, 225-267.

Walsh, V. (1984). Invention and innovation in the chemical industry: demand-pull or discovery-push? *Research Policy, 13*, 211-234.

Williamson, O.E. (1970). *Corporate Control of Business Behavior*, Prentice-Hall, Englewood Cliffs, N.J.

Williamson, O.E. (1975). *Markets and Heirarchies: Analysis and Antitrust Implications*. Free Press, New York.

Williamson, O.E. (1981). The modern corporation: Origins, evolution, attributes. *Journal of Economic Literature, 19*, 1537-1568.

Williamson, O.E. (1985). *The Economic Institutions of Capitalism*. The Free Press, New York.

TEN

Dimensions of Skilled Migration from Developing Countries

M.C. MADHAVAN

INTRODUCTION

Migration of skilled and talented people from developing countries on a scale never before encountered is an outgrowth of the opening up of employment opportunities in developed countries in the post-Sputnik era, increased access to higher education facilities in developed countries, improved communication among countries and increased skilled employment opportunities in some developing countries. In the late 1960s there arose an International Career System in which the opportunities for upward mobility and achievement went far beyond the boundaries of any one society (Richmond, 1968). The flow of educated and talented people from developing to developed countries, some of whom received Nobel Prizes for their monumental contributions in ever increasing numbers and the non-return of students sent to developed countries for education created such international concern that a new term, "brain-drain", was coined to reflect that concern.

Though there is still concern about the flow of skilled and talented people from developing countries, the movements so far are not viewed as something detrimental to the long-term interests of many developing countries. The late Prime Minister of India, Mrs. Indira Gandhi, viewed the talented people of Indian origin living outside of India as a "Brain Bank". Such changes in perceptions have created an international environment conducive to tackle the issue.

Statistics on Migration of Skilled and Talented People

The word "skill" has a spectrum of meaning ranging from practical abilities acquired through non-formal education (Arrow-type learning-by-doing process) to high level of abilities imparted through formal education over a long gestation period involving heavy, private as well as social, investment (UNCTAD, 1987, 3). The difficulty associated with defining "skilled" has led to the use of occupational characteristics of immigrants to get a handle on the problem. But even such data with varying degrees of accuracy exist only for a few countries.

In summary, the state of skilled immigrant flow statistics is far from satisfactory. The lack of comprehensive and standardized migration statistics continues to be an obstacle in assessing the dimensions of skill flows, even though the United Nations formulated recommendations in this respect almost 35 years ago (U.N. Statistical Paper Series M. No. 38, 3-8). Skilled migrant data presently available have a downward bias, from the point of view of a developing country, owing to the exclusion of qualified housewives at entry in estimating skilled migrant flow and the use of last permanent residence instead of country of birth in determining the origin of the immigrant. There is also an upward bias due to the lack of net flow data for almost all countries. Also when a country classifies the occupation of a person at the time of granting resident status rather than the time of entry, upward quality bias may creep in, particularly in those cases where a resident status seeking person has already had the benefit of education and training in the country.

Skilled Migration Flow to Selected Developed Countries

However, inadequate the available statistics may be, it is still possible to paint a broad picture of developing country skilled migrant flow situation in general, and discuss in particular those countries which do provide better statistical coverage. It may be seen from Table 10.1 that the gross inflow of skilled migrants into the United States, Canada, the United Kingdom and continental Western Europe might be of the order of 1.2 million in the last 27 years. The USA accounted for over three-fifths of the total, the U.K. over one-fifth, Canada over one-eighth and the rest by continental Europe. Japan receives only a very small number of developing country migrants, mainly entertainers from the Philippines. Australia has been receiving increasing number of Asian-Pacific skilled persons during 1976-82, but no estimate of the total skilled migrant flow seems to exist. Skill flows to New Zealand should be very minimal as dictated by its immigration policy of excluding skilled persons from developing countries unless skills are needed in New Zealand, are not in demand in their country of origin and are not obtainable from a developed country (TRLIN, 1984). The above overall review indicates that legal gross flow of skilled immigrants from developing countries to all developed countries would be of the order of 1.3 million in the last 27 years.

Some developing countries, notably Saudi Arabia, Kuwait, Qatar, Oman, United Arab Emirates and Venezuela were major recipients of skilled immigrants from other developing countries such as Egypt, the Philippines, Pakistan, India, Bangladesh, Korea, Sri Lanka, Thailand, Peru and Ecuador. These were mainly contract immigrants. It is not clear, however, how many of these people were residing in those countries at different points in time. A recent estimate suggests that the proportion of skilled Asian Contract Immigrants in the total flow into these countries varied between 1.9 per cent in the case of Sri Lanka and 10.4 per cent in the case of the Philippines, with proportions for Pakistan and Bangladesh being 4.3 and 5.5 per cent, respectively, (Demery, cited in UNCTAD 1987: 5). Recent data for the Philippines, however, suggest a higher percentage (16.2 during 1982-85) of skilled people in the total flow from the Philippines to Middle Eastern countries.[1] A very large proportion of 400,000 talented Egyptians residing abroad is likely to be working in Middle Eastern countries. Since many of these people are going to Middle East on contracts of varying duration, it is very difficult, if not impossible, to develop a series of skilled contract immigrants residing in different migrant receiving Middle Eastern countries. Hence we will confine our discussion to skilled migration to selected developed countries.

United States

The USA is the largest recipient of developing country skilled immigrants since 1960. After the 1965 law emphasizing skill rather than national origin as the major determinant of immigration, annual average inflow increased rapidly by 170 per cent during the rest of the 1960s, and kept increasing at a very much reduced rate in the 1970s (see Table 10.1). The trend was reversed somewhat in the 1980s. Of the 700,000 people who were admitted during 1960-86, some would have certainly returned to their country of origin, but there is no mechanism in place that will provide the estimate for returning immigrants. Though attempts have been made to estimate the number of overall returning immigrants for certain period (see Warren and Peck, 1980) no such attempt seem to have been made specifically to estimate cohort loss rate for skilled immigrants. UNCTAD (1979: 4) pointed out that "reverse flow and to-and-fro migration" may be about 25 per cent of gross flows.

TABLE 10.1: **Estimates of Skilled Immigrant Flows (Total) from Developing Countries to Selected Developed Countries: 1960-86**

	Annual Average Flow						
Country	1960-65	1966-70	1971-75	1976-80	1981-86	Total	Per Cent
USA	9,476	25,478	33,083	32,849 [a]	30,852 [b]	699,018	61.5
Canada	1,217	7,028	8,462	5,477 [c]	4,824 [d]	141,102	12.4
U.K.	10,205 [e]	9,391	8,338 [f]	13,072 [a]	12,933 [g]	(233,175)	20.5
France	n.a.	800 [h]	1,200	350 [i]	n.a.	(11,750)	1.0
Other Western Europe	⟶	400	⟵	n.a.	n.a.	(50,000)	4.4
		Total				1,136,045	100.0

Sources:

1. Average skill flows into the USA and Canada were computed from data in UNCTAD (July 1987), Annex Tables 1 & 2. Developing countries are defined to include Romania and to exclude Israel.
2. Average skill flows into the U.K. were computed from data in UNCTAD (1979), and International Migration Statistics Series MN.
3. Average skill flows into France are based on "high level" Cadres and Technician category proportions given in Anicet le Pors (1977), cited in UNCTAD (1979).
4. Average percentage of 2.1 estimated for France for the period 1969-75 was applied to an estimated 235 million immigrants in other West European countries in early 1970s.

Notes:

a	=	Average for 1976-79	b	=	Average for 1982-86
c	=	Average for 1976, 77, 79 & 80	d	=	Average for 1981-84
e	=	Average for 1964-65	f	=	Average for 1971 & 72
g	=	Average for 1981-83	h	=	Average for 1969 & 70
i	=	1978 only	N.A.	=	Not available

If we assume a 5 per cent cohort loss rate of skilled immigration for 1980s, 10 per cent for 1970s and 20 per cent for 1960s, there should be now in the US around 600,000 (out of 700,000 admitted during 1960-86) skilled immigrants from developing countries. But available evidence suggests that there may be more than 700,000 skilled persons born in developing countries. Also there may be much more skilled people of developed country birth than those who were admitted.

Table 10.2 is an attempt to understand whether there were less number of skilled immigrants in 1980 than the number admitted during 1970-80. According to 1980 census, there were 537,141 skilled immigrants who were born in developing countries and admitted during 1970-80. This is about 93,000 more than what US Immigration and Naturalization service reported it had admitted during that period. For every 100 skilled immigrants from developing countries who were admitted, there were 113 in 1980. For every 100 skilled immigrants from developed countries, there were 105.

Among the developing country groupings, if we compare the INS data with census data for Asia after adjusting it for the inclusion of Israel and Japan, they are approximately equal (Table 10.2.) On the other hand, for every 100 skilled people admitted during 1970-80, there were 134 from Latin America and 123 from Africa. The difference could be attributed to people staying illegally in the US. Some countries could have experienced a cohort loss as was the case in India.[2] (Table 10.2). This does not mean, however, that there are no skilled immigrants from India staying illegally. There is no way of exactly knowing how many are illegally overstaying by comparing INS data with census data, but it will be the first step.

The share of developing countries in the skilled migration to the US more than doubled following the enactment of the 1965 Law, cutting down developed country share to about one-third of what it was in the pre-1965 period. Thereafter, the shares of the latter have risen to over 25 per cent, and the former slightly declined to about 75 per cent (Table 10.3). Asia became the most important source of skilled immigrants in the late 1960s, reached the peak of about 60 per cent during 1971-75, and then it declined to the present level of over 50 per cent. The contra trend is evident in the case of skilled immigrants from Latin America, but its share of 18.5 per cent is still far below its share in the early 1960s. Even though Africa share is very small, it has grown consistently and now accounts for over 4 per cent.

TABLE 10.2: **A Comparison of 1980 US Census Data with Immigration and Naturalization Service Estimates of Skilled Immigrant Flows During January 1970 to March 1980**

(In thousands)

Country or Region of Birth	1980 Census Data Professional	Technicians	Managerial	Total	%	INS Data Total	%
Asia[a]	138.7 (50.6)	48.8 (55.3)	74.6 (42.6)	262.1	48.8	266.5[b]	55.5
China	8.9	3.9	7.9	20.6	3.8		
India	35.2	8.5	10.1	53.8	10.0	63.114.2	
Korea	11.8	3.5	20.6	35.9	6.7		
Philippines	32.0	12.2	13.3	57.6	12.6		
South America	12.9 (4.7)	3.9 (4.4)	9.8 (5.0)	26.5	4.9 }	66.214.9	
North and Central America	27.2 (9.9)	10.4 (11.8)	24.7 (14.1)	62.3	11.6 }		
Dominican Rep.	1	Neg	1.2	2.3	0.4		
Haiti	1.6	1	1	3.0	0.6		
Jamaica	4.6	1.8	2.7	9.1	1.7		
Mexico	8.2	2.8	9.3	20.4	3.8		
Africa	12.3 (4.5)	3.1 (3.5)	7.3 (4.2)	22.7	4.2	18.44.1	
Developing Countries	191.1 (69.8)	66.1 (75.0)	116.5 (66.5)	373.7	69.6	331.174.5	
Developed[c] Countries	59.8 (21.8)	13.8 (15.7)	45.3 (25.9)	118.9	22.1	113.325.5	
Others[d]	23.0 (8.4)	8.2 (9.3)	13.3 (7.6)	44.6	8.3		
Total — All Countries	273.9 (100.0)	88.1 (100.0)	175.1 (100.0)	537.1	100.0	444.4100.0	
Total for U.S. Population (in millions)	12.0 (47.8)	3.0 (12.0)	10.1 (40.2)	25.1 (100.0)			

Sources: INS data as compiled in UNCTAD (1987), Census data from U.S. Bureau of the Census (1984) Detailed Population Characteristics, Table 225.

Notes:
a = Census data for Asia includes Japan and Israel. There were over 47,000 immigrants from Japan and 26,000 from Israel who came into the USA during 1970-80, including about 18,000 skilled migrants.
b = Excludes Israel and Japan.
c = Includes Yugoslavia, Romania and Malta (which are excluded from this category in INS data reported here) but excludes Israel and Japan. Over 42,000 persons of Yugoslav origin and over 17,000 of Romanian origin were admitted during 1971-80. Australia and New Zealand are excluded in INS data.
d = Soviet Union, Oceania, Australia and New Zealand
neg = less than 500.

TABLE 10.3. **Share of Developing Countries in Skilled Migration into the USA Canada and the U.K. 1960-86**

(Percentages unless otherwise stated)

Region of Birth or Last Permanent Residence	1960-65	1966-70	1971-75	1976-80	1981-86	1960-86
United States						
Skilled Immigrants Admitted from All Countries - Annual Aver.	25,430	41,404	42,572	43,611[a]	41,278[b]	38,128
Developed Countries	62.7	38.5	22.3	24.7	25.3	33.3
Developing Countries	37.3	61.5	77.7	75.3	74.7	66.7
Africa	1.3	3.3	3.6	4.2	4.1	3.4
America	25.6	21.3	12.9	17.4	18.5	18.8
Asia	8.3	34.4	59.5	52.1	50.5	42.5
Europe	2.0	2.6	1.6	1.4	1.5	1.8
Oceania	0.1	0.1	0.1	0.2	0.2	0.1
Canada						
Skilled Immigrants Admitted from all Countries - Annual Aver.	11,254	29,279	23,338	15,017[c]	13,164[d]	15,659
Developed Countries	89.2	76.0	63.7	63.7	63.4	68.5
Developing Countries	10.8	24.0	36.3	36.3	36.3	31.5
Africa	1.6	2.0	4.8	4.5	4.0	3.8
America	3.3	5.6	8.8	8.1	6.2	7.7
Asia	5.5	15.6	21.4	22.1	23.8	19.0
Europe	0.4	0.9	1.0	1.5	2.5	1.2
Oceania	Nil	0.1	0.2	0.2	0.2	0.2
United Kingdom						
Skilled Immigrants Admitted from all Countries - Annual Aver.	39,250[e]	42,398	45,030[f]	24,500[a]	23,966[g]	34,403
Developed Countries	74.0	77.9	81.5	46.6	46.0	68.4
Developing Countries	26.0	22.1	18.5	53.4	54.0	31.6
New Commonwealth	N.A	N.A	N.A	28.1	27.5	N.A.

Sources: Computations were based on data in UNCTAD (1987) for United States and Canada; UNCTAD (1979) page 5 and International Migration Series MN. Tables 3.4 and 3.10 for 1976, 77, 78, 79, 81, 82 and 83 for the United Kingdom.

Notes:

a = Average for 1976-79
b = Average for 1982-86
c = Average for 1976, 77, 79 and 80
d = Average for 1981-84
e = Average for 1964 and 65
f = Average for 1971 and 72
g = Average for 1981-83
N.A. = Not available

The ratio of skilled to total migration was higher for developed than for developing countries for all but one period (Table 10.4). However, comparable ratios for African and Asian developing countries were higher than those for developed countries. An interesting feature of the data in Table 10.4 is that an average African immigrant is much better qualified professionally than an average person in any other group.

TABLE 10.4: **Ratio of Skilled Migration to Immigrant Flows into the USA, Canada and the U.K., 1960-86**

Region of Birth or Last Permanent Residence	1960-65	1966-70	1971-75	1976-79	1982-86	1960-86
United States						
All Countries	11.5	11.5	11.0	8.6	7.2	9.6
Developed Countries	14.8	11.8	10.4	11.5	12.9	12.5
Developing Countires	8.4	11.2	11.2	8.0	6.3	8.6
Africa	14.8	31.5	26.1	19.7	11.9	18.7
America	7.4	5.5	3.3	3.7	3.8	4.5
Asia	10.0	26.2	22.0	12.0	7.8	13.2
Europe	18.0	16.3	9.1	11.8	12.5	11.3
Oceania	6.3	6.5	3.8	3.7	4.0	4.3

Canada	1967-70	1971-74	1975-77	1983-84	1967-84
All Countries	17.2	13.8	13.8	10.0	15.1
Developed Countries	17.7	15.9	18.7	18.7	7.3
Developing Countries	16.1	11.2	9.5	6.2	12.0
Africa	16.4	13.9	13.5	11.4	14.4
America	10.0	8.2	6.8	4.1	8.3
Asia	23.6	13.4	10.5	6.1	12.9
Europe	5.7	8.0	13.4	23.5	—
Oceania	6.2	3.1	3.3	1.9	3.7

United Kingdom	1971-72	1976-79	1981-83	1971-83
All Countries	29.3	19.4	19.1	21.7
Developed Countries	39.5	21.8	19.5	26.5
Developing Countries	15.3	17.7	18.7	17.5
New Commonwealth	N.A.	16.5	17.3	N.A.

Sources: Computed from data in UNCTAD (1979), UNCTAD (July 1987), International Migration Series MN, U.S. Immigration and Naturalization Service *Statistical Year Books and Immigration Statistics*, Canada.

Canada

Over 140,000 skilled immigrants have been admitted into Canada in the last 27 years. The flow followed the same pattern as was noted in the case of the USA. There was a big spurt in the flow in 1967 when new policy emphasizing skill was implemented. After almost a five-fold increase in the flow in the second half of 1960s, momentum was maintained, but at a lower rate of growth. The upward trend was reversed in 1975 when the labour market concerns played an important role in implementing the immigration policy. Thereafter the skill flow dropped in successive periods (Table 10.1), reaching slightly above 1966 level. Now the intake of immigrants responds mainly to humanitarian concerns and a bona-fide economic immigration of all races and nationalities have become quite small. One exception of this trend is an active recruitment of entrepreneurs importing financial capital into Canada (Kubat, 1984).

After an increase in the share of developing countries in the total skill flows during 1967-75, it remained approximately at the same level in the subsequent periods. Two out of three skilled migrants to Canada come from developed countries as against nine out of ten before 1967. Among the developing countries, Asian region accounted for 60 per cent of developing country share. An interesting phenomena during 1981-84 was the developing country share increased from 32 per cent to 46 per cent, but at lower levels of flow. It might signify that developing country share may increase, but absolute numbers might decline because of decrease in overall flow from all sources.

Developed countries send proportionately more skilled immigrants than developing countries (Table 10.4). What is interesting is that relative importance of skilled migrant in the total flow has continuously declined over 1967-84 in almost all developing regions, while it has slightly moved up and remained high in the case of developed countries.

United Kingdom

Information from different sources is pieced together to estimate the skill flows from developing countries to the United Kingdom. The total skilled migrant flow during 1964-85 may be estimated between 230,000 and 240,000 (Table 10.1). Average inflow in 1980s was around 13,000, about 25 per cent higher than the average for early 1960s. Unlike the U.S. and Canadian experience, the inflow decreased during 1964-75, increased in the second half of 1970s and remained at about the same level during 1980s. The initial decline was perhaps due to the restrictions first introduced with the 1962 Commonwealth Immigration Act and strengthened with the 1971 Immigration Act.[3]

The above trend is also reflected in the share of developing countries in the gross inflow of skilled immigrants into the U.K. from all sources. Developing country share dropped from 26 per cent in 1964-65 to 18.5 per cent in 1971-75, and then almost trebled to 54 per cent in early 1980s. Yet the proportion of skilled persons in the total flow from developed countries, though declined by half to 19.5 per cent in the early 1980s, is still marginally higher than the corresponding figure for the developing countries (Table 10.4). During 1971-83, one out of four immigrants from developed countries was a professional compared to one out of six in the case of developing countries.

Not all of the skilled immigrants would, however, still be living in the United Kingdom, as many might have returned to their country of origin or moved on to other destinations such as the USA and Canada. Though no comprehensive data on return migration are available, scanty skilled migrant inflow and outflow information published in migration statistics [4] would throw some light on this issue. During 1976-83, gross inflow of skilled immigrants (professional and managerial category) from New Commonwealth countries amounted to 27,500 and from alien (which included Pakistan, Middle East and other developing countries) group 97,000. Outflows were reported to be 20,000 from New Commonwealth and 74,000 from the alien group. Since the net immigration flow from Pakistan, Middle East and other developing countries accounted for 77 per cent of the net immigration flow of alien group, the net skilled immigrant flow from developing countries may be estimated at around 25,000 during 1976-83. It is not unreasonable to conclude that 27 per cent[5] of the skilled immigrants from developing countries who migrated to the U.K. might have remained there.

Continental Western Europe

Though this region is an important recipient of skilled immigrants from developing countries, skill flows data are not easily accessible. Estimates are often sketchy, and sometimes contradictory. Estimates of skill flows to France were made here on the basis of skill migrant proportions suggested in Anciet Le Pors study and cited in UNCTAD (1979). Our estimate indicates an inflow of approximately 7,600 during 1969-75. The 1978 inflow might have been about 350 as determined from source data. However, UNCTAD (1987) refers to a skill flow (equivalent to Cadre and Technicians) estimate of 6,187 during 1967-84 by A.B. Zahlan. It is not clear whether it is a net flow or gross flow. In any event, there is need for making data accessible and comparable.

Based on Anciet Le Pors study, French weighted average skill flow rate for 1969-75 was of the order of 2.1 per cent of the labour force. Applying this rate to an estimated developing country immigrant labour force of about 2.35 million in the early 1970s in the rest of continental Western Europe, the stock of skilled migrants from developing countries may be placed at about 50,000. Fragmentary data about inflow into France from individual developing countries suggest that while 20-50 per cent of immigrants from Argentina, Brazil, India and Lebanon are skilled, less than 5 per cent of immigrants from Morocco, Senegal, Chile, Laos, Cambodia and Vietnam are skilled.

Regional Distribution

Table 10.5 reinforces the earlier conclusion that Asia is the largest source of skilled migrants for the USA and Canada, followed by Latin America and Africa. As regards Asia, the same seems to hold true for the U.K., but the order is reversed between the other two.[6] What is disturbing is the magnitude of skill flow from Africa and small Caribbean countries such as Jamaica, Dominican Republic and Haiti.

According to UNCTAD (1975) estimate, the total outflow of professionals from Africa during 1961-72 was over 17,000, nearly 60 per cent of which going to the U.K., followed by the USA and Canada. There seems to have been some accelaration in the skill flow from Africa to the USA during 1970-80 when approximately 23,000 professional, managerial and technical people migrated (U.S. Bureau of Census, 1984 – Table 255). The flow of highly skilled professional speciality occupations such as doctors, engineers, scientists, university professors, and teachers was 12,347 which was approximately the same as was for South America, and 150 per cent more than the combined total skill flow from Greece, Italy and Portugal. Skill flow from Jamaica at over 9,000 to the USA during the same period was 50 per cent more than the comparable flow either from Greece or Italy, and flow from Portugal (1,800) was smaller than those either from Haiti (3,000) or from Dominican Republic (2,300).[7]

The outflow of talent from developing countries is related to the non-return of students who went to developed countries for higher studies either on their own or some sort of scholarship. A sample survey conducted among Jamaicans, (Brown, 1981) suggested that approximately 50 per cent of Jamaican students studying overseas intended to remain abroad.[8] As the period of domicile away from home increases, so does the likelihood of remaining away. Indian experience is also in the same view. Madhavan (1988) estimated that the total number of persons of Indian birth in the USA who got their student, exchange visitor and temporary trainee visas status adjusted to immigrant category during 1966-85 (excluding 1980-81) amounted to over 38,000, which was 46 per cent of all skilled immigrants admitted from India during the same period.

This group's share in the total immigrant flow varied. It increased from over 6,000 during 1966-69 to over 16,000 in the first half of the 1970s, but the share declined from 34 per cent to 24 per cent. Since then, both the absolute numbers and relative shares have declined, reaching about 6,000 during 1982-85 and accounting for 6 per cent of the total immigrant flow. This downward trend may partly explain the declining share of professional, managerial and technical people in the total immigrant flow in recent years from India to the USA.

Some African countries have also had similar experience. It has been estimated that in the 1960s, when the demand for physicists and chemists was very great in the West, more than half of the African students sent abroad for advanced studies in these areas did not return to their home countries. "The situation improved thereafter, but by 1977, 17 per cent of former students were working in industrialized countries and 3 per cent in developing countries other than their own" (UNESCO, 1984: 433).

TABLE 10.5: **Regional Distribution of Skilled Migration to the USA and Canada, 1960-86**

(In thousands)

Developing Region of Origin or Last Permanent Residence	Average Annual Flows															Estimated Total Flows		
	1960-95			1966-70			1971-75			1976-80			1981-86					
	U	C	T	U	C	T	U	C	T	U	C	T	U[a]	C[b]	T	US	Canada	Total
Africa	0.3	0.2	0.5	1.4	0.6	2.0	1.5	1.1	2.6	1.8	0.7	2.5	1.7	0.5	2.2	35.7 (5.1)	16.1 (11.4)	51.8 (6.2)
America	6.5	0.3	6.8	8.8	1.6	10.4	5.5	2.0	7.5	7.6	1.2	8.8	7.6	0.8	8.4	19.4 (27.8)	31.7 (22.5)	226.1 (26.9)
Asia	2.1	0.6	2.7	14.2	4.6	18.8	25.3	5.0	30.3	22.7	3.3	26.0	20.8	3.1	23.9	449.0 (64.2)	86.9 (61.6)	535.9 (63.8)
Europe	0.5	Neg	0.5	1.1	0.2	1.3	0.7	0.2	0.9	0.6	0.2	0.8	0.6	0.3	0.9	18.7 (2.7)	5.7 (4.0)	24.4 (2.9)
Oceania	Neg	Nil	Neg	Neg	Neg	0.1	0.1	Neg	0.1	0.1	Neg	0.1	0.1	Neg	0.1	1.5 (0.2)	0.7 (0.5)	2.2 (0.3)
Total	9.5	1.2	10.7	25.5	7.0	32.5	33.1	8.4	41.5	32.8	5.4	38.2	30.9	4.8	35.7	699.3 (100.0)	141.1 (100.0)	840.4 (100.0)

Sources: Computed from data in UNCTAD, "Trends and Current situation in Reverse Transfer of Technology". (July 1987).

Notes:
U = United States
C = Canada
T = Combined Total
neg = Less than 50
a = refers to 1982-86
b = refers to 1981-84.

Quality Characteristics

One statistic that would capture the overall skill embodies in the immigrant from developing countries is the educational level attained by them. Among 25 years old who entered the USA during 1970-80, over 22 per cent had completed at least 4 years of college and about 13 per cent, at least 5 years of college, compared to only 16 per cent and 7.5 per cent, respectively, for US born persons. Surprising as it may sound, the best qualified immigrants are from Africa, 43 per cent of whom had completed at least 4 years of college and 27.5 per cent at least 5 years of college (Table 10.6). They also had the highest per cent of labour force employed in professional occupations. Among the individual countries for which data are available, immigrants from India have distinguished themselves with 46 per cent of them having completed at least 5 years of college, and over 50 per cent were in professional occupations. Immigrants from the Philippines had the next best educational achievement. In general, immigrants from Asian and African countries had better educational accomplishments than those from Europe (excepting the U.K.) and Latin America. Comparable data are not available for Canada and the U.K. Sketchy information that are available seem to suggest that immigrants from India, the Philippines, China and Egypt are well educated, but the extent of difference in educational achievement between them and others may not be striking as it is found in the USA.

The educational level of developing country immigrants in the USA is also reflected in the occupational structure. Fifty one per cent of the skilled immigrants who entered the USA during 1970-80 were employed in professional speciality occupations such as doctors, engineers, scientists, university professors, nurses and school teachers, ranging between 33 per cent[9] for Korea and 66 per cent for India. Proportionately there are more developing country immigrants in professional speciality occupations than the corresponding ratio for the U.S.-born persons (Table 10.2). While Canadian experience may approximately be the same as that of the USA, in the U.K. the proportion of immigrants in professional occupations is likely to be lower than the ratio for British-born persons.

An interesting feature of developing country immigrant labour force in the USA is the number of women in professional speciality

TABLE 10.6: **Selected Quality Characteristics and Mean Family Income of Immigrants to the USA During 1970-80**

Country or Region of Birth	Number Immigrated (000s)	% over 25 yrs of age	% having at least: High School	% having at least: 4 yrs. of College	% having at least: 5 yrs. of College	% of Labour Force in Professional Occupation	Mean Family Income ($)
All Countires	5,560	55.5	56.9	22.2	12.5	17.7	18,626
Europe	742	63.2	60.4	20.4	12.4	22.7	23,568
Greece	67	67.1	41.5	10.6	6.0	15.7	18,575
Italy	100	64.0	33.4	8.2	5.1	9.7	21,149
Portugal	83	59.0	19.3	2.8	1.5	3.1	19,907
United Kingdon.	132	60.6	88.6	30.5	17.6	42.9	29,872
Asia	1,763	59.2	74.5	34.4	19.8	27.7	21,364
China	136	82.4	59.7	27.6	14.0	21.5	18,792
India	158	72.1	87.2	63.1	46.1	50.5	28,061
Korea	243	55.6	74.4	31.6	9.6	20.7	21,316
Philippines	319	67.1	77.1	47.9	21.4	26.0	26,704
Central and North America	2,153	49.6	33.2	6.9	3.9	7.2	15,692
Canada	123	52.3	78.0	30.0	17.6	41.6	29,777
Cuba	163	67.5	40.2	10.3	5.7	10.7	16,795
Jamaica	115	53.9	60.7	9.7	4.8	12.2	17,976
Mexico	1,207	47.8	17.0	2.7	1.7	3.0	13,512
South America	316	59.9	66.2	18.3	11.9	15.5	18,058
Africa	130	63.1	88.5	43.3	27.5	33.6	19,574

Source: Computed from data in the U.S. Bureau of Census (March 1984) *Detailed Population Characteristics*, Table 255.

occupations. Though there are no such comprehensive information available at present, data on occupations of employed Asian-origin women (excluding Japanese origin, most of whom were born in the USA) the 1980 census may throw some light on the role of developing country women in highly skilled occupations. According to the census, there were over 12,000 Asian-origin women in health diagnosing field, 8,000 natural scientists, 38,000 executives, administrators and managers, 44,000 nurses, 8,000 college and university professors, librarians and counsellors and 2,000 engineers. They accounted for over 20 per cent of women physicians and dentists in the USA in 1980, and 10 per cent of women employed in natural science fields.[10] This is noteworthy, particularly when developing country Asian-origin women constituted less than 2 per cent of the total employed women in the USA.

Asian-origin men in professional speciality occupations numbered about 221,000. Of this, 87,000 were managers and executives, 50,000 engineers, 35,000 doctors, 20,000 natural scientists and 17,000 university and college professors, librarians and counsellors. They accounted for 6.4 per cent of male doctors in the USA, 6.7 per cent of natural scientists and 2.5 per cent of college and university professors.

As stated earlier, in the U.K., the net flow of developing country migrants in the professional and managerial occupations was of the order of 28,000 during 1976-83 (excepting 1980), one-fourth of whom were women.

Valuation of Skill Flows

The foregoing analysis indicated that more than 1.2 million skilled persons would have migrated from developing to developed countries during 1960-86, and many of them have chosen to settle permanently in the country of destination. Skills they acquired while in the country of origin are now embodied in them. Part of the cost of acquiring such skills was met out of public funds. When they move out of the country of origin permanently they are transferring a resource produced and nurtured in the country of origin to the country of destination. They are the agents through whom some value is added to the country of destination while, at the same time, corresponding value is withdrawn from the country of origin.[11] Valuation of this skill transfer could be necessary to construct an international resource flow accounting.[12]

In the past, researchers have used principally three approaches – Historical Cost, Present Discounted Value and Replacement Cost – to impute a monetary value to the skills of immigrants. There are many difficulties in using any one of them. Historical cost approach suffers from the problems of obtaining all the relevant historical data on the cost of education and training, while PDV necessitates making arbitrary assumptions in regard to lifetime income profiles and distribution, trends in productivity and the discount rate (UNCTAD, 1987). The Replacement Cost Approach enables one to impute the value loss, with some accuracy because of the use of current data, in the case of a spending country, and the value saved in the form of educational expenditure by the receiving country. In practice, however, "the imputation concerning the same group of migrants made in the two countries concerned hardly yield similar results, as the cost of education and training may vary substantially as between the countries. Moreover, it should be noted that there might also be considerable qualitative differences in the educational systems and that the productive capability of an individual depends also on other important factors apart from education and training". (UNCTAD, 1987: 9).

However, imperfect these methods of imputing monetary value of skilled migrants may be, they have nevertheless, been used to estimate the transfer implied in the migration of skilled people from developing to developed countries. Some of the significant studies in the area are summarized in Table 10.7. There is a wide variation in the estimated values for the same year. Even after allowing for differences in skills covered, the results have highlighted the imprecise nature of these approaches. For example, the congressional research service estimates the average benefit for the USA during 1971-72 to be less than $1 billion a year as against an estimate of over $2 billion a year made by UNCTAD for the period 1961-72. Policy-makers would like the economists to come up with a method less objectionable to all actors who would use these estimates in their negotiations with others.

Perhaps a new approach to impute the monetary value of skill may be considered. Skill embodiment in an individual is the result of investment of time, effort and money made by the individual as well as the government of the country of birth. Since the migrating individual enjoys the benefit of his or her effort in the form of emoluments received in the immigrating country, it is the country of birth that loses its educational investment made in the emigrating person. How do we measure it?

TABLE 10.7: **Imputed Value of Selected Skilled Immigrant Flows from Developing to Selected Developed Countries**

Country	Reference Years	Kinds of Skills Valued	Method of Estimation,	Estimated Value
USA	1966	S,E, & P	Cost of training	$ 88 million
USA	1967	-do-	in the developing	$ 150 million
USA	1971-72	-do-	country, $ 20,000 per person.	$ 565 million
USA	1971-72	-do-	Historical cost	$ 1,697 million
Canada	1967-73	-do-	-do-	Can. $1 billion 2.4 billion at 1968 prices
Switzerland	1979	-do-	-do-	Swf. 237 million
USA	1961-72	S[1], E & D	PDV	$ 28, 233 million
Canada	1963-72	S[2], E, D & Others[3]	PDV	$ 9, 556 million
U.K.	1964-72	E, S, D & Others[4]	PDV	$ 4, 603 million

Sources· U.S. Library of Congress, Congressional Research Service (1974); De Voertz and Maki (1980); Guntram Rehsche (1981) cited in UNCTAD (1987 & 1979).

Notes:
S = Scientists; E = Engineers; P = Physicians;
D = Doctors;
S[1] = Social and Natural Scientists;
S[2] = Natural Scientists, Biologists and Agricultural Professionals;
Others[3] = Professors, teachers, nurses, medical technicians and managerial and other professionals;
Others[4] = Teachers, nurses, medical technicians, and managerial and other professionals;
PDV = Present Discounted Value approach, using immigrant's actual earnings.

From the current information available on government and non-profit institutional expenditures on education in top representative schools, colleges and universities in the country. It may be possible to calculate the average expenditure per student from secondary level of education on to college and university level for every skilled profession. This could then be used to calculate the total amount of educational investment by the government and non-profit instutu-tions in those migrating to another country. Once monetary value of skill migration at current prices is established, purchasing power dollar values can be calculated using purchasing power conversion rates developed for most countrics by International Comparison Project (Kravis, Heston and Summers, 1982). The monetary value, measured in ICP dollars may be viewed as the opportunity cost of educational investment incurred by the country of emigration. Of course, this approach does not cover all the bases, but it is a step in the right direction.

Causes of Skilled Migration

The question of what causes migration has been analysed for many years, but there have not emerged any definitive conclusions about the determinants of skilled migration (see UNCTAD, 1987). The probable causes of skilled migration are as follows.

It is commonly assumed that income differential between developing and developed countries is an important cause of skilled migration from the former to the latter. Studies by Krugman and Bhagwati (1976), Psacharapoulos (1975) and Glaser and Herbers (1973), and Rudd and Hatch (1968, cited in Krugman and Bhagwati), suggested that income or discounted value of lifetime earnings influences migration decision, but there is not enough accumulated evidence to pinpoint income differential as a major determinant of skilled migration.

Another factor that seems to be a cause of emigration of skilled people from developing countries is the existence of surplus in certain fields.[13] This is perhaps due to the production of professional college graduates most of whom would have been employed if economic growth projections had materialized.[14] With long lead time required for the development of technical and professional education, it might be unavoidable to have more graduates in any given year than the economy could absorb, when development programmes go hay wire due to lack of funds or factors beyond the control of the country. Persistence of acute surplus is due to poor manpower planning in the initial stages. In certain disciplines such as medicine, however, the "surplus" is due to the unwillingness of the graduates to serve in rural areas where a large portion of medical needs are unmet. When science, engineering and agriculture graduates do not simply want to move out of their known surroundings to work in other parts of the country, educated unemployment swells. The persistent unemployment of skilled people and frustration associated with it create conditions that make people take risks that they might otherwise shun. High unemployment and underemployment situations among skilled people in India, Pakistan, the Philippines and Jamaica would have contributed to them becoming hatchment areas of skilled migration to developed countries.

Family considerations to enter into the decision-making process, but they may act both as a deterrent to, and incentive for, skilled migration. Glaser study found that family interests appeared as reasons for staying at home (Krugman and Bhagwati, 1976: 46). On the other hand, if the prospective skilled emigrant is the first or second child of a large family whose scarce resources were used to educate the person, he or she may feel that obligations to the family cannot be fulfilled with the opportunity he or she faces at home. Hence the decision may be made to migrate to a country where potential pay-off will be large. Thus the need for high income to meet one's obligations to other members of the family may act as an incentive for skilled migration.

One of the serious professional motivation for emigration appears to be an effort to avoid isolation (UNESCO, 1984: 428) loss of contact with colleagues through inability to travel, lack of equipment, instruments and libraries, lack of government support for research, access to new techniques of analysis and such others are some of the specifics that contribute to the emigrating process. It is, however, not clear how important these factors are. Glaser's analysis found professional needs to be weakly associated with the decision on migration. Commenting on this result, UNCTAD (1979: 11), observed that "it is, however, possible that while a small number of people may be affected by working conditions or professional needs, those affected may be the more important ones from the society's viewpoint".

Another reason for skilled migration to developed countries is the lack of challenging research and development opportunities in many developing countries.[15] In 1973, the developing countries spent less than 3 per cent of the Global Research and Development Budget, and employed 13 per cent of the world's scientists and engineers (Norman, 1979). Since that time, the share of the developing countries in the Global R & D Budget has risen to 6 per cent

(UNESCO, 1985). Yet R & D expenditure as a proportion of GNP is so low that they could not utilize the available talents. It was about 0.2 per cent in Pakistan, the Philippines and Argentina and 0.3 per cent in Nigeria. India and Korea are the exceptions to this dismal situation. But an increase in R & D does not mean optimum use of the resource. There is wastage in government supported R & D organizations[16] and private R & D organizations in India which are helped by the tax policy of the government of India.

Sometimes actions taken to encourage emigration by forward looking government will improve the welfare of its citizens in the long-run. For example, Korea has adjusted part of its emigration policy to meet changes in receiving countries' demand for certain types of immigrants (Kim, 1984). For business emigrants to Canada, for instance, the Korean government has lifted the relevant provisions of the foreign exchange regulations limiting the maximum amount of foreign exchange to $ 100,000 that an emigrant family can take overseas, and has also taken measures to ease the issue of passports for those travelling to Canada to explore business prospects there.

Other factors of significance that enter into the equation of emigrating process are unstable economic and political conditions, tensions between ethnic groups, shortage of consumer goods, life-styles prevalent in the country of destination, foreign spouse and better education for the children (UNESCO, 1984: 435 & Oguzkan, 1985: 16).

Skill inflows from developing countries are very much affected by the policies of immigrant receiving countries. These policies have changed over time and they are reflected in the inflow of skilled persons from developing countries. In the late 1950s and early 1960s, there was a slow down in the flow of skilled people from traditional sources in to the USA and Canada at a time when skill shortages were noticeable in some sectors of the economy. These were partly overcome by opening up the immigration process to all skilled people irrespective of national origin. Besides eliminating the discrimination inherent in the earlier immigration laws, these new laws also provide them with skilled immigrants who had already proven their ability while they were students. In recent years, there have been conscious efforts in Canada, as stated earlier, to respond only to humanitarian concerns, leading to substantial decline in bona-fide economic immigration of all races and nationalities. The USA has also tightened up the procedures. But the business interests prevail when they find the right person for employment. As referred to earlier, there is no significant decline in the inflow of skilled immigrants from developing countries.

Consequences of Skilled Migration[17]

Any attempt to determine the consequences of skilled migration for sending as well as receiving countries may have to be illustrative because of data and conceptual problems.

Consequences for Developing Countries of Origin

Skilled migration could contribute to a reduction in the unemployment level in the short-run among science, engineering and medical graduates. It would, however,undermine the ability of countries to reach the critical mass needed for scientific and technological breakthroughs. In the case of countries with a small size of professionally-oriented labour force, skill outflow would create shortages in the short-run and adversely affect the implementation of development programmes. In the first group are countries such as India, the Philippines and Egypt, and in the latter are Bangladesh, Sri Lanka, Jamaica and Yemen Arab Republic.

The total number of Indian born professional, technical and kindred workers who migrated to different parts of the world up to 1980 was approximately 233,000 (Madhavan, 1985). This was equivalent to 12 per cent of economically active persons in science, engineering and medical fields in India.[18] To put it in another way, these skilled migrants were equivalent to 45 per cent of job seekers on the live registers of employment exchanges in 1980.[19] In the Philippines, nearly 40,000 skilled persons emigrated during 1975-81, 80 per cent of whom went to the USA (Tidalgo, 1984: 34). Approximately 100,000 skilled people also left on contract to work mainly in the Middle Eastern countries (Republic of the Philippines, NEDA 1986: 486-487). These two groups together accounted for about 13 per cent of total professional, technical, and kindred workers employed in the Phillipines in 1981. There is no unemployment data available for professional, technical and kindred workers. Viewing against educated unemployment, skill migrants during 1975-81 are equivalent to almost two-thirds of unemployment people among college graduates in 1978.[20]

The impact of skill flows on developing countries can best be seen in relation to the domestic stock or flow of certain skill categories. On the basis of the number of skilled Indian immigrants residing in the USA in 1980 and assuming that was equivalent to 45 per cent of the total flow from India, the number of doctors born and educated in India, now residing outside, may be estimated around 33,000; engineers 36,000, and natural scientists 13,000.[21] As a proportion of economically active people in these categories in 1980, they were 21 per cent, 16 per cent and 6 per cent respectively. Since average quality of training of those migrated is likely to be superior to average quality of training of those in India, the real loss to India would be higher than the above percentages indicate. Still outflow would have certainly delayed the creation of critical mass necessary for scientific and technological breakthroughs in many fields of research and development activities.

Skilled Filipinos settled in the USA as of 1980 are about 91,000 (U.S. Bureau of the Census, 1984), of whom 28,000 were in managerial occupations; 6,000 engineers; 11,000 doctors; 5,000 natural scientists and 28,000 nurses. Since roughly 80 per cent of those who migrate to the USA, the total flow of certain categories of skilled people for permanent settlement may be estimated as follows: doctors – 14,000; engineers – 7,500 and natural scientists-6,250. The number of doctors who migrated were approximately equal to those who passed the board examination in medicine during 1970-80.[22] Such a large outflow had its toll on the availability of physician services, increasing the number of people per physician substantially from 1,310 in 1965 to 2,150 in 1981 (World Bank 1986:234). The situation in engineering is not as bad as it is in medicine. The number of engineers who migrated permanently up to 1980 would be around 10 per cent of all types of engineers who passed the board examinations during 1970-80.[23] The flow of scientists and engineers seemed to have slowed down the research and development activity in the Philippines which is still in its early stage of development.

Skilled migrants from Egypt seemed to have deprived the country of considerable part of its talented people. Alarmed by this situation, Egypt "has taken appropriate measures to regulate the outflow of manpower" (UNCTAD, 1983). To appreciate the gravity of the situation, one has to remember that between 1966 and 1976 more than 33,000 Egyptian research scientists and engineers emigrated, 40 per cent of whom were highly specialized scientists (UNESCO, 1984: 435). Nearly 70 per cent of Egyptian highly emigrants had Doctorates and 17 per cent Masters' Degree (Salman, 1980). This flow would have adversely affected the creation in Egypt of critical mass of scientists and engineers necessary for high level research and development activity.

In countries with meagre skilled human resources, skilled emigration can have an adverse effect on the country's ability to implement development projects. The planning institute of Jamaica estimated that nearly 8,800 Jamaican professional and managerial workers migrated during 1976-80, the proportion of skilled migrants to North America increasing from 16 per cent in 1970 to 27 per cent in 1980 (UNCTAD, 1987). According to the Prime Minister of Jamaica, his country has lost through migration to North America, the equivalent of almost 60 per cent of those who graduated as professional or skilled workers during the period 1977-80.

In Sri Lanka, the outflow of skilled labour has aggravated labour market imbalances in recent years so that, for example, nearly 2,000 additional engineers were required in 1984-85, and the shortage of 800-850 doctors was reported in 1977 (UNCTAD, 1987). In Bangladesh, for example, professional and technical personnel constituted 17 per cent of total emigration in 1976-78, giving rise to personnel shortages in these fields. After reviewing the impact on emigration from Yemen Arab Republic to the Middle East (Fergany, 1982), concluded that emigration was detrimental to Yemen's economic development.

One major benefit to migrant sending countries from International Migration for Employment is the sizeable inflow of private unrequited transfers from those who migrated. These transfers to many countries have more than doubled between 1976-80 and 1982-86. They even exceeded the foreign exchange earnings from merchandise exports in Pakistan during 1982-86.[24] Remittances amounted to two-thirds of export earnings in Egypt, Turkey and Burkina Faso. Pakistan received $ 2.8 billion a year during 1982-86, India $ 2.5 billion, Bangladesh 500 million, Sri Lanka 250 million and the Philippines 220 million, (Asian Development Bank, 1987). These receipts helped them to reduce current account deficit by more than 75 per cent in Pakistan, about 50 per cent in India and Bangladesh, 40 per cent in Sri Lanka and 15 per cent in the Philippines.

Discussing the impact of private unrequited transfers on Indian economy, (Madhavan, 1985: 474) concluded that "emigrant remittances and deposits held in non-resident accounts in Indian-owned banks have played a significant role in improving India's balance of payments position. These remittances have contributed to the growth in household savings in India, accounting for 8.25 per cent of the total household savings in 1980-81. Besides improving the income of emigrant households significantly, in Kerala remittances are likely to have contributed to the reduction of inequality in income distribution".

It is generally contended that the bulk of the remittances are from non-skilled or unskilled migration to Europe and the Middle East and the transfer by skilled migrants are likely to be only marginal.[25] Though this might have been truc in the early 1980s, some changes are already beginning to emerge in India. The capital account of the balance of payments is fortified by the inflow of deposits in non-resident accounts maintained in Indian-owned banks by non-resident Indians (and people of Indian origin who are citizens of other countries) living outside India. U.S. Dollar Denominated Foreign Currency Non-resident account deposits more than quadrupled in 21 months ending December 1986 to $ 2.2 billion. Pound Sterling Accounts increased by 30 per cent to 441 million, Pound Sterling and Non-resident External rupee account by over 40 per cent to 41 billion Indian rupees (Government of India, Ministry of Finance 1987: 91). Though there are no data about the ownership of these deposits, it will not be incorrect to conclude that considerable part of the growth in dollar dominated account deposits would have come from the USA where 43 per cent of Asian Indians in the labour force are employed in professional speciality occupations. Also under two investment schemes available to non-resident Indians (Direct Investment 40 per cent Scheme and Direct Investment 74 pcr cent Scheme), over 4 billion Indian rupees have been invested by non-resident Indians (Datta, 1986: 40). A substantial part of this amount would have come from skilled immigrants.

Consequences for Developed Countries of Immigration

In the fairly extensive literature on the consequences of international migration for the immigration (receiving) countries, relatively little attention has been paid to the particular effects of skilled migration

(UNCTAD, 1987: 16). The attempt made here is one of explorative nature.

As stated earlier, nearly 700,000 skilled migrants were admitted into the USA during 1960-86; nearly half of them in 1970s. According to the 1980 U.S. census, however, there were 373,700 skilled persons of developing country origin on April 1, 1980, who were admitted during January 1, 1970 – March 31, 1980. This was about 22,000 more than the figures reported by the US Immigration and Naturalization Service. Over 50 per cent of the skilled persons were employed in professional speciality occupations such as doctors, engineers, scientists and university professors, over 30 per cent in managerial occupations and about 20 per cent as technicians. They accounted for 1.6 per cent of all those in professional speciality occupations, 1.2 per cent of managerial occupations and 2.2 per cent of all technicians (Table 10.2). These proportions would be at least 50 per cent higher when adjustment is made for the skilled immigrants who were admitted during 1960-70. The actual proportions as of April 1980 are likely to be 2.5 per cent of all those employed in professional speciality occupations, 1.7 per cent of managerial occupations and about 3.0 per cent of technicians. Since immigrant population from developing countries was about 3 per cent[26] of the total U.S. population, the contribution of developing countries to the skilled U.S. labour force development may not look very impressive. Yet there are some professional occupations where their entry had some significant impact.

The number of physicians from developing countries who are admitted into the USA during 1961-72 was 40,876 (UNCTAD, 1979: 6), about 14 per cent of the active physicians in the USA in 1972. The number of active physicians rose from 230,000 in 1960 to 281,000 in 1970 (U.S. Department of Commerce, Bureau of the Census, 1986: 90). The entry of developing country physicians certainly helped to relieve the acute shortage that might have otherwise developed. If the developing country physicians had not been admitted during the 1960s, the number of active physicians per 100,000 population in the USA would have declined from 126 in 1960 to 117 in 1970, instead of 137 that was achieved due to the inflow. The inflow reached its peak in 1973 when about 5,600 physicians of developing country origin were admitted.[27] Since that time their numerical growth seemed to have slowed down during the 1970s. The total number of active physicians between 1970 and 1980 increased by 134,000, of which 28,000 were foreign medical graduates. Of these physicians, 70 per cent is likely to be from developing countries. That means the immigrant physicians from developing countries would have accounted for only 15 per cent of the growth in the number of active physicians during 1970-80, a remarkable slowdown from the 1960s, when over 75 per cent of the growth needs was met by immigrants from developing countries. In 1981 there was a sharp increase of 8,000 foreign medical graduates in the active list and the flow had declined to 6,000 and 4,000 in the subsequent period. In the early 1980s, foreign medical graduates accounted for one-third of the growth in active physicians. Approximately one in four active physicians in the USA is a foreign medical school graduate. Probably one in six is likely to have come from a developing country.

Developing country immigrant scientists and engineers in the USA have done well. They have brought honours to the USA in the form of Nobel Prizes for their monumental contribution, contributed to knowledge immensely as reflected in the frequent citations of their research work and invented many devices. Some of them have become entrepreneurs. One out of every 16 natural scientists in the USA is of Asian origin, as well as one in every 12 doctoral scientists and engineers, (U.S. Department of Commerce, 1986 : 572). Asian origin persons received 22,500 doctoral degrees in science and engineering fields during 1975-85, accounting for one in six doctoral degrees conferred.

The developing country skilled immigrants have also contributed to the growth and development of the U.S. economy. Besides the obvious benefit of saving the cost of earlier education of skilled immigrants and the timed needed for the training process, their contribution is significant in many respects. In an interesting study on "The Economic Effects of Immigration", the Council of Economic Advisers (1986) have concluded that:

(i) economic benefits are spread throughout the economy, including increased job opportunities, higher wages for some workers, lower product prices and higher profits;
(ii) the employment of skilled persons from developing countries in bottleneck positions might have held down inflationary pressures and allowed economic expansion ; and
(iii) immigrants are not heavy users of public services and, in

fact, skilled immigrants are often paying more in taxes than they use in services.

However, the earnings of developing country immigrants, other things remaining constant, are lower than those immigrants from the U.K. and Canada (Table 10.6). Chiswick (1986) estimates immigrants from some parts of Europe, the Middle East, South Asia and other Asian countries have earnings 11 to 17 per cent below those of U.K. immigrants. The lowest earnings group includes immigrants from parts of Asia (China, the Philippines, Vietnam), Latin America, the Caribbean and Africa, with earnings of 24 to 32 per cent below those from the U.K. It may take 10-15 years for developing country immigrants to bring parity in earnings with immigrants from the U.K.

Policies and Proposals to Ameliorate Adverse Consequences

Skilled migration, permanent settlement types as well as temporary contract workers from developing to developed and other developing countries, would have now reached a staggering level of 1.6 to 1.8 million, a third of which may be contract migrants. Such a large outflow in a relatively short span of about 25 years has given rise to many structural problems in the sending countries and social problems in some receiving countries. To tackle these problems, many policies have been instituted both by the sending and receiving countries, many resolutions have been adopted in the international forums calling for concrete measures to attenuate the effects of skilled migration,[28] three major proposals for multilateral action have been made, and two major international programmes are in place to mitigate some of the negative effects of skill flows.

The policies have to be formulated within the framework of United Nations Charter on Human Rights. It should, however, be necessary to reconcile the individual need with national requirement.[29]

Developing Country Measures

To stem the unacceptable levels of skill flows and to encourage the return of talents, many developing countries have implemented measures, some of which are regulatory and restrictive and others are incentives. Regulatory and restrictive policies take the forms such as limits on the availability of foreign exchange service requirements for professionals such as doctors, service bond requirements for government and semi-government employees, regulation in the issuance of passports and exit visas, compulsory remittances and others. It is not clear how far these regulatory and restrictive policies were successful in achieving their goals in various countries. Since many of the above practices are aimed at student population, government or semi-government employees and professionals desiring to go to the USA and other countries for higher studies and training, one indicator that could be used to evaluate the effectiveness of the policies might be the number of people who get their status adjusted to immigrant category after their studies or training.

In the case of Indian students and others who went on student (F1) and exchange visitor (J1) visas to the USA there has been a declining trend in the number of those F1 and J1 visa holders who are adjusted to permanent resident status from about 14,000 during 1970-74 to less than 5,000 during 1982-86 (Madhavan, 1988). As a proportion of the current inflow of respective categories, F1 visa conversions have fallen steeply from 47 per cent to 13 per cent and J1 visa conversions from 46 per cent to 9 per cent. Besides the regulatory practices of the Government of India, lower rates of growth in professional employment opportunities and strict enforcement of immigration laws in the USA seem to have contributed to the above declining trend. At the same time, however, the loopholes in the Immigrations Laws have been utilized by the employers of Indian trainees and the students themselves to perpetuate their stay in the USA, this is reflected in the six fold increase in the H1 (temporary workers and trainees which is used as an intermediate step by students and others) adjustment to resident status. It is also not known what proportion of the students who go for training in engineering and sciences return to India.[30] It remains to be seen whether the relative success that Indian seemed to have had in the return of those who went to the USA for studies will continue in the future. (There is a substantial increase in the number of Indian students enrolled in the U.S. Universities from 9,000 in 1980 to 15,000 in 1985.)

In spite of the difficulties in getting U.S. student's visa, foreign student enrolements in the U.S. Universities have almost doubled between 1976 and 1985 when they were 342,000. Almost two-thirds of this growth is due to Asian students population (U.S. Bureau of the Census 1987: 140). Only time will tell what effect this would have on the skilled migration from developing countries.

Incentive policies of various hues have been adapted by developing countries to encourage the return of expatriate professionals. The first country to introduce this type of policy is India – through the establishment in 1958 of Scientists' Pool. Similar programmes were also implemented in Argentina, Colombia, Iran, Iraq, Jordan, Peru, the Philippines and Sri Lanka. Of all these schemes, India's Scientists' Pool seems to be the most successful.

Nearly 16,000 persons were selected to join the Pool up to March 1986, 83 per cent of whom, were residing outside of India at the time of selection (Government of India, Ministry of Science and Technology, 1986: 77). Almost 9,000 of the selected persons returned to India. About one-third of those who returned secured regular employment soon after their arrival and did not join the Pool. Over 70 per cent of those who joined the Pool from foreign residence were from the USA and the U.K. Only 5 per cent left the Pool to return to their previous foreign residence; an excellent achievement. This underscores the satisfaction level prevalent among Pool scientists which was revealed in an opinion survey of 400 ex-pool scientists.

Developed Country Efforts

Developed countries have undertaken programmes individually or in cooperation with others to facilitate the return of talents to developing countries.[31] For example, the Bonn Ministry of Economic Cooperation promotes reintegration seminars for graduates and those about to graduate and provides information on economic, social and labour market conditions and employment opportunities in their homelands. Also it has set up a scheme to encourage entrepreneurial activities in developing countries by giving individuals or groups limited financial incentives to start up independent industrial projects. Another interesting project is the Swedish International seminars in physics and chemistry at the University of Uppsala, where stress is laid on problem-solving geared to the specific needs of developing countries. The U.K., Sweden, the Netherlands and West Germany are cooperating with developing countries in defining training needs.

An interesting cooperative effort between developing and developed countries, under the auspices of the Intergovernmental Committee for Migration (ICM), to foster the return of talent to the countries of origin has yielded significant dividends.[32] ICM's interest in helping the developing countries to overcome the shortage of human resources goes back to the mid-1960s, and the plan of action for the return of talent was launched in 1974. "The ICM's activities have had a decisive impact on the exodus phenomenon. The figures speak for themselves: almost 30,000 executives and technicians have been transferred by the ICM since 1965. This figure includes more than 3,500 nationals transferred since the first return programmes were set up in 1974" (Ardittis, 1984: 45).

ICM is currently running three major return assistance programmes – the return of talent programme, the Latin American reintegration assistance programme and the return of talent from the U.S. programme – and six ad hoc programmes to meet priority needs of some countries. Though both developed and developing member countries (29 member governments and 16 observer governments) make contributions, major part of the funding comes from developed countries, especially West Germany.

These programmes operate in Latin America, Africa and Asia. Its activities involve executives, technicians and expatriate skilled workers and benefit both the public and private sectors in the countries of origin. Its services are free to public institutions, but private sector employers make a flat rate contribution for every emigrant recruited. These programmes provide various types of benefits to facilitate the return of qualified emigrants to their countries of origin. These benefits vary from one programme to the other. Generally they provide for full or part of the travel cost, part of medical insurance, small salary supplement, accommodation and food allowance and reinstallation grant.

The return of talent to Latin America is by far the most important activity of ICM. Of 3,421 who returned to Latin America, over one-third went back to Chile. Columbia, Argentina and Peru are other major beneficiaries of the programme, accounting for 30 per cent of the total returns. The largest number of emigrants were from West Germany (1,138), followed by Spain (1,082), the USA (446), France (217) and Belgium (117). Twelve per cent of those who returned were doctors and dentists, 14 per cent engineers, 4 per cent scientists, 25 per cent university and college teachers and 5 per cent economists.

Though the success of the ICM programme was a great success, the number of scientists, technologists, engineers and doctors returning to the countries of origin in Latin America seems to be small compared to India's Scientists Pool programme. During the same period, the number of Indian scientists, engineers, technologists and doctors who returned to India under the Pool programme would have been around 2,000[33] which is about twice as many as those who returned to Latin America under ICM programme. However, all these returns of skilled emigrants to countries of origin for possible permanent settlement is not significant viewed against the magnitude of skill outflow. This has led to two categories of proposals for multilateral action.

Proposals for Amelioration of Adverse Consequences

The first category of proposals aim at compensating the emigrating countries for the loss incurred by them. The other relates to the establishment of international funds for vocational training and recruitment of skilled manpower. In the first category are proposals by Prince Hassan of Jordan (1977); Bhagwati (1978); Pomp and Oldham (1978) and Bohning (1982). In the second category are proposals by President Mubarak of Egypt (1983) and Prime Minister Seaga of Jamaica (1984).

Prince Hassan proposed the establishment of an International Labour Compensatory Facility along the lines of existing International Monetary Fund facilities, drawing its resources mainly from immigrant receiving countries. The accumulated resources would then be utilized to the development of immigrant sending countries in proportions relative to the estimated cost incurred due to the loss of labour. Bhagwati proposed levying a surtax on income of highly skilled immigrants in developed countries. These levies will be collected by developed countries and the receipts would then be transferred to the developing countries. Pomp and Oldham suggested developing countries levying a tax on their nationals residing abroad and the taxes will be collected with the cooperation of immigrant receiving countries. Bohning proposed that the government of the receiving country would make the sending country a lump sum payment for each immigrant on the basis of once-and-for-all assessment at the time of entry. Though these proposals were made five to ten years ago, there is not much concrete action on these proposals due in part to the lack of their attractiveness to the receiving countries.

President Mubarak proposed the establishment of an International Fund for Vocational Training. The proposed fund would enable those countries which suffer manpower outflows to implement programmes for training substitute elements, thus filling the gap left behind by emigration. Prime Minister Seaga's proposal would help finance recruitment of the skilled manpower on a medium-term basis.

Programmes of UN Agencies

Schemes have been initiated by the international organizations to counteract or prevent the loss of skills suffered by immigrant sending countries. The first programme of this kind was initiated in 1977 by the United Nations Development Programme (UNDP) in collaboration with the Turkish government to transfer knowledge acquired by Turkish expatriate nationals for Turkish development. This programme was christened as "Transfer of Knowledge Through Expatriate Nationals," popularly known as TOKTEN. The United Nations Education, Scientific and Cultural Organization (UNESCO) has also initiated a programme similar to TOKTEN to assist developing countries to bring home, on short duration, expatriate professionals. While the UNESCO programme is still in the beginning phase, TOKTEN has completed 10 years.

UNESCO has collaborated with Egypt in establishing the Centre for Scientific Research in Alexandria, which will be completed in 1989, with the explicit objective of motivating the scientists and professionals who emigrated, especially to North America, to return (UNESCO 1984: 438). The initial experience of UNESCO in motivating the scientists to return has not been all that encouraging. UNESCO has also initiated a programme to arrange visits of expatriate scientists to their countries of origin to help strengthen national research institutions. The visits of this nature already took place in Bangladesh, Chile and other countries. Programmes of regional exchange among advanced research personnel and university professors are also being considered.

The TOKTEN programme is now in operation in 24 countries and 12 more countries have expressed their desire to start it. Up to December 1987, about 1,700 expatriate consultants would have visited TOKTEN countries at a cost of $ 9 million in UNDP/IPF funds, covering a wide spectrum of disciplines such as architecture, bio-technology, micro-electronics, alternative power sources, remote sensing, machine and tool design, industrial hygiene and safety, telecommunications and water resource development. These consultancies have resulted in the introduction of new techniques and new processes of product development, have given a Fillip to research and development activities and have provided new information on many areas pertinent to development.

The uniqueness of TOKTEN lies in the voluntary service of expatriate nationals, timeliness of consultancy, cost-effectiveness of the programme and the desire of expatriate nationals to establish links for continuous contact between individuals and institutions in their countries of origin and counterparts in their countries of residence. Experience to date seems to confirm that such links are being establish to serve their countries of origin.

Summary and Conclusions

The International migration has now reached gigantic proportions, and the number of persons living outside their country of birth will be around 55 million, 60 per cent of which are likely to have originated in developing countries.

Unlike in the earlier period when developing country migrants were recruited for plantation development in colonial territories, the growth in the size of developing country migrants in the post-Second World War period, was brought about by other factors. These have brought about significant changes in the magnitude, geographical distribution and skill composition of migrant flows. The shares of European immigrants in the USA, Canada and Australia declined dramatically while those of Asians soared. In the U.K., the share of the New Commonwealth countries increased, while those of Europe, Australia, New Zealand and the USA declined. Oil exporting countries have become important immigrant receiving countries.

Skilled Migration

Migration of skilled and talented people from developing countries, on a scale never before encountered, is an outgrowth of the opening up of employment opportunities in developed countries, increased access to higher education facilities in developed countries, improved communication among countries and increased skilled employment opportunities in some developing countries. The outflow was so large that a new term, "Brain drain" was coined to reflect that concern. Lately, this seems to have given way to "Brain Bank".

The word "skill" has a spectrum of meaning and the difficulty associated with defining "skilled" has led to the use of occupational characteristics of immigrants to get a handle on the problem. But even such data with varying degrees of accuracy exist only for a few countries. The state of skilled immigrant flow statistics is far from satisfactory. However, inadequate the available statistics may be, it is still possible to paint a broad picture of developing country skilled migrant flow situation.

The gross flow of skilled migrants from developing to all developed countries for possible permanent settlement would be of the order of 1.3 million in the last 27 years. The USA accounted for about five-ninths, Canada one-ninth, the U.K. two-elevenths and the rest by all other developed countries. Besides, there have been movements to other developing countries, notably to oil exporters. On a net flow basis (including illegal stays), the figures may be approximately the same both for the USA and Canada as their respective gross flows, but substantially lower for the U.K..

The developing countries have increased their shares in the total skilled migration to the USA, Canada and the U.K. to 67 per cent, 37 per cent and 54 per cent, respectively, in the last 27 years. However, proportionately developed country migrants are more skilled than those from the developing countries. (In the USA comparable ratios for Asian and African migrants were higher than those for developed countries, and an average African immigrant is much better qualified professionally than an average person in any other group).

Asia is the largest source of skilled migrants for the USA, Canada and the U.K., followed by Latin America and Africa to the USA and Canada; but the order is reversed in the case of the U.K. What is disturbing is the magnitude of skill flow from Africa and Caribbean countries such as Jamaica, Dominican Republic and Haiti.

The flow of highly skilled, professional speciality people from Africa to the USA during 1970-80 was approximately the same as was from South America. Skill flow from Jamaica was 50 per cent more than the comparable flow from Greece or Italy, and the flow from Portugal was smaller than those from Haiti or Dominican Republic. The outflow of talent is related to the non-return of students who went to developed countries for higher studies.

Surprising as it may be, the best qualified immigrants coming from any one continent are from Africa. Among the individual countries, people from India are the best qualified, followed by Filipinos. Comparable data are not available for the U.K. and Canada. Sketchy information that are available seem to suggest that immigrants from India, the Philippines, China and Egypt are well educated, but the extent of difference in educational achievement between them and others may not be striking as it is found in the USA.

Educational level of developing country immigrants is reflected in the occupational structure. Proportionately there are more developing country immigrants in professional speciality occupations than the corresponding ratios for U.S. and Canadian-born persons. In the U.K. the proportion of immigrants in professional occupations is likely to be lower than the ratio for British-born persons.

An interesting feature of the developing country labour force in the USA is the number of women in professional speciality occupations. Asian origin women accounted for over 20 per cent of women physicians and dentists in the USA in 1980 and 10 per cent of women employed in natural science fields. Asian origin men accounted for 6.4 per cent of male doctors in the USA and 6.7 per cent of natural scientists.

In the U.K. the net flow of developing country migrants in the professional and managerial occupations was of the order of 28,000 during 1976-83, one-fourth of whom were women.

The valuation of skill flows is a hazardous activity. The imprecise nature of the earlier value estimates of skill flows has led the author to suggest a new approach.

Causes of Migration

The question of what causes migration has been analysed for many years, but there has not emerged any definitive conclusions about the determinants of skilled migration. Skill flows from developing countries are very much determined by the policies of immigrant receiving countries. The probable causes from the perspective of developing country migrant are differences in income or discounted value of lifetime earnings, persistent unemployment and frustration associated with it, considerations to meet one's familial obligations, need to avoid isolation, lack of challenging research and development opportunities, policies by developing country governments to encourage emigration of certain types of people which might be beneficial in the long-run for the country and others.

Consequences for Developing Countries

Skilled migration could contribute to a reduction in the unemployment level in the short-run among science, engineering and medical graduates. It would, however, undermine the ability of the countries to reach the critical mass needed for scientific and technological breakthroughs. In the case of countries with a small size of professionally oriented labour force, skill outflow would create shortages in the short-run and adversely affect the implementation of development programmes. In the first group are countries such as India, the Philippines and Egypt, and in the latter are Bangladesh, Sri Lanka, Jamaica and Yemen Arab Republic.

The impact of skill flows on developing countries can best be seen in relation to the domestic stock or flow of certain skill categories. The number of doctors born and educated in India, now residing outside, is equivalent to 21 per cent of economically active doctors in India in 1980; engineers 16 per cent of economically active; and natural scientists 6 per cent of economically active. In the Philippines, the number of doctors who migrated during 1970-80 were approximately equal to those who passed the board exam. in medicine during 1970-80. The number of engineers would be around 10 per cent of all types of engineers who passed the board exam. In Egypt, between 1966 and 1976, more than 33,000 research scientists and engineers emigrated, 40 per cent of whom were highly specialized scientists. Nearly 70 per cent of them had doctorates. In all the three countries, skill outflow would have certainly delayed the creation of critical mass necessary for scientific and technological breakthroughs in many fields. In the Philippines, such a large outflow of doctors had its toll on the availability of physician services, increasing the number of people per physician substantially from 1,130 in 1965 to 2,150 in 1981.

In countries with meagre skilled human resources, skilled

emigration has aggravated labour market imbalances. According to the Prime Minister of Jamaica, his country has lost through migration to North America, the equivalent of almost 60 per cent of those who graduated as professionals or skilled workers during 1977-80. In Sri Lanka and Bangladesh, emigration gave rise to shortages in professional and technical fields. The emigration was detrimental to the economic development of Yemen Arab Republic.

One major benefit to migrant sending countries from international migration for employment is the sizeable inflow of private unrequited transfers. It is generally contended that transfers by skilled migrants are only marginal. Though this might have been true in the early 1980s, some changes are already beginning to emerge in the case of India.

Consequences for Developed Countries

In the fairly extensive literature on the consequences of international migration for the receiving countries, relatively little attention has been paid to the particular effects of skilled migration. It is generally felt that since immigration is so small a portion of the total labour force of the USA, Canada or the U.K., immigrants contribution to the receiving country is not likely to be significant. Yet there are some professional occupations where immigrants entry had some significant impact.

The entry of developing country physicians into the USA during the 1960s had helped not only to relieve acute shortage but also to improve physician services. If developing country physicians had not been admitted, the number of active physicians per 100,000 population would have declined from 126 in 1960 to 117 in 1970, instead of 137 that was achieved due to the inflow. Now one in four active physicians in the USA is a foreign medical school graduate. probably one in six is likely to have come from a developing country. Among scientists and engineers, one in 12 doctoral scientists and engineers is of Asian origin. These people received 22,500 doctoral degrees in science and engineering fields during 1975-85, accounting for one in six doctoral degrees conferred.

The developing country skilled immigrants have contributed to the development of the U.S. economy in many ways which have been noted by the Council of Economic Advisers to the U.S. President. However, the earnings of developing country immigrants, other things remaining the same, are lower than those immigrants from the U.K. and Canada. A recent study has estimated some developing country immigrants earn 11 to 17 per cent below those of U.K. immigrants, and still others 24 to 32 per cent below.

Policies and Proposals

Skilled migration, permanent settlement as well as temporary contract workers from migrant sending developing to developed and other migrant receiving developing countries would have now reached a staggering level of 1.6 to 1.8 million, a third of which may be contract migrants. To stem the unacceptable levels of skill flows and to encourage the return of skilled migrants, many developing countries have implemented regulatory and restrictive policies as well as incentive measures. The regulatory and restrictive policies are aimed at student population, government or semi-government employees and other professionals who go for higher studies and training. One indicator that could be used to evaluate the effectiveness of the policies might be the number of people who get their status adjusted to immigrant category after their studies or training. In the case of Indian students and exchange visitors, conversion of F1 and J1 to resident status have declined substantially both absolutely and as a proportion of current inflows of these categories. It remains to be seen whether the relative success (partly due to the U.S. policies and economic conditions), India seemed to have had in the return of those who went to the USA for studies will continue in the future.

The incentive policies have been adapted by many developing countries to encourage the return of expatriate nationals. Of all these schemes, India's Scientists Pool seems to be the most successful. Up to 1986 almost 9,000 scientists, engineers, and doctors returned to India. Only 5 per cent of them emigrated again.

Developed countries have undertaken programmes individually or in cooperation with others to facilitate the return of talent to developing countries. An interesting cooperative effort between developed and developing countries, under the auspices of the Intergovernmental Committee for Migration has yielded significant dividends. More than 3,500 nationals have returned to their countries of origin since 1974 when the return of talent programme was launched. Of the 3,421 people returned to Latin America under the programme, 30 per cent were scientists, engineers and doctors, 25 per cent university and college teachers and 5 per cent economists. However, all this return of skilled migrants to countries of origin for possible permanent settlement is not significant, viewed against the magnitude of skill outflow. This has led to two categories of proposals for multilateral action.

The first category aims at compensating the emigrating countries for the loss incurred by them as a result of skill emigration. The other relates to the establishment of international funds for vocational training and recruitment of skilled manpower. In the first group are proposals by Prince Hassan of Jordan, Bhagwati, Pomp and Oldham and Bohning. In the second are proposals by President Mubarak of Egypt and Prime Minister Seaga of Jamaica. Though some of these proposals were made 10 years ago, there is not much concrete action on them due, in part, to their unattractiveness to the receiving countries.

Programmes by U.N. Agencies

Schemes have been initiated by international organizations to counteract or prevent the loss suffered by immigrant sending countries. The UNDP programme, known as TOKTEN, was the first attempt of this. UNESCO has also initiated a programme similar to TOKTEN to assist developing countries. While UNESCO programme is still in the beginning phase, TOKTEN has completed 10 years. TOKTEN consultancies have resulted in the introduction of new techniques and new processes of product development activities and have provided new information on many areas pertinent to development.

In conclusion, skilled migration is a historical phenomenon that will be with us for years to come. It becomes a problem when the outflow from a country reaches an unacceptable level. This level will vary from one country to the other, and from one time period to the other. It should be prevented by proper coordination of policies within the country and of policies between immigrant sending countries and immigrant receiving countries.

The outflow level becomes unacceptable at a point when the benefits received from the nation's point of view are less than the cost incurred by the nation to embody human capital in the persons who emigrate.

Historically speaking, there were times when many Italians and Irish people migrated in large numbers to the USA. The flows from these countries seemed to have dwindled in recent years, due in part to the greater opportunities for professional fulfilment in those countries. Skill flows may be cyclical.

It is important to have programmes in place to reduce the adverse effects of the flow. If the expatriate are viewed as a "Brain Bank" and they have the love for the country of origin and the desire to repay the debt they owe it, ways could be found to repay the country of origin for the loss of service the emigration entailed. TOKTEN, India's Scientists' Pool and the Inter-governmental Committee for Migration are only the beginning of the journey and we have miles to go.

NOTES

1. See Republic of Philippines, National Economic Development Authority, *Philippine Statistical Year Book*, 1986, pp. 486-87. The proportion of skilled migrants in the total contract flow has risen from 11.4 per cent in 1982 to 22.5 in 1985, and the share of Middle East in the total flow during 1982-85 was 83 per cent.
2. Experience of other countries will be discussed when the relevant data become available.
3. The 1962 Act took away the right to enter from all Commonwealth citizens except those issued with vouchers and wives and children under 16 of those already in the U.K., Ermisch (1983: 44) observed that immigration from the Indian subcontinent peaked in 1968, was reduced by 75 per cent by 1973. It stabilized thereafter, and exhibited a small recovery in 1978 and 1979.
4. Data are drawn from International Migration Statistics. These relate to the years 1976-79 and 1981-83.
5. This was arrived at by dividing 25,000 by 91,000 which was the gross flow during 1976-79 and 1981-83.
6. The Indian subcontinent and Sri Lanka are the largest source of skilled migrants for the U.K., followed by African Commonwealth and Caribbean area.
7. Highly skilled professional speciality immigrant flow during 1970-80 to the USA – from Jamaica was over 7,300; almost 2,400 from Haiti; over 2,000 from Dominican Republic, Italy and Greece; and 700 from Portugal.
8. Brought to my attention by UNESCO (1984).
9. Korea had 57 per cent of its skilled people in managerial occupations. (See Table 6).
10. There were 54,300 women physicians and 8,400 dentists and 69,000 natural scientists in 1980, U.S. Department of Commerce, *Statistical Abstract of the United States*, 1987, pp. 91 and 385.
11. See U.S. Library of Congress, Congressional Research Service, Foreign Affairs Division (1974) which stated that "migrating professionals have a value in themselves . . . and whatever that value may be, it is added to the receiv-

ing country, and correspondingly withdrawn from the sending country." Also see D.G. Papadetriu (1984).

12. For discussion of this issue, see Jagdish N. Bhagwati (1976).
13. See Salman (1980). Lack of appropriate manpower planning in Arab countries, he contends, especially in terms of tertiary educational training, resulted in an over-supply of trainees specialized in "surplus disciplines".
14. In India, unemployment rate for engineering graduates was 7 per cent in 1985; engineering diploma holders 20 per cent; medical graduates 7 per cent; agricultural science graduates 11 per cent; and basic science graduates 20 per cent (Madhavan, 1985: 470).
15. See for sample Tabbarah (1981:30) funds for research in the Arab region have been extremely inadequate and an appropriate institutional structure for scientific research does not exist.
16. In an in-depth analysis of the CSIR, the Review Committee stated that "CSIR has responded well in times of need when it has been set a task. Some of its laboratories have made significant. . . nevertheless there has been disproportionate emphasis in terms of work on known products and known processes akin to reinventing the wheel. . . . The blame for what has gone wrong cannot be laid at the door of the CSIR alone. It is a collective responsibility. It is as much a failure of other two major actors on the stage: the industrial system and the regime of policies" (Report of the CSIR Review Com. 1986: ii).
17. The format of this section is influenced by UNCTAD (1987).
18. Awasthi (1985: 217) reports there were 917,000 graduates in science who were economically active in India in 1980; 218,000 scientists above post-graduate level; 329,000 diploma holders in engineering and technology; 155,000 medical graduates; 221,000 engineers and technologists with bachelors degree and above; and 97,000 graduates and above in agricultural and veterinary sciences.
19. There were 506,000 job seekers in various fields as follows: medical graduates — 17,000; engineering — 110,000; science — 336,000; and others — 12,000, (Government of india, Dept. of Science and Technology, 1986: 73).
20. Tidalgo (1984: 18) reports that 24.9 per cent of 811,000 unemployed in 1987 were college graduates.
21. U.S. estimates were made from data in the 1980 census. In arriving at the Indian-born skilled persons, the ratio of Indian-born to Asian Indian origin was used. In 1980, 14.3 per cent of the people of Asian Indian origin in professional speciality occupations are born outside of India.
22. The number of people who passed the board exam. in medicine during 1975-81 was 7,872, averaging 1,312 a year (Republic of Philippines, NEDA, 1986: 460-61); see also UNCTAD (1979: 6) and Swamy (1984: 72).
23. Over 48,000 passed board examinations in various fields of engineering during 1975-81, averaging over 8,000 a year.
24. During 1982-86, Pakistan's exports amounted to $ 13,004 million compared to private unrequited transfers of $ 14,046 million (Asian Development Bank, Economic Office, 1978: 244-245).
25. For example see UNESCO (1984:430), and Russel (1986).
26. There were 7 million immigrants born in developing countries in April 1980 out of the total U.S. population of over 226 million.
27. This figure was arrived at from the following quote attributed to a Commonwealth Secretariat Study of 1976. "In the USA in 1973, it would seem that out of 16,700 newly licensed doctors, 44.5 per cent (7,400) were graduates of foreign medical schools. Out of the latter only one-fourth or

less than 2,000 came from developed countries" (UNESCO, 1984: 432).

28. For a detailed examination of the different plans of action proposed within the framework of the United Nations, see UNCTAD (1983, June).
29. UNESCO (1984: 427) states further that "in our increasingly interdependent world, a balanced exchange of talent can take place between countries".
30. Two-thirds of the students from India are enrolled in engineering, science and business administration fields (U.S. Bureau of the Census 1986: 140).
31. See UNCTAD (1983, June); also UNESCO (1984).
32. Material for this section is mainly drawn from Ardittis (1984).
33. Actually over 5,700 persons were selected to join the pool during 1974-83. (Government of India, Ministry of Science and Technology, 1986: 78).

REFERENCES

Ardittis, Solon (1984). "the assisted return of qualified migrants to their countries of origin: the UNDP and ICM multilateral programmes, *International Migration for Employment Working Paper No. 17,* (Geneva, ILO).

Asian Development Bank (1987). *Key Indicators of Developing Member Countries of ADB* (Manila, the Philippines).

Awasthi, S.P. (1985). "Indicators of Scientific and Technical Manpower Development", in S. Pruthi and P.S. Nagpaul (Editors), *Science and Technology Indicators for Development,* (New Delhi, India, Workshop Proceedings, February 21-26).

Bhagwati, Jagdish (1978). "The Brain Drain, Compensation and Taxation". Paper prepared for the Conference on "Economic and Demographic Change: Issues for the 1980s", International Union for the Scientific Study of Population (Helsinki, August 28 to September 1).

Bohning, W.R. (1982). "Towards a System of Recompense for International Labour Migration", *International Migration for Employment, Working Paper No. 2,* (Geneva, ILO).

Brown, A. (1981). The Emigration of Highly Educated Personnel from the Caribbean Commonwealth during the 1970s, (Paris, UNESCO).

Chiswick, Barry R. (1986). "Is the New Immigration to the United States Less Skilled than the Old?", *Journal of Labor Economics,* April.

Council of Economic Advisers (1986). *Economic Report of the President: Transmitted to the Congress* (Washington, D.C., U.S. Government Printing Office).

De Voretz and Maki (1980). "The Size and Distribution of Human Capital: Transfers from LDCs to Canada", *Economic Development and Cultural Change,* 28 (4), July.

Ermisch, J. (1983). *The Political Economy of Demographic Change: Causes and Implications of Population Trends in Great Britain* (London, Heinemann).

Fergany, N. (1982). "The Impact of Immigration on National Development in The Case of Yemen Arab Republic, *International Migration Reveiw* 16 No. 4 (Winter) 757-780.

Glaser, William with G.C. Habers (1978). *The Brain Drain: Emigration and Return,* UNITAR Research Report No. 22 (Elmsford, New York, Pergamon Press).

Government of Canada, Department of Manpower and Immigration, *Immigration Statistics,* various issues.

Government of France, *Immigration Des Travailleurs Permaneurs: Nationalites.*

Government of India, Department of Science and Technology (1986). *Research and Development Statistics* (New Delhi, India, Government of India Press).

———, Ministry of Finance (1987). *Economic Survey, 1986-87* (New Delhi, India,

Government of India Press).

———, Ministry of Science and Technology (1986). *Project TIES: Report of the Committee on Indian Scientists and Technologists Working or Settled Abroad*, (New Delhi, India).

Gunatilleke, Godfrey (Ed). (1986). *Migration of Asian Workers to the Arab World*, United Nations University (Tokyo).

International Labour Organization (1986). *World Labor Report*, (Geneva).

Kim, Jung Keun (1984). "The Trends and Polices of Korean Immigration", Paper presented in the East-West Population Institute Conference on "Asian-Pacific Immigration to the United States", Honolulu, Hawaii, 20-25 September.

Kravis, Irving, Alan Heston and Robert Summers (1982). *World Product and Income: International Comparisons of Real Gross Product* (Baltimore, John Hopkins University Press).

Krugman, Paul and Jagdish Bhagwati (1976). "The Decision to Migrate" in J. Bhagwati (Ed), *The Brain Drain and Taxation II: Theory and Empirical Analysis* (Amsterdam, North Holland Publishing Co.).

Kubat, Danial (1984). "Canada and Immigration of Asian Nationals: Development of an Immigration Policy", Paper presented to the East-West Population Institute Conference on "Asian Pacific Immigration to the United States", Honolulu, Hawaii, September 21-25.

Madhavan, M.C. (1985). "Indian Emigrants: Numbers, Characteristics, and Economic Impact", *Population and Development Review*, Vol. II, No. 3, September.

———, "Asian Indians in America — Growth, Quality and Change", Mimeo.

Norman, C. (1979). "Knowledge and Power: The Global Research and Development Budget", World Watch Paper 31 (Washington, D.C.).

Oguzkan, Turhan (1985). "A Global Perspective of the Brain Drain from the Developing Countries", United Nations Development Programme, TOKTEN Workshop, Cairo, Egypt, January 12-17.

Papademetriu, D.G. (1984). "International Migration in a Changing World". *International Social Science Journal*, Vol. XXX No. 3.

Pomp, Richard and Oliver Oldham (1978). "Legal and Administrative Aspects of Compensation, Taxation and Related Policy Measures: Suggestion for an Optimum Policy-Mix": A Study for UNCTAD.

Price, Charles A. (1984). "Asian Pacific Immigrants in Australia", Paper presented at the East-West Conference, Honolulu, Hawaii, September 21-25.

Psacharapoulos, George (1975). "Estimating Some Key Parameters in the Brain Drain Model", *Journal of Development Economics*, Vol. 2 No. 3.

Recommendations on Statistics of International Migration, (United Nations Publications,) *Statistical Papers*, Series M, No. 58.

Report of the CSIR Review Committee (1986). Towards a New Perspective (New Delhi, India).

Republic of the Philippines, National Economic Development Authority (1986). *Statistical Yearbook of the Philippines*, 1986 (Manila, the Philippines).

Richmond, A. (1986). *Migration to Industrial Societies* (London, Cambridge University Press).

Russell, Sharon S. (1986). "Remittances from International Migration: A Review in Perspective", *World Development*, Vol. 14, No. 16, June.

Salman, R. (1980). "A Preliminary View of the Arab Brain Drain", Economic Commission for West Asia, *Seminar on the Brain Drain*, Beirut, Lebanon, February 4-8.

Swamy, Gurushri (1984). "Population and International Migration", World Bank, Staff Working Paper, No. 689, Population and Development series No. 14

(Washington, D.C., The World Bank).

Tabbarah, R. (1981). "Population, Human Resources and Development in the Arab World" *Population Bulletin of ECWA*, No. 20, June, pp. 5-38.

Tidalgo, Rosa Linda F. (1984). "Labor Market, Structural Adjustment in the Philippines" ASEAN – Australia Working Papers No. 13.

Trlin, Andrew (1984). "New Zealand: An Alternative Destination for Asian and Pacific Immigration", paper presented in East-West Population Institute Conference on "Asian Pacific Immigration to the United States", Honolulu, Hawaii, September, 21-25.

United Nations, Department of Economic and Social Affairs (1979). *Trends and Characteristics of International Migration Since 1950*, (New York).

———, Department of International Economic and Social Affairs (1982). *World Population Trends and Policies: 1981 Monitoring Report, Vol. 11, Population Policies*, (New York).

United Nations Conference on Trade and Development (1975). *The Reverse Transfer of Technology: Economic Effects of the Outflow of Trained Personnel from Developing Countries*, (New York).

——— (1979). *The Reverse Transfer of Technology: A Survey of its Main Features, Causes and Policy Implications,* (New York).

——— (1983). "Report of the Meeting of Governmental Experts on the Reverse Transfer of Technology", September, (Geneva).

——— (1987). "Trends and Current Situation in Reverse Transfer of Technology", paper prepared for the Fourth Meeting of Governmental Experts on Reverse Transfer of Technology, 31 August, (Geneva).

UNESCO (1984). "Brain Drain or the Migration of Talent and Skills" in the United Nations Department of International Economic and Social Affairs, *Population Distribution, Migration and Development* pp. 427-441, (New York).

——— (1985). *Statistical Year book, 1985,* (Paris, UNESCO).

U.S. Bureau of the Census (1984). *Detailed Population Characteristics* (Washington, D.C. March).

——— (1984). General Economic and Social Characteristics, (Washington D.C.).

——— (1986). *Statistical Abstract of the United States* (Washington, D.C.).

United States Immigration and Naturalization Service, *Annual Reports,* Various Issues (Washington, D.C., U.S. Government Printing Office).

———, *Statistical Yearbook of the Immigration of Naturalization Service*, Various Issues, (Washington, D.C.).

United States of America, Library of Congress, Congressional Research Service, Foreign Affairs Division (1974). *Brain Drain: A Study of the Persistent Issue of International Scientific Mobility,* prepared for the Sub-Committee on National Security Policy and Scientific Development of the Committee on Foreign Affairs, U.S. House of Representatives, (Washington, D.C., U.S. Government Printing Office).

Warren, R. and S. Passel (1983). "A Count of the Uncountable: Estimates of Undocumented Aliens Counted in the 1980 United States Census", Population Association of America Meeting, Pittsburg, Pennsylvania.

Warren, R. and J.M. Peck (1970). "Foreign Born Emigration from the United States" *Demography*, 17 No. 1 (February) 71-81.

World Bank (1986). *World Development Report*, (Washington, D.C.).

ELEVEN

Education and Rural Transformation in Developing Countries

T. R. LAKSHMANAN & R. P. MISRA

The contemporaneous view of rural development is not simply one of agricultural and economic growth in the narrow sense but one of balanced social and economic development. This view equates rural development with far-reaching transformation of the social and economic structures, institutions, relationships and processes in any rural area, leading to an equitable distribution as well as the creation of benefits. Among the long-term goals are more equitable access to land and other assets, generation of new employment, general improvements in nutrition, health and shelter, and greater opportunities for rural people to realize their full potential through education; and a participatory role for ruralites in shaping decisions and actions governing their lives. .

In view of its importance to the present as well as to future generations, education has been viewed traditionally as an important instrumental variable towards achieving the long-range goals reviewed above. Consequently, there has been, in the last two or three decades, a rapid quantitative expansion of the existing education largely in its old image, under the assumption that this would equalize opportunity and develop technical and leadership skills needed for development. This expectation has not materialized in view of the misfit between the attributes of inherited education systems and the realities of rapidly changing societies. The maladjustment has been particularly severe in rural areas, which were neglected in the allocation of scarce national educational resources, and where the incompatibility between the output of the educational system and the learning needs of children and adults outside schools is more severe. This set of circumstances has predictably stimulated a strong new interest in restructuring the educational system with a view to increasing its contribution to rural transformation.

How does education fit into the newer broader concept of rural transformation? Even to begin to address this question, one needs a realistic notion of the rural development process. The rural development is a systematic process whose outcomes are determined by the interactions between four system components. The first three components – asset distribution, organizations and institutions, and the incentive system – define the "inside" of the system and the last – external linkages – is the "environment" of the system (Fig. 11.1). Assets are viewed as including not only physical assets such as land or physical capital but also a variety of skills embodied as human capital. The character of the institutions and organizations which make the "allocative" choices and determine the types of technologies and goods and services to be produced will be consistent with the type of asset concentration. Similarly, in a functional rural development system, the type of incentives–private collective or sectorial–in place would be consistent with the organizational structure. Finally, all the "inside" components interact with the external world in complex ways, resulting in two-way flows of ideas, standards, labour, capital, materials, and so on.

Investments in education in such a rural system affect the various components differentially and thus may cause changes in the nature and distribution of rural goods and services. Improved education will naturally alter the asset distribution in a region and consequently the incomes deriving from the ownership of assets. Improved education and training will augment the "allocative" skills of individuals in organizations and institutions, who make choices on the type, location and quantity of production and consumption activities.

Again, education leads to direct enrichment of the lives of those who obtain it. Further, it contributes to improvements in nutritional levels, child health and lower fertility. Through such changes, education helps individuals to take greater advantage of the incentives in the system and forge beneficial links between the region and the rest of the world.[1]

In order that education can be responsive to rural transformation needs in this fashion, it must meet the following types of needs: (Nichoff and Neff, 1977; Coombs and Ahmed, 1974)

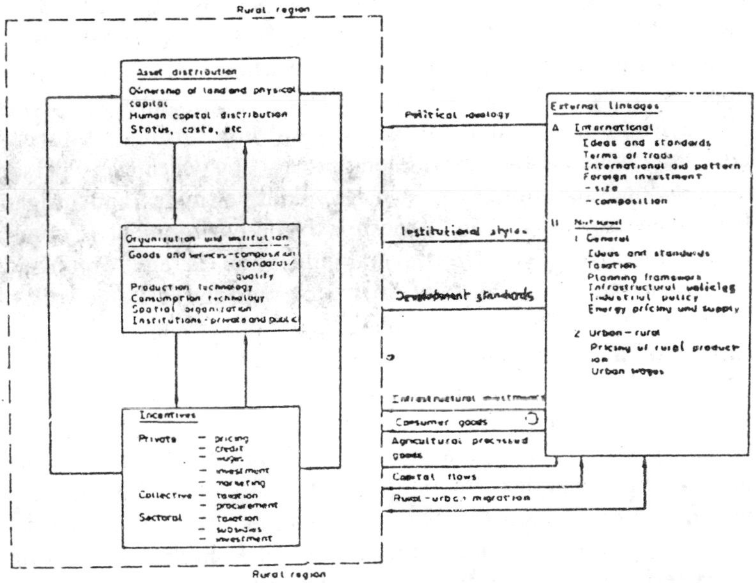

FIG. 11.1: Components and "environment" of a Rural Development System

1. *Basic or General Education* – focused on literacy, numeracy and a basic understanding of the environment, e.g. primary and secondary schools.
2. *Work-Directed or Occupational Education*–specially dispersed to impart particular skills and knowledge associated with renumerative work opportunities. These opportunities may be in (a) primary activities–farming, animal husbandry, forestry, fishing, etc.; (b) off-farm production and commercial activities–artisans, light manufacturing, construction, retail, repair shops, etc.; and (c) general service personnel–rural planners, administrators and technical experts.
3. *Family Betterment Education* – here the focus is on skills and knowledge pertaining to health, nutrition, family planning, etc.
4. *Community Betterment Education* – the focus here is on training in political participatory activities, community projects, etc.

Very few rural areas provide these four types of educational needs. Indeed, educational services available to many rural areas are a blend of formal and informal education. A useful way to characterize the type of educational environments in rural areas appears in Fig. 11.2 (La Belle, 1977). Here we recognize three types of environment–formal, informal and non-formal. Informal education is defined as "the lifelong process" by which every person acquires and accumulates knowledge, skills, attitudes and insights from daily experiences and exposure to the environment (Coombs and Ahmed, 1974). Non-formal education is any organized, systematic educational activity carried on outside the framework of the formal system to provide selected types of learning to particular subgroups in the population, adults as well as children. Formal education is the institutionalized hierarchically structured education system from primary school to university. In Fig. 11.2 the above three types of education are viewed as predominant educational modes rather than discrete entities. In the case of formal education mode, if formal characteristics are taken, we arrive at the graded hierarchy schools. Within the non-formal mode, the formal characteristics may lead to granting of certificates, the non-formal characteristics to institutional participation (La Belle, 1977). The advantage of Fig. 11.2 is not to be constrained by the instructional aspects of non-formal education but also with the secondary and potentially more important participatory experiences in terms of learning outcomes.

Given these broad characterizations of the rural transformation, educational needs and learning environments, our objective is to formulate a research project that would critically and systematically analyse past experience, current evidence and new ideas, if any, so as to develop information, analytical capability and guidelines for planning education in the service of rural transformation. Since the scope of such a study would be large, we limit ourselves to education programmes directed at occupational education (geared to farmers, small businessmen, etc.) and to general education for the children.

In developing this project, we try to address the following questions. For convenience, we group them into three groups of questions. First what attributes do people need to carry forward the process of development and in what ways can education enhance these attributes? Since people with more education earn larger incomes, is this case of education's contribution or merely its capacity to sort out people according to future productivity? What alternative approaches have analysts taken to assess the contribution of education to economic growth? What is the mechanism through which education has its economic effects–how much is due to modernity, adaptability, work discipline, and how much due to literacy and numeracy? Do these studies provide an insight into the *Processes* of development? In the latter case, what is needed is more understanding of the nature of interactions between educational achievement, learning-by-doing, and new training investment? What are the effects of education in the labour market–on earnings, labour force participation and employment.

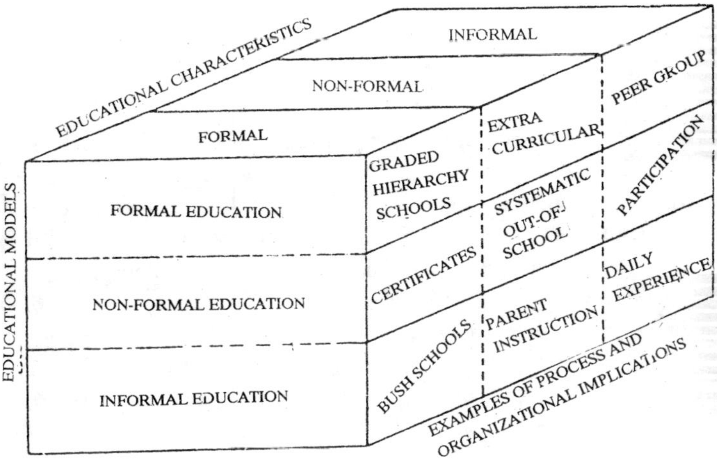

FIG. 11.2: Formal, Non-formal and Informal Relationships

Second, what has been the pattern of educational investment in countries distinguished by high level of development? How have the different educational environments faired relatively in enrolment, physical inputs, teachers and overall resources? What is the nature of differential participation in the educational system and its effects on income distribution.

Third, what alternative educational approaches would be possible to support rural transformation as defined here? If the focus is on improving rural incomes, what choices exist for reinforcing and supplementing educational and developmental opportunities in the rural areas?

We provide in the next section a preliminary discussion of these issues. In the third section, we identify a research project for our international comparative analysis of education experiences and synthesize preliminary responses to issues raised here.

ROLE OF EDUCATION IN RURAL TRANSFORMATION

A Review of Analytical and Policy issues

We attempt here to provide a brief review of:

(a) the state of current knowledge about the effects of education on national and regional development; and
(b) the broad features of the educational system in developing countries as viewed from a functional perspective and its relevance to improving rural productivity and employment.

The purpose of these reviews is to set the stage for a discussion of key analytical and policy issues pertaining to the role of education in rural transformation. From such a discussion we propose the outline of a research project UNCRD could undertake.

Education and Rural Transformation

Some Perspectives

As noted earlier, education has multiple claims on national resources: first, it improves the quality of life of the recipients. Second, it leads to improvements of nutritional levels, health care and to reductions in fertility. Third, education contributes to productivity and growth in incomes and, in many cases, to an improved distribution of income as well.

Much of the research carried out to substantiate these claims has focused on the effects of education on income. Several strands of inquiry are evident in such studies.

1. Cross-national analyses of role of education in explaining GNP gap among countries;
2. Aggregate production functions and growth accounting;
3. Microlevel production functions;
4. Rates of return and earnings functions; and
5. Studies of incidence of education benefits.

Cross-national Analyses

Among the many attempts to specify the extent to which human factors might explain income gaps among countries, the work of Anne Krueger is noteworthy (Krueger, 1968). Assuming an underlying aggregate production function with constant returns to scale, she estimates the effects of education as a proportion of the per capita income gap between the USA and each of many countries (Table 11.1). The largest contributions of education are associated with lower levels of per capita income. The striking deviance for Japan suggests that it was ready for rapid growth in production with post-war accumulation of investment in machinery and equipment.

In analysing differences in incomes per capita among 23 countries, Fallon and Layard (1975) tested through the use of two-level CES production function the hypothesis that skills and physical capital are complementary. Their model attributed the greater part of the gap in per capita incomes between the USA and most developing countries to physical capital and the "efficiency parameter." Education is important, but so are physical capital and organizational efficiency. Somewhat similar results were obtained by other cross-national studies (Correa, 1970; Maddison, 1970).

Aggregate Production Functions and Growth Accounting

Much of the work on production functions to explain role of education was stimulated by the work of Schultz (1961), who himself focused on the rate of return of education. Nothing that the stock of education in the USA rose approximately by 850 per cent between 1900 and 1956 as compared with an increase in reproducible capital of 450 per cent (in same period) he argued that the return to investment in education is at least as large as, if not larger than that to non-human capital.

TABLE 11.1: **Education and Gaps in Per Capita Incomes between the United States and other Countries as Measured by Anne Krueger**

Country	Per capita GDP as percentage of U.S. value	Per capita attainable income with present human	Percentage by which attainable income is reduced by gap inresources		Percentage of gap explained by education
	(1)	(2)[a]	(3)[b]	(4)[c]	(5)[d]
U.S.A.	100.0	—	—	—	—
Canada	72.6	100.5	8.1	7.9	28.8
Israel	38.3	83.8	13.6	13.9	22.5
Japan	14.4	93.2	3.7	4.3	5.0
Puerto Rico	23.2	59.8	12.6	16.5	21.5
Jamaica	16.2	56.7	16.0	21.1	25.2
Panama	15.0	51.5	16.0	21.5	25.3
Mexico	14.2	45.6	22.9	29.5	34.4
Greece	12.5	71.2	28.6	29.8	34.1
Portugal	11.6	67.1	29.9	31.3	35.4
El Salvador	7.5	45.5	24.1	30.5	33.0
Honduras	7.5	36.6	23.9	33.3	36.0
Peru	7.3	51.0	18.3	23.3	25.1
Iran	7.2	39.8	33.2	40.0	43.1
Jordan	6.9	38.7	23.3	31.3	33.6
Malaysia	7.9	44.2	25.0	31.5	34.2
Indonesia	3.1	37.3	32.2	38.8	40.0
South Korea	4.7	44.3	24.8	30.8	32.3
Taiwan	3.9	48.5	21.6	27.2	28.3
Thailand	3.6	46.5	21.4	27.6	28.6
India	3.0	34.1	32.6	39.3	40.5
Ghana	7.7	38.0	30.3	37.4	40.5

— = No data available

Source: Bowman, 1980.

[a] = Per capita income attainable with present human resources if the country has U.S. per capita non-human resources. Human resources as defined by Krueger included age structure, education and rural-urban sectoral composition.

[b] = Controlling for age and sector.

[c] = Including half of the age-education-sector interaction. (Controlling for age and education, sector had a very small effect.)

[d] = Column (4) divided by [100 - column (1)].

The production function traditionally used is the Cobb-Douglas Variety. In a general and simple from, the following versions appear in the literature:

$$X = X(A, K, L) \quad (1)$$
$$X = X(A(t)K, L) \quad (2)$$
$$X = X(K, A(t)L) \quad (3)$$
$$X = X(K, L, A(t)) \quad (4)$$

Where X is national output, K is capital, L, Labour input and A stands for an index of technology (or "technological progress" or "organization", etc.). Model (1) is one in which technological progress is a "residual" (the part of the observed growth in X not explained by the Cobb-Douglas production function), that is independent of K and L and not a function of time. This is the form most used in most aggregate growth accounting studies that explain the role of education or other "nonconventional" factors of production (Denisn, 1967; Jorgenson and Grileches, 1969).

Model (2) is the vintage model of Solow (1960) which views technical progress as capital augmenting, leaving the marginal productivity of labour (viewed as homogenous) unchanged. In Model (3) is the labour augmenting variety required for Harrod's neutral technical progress. In Model (4), technical progress is a shift in the production function that is systematically associated with time.

David Wheeler (1980) in implementing "a simultaneous model of Human Development and Economic Growth" for 88 developing countries in the 1970s, found literacy to be consistently labour augmenting to faster growth in manufactured exports, and to contribute significantly to the improvement of other welfare indicators. Increases in the adult literacy had a significant positive effect in the equations explaining rates of investment growth over 1960-77. In extensive simulation experiments with different schooling intensities, Wheeler noted that unless the primary school enrolment ratio is over 80 per cent, "the performance of the socio-economic system seems fundamentally constrained in the long run".

Nadin (1972) in a survey of production function studies (Model 1 above) concludes that except for fast-growing countries of Japan, Israel and Mexico, the contribution to measured growth of total labour-input growth is greater than the contribution of capital-input growth. From the disaggregation of the labour-input contribution into various components (Table 11.2) one can note that education is responsible for about one-third to one half of labour's contribution to the growth of output. The contribution of education is very large in slow-growing economies such as the USA and the U.K. While in some fast-growing economies (e.g. FRG) it is also low. In developing countries except for Argentina, the contribution of education is relatively much smaller. Indeed the smaller contribution of education in developing countries may be due to the low rate of return on education as compared to that in physical capital.[2] While the growth accounting aggregate production function studies have been broadly suggestive, too much faults in them is not warranted for a variety of biases inherent in them (Bowman, 1980). Among these are the omission of "maintenance component," the use of a Cobb-Douglas form (with its a priori restrictions on elasticities of substitution), static specification, etc. More appropriate specifications are available in some micro studies to which we turn next.

Microlevel Production Functions

The aggregate studies reviewed above do not provide much insight into the processes of interaction between education–formal or non-formal and new investment or growth in a region. Micro behavioural data on the performance of production units–farmers, light industry manufacturers–could provide much greater insights into these processes linking education and economic development.

The two micro analytical studies are worth noting in this regard. Saxonhouse (1977), in an analysis of data on individual cotton spinning firms in Japan for the five decades prior to 1935 used a generalized production function.

$$X = X\left(K, L, X_3 \ldots\ldots X_m, X^*_{mti} \ldots\ldots X_r\right) \qquad (5)$$

Where X is output quantity

K and L are capital and labour service respectively

X_i is conventional input i

X_j is nonconventional input j

TABLE 11.2: **The Contribution of Labour Input Components to Economic Growth**

Country	Period	Contribution of Labour Input Type			
		Education	Health and Nutrition	Employment Growth	Total Labour Input
Argentina	1950-62	0.53	0.12	0.93	1.58
Brazil	1950-62	0.18	0.43	1.83	2.44
Chile	1950-62	0.20	0.20	0.65	1.05
Colombia	1950-62	0.20	0.49	1.66	2.35
Ecuador	1960-62	0.23	0.32	0.92	1.47
Honduras	1950-62	0.29	0.82	1.06	2.17
Mexico	1950-62	0.05	0.93	1.43	2.41
Peru	1950-62	0.14	0.57	0.67	1.40
Venezuela	1950-62	0.19	0.21	2.19	2.59
India	1950-60				1.86
Philippines	1947-65				2.24
Netherlands		0.24	0.04	0.78	1.06
USA	1950-62	0.49	0.02	0.90	1.41
W. Germany	1950-62	0.11	0.28	1.49	1.88
France	1950-62	0.29	0.15	0.07	0.51
Belgium	1950-62	0.43	0.09	0.40	0.92
U.K.	1950-62	0.29	-0.03	0.50	0.76
Japan	1950-62	0.31	n.a	2.48	

Source: Correa, 1970, Nadiri, 1972.

In this formulation, a change in a "non-conventional" input such as education would affect the marginal rates of substitution between capital and labour; there is not a priori specification of the directions of technological bias. He used a CES production function for (5).

$$X = \left[(ad)^c + (b\,1)^c\right]^{i/c} \qquad (6)$$

Parameters a, b, c in (6) are viewed as dependent on non-conventional inputs. Thus,

$$a = u_0 + a_3 x_3 + asub4x_4 \ldots\ldots + a_8 x_8^*$$

$$b = b_0 + b_3 x_3 + b_4 x_4^* \ldots\ldots + b_8 x_8^* \qquad (7)$$

$$c = c_0 + c_3 x_3^* + b_4 x_4^* \ldots\ldots + b_8 x_8^*$$

From his analysis, Saxonhouse showed that workers' experience, education and working conditions had large and pervasive effects on better productivity improvements and absorption of labour. Management's education had little effect and management's experience and age of equipment had no effect at all. A change in the incidence of primary education had an output augmenting effect (through its influence on labour and capital) and on returns to scale.

A number of other micro studies of the role of education on the productivity of small farmers have been reviewed by Lockheed, Jamison and Lav (1980). On the whole, their findings suggest that education had a positive effect–on an average farm productivity increases by 7.4 per cent as a result of the farmer completing four additional years of elementary education rather than one. A few studies suggest a threshold number of years (4-6) at which the effect of education became more pronounced. Further, the studies suggested that the effects of education were more likely to be positive in modernizing environments rather than traditional environments. However, none of the studies explored the issue of how (i.e. via literacy, numeracy or modernity) education affects productivity.

Rates of Return and Earnings Functions

Empirical cost-benefit analysis was first proposed by a Soviet scholar Strumilin (1929). Much of the work has actually followed the work of Schultz (1961) and Becker (1960). In the sixties, the popular procedure was to estimate the rate of return to education as in the following example: if one is interested in the private rate of return to investment in higher education, assume Y stands for labour earnings, V and S are subscripts representing university and secondary education, the rate of return (v) is obtained from solving the following:

$$\sum_{t=1}^{n}(Y_u - Y_s)_t(1+v)^{-t} = \sum_{t=1}^{c}(Y_s)_t(1+r)^t \qquad (8)$$

Where there are c years when education costs are incurred beyond the age of 18, and n benefit years [Equation (8) is solved iteratively].

In the seventies the benefit cost analysis of education is investigated more often by the use of earnings functions:

$$\ln Y_i = a + bs_i + cEx_i + dEs_i^2 \quad (9)$$

Where s represents years of schooling for individual i Ex_i represents years of labour market experience. Equation 9 is based on human capital theory and the parameter B is the average private rate of return to one year of extra schooling.

The returns to education by level of education and by type of regions are displayed in Table 11.3, drawn from Psacharopoulos (1980).

It must be evident that returns to primary education are the highest, suggesting that top priority should be given to primary education as a form of investment in human resources. The returns to education are higher in developing countries relative to affluent economies. The private returns to education are much higher than social rates of return especially at the university level, indicating that some university education can be shifted to the private sector without becoming a disincentive to university higher education.

TABLE 11.3: The Returns to Education by Level and Region or Country Type

(in percentages)

Region or country type	N	Private			Social		
		Primary	Secondary	Higher	Primary	Secondary	Higher
Africa	(9)	29	22	32	29	17	12
Asia	(8)	32	17	19	16	12	11
Latin America	(5)	24	20	23	44	17	18
Average	(22)	29	19	24	27	16	13
Intermediate	(8)	20	17	17	16	14	10
Advanced	(14)	a	14	12	a	10	9

Source: Psacharopoulos, 1980.

N = Number of countries in each group.

a = Not computable because of lack of control group of illiterates.

Incidence of Education Benefits

Educational benefits are greater for some groups than for others (Fields, 1980). Given the same measured skills and education men earn more than women in most developing countries; some racial groups do better than others inmigrants do as well as lifelong residents of an area. Modern sector workers fare better than traditional sectors in Colombia and Singapore. White-collar group do better than blue-collar workers in Malaysia.

Further, studies suggest that the educational opportunities differ among group–stratified by sex, race, tribe–in developing countries. Such differential participation in educational system is an important cause of income inequality. Among the reasons why poor invest in education of their children are market conditions that work against the poor and limitations of opportunities imposed by class structures in those societies.

Before completing the review of the effects of education on incomes, one must enter a cautionary note about the results reviewed so far. Since social rates of return are often used for countries' past educational performance and in planning education for the future, criticisms of the methods of estimating social rate of return (SRR) need to be heeded. The assumption behind the computation of SRR of education is that differences in incomes among individuals with different educational attainments reflect differences in their social marginal productivity and those differences are traceable to their education (Fields, 1980). Such assumptions of the labour markets in developing countries are not always plausible, so that estimates of SRR need to be treated with caution.

Clearly, there are social benefits of education in terms of reduction of poverty, higher incomes, etc. Nationally, or regionally, we observe as education goes up, so does income. It is a fact that higher education *causes* higher national income and higher national income *permits* a high level of education. Researchers have not yet established to what extent education *causes* higher income and to what extent is a *result* of higher incomes.

An Overview of Rural Educational Systems

We survey here the state of the rural educational systems in developing countries, identifying their objectives, their modes of delivery, their quantitative achievements, their distributional outcomes, and their relevance to the rural transformation requirements. From such a discussion we attempt to highlight the focus and key issues that must engage planners concerned with using educational (along with other complementary) strategies for rural transformation.

Goals and Types of Learning Environments

In the 1950s and 1960s most developing countries launched a massive expansion of their educational systems. The objectives were to increase the enrolment of students and reduce the non-schooling gap – the difference between school-age population and actual enrolment. Their achievements in terms of enrolment are impressive, the enrolments very from 96.4 million in 1960 to 193.3 million in 1975, though the enrolment gap has widened to some degree (Table 11.4). The enrolment in higher education has expanded in these countries at a greater *rate* than enrolment in secondary education, while the latter, in turn, expanded at a faster rate than enrolment at the primary level.

TABLE 11.4: **No. of Children of Ages 6-11 Enrolled and out of School in Developing Countries, 1960-75***

(In millions)

	1960	1965	1970	1975
Population	205.7	242.1	279.8	313.8
Number enrolled	96.4	131.9	161.1	193.3
Number out of school	109.3	110.2	118.7	120.5

Source: World Bank 1980 Annex 4.
Not including China, North Korea and Vietnam.

Much of this educational expansion has taken place in the public sector, though in some countries in Latin America and Africa, a significant percentage of children continue to be enrolled in private schools. Such private schools financed by tuition fees are largely serving the higher income groups. The public educational systems are heavily subsidized by government, whose income derives from the tax structure, which is often proportional. The distribution of benefits from education in developing countries appears to be highly inequitable by the criterion of equal opportunity (Fields, 1980). In an analysis in Colombia, it was noted that the positive effect of public financing of education for the poor is only due to the financing of primary education, which strongly helps the poor. On the other hand, the public financing of secondary and higher education helps the lower and upper middle class. If the criterion of equal opportunity is applied – that is, the proportion of overall benefits received by the poor is compared with their share of the population – the poor share less than proportionately in the benefits of education (Table 11.5) (Jallade, 1974).

TABLE 11.5: **Distribution of Public Subsidies for Education by Households' Income and Per Capita Income—Colombia**

Household Income ('000 pesos)	Distribution of Households (%)	Distribution of Subsidies (%)
0 - 6	19.0	5.9
6 - 12	20.2	9.5
12 - 24	24.9	23.7
24 - 60	22.9	38.7
Over 60	13.0	22.2
Total	110.0	100.0

Source : Jallade, 1974.

However, this rapid expansion of the educational systems inherited from earlier elitist orientations, have been irrelevant to the needs of the majority of the population. The emphasis was on the requirements of the modern urban industrial sector and its elite employees, with the education delivered in an institutional, hierarchically structured environment. The resulting irrelevance of education has become more severe in rural areas for several reasons. First, rural areas have been denied their share of national resources for education (as in other dimensions of development in the 1960s and 1970s). Secondly the misfit between the output of the school system and what was required for functioning effectively in rural occupations was most severe. Further, since formal schooling was largely seen as education, the learning needs of children and adults outside school were largely ignored.

This situation has stimulated considerable interest in understanding the "external" relations of education, that is, how education relates to the world of work. In other words, how does general education relate to vocational education and how do schools prepare students for future occupations and what types of learning are possible in and out of schools? When the issue is framed in this fashion, one has a functional view of education distinct from a structural or institutional approach used traditionally. In this view, the needs of the learners are identified first and a set of educational (equated with learning) means appropriate for these needs is defined. As UNESCO suggested, education can no longer be viewed as a time-bound, place-bound process confined to schools and measured by years of exposure (ICDE, 1972). Education is a continuous process, stretching from childhood to the adult years involving a variety of means and learning environments. Earlier, three such learning environments – formal, non-formal and informal – were identified.

There is increasing agreement that ideally countries and regions should try to develop over time "lifelong learning systems" or recurrent education and training systems, so as to promote a diversified range of useful learning options through life. Any such system would obviously have to define carefully the links between education and work, a subject we turn to in the case of rural development.

Educational Requirements for Rural Transformation

Change in a rural region viewed as a system (Fig. 11.1) takes place in a desired direction if a consistent set of actions on the institutional-organizational-incentive-relational milieu are taken. One such action naturally involves appropriate education and training.

Two kinds of educational needs are required for rural transformation. One is the rural school, where general education can be provided. As noted earlier, completion of four years of school improves farm productivity. However, it is important to remove the urban bias in school curricula.

Our focus is on the second educational need – the learning needs of the occupational groups in the rural area. We recognized earlier three types of such groups:

(i) persons engaged in primary activities (farming, animal husbandry, fishery, etc.);

(ii) off-farm production and commercial activities – artisans, light manufacturing construction, retail, repair shops, etc.;
(iii) general service personnel – rural planners, administrators and technical experts.

An idea of the learning needs of these groups can be obtained from Table 11.6 taken from the work of Coombs and Ahmed (1974). It must be clear that these needs can be met by a combination of different learning environments identified earlier. The various components of such a programme must be viewed as parts of an overall *knowledge-generation and delivery* system, whose mission is to help farmers, artisans, and other ruralites. Second, they must be seen as a part of a rural development system, involving, with educational elements, a number of non-educational elements.

TABLE 11.6 : **Illustrative Rural Occupational Groups and their Learning Needs**

Groups	Types of Learning Needs (at varying levels of sophistication and specialization)
A. Persons directly engaged in agriculture	
1. Commercial farmers 2. Small subsistence and semi-subsistence farm families 3. Landless farm workers	* Farm planning and management; rational decision-making; record keeping; cost and revenue computations; use of credit * Application of new inputs, varieties, improved farm practices * Storage, processing, food preservation * Supplementary skills for farm maintenance and improvement, and sideline jobs for extra income * Knowledge of government services, policies, programmes, targets * Knowledge and skills for family improvement (e.g., health, nutrition, home economics, child care, family planning) * Civic skills (e.g., knowledge of how co-operatives, local government, national government function)

(Contd.)

B. Persons engaged in off-farm commercial activities	
1. Retailers and wholesalers of farm supplies and equipment, consumer goods and other items 2. Suppliers of repair and maintenance services 3. Processor, storers and shippers of agricultural commodities 4. Suppliers of banking and credit services 5. Construction and other artisans 6. Suppliers of general transport services 7. Small manufacturers	* New and improved technical skills applicable to particular goods and services * Quality control * Technical knowledge of goods handled sufficient to advise customers on their use, maintenance, etc. * Managementment skills (business planning; record keeping and cost accounting; procurement and inventory control; market analysis and sales methods; customer and employee relations; knowledge of government services, regulations, taxes; use of credit)
C. General services personnel:	
Rural administrators, planners, technical experts 1. General public administrators, broad-gauged analysis and planners at subnational levels 2. Managers, planners, technicians, and trainers for specific public services (e.g., agriculture, transport, irrigation, health, small industry, education, family services, local government, etc.) 3. Managers of cooperatives and other farmer associations 4. Managers and other personnel of credit services	* General skills for administration, planning, implementation, information flows, promotional activities. * Technical and management skills applying to particular specialties * Leadership skills for generating community enthusiasm and collective action, staff team work and support from higher echelons

Source: Coombs and Ahmed, 1974.

The philosophy underlying such a design can be best described by the following. What types of learning have to take place so that people are adequately prepared for occupations? What are the functional roles in this learning process of general education, occupation-oriented education, specific training and work experience? When should the individual begin his occupational preparation and in what sequence?

A Summing Up

From this review, what analytical and policy issues emerge? First, there is broad-based evidence that education has beneficial effects on development. Private and social rates of return are impressive in developing countries. Such studies of human capital investments, aggregate production functions and growth accounting, however, do not provide much insight into the processes of interaction between education (formal or non-formal) and new investment in a region. A few microanalytical studies provide more insights into the education-growth relationships. However, what is really needed is a production function of skills and knowledge. Such a function would relate the level of skills and performance of a person over time to the level and timing of the inputs of formal schooling, work experience, abilities, interests, leisure and other interactions.

Second, while the performance of educational systems in developing countries has been remarkable in quantitative terms, such as enrolment, these educational opportunities are *inequitably* distributed among individuals distinguished by sex, racial composition, rural-urban location, and modern or informal sector.

Third, the extant education system is largely inappropriate to the needs of the workplace, particularly in the rural sector. The principal issues revolve around: (a) *kind of education* or training that is best suited for rural occupational opportunities – farming, animal husbandry, fishing, light manufacturing, artisanry, etc.; and (b) the *institutional forms of delivery* of such training. This calls for various blends of formal and non-formal education and training. These combinations could include general education, professorial education, on-the-job training and a mix of education and work.

Fourth, the internal organization of education could be improved in terms of optimal use of resources, so that quality education is equitably available to all. Since the resources for education are scarce, careful analysis of the costs and financing of education should be carried out, to assume efficient and equitable outcomes.

NOTES

1. While education — taking many forms and reaching many people — is clearly a key factor of rural transformation, it must be noted that rural development is the outcome of many interacting forces. In the absence of many complementary forces, education, least of all traditional schooling, cannot alone stimulate a dynamic transformation of rural life (Lakshmanan, 1982).
2. In India, the rates of return for education vary from 7 per cent (for higher

education) to 17 per cent (for primary education), while they range between 17.2 per cent and 26.1 per cent for physical capital. This could result from the government policy of over-investing in education regardless of demand and by the type of education emphasized (Nadiri, 1972).

REFERENCES

Adelman, C., et at., (1977). "Rethinking Case Study: Notes from the Second Cambridge Conference," *Cambridge Journal of Education* 6, 1977. pp. 139-150

Becker, Gary S., (1962). "Investment in Human Capital: A Theoretical Analysis," *Journal of Political Economy*, October.

Bowman, Mary J., (1980). "Education and Economic Growth: An Overview," in *Education and Income* (ed.), T. King. World Bank Staff Working Paper No. 402, pp. 1-71.

Case, Harry L. and Niehoff, Richard O., (1976). *Educational Alternatives in National Development: Suggestions for Policy Makers* East Lancing, Mich.: Institute for International Studies in Education, Michigan State University, (Programme of Studies in Non-Formal Education. Supplementary Paper No. 4.)

Colletta, Nat J., (1982). *Worker-Peasant Education in the Peoples' Republic of China* World Bank Staff Working Paper No. 527.

Coombs, Philip H. and Manzoor Ahmed, (1974). *Attacking Rural Poverty: How Non-formal Education can help* The Johns Hopkins Press, London.

Correa, Hector, (1970). "Sources of Economic Growth in Latin America," *Southern Economic Journal*, July, pp. 17-31.

Denison, E. F., (1967). *Why Growth Rates Differ: Post-war Experience in Nine Western Countries* Washington D.C.: Brookings Institution.

Fields, Gary S., "Education and Income Distribution in Developing Countries," in *Education and Income* (ed.), T. King. World Bank Staff Working Paper No. 402. pp. 231-315.

Harbison, Frederick H., (1973). *Human Resources as the Weather of Nations,* New York: Oxford University Press.

Hayami, Y. and U. W. Ruttan, (1971). *Agricultural Development: An International Perspective* Baltimore: The Johns Hopkins University Press.

ICDE (International Commission on the Development of Education), (1972). *Learning To Be: The World of Education Today and Tomorrow* Paris: UNESCO, London, George G. Harrap. Co.

ILO, (1971). *Matching Employment Opportunities and Expectations: A Programme of Action for Ceylon* (The report of an inter-agency team organized by ILO).

Jallade, Jean-Pierre, (1974). *Public Expenditures on Education and Income Distribution in Columbia* World Bank Staff Occasional Papers No. 18. Baltimore: Johns Hopkins University Press.

Kruger, A., (1968). "Factor Endowments and Per Capita Income Differences among Countries," *Economic Journal* September, pp. 641-659.

La Belle, Thomas J., (1977). "Liberation, Development and Rural Non-Formal Education," in *Non-Formal Education and the Rural Poor* (ed.) R. O. Nichoff. Michigan State University, Lansing. pp. 211-226.

Lakshmanan, T. R., (1982). "A System Model of Rural Development," *World Development* October.

Lockhead, M. F., D. J. Jamison, and L. J. Lau, (1980). "Farmer Education and Farm Efficiency: A Survey," in *Education and Income* (ed.) T. King. World Bank Staff Working Paper No. 402, Washington D.C., pp. 111-151.

Meddison, A., (1970). *Economic Progress and Policy in Developing Countries,*

London: Allen and Urwin.

Milliken, Max and David Hapgood, (1967). *No Easy Harvest,* Boston: Little Brown & Col.

Nadiri, M. Ishaq, (1972). "International Studies of Factor Inputs and Total Factor Productivity: A brief Survey," *Review of Income and Wealth* 18, pp. 129-148.

Nichoff, Richard O., (1977). *Non-Formal Education and the Rural Poor,* Michigan State University Press.

Psacharopoulos, G., (1980). *Higher Education in Developing Countries: A Cost-Benefit Analysis,* World Bank Staff Working Paper No. 440.

______________, (1973). *Returns to Education: An International Comparison,* New York: American Alsevier Jossey-Bass.

Saxonhouse, G. R., (1977). "Productivity Change and Labour Absorption in Japanese Cotton Spinning 1891-1935," *Quarterly Journal of Economics,* No. 2, May, pp. 195-220.

Schultz, T., (1961). "Investment in Human Capital," *American Economic Review,* March.

Stewart, Frances (ed.), (1975). *Employment, Income Distribution and Development,* London: Frank Cass.

Staley, Eugene, (1971). *Planning Occupational Education and Training for Development,* New York: Praeger.

Stoikov, Vladimir, (1975). *The Economics of Recurrent Education and Training,* ILO. Geneve.

Strumilir, S. G., (1968). "The Economic Significance of National Education," *The Planned Economy*; reprinted in UNESCO. Readings in the Economics of Education. New York.

Wheeler, D., (1980). "Human Resources Development and Economic Growths in LDC's: A Simultaneous Model" World Bank Staff Working Paper No. 407, Washington D.C., July.

World Bank, (1980). *Education: Sector Policy Paper,* Washington D.C., August.

TWELVE

Regional Disequilibrium and Supranational Organization in Japan

YASUO MIYAKAWA

The regional disequilibrium in Japan became less and less in response to the growth of Japan's economy, especially after the Second World War. Looking after the changing phase of regional disequilibrium in Japan, it generally became enlarged in the time of high economic growth and became less in the stable economic time, although new driving forces for enlarging regional disequilibrium were accumulated in the leading metropolitan areas as ever. That is to say, the regional disequilibrium in Japan has been fundamentally enlarged by the economy of urbanization and agglomeration especially in the old and new capital regions (Kyoto and Tokyo), in spite of the comprehensive national land development plans and other regional development plans (Miyakawa, *Regional Development Alternative,* edited by A. L. Mabogunji and R. P. Misra from UNCRD).

In Japan, we could not find direct influences on the regional disequilibrium by the supranational organizations; however, they exerted great invisible and fundamental influences on the change of regional disequilibrium, especially at the three important epochs of Japan's metamorphosis – the opening of the country and the Meiji restoration after the Treaty of Commerce with the United States and the four major European countries in 1858 up to their reversion of unequal treaties in 1894. , the General Head Quarters (GHQ), control and democratization of Japan's economy and policy after the Second World War up to the abolishment of GHQ in 1952. , the liberalization of trade and investment started in 1960 up to 1973, when the yen floated and Japan suffered very much from the Oil Crisis.

After the first epoch, Japan introduced foreign investment according to the amended Meiji Commercial Law enacted in 1899, which enabled the establishment of joint concerns with foreign companies. It gradually promoted the establishment of joint concerns such as Nippon Electric in 1899 and Ford Motors in 1923, which evoluted much Japan's industrial system. Rebirths of these joint concerns after the Second World War had been gradually brought since the promulgation of Foreign Capital Introduction Law in 1950. In spite of the announcement of the fifth liberalization of capital investment, foreign pressures on Japan's exports and self-control of Japan's export in response to succeeding movements towards limitations of imports from Japan, Japan was obliged to establish its overseas factories. Most of them, especially small subcontractors, who were urged to follow up their parent overseas subsidiary companies, could not have enough revenue and revenue and gradually suffered from decrease not only of exports but also of domestic demands due to increased imports of parts, although most of the foreign companies in Japan have got enough revenue, because of change of industrial structure caused by the Oil Crisis and by large fluctuation of floating yen rate in a short time. In 1983, the United States President asked for the liberalization of Japan's financial market and internationalization of Japanese yen and, in 1986, the decision of five Ministers of advanced countries caused extreme increase of exchange rate of yen on the U. S. dollar, accelerated the Japan's foreign investment to keep its foreign markets on the one hand and on the other, it caused a big damage on local industrial areas composed of small businesses, which are not able to export their products and suffered very much from increase of imports. Thus, a decision of a sort of supranational organization gradually exerts a great influence on the regional disequilibrium in Japan.

In this paper, as effort has been made to clarify the invisible relation between the regional disequilibrium and supranational organization, paying due regards to the location of multinational companies, in each stage of Japanese economic development. In a postscript, I will refer to the Japanese investments in a supranational organization's areas – EC and Asian countries, which will contribute a little to the main discussion subjects on this committee's meeting.

Modernization of Japan's Industry and Unequal Treaties

In 1792, a Russian envoy came to Hokkaido, requesting for opening of trade relations, which was turned down by the Shogunate. Russia was very much interested in Japan, especially in Hokkaido, which already had established its Japan Navigation School in 1762 and Japanese language school in 1768 at Irkutsk and had requested for the opening of trade relations to a lord Matsumae governing the southern tips of Hokkaido in 1779. Following Russia, its rival England also approached Muroran in a southern part of Hokkaido in 1792. Due to these menaces to the Shogunate, it was obliged to strengthen the nation's coastal defence, especially Hokkaido and Kyushu islands, where Russian envoy also visited at Nagasaki, only one foreign trade port for Hollanders and non-Christian Chinese. As a result, two peripheral islands were gradually developed. In 1837, Americans visited Uraga on the mouth of Edo Bay (today's Tokyo Bay) and then in 1844, French succeeded in opening international trade with Satsuma clan only at Rukyu island (today's Okinawa prefecture), which governed Rukyu Kingdom at that time and could succeed in gathering latest information of foreign countries and world new trends for promotion of modernization of its economy, especially industry.

At last, in 1853, a naval squadron of the United States entered directly in Tokyo Bay, disregarding the Shogunate's isolation policy in 1853 and a subsequent visit in 1854 compelled Japan to end its state of isolation. The treaty of amity with the United States was followed by the conclusion of similar unequal ones with Russia, the United Kingdom and the Netherlands in the same year and with France the next year. The changes in the feudal economy caused by the opening up of Japan to international trade undermined the rigid foundations of the feudal structure and the feudal industrial system, which had been sustained by feudal lords and the Shogunate through special privileges, and resulted in relatively equal regional developments (Y. Miyakawa, 1981, EKISTICS vol 48) . In other words, an invisible league of suzerains, a quasi-supranational organization urged Japan to open its country and caused new regional disequilibriums led by the newly opened international trade ports, especially near the centre of economy, Osaka, and near the centre of administration, Edo (Tokyo) .

Due to these unequal treaties, its import tax was reduced to only five per cent in 1866, and new treaties were amended as a result of the defeat in the Shimonoseki attack by the four countries' Navy. It accelerated the import of cotton textiles which led to the demolition of Japan's cotton cultivation areas such as Senshu near Osaka and Mikawa near Nagoya. As the free activities of foreign traders in foreign settlements led to the opening of the first port, Yokohama, which became a centre of international trade, and silk and tea manufacturers developed remarkably on the fringe of today's Tokyo metropolitan area. However, as a whole, Japanese traditional industries suffered very much from the increase in imports and were almost demolished. In response to the increase in international trade, Japan opened Hyogo (today's Kobe) port according to the aforementioned unequal treaties in 1867, which helped redevelopment of the Osaka metropolitan area, the most important centre of economy during the Edo era, as was seen in the establishment of the second modern cotton mill by the Satsuma clan, who established the first at Kagoshima illegally in 1865.

Growth of industries in the two huge metropolitan areas had been accelerated by the construction of government owned factories, some of which were originally constructed in the Edo era, such as the aforementioned Sakai Cotton Spinning Mill and Ishikawajima Shipyard in Tokyo and then were requisitioned by the Meiji Government. The largest Naval yard, Yokosuka, was also constructed by the Tokugawashogunate in 1865 as the most important yard against the advanced countries in the Tokyo metropolitan area. Similar to The Ishikawajima shipyard in 1876, Hyogo shipyard at Kobe was also transferred to Kawsaki and became an important shipyard in Japan in 1887. Near Kobe, an English trader, E. H. Hunter, constructed its shipyard, Osaka Iron Works (Hitachi Shipbuilding & Engineering) at Osaka in 1881, thanks to the revenue from transportations in the Civil War in 1877. In 1881, Japan Railway Co. Ltd. was also established to construct national railway system, originally started in 1872 between Shinbashi (Tokyo) and Yokohama constructed by English bonds and then between Osaka and Kobe in 1874 and between Kyoto and Osaka in 1876. At last in 1889, when the Meiji Constitution, patterned after the Prussian one, was promulgated, the Tokaido railway between Tokyo and Osaka was opened and in 1892, when the Reversion committee on Unequal Treaty started, the Railway Construction Law was enacted.

In 1894, conflicting interests in Korea led to the outbreak of Sino-Japanese war and the Treaty of Commerce and Navigation with the United Kingdom was signed, which was the first step of treaty reversions. Due to victory for Japan in this war in 1895 Japan was able to adopt the gold basis in 1897 and succeeded in the reversion of unequal treaties in 1899. And as a result of amendment of the Meiji Commercial Law in 1899, the establishment of joint concern with foreign capitals was enabled. Nippon Electric with American Western Electric was the first foreign company established in Japan in this year, when telephones came into use in Tokyo and Osaka. Its rival, General Electric, was also in corporation with Tokyo Electric (Toshiba) in 1905, when Japan emerged victorious in the Russo-Japanese War. Thus, an international oligopolitic industrial structure exerted a great influence on the evolution of industrial system in underdeveloping country and on the regional industrial development. The location of sheet glass industry may be quoted as another good example. The first sheet glass maker, Asahi Glass, was established by Iwasaki, founder of Mitsubishi Financial group, with the help of Belgium technology in 1909, a year before the annexation of Korea and recovery of tariff autonomy in 1910. In 1914, its second factory was constructed at Makiyama in Kitakyushu, which developed remarkably owing to the decrease of imports due to the outbreak of the First World War and became an important exporter of sheet glass not only to Asia but also to southern Africa. In 1918, Nippon-America Sheet Glass (Nippon Sheet Glass) was established by Sumitomo group and Libbey Glass of the United States with Asahi Glass in Futajima near Makiyama in Kitakyushu, a new modern industrial area after the construction of Yawata Iron Works in 1901 by the government. On the other hand, these two sheet glass makers constructed their factories in the Tokaido Megapolis, Tsurumi of Asahi Glass in 1916 and Yokkaichi of Nippon Sheet Glass in 1935, in response to the growth of domestic market. After the Great Earthquake in the Tokyo metropolitan area in 1923, Ford Motors constructed its factory at Yokohama for demand caused by the rehabilitation of transport system in Tokyo. Following Ford, General Motors constructed its factory at Osaka in 1926 attracted by the Osaka city industrial policy for introduction of foreign investment. The location of these two multinational companies developed remarkably Japan's infant automobile industry, but on the other hand, it became a menace to the existence of Japan's automobile industry and was considered a threat to the security of the nation by the Army and MITI. And they promoted the promulgation of Automobile Industry Law in 1936, which encouraged the development of Japan's automobile industry such as Nissan and Toyota and succeeded in the close of these two foreign factories in 1939, although they tried again and again to establish their joint concerns with Nissan and Toyota. In response to the formation of War Economic system, Tokyo gradually became the centre of industry instead of Osaka and Kyoto. After the relocation of the Capital from Kyoto to Tokyo in 1868, Kyoto lost its ground remarkably, although it surpassed all the cities in industrial output in 1874, with 7.9 per cent of the total output, followed by Osaka (5.8%); while the industrial output in Tokyo was then only a quarter of Kyoto's. With the decline of Kyoto in industry and in population, Osaka gained ground. By 1909, Osaka was the most important industrial centre with 17.4 per cent of the total output, followed by Hyogo (12.5%), Aichi (6.8%), Tokyo (5.9%) and Kyoto (4.2%) . The population of Osaka in 1908 was over 1 million (1, 227, 000), next to Tokyo (2, 186, 000) and followed by Kyoto (442, 000). And in 1939, a year after the National Mobilization Law, Tokyo surpassed Osaka in industrial output with 16.9 per cent of the total, followed by Osaka (15.4%), Hyogo (8.8%), Fukuoka (8.4%), Kanagawa (8.1%) and Aichi (7.4%) . Kyoto accounted only for 2.1 per cent. According to the census of 1940, the population of Tokyo had reached 6, 779, 000, followed by Osaka (3, 252, 000), Nagoya (1, 328,000) and Kyoto (1, 090, 000) . The two international ports near the huge cities of Yokohama (968, 000) and Kobe (967, 000) were approaching a million inhabitants. Nagoya situated between Tokyo and Osaka became the third important metropolis, especially in manufacturing activities, largely owing to the development of aircraft industry.

Government by GHQ and Changes of Eco-Political System

With surrender, the Allied occupation of Japan began, whose General Head Quarter's orders insisted Japan to change fundamentally its eco-political system and exerted a great influence on the regional development directly and indirectly. In 1945, GHQ of SCAP announced its initial occupation policy and asset freezing and dissolution of 15 zaibatsu (large financial and industrial groups such as Mitsubishi, Mitsui and Sumitomo). And GHQ ordered emanicipation of farmers and farm land reform, which exerted a great influence on Japan's regional development after the Second World War. In 1946, new Japan Constitution was promulgated. GHQ ordinance for special measures on trade was issued and the law for

Reconstruction and Improvement of Corporations and law on Special Measurement for Creation of Owner Farmers were also promulgated. Under the control of GHQ, the Cabinet adopted the 4th Quarter Supply Demand Plan for Goods, according to which the priority production formula started. For promotion of this formula, the Reconstruction Finance Bank was inaugurated in 1947 with Government capital and it supplied equipment funds and working funds required for post-war reconstruction to key industries, especially the coal and steel industries and working funds to public corporations. Owing to this policy, the coal production increased from 22.5 million tons in 1946 to 34.8 million tons in 1948, a remarkable development in the coal producing areas in Hokkaido and in the northern part of Kyushu islands having taken place. Iron and steel industries were also rehabilitated, and according to this policy and to the research report of American Army in 1948, all works could survive, although Nippon Steel was divided into Yahata Steel with Yahata, Tobata and Hikari works and Fuji with Muroran, Kamaishi and Hirohata due to the Deconcentration Law. Thanks to the technical advice by U.S. Steel, Muroran works invented a new technology for production of coalite from domestic coal, which accelerated the recovery of iron and steel industries in these coal-producing areas.

For the reconstruction of iron and steel industry, GHQ gave a special permission for imports of heavy oil 1947. GHQ also promoted the establishment of Japan Oil Storage together with multinational oil enterprises such as Standard, Shell and Cartex in 1948, which ordered refining on commission to the Yokohama of Nippon Oil and Wakayama refinery near Osaka of Toa Nenryo Kogyo. In succession, GHQ of Supreme Command for the Allied Powers (SCAP) issued orders for re-operation of oil refinery on the Pacific and for imports of crude oil and promoted the establishment of joint concerns such as Toa with Standard, Nippon Oil with Cartex and Mitsubishi with Tide Warter in 1949. It was one of the main driving forces for recovery of the industrial areas and development on the Pacific side.

General Head Quarters had controlled almost all activities, not only in production but also in sales as was seen in the prohibition of domestic sales of field glasses, which resulted in developments of field glass industry as an export-oriented industry, mainly towards the United States. Therefore, most of all Japanese companies established and relocated their head offices in Tokyo where they could easily get the latest information on GHQ activities. As a result, Tokyo became the most important centre of business (Y. Miyakawa *Ekistics* 50, 1983) . The Korean War in 1950 urged the change of occupation policy and accelerated the recovery of Japan's economy. In 1950, Tokyo topped all the rest with 12.5 per cent of the total industrial output of Japan, followed by Osaka (12.3%), Hyogo (8.1%), Aichi (12.3%) and Kanagawa (6.1%). Special procurement contracts since the Korean War enabled the recovery of Japan's economy and politic's autonomy. In 1950, the Foreign Capital Induction Law was promulgated and in 1951, the San Fransisco Peace Treaty and Japan-U.S. Security Treaty were signed and at last, in 1952, GHQ was abolished.

Liberalization of Japan's Economy and Quasi-supranational organization

After the Second World War, advanced capitalistic countries established quasi-supranational organizations for accelerating the rehabilitation of world economy: IMF (International Monetary Fund) and International Bank for Reconstruction and Development (World Bank) were set up in 1946. In 1947, ECAFE (Economic Commission for Asia and the Far East) and GATT (General Agreement on Tariffs and Trade) were inaugurated and, in 1948, OEEC (Organization for European Economic Cooperation) was established. In these organizations, Japan became a member after 1952; IMF and IBRD approved Japan's membership in 1952, ECAFE in 1954 and GATT in 1955, when the government formulated five year plans for economic independence. Especially, the World Bank exerted a great influence on the development of Japan's heavy chemical industry and on the construction of Tokaido Megalopolis through its impact loans, as were seen in the following loans – Yahata Steel in 1955, Kawasaki Steel in 1956, Sumitomo Metal and Kobe Steel in 1958, Yahata Steel and Fuji Steel in 1959 and Kawasaki Steel and Sumitomo Metal in 1960. As a result, Japanese iron and steel industry developed remarkably by means of construction of integrated iron and steel works within the Pacific Industrial Belt, especially in the Tokaido Megalopolis' large metropolitan areas in response to the first (1951-1955) and second (1956-1960) rationalization plans for iron and steel industry on the one hand and on the other, it developed remarkably production technologies as was seen in the technological aids contracts with Taranto Iron and Steel Works in Italy in 1965. Another example is Toyota Motors in the Nagoya metropolitan area, which used WB loan in 1956, when Toyota Motors started its mass-production system, using imported machine tools. IMF loans (125 million dollars) also helped much Japan's economic growth, which was approved in 1957, when the EEC Treaty was signed. In 1959, the government offered 30 million bond issue in New York for public subscription, the first foreign bond after the Second World War, and the Finance Ministry adopted policy for liberalization of foreign trade and exchange transaction in response to the decision of GATT Tokyo Conference to promote liberalization of imports of 10 products such as pig iron. Regionally, WB loans for construction of Japan's first highway, Tomei-Mishi highway between Tokyo and Osaka, exerted a great influence on the agglomeration of economy and population into the Tokaido Megalopolis, the together with the construction of Tokaido bullet railway between them in 1964.

In 1960, when Latin America Free Trade Association was established and New Japan-U.S. Security treaty was signed, the Japanese Cabinet adopted basic policy for trade and exchange liberalization, aiming at achieving 80 per cent decontrol in three years. In this year, the income-doubling programme was announced and the Overseas Economic Cooperation Fund Law was promulgated, which exerted a great influence on industrialization of underdeveloping countries and, in turn, internationalization of Japanese industry. In this year, 20 Western nations signed OECD Treaty (revised and enlarged OEEC), which approved Japan's membership in 1963, when IMF recommended Japan to become Article 8 nation and GATT also to Article 11 nation, in response to liberalization of Japan's trade. It accelerated rationalization of Japanese industry and promoted reorganization of industrial structure, which exerted a great influence on the construction of New Industrial Cities but led to depression of textile areas due to the MITI's instructions to cotton spinners to impose production cutback ration urged by the agreement between Japan and the United States. In 1963, a Revised Foreign Exchange Control Ordinance was issued for the purpose of liberalization of capital transaction, which promoted foreign investments in Japan too. In response to internationalization, the government decided to construct Tsukuba academic town for technological development on the one hand and on the other, it accelerated scrap and built formula of coal-mines.

As a result of the Central Bank heads conference of seven nations on the gold pool system in 1968 and so-called dollar shock in 1971, the Japanese Government decided to shift yen in floating system. It accelerated the change of industrial system and structure, especially after the Oil Crisis, as was seen in the metamorphosis of coastal industrial complexes. And in 1974, National Land Utilization Planning Law was enacted and National Land Agency was established for promotion of regional development. Japan gradually overcame depression caused by the Oil Crisis and became the world centre of manufacturing production and a centre of world economy as was seen in the establishment of a branch of the World Bank in 1970, when Japan turned its position to be a supporter. The Japanese automobile industry may be a good example of this case. Owing to developments in the automobile industry in 1977, Aichi prefecture, including Nagoya metropolitan area, topped all others with 9.5 per cent of total output, followed by Kanagawa (9.1%), Osaka (9.0%) and Tokyo (8.6%) . However, most of all other important economic activities such as financial, information and trade are concentrating into the Tokyo metropolitan area, especially Tokyo, where a lot of foreign companies' offices and factories with high technology are agglomerated, in response to changed industrial structures by liberalization of finance and information in 1985. At present, Japan suffers very much from depression due to the rapid yen-up valuation in a short time, caused by the decision of the meeting of Five Finance Ministers in 1985 which depressed local industrial areas and also caused metamorphosis in leading industrial areas due to increased Japanese foreign investments and expansion of overseas production.

Conclusion and Postscript

In Japan, a supranational organization, GHQ, changed fundamentally Japan's industrial structure and system, just after the Second World War, which exerted a great influence on the regional development, especially in agricultural areas and in coal producing areas. And quasi-supranational organizations such as IMF, World Bank, GATT also exerted their influence on rehabilitation of Japan's economy and on development of Tokaido Megalopolis. The Liberalization policies urged by GATT also changed Japan's industrial system and promoted metamorphosis of regions.

Concerned with Japan's investment in EC and ASEAN, please refer to the *International Economic Restructuring* (1985, Y Miyakawa, UNIDO)

THIRTEEN

Land Development and its Impact on Land Prices: Seoul, Korea

YEONG-HEE JANG & LATA CHATTERJEE

INTRODUCTION

Rapid expansion of the urban population in the developing countries, particularly in the last two or three decades, has posed a major challenge to their urban and national planners. The rapid growth rates have placed an inordinate pressure on the limited supply of the urbanized land and the demand has dramatically and consistently driven up land prices. Two strategies have been adopted in these countries to reduce the gap between the demand for and supply of urbanized lots; the improvement of the efficiency of land use in the existing built up areas, and the rapid expansion of urban boundaries through peripheral land development. The land development in built up areas is an expensive and complex process that entails land assembly, demolition of existing structures and capital investment to change the current patterns and uses. Consequently the major source of new urban land in rapidly growing metropolitan areas is the rural to urban land conversion in the periphery. Peripheral expansion requires the provision of roads, sewers, water supply and utilities on rural land. As the installation of these services has been expensive, the supply of urbanized land has not kept pace with the expanding demand.

The increasing gap between the demand for and the supply of urbanized land has resulted in high land prices. Several factors explain high prices. First, there is this scarcity of urbanized land with good access to employment opportunities and urban amenities. Second, urban land ownership is recognised as a lucrative form of financial investment in developing countries. In the absence of the limited existence of profitable investment alternatives a substantial amount of household savings is channelled to land ownership. Since there is too much money relative to available land this has had inflationary impacts. Third, given this rate of inflation speculative gains can be made through land ownership and this further accelerates the demand for urban land fuelling a process of cumulative inflation of land prices.

Rapid inflation in land prices has promoted government intervention in the provision of urban land. Government intervention in urban land markets is commonly justified on grounds of efficiency, such as the protection of valuable agricultural land, curtailment of urban sprawl or the achievement of the "highest and best use" of the land in planning terms. In addition, substantial amounts of initial investment are required for the provision of basic infrastructure facilities. These development costs are not always immediately recoverable from the price of developed land. While the private sector may recover the costs of onsite infrastructure in selected upper income projects, for the most part the public sector has to install off site infrastructure as well as the onsite infrastructure for moderate and lower-income households.

The high initial investment in land development has imposed severe constraints for the public sector. The Local governments have limited financial capabilities and this has restricted urban land development. Different countries have responded to the need for public intervention in a variety of ways. Some important new policies for land use management which have been employed recently include environmental conservation planning (U.K., USA, Switzerland), the adoption of various land use regulations such as the right of first priority given to public authorities (Sweden, Germany) and land readjustment schemes (Japan, Korea, India, Taiwan and Australia). The Land Readjustment Method is a mechanism that attempts to minimize the financial constraints faced by land development agencies. This method not only permits self-financing of urban land development, it also facilitates the acquisition of land for the provision of public facilities such as schools, parks and community facilities.

This paper discusses the implementation of the land readjustment method in South Korea. This method has accounted for approximately 90 per cent of the new land developed in urban areas in the last two decades. In Korea the areas developed or that are being developed by this method accounted for 14.4 per cent of the total urban area (138 sq. miles or 357.58 sq. km). However, in Seoul 58 per cent of the urban area (47 sq. miles or 121.96 sq. km) had been developed through Land Readjustment Projects (LRP) by 1978 (City of Seoul 1978).

The purpose of this paper is to examine the land readjustment method and its influence on land prices in Korea. In section 2 some distinguishing features of the LRP's in Seoul will be highlighted. Its effects on the land prices will be considered in section 3.

Land Readjustment as an Urban Development Mechanism in Seoul

Land Readjustment Method is distinctive in its means of raising funds for urbanizing land. The land readjustment procedure includes the compulsory seizure of land from existing land owners until the planning and development are finished. After development a portion of the urbanized land is redistributed to the original owners in the form of urbanized plots in the same area. Land owners who benefit from the improved value of the land bear all the cost for the urbanization of their land. The self-financing mechanism of the LRP addresses the serious problems of inadequate public finance and conflicts in capital budgeting that are common to governments in developing countries. Under alternative procedures employed in other countries, infrastructure costs are imposed on a large group of tax payers, who are then motivated to oppose development. It can also be contrasted to the method of betterment levies for recovering the costs. Poor collection of betterment levies has posed a severe constraint for a continuous process of land development in urban areas.

The roots of land readjustment lie in the law concerning land transfer (Lex Addickes) that was first adopted in Frankfurt-am-Main; Germany in 1902 (NULRA 1966). Since then it has been adopted in Japan, South Korea, and other countries. In Japan it became the most important mechanism for urban land development since the concept was formally incorporated into the city planning act of 1919. It was particularly important in the rebuilding of Japanese cities after the great earthquake in 1923, the bombing of Second World War and typhoons and other natural disasters

(Doebele 1982). By 1965 about 27 per cent (580 sq. miles) of the total urban area in Japan had been or was under the land readjustment scheme.

In contrast to Japan, where the system has been much more dependent on private landowners voluntarily organizing themselves, often with the help of land readjustment organizations to make their own site plan for their collective holdings, the South Korean scheme has largely been initiated and implemented by the government (NULRA 1966, Doebele 1982). Although the Land Readjustment Law specifies four groups who can implement a LRP: namely the Korea Housing Corporation, Construction Ministry of the central government, the local (city) government, and an individual owner or group of land owners (either as a group or as an incorporated body)[1], most of the land readjustment projects done so far were undertaken by the local government.

The city government accounted for 38 of the 43 Land Readjustment Projects in Seoul by 1977, and approximately 93 per cent of the total developed area (Table 13.1). The average size of the government sponsored Projects was also larger than the private development. Whereas the average size of privately sponsored projects was 564 pyeongs, the average size of the government sponsored projects was 904 pyeongs.

TABLE 13.1: **Percentage of Korean Land Readjustment Projects in Seoul by Various Institutions**

Implementing Agency	Number of Projects	Area of Projects (Pyeong)	Per cent
Private or Association	3	1,693,115	4.58
Korean Housing Corporation	2	923,001	2.50
City of Seoul (local Govt.)	38	34,344,232	92.22
Total	43	36,960,348	100.00

Source : Ministry of Construction, 1977.

The public authorities have three main roles in LRPs: area selection, layout planning, and actual development. Development activities consist of rearranging the shape of plots, land grading, constructing basic infrastructure such as roads, water and sewage systems, providing recreation areas like parks and play grounds and reallocating housing sites on the basis of the new layout. The initial infrastructure costs in the land readjustment scheme are financed by a special government account. However, the costs after development are recovered through an appropriation of a portion of the urbanized land prior to land disbursement. This acquired land is sold through auctions and the special government account is replenished. The amount of land appropriated for cost recovery is expressed through a reduction rate in each project which varies by project.

There, are two mechanisms through which the government recovers costs: (1) through public land acquisition; (2) through cost equivalent acquisition. Public land is acquired for roads, parks, markets, and schools. They account for approximately 25 to 30 per cent of the total project area. Cost equivalent acquisition allows the recovery of the costs of installation of public facilities and administrative expenses. In the 38 L.R. projects in Seoul cost equivalent acquisition ranged from 6 to 20 per cent of the total project area. This large variation in land acquired by the project authorities for recovering costs partly results from the variation in the actual costs of development caused by topographic differences. The amount of serviced lots that the land readjustment agency must take over and sell to recover the project expenses also depends on the market value of serviced land. Therefore, in order to recover its development costs, the agency uses an elaborate strategy to develop and sell the land at the highest price it can get. In order to get the highest price the readjustment agency invests in community facilities, stimulates high income housing, and provides various tax exemptions to buyers. In addition, the agency auctions the highest value land–thus they adopt a type of mini growth centre strategy, with several mini-growth poles designated within a project area. These centres have the highest value land, as they have commercial use.

Land Readjustment and its Impact on Land Prices in Seoul

The scale of contributions of LRP's to total developed area is shown in Table 13.2. The readjusted area accounted for approximately 58 per cent of the total developed area in 1973. About 80 per cent of the readjusted area was set aside for residential purposes and Hwang (1976) estimates that this was equivalent to 430,000 dwelling sites.

During the 1960s when a variety of city development programmes such as the construction of major radial highways into the capital and the accompanying rearrangement of land along these roads were actively carried out, project areas were selected with the primary intention of securing land for arterials. This is illustrated in Figure 13.1.

TABLE 13.2: **Contributions of LRP to the Development of Seoul**

	in km^2
Total area (1973)	613.00
Total developed area (1973)	193.37
Total Residential area (1973)	118.62
Total Readjusted area	112.47
Readjusted area for residential purpose (1960-73)	94.45

Source: *Seoul Statistical Yearbook*, 1975.

These arterials also facilitated transportation and most of the projects are currently well connected to the central city. Areas developed before the 70's were within a 10-km. ring. Due to the rapid utilisation of the vacant land within the ring the post seventies projects are primarily in the 10 to 15 km. ring. The newer projects are predominantly in the southern part of the city.

Twelve projects were selected for analysing the pattern of land uses. The land returned to the land owners varied from 40 per cent to 73 per cent (Table 13.3). Thus there is considerable variation between projects. Land retained for public use accounted for approximately 30 per cent of the total area. While there is not much variation around this mean (with the significant exceptions of Kuro and Jamsil) a time trend can be discerned. Since 1967 there has been an increase in the amount of land retained for public use. In the projects designed in 1967 an average of 25 per cent of total land was retained for public use. The corresponding figures for projects initiated in 1968 and post-1974 are 31 per cent and 37 per cent respectively. The increase is most marked in land set aside for parks and schools. The increase in public lands reflects the economic and social needs at the time of development, particularly the increasing standards of public facilities that follow the rise in per capita incomes. A similar trend can be seen in the amount of land retained for cost recovery. In the projects initiated in 1967 an average of 5.5 per cent of land was retained as cost equivalent acquisition.The figures for projects initiated in 1968 and post-1974 are 9.5 per cent and 19 per cent respectively. This increase reflects the increasing costs of land development in this period. As can be expected the original landowners shares in the 1967-80 period have also declined from 69 per cent in the 1967 project, to 47 per cent in the post-1974 projects.

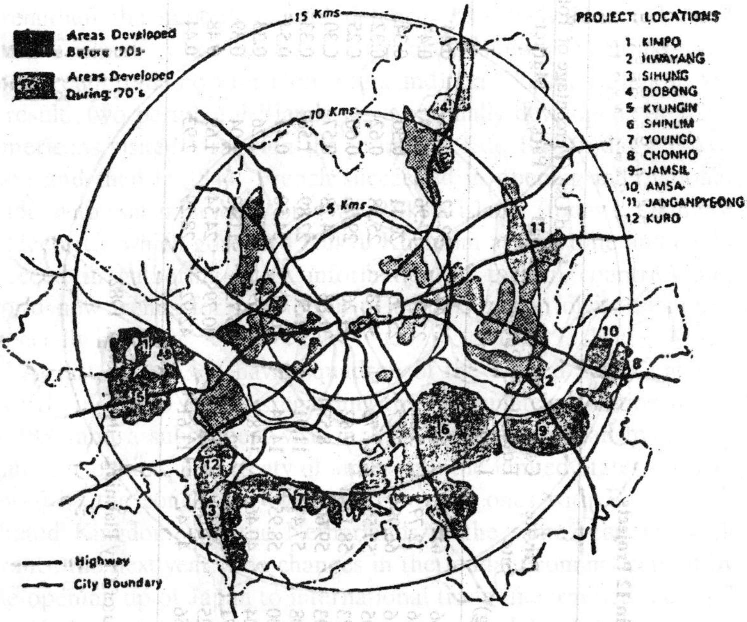

FIG. 13.1: Land Readjustment Projects in Seoul, Korea

Source: Readjustment Department Bureau of City Planning, City of Seoul, 1982.

While the landowner's share of land has declined since 1967 this is not reflected in the landowners' share of value increment. Due to the rapid inflation in land prices in Seoul the landowners have made and are making substantial windfall gains, even though they are getting back a smaller share than in the earlier projects. These windfall gains have created equity problems and have had political and

TABLE 13.3: **Variation in Land Use in 12 Projects**

Projects	Development Period	Total Area (Pyeong)	Private Site	Cost-Equivalent Land	Total Public Land	Land Use (Percentage of Total Developed Area)						
						Road	Park	Market	School	Others	Total	Reduction Rate.
Kimpo	1967-79	1,423,666	65.75	6.38	27.87	22.52	0.63	0.44	1.60	2.68	100.00	32.5
Hwayang	1967-72	1,066,826	72.77	5.04	22.19	17.96	0.53	0.47	1.06	2.17	100.00	29.4
Sihung	1968-79	1,736,416	66.98	7.27	25.75	23.41	0.30	0.34	0.64	1.06	100.00	31.0
Debong	1968-78	812,405	57.55	11.72	30.73	25.58	0.62	0.32	0.43	3.78	100.00	36.3
Kyungin	1968-78	2,212,373	58.12	7.62	34.26	29.76	0.60	0.25	0.68	2.97	100.00	32.0
Shinlim	1970	1,651,603	59.60	8.57	31.83	24.28	0.57	0.30	1.09	5.59	100.00	32.0
Youngdong	1968-79	9,620,008	57.41	11.01	31.58	22.89	1.58	0.33	1.04	5.75	100.00	39.6
Chonho	1972-79	785,000	58.95	14.24	26.81	24.50	0.41	0.54	1.36	0.00	100.00	39.4
Jamsil	1974-78	3,374,804	40.46	13.85	45.69	17.61	1.26	0.33	3.79	22.71	100.00	52.9
Amsa	1976-79	513,371	51.19	22.09	26.72	11.43	1.04	0.39	4.01	9.85	100.00	56.0
Janganpyung	1976-80	584,525	42.00	27.21	30.79	24.54	1.69	0.48	1.56	2.52	100.00	53.8
Kuro	1979-	446,156	45.47	11.61	42.92	28.29	2.93	0.44	7.43	3.84	100.00	54.4

Source : Readjustment Dept., Bureau of City Planning, City of Seoul, 1982.

administrative implications. In the following section trends in land prices are analysed and the equity implications are highlighted, in the concluding section.

Trends in Land Prices

Although the land prices vary with the location and level of facilities found in a project, a smaller serviced lot has a value several times higher than a larger unserviced one. For this reason land owners in the fringe areas are very eager to have their land involved in a LRP, inspite of the fact that 35 to 55 per cent of their land is withheld by the planning agency for public use and cost recovery. Moreover, the inflation in land prices has increased the gains made by the original landowners, particularly when they are able to hold on to the land in the post-development period.

While the land prices have increased in all areas of Seoul, the highest increase was recorded in the outer zone of the city which is located between 10-15 km. ring from the centre (see Figure 13.1). If the city is divided into 0-5, 5-10, 10-15 km. rings (using direct distance from the centre), the average price increases of each ring during the period of 1965-80, were 44, 122, and 140 times respectively (KRIHS, 1982). The rates of increase considerably exceed the CPI (consumer price index) increase of 8 times and the increase in per capita GNP of 14 times during the same period.

To what extent has the LRP contributed to the increase in land prices? As noted earlier increase in land prices result from several factors. A major factor is the undersupply of land relative to demand. The city of Seoul has de facto (though not de jure) monopoly powers over land development. The supply of urbanized land, through the readjustment mechanism has not kept pace with the demand generated by the expanding Korean economy, the rise in per capita incomes and the increased migration to the metropolis. The Government's unwillingness to permit enough rural-urban land conversion to meet the need of rapid demographic and economic growth of Seoul is viewed by many as a major cause of this inflationary spiral in land prices and the consequent rise in windfall gains made by the landowners. From Figure 13.2 it is evident that 50 to 100 per cent annual increase in land prices is found in several years during the 1965-78 period.

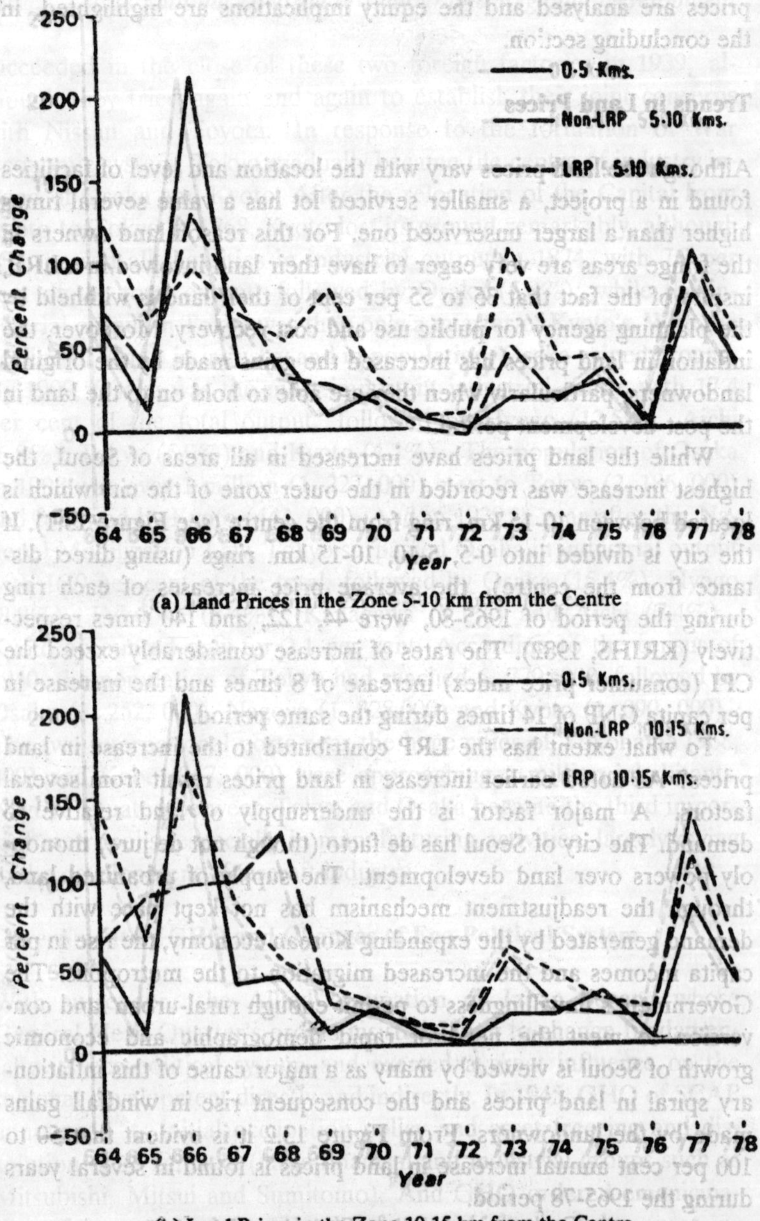

(a) Land Prices in the Zone 5-10 km from the Centre

(b) Land Prices in the Zone 10-15 km from the Centre

FIG. 13.2: Land Price Fluctuations in Seoul; 1963-78

Source: Housing Information, Korean Housing Business Association, 1981.

Some of the peaks in Figure 13.2 indicate that the land prices are very sensitive to changes in general economy. For example, the initiation of 5 Year Economic Development Plan in early 1960s and the money flow from the Middle East in late 1970s corresponds with the two culminating points in land price increase in 1962-67 and 1967-78 respectively. The other two peaks in 1967-69 (Fig. 13.2a) and 1972-73 (Figs. 13.2a and 13.2b) were largely caused by the commencement of large scale urban development in outer ring areas. The two peaks in 1967-68 and 1976-77 in non-LRP areas (Fig. 13.2b) can be attributed to the speculative activities which spread to non-LRP areas, from surrounding areas of LRP.

Is there a difference, in land price increase, between LRP and non-LRP areas? LRP's can be subdivided into smaller areal units called precincts. Average rates of price increase in 25 sampled precincts were examined for the purpose of distinguishing the difference in price increase between LRP and non-LRP areas. Five precincts were randomly selected among LRP and non-LRP areas each in the 5-10 km and 10-15 km ring and only non-LRP precincts were included for the 0-5 km-ring. The price fluctuations in the 5-10 km rings showed that the LRP areas had a higher rate of price increase in comparison to non-LRP areas during the 1965-78 period, except for the 1966-67 period. However, LRP's were not well developed and were a new experiment in that period. In the 10-15 km ring the pattern of price differences is not so clear and in the 1967-69 and 1976-78 period the price increase in non-LRP areas was higher than in the LRP areas.

In order to assess the price trend in areas developed by LRP, 63 precincts mostly belonging to outer ring, were examined to determine the average rate of increase and standard deviation for the period of 1970-81. Three kinds of prices, highest, medium, lowest price within the precinct, were analysed. This is illustrated in Table 13.4. There are some clear variations in the average rate of price increase and the standard deviations. First, the higher rates of price increase are generally found in areas that also have higher standard deviations. Thus these areas have the largest variations as well as the largest increase in prices. The areas with the highest land values also have lower standard deviations, indicating that these areas remained relatively stable compared to the lower price areas. Medium and lowest price areas, in many projects, show a tendency for a higher rate of price increase as well as a wider range of standard deviation. This implies that people tend to invest more in the fringe areas where the prices are still low in comparison to the core areas of the projects. In fact speculation activities in the peripheral areas within the LRP's have been observed for the past few years.

TABLE 13.4: **Average Rate of Land Price Increase in LR Projects by Standard Deviation**

Standard Deviation	Land Price Classification					
	*Highest Price Projects (in %)		Medium Price Projects (in %)		Lowest Price Projects (in %)	
$\sigma<5$	2	29.51	2	33.56	4	40.46
	3	31.52			10	74.15
	4	41.11			11	55.88
	7	35.01				
	10	29.01				
$5\leq\sigma<10$	1	38.03	1	46.85	2	52.79
	5	37.07	3	38.46	3	49.86
	6	51.08	4	48.26	5	66.47
	8	41.67	5	45.19	7	47.45
	11	33.63	9	56.82	8	68.54
	12	27.32	12	31.51	12	59.79
$\sigma\geq10$	9	54.72	6	65.57	1	65.09
			7	67.50	6	85.84
			8	53.45	9	95.28
			10	45.94		
			11	46.41		

*see Figure 13.1 for the location of the projects.

Source : *Land value Survey*, Korea Appraisal Board, 1967-1982.

Concluding Comments

While South Korea is commended internationally for its efficient urban land development in the context of limited financial resources of a developing country, the city of Seoul is domestically under attack for the high price of land. The timing and scheduling of land development and its marketing policy in LRP's has raised questions about equity. First, the landowners fortunate enough to have their lands involved in LRP projects have realised economic rents due to the scarcity value of urbanized land. They have made windfall gains.

In order to recover costs the development of low cost sites has also been neglected, consequently low income households have not benefited from the LRP's. Further the slow pace of land development relative to need has increased land prices even in non-LRP areas and thus low income households are priced out of the market in non-LRP areas as well. The desire to keep the LRP prices high so as to recover costs and the pace of land development have combined to increase the hardship of low income households.

In order to increase equity two solutions have been proposed by an international study group (Shoup, 1978). First more of the developed sites should be retained for cost recovery, that is the reduction rate should be even higher. A higher reduction rate will permit lower income households to be cross subsidized. Moreover a higher rate of withholding will reduce some of the windfall gains made by the large landowners. A higher reduction rate would allow the Government to provide sites for low income housing.

Second, the Government should increase the pace of land development so as to put a downward pressure on the price of serviced land. Speculative gains will be reduced when the gap between the demand and supply of urbanized lots are minimized.

The LRP has considerable potential applicability for providing low cost sites through the revision of the policy in the future. As Doebele puts it:

> If land readjustment projects are properly conducted, their net result is to create new urbanization for the city at no expense to itself, and at a reasonable profit to the owners involved.

In almost every major city in developing countries of the world, rapidly rising urban land values appear to be a serious problem. The urban land requires a high level of public services and consequently there is a gap between the need for urban land and its supply. This gap results partly from the limited level of investment available for the provision of public services.

The development of sufficient urban land to meet the urban needs has frequently been restricted by the requirement for large amounts of public investment. Shortage of municipal resources in most developing countries has deterred urban development causing public services to fall behind the demands made by the continuously increasing population. The experience of Korea shows that the LRP is an important tool for land development. Its advantage lies in the self-financing characteristics of the process and the limited financial demands made on the public sector. Its weakness has been the high price increase, which partly results from a slow process of land development for which the government has had a monopoly power. This high increase in land prices has had an adverse effect on low income households and attempts are being explored to address these weaknesses through cross subsidies. If the disadvantages of high prices are minimized, then the LRP can be viewed as a useful mechanism for urban development in developing countries that have a shortage of public finance.

NOTE

1. They are required to obtain an agreement on the proposed plan from two thirds of the land owners involved and an approval from the appropriate government agencies.

REFERENCES

City of Seoul, (1978). "A study of Land Reallocation Method",

Doebele, W.A., (1977). "Land Policy in Seoul and Gwanju, with Special Reference to Land Readjustment", World Bank Draft Report.

Doebele, W.A. (ed), (1982). *Land Readjustment*, Lexington BooKs.

Hwang, M.C., *Self Help Site Development in Korea: An Overall Evaluation*, Korea Research Institute for Human Settlement, Seoul.

KRIHS Data for the First National Development Plan 1982.

NULRA Tochi Kukaku Seiki (Land Readjustment in Japan) 1966.

FOURTEEN

Regional Development, International Division of Labour and the South of Italy

ATTILIO CELANT

Introduction or the Explicit Formulation of a Few Problems

The present paper aims at analysing the economic effects of progressive economic internationalization and the specific influence international division of labour has on backward areas in advanced countries; it shall deal, at the same time, with the adjustment that regional development policies must undergo as a consequence of these effects. Indeed, it is well known that if strong and weak regions establish consistent relationships and no specific action is undertaken to support fragile economic structures, this produces grievous consequences on the latter, and favours stronger regions. This introductory consideration implies that policy in favour of backward regions requires progressive reappraisal and updating as the economic integration process takes place. Indeed, traditional instruments to control and stimulate an economy may become too old or inadequate in dealing with economic conditions that are different from – more complex than – those where such instruments were originally studied and put into practice. A changed context requires an appropriate correction of policy measures.

The experience of the last 15 years, however, shows that under-developed areas are affected by problems that are even more complex and delicate than those related to economic and territorial integration. The internationalization of economic systems or, better, the particularly advanced stage reached by the ubiquitous diffusion of industrial production (which process receives a major thrust by technological progress in the transport sector) produces a clear cut reduction of distances. In economic terms, this means that the cost of transportation has an increasingly minor incidence on total cost of production. This implies that competition among regions or among industrial structures tends to be increasingly based on relative productivity or, better, on the degree of efficiency achieved by the specific combination of the productive factors employed, indpendently of transport costs, that is, of distance. Thus, the internationalization of economic systems clearly favours stronger countries; but it is also going, to favour those economies that will have the possibility and the capability to control costs of production. An increasing role in such a productive rationalization will be played by the cost of labour and, consequently, by the international division of labour.

It is also worth noting that productive integration within macro-spaces and differing degrees of efficiency do not only produce conflicts and push weaker structures into having a marginal role within the international economy – these effects can be deduced by means of instruments of static analysis such as indifference curves, costs of production, research on industrial agglomerates, externalities etc.; they also lead to and progressively favour, the new role of dynamic economic factors, that is, economic processes. Giant productive structures are not as important as they previously were or, at least, they are not the only ones to exert a positive effect on economic growth. There are highly dynamic productive structures catching up and sometimes taking their place, forms of production or regions that are in the best conditions to introduce and produce technical progress and technical innovation. Recent history of great industrial areas in Europe and North America provides quite a few examples : the rapid de-industrialization of regions that were defined strong up to a few years ago, the deadlock in some basic goods industries and, conversely, the rise of new industrial regions, the growing competition by NICs : all these elements prove that there is a structural crisis in our industrial pattern of growth, if not in our industrial "culture" as a whole. But they also show the importance and the dynamic role of recently developed productive sectors which consist in new kinds of equipment that use highly sophisticated technology, computers and robots.

The economic upswing in some regions and the extraordinary vitality of the new industrial sectors should render us quite optimistic about a take-off in European underdeveloped areas such as Italy's South but some elements force us to be a little more cautious. In the first place, backward areas in advanced countries are affected by forms of inelasticity that do not allow a growth process to begin. The cost of factors of production is not always spatially differentiated : the cost of capital, the cost of labour, etc., in a country's weaker regions are, in spite of all incentives introduced, substantially the same as in its stronger regions. Different conditions could hardly exist and it is, therefore, important to stress how all this implies quite a few negative consequences for the weaker areas. Indeed, such areas suffer (and will support the increasing losses coming from) the harsh competition by other peripheral areas, where some of the costs can be cut down – consider, for instance, the low cost of labour in Third World countries. Furthermore, contrary to what occurs in backward countries – where development strategies consist in importing mature technologies and in compensating the diseconomies related to obsolete productive processes with lower wages – this behaviour is not possible in underdeveloped areas because of the above mentioned forms of inelasticity. The forms of inelasticity practically prevent the substitution of cheap factors for more expensive ones (as we previously noted, the cost of labour in advanced countries is substantially the same all over their territory), so mature technology only means a higher cost of production and uncompetitive products. On the other hand, advanced technology implies, for well known reasons, a high level of investment and priority to industrial sectors that are characterized by a high or higher (K/L) ratio and little use of manpower. This situation clashes with the most common features of weak regions : abundant labour and little capital.

There is a second important reason for the bad performance of backward areas in advanced countries when compared with NICs and with the more dynamic and active countries of the Third World. Under-development in Third World countries, as well as in some European regions (including also a part of Italy's South) is very difficult to overcome because productive structures are weak and do not take off but the major reason is that the nature of these societies is intrinsically very static and has crystallized social patterns. This is the major and the crucial obstacle to be removed : human society has to become dynamic.

If we accept this principle, we realize that the development of a region is a phenomenon only partially related to economic policies and strategies. Action for regional development can be defined as a necessary but not sufficient condition. Indeed, it is absolutely necessary, in these cases, to go beyond economic action, to try to initiate mechanisms that may produce territoriality and introduce society into dynamic phenomena such as cultural growth, a greater tendency to acquire new technologies, the identification of goals to be pursued. Economic thought can achieve very few goals unless the principles it is based on are accepted and assimilated. The development policy, therefore, requires a preliminary action, which must aim at ideological involvement, at providing a behavioural philosophy, at initiating a process of social evolution and promotion, in order to permit economic mechanisms to be understood and to stimulate interest in participation – in the absence of which there can be no growth.

It is less from per capita income or from the structure of the active population than from the comparison between the static nature of some social and productive structures and the dynamic nature of other developed or developing countries that existing gaps show up and become clear. Only the comparison between different processes, the analysis of different growth patterns, the study of territoriality, thus of the society – space – time triad, will provide indications and guidelines so that development policies may have an adequate background and a chance of success.

Underdeveloped Areas and Economic Internationalization

A Few Preliminaries on Italy

The economic backwardness of Italy's South and the regional policies to reduce productivity gaps between different territories constitute two issues that can be interpreted and dealt with only within a national framework. From this point of view underdevelopment in Italy's South is first of all an Italian problem, which can be substantially solved only through Italy's overall economic policy.

This does not mean that the national economy is the only context where these problems are originated and become so relevant and where corresponding solutions may be identified. Indeed, there is no doubt that – independently of national causes or of possible responsibilities of the State authorities – Italy's economically backward regions suffer the consequences of various elements related to the progressive introduction of such regions into supernational productive contexts. Positive effects do exist, even though they can be usually noticed only in the long period, but negative effects prevail in the short period. The internationalization of economic systems favours stronger and more advanced productive structures and areas, at the expense of late coming regions which are witnessing to the formation of new types of colonization and of economic dependence. The greater the freedom of the productive structures within these territorial systems – that is, the more competition without appropriate protection of weaker structures there is – the more intensive is the phenomenon. These considerations are well known to all those who deal with these issues. Obviously the weakness and scarce firmness of the productive pattern in economically peripheral areas, the technological backwardness and the scarce efficiency of marginal territorial structures favour strong regions, which extend their markets, thus contributing to the elimination of all those competing firms that suffer local conditions and cannot but carry out their productive activity at definitely higher costs.

We must not fail to consider the consequences that the institution of the EEC and the enhancement of its policies had on Italy's South. The regions of Southern Italy constitute the major problem area of the European Economic Community and the scarce economic protection they had up to now certainly contributed to retard their development.

Even though the major responsibility lies in the Italian authorities, we cannot disregard that the development of the European economy as a whole implies at least two drawbacks for the South. First, as we previously noted, the South pays for the weakness of its productive (as well as social) structures, which clash with those of Central Europe and are thereby extruded and rendered more peripheral, with probably fewer chances of recovery. Second, measures taken at a European level – which are not just by change the result of complex negotiations between the representatives of member countries – differ from those that would have been taken at a national level. Here too, the highest price is paid by the weaker regions (if not for objective reasons, for the intrinsic incapability to support further burdens) and the South suffers worse consequences than it should. There are many cases that provide evidence for what is being said here and it is not really worth presenting them here.

However, the issue will be better understood if we keep in mind the solutions recently provided to the problems of the steel industry, to those – dating up to some years ago – of the Regional Development Fund and to those concerning agriculture.

Undoubtedly economic integration has positive effects on backward regions, due to the drag effects that, in one way or another, favour the economic growth of a macro-area as a whole. However, 30 years after the institution of the European Economic Community we can see that all regions grow but at different rates, and slow-developing areas keep on falling behind. We may conclude that, if there will be no specific action for the recovery of weaker areas, productivity gaps will not be reduced and those areas will become more and more peripheral.

Regional Policies and the Constraints arising from International Division of Labour Constraints

Progressive economic internationalization is not restricted to a merely continental level, nor does it only imply a negotiated integration of national economies. Since quite a few years ago, an advanced process of internationalization of productive structures has been taking place, which has produced its effects on underdeveloped regions and, consequently, on regional policies aiming at their recovery. So all action to develop the South and all attempts to identify appropriate strategies to overcome underdevelopment in this vast area of Europe absolutely must not consider only European economic integration but also what is occurring in the economies of Mediterranean countries and, in general, in the Third World countries. The reasons for this are all very well known.

It is some time now, at least twenty years, that we are witnessing to a slow, discontinuous yet progressive and probably unavoidable and irreversible transfer of industrial activities from developed regions onto some of the developing areas. It is an apparently linear and obvious phenomenon since it seems to reflect a fundamentally liberistic rationale, where an absolute mobility of productive factors is assumed. Things are not exactly like this, and not just because actual events are always a bit more complex than theoretical models. The point is that the location of industrial plants in Third World countries is a phenomenon we may easily compare to the top of an iceberg, it is hard to interpret and its dynamic and evolution are determined by multiple causes.

Things may appear clearer if we remember that we are discussing an economic phenomenon which is, therefore, related to the operating of economic principles; from this point of view, a good theoretical approach may be provided by Weber's location theory. Industrial location in a free-trade economy cannot disregard cost factors, so transnational firms–at a continental when not intercontinental level–tend to set up new industrial activities in regions where they manage to spend less. From this point of view, the low cost of labour in the Third World countries is a particularly inviting element for entrepreneurs–particularly with respect to goods that have a high incidence of labour costs over total costs.

Truly the condition of a balance between higher costs for transportation and lower costs for labour, however, necessary, is luckily not sufficient and does not produce significant transfers of industrial activities. The relevant changes in the way new industrial sites are chosen require much more, including political stability, a social and cultural environment capable of perceiving modern forms of production, etc. There is no doubt, however, that decentralization is actually taking place and this proves that some regions of the world have become particularly favourable from an economic point of view.

All these cases show a somewhat unusual convergence between the action of transnational firms and some stimulating approaches to development strategies in underdeveloped areas of the world. Every body knows the Brandt Report and the "New International Order" approach which expected a growing role and economic involvement of developing countries. In fact, as far as the "New International Order" approach is concerned, assumptions are extremely vague and appear to be much more a list of what is derivable than a somewhat operative proposal. This approach foresees an eminently economic process whereas it pursues goals that are of a more political and humanitarian nature.

A deeper analysis shows that, inevitably, the policies of transnational firms and the assumptions of the Brandt Report go different ways, in spite of their apparently common goal, i.e. the industrialization of the Third World. It is not worth going into the details of this issue since the aim of the present paper is to identify regional development policies tnat take into account the influence exerted by international division of labour; a preliminary assessment may, therefore, be sufficient. It is certainly true that the identification of an appropriate regional policy would require the assumptions underlying the perspective of the New International Order to be very clear and it would, therefore, be better if the latter were more precisely defined. Truly the analysis carried out by the Brandt Report (and, to some extent, by the previous U.N. Report edited by W. Leontieff) on the chances for stronger North-South trade and for a new economic role of developing countries, does not provide a clear outlook on the future order of the world economy. More precisely, what is still indefinite is the industrial role of the developing countries and the red issue one feels like raising is not what configuration the New International Order will have but whether there will actually be such an order or not. The New International Order proves to be, at present, a very remote and abstract goal even when we look at the development of industrial location and of the productive sectors it affects, which are much closer to the logic and the interests of transnational firms than to the utopistic principles that should act as guidelines for a planned growth of backward countrie

Aside from this, a pro‹ ‹s aiming at a New International Order implies the solution of ‹ ‹me not irrelevant preliminary problems. Let us dismiss internat‹‹nal issues and concentrate on the specific features of developing countries : these countries would have to provide a solution to : previously domestic conflicts between modernizing groups and traditional society; the problem of the legitimation of classes in power and, more generally, of the central government's power; religious conflicts – mostly due to the diffusion of Islam, etc. These problems still have to be solved and economic development in some of these countries appears to be much closer, linked to, and may be also determined by, the interests of the multinationals than to the unlikely growth expectations of the Brandt Report.

It is also worth noting, that, as Sylos Labini (1983) pointed out, the location by transnational firms of new industrial activities in the backward regions of the world is, in one way or other, a way to set-off deveıopment – however slow the latter may be. Consequently, foreign investment by transnational firms has to be considered a positive factor for these countries. But the major element influencing international capital movement consists in potential profit margins and, therefore, the allocation of capital considerably depends on the cost of productive factors, particularly of labour.

No philanthropic motives are leading to the establishment of a New International Order or providing the guidelines for a successful emergence of the Newly Industrialized Countries. It is through the iron law of private interests and the prevailing, unambiguous and straightforward rules of the market that the transfer of mature industrial activities onto specific and restricted underdeveloped regions clashes both with expected economic growth in underdeveloped areas of advanced countries and with traditional regional policies for backward countries.

International industrial location mechanisms that have no reference to a specific idea of Third World development and are much more related to the curbing of production costs, check many regional policies. This occurs while a drastic reduction in potentially propulsive sectors and in the possibilities of intervention is taking place.

While industrial reconversion within highly industrialized areas is producing delocation and displacement of all activities that use low-technology, competition by demographically intensive regions is altering the previously established pattern of growth – which consisted in extending production to neighbouring territories. This forces whoever deals with regional policy in underdeveloped areas to acknowledge that it is impossible to introduce productive sectors that are already involved in the International Division of Labour into these areas' development programmes.

Italy's South, a vast peripheral area within economically developed Europe, is greatly affected by these changes. Ubiquitous industrial location, that is, the building of industrial plants wherever, productive conditions are most favourable independently of transport costs which are definitely low, renders the development outlook on Southern Italy's regions quite negative, because of inelasticities which can hardly be eliminated Competition by emerging areas of the world is particularly strong because lower factor costs go along with a remarkable economic vitality, practically no social conflicts and a substantial political stability.

The influence of International Division of Labour – which is quite different from the case of a New International Order – is going to affect the evolution of the world economy in a considerable way (cf. the estimates made by W. Leontieff in the above-mentioned book) and growth in some Third World countries will be prejudicial to growth in underdeveloped areas of Western Europe and North America. The issue, in the latter, is to realistically search for alternatives and rapidly put them into practice.

As to the South of Italy, its development outlook is definitely negative. Undoubtedly, a considerable part of Southern Italy has – in one way or the other–undergone a take-off process, since government action did achieve some results in the last 30 years, and Italy's underdevelopment has definitely undergone some changes since the end of the First World War. However, estimates show that at least a million new jobs will have to be created in the peripheral areas of the South. Some jobs may eventually be created by the service industry, especially that part of the industry that uses high technology and that deals with the manufacturing industry (as opposed to households) and with tourism. But it is the manufacturing industry that will have to actually provide a solution to unemployment. The question, here, is which sectors have to be enhanced. Fig. 14.1 and Fig. 14.2 show the evolution of the official discount rate and of the cost of labour (*source*: IMF) during a significant time interval. Let us immediately point out: (1) the extremely high cost of capital in Italy (thus also the South) – note that the prime rate exceeds the Bank of Italy's discount rate by at least two point – and the exponential trend in the cost of labour (the index number 1980=100 is based on the weighted average of nationally negotiated wage-rates); (2) the cost of capital could be lowered (it is worth recalling that high interest rates are due to the government's need to finance its enormous debt, which is one of the major causes for inflation: should government debt be curbed, the cost of capital would go down) but this is not the case for the cost of labour. Thus, in spite of a great deal of unemployed or underemployed labour, capital is considered more convenient, just as in the past, and capital intensive sectors are believed to be more favourable. As the incidence of labour increases, the competitiveness of the output decreases, unless wages go well below negotiated minimums (a phenomenon that is actually occurring in some Southern and Mid-Northern areas and that is a major factor for the spread of a "submerged" economy). This is true both for industries supplying domestic markets and–above all–for export-oriented industries incentives to capital-intensive industrial sectors are, however, precluded by the high level of government debt. Indeed, public expenditure must not go on growing: this would produce grievous consequences, both on inflation and on economic recovery. What is necessary is that, given the same amount of public debt, the share of current expenditure decrease in favour of productive investment; this would entail a rise in the public sector's overall efficiency and productivity, which is a primary condition to be fulfilled if regional policies in depressed areas are to be financed and if incentives for capital-intensive industrial sectors have to be provided.

Not all capital-intensive sectors can be indiscriminately used in regional policies since most of them are affected by a marked slack in demand and suffer the effects of international division of labour and of harsh competition by developing countries. The iron and steel, metallurgical, petroleum and chemicals, and non-ferrous metal industries are clear examples of sectors that are going to be important for countries that are now producing only the raw materials for those industries. These countries might not be able to deal with the entire productive cycle but they will certainly carry out its first phases. However, in the latter case the basic commodity industries will not be able to have a propulsive effect on backward regions, as was once the case. Note that the location of plants for the transformation of raw materials in emerging countries does not rely so much on capital coming from the multinationals of the West as on "self-centre" development or on capital coming from the OPEC countries. So, paradoxically only sectors with a high K/L ratio, sectors that innovate, advanced industries, new activities based on an intensive use of electronics and of computers, will be able to shield themselves from the competition deriving from the international division of labour.

However, this prospect of development in underdeveloped areas does not appear to be conceivable and practicable since it is well known that Society needs a great deal of energy and vitality if these sections of the economy are expected to emerge. The static nature of the economic environment in the backward regions of the south clashes with these requirements and show that the main issue is above all social and does not consist in the mere development of the south's economy. There probably are no priorities in the measures to take. The economic context and social environment are strongly linked and exclusively economic measures will produce very limited

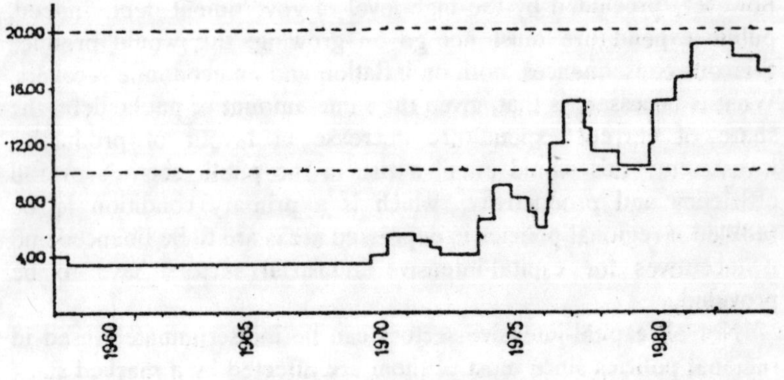

FIG. 14.1: Discount rate's evolution

FIG. 14.2: Contractual wages evolution (1980 = 100;
Source : IMF, 1983)

effects. Underdevelopment tends to be hypocritically considered as a merely productive issue. The truth is that its roots delve deep in the society, culture, structures and territory of backward regions. Surely, economic measures have to be taken but there must also be policies to promote the social growth of all the people living in backward areas. In this sense, underdevelopment is a phenomenon that goes beyond economics and that involves many more disciplines.

REFERENCES

Brandt, W. (ed.) (1980). *North-South: A Programme for Survival*, ICIdI.

Comito, U. (1977). L'industria italiana e la divisione internazionale del lavoro, *Economia e politica 4*, pp. 21-30.

Vassal, S. (1982). Le changement economique modial, *L' Information Geographique*, 46, pp. 156-161.

Muchalet, C. A, (1976). Le *capitalisme mondial*, PUF, Parigi.

Leontieff, W., (1976). *The future of world economy*, United Nations, (New York).

D'aponte T. (1982). Evoluzione degli insediamenti e divisione internazionale del lavoro. Considerazioni sui relativi effetti territoriali nel caso di regioni periferiche marginali : l'esempio del Mezzogiorno italiano., *Bollettino della Societa Geografica, Italiana* suppl. Vol. XI Serie X, pp. 153-157.

Sylos Labini P. (1983). *Il sottosviluppo e l'economia contemporanea*, Bari, Laterza.

FIFTEEN

Regional Imbalances in Business Cycle Sensitiveness and Multiplant Enterprises

MATHIAS HOLST

Business Cycle Sensitiveness - and often Neglected Short-term Aspect of Regional Economic Development

When we are discussing regional imbalances in the regional sciences, normally two dimensions are at special issue: the first refers to the level of regional development, e.g. the level of production or income, the equipment with physical or social infrastructure, etc., the other dimension refers to the regional development itself: "Are there increasing or decreasing imbalances?" is the usual question. This consideration, which is in my opinion a more long-termed one, should be supplemented by a more short-termed one: the phenomenon of regionally differing business cycles. For want of data or adequate methods this aspect has often been neglected. At the same time the stability goal is – as, e.g. in the Federal Republic of Germany – an important objective of regional economic policy.

First I would like to place the phenomenon of regionally differing business cycles in the more general research context that has given work to regional economists respectively to economic geographers in the 1980s. In this research context the relevance of supranational or simply multiplant enterprises for regional development is introduced, and reference is made to the (new) international division of labour (Fröbel/Heinrichs/Kreye 1986). In the next part of the paper I will overview theoretical approaches in respect to regional cyclical movements. The presentation of the methodical approach used here and of the results produced by the empirical analysis round off the paper. In this context it is important to mention that the empirical analysis is dedicated to the manufacturing industry of the Federal Republic of Germany and to the period between 1978 and 1984.

Recent Trends in the Theory of Regional Economic Development and Explanatory Approaches to Regionally Differing Business Cycles

New Structural Features in Regional Economic Research

Basic principle of the following ideas is that the economic development of a region is essentially the result of the development of the region's plants. Thus the structural composition of a regional economy becomes the focal point of interest. In regional research the structural dimension was reduced to branches or sectors for a long time: Regional development was a function of a region's industrial mix. Indeed in the last few years one can observe that "new structural features" have found attention:

- A first group of research deals more intensively with the distribution of plant size and in particular with the question of the contribution of small and medium as well as young enterprises to the regional growth of employment – as a special aspect of regional development (Birch, 1979; Fothergill/Gudgin, 1982; Ewers/ Fritsch/Kleine, 1984 and Aiginger/Tichy, 1985).
- A second group of investigations deals with the functional structure of enterprises and establishments as well as the distribution of single enterprisal functions – as production, research and development or administration – among different regions and with the effects of such distributions on the economic development of these regions (Bade, 1979; Müller, K., 1981; Bade/Eickelpasch, 1983 or Bade, 1984).
- A third group finally deals with the distribution and the influence of spatial control networks among establishments and enterprises. In the spatial context the so-called external control is the most important factor (see the summaries of literature and the empirical results in Bade, 1981; Tödtling, 1983; Schackmann-Fallis, 1985 and Gräber/Holst/Schackmann-Fallis/Spehl, 1986).

This last group of research studies refers especially to the relevance of multiplant respectively of supranational enterprises for regional development. Therefore it is useful to have a little bit closer view of their theoretical considerations (see in detail Gräbar/Holst/Schackmann-Fallis/Spehl, 1984).

Multiplant enterprises arise in the course of the enterprisal growth. Ideal typically the growth path starts at the stage of a successful single plant enterprise. In this stage all enterprisal functions are concentrated at one location. The end of the growth path is reached with the supranational organization of a world enterprises. In the (worldwide) headquarter the strategic functions, in the (nationwide) main plant the administrative functions and in the (spatially dispersed) branch plants respectively in the subsidiaries the operative enterprisal functions are located (e.g. the models of corporate growth and corporate organization in Lloyd/Dicken, 1977, p. 367 or Watts, 1981, p. 7). Finally all the plants or establishments of an enterprise are specialized on certain enterprisal functions.

This functional division of labour between the plants of a multiplant enterprise is then of particular relevance for regional development, if the single functions are spatially dispersed in a way, that plants or establishments with certain functional characteristics are concentrated in special types of regions respectively in special types of nations. Normally each enterprisal function has indeed its particular locational requirements: Strategic planning and control functions are depending on information supply and on information processing (Bade, 1979). These locational requirements are especially to be found in the industrial centres, the agglomerations. Administrative activities of lower responsibility are usually more dispersed in space. For the allocation of production activities, there follows a similar hypothesis from the product-cycle-theory: highly standardized productions with particular requirements for labour education and quality are expected to be located in the peripheral areas, whereas hardly standardized productions with particular requirements for labour supply are especially situated in regions or nations with higher education standards or rather with higher development status (see the basic work of Vernon, 1966 and 1979 as well as the younger references in Schackmann-Fallis, 1985, p. 106ff).

Finally the functional division of labour between the establishments of a multiplant enterprise is thus expanding to a spatial and functional division of labour first of all between the regions of a country and afterwards between countries, too (see the idea of worldwide sourcing in Fröbel/Heinrichs/Kreye, 1986). In the central areas headquarters as well as main plants and with them headquarter functions are concentrated, in the peripheral areas on the contrary only producing establishments or branch plants and with them enterprisal functions of lower quality are accumulated – this in an ideal typical manner and naturally above all, if the importance of multiplant enterprises in relation to the whole economic activity is a great one. Nowadays this should be the case in every industrial country.

Starting-point for the evolution of the functional division of labour between regions was the formation of multiplant enterprises due to enterprisal growth as well as the fact that multiplant enterprises have to rationalize the spatial organization of production processes in consequence to structural changes in the world economy and in consequence to the intensified national and international competition. Within the multiplant enterprises we have the formation of different types of establishments in the corresponding types of regions – as has been mentioned before: Headquarters or main plants on the one hand, only performing subsidiaries or branch plants on the other. The essential distinguishing feature for these types of establishments is their control status, that is, the degree by which the establishments are mastering other establishments or are depending on the decisions of other establishments. The control status usually determines the functional equipment of an establishment, that is, the quantity and quality of functions that are to be executed by the establishment. Furthermore the products that are to be manufactured, and the production techniques that are to be used depend partly on an establishment's control status.

Summing up and bearing in mind the other structural variables and causal relations the chain of effects on the microeconomic level is illustrated in Figure 15.1. I do not want to present the effects besides the relations to the control status. Otherwise the frame of this paper would be split up (see the literature cited in connection with plant size as well as Strassert, 1976; Ertl/Hübl, 1978; Müller, J., 1983 in regard to the sector structure).

The presented general micro-economic interrelations now are to be adapted to the phenomenon of stability of a typical enterprise's development. Furthermore they are to be seen spatially and to be related to the problem of regionally differing business cycles. This refers to the macroeconomic level of effects.

Theoretical Approaches to Regional Business Cycle Fluctuations

The most important theories in respect to regional business cycle movements will now be briefly reviewed. It will become apparent that not all determinants considered essential for the regional business fluctuations can be included in the empirical analysis because the corresponding data are not available.

A first group of theoretical approaches – in principle it can be seen in accordance with this study – emphasizes the composition of establishments in a region. Typically for the traditional research in regional economics the sector structure is analysed, but the control and the plant size structure are also mentioned as relevant dimensions.

(1) *Sector structure*: A varying intensity of business cycle sensitiveness exists without doubt between sectors. The sector structure of a regional economy is an important explanatory variable for regional business cycle sensitiveness, because there are different "regional mixes" of stable and unstable sectors (e.g. Ertl/Hübl, 1978). The classification of sectors that was carried out for this research by the "Federal Statistical Office" is, however, based on the growth dynamics of the sectors and leads to a classification, which is not very suitable as indicator for "business cycle sensitiveness". Nevertheless it is used in the empirical analysis.

(2) *Plant size structure:* The majority of the research related to plant size argues that larger enterprises have a stabilizing influence. Especially investment and employment behaviour is examined (ABmann/Schmitt, 1975; Gruhler, 1979; Kalfass, 1982), an analysis of production development is not to be found.

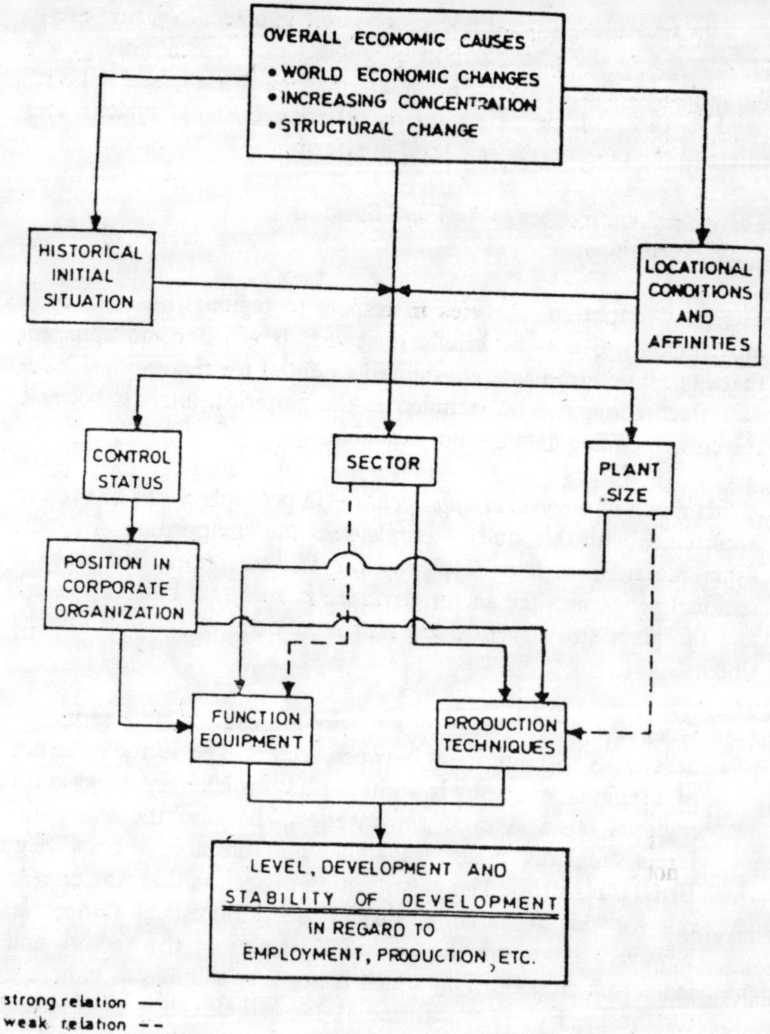

FIG. 15.1: Micro-economic Context of Effects

Central arguments for the stabilizing influence of bigger enterprises are better quality and longer terms of investment plans; less dependence on short term moods, expectations and evaluations, that are strongly related to the business cycle; assumed higher significance of in-company labour markets that lead to more stable employment conditions (for differentiation of internal and external labour markets see Freiburghaus/Schmid, 1975, p. 420ff); larger segments of the in-company labour market, in which qualifications are predominant, that are related to the company's needs. Because of the return of the human capital investments undertaken by the enterprise relatively stable employment conditions can be expected for these employees; correlations with the effects of concentration (it is generally assumed, that large enterprises possess a stronger market power than smaller enterprises – see Fassing, 1982, p. 139); greater probability of receiving subsidies from the State in times of crisis; minor importance of newly-founded companies – especially those inclined to insolvency – in the class of larger enterprises; higher degree of diversification in big enterprises and therefore the possibility of "spreading market risks" during periods of fluctuation in manufacturing of different products (Küting, 1980 and Schwalbach, 1985).

But there are also arguments against the stabilizing effects of big enterprises, which, for example, reveal the management behaviour of capital companies (see Kalfass, 1982). According to this the management is interested in a constant distribution policy in order to preserve a certain autonomy in the face of the shareholders. This leads to a procyclic investment behaviour, if the high profits in times of boom are invested in the enterprise, while the distributions in times of crisis have to be partly financed by the reduction of investment projects.

To sum up it can be said that the overwhelming majority of arguments indicates a positive relation between the size of an enterprise and business cycle stability. Nevertheless it is obvious, too, that the size may not be a real determining factor, but that along with the size of an enterprise other influencing variables – legal form, range of products, age, etc., are taken into consideration. Indicators for a region's plant size structure are therefore included in the empirical analysis. Plant size is measured via a company's employees.

(3) *Control Structure*: The significance of control structure for the regional business cycle sensitiveness is dealt with in the relevant literature especially concerning main plant and branch plant as different types of control status.

Single plant enterprises are not often mentioned explicitly; since single plant enterprises are often small enterprises, the corresponding considerations can be transferred from the size hypothesis.

For a long time branch plants were called "extended work-benches" or "rucksack enterprises". These terms indicate a particular business cycle sensitiveness of this control status type. Of course they have to be seen in front of the boom of plant openings from the middle till the end of the sixties and the beginning of the seventies in the Federal Republic of Germany, where the newly opened plants in sectors that were negatively affected by the structural changes in the world economy turned out to be less persistent (Gräber, 1979, especially chapter 6 and 7).

In the meantime a qualitative consolidation of the still existing branch plants can be assumed. Nevertheless there is a chain of arguments that suggests a special business cycle sensitiveness of branch plants with the corresponding consequences for their region. They will be summarized briefly (for closer information see Gräber, 1979, p. 178 f; and also Gerlach/Liepmann, 1973 and Ertel, 1976, especially p. 179f).

- Branch plants are often said to have the function of serving the production peaks and to be used as business cycle buffer by the main plant. A strategy of this kind will be suitable for the enterprise, if the employees in the branch plant have a low level of qualification, if there is only a weak relation between existing qualifications and the plant's needs, if the degree of union organization is low and the probability of re-employment after dismissal is high. These conditions are generally fulfilled – especially in the case of branch plants in peripheral regions.
- The low degree of functional completeness of the branch plants will in case of demand disturbances lead to a burdening of the local labour market, because the possibility of changing the qualification of the employees and the transformation of production are missing to a large extent (Buttler/Gerlach/Liepmann, 1977, p. 101).
- Branch plants show a stronger production orientation than the other control status types. Business cycle movements become more apparent in the production than in the administrative division of enterprises.
- The employees are assigned to a great extent to the so-called "non-specific everyman's market", in which the demand of the enterprises is restricted to non-specific knowledge and

abilities such as a certain degree of physical and intellectual disposition as well as basic intellectual knowledge. Therefore these jobs do not demand a stable labour market behaviour (Lutz/Sengenberger, 1974).

These arguments indicate that an evaluation of the branch plants depends primarily on their production connections with the main plant. Georgi and Giersch emphasized in their research concerning the Saar that the negative aspects of branch plants are related most of all to branch plants with"parallel production", whereas branch plants with an "integrated production" or with "independent production" programme are to be judged more favourably (Georgi/Giersch, 1977).

Furthermore it becomes clear that the arguments assume a dominance of late production cycle phases in the branch plants with the corresponding negative consequences for conditions of location. Unfortunately we are not able to further differentiate the branch plants according to these criteria.

Following these considerations a high proportion of externally controlled branch plants should lead to high business cycle sensitiveness of regions, whereas a high proportion of main plants should result in a low regional business cycle sensitiveness.

Further differentiations of the mentioned hypothesis are possible by including reasons for relations of dependence and dominance between plants and enterprises (legal relations, strongly one-sided supply and customer relations, etc.). But the empirical analysis is restricted to the numbered control status types since our statistical sources do not allow for such a differentiation.

A second group of theoretical approaches emphasizes the aspects of demand. On the one hand the basic non-basic concept is applied. According to this regional business cycle movements are initiated by changes in the demand for products of a region. First they affect only the export-oriented economic sectors. Then they spread by way of delivery networks and distribution of income to the regional-oriented economic sectors (Stöckmann, 1970, p. 48). It becomes quite apparent that the dependence on external impulses is corresponding to the quantity of the export flows of a region.

Different regional business cycles can then be deduced from different regional basic non-basic ratios and from different regional consumption functions (see the interregional multiplier models by Airov, 1963).

On the other hand the structure of demand can be taken into account. The components of the global economic demand show a different business cycle sensitiveness. Investment – especially inventory investment – shows relatively strong cyclical movements; the demand for consumer products is characterized by relatively low fluctuations. In addition in nearly all post-war business cycles in the Federal Republic of Germany periods of increasing business activity started by expansion of foreign and/or state demand. The importance of these influences for the intensity of regional business cycle movements and for regional lead-lag-structures should be obvious.

The theoretical approaches mentioned above can be examined only in a rudimentary way within the limits of this empirical study. The demand structure has to be deduced from interregional Input-Output tables which are not available in the Federal Republic of Germany. The external demand can be included in respect to foreign trade of regions and its development, but data concerning interregional trade relations are not available. Nevertheless in this way some of the mentioned theses can be checked.

A last group of theoretical approaches emphasizes the importance of cost of supply factors which lead to regionally differing competitiveness. If, for instance, certain regions have high proportions of marginal suppliers, periods of increasing economic activity are supposed to become apparent relatively late and periods of decline relatively early in respect to other regions. It is obvious that in this context the regional factors are of special importance (manpower, commodity capital, infrastructure, tax burden, etc. – see Siegel, 1966, p. 57ff). These cost and supply factors have to be reduced in the empirical analysis. Data are only available for the regional reachability by public and individual transport. Finally indicators for settlement structure complete the independent variables.

A Methodical Approach to Measure Business Cycle Sensitiveness on a Regional Level

The cyclical movements of the regional activity have to be measured by suitable variables. Necessary characteristics of such variables are:

- explanatory value in the context of regional business cycle theories;
- relatively stable relation to the business cycle fluctuations;
- availability on a quarterly, or better monthly basis;
- not too long temporal delays, no leads or lags to the business cycle (Keinath, 1978, p. 79ff and Porschen *et al.*, 1983, p. 13ff).

In principle the gross domestic product would be the most comprehensive indicator for the economic development of a region. But for regions below the level of the 11 States, the "Länder" of the Federal Republic of Germany this figure is only available every second year. A similar indicator – the index of the industrial net production – is registered monthly, but only for the "Länder", too. For data reasons these two best indicators must be ruled out in the context of a regional business cycle analysis. One has to look for indicators that are closely linked up to them and that are available! From the possible indicators – unemployment ratio, employees, blue-collar manhours and sales – the blue-collar manhours were taken as the second best solution for theoretical and empirical reasons: the workers cover nearly 70 per cent of the total labour force, and they are of special importance for the production. Furthermore the volume of overtime/short-time work is included in the indicator. The development of productivity by the hour is finally subject to relatively small fluctuations in the business cycle.

A comparison between the time series of the indices of industrial net production and blue-collar manhours was carried out for the State of Rheinland-Pfalz. Without any corrections the two time series correlate by 67,2 per cent between January 1978 and April 1984 (for the whole of the Federal Republic of Germany the correlation coefficient is above 75 per cent). After the application of a newly-developed procedure of season adjustment described below the coefficient for Rheinland-Pfalz rises to 72.1 per cent, so that a sufficiently high adjustment of the two indices can be assumed. It is for these reasons that we will use the time series of "blue-collar manhours" to define the regional business cycle movements

Once the indicator is chosen one has to take into account that it is not only the business cycle that has an effect upon the time series of the chosen index; the medium-term growth rate (trend) and the short-term seasonal fluctuations (season) of the regional economy are reflected as well. Therefore, an adjustment of the time series for the trend and seasonal influence is necessary to define the intensity of business cycle fluctuations. The usual procedures of time series analysis were developed for nationwide analyses and cannot be readily applied to small-sized regions. Thus the usual procedures of seasonal adjustment presuppose an equal seasonal influence for all regions. But this assumption is not valid for the States of the Federal Republic of Germany, because each State has specific holidays and holiday seasons in the schools. We have, therefore, developed a special seasonal adjustment procedure. First, the influence of working days, summer holidays and other holidays on the time series of blue-collar manhours is determined for each State of the Federal Republic of Germany by regression analysis. Thus we get coefficients, which show the significance of differences in working time by States for the time series of blue-collar manhours.

For every planning region the time series of working hours was adjusted correspondingly on the basis of state-specific coefficients for working days, summer holidays and if necessary rest holidays. Remaining small coincidental variations were eliminated subsequently by the calculation of a gliding three months average.

After this adjustment only the trend and business cycle components remain in the time series of blue-collar working hours and have to be separated. This separation was achieved by the estimation of a linear trend function for each of the 75 planning regions. The deviation from the trend was then regarded as the business cycle component. The standard deviation of residuals is taken as a measure for the intensity of regional business cycles and illustrates therefore whether a region is more or less susceptible to business cycle fluctuations (similar approaches of Keinath, 1978 and Porschen, *et al.* 1983).

Regionally Differing Business Cycle Sensitiveness in the Federal Republic of Germany and some Causal Relations

Business Cycle Sensitiveness in the Planning Regions of the Federal Republic of Germany

First we look at the monthly development of the season-adjusted net production index of the manufacturing industry from January 1978 to April 1984 of the whole Federal Republic of Germany. A slightly negative medium-term trend with a relative peak at the turn of the year 1979/80 and a relative bottom at the turn of the year 1982/83 is to be seen (see Fig. 15.2). The development of the working hours that were adjusted by the abovementioned procedure shows relatively similar tendencies in the comparative period. The two relative turning points, however, appear with a small time lag.

As discussed above the index "blue-collar manhours" is used to analyse business cycle movements on the level of individual planning regions. The planning regions are clustered according to their settlement density and industry mix into four groups. The first group includes planning regions with a high population density and a favourable industrial structure (type A), the second group comprises planning regions with a high population density and a large share of declining industries – the so-called old industrial areas (type B), the third group includes the peripheral or rural regions (type C) and the fourth group consists of planning regions with increasing settlement density (type D). The investigation of these groups resulted in the following major tendencies (see Table 15.1):

TABLE 15.1: **Business Cycle Sensitiveness* of Planning Regions on the Basis of Types of Planning Regions between January 1978 and April 1984**

	Index Average Value	Number of Regions	Significantly different from (on 5% - Level)	(on 10% - Level)
Type A	0,460	21	C	C and D
Type B	0,444	6	–	C
Type C	0,611	20	A	A and B
Type D	0,574	26	–	A
	0,541	73		

* Standard deviation of the residuals of a regression on function A = b * t
with A = season-adjusted standardized blue-collar manhours
and t = time index.

The regions with a high population density – the ones with a favourable industrial structure as well as the old industrial areas – show a very similar development during the research period. Their business cycle sensitiveness was essentially lower than the regional average. On the contrary the peripheral and rural areas are characterized by significantly larger amplitudes of business cycle movements. Apparently the more favourable development trend of the manufacturing industry in the less densely populated regions of the

Federal Republic of Germany, that has been reported in recent research (Gräber/Holst/Schackmann-Fallis/Spehl, 1986, chapters 2 and 4), is attented by stronger fluctuations in the business cycle.

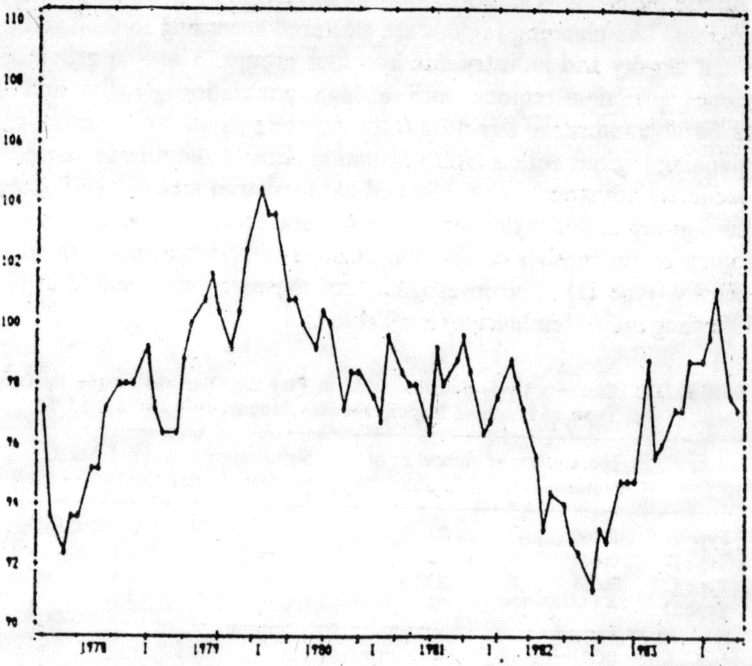

Fig. 15.2: Development of the Net Production Index of Manufacturing Industry of the Federal Republic of Germany from January 1978 till April 1984 (1980 = 100).

Source: Statistische Beihefte zu den Monatsberichten der Deutschen Bundesbank, Reihe 4 — Saisonbereinigte Wirtschaftszahlen. Several years of publication.

The hypothesis regarding the regional imbalances in business cycle sensitiveness, which have been presented in the course of the theoretical discussion, are now to be reconsidered in relation to the existing data.

The Relevance of Multiplant Enterprises and other Factors for Business Cycle Sensitiveness

First of all the significant correlations between the independent variables presented above and the dependent variable "business cycle sensitiveness" are to be analysed (see Table 15.2).

TABLE 15.2: **Correlation Analysis with Business Cycle Sensitiveness**

	Variable	Pearson's R	Level of Significance
Settlement Structure	Reachability by		
	- individual transport	-0,40	*
	- public transport	-0,36	*
	Population Density	-0,33	*
	Share of inhabitants in the biggest town (degree of agglomeration)	-0,40	*
Control structure	Share of employees in		
	- main plants	-0,25	**
	- branch plants	0,15	+ (11 %)
	Index for mastery	-0,22	**
Plant size Structure	Share of employees in		
	- establishments < 50	0,31	*
	- establishments > 500	-0,14	+ (12 %)
Functional Structure	Share of employees in		
	- production functions	0,24	**
	- dispositive functions	-0,15	***
	- administrative functions	-0,20	**
External Demand	Development of the foreign sales percentage	0,45	*

There is a relatively strong relation between the variables concerning the settlement structure and the regional business cycle sensitiveness. Poor Reachability by transport, low population density and an unimportant degree of agglomeration are connected with strong fluctuations in the business cycle during the research period. Between the indicators referring to the control structure there are only two with a significant correlation: the share of employees in main plants and the index for mastery. As expected the correlation is both times a negative one. Therefore, regions with lower business cycle sensitiveness are characterized by main plants and mastery – that is to be seen in analogy with the results regarding the settlement structure. Pearson's R with the external dependence on the contrary illustrates only a weak relation. As expected the sign is positive nevertheless. The reason – one can assume – is to be seen in the relatively proportionate distribution of branch plants in space which indeed has not been expected in front of the outlined theoretical background.

The indicators for the functional equipment, respectively, the functional structure of a region, show the relations that had to be expected: a strong orientation on production coincides with more intensive business cycle fluctuations; a higher share of employees in headquarter or simply dispositive functions is linked with smaller fluctuations. Indeed the correlation coefficients are not very high!

The hypotheses regarding the plant size structure are verified in principle: a high share of employees in small establishments is connected with relatively strong business cycle fluctuations, whereas big enterprises tend to stabilize the business cycle. This relation again is not very significant.

The indicators for the sector structure do not show any significant relations to the business cycle. This result should not be interpreted in a way that the regional mix of relatively stable and instable sectors is not relevant for business cycle sensitiveness. As mentioned above it was not possible to specify the sector structure in an adequate manner.

Likewise there is no significant correlation between the level of the foreign sales percentage and the business cycle sensitiveness, although the foreign demand is generally subject to stronger fluctuations as the domestic demand (see, e.g., received orders, sales, etc.). Perhaps this indicator is relevant for special lead-lag-relations: after the Second World War nearly every boom in the Federal Republic of Germany was introduced by an expansion of foreign demand. But these relations could not be analysed in this study. In this context it should be mentioned that, if only the regions with a high population density and with a favourable economic structure (type A) are included in the analysis, the foreign sales percentage correlates – as expected – positively with the business cycle sensitiveness. Beyond the development of the foreign sales percentage shows a very high positive correlation with the business cycle sensitiveness. Obviously regions that became strongly integrated in foreign trade could realize that only in connection with more intensive business cycle fluctuations. This concerns particularly the peripheral and rural regions of type C.

The independent variables that have been discussed before one by one are now introduced simultaneously in a model for regional business cycle sensitiveness. The ideas and hypothesis regarding the network of the single variables and the level of effects (see the microeconomic chain of effects in Figure 15.1) seem to make the application of path analysis useful. A Path Analysis is consisting of a system of multiple regression that the linked in hierarchical series (Holm 1977 or Lange 1978). The result is presented in Figure 15.3.

The variables referring to the settlement structure have effects on each level of the analysis. On the first one (explaining the business cycle sensitiveness) the reachability by individual transport as well as the population density are included. Obviously locational effects are of particular relevance for stable business fluctuations: The worse the reachability by individual transport and the less the population density, the higher was the business cycle sensitiveness during the research period. More important, however, was an increase in the foreign sales percentage. Those regions that became stronger integrated in the foreign trade, therefore, suffered greater business cycle fluctuations.

Of special relevance for an increase of the foreign sales percentage was the control structure and with it the economic activities of multiplant enterprises. A high share of main plants led to a decrease of the foreign sales percentage, whereas a strong orientation on production functions caused an increase. A strong production orientation, however, is on its part seriously affected by the control via multiplant enterprises (the influence of the mastery index is a negative one) and furthermore by the external dependence (positive influence). The chain of causal relations in the path model thus illustrates the particular importance of the external control by multiplant enterprises in regard to the regional business cycle sensitiveness.

Besides the control structure there is the sector structure as traditionally influencing factor, that has an effect on the development of the foreign sales percentage – partly via the production orientation, too. A high share of recessive sectors is linked with an increase of the foreign sales percentage and vice versa. But the effects of the sectorial mix are of relatively less significance when compared with the effects of the external control.

The variables referring to the plant size structure are not included in the path model. The effects of these variables seem to be dominated by the effects of other independent variables – especially those presenting the settlement structure. Where settlement density and reachability by public or individual transport is low, there should be working a very high share of employees in small establishments. This situation again causes a higher business cycle sensitiveness.

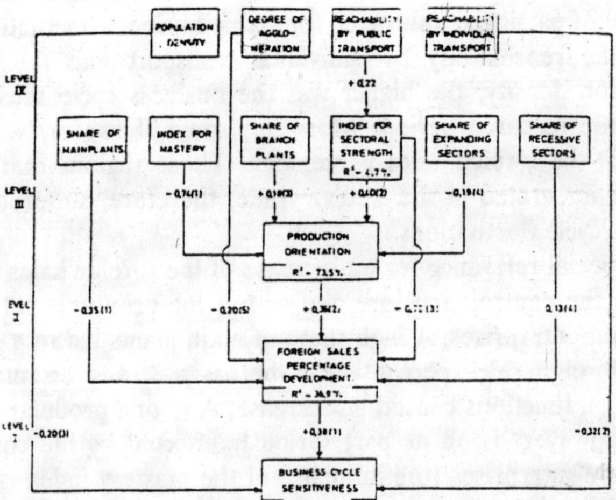

FIG. 15.3: Path Model to Explain Business Cycle Sensitiveness

Legend: R^2 = R square of the dependent variable
+/-0,... = Gradient of the linear multiple regression function
(...) = Order of the significance of the independent variable

Summing up I would like to state that by introducing the phenomenon of functional division of labour within multiplant enterprises a certain progress in explaining regional imbalances in the business cycle sensitiveness is to be achieved. The theory concerning the spatial and functional division of labour on the one hand illustrates that an influence of multiplant enterprises on regiona' development and with that on business cycle fluctuations via external control is evident. On the other the presented empirical study for the manufacturing industry in the Federal Republic of Germany was able to demonstrate sufficiently the effects of the external control in spite of the methodical problems.

Finally there remains the impression that the introduction of multiplant enterprises into the discussion of regional economic development is still at the beginning. First references are already existent, a theoretical systematization is still missing – just as empirical research in the international context.

REFERENCES

Airov. J. (1963). "The construction of interregional business cycle models", *Journal of Regional Science*, Band 5, pp. 1 - 20.

Aiginger, K., Tichy, G. (1985). *Die GröBe der Kleinen. Dieüberraschenden Erfolge Kleiner und mittlerer Unternehmungen in den achtziger Jahren*. Wien.

ABmann, K., Schmitt, K.H. (1975). *Die Konjunkturabhängigkeit der Klein – und Mittelbetriebe* Göttingen.

Bade, F. J. (1979). "Funktionale Aspekte der regionalen Wirtschaftsstruktur", *Raumforschung und Raumordnung*, Heft 6, pp. 253 - 268.

Bade, F. J. (1981). "Die Standortstruktur groBer Industrieuntenehmen – Eine explorative Studie zum EinfluB von GroBunternehmen auf die regionale Wirtschaftsentwicklung", *Jahrbuch für National ökonomie und Statistik*, Bd. 196/4, pp. 341 - 366.

Bade, F. J. (1984). *Die funktionale Struktur der Wirtschaft und ihre räumliche Arbeitsteilung*. Berlin, = IIM/IP 84 - 27.

Bade, F.J. Eickelpasch, A. (1983). "Funktionale Arbeitsteilung und regionale Beschäftigungsstruktur", in Garlichs, D., Maier, F. und Semlinger, K. (eds.), *Regionalisierte Arbeitsmarkt – und Beschäftigungspolitik*. Frankfurt.

Birch, D. (1979). *The Job Generation Process*. Cambridge, Mass.

Buttler, F., Gerlach, K. und Liepmann, D. (1977). *Grundlagen der Regionalökonomie*. Reinbek near Hamburg.

Ertel, R. (1976). *Regionale Konjunkturpobleme und mögliche wirtschaftspolitische Konsequenzen*. Berlin.

Ertel, R., Hübl, L. (1978). Aspekte und Konsequenzen regional differenzierter Konjunkturentwicklungen, *WSI-Mitteilungen*, Heft 1, S.12ff.

Ewers, H.J., Fritsch, M., Kleine, J. (1984). *Bildungs- und qualifikationsorientierte Strategien der Regionalförderung unter besonderer Berücksichtigung Kleiner and mittlerer Unternehmen*. Bonn, = BMBau 06.053.

Fassing, W. (1982). *Wettbewerb. Unternehmenskonzentration und Investitionsverhalten*. Berlin.

Fothergill. S., Gudgin, G. (1982). *Unequal Growth*. London.

Freiburghaus, D., Schmid, G. (1975). "Theorie der Segmentierung von Arbeitsmärkten", *Leviathan*, pp. 417 - 448.

Fröbel, F., Heinrichs, J., Kreye, O. (1986). *Umbruch in der Weltwirtschaft — Die globale Strategie: Verbilligung der Arbeitskraft/Flexibilisierung der Arbeit/Neue Technologien*. Reinbek near Hamburg.

Georgi, H. and Giersch V. (1977). *Neue Betriebe an der Saar. Bestandsaufnahme — Analyse — Perspektiven*. Saarbrücken, = Staatskanzlei des Saarlandes und der IHK Saarbrücken (eds.).

Gerlach, K. and Liepmann, G. (1972). "Konjunkturelle Aspekte der Industrialisierung peripherer Regionen — dargestellt am Beispiel des ostbayerischen Regierungsbezirks Oberpfalz", *Jahrbücher für Nationalökonomie and Statistik*, Bd. 187, pp. 1-21.

Gräber, H. (1979). *Die Persistenz von Industrieansiedlungen. Theoretische Überlegungen und empirische Ergebnisse für die Bundesrepublik Deutschland*. Bochum, — Beiträge zur Struktur und Konjunkturforschung, eds. Klemmer, P., Bd. VIII.

Gräber, H., Holst, M., Schackmann-Fallis, K.-P., Spehl, H. (1984). "Multiregional enterprises in manufacturing industry, regional development and regional policy in the Federal Republic of Germany". Paper presented at the 24th European Congress of the Regional Science Association, Milan, August 28-31.

Gräber, H., Holst, M., Schackmann-Fallis, K.P., Spehl, H. (1986). *Regionale Wirtschaftsstrukturen im Verarbeitenden Gewerbe unter besonderer Berücksictingung der Kontrollstruktur — Bestandsaufnahme, Wirkungsanalyse und regionalpolitische Einschätzung*. Trier.

Gruhler, W. (1979). *Unternehmensgröße und Beschäftigung in der Industrie*. Köln.

Holm, K. (ed.). (1977). *Die Befragung 5*, München.

Kalfass, H. (1982). "Großunternehmen und die Stabilität der Investitionen im Konjunkturverlauf". *Konjunkturpolitik*, Heft 1, pp. 36-54.

Keinath, K. (1978). *Regionale Konjunkturschwankungen*. Tübingen.

Küting, K.H. (1980). *Unternehmerische Wachstumspolitik*. Darmstadt.

Lange, E. (1978). Determinanten der Entscheidung für das Studium der Soziologie — Eine Anwendung der Pfadanalyse. *Zeitschrift für Soziologie*, 7, Heft 1, pp. 72-86.

Lloyd, P.E., Dicken P. (1977). *Location in Space. A Theoretical Approach to Economic Geography*. 2nd ed., London.

Lutz, B., Sengenberger, W. (1974). *Arbeitsmarktstrukturen und öffentliche Arbeitsmarktpolitik. Eine Kritische Analyse von Zielen und Instrument*. Göttingen.

Müller, J. (1983). *Sektorale Struktur und Entwicklung der industriellen Beschäftigung in den Regionen der Bundesrepublik Deutschland*. Berlin, = Beiträge zur angewandten Wirtschaftsforschung, Bd. 12.

Müller, K. (1981). *Wirtschaftlicher Strukturwandel und räumliche Entwicklung. Fallstudien — Ergebnisse zum Ausmaß sowie zu den Ursachen und Wirkungen funktionaler Konzentration in der Schweiz*. Bern und Stuttgart, = Publikationen des Schweizerischen Nationalfonds aus den Nationalen Forschungsprogrammen, Bd. 10.

Porschen, D. et al. (1983). *Konjunktur und Wachstum in Lande Bremen*. Bremen.

Schackmann-Fallis, K.P. (1985). *Externe Abhängigkeit und regionale Entwicklung. Theoretische Grundlagen und empirische Ergebnisse für die Region Trier*. Mannheim.

Schwalbach, J. (1985). "Diversifizierung von Unternehmen und Betrieben im Verarbeitenden Gewerbe". Discussionpaper des Intenationalen Institutes für Management und Verwaltung, IIM/IP 1985/5, Berlin.

Siegel, R.S. (1966). "Do regional business cycles exist?". *Western Economic Journal* 5, pp. 48-60

Stöckmann. W. (1970). *Die regionalen Konjunkturprobleme – Das Beispeil der norddeutschen Küstenländer*. Göttingen.

Strassert, G. (1976). *Regionale Strukturpolitik durch Wirtschaftsstrukturförderung – Ansatzpunkte und Probleme einer sektoralen Differenzierung der Regionalen Wirtschaftsförderung*, Hannover, = Veröffentlichungen der Akademie für Raumforschung und Landesplanung, Abhandlungen Band 73.

Tödtling, F. (1983). *Organisatorischer Status von Betrieben and Arbeitsplatzqualität in peripheren und entwicklungsschwachen Gebieten Österreichs*. Wien (VWGö), = Dissertationen der Wirtschaftsuniversität Wien 37 (= Wien).

Vernon, R. (1966). International Investment and International Trade in the Product Cycle. *The Quarterly Journal of Economics*, Jg. 80, pp. 190ff.

Vernon, R. (1979). The Product Cycle Hypothesis in a New International Environment. *Oxford Bulletin of Economics and Statistics*, 41, pp. 255-267.

Watts, H. D. (1981). *The Branch Plant Economy: A Study of External Control*. London.

SIXTEEN

Multinational Establishments and Regional Development in Nigeria

JOSEPHINE OLU ABIODUN

INTRODUCTION

The past few decades have witnessed increased concern about the impacts which multinational establishments generate on the economic development of the less developed countries. One of the legacies of colonialism was the control which the various multinational corporations, operating from the advanced metropolitan countries, exerted on the economies of the colonies. Even after political independence, the various forms of influences of the multinational corporations are still evident. Corporations of rapidly expanding economies like Japan, USA, Korea and the communist countries, which were not important colonial powers, have, of late, begun to exert considerable influences on the development plans of the less developed countries as well.

Until recently, the multinational corporations were embraced by the developing countries as the *sine qua non* of their development. They were seen as the prime movers of their economies, for through the various links which they established in the host countries, they helped to accelerate their development processes. (UN., 1978, p. 4). More recently, however, the roles of the multinational corporations have come under closer examination. Various yard sticks are being used in their assessment. These include the conditions under which they exploit the resources of the host countries and the living levels of the population in which multinational corporations operate. It has thereby been realized that the multinational corporations operate largely to the benefit of the parent companies in the advanced countries. In fact, under uncontrolled conditions, multinational corporations could actually contribute adversely to the overall development efforts of the less developed countries through excessive siphoning out of resources, such as profits, and excessive exploitation of the natural resources of the host countries. For these reasons, developing countries like Nigeria now devote more attention than hitherto to the activities of the multinational corporations in their economies (Lall and Streeten, 1977).

This study examines the roles of multinational corporations within the framework of regional development in Nigeria. The Nigerian Enterprises Promotion Decree (NEPD) 1972 and its amendment in 1977 still forms the basic instrument regulating the activities of multinational corporations in the country. The structure of industrial, service and commercial activities as they relate to the NEPD are examined in the selected states of Lagos, Kano and Ondo on which data is presently available. This study is, therefore, by no means exhaustive. It is hoped, however, that as more data become available, a fully dimensioned view of the pattern of activities of the multinational corporations in the regional development context within all the States of the Federation will be possible.

Theoretical Background

Regional development impulses have been attributed largely to two different theories. One is the unbalanced growth model which views regional development as resulting largely from the activities of localized key establishments which through their spread effects ultimately produce balanced regional development in the long run (Hirschmann, 1958). The activities of the multinational corporations, therefore, belong to this school. The multinational corporations could, in this sense, be regarded as constituting prime movers in the development of the less developed countries. Proponents of this school, therefore, contend that, under the free market economy, the operations of the market mechanism would, through the numerous linkages, accelerate the development of the less developed countries. Any initial inequalities between the developed and developing countries (and at a lower scale, among different regions within each developing country) could, therefore, by this reasoning, be regarded as temporary.

There is, however, another school of thought which asserts that the backwash effects of development tend to be stronger than the spread effects, and that the cumulative and circular (Myrdal, 1957) effects of the early starters in the development race tend to accentuate inequalities between the more developed and the less developed regions. The universality of the increasing problem of inequalities has now been accepted and developing countries, which are more adversely affected by the core-periphery relationships among their economies and those of the more advanced nations, have lately formulated various policies to control the activities of the multinational corporations. The various policies are aimed at minimizing the negative effects of the activities of the multinational corporations and maximizing their positive effects in the economies of the developing countries

Multinational Corporations in the Regional Development of Nigeria

Multinational corporations may be defined as enterprises which own or control production or service facilities outside the country is which they are based. Such enterprises are not always incorporated or private, they can also be "cooperatives or State-owned entities" (UN. 1978, p. 158). The multinational corporations have their head offices in the developed countries and their ancillaries are largely in the developing countries where lower costs of production have been the major factors attracting them to operate outside the metropolitan areas. The corporations operate in the various sectors of the economies of the less developed countries employing advanced production technologies.

The large population and abundant natural resources have over the years combined to attract several multinational corporations into Nigeria. In keeping with the global trend of controlling the activities of the multinational corporations in the developing countries Nigeria promulgated the Nigerian Enterprises Promotion Decree in 1972 to reserve certain sectors of her economy for Nigerians. The Decree also gave guidelines for regulating the activities of the multinational corporations, in consonance with national development objectives. The 1972 Decree was amended subsequently to cover all sectors of the Nigerian economy. An assessment of the role of the multinational corporations in the regional development of Nigeria can, therefore; be undertaken within the framework of the Nigerian Enterprises Promotion Decree (NEPD).

Under Schedule I of the NEPD, 40 activities were reserved exclusively for Nigerians. Under Schedule II, 56 activities were classified as partnerships in which Nigerians could operate with multinational firms but at least 60 per cent of the share had to be for Nigerian shareholders. Under Schedule III, 40 activities could also be operated as partnerships between local and foreign firms with at least 40 per cent of the shares belonging to Nigerians. The rationale behind the classifications is that some sectors are regarded as strategic to the Nigerian economy and they have accordingly been reserved for Nigerians. The partnerships, on the other hand, is a recognition of the potential contributions of both the foreign and domestic partners in collaboration, the foreign firms contributing technology and initial management expertise and the latter participating with special knowledge of domestic market conditions, laws, labour management and other local information.

TABLE 16.1: **Spatial Distribution of Companies affected by the Nigerian Enterprises Promotion Decree, 1981**

	Distribution by Schedule				%
State	Schedule I	Schedule II	Schedule III	Total	of Total
Anambra		2	5	7	0.4
Bauchi		1	1	2	0.2
Bendel		19	6	25	2.2
Benue					0.0
Borno		6		6	0.5
Cross River	1	2		3	0.3
Gongola					0.0
Imo		2		2	0.2
Kaduna	1	10	12	23	2.0
Kano	16	94	25	135	12.0
Kwara	3			3	0.3
Lagos	40	576	209	825	73.1
Niger					0.0
Ogun	1	1	2	4	0.4
Ondo					0.0
Oyo	5	29	7	41	3.6
Plateau		18	3	21	1.9
Rivers	2	16	7	25	2.2
Sokoto	1	6	1	8	0.7
Total	70(6.2%)	782(69.3%)	276(24.5%)	1,128	100.0

Source: Akintola-Arikawe (1983, p. 48).

As at July, 1981 a total of 1,128 companies were affected by the NEPD. The distribution of the companies in the States, according to the schedules, appears in Table 16.1.

The companies under Schedule I which are exclusively reserved for Nigerians are engaged in advertising and public relations, blending and bottling of alcoholic drinks, commercial transportation, retailing, garment manufactures and wholesale distribution of local manufactures. In all 40 activities fall under schedule I.

Schedule II comprises 56 activities in which Nigerian equity content could not be less than 60 per cent and covers banking, various forms of manufacturing to the operation of photographic studies including commercial and aerial photography.

Schedule III covers 40 activities requiring a Nigerian equity of at least 40 per cent and involving a wide range of manufacturing and other activities.

From Table 16.1 it is clear that most of the effected enterprises fall into schedule II. It could also be observed that Lagos State has the bulk of the multinational corporations operating in Nigeria. Four other States do not have any of the multinational firms operating within their territories. The location of the multinational corporations cannot be separated from the overall spatial distribution of urban centres with their modern manufacturing industries, social services and population concentrations. The spatial distribution of the corporations, therefore, gives a useful index of the levels of development of the States in terms of infrastructure and other favourable locational factors in different parts of the country. Table 16.1 also gives a useful index of the magnitude of the impacts of the multinational corporations in terms of potential employment opportunities, skills and incomes generated in each State. The Federal Government has recently drawn up policies aimed at ensuring maximum utilization of domestic natural resources in the operation of the multinational corporations. Training schemes have also been suggested as a way of replacing the foreign employees with local personnel. The combination of these measures is expected to increase the local impacts of the corporations. In the following sections the operations of the multinational corporations in Lagos, Ondo and Kano States are examined.

Lagos State

As has been observed in Table 16.1 Lagos State has the bulk of the branches of multinational corporations in the country. Till 1977 there were 645 such firms in Lagos. By 1981, the number had increased to 825. The locations of these firms in Lagos in 1977 are indicated in Table 16.2.

TABLE 16.2: **Location of Multinational Firms in Lagos State, 1977**

Area	No. of firms
Lagos Island & mainland	553
Mushin	8
Ikeja	84
Total	645

An important aspect of the corporations relates to their ownership characteristics by nationality. Table 16.3 indicates that British firms are still important. However, most of the firms are made up of partnerships between Nigerians and foreigners, which indicated the Nigerianization policy has progressed.

TABLE 16.3: **Ownership of Multinational Firms by Nationality**

British	44	6.82%
American	13	2.01%
European	24	3.72%
Asian	31	4.80%
Foreign Partners	30	4.65%
Foreign & Nigerian	503	77.98%
Total	645	99.98%

Source: Lagos State Ministry of Trade and Industries.

Branches of Multinational Corporations are, generally, large-scale units with large capital outlays. Table 16.4 indicates that a significant proportion of the firms in Lagos State had investments of over ₦ 250,000 each. In fact about 90 of the firms had a minimum of ₦ 1 million in fixed capital.

Only an insignificant proportion of multinational firms came under Schedule I – which has to be 100 per cent Nigerian. The extent to which the multinational firms are concentrated under Schedules II and III can be seen from Table 16.5. As noted earlier with respect to firms under Schedule III, at least 40 per cent of the shares should belong to Nigerians. Under Schedule II at least 60 per cent of the shares should be subscribed by Nigerians.

TABLE 16.4: **Paid-up Capital of Multinational Firms in Lagos**

Paid-up Capital	No. of Enterprises	% share
Less than ₦ 10,000	55	8.52%
₦ 10,000 - ₦ 49,999	83	12.87%
₦ 50,000 - ₦ 249,999	174	26.97%
₦ 250,000 - ₦ 499,999	145	22.48%
₦ 500,000 - ₦ 1 million	98	15.19%
Over ₦ 1 million	90	13.95%

Source: Lagos State Ministry of Trade and Industries, 1977.

TABLE 16.5: **Nigerian Participation in the Multinational Firms in Lagos, 1977**

% Shares	No. of firms	% of firms reporting
Schedule II (60%)	394	73.92%
Schedule III (40%)	110	20.64%
61%-99% Nigerian	28	5.25%
100% Nigerian (Schedule I)	1	0.18%
Total firms responding	533	99.99%

Source: Lagos State Ministry of Trade and Industries, 1977.

As can be deduced from Table 16.5, most of the firms are set up as partnerships between Nigerians and overseas companies.

TABLE 16.6: **Period of Establishment of Multinational Commercial Establishment in Kano State**

Period	No. of Establishments
Pre-1960	33
1960-1975	20
1976-1985	25
Total	78

Source: Ministry of Trade and Industries, Kano, 1986.

Kano State

Information on multinational commercial activities in Kano State is rather sketchy. In 1977, there were a total of 78 of such firms all located in Kano city. The firms employed a total of 9,377 workers. Table 16.6 indicates the years of establishment of the companies.

In the case of the manufacturing sector, there were 230 firms all located in Kano city employing a total of 27,787 workers. Table 16.7 indicates the years of establishment of the firms.

TABLE 16.7: **Period of Establishment of Industrial Firms in Kano State**

Period	No. of Establishments
Pre-1960	16
1960-1975	82
1976-1985	132
Total	230

Source: Ministry of Establishment of Industrial Firms in Kano State.

The number of the industrial firms according to the Schedules are as follows:

TABLE 16.8: **Percentage Participation by Nigerians in Multinational Firms in Kano State**

Up to 40% (Schedule III)	8 (7%)
41% to 60% (Schedule II)	38 (33.6%)
61% to 99%	8 (7%)
Wholly Nigerian (Schedule I)	59 (52.2%)
Total responding	113 (99.8%)

Source: Based on data from Kano Ministry of Trade and Industries, 1986.

A comparison with Table 16.5 will lead us to conclude that a greater degree of Nigerianization has been achieved in the manufacturing activities in Kano State than was the case in Lagos. However, it should be noted that only 113 of the 230 firms (i.e. about 50 per cent) in Kano State actually responded to the survey.

Ondo State

Ondo State is one of the new States created in 1976. As has already been observed in Table 16.1, Ondo was one of the States which did not have any multinational corporation operating in it in 1981. Multinational corporations are very demanding in their requirements of infrastructure, skilled labour supply and other agglomeration factors. They, therefore, rarely operate in relatively poor States with regard to manufacturing and trading. Of the total of 280 manufacturing establishments in the State in 1981, none was a multinational establishment.

Table 16.9 gives information about the paid-up capital of the industrial establishments in 1981..

TABLE 16.9: **Paid Up Capital of Industries in Ondo State, 1981**

Paid-up Capital	No. of Enterprises	% Share
Less than ₦ 10,000	53	22.3
₦ 10,000 - ₦ 49,999	64	26.9
₦ 50,000 - ₦ 249,999	100	42.0
₦ 250,000 - ₦ 499,999	17	7.1
₦ 500,000 - ₦ 1 million	2	0.8
Over ₦ 1 million	2	0.8
Total	238	99.9

Source: Author's Fieldwork, 1981.

Table 16.9 indicates the embryonic stage of industrial development in Ondo State. Most of the industries have low paid-up capital. They are largely small-scale units with individual sole proprietorships. This contrasts with the situation in Lagos State. The period of establishment of the industries in Ondo State is shown in Table 16.10.

Table 16.10 further emphasizes the fact that industrialization in Ondo State is of very recent origin, mostly a post-independence (1960) phenomenon.

Implications for Regional Development

Multinational corporations exert considerable influences on the pattern of regional development in various countries, particularly in the less developed countries (Arikawe, 1983). The regional impacts of the multinational corporations may be assessed in terms of the following factors:

TABLE 16.10: **Period of Establishment of Industries in Ondo State**

Time Period	No. of Industries	%
Pre-1960	3	1.2
1960-1975	84	34.3
1976-1985	158	64.5
Total	245	100.0

Source: Author's Fieldwork, 1981.

Exploitation of Natural Resources

This activity can create employment and generate income in the natural resource area. None of the corporations investigated was, however, engaged in natural resource exploitation. Those that are so engaged have their head offices in Lagos or other towns, while they actually operate elsewhere in the country. Such companies include those engaged in oil exploitation and other mining activities. The Federal Government has through the promulgation of different edicts attempted to reduce the negative effects associated with extractive or mineral exploitation. The ecological problems and the problems of providing social amenities and employment opportunities in the rural areas of operation have often been the focus of attention.

Employment and Skill Generation

This is an area where multinational corporations could contribute to regional development. The opportunity to train indigenous skilled manpower, especially in technical and administrative spheres, has been an immense contribution to regional and national development. The trickling down effects of employment and acquired skills to the rural areas has generally been very minimal. On the other hand, the polarization effects of the activities of the multinational corporations are dominant. This feature is particularly evident in Kano State, where all the corporations are located in

Kano city with minimal linkages with the rural areas of the State.

Forward Linkage Effects of the Corporations

Little information was directly available from the available data. Generally, however, corporations dealing in capital goods and related activities which establish production links with other activities are few. In all, about 58 firms were found to be in this category. This category excludes linkages with the marketing sector.

Impact of the Multinational Corporations on Rural Industries and Other Rural Activities

One of the negative impacts of the multinational corporations relates to their advantages over rural activities in terms of capital, management skill, employment potentials, superior final output and marketing organization. Moreover, these corporations are primarily urban-based. Even among the urban centres multinational corporations in Nigeria have the tendency to locate in the large urban units and metropolises. In consequence, they indirectly contribute to the drain on the rural areas by luring to themselves the young, educated and skilled members of the rural communities. They, thus, contribute to the intensification of rural-urban migration and regional imbalance and disparities.

Conclusion

This study has focused on the role of multinational corporations in regional development in Nigeria. The specific cases of Lagos, Kano and Ondo States were examined as it was observed that generally the multinational corporations are important channels for the diffusion of the innovations needed in the development process. To benefit optimally from the advantages that the corporations could transmit to the population and the economy as a whole, the following are proposed. Firstly, the activities of the multinational corporations should be seen as complementary to those of the rural population. Therefore, efforts should be made to integrate these activities. For example, backward linkages should be established between urban multinational industries and rural agricultural activities. The success of the Nigerian Tobacco Company in encouraging the emergence and integration of small tobacco growers in its production chain is worth emulating by other establishments.

Secondly, as Arikawe (1983, p. 56) has observed, there is also the need for the Government to monitor the activities of the multinational corporations with a view to ensuring that, inter alia, they comply with those government directives which are related to rural development.

Overall, more research is needed to reveal the changing nature and impacts of the multinational corporations in all the States of the Federation.

REFERENCES

Akintola-Arikawe J.O. (1983). "Foreign Investment and Public Policy: The Canadian and Nigerian Experiences" in *U.B.C. Planning Papers: Comparative Urban and Regional Studies* CS N 8. UBC. Vancouwer B.C.

Hirschmann A.O. (1958). *The Strategy of Econòmic Development.* New Haven. Connecticut: Yale University Press.

Lagos State Ministry of Trade and Industries. The Secretariat, Lagos. Nigeria.

Lall, S. and Steeten, P. (1977). *Foreign Investment, Transnationals and Developing Countries.* London: The Macmillan Press Ltd.

Kano State Ministry of Trade and Industries. The Secretariat, Kano. Nigeria.

Myrdal, G. (1957). *Economic Theory and Underdeveloped Regions.* London: Duckworth.

United Nations Economic and Social Council (1978). "*Transnational Corporations in World Development: A Re-examination*". New York. UN.

SEVENTEEN

Dependence and Regional Development : An Analysis of the Political Economy of Industrial Change in Nigeria

JERRY GANA

The Creation of Dependency Relations

To effectively analyse the impact of the international division of labour on the regional development process in Nigeria, it is important to grasp the dynamic process which transformed the industrialized countries into the centre of a world economic system into which the other regions were subsequently incorporated in accordance with the requirements and growth dynamics of the centre. In other words, production in the peripheral countries was organised in response to external markets for raw materials. During the first phase of the creation of a centre-periphery structure of the world economy, technological and scientific progress was concentrated in the centre countries. The growth mechanism of the countries at the "centre of the system" was, largely, the overall rate of domestic investment in industrial production and technological innovation.

In the peripheral countries, however, "exports were the dynamic factor, and the constraint was to maintain the flow of investment needed to permit and expand the rural sector in order to render it capable of meeting the requirements of external demand...". (Ikonicoff, 1981, p. 8). In response to the massive demand for raw materials, the economies of such peripheral countries like Nigeria became transformed into producers of agricultural and mineral raw materials. For instance, in Nigeria the production of such crops as cocoa, groundnuts, cotton, etc., grew rapidly (Table 17.1).

TABLE 17.1: **Commodity Exports, 1955-1974**

(in millions of Naira)

Commodity	1955	1960	1965	1970	1973	1974
Cocoa	52.4	73.6	85.4	133.1	112.4	160.0
Groundnuts	55.4	59.8	106.2	77.8	85.5	21.2
Palm Oil	26.4	19.6	28.0	1.1	—	—
Palm Kernels	38.4	52.2	53.0	21.7	18.9	43.7
Cotton	18.8	12.4	6.6	13.1	4.7	2.0
Rubber	11.2	28.4	22.0	17.6	19.4	29.0
Timber and Plywood	11.2	16.2	15.4	8.1	14.7	14.1

Nigeria entered the world cocoa market in about 1892. From 1905 cocoa production expanded rapidly, so that by 1915 cocoa exports had increased to about 9,000 tons. World cocoa prices remained fairly steady from 1900 until the Great Depression of the 1930s, when producer prices tumbled. For instance, the export price for cocoa in 1934 was less than 1/3 of the 1928 price. Although there was slight recovery in the 1936-37 season, cocoa prices further collapsed in 1938-39. Commodity prices were kept low during the Second World War, but they promptly skyrocketed after the war. "By 1947, the Nigerian cocoa export price had reached a new record level, over six times that of 1939, and roughly double that of the pre-Depression years. This was the result of the sudden release of a greatly increased, though previously pent-up, world demand faced by a virtually unchanged world supply." (Helleiner, 1966, p. 85).

As shown in Table 17.2, the vastly increased producer prices after the Second World War raised income flows to producers. Although producer prices fell in the early 1960s owing to increased world supplies of cocoa, the increase in real producer incomes was maintained by vastly increased output. It should be pointed out, however, that a substantial part of the real income due to producers was withheld from them via export duties, Marketing Board trading surpluses and the produce purchase tax.

As pointed out elsewhere (Gana, 1981), income flows from cocoa exports greatly influenced the development policies of the then Western Regional Government. Regional development expenditures in the western Region were substantially greater than in both the Eastern and Northern Regions. During the period of substantial price increases for cocoa, producers enjoyed some measure of relative prosperity. However, there was a sharp reduction in cocoa farmers' prosperity following drastic (45%) price reductions from the 1965-66 season. The reductions were so drastic that the price levels fell below those of the Great Depression. Combined with the effects of petroleum production on Nigerian agricultural productivity, cocoa farmers have not really recovered from the effects of such drastic world price fluctuations.

TABLE 17.2: **Indexes of Real Producer Prices and Incomes : Cocoa 1948-100**

Period	Real Producer Price	Real Income
1914-1917	229.9	—
1923-1930	133.1	20.4
1931-1934	80.9	61.9
1935-1937	114.5	105.2
1938-1948	58.6	74.8
1949-1952	179.0	278.7
1953-1956	242.3	335.2
1957-1961	178.2	338.9
1962-1964	110.1	299.6

Source: G.K. Helleiner, 1966, p. 90.

Just as cocoa exports promoted regional development in the then Western region of Nigeria, groundnut production had some impact on the economy of the Northern region. Groundnut exports grew rapidly after the rail link from the coast to the groundnut growing areas of Northern Nigeria. By 1929 groundnut exports reached 147,000 tonnes per year. The growth of groundnut exports was not seriously affected by the Great Depression. For instance, groundnut exports rose to 326,000 tonnes in 1937. Lower producer prices during the war years affected production levels, but growth was resumed after the war. Groundnut exports rose from 428,000 tonnes in 1954 to about 614,000 tonnes in 1963. In addition, Marketing Board purchases of groundnut oil rose from 430,000 tonnes in the 1952-53 season to over 870,000 tonnes in 1963.

World groundnut prices rose in the 1920s but fell off during the Great Depression. World prices rose rapidly after the second world war. In the post-war years, Nigeria and Senegal came to dominate the world groundnut market because of the withdrawal of India from the market. According to G.K. Helleiner (1966), "the early post-war period was marked by a tremendous increase in export value. Even though a large proportion of increase in world oilseed prices was withheld from Nigeria by the British Government through the west African Produce Control Board, sufficient increases were passed along, together with increases in export volume, to produce an increase in the value of groundnut exports from £ 2.7 million in 1945 to £18.9 million in 1949 and a peak of £29.9 million in 1954" (p. 116). Perhaps the impact on producer incomes would have been substantially greater if the full price increases had been passed on to farmers.

Groundnut exports collapsed in the early 1970s, especially following the Sahellian drought of 1972-73 season. In fact, Nigeria is currently a net importer of groundnuts to the tune of 107,892 tonnes in 1978 and 170,190 tonnes in 1980 (*Nigerian Ports Authority*, 1981, p. 155).

Other major agricultural exports include cotton, rubber, and palm oil. As clearly indicated in Table 17.3, the dependence on agricultural exports has since 1971 shifted to a dependence on crude oil exports. Like agricultural exports, petroleum exports have also been greatly affected by world price fluctuations. In fact, Nigeria is currently facing a huge financial crisis partly as a result of the fluctuations of the world oil market.

Whereas the first phase of the functioning of the international economic system was characterized by exchange of primary commodities for manufactured goods, the second saw a "restructuring of the productive system on a world scale with the location of industrial activities in the periphery", (Ikonicoff, 1981, p.19). The key factors that promoted the redeployment of industrial production were strongly related to both international competition for consumer markets and internal dynamics within peripheral countries such as Nigeria.

At the international level the process was propelled by the fact that firms came to compete more through the speed innovation and product differentiation than through consumer prices. However, as Ikonicoff has rightly argued, "a growth mechanism of which a key component is oligopolistic competition based on product differentiation tends to shorten the product's market life-span drastically, with a resulting rise in costs for the producer firm," (1981, p. 20). Therefore, to offset the drastic reduction of the product's life cycle, firms struggled to expand the geographical market area. In other words, firms tended to "multinationalize" their sphere of economic production and distribution by establishing new plants and warehouses in other countries to facilitate effective product circulation.

TABLE 17.3: **Petroleum Sector's Contribution to Federal Revenue**

Fiscal Year	Federal Government Revenue (000 Naira)	Revenue from Petroleum (000 Nairá)	Share of Petroleum in Total Revenue (%)
1958/59	154,632	122	0.80
1959/60	177,648	1,776	1.00
1960/61	223,700	2,452	1.10
1961/62	228,962	17,070	7.46
1962/63	231,638	16,938	7.31
1963/64	249,152	10,060	4.04
1964/65	299,132	16,084	5.38
1965/66	321,870	29,175	9.06
1966/67	339,196	44,967	13.26
1967/68	300,197	41,884	13.95
1968/69	299,986	29,582	9.86
1969/70	435,908	75,444	17.31
1970/71	755,605	196,390	25.99
1971/72	1,410,911	740,185	41.45
1973/74	2,171,370	1,549,484	71.36
1974/75	5,177,063	4,183,816	80.81
1975/76	5,252,297	4,568,425	86.98
1976/77	5,756,328	4,833,713	83.97
1977/78	7,652,500	6,459,000	84.04
1978/79	6,815,200	5,458,800	80.01
1979/80	11,809,100	9,869,500	83.57

Sources:
(1) Ministry of Petroleum Resources, Lagos Official Records, 1977.
(2) Central Bank of Nigeria, Annual Report and Statement of Accounts for the year ended Dec. 31, 1979, p. 60.

Internal Dynamics of Redeployment

In addition to the international process outlined above, a national policy of industrialization through import substitution became operative in Nigeria as from 1957, and particularly after political independence in 1960. As shown in Figures 17.1 and 17.2, manufacturing industries were concentrated in only a few centres, such as Lagos, Ibadan, Sapele, Kano and Kaduna, Zaria, Aba and Port Harcourt. The main branches of industry at this early period

(1950-57) included food and beverages, textiles, tobacco manufacture, leather and footwear, paper, printing and publishing, furniture, etc.

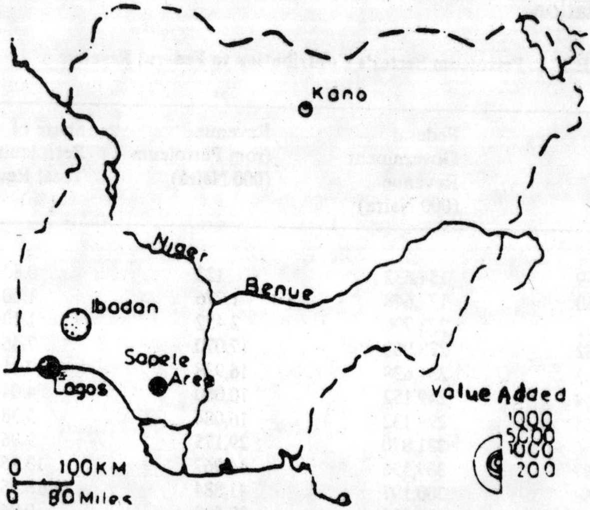

FIG. 17.1: Location of Manufacturing industries in Nigeria, 1950

To facilitate industrial growth, both the Federal and the then regional governments derived a set of industrial incentives to attract manufacturing firms to certain locations in Nigeria. The most important of such incentives were the Industrial Development (Import Duty Relief) Act and the Industrial Development (Income Tax Relief) Act of 1958. According to P.C. Asiodu;

> Under the Income Tax Relief Act, an industry can be declared a pioneer industry and a firm wishing to start activity in that particular field can obtain a pioneer certificate. This certificate would entitle the firm to a tax holiday for a period extending from three to five years, depending upon the amount of capital invested. Losses incurred during this period can be offset against profits earned when the tax holiday period expires. (1967, p. 162)

Other incentives included the creation of industrial estates at urban centres with facilities as electricity, water supply and other essential amenities; provision of funds for direct participation in manufacturing industries; establishment of development corporations; and the guaranteeing of external loans for new industrial projects. These industrial incentives plus agglomeration advantages promoted the formation of industrial agglomerations at such centres as Lagos, Kano, Ibadan, Kaduna, Jos, Enugu, Aba, Port Harcourt, Sapele, Onitsha, Gusau and Zaria (Fig. 17.3).

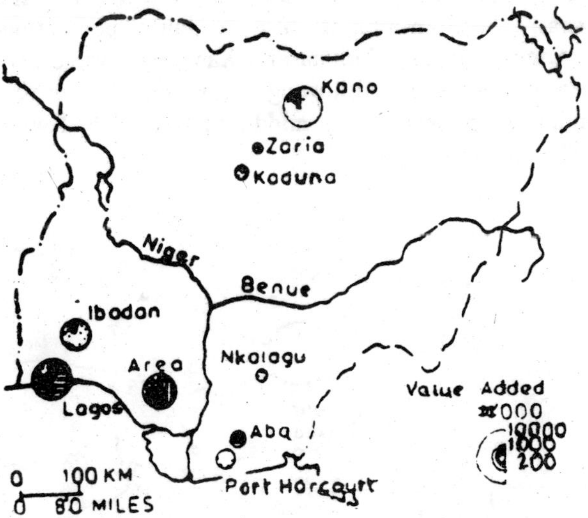

FIG. 17.2: Location of Manufacturing Industries in Nigeria 1957

A powerful factor which has influenced the spread of industrial agglomerations is the force of material orientation. Industries using a substantial amount of domestic raw materials have tended to be rooted to sources of such bulky raw materials. Such material oriented industries include cement manufacture, sugar processing, cotton ginneries, tobacco processing; and other agro-processing industries. Through this mechanism, important industries have been recently deployed to the formerly neglected middle Belt region of Nigeria. Such industries include the Bacita Sugar processing factory near Numan; Benue Cement factory at Yandev near Gboko; and the massive Ajaokuta Steel production plant near Okenne in Kwara State. The establishment of these large-scale industrial plants has necessitated the investment of substantial financial resources in a previously neglected region. For instance, over a billion Naira has been invested in the Ajaokuta Steel Factory; about Naira 47 million in Benue Cement Factory and over Naira 400 million in the Savanna Sugar Company. These relatively massive investments have created new job opportunities to which labour from the major industrial agglomeration has been attracted. A significant process of population redistribution has thus been set in motion. Perhaps it is important to point out that the middle belt region of Nigeria has, until recently, been an area of out-migration of population to such cities as Lagos, Ibadan, Kaduna and Kano. A reverse process has now been set in motion following recent massive investments in major industrial projects in the middle belt States of Kwara, Niger, Benue, Plateau and Gongola.

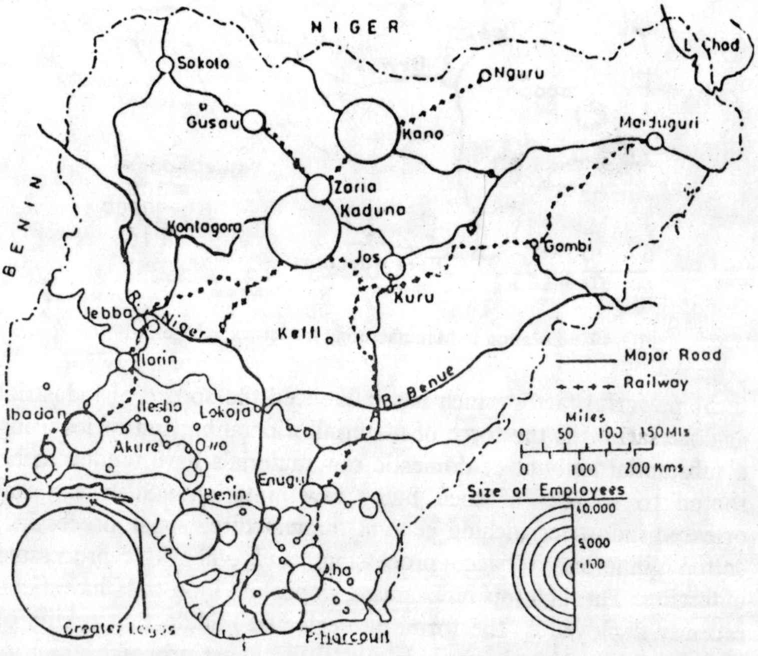

FIG. 17.3: Location of Raw Material oriented industries in Nigeria 1969 (After Schatzl, 1973)

In addition to these industrial investments the recent relocation of Nigeria's Federal Capital from the Port city of Lagos to Abuja, has occasioned new investments in infrastructural facilities to serve the new City. Between 1979 and 1982 about Naira 2 billion has been spent on projects at Abuja. Such new investments have created a new potential for regional economic development in a previously isolated and neglected region.

Productive Investments and Regional Growth

Productive investments play a crucial role in the dynamics of regional growth (Richardson, 1978). It is argued that the flow of productive investments into a regional economy creates a capacity for regional growth through capital accumulation, expansion of demand, diffusion of technology and a calculus of multiplier effects of cumulative causation processes. For instance, it is argued that new investments in a manufacturing industry within a regional economy could set in motion a chain of interacting growth processes. The basic logic is that a new investment would create employment opportunities for labour, thereby generating labour migration into the region. Population concentration would raise the crude demand for goods and services, and so service industries would be attracted to locate within the region to satisfy the expanding demand for consumer goods. Such service industries would create further employment opportunities leading to additional population concentration through labour migration. Apart from providing demand for service industries, labour migration provides the necessary work force for expanding industries. The regional economy would also gain from the transfer of labour skills and technical innovation through inter-regional labour migration.

The salaries and wages paid to industrial workers would not only provide effective demand for goods and services but would also raise the tax base of the regional government. Improved revenue would enable the regional government to provide better infrastructure such as roads, water and power supplies, schools, etc. Such improvements of regional infrastructure, it is argued, would make the regional economy even more attractive to other productive firms to locate, thereby setting in motion further growth processes.

It is argued that through such flows of productive investments and the attendant multiplier effects, internal structural changes would occur within a regional economy, such as an increase in the proportion of the labour force engaged in manufacturing industries; expansion of agricultural production to meet growing demands for industrial raw materials and services. It is held that gradually the regional economy would cross one threshold after another, leading to diversification of economic and business operations. Eventually, these growth processes could propel the regional economy into a stage a sustained and cumulative growth (Myrdal, 1957; Perloff *et al.* 1960 and 1964; North, 1964; Richardson, 1973 and Siebert, 1969). It would thus be interesting to study the kind of growth processes that new Investments would generate within the middle belt States of Nigeria in the next decade.

The Impact of Transnational Corporations

The process of the transnationalization of industrial production has had a profound effect on the structure of the Nigerian economy. During the first phase of the functioning of the integrated world economy, Nigeria like many developing countries was reduced to a producer of agricultural raw materials. The majority of the nation's labour force was located within a traditional sector which became functionally integrated into the "modern" system as a reservoir of cheap labour. The production costs of several agricultural commodities were, therefore, low and this facilitated the creation of economic surplus with increased productivity. The benefits of increased productivity were, however, appropriated by foreign trading firms and a minority elite such as landowners, civil servants, commercial intermediaries, etc. Such new income was rarely re-invested in local production of goods but spent on imports of consumer goods.

During the second phase, what was supposed to be industrialization through import substitution became a process of "industrialization through consumer pattern substitution". As Table 17.4 reveals, the structure of industrial production placed emphasis on processing and consumer service industries. The critical manufacturing sector constituted only 5 per cent of production in 1960 and 9 per cent in 1978. On the other hand, processing industries rose from an 11 per cent share of production in 1960 to 43 per cent in 1978.

In an attempt to break this pattern of dependent industrialization the Nigerian Federal Government has played a significant role in the sphere of industrial development since 1970. Backed by substantial revenue from oil as shown in Table 17.5, the Federal Government invested considerable resources in such basic industries as iron and steel, petrochemicals and essential infrastructure. In the area of steel development, industrial complexes have been established at Ajaokuta in Kwara state and Aladja in Bendel State. Steel rolling mills have also been established at Jos, Katsina and Öshogbo.

TABLE 17.4: **Growth and Structure of Production in Nigeria, 1980**

Sectors	Growth of Production (% Annual Growth Rate)		Structure of Production	
	1960	1978	1960	1978
Agriculture	-0.4	-1.5	63%	34%
Processing Industry	16.0	10.3	11%	43%
Manufacturing	9.3	13.4	5%	9%
Services	0.2	8.6	26%	23%

Source: World Bank, *World Development Report*, 1980, pp. 112-155.

TABLE 17.5: **States' Share of Federal Revenue. 1970-1978**

(Naira million)

Year	Total Revenue	Total Statutory Allocations to States	% of Total	Revenue Retained by the Federal Government	% of Total
1970	633.2	267.6	42.3	365.6	57.7
1971	1,169.0	330.8	28.3	838.2	71.7
1972	1,404.8	331.0	23.6	1,073.8	76.4
1973	1,695.3	307.3	18.1	1,388.0	81.9
1974	4,537.0	643.0	14.2	3,894.0	85.8
1975	5,514.7	1,039.9	18.9	4,474.8	81.1
1976	6,765.9	1,142.8	16.9	5,623.1	83.1
1977	8,042.4	1,202.7	15.0	6,839.7	85.0
1978	5,275.1	908.3	17.2	5,274.8	82.8

Source: Computed from *Statistics in Economic and Financial Reviews*, Central Bank, Lagos, (1970-1978).

Progress in the field of petrochemicals has not gone beyond the setting up of refineries at Port Harcourt, Warri and Kaduna. However, the latest refinery at Kaduna produces a considerable range of petroleum products. The key objective of the government is to establish integrated petrochemical industries which would facilitate the manufacture of a wide range of hydrocarbon by-products.

It is interesting to note that in the struggle to break the pattern of consumer industrialization imposed by the transnational corporations, we seem to have moved into even deeper technological dependence. This situation has arisen from the fact that the new strategy of industrialization inevitably requires the importation of advanced technology. Four major consequences may be identified. First, the capital-intensive nature of the new industries means a relatively small capacity to absorb indigenous labour. The proportionately small number of nationals that may be employed are often in the lower cadres of the hierarchy, although a few may hold key management positions. Thus the new industries cannot be used as instruments for solving the nation's unemployment problem. The new regime in Nigeria has directed that emphasis be placed more on labour intensive projects in the implementation of industrial programmes. This policy is aimed at creating new jobs for a growing "army" of unemployed youths, including University graduates.

Secondly, apart from their high technology content, a number of the new industries, especially vehicle assembly plants, depend largely on imported raw materials. Consequently as soon as the country faced the recent foreign exchange crisis and was, therefore, unable to import adequate raw materials, several manufacturing plants had to either close down or had to drastically reduce the size of their operations. This situation increased the volume of unemployed workers who had to be laid off due to lack of raw materials. It is important to note that had the imported technology been suited to local raw materials, perhaps this problem of rising unemployment could have been reduced.

Thirdly, there is the heavy dependence on international engineering firms in the construction or assembly of new industrial plants. This resort to "turnkey contracts" in which foreign engineering firms assume entire responsibility for the setting up of new production plants, has serious implications. The most critical implication is that although the indigenous labour force may be able to "master production without foreign intervention,. . . it rarely masters maintenance and servicing and still less reproduction" of the new machinery (Ikonicoff, 1981, p. 39). Indeed it can be shown that;

> ... "the big firms are still frequently in a position to impose directly or indirectly the industrial projects carried out in the peripheral countries. They suggest an idea for a project, a type of

> product, a volume of output, a technological process. They provide a ready-made study of the project free. Finally, they impose through a particular orientation and organisation of industrial development a certain pattern of social change"(*ibid,* p. 39).

Fourthly, the new strategy of industrial development tends to have a substantial foreign exchange component leading to massive external debts currently over Naira 8 billion dollars.

Thus the new strategy of industrial development has only helped to deepen our technological dependence, in the short term. Perhaps the most devastating aspect of our technological dependence is the loss of self-confidence in our own creative capacities. Indeed as Professor Mabogunje has rightly observed, "the situation is almost such that many Nigerians today hardly believe that any Nigerian can invent anything that needs to be taken seriously, When we have to deal with problems of our environment, the tendency has been to believe that only foreign expertise and know-how can help" (1978, p. 77). Herein lies the real tragedy of our dependent strategy of industrial development. Surely genuine development cannot but be an essentially human issue. It concerns the capacity of a people to effectively transform the natural resources of their environment into goods and services through the imaginative application of their own creative powers. This is not to say that a developing country like Nigeria should refuse to draw upon the scientific and technological achievements of the industrialised nations. Rather, the call is for an imaginative policy of scientific and technological adaptation relevant to the needs of Nigeria. Such a technological transformation would make it possible for our technical manpower not only to efficiently operate new machinery but to have the technical ability to maintain, service and reproduce such machinery. The new system of technology transfer being advocated would also require the fashioning for new modes of labour organization for production which emphasize cooperative solidarity rather than ruthless, competition

Indigenization Policy

Indigenization has recently been used in Nigeria as a policy instrument for achieving a more acceptable economic autonomy.

Professor Adebayo Adedeji, who contributed immensely to the formulation of Nigeria's indigenization policy, has identified four types of indigenization, namely; (a) the indigenization of ownership; (b) the indigenization of control; (c) the indigenization of manpower; and (d) the indigenization of technology, (Adedeji, 1981). Nigeria's indigenization policy promulgated in 1972 appears to have concentrated on the first three forms of indigenization. Yet, the indigenization of technology is clearly the most crucial step in any self-reliant strategy of industrial development. Studies have revealed the relative success of the indigenization policy in Nigeria (Nigerian Economic Society, 1974), but technological dependence continues and cruel poverty remains endemic.

Towards a New Development Strategy

If indeed the "release of the creative energies and potentialities of the rural masses" lies at the heart of a progressive development process, (Baran, 1973), then there is a need for a new development strategy in Nigeria. The current strategy places too much emphasis on the creation of industrial growth poles with the power to create a matrix of growth impulses and a calculus of linkages within the economy. The hope is that such development impulses would "trickle down" and transform the vast rural economy as well. This growth pole strategy has clearly failed. It is, therefore, necessary to effect a radical integration of industrial growth with a sound strategy of rural development. The details of such an integrated policy have been presented elsewhere (Gana, 1982). Quite central to the new strategy is a rural development policy which places emphasis on the transformation of natural resources and human skills for a people-centred development process. It is argued that such a strategy would require the creation of effective local instruments for the mobilization and cooperative organization of our people to enable them participate fully in the development process.

REFERENCES

Adedeji, A. (1981). *Indigenization of African Economies*, Hutchinson University Library for Africa, London.

Asiodu, P.C. (1967). "Industrial Policy and Incentives in Nigeria", *The Nigerian Journal of Economic and Social Studies*, Vol. 9, No. 2, pp. 161-174.

Baran, P. (1973). *The Political Economy of Growth*, Penguin Books.

Gana, J.A. (1982). "Development from Above or Below? Towards a new development strategy for Nigeria", *Nigerian Geographical Journal*, Vol. 25, 1982.

Helleiner, G.K. (1966). *Peasant Agriculture, Government, and Economic Growth in Nigeria*. Richard D. Irwin, Inc., Homewood Illinois.

Ikonicoff, M. (1981). *Multinationals and Development*, Paper presented at the General Conference of the European Association of Development Research and Training Institutes held at Budapest, November, 11-14, 1981.

Mabogunje, A.L. (1978). *On Developing and Development*. Ibadan University Press, Ibadan.

Mabogunje, A.L. (1980). *The Development Process; A Spatial Perspective*. Hutchinson University Library, London.

Myrdal, G. (1975). *Economic Theory and Underdeveloped Regions*. Duckworth, London.

Nigerian Economic Society (1974). *Nigeria's Indigenisation Policy*. The Caxton Press, Ibadan.

Nigerian Ports Authority, (1981). *Bi-Lingual Magazine*, 1981, Lagos.

North, D.C. (1964). "Location Theory and Regional Economic Growth", in Friedmann and Alonso.

Perloff, H.S., Dunn, Jr., E.S., Lampard, E.E. and Muth, R.F. (1960). *Regions, Resources and Economic Growth*. Johns Hopkins Press, Baltimore.

Perloff, H.S. and Wingo, L. (1964). "Natural Resource Endowment and Regional Economic Growth" in Friedmann J. and Alonso, W. (1964). *Regional Development and Planning: A Reader*. The M.I.T. Press, Cambridge, Mass.

Richardson, H.W. (1973). *Regional Growth Theory*. Macmillan, London.

Richardson, H.W. (1978). *Regional and Urban Economics*. Penguin Books.

Siebert, H. (1969). *Regional Economic Growth: Theory and Policy*. International Textbook Company, Scranton.

EIGHTEEN

The Redeployment of Functions in the Sugar Economy of Cuba

FRITZ HOENSCH

The International Division of Labour in the Sugar Economy

For more than 100 years Cuba has been the most important exporter of sugar in the world despite a relatively high own consumption of presently about 57 kg per inh. For that reason changes in the international sugar market are of immediate influence on the economic and social development policy of the country. What do these changes consist in? The changing international sugar market is characterized by

(a) decreasing rates of sugar consumption from 3.4 per cent on the average between 1951 and 1955 to 1.3 per cent between 1978 and 1982 on a global scale;

(b) a considerable regional differentiation in these rates according to groups of countries

  (i) with *increasing consumption* in some socialist countries and developing countries with low consumption rates per head and increasing numbers of population ;

  (ii) with *stagnation* in many European countries where the share of indirect or industrial consumption exceeds that of direct sugar consumption and natural or chemical substitutes increase in importance ;

  (iii) with *decrease,* mainly in the USA where synthetic sweeteners made from corn increase in importance;

(c) the spread of other natural sweeteners since the middle of the seventies with an increasing tendency. This refers to fructose in wheat, rice, potatoes, and above all corn. Already in 1982, the production of corn syrup JMRF amounted to 3 million tonnes and made up 26 per cent of the U.S. American market. For 1984, 4 million tonnes are expected. Since 1981 similar trends have occurred in Japan, the EC and Canada, too ;

(i) the promotion of these replacement effects by protectionist-fiscal measurements in some countries with an orientation to self-supply. Thus the rate of self-supply (as relation production : consumption in %) in the EC, the USA, and Japan changed as follows:

	ø 1951-55	ø 1978-82
EC	66.8	132.8
USA	55.3	59.3
Japan	4.0	25.5

The EC changed from an importer of sugar into an important exporter, in particular of refined sugar with higher export profits.

These changes are not the result of a planned international division of labour. For Cuba, as well as for other sugar-exporting developing countries, this sets limits to a long-term export policy. The export of sugar, however, is an indispensable precondition for the realization of the economic and social policy of Cuba.

Redeployment of Functions in the History of the Sugar Economy of Cuba

In a study on "Sugar Regions of Cuba" from 1956 D. Dyer wrote : "Truly, sugar is king in Cuba : for, however, sugar goes, so goes Cuba." As particularly favourable factors he mentioned the productive soils, the tropical climate with its dry season, the topography, good harbours, the U.S. market with preference clauses, the availability of U.S.-American money for investments in production and transport as well as an ample supply of good labour, and favourable political relations. Favourable for whom? The answer led up to the revolution of 1959.

This dogmatization of Sugar was an attempt to justify a division of labour the effects of which meant for Cuba a structural deformation of the national economy, marked regional disproportions, deforestation and for the majority of the population seasonal unemployment, poverty, analphabetism, high mortality of children, and a low life expectancy.

Sugar was not always king on Cuba. In contrast to other "sugar Islands" of the Caribbean from the beginning of the 16th to the middle of the 18th century sugarcane played a minor role on Cuba. The main factors of influence on the trend and intensity of land use were the interests of the Spanish Crown and the conquistadors in the order of rank : animal husbandry, tobacco; coffee, fine wood, and finally sugar. For the realization of the economic utilization and the protection of possessory interest in "donated" areas (mercedes) in this Spanish colony between 1550 and 1729 circular portions of land were formed: "hatos" with a radius of 11 km and "corralles" with a radius of 5 km ; the first ones devoted to breeding cattle, the latter to hogs, which were much greater in number. Although the slave-colonial or later capitalist sugarcane landscape had nothing to do with these original pattern of property and its use during the 16th and 17th centuries, the regional effect of these circles can be seen in part still today : in the settlement network, the arrangement of paths, roads and railways, as well as in the pattern of land use.

About 1620 there were 25 small enterprises cultivating and processing sugarcane (trapiches or ingenious respectively) around Havana and 37 in Oriente concentrated in the Bay of Santiago de Cuba or Bayamo respectively. These plants provided mainly for the demands of the local population or animal husbandry. These functions determined the location of the plants close to the consumers. Only by the end of the 17th century some export started, when the consumption of sugar in Europe increased and the Spanish Crown took an interest in its import. In 1670 84,000 arrobas (about 100 tonnes) of sugar were supplied to Spain.

In the middle of the 18th century, supported by protectionist measures, an upward tendency in the sugar economy of Cuba set in. It was caused by an increasing national demand, the seizure of Havana by the British army, the opening of new markets in the

British colonies in North America, the revolution of the neighbouring island of Haiti, and last but not least the slave trade. This jump in development is not by chance in correlation with the development of capitalism in Europe, it forms one of the sources of the accumulation of capital for this process. These factors led to a wavelike development of the country beginning in the original areas of concentration. In the course of the "occupation" of a zone by ingenious with an areal demand of about 150-160 ha. each the sugar economy spread from Havana to the east to Matanzas and further along the coast up to Cardenas. This process ended with the development of the north of the province of Oriente in the first third of the 20th century. In the beginning, the territorial expansion of the sugar economy was an extensive process without agro-technical measures for the preservation or improvement of the natural conditions of production. The small size of areas and installations made it possible to change the place when the local conditions worsened. The landscape was impacted by the clearing of vast forests and their conversion into sugarcane fields. The number of ingenious increased.

The expansion of the sugarcane economy towards the east resulted not only from the exhaustion of areas available around Havana, but also from increasing ground prices and replacement by suburban agriculture and competing cultures like tobacco and coffee.

An important driving force behind this structural and spatial redeployment was the colonial slave regime. Due to a low standard of production technology in the cultivation and processing of sugarcane production was dependent on the number of workers available. By 1620, however, the island had altogether hardly 20,000 inhabitants. Therefore, an essential increase in production could only be obtained by the import of slaves, i.e. while in the phase of evolution between 1521 and 1761 altogether about 60,000 slaves were brought to Cuba, in the following 8 decades almost 60,000 people were enslaved. This brought about a basic change in the demographic structure and its regional differentiation.

With the extension of export by the end of the 18th century the Cuban sugar producers were confronted on the world market with the price mechanism and the necessity to produce even more. For the time being, both problems were solved extensively by an increased exploitation of slaves and a constant spatial expansion of the sugarcane economy.

In the second half of the 19th century again greater functional changes took place in the sugar economy of Cuba with effects on the national, regional, and local levels. With the extraction of sugar from sugar-beets now competitors of cane-sugar turned up, mainly in Europe. After the suitability of the sugar-beet for an economic utilization had been proved in France in the first quarter of the 19th century, in other European countries, too, the growing of sugar beets increased. Between 1830 and 1840 in Bohemia alone 54 sugar plants were established. The development of European competitors forced the Cuban producers to make use of technical innovations of the industrial revolution, in particular the application of the steam engine. An increase in production could no longer be realized by horizontal expansion, i.e. by a simple addition of plants, labour and land without an increase in labour productivity. On the contrary, with the beginning of the industrial revolution the number of producers decreased and capacity increased : *a process of concentration* started that was .basically finished by 1925. The number of ingenious diminished:

1780 about 480	ingenious	1878	about	1,190 ingenious
1827 about1,000	ingenious	1891	about	850 ingenious (among them already 150-200 so-called "ingenious centrales")
1850 about1,500	ingenious			
1860 about1,360	ingenious	1899	about	270 ingenious

The process of concentration was promoted by the first war of independence (1868-1878), in the course of which many ingenious were destroyed, and by a lasting depression in the sugar economy with an absolute low point about 1883-84. The driving force behind these processes was the transition from the slave-colonial regime to capitalism. It changed the traditional social structures in the sugarcane agriculture. The dissolution of the "ingrated ingenious" based on slave labour into sugarcane latifundia (colonos)on the one side and sugar producers on the other. The sugarcane latifundia were concentrations of sugar-growing property and were distributed over the country irregularly with a distinctly greater number of them in the eastern parts of the country where the revolutionary movement was strongest.

The separation of sugar production from sugarcane agriculture was not purely a capitalist division of labour but also a subordination of the "colonos" under the sugar factories. The "colonos" with an average acreage of ca. 1,000 ha per ingenious supplied the larger modernized "ingenious centrales" or short "centrales" by contract. The first centrales developed after 1880. Between 1884 and 1891 in the region of Cienfuegos alone 13 centrales were established, among them centrale, "Constancia" as the biggest sugar plant of the world at that time.

The second war of independence of Cuba against Spanish colonial rule (1895-98) accelerated the process of concentration in the sugar economy and the transition to the *monopolistic phase of develop- ment.* The engagement of the USA in the war of independence paved the way for a direct economic intervention of U.S.-American capital in the sugar economy of Cuba. While in 1895 U.S. investments in Cuba amounted to about 50 million dollars, there was an increase to 700 million by 1929. Already in 1903 U.S.-American companies effected more than 23 per cent of all capital investments in Cuba. The extensive reconstruction of the sugar economy influenced also the international "division of labour." On the international sugar market beet sugar had reached already a ratio of 59 : 41 1890-91. The season of 1901-02 showed a ratio of 50 : 50 and in 1911 the ratio had changed again to the advantage of cane sugar and was 41 : 59. First World War brought a temporary increase of 20 : 80 and at that time Cuban centrales provided 25 per cent of world sugar production.

Compared with international developments, the expansion of the Cuban sugar economy as a consequence of the transition to the monopolistic phase of development between 1898 and 1926 was an exceptional process. Between 1898 and 1926, 75 centrales were established, the actual "boom" starting after 1909 and being promoted by First World War. The new centrales sprung up mainly at Camaguey and Oriento, to the east of the "gran zona azucarera central" of Matanzas-Cardenas-Colon. This led to a shift of the centre of production to the east, to the opening of suitable areas and increased deforestation. With centrales producing more than 300,000 sacos (sacks) per zafra (cane harvest), the so-called "Colosos" the limits of technological efficiency were reached. Partly, these "Colosos" had cane fields, ports and railway lines of their own,which made them nearly enclaves. In the region of the Nipe Bay the United Fruit Company bought 75,000 ha. for the establishment of the centrale "Preston", and for the centrales "Francisco" and "Chaparra" 32,000 or 27,000 ha. respectively passed into foreign hands. The process of concentration of the Cuban sugar economy influenced greatly the pattern of distribution of the rural population and of infrastructure. Numerous settlements developed as company-owned settlements ("bateys"), rural settlements and dispersed individual farms in the regions of the sugarcane plantations. After great numbers of Chinese workers had been recruited already in the second half of the 19th century, between 1913 and 1921 81,000 Haitians and 75,000 Jamaicans were used as cheap labour in the Cuban sugar economy.

The practically exclusive orientation on the one-crop system of sugarcane growing led to a deformation of the sectoral and territorial structure of Cuba, to political dependence, social polarization, and ecological destabilization. The Cuban L. Abad wrote on this development in 1945 :

> "... y creo que debemos pedir a los Santos patronos que nos protegen, que ese exido no siga porque en un futuro, mas o menos remoto, pudiera ser de efectos desastor para la economia, la politica y la sociedad cubana" (8-403).

Spatial Effects of the Redeployment of Functions After 1959

With the revolution of 1959 and the land reforms of 1959 and 1963 as well as the nationalization of the sugar industry a far-reaching process of socio-economic transformation of the national scale started, which included regional and local effects, too. Does sugar remain king in Cuba? – that was one of the main questions of economic policy.

When assessing downward tendencies in the sugar economy in the first period of 1959-1964, several factors have to be considered. They include the necessity of a home production of agricultural produce and the restriction of respective imports, the breakdown susceptibility of old-fashioned plants, the lack of ancillary industry, the low standard of mechanization in agriculture, as well as concepts of industrial diversification that could not yet be realized at that time.

In 1964 FIDEL CASTRO formulated the position of the revolutionary government with regard to the sugar economy : Concentration of all forces on the reconstruction, extension and modernization of the sugar industry, of the sugarcane agriculture and of transport facilities, as well as humanization of work in all phases of the production circle. The was the beginning of the second period of development. As a result of these efforts the production of sugar increased and reached a temporary climax in 1970 with a record crop of 8.5 million tonnes.

At present the driving forces of sectoral and spatial changes in the sugar economy of Cuba are ;

- the necessities of the international sugar market;
- the possibilities of scientific-technological progress;
- the social conditions and tasks of the socio-economic development of the country.

These factors have an effect on the 3 main trends of redeployment and intensification of functions.

Changes on the International Sugar Market

These require the protection and improvement of the competitiveness of Cuban sugar, i.e. continued modernization of the agro-industrial cycle and limited establishment of new centrales up to 1990 to obtain an output of 8-9 million tons of sugar during a zafra of 150 days.

From the 152 centrales working in the provinces of pinar del Rio, Matanzas, Villa Clara, Cienfuegos, La Tunas, Granma, and Camaguey. These new establishments will not lead to an essential restructuring of the historically developed and fairly stable locational pattern on the national scale. They will, however, influence the regional pattern of location, above all in the province of Camaguey, and in any case the spatial structure on the local levels.

Scientific-Technological Progress

It can be seen mainly in the diversification of the sugar economy. It takes place by way of the erection of a material-technical basis of its own and the development of an "industry of transformation. "At Manzanillo a factory for sprinkle equipment was built, at Cardenas one for railway installations, and at Santa Clara one for boilers. In 1980 the plant producing sugarcane combines at Holguin reached its annual capacity of 600 combines.

The sole interest in exporting sugar hindered the development of a derivative industry, though already in 1908 there had been attempts to make paper from bagasse. A derivative industry would include alcohol and sugar chemistry, general and luxury food industry, the production of animal fodder, as well as paper and cellulose industry. It may produce intermediate products for detergents, herbicides, polymers, rubber, pharmacentics, insecticides, synthetic fibres, blockboards, and many others. Though some side-products of sugarcane processing have still to be burnt to compensate oil, derivative industry has become a dynamic and promising branch of industry.

The Main Tasks of the Socio-economic Development of the Country

These are the improvement of the material, social and cultural standards of living, the gradual removal of spatial disparities and a further increase in production and diversification of industry and agriculture. The sugar economy is an integral part of this development and at the same time a precondition of its realization. The consistent utilization of the *new social conditions* can be seen on the regional and local levels mainly in agro-industrial integration.

Already in the twenties and thirties there had been a vertical integration in Cuba in the production line "plantation-centrale-port". It was, however, solely oriented to export (transfer of profit) and did not serve a complex spatial development. Owing to predominantly government and cooperative property involved in sugarcane production and an increase in industrial forms of production since 1980, there have been increased efforts for agro-industrial integration in regional and local levels. "Agro-industrial complexes" (CAI) connect centres of material-technical equipment for the production and processing of sugarcane and sugar, the actual production of cane and sugar, the chemical and food industries based on derivates, the fuel, cellulose and fodder industries for the utilization of side-products, storage and transport, as well as housing and public constructions, social and cultural provision and qualification, and basic and applied research. Thus, besides their economic function CAI have an important social function in the regions. By way of common funds they support the erection of new settlements and in doing this the concentration of the rural population. This concentration is a prerequisite for an improved social and cultural provision. By the policy of "autoconsumption" the CAI make use of the possibilities for growing foodstuffs for local demands existing in the regions.

Since 1965 the connection of the specialized growing areas with the centrales has been ever more realized by "centres of collection or purification" respectively (in 1985 there will be about 720 centros de acopio or 58 estaciones de limpieza respectively). They have three functions: improving the productivity of macheteros (cutters) and combines, reducing impurities for a better processing in the centrales, and supply of fodder. In order to safeguard the legal bases for the formation of CAI, in 1980 the Ministry of Agriculture had to transfer the rights and duties connected with the production of sugarcane to the Ministry of Sugar Economy. This act was the end of a long way leading from the "integrated" plantation based on slave work over the separation of centrales and latifundia and the subordination of the latter to cooperation and finally to amalgamation to form a homogeneous spatial administrative economic organism.

Summary

The redeployment of functions in the sugarcane economy of Cuba is considered as a historical process.

As a result of the historical process of division of labour the spatial structure of the Cuban sugar economy is characterized by a high rate of concentration and specialization, by an effective regional-administrative integration of the social division of labour between cane-growing and processing, and by a typical regime of land use with a characteristic social and technical infrastructure and a close connection with ports as well.

REFERENCES

Abad, Luis V. de, (1945). *Azucar y cana de azucar*. Habana : Ed. Mercantil Cubana, S.A.

Anuario Azucarero de Cuba (1958). Vol XII, La Habana : Cuba Economica y Financiera.

Cabrisas Ruiz, R., (1984). El mercado Internacional Azucarero. Situacion actual. *Cuba Socialista* 10, Marzomayo : 57-91.

Charadon Lopez, F., (1982). *La industria azucarera en Cuba*, La Habana : Editorial de Ciencias Sociales.

Dyer, Donald R., (1956). Sugar regions of Cuba, *Economic Geography*, 132, 2 : 177-183.

Gonzales Sousa, R., (1981). *Ekonomiko - geograficeskij analiz territorial 'noi organizacii trostnikogo-sacharnogo agrarnopromyslennogo kompleksa Kuby'*. Moskva : MGU. Kand. Diss.

Le Riverend, J., (1973). *Historia economica de Cuba*. La Habana : Edicion Revolucionaria, Instituto Cubano del Libro.

Maergoiz, I.M., (1964). Cechoslovackaja Socialisticeskaja Respublika, Moskva : Mysl.

Moreno Fraginals, M., (1977-78). El *ingenio*, La Habana : Editorial de Ciencias Sociales.

Perez de la Riva, J., (1979). *El monto de la inmigracion forzada en el siglo XIX*, La Habana : Editorial de Ciencias Sociales

NINETEEN

The Role of Planned Colonization in the Expansion of the Frontier in Amazonia

MARIANA MIRANDA

INTRODUCTION

In its occupation and expansion, the Amazonian frontier represents a historically specific process of occupation of new lands in which different social interests come face to face and where the action of the State, in promoting this occupation and making it possible, takes on contradictory characteristics which reflect these different social confrontations. As such, this occupation of lands turns from being a purely economic process to becoming a political one as well, and it will be seen to be carried on via specific forms which are mutually opposed but which, by virtue of the role played by the State, appear not as excluding but rather as complementing one another.

Thus planned colonization, as one of these specific forms of the occupation of space on the Amazonian frontier, acquires a character of its own, different from similar experiments in other areas, owing to the rate at which occupation takes place and the degree to which State interference occurs.

Although from the point of view of time the period in which it was put forward as the model form of occupation was a short one, planned occupation appears as an alternative form of expansion of the frontier in Amazonia and of the land policy developed by the State, and this is proved by the new undertakings of this kind which are installed there and by the continual investment of public funds.

The purpose of the present study is to clarify the significance of planned colonization in the expansion of the frontier in Amazonia, on the basis of an assessment of concrete experiments carried out there.

The analysis focuses on two questions: a theoretical and a methodological one. The theoretical one is based on the presupposition that planned colonization is carried out as complementary form of expansion of the frontier centred on the presence of monopoly capital as defined and supported by the State. And as such, although the settlement projects often do not attain their proposed objectives, i.e., uniform occupation by small proprietors inserted into a process of capitalization, they do contribute not only to capital accumulation on the frontier but also to a real occupation of space, offering effective access to the means of production, among which more particularly is the land itself for the small producer (Miranda, 1982).

According to Foweraker (1982), the concrete achievements of settlement have probably contributed little to giving shape to the expansion pattern of the frontier, but settlement nevertheless offers another context in which to investigate the forms of political mediation in the struggle for the land and capital accumulation on the frontier. It is in this direction that an examination of the real achievements of settlement should turn, not so much to see whether the objectives have been attained as to discover the significance of the experiment carried out in relation to the socio-spatial agents involved: population, settlement enterprises, State and region.

From the methodological point of view, the question comes down to the supposition that settlement can be manifested in spatially different economic and social forms, depending on the elements which have a concrete part to play in the process and their interactions and the conditions of the places concerned. Since places have the power to influence the role and value of those elements, and the elements have their value dictated by the dynamic of relationships, it is to be expected that each experiment will have its own particular characteristics and that the results will show differentiation. Therefore, the role of planned colonization is much more clearly perceived when it is assessed on the basis of the concrete results in the places where it has been established.

In the development of the present paper, the focus will be on the process occurring in the state of Mato Grosso and, as it is impossible to include all the settlement projects in the study, analysis will be restricted to three plans for the north of the state, in a region which covers the present-day municipalities of Sinop, Colider and Alta Floresta. All three have been the object of a field survey.

The area concern is cut by the main highway from Cuiaba to Santarém; the process of its occupation was bound up with the period when the Brazilian Government was stressing the policy of planned colonization, i.e., from 1970 onwards, and particularly the policy of support for private settlement projects.[1]

During this phase, private enterprises from the South began effective occupation of this space. By taking advantage of a fortuitous combination of circumstances which allied the existence of large areas of land capable of being appropriated and practically free from disputes to the pressure being exerted on the lands on the former agricultural frontiers in the South, these enterprises were able to launch out into developing settlement projects in northern Mato Grosso. Parallel with this came the simultaneous settlement projects on government initiative.

Of the three settlements studied, two are private ones begun in the seventies. They are the projects developed by Sinop Colonizadora S.A. and Indeco (Integracao, Desenvolvimento a Colonizacao), in Sinop and Alta Floresta respectively. The third one is more recent and was the result of government initiative in the execution and administration of a project carried out jointly with the Cooperca na (Cooperativa Agropecuaria Mista the Canarana Ltda.)in Terra Nova, in the municipality of of Colider.

These colonization projects each have their own characteristics and, although similar situations occur within them, they fit into the framework of a special process which deserves to be described.

Private Colonization: The Selective Occupation of Space

The settlements developed in Sinop and Alta Floresta have in common the fact that both are the result of private initiative which has as its strategy not only, as formerly happened, extractive activities and speculating with the sale of lands, but also the development of occupation projects representing long-term investments connected with the control of the land market, agricultural production and associated activities.

As such, these settlement enterprises not only looked for suitable lands where their strategy could be carried out, but also took the responsibility for the whole undertaking, including the installation of infrastructural works, with the surveying and demarcation ot the lands, the opening of local roads, the establishment of urban nuclei and the setting up of health and education services.

Another aspect they have in common is that both undertakings not only started at more or less the same time, but used identical methods of attracting occupants to the area. Using advertising and land agents, they both confined their activities to one and the same region – the South, with a preference for the state of Parana – paying likely purchasers to come and competing with each other for custom. These two companies also had a complete monopoly of the settlement schemes and the power of decision, obtaining political control of their areas through representation and competition at State and federal level. Recently, with the politico-administrative emancipation of the areas where the projects are registered and the heavy cost of dues and taxes, they have been transferring these dues to the appropriate organs, but have continued to maintain economic and political control.

These similarities, however, have not led to identical manifestations of the process, and each of the settlements has special features connected with the organizational and operational characteristics of each enterprise and its area of occupation.

The Sinop settlement

The first enterprise to begin its activities in region under review was Colonizadora Sinop S.A. (Sociedade Imobiliaria Noroeste do Parana) which in 1970-71 came to occupy, through purchase from a third party, a stretch of forest land initially 369.017,1 hectares in area-named Gleba Celeste along the Cuiaba Santarém highway, on the right bank of the river Teles Pires. Subsequently the Sinop group expanded its area of settlement by incorporating a new area of 113.146,48 hectares separated from Gleba Celeste by a strip of large ranches, which were partially exploited. Today the area settled by the Group covers approximately 550.000 hectares.[2]

Occupation began with the establishment of the physical structure of the project and the sale of the first lots through advertising campaigns and the work of real estate agents in the south of Brazil. Seeking to integrate its activity with the official government policy programmes for the occupation of Amazonia, the Company introduced into its settlement area a structure that fitted in with the kind advocated by the rural urbanization schemes defined by INCRA, but with some adaptation. Thus Gleba Celeste was organized territorially on the basis of a division into sectors comprising *chacaras* (i.e. implying small rural properties with vegetable gardens, orchards, etc.), rural lots, and a centre called the convergence or community centre. The urban base of the area was made up of the so called settlement nuclei, i.e. urban centres with political and administrative functions and provision of services.

The communities were responsible for the socialization of the settlers in the sector, who lived at an average distance of 3 km from the lots they worked on and had a church, a school and a small grocery store to attend their needs. The *chacaras* and lots were planned so as to be served by road and water.

The occupation of the whole area was carried out in successive stages.[3] The first centred on the Vera nucleus, opened in 1972 and planned to be a small town, the nucleus marking the start of the occupation. Then, in 1974, the nuclei of Carmem and Sinop were founded in Glebe Celeste· Sinop alongside the BR-163 highway from Cuiaba to Santarem, which already had its route traced out. Sinop's strategic position give it the leading place among the urban nuclei: it was there that the commercial, industrial, and service activities of the area became concentrated and, on account of its functions, it also began to command relations in the area. The other centres, Vera, Carmem and Claudia, the last-named established in 1978 with the expansion of the project, form smaller centres. Possessing a few shops, sawmills, health and education services, and technical assistance facilities for the settlers, they correspond to *vilas* (villages) or, by analogy with the rural urbanization plan, to the *agropolis* (agricultural village).

In the land structure, the distinction between *chacaras* and rural lots is a question of size and distance from the settlement nuclei. The *chacaras* are about 10 hectares in area and are situated around the settlement nuclei and, although they were planned to form a green belt round the nuclei, in practice their owners also carry on permanent crop-growing in them. An example of this was one of the first and most successful settlers in Sinop who grows coffee on his *chacara.* The rural lots are larger, though they rarely attain or exceed 300 hectares except in the most recent part of Gleba Celeste and also in part of the expansion area centred on the nucleus of Claudia.

The project is basically concerned with small units of ownership, averaging 60 hectares in area, and although there has not been any obstacle to purchasing more than one lot, the situation has remained practically unchanged, so that small properties now comprise as much as 80 per cent of the settlement lots.

The relationship of the settler to the land, expressed in the fact of ownership, is defined to a certain extent. Excluding the lots belonging to the settlement company and kept in reserve, practically 50 per cent of the settlers already possess the definitive title deeds to their lots. The rest, who have sale and purchase contracts, do not yet possess title deeds to their property, either because they have ceased paying or because they have not attempted to get their situation as owners regularized.

Although the whole area is divided into lots and almost all sold, except for the part held in reserve by the Company, only 20 per cent of the lots are occupied productively.

This shows that in this occupation by way of settlement, both the process of flight from the lands and draining away of capital and the purchase of lands without subsequent exploitation have been taking place, bearing witness to speculative acquisition carried on with the connivance of the Company.

As the Company's biggest concern was the success of the project, in a certain sense this speculation served its interests because it guaranteed the image of an occupied space and, therefore, of settlement as a successful social investment. There was, then, no interest on the Company's part in taking back the lots after they had remained three years without being exploited, as INCRA allowed them to do. In abdicating their right to take back and resale the lots, the Company was not losing, but simply not gaining, and thereby freeing itself from the bureaucratic dues and fees bound up with real estate transactions. At the same time, resale was already going on in the area, resulting from a natural process of selection, via evasion/succession which guaranteed the occupation and maintenance of the project within a small property land system.

The occupation of the space settled was carried out with people from the south of Brazil, particularly form Parana, the state of origin of the colonization group and scene of its most notable activity. Though many of the settlers who came from Parana had made their homes there, they had actually originally come from other parts of the country and formed a body of small proprietors, sharecroppers (*Parceiros and meeiros*)who now come in search of more land or their own land to till. The first to arrive were able to buy land cheaply to start their activities but they did not all remain. About 50 per cent of them sold their lands, and either went on to other places, such as Rondonia, or to the urban nuclei and there changed their activities. The initial difficulties of getting acclimatized to a place where natural conditions, despite the presence of woodland, were different from those in the south, with poor soils requiring enrichment techniques that had not been practised before, plus the failure of the coffee crop (the traditional resources of the small migrant producer) and the shortage of funds of many of the settlers who had invested all their money in purchasing the land without leaving anything in reserve and with no financing – such were the factors that determined many to give up. Even those who came to take their place were hit by the inherent difficulties of agriculture that especially affect the small producer and went through the same problem, many of them ending up by becoming decapitalized and excluded from the productive process. In this way, other social relations of production began to be introduced, such as leasing, which, by maintaining family labour, prevented many settlers who had transferred to other activities from losing ownership of the land, while at the same time it enabled those who managed to set up a production structure to use their operational capacity without immobilizing capital. However, though present, this form of land exploitation is not yet significant in relation to the whole, and it is direct exploitation by the owner of the land together with his family that continues to predominate. With a view to guaranteeing their continued stay as producers, many settlers or members of their families also exercise other activities at the same time, either in trade or industry or even in government jobs.

The differentiation that grew up among the settlers created the conditions for leasing, and simultaneously made it possible for other work relations to be introduced side by side with family labour as dominant form. Thus there appear both wage labour, more commonly found in the form of temporary work, paid either at a daily rate or as piecework, and the practice of exchange of services. As ways of using the work force among the settlers, wage labour and exchange of services occur most commonly at the most intensive periods of agricultural activity.

As for agricultural production, since the time when the project was first set up special emphasis has been placed on coffee growing as being of higher commercial value and as an attraction for the settlers in view of their tradition as coffee-planters.

At present, owing to the fall in the coffee yield, coffee is losing its importance and is being replaced by other crops. Of these, rice has become the dominant one and mechanization has been introduced. The cultivation of manioc, traditionally a subsistence crop, is being encouraged in order to supply the anhydrous alcohol plant belonging to the Sinop group.

The alcohol plant thus represents one of the forms in which accumulation takes place on the frontier.

In order to make their undertaking more profitable, the economic group, led by Enio Pippino, has diversified its activity via other enterprises, among which is Sinop Agro-Quimica S.A. (SAQ), expressly set up to produce anhydrous alcohol from manioc.

The alcohol production plant was begun in 1975 and went operation in 1981. Its aim is to facilitate capital investment and at the same time guarantee the continuing stay of the settlers in the area and promote the industrialization of agricultural products so as to meet the needs not only of the local market but that of other parts of the country as well.

To meet the demands of the plant, whose size requires a supply of manioc larger than what is at present being produced within project limits, there is a whole policy of incentives to encourage farmers to grow more. But this policy still comes up against a certain unwillingness on the part of producers who, despite total Banco do Brasil support in making loans available for the pro-alcohol programme and the plant's guarantee to consume the local production, are afraid of the financing, the price fixed for the product and their dependence on the enterprise.

The marketing of production for local, regional and even the national market is done by the Cooperativa Agricola Mista Celeste Ltda. (COMICEL), an enterprise set up when the project was installed, already included in the settlement plans, and following a scheme of compulsory membership, which goes against the guiding principles of the cooperative system of voluntary membership.[4]

The Cooperative sells farming production and supplies utensils, machinery and inputs. In exchange for crop processing and for cash advances based as future of product the Cooperative is responsible for production storage in its own storehouse and as those belonging to Cibrazem. From the start it was also responsible for drawing up fund-raising projects. This function was abandoned since an EMATER office was installed in the area and because producers start to obtain individual credit directly from the banking system.

Although all the owners of lots are members of the Cooperative, not all who are included in the production process use the services of it, but may prefer to market their products via private individuals, local merchants. Those who act in this way do so either because they do not agree with the Çooperative's way of acting or because they have stopped trusting the Cooperative system after previous negative experience of it, or again because it has become disadvantageous for them to take their products to the Cooperative.

This non-participation of members makes matters difficult for the Cooperative, which also has to face financial problems connected with the shortage of capital. Although thc Cooperative serves the settlers, the advantages arising on each side will be greater for the Cooperative. According to a statement by one of its directors, it is not serving the members as well as it should be, but for some time it did provide the basic support for the project and its success.

Bearing in mind that the majority of the directors of the Cooperative are people connected with the colonization group, the Cooperative is beginning to be a way for the group to retain control of initiative and economic power.

The settlement company does not maintain control only via the enterprises belonging to the group, but also by many of the Cooperative.

The economic development of the Sinop region, made possible by the settlement process, is not getting support from rural activities. The difficulties experienced by the settlers as producers, stemming from the price of products, problems connected with the shipment of products, and the high rates of interest on financing – when it can be obtained – do not guarantee agriculture a return which can allow it to play this role. The various activities introduced with the colonization project, chief among them being the timber industry which has in its increasing expansion already passed from the processing stage to that of manufacture, are responsible for the growth of the town of Sinop and for the ongoing development.

The Alta Floresta Settlement

The occupation of the space which was to form the municipality of

Alta Floresta originated in the public auction of unoccupied public lands for settlement projects that was held by the state of Mato Grosso in July 1973, and in the purchase by Indeco S.A. of an area of 400.000 hectares in open bidding. Indeco, with its head office in Sao Paulo, purchased these lands in order to carry out an Integrated Colonization Programme (there being a time-limit of 5 years for implementation of the programme) and establish the infrastructure. From this time on, the company, presided over by Ariosto da Riva, who had experience of settlement projects in northern Para and southern Mato Grosso, began its studies to develop the project and undertook a forest-clearing scheme.

The actual occupation of this area, which is on the west side of the Cuiaba-Santarém highway but has a privileged geographical position in relation to its own state and Para and Amazonas, began in 1976 with the arrival of the first settlers to Gleba Alta Floresta and the inauguration of the urban nucleus of the same name.

The occupation took place in accordance with the guidelines drawn up by the enterprise for its settlement projects. Though it used the same system to regiment the population as its sister settlement of Sinop, it did, however, put forward a different territorial organization.

In the Gleba Alta Floresta, as in the other stretches of land where the enterprise carried out its settlement activity in the region, the physical structuring comprises an urban zone surrounded by an area of settlement lots and peripheral area of autonomous farming lots.[5]

The urban base of the project is centred on a single nucleus, the town of Alta Floresta, while its rural base covers many miscellaneous-sized areas earmarked for various purposes. Thus, in the area intended for settlement by small producers on family bases, the lots vary from 100 to 300 hectares in size, while in the farming project area the sizes are much larger and may even reach over 10.000 hectares.

With this land structure the settlement company sought to guarantee the success of the undertaking, because on the one hand it opened up access to the land to different levels of producers, bringing the medium and large investor to the area, while on the other hand it built on the principle of complementarity to ensure that the settlers would remain there: they would provide manpower and the production of means of subsistence and also have the opportunity to supplement their family earnings.

To Alta Floresta also came settlers from the south of the country, many of them from areas that had been opened in Parana and Santa Catarina less than thirty years before. In moving. they were seeking to escape from a land structure that was hampering their growth.

The whole territorial organization of the settlement arranged by Indeco was devoted to creating the spatial conditions that would make occupation possible, whether by determining that all the lots should be served by roads, or by benefiting the rural environment with a school network which would be a factor in the settlement area to encourage the settler and his family to stay, and also be the physical base for the functioning of the rural community.

Not all the lands purchased were occupied. Although the settlement company wanted the land occupied as a means of carrying out the project and the settlement process, since it was a private undertaking there could be no legal basis for making occupation a requirement, and at the same time it would not serve the interests of the enterprise itself if a limit were set to the demand. Thus, once an occupation had begun that would project a successful image of the undertaking, it did not matter that many purchases were merely speculative ones. Quite on the contrary.

In Alta Floresta the attitude adopted by the settlement company in Sinop is reproduced.

The enterprise itself, in its strategy not to exhaust the land market and guarantee control of it, not only left areas in reserve, but also took advantage of the motivation of the initial project to expand its activity in the remainder of the area acquired by auction and in another area purchased by the group.

Starting from Alta Floresta, 58 km to the west the establishment of a new project–Paranaita–was begun. Occupation commenced on the same lines in 1979, with the urban nucleus of Paranaita as its centre. Paranaita today has developed a life of its own. It is a smaller centre than Alta Floresta. Now the enterprise has also begun the carrying out of Project Apiacas, 200 km from Alta Floresta, and is marketing its lands.[6]

In this process of occupying the space divided into lots by Indeco, particularly in the Alta Floresta part, many settlers who had bought 100 hectares. lots and later found they had insufficient capital to develop agricultural production, redivided their lots and sold them to third parties by private deed. As legal registration is only given by the Company after the purchaser has fulfilled his obligations, these redivisions brought problems with them in regulating the land situation. But it was the way the settlers found to preserve themselves as producers and owners of the land. Those who regarded the purchase of land in this new area as a profitable investment and did not wish to leave it immobilized or think of moving from their place of origin, sent agents mostly farmers lacking means of production, to occupy these lands as share-croppers.

This situation, allied to the fact that coffee was the principal crop grown in the area and needed plenty of labour made share-cropping a frequent relationship. Many settlers needing labour brought other families along to work on their lands under the same system of share-cropping. To these families this mode of work began to be a chance for them to convert themselves into owners too, and this made them potential purchasers from the Company, who stimulated, this relationship. The fact is that those who managed, one way or another, to accumulate capital became purchasers in the settlement.

Since private colonization companies use their mechanisms of control to prevent their lands being invaded, those share-croppers who have not been able to change their situation or who, as share-croppers, no longer have the means to subsist, appeal to the government land agency INCRA for support for their claims to access to the land.

In order to answer these appeals, a strategy has been established by INCRA to place the settlers in a small stretch of land–the PAC Carlinda–as part of a process associated with the Cotia Cooperative. For this stretch of land, which is contiguous with the area settled by Indeco, the largest and most needy families are selected. This move by the State to absorb families supports the settlement company in its control of the land market while at the same time it guarantees the presence of a potentially available work force in the neighbourhood of the Project area.

From the time it was formulated, the Project specified that the agriculture to be practised should be deversified by associating crop-farming with stockbreeding and orienting the activities with regard to the size of the properties concerned.

Alta Floresta has more fertile land than Sinop and permanent crops–coffee, cocoa, guarana–were introduced. Coffee, as a result of its being a crop traditionally practised by the settlers, was grown on the biggest scale, but has been showing a fall in yield which has discouraged many settlers from keeping it up. Temporary crops are planted to try and guarantee the production of basic foodstuffs–rice, beans, maize–rice being the biggest in terms of production and market value. Stockbreeding is carried on the large properties, or among settlers with the larger lots, jointly with crop farming, although even settlers with small properties are trying to introduce it as a form of defence against the vicissitudes of subsistence cropfarming or the low coffee yield.

The differentiated use of the land by the settlers, both qualitatively and quantitatively, will be seen to reflect the socio-economic differentiation that exists among them.

Settlement is not a satisfactory process for all of them, and this confirms their selectivity, although they all face both the general problems of agriculture and the particular ones connected with the district where they have settled, such as transport, the price of product, and the cost of processing and storage.

Besides those who use that they can accumulate to try and reproduce themselves, there are also a good number who only manage to survive as settlers or have already given up farming and turned to other forms of subsistence, especially prospecting, which–alongside temporary work–also represents a way of supplementing their earnings.

Nevertheless, the area is undergoing largescale development which, just as in Sinop, is not sustained by agriculture.

Indeco S.A. acted differently from Sinop S.A. in not itself assuming the running of a series of undertakings in the area, but it did stimulate private initiative to come, creating the material conditions and/or guaranteeing the financial companies necessary for getting them installed, on the principle that to bring investors into the area meant an opportunity for progress and the generation of new jobs. Among the undertaking which became established in the area are those of the NB Group, which possesses among other enterprises the Companhia de Armazens Gerais (General Storage Company)–COAG. This company, jointly with a storehouse on Fazenda Caiabi belonging to the Indeco group, and with

CIBRAZEM and CASEMAT (which are state and federal government enterprises) is responsible for storage of produce in the area.

The development of town of Alta Floresta, whose varied functions have led to its assuming the role of a regional centre in this part of the state, is much more bound up with the presence of these investments and the circulation of money generated by goldmining, which is an important economic activity in this part of Mato Grosso, than with the agricultural activity for which it constitutes a focus of services.

The Alta Floresta settlement group, like that of Sinop, in a capital/State link up using political and administrative mediation, has obtained for its area the supporting infrastructure which enables it to continue with its project, thus guaranteeing the initial and future investment and control over the settlement's space.

Direct State Action : the Settlement Process in Terra Nova

Unlike what happened in Sinop and Alta Floresta, the settlement of Terra Nova developed from government initiative with the main aim of resolving the calamitous situation created by the expulsion of settlers from the Nonoai and Guarita reserves in Rio Grande do Sul in 1978. To meet the needs of this surplus landless rural population and so eliminate a focal point of social tension, the federal government decided to use the public lands situated in what is today the municipality of Colider for a colonization project, thus offering access to the land to these small farmers from the south.

In order to implement this emergency programme, the Coopercana Cooperative[7] was called in to collaborate on executing and administering the project on the lines of the policy adopted by the government. Coopercana was chosen on account of the experience gained by its directors in colonization projects in the state of Mato Grosso. Thus Coopercana, constituted to act as a production and consumption Cooperative, took on the role of a settlement company, different to a certain extent from the others, since its activity was delimited by government resolutions.

The Cooperative was given the credentials to undertake the development of the programme within the official policy for a settlement project, and was given power to establish it, sell lots and execute the transfer and placing of the settlers. Initially, the lands would be transferred to the Cooperative, who would sell them to the settlers via a land credit project.

Subsequently, with the project already under way, the federal government revoked this resolution and made a contract with the Cooperative for concession of the use of public lands. For the Cooperative, this represented losses in comparison with the initial advantages of the appropriation of the unoccupied public area, since it limited the return on the capital invested.

It can be seen from this how changes in government guidelines can alter a whole process the State itself has unleashed, with direct reflexes on the aims proposed and on the other agents involved.

The purchase of lots by the settlers re-established in the area was effected by means of financing via Proterra credit facilities over a period of 12 years, with 3 of grace and 9 for repayment at an interest rate of 12 per cent per annum.

The programme as it appears today comprises two projects, Terra Nova I and II, and is the result of alteration made to the initial project which were dictated by the actual carrying out of the work of establishing it and by events that subsequently occurred in the area, such as invasion of lands and prospecting.

With a total area of 207.000 hectares, the overall project at the moment actually occupies 186.00 hectares in a physical structure comprising 9 rural sectors, each of which has an *agrovila* functioning as a secondary urban nucleus and in which the homes of the settlers are located on *chacara*-type lots, and a main urban nucleus–the town of Terra Nova itself–following the official model.

The occupation of the area began in 1978, when the first families were brought in and placed. By 1979 there were already 632 families installed. From the initial period up to June 1982 more than 1,000 new families had been settled within the area of the programme, almost all of them from Rio Grande do Sul, but some also from Parana and the areas of social tension in Mato Grosso; Caceres, Parabuburi and Sete Quedas.

As the measure to relocate the settlers from the south included all those who had been dislodged from the Indian reserves, there was no real selection. Thus lots were granted not only to farmers but also to people with no agricultural background, which meant a contradiction between the objectives and the actual settlement, but was in harmony with political imperatives.

In this way what had occurred in other places was reproduced in this area, and the process of natural substitution was also helped on via the giving up and/or transfer of lot.

This process results from various causes, but in the case of Terra Nova the most important was the inability of many settlers to cultivate crops to guarantee their reproduction or to direct an agricultural undertaking, the result of having come without any previous agricultural experience.

To this should be added financial and health problems among them that of malaria, hitherto unexperienced by the majority of the in-migrants. Delay in releasing financing, both for settlers to develop their activities and for the Cooperative to supply them, had the result that families who did not have the initial capital needed for exploiting the land were forced to transfer their lots and seek a different activity in order to subsist. The unreliability of the health services, their high cost, and the difficulty of access to the centres which could provide them led many settlers to abandon their activity and leave the area. It is calculated that 35 per cent of the settlers gave up, abandoning or selling their lots to third parties. All this reveals the bureaucratic blunders of the settlement undertaking and the ambiguous part played by the State apparatus.

The present situation shows that, although the programme in regard to the two projects has its physical structure defined and the settlers officially placed and possessing the title-deeds granted by INCRA (in 1982 there were 1,062 registered lot owners), there are still a number of difficulties that have to be faced by those who have come to occupy the area.

Occupation via official colonization was not a tranquil process differing from the two previous ones. Moments of tension were and continue to be experienced in the area owing, on the one hand, to problems connected with the implementation of the project and, on the other, to occurrences recorded during the process. Since it was a government undertaking, it might have been expected that the process would develop harmoniously, but that was not the case, paradoxically enough. This sprang from the very ambiguity of the policy and action of the State. The failure of the parties involved to fulfil agreements and responsibilities (government/cooperative, cooperative/community, government/community) plus the natural difficulty of adaptation to a new region were the first causes.

Invasions and landgrabbing–which were not taken into account in the system adopted–came along to help worsen the problem.

One result of the official planned process was the coming of other families, many of them relatives of settlers, who made their homes in *agrovilas* and invaded the remaining areas, as they had their claims to lots answered. Attempts to regularize the situation were made but came up against the dynamic nature of the process.

The growing prospecting activity in the tributaries of the river Peixo to Azevedo led to the invasion of one area of the project and the formation of an urban nucleus which rapidly expanded. At the same time, landgrabbing within the project area generated conflict. The action of these landgrabbers, placing squatters in the area with the support of state politicians, clashed with the role of the Cooperative as executor of the settlement project and was weakly supported by the federal organs. Both conflict and complicity of interests are thus well in evidence, as well as the contradiction of the bureaucratic machine in the process of mediation.

One important point to be stressed in the whole problem is that the producers hardly manage to get a surplus, and for many it is only an insignificant one. Devoted basically to producing rice and maize and some coffee, whereas it is better-priced products such as guarana and latex that are now being incentivated, the settlers come across the problem of the price of the product, the cost of transport, and the cost of processing, credit here too frequently forcing them to seek another source of income. In the present case, prospecting is the most frequent alternative.

The Cooperative does not act in the area only as the executor of an official settlement plan, but also has the function of marketing, processing and storing production.

In this way a link is established between the settler as producer and the cooperative as marketing agent for his produce, which makes it possible to appropriate the small surplus created and accumulate capital.

The situation as seen in Terra Nova reveals that the official settlement model reproduces similar situations in different places. Thus we shall find, in the same form as already identified in the case of the Transamazon Highway (Miranda, 1982), a spontaneous occupation process imposing itself on what had been planned; stagnation and/or abandonment of most of the *agrovilas* alongside the growth of others because of their position in the area; the exodus to the urban nucleus, so generating the development of the town; differentiation of the settlers with the permanences and growth of those who overcame the risks and uncertainties in the process of selection. But this reproduction takes place at a rate and a time peculiar to the place and also adopts its own peculiar form.

Planned Colonization and the Expansion of the Frontier

Final Considerations

Settlement in northern Mato Grosso expressed concretely in the three projects studied has not produced a whole that can be considered homogeneous. Although the experiments represent identical forms of occupation and have common objectives, each of them reflects a differentiated pattern of occupation dictated by the intrinsic internal contradictions.

But while each project constitutes a concrete reality with different results in each case, taken as a whole they represent a mode of private enterprise and State operation in the expansion of the agricultural frontier.

Although as colonization plans in response to economic incentives and definite political objectives, these projects do not imply effective productive occupation of the lands and do not ensure the insertion of all the families of small proprietors into a process of capital accumulation or their reproduction in the conditions idealized, they have encouraged the occupation of the region and do constitute the form responsible for the unleashing of the development process there, so contributing to the forging of changes and new realities, in Amazonian space.

In this sense, even if planned colonization, whether private or government directed, is a long way from being the success that the settlement organizers wish to believe, it is at the same time by no means the failure that many make it out to be. It is between these two extremes that the relations which take shape via the settlement process appear materialized in the space of the frontier.

The planned çolonization, which is a process aimed at offering effective access to the land to rural workers and their families, makes it possible, through labour on the land and production for a market, to create a surplus which is appropriated directly by those who hold capital in the settlement area, and indirectly by the State.

Although the settler is the owner of the means of production, in most cases he only manages to guarantee his reproduction. Cases of keeping the wealth produced, the surplus, are in a minority, which points to the heterogeneousness and the selectiveness of the process and does not confirm the optimistic discourse either of the settlement enterprises or the State.

To the extent that planned settlement, irrespective of its success, stimulates the search for more land for production via the entry of new people into the area in quest of similar conditions and/or the abandonment of them for other areas (an exodus/succession movement), it maintains a constant association of land and work and therefore the appropriation of the surplus created, generating accumulation for the investors and particularly for the settlement enterprises. The events recorded in northern Mato Grosso, exemplified by what is occurring in Terra Nova; by the relations of the Sinop settlers with the Group's enterprises, especially the cooperative and the alcohol plant; by the action of Indeco in bringing investors into the area and also widening their area of settlement to include Paranaita and, more recently, the new front at Apiacas; or by the new projects in the area, like the Bandeirantes one-all well illustrate situations in which accumulation is achieved.

The private settlement companies acting in the region, identified as development companies, related to the capitalist stage of expansion of the frontier, and belonging to the monopoly fraction of capital, need to have a guaranteed return on their investments. For this reason they need not only to appropriate the value created by economic activity but also maintain control of the land for as long as possible. What has been noticed is that, in the case of economic control, this has been done through domination of the land market and the commercial and credit networks linked with settlement.

In the second case, that of political control, they will seek support outside the local sphere, in the various echelons of the federal administration. In this way, the political support offered to the private settlement enterprises is inserted into the context of State activity and the relations between the State and the enterprise materialize through a policy of connections between private enterprise and the public administration.

From what has been noted in the study area it can be inferred that in the settlement process, whether public or private, bureaucracy plays such a fundamental mediating role that one can agree with Foweraker (1982) when he asserts that the mediation of bureaucracy is essential for making profits on the frontier.

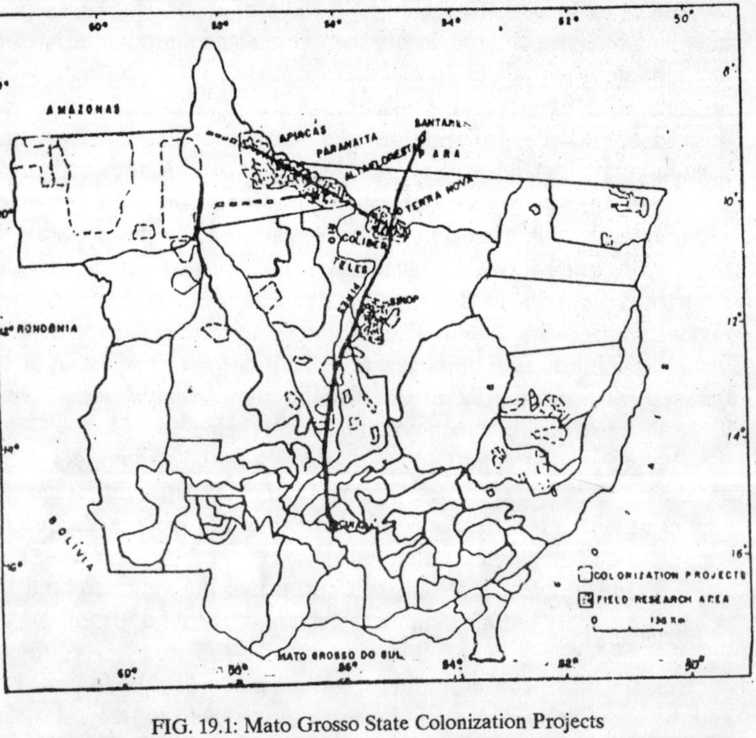

FIG. 19.1: Mato Grosso State Colonization Projects

As for planned colonization, it can also be inferred that, though oriented by definite common principles, it appears with well-marked special characteristics depending on whether the process is linked with the action of the government or private groups. One of these specific features is the degree of selectivity of the process, which is much more accentuated in private settlement. In this form of settlement, access to the land implies the pre-existence of resources, which will be more and more required as the land gains in value during the development of the process. Another point is that of the presence of a spontaneous process going on parallel with the planned one, and its implications for the land in question. In the official settlement the planned process has generally induced a spontaneous search for land in the settlement areas, and this has, resulted in conflicts and disputes over the land in question. The events observed in Terra Nova and those recorded during the occupation process in Altamira in the Transamazon region from 1974 onwards are very expressive of this specific feature of official settlement. In private settlements, on the other hand, on account of the need for a return from the investments and the appropriation of the surplus, control over the land is maintained by the settlement authority, who guards his area from invasion by his own mechanisms, which comprise not only control and inspection but also the incentive to adopt social relations of production that guarantee the work on the land and/or to protect his interests through contact with government agencies.

Thus, from the reality studied and from what had previously been seen in studying the official colonization area in the Transamazon region (Miranda, 1982), a number of conclusions can be drawn as to the role of planned colonization in the expansion of the Amazonian frontier.

In the first place official planned or private colonization has contributed to the movement of frontier expansion, showing itself as an alternative form for this and as a complementary form of occupation, partly responsible for the spatial pattern of expansion in that region. It constitutes a point of equilibrium in the question of the struggle for the land, in that on the one hand it offers the State the chance of solving conflicts in the rural area, so preserving the character of the land as private property, and, on the other hand, guarantees the small farmer access to the land and the chance of improving his condition as a producer even if it is through a selective process, with unequal effects and subordination to capital. Besides this it constitutes one of the forms by which the process of capital accumulation of the frontier is made possible.

From the point of view of the purpose of the theme in question, however, other realities also need to be assessed and new inquiries formulated for a better understanding of them.

NOTES

1. Private settlement represented a way in which the State could attract private enterprise by creating the conditions for the expansion of capitalism and accumulation on the frontier.
2. According to the map provided by the colonization company and information obtained from field interviews.
3. The settlement took place in parts, covering areas of various sizes. The first four parts covered respectively 67.597,68 ha, 71.826,96 ha, 67.274,82 ha, and 129.359,62 ha, according to data supplied by INCRA.
4. On becoming a member, each purchaser in the settlement area promised to pay dues corresponding to 1 per cent of the value of the lot or *chacara* to make up his shares in the social capital of the cooperative.
5. In Alta Floresta the project covers 211.916,05 hectares, of which 3.618,04 hectares are for the urban area, 95.209,24 hectares for settlement, and 112.453,03 hectares for farming lots.
6. According to plans provided by Indeco, the areas occupied by Projects Paranaita and Apiacas cover 183.033,36 ha and 164.800,00 ha respectively.
7. Cooperativa Agropecuaria Mista Canarana Ltda.

REFERENCES

Almeida, Ana Luiza Osorio de (1981). *Tipos de fronteiras e modelos de colonizacao na Amazonia : revisao de literatura e especificacao de uma pesquisa de campo.* Rio de Janeiro : IPEA/INPES.

Arezzo, Dryden Castro de (1982). *Colonizacao.* Brasilia, D. F. Fundacao Petro nio Portela.

Arruda, Helio Palma (1978a). *Amazonia Legal : Panorama Fundiario e Ocupacao.* Sao Luis : INCRA.

Arruda, Helio Palma (1978b). *Colonizacao oficial e particular.* Brasilia : INCRA.

Becker, Bertha K. (1983). *A fronteira em fins do seculo XX. Proposicoes para um debate sobre a Amazonia.* Uberlandia, MG: UFB

Castelo Branco, Joao (1951). Planejamento e Colonizacao em Mato Grosso. *Revista de Servico Publico :* DASP.

Coopercana (1982). *Programa Terra Nova: relatorio geral* 01/82. Barra do Garcas: Cooperativea Agropecuaria Mista Canarana Ltda.

Foweraker, Joe (1982). *A luta pela terra: a economia politica da fronteira pioneira no Brasil de* 1930 *aos dias atuais* Rio de Janeiro; Za har Editores S.A.

Goodman, David Edwin. (1971). Expansao da fronteira e colonizacao rural : recente politica de desenvolvimento no Centro-Oeste do Brasil. In : *Dimensoes do desenvolvimento brasileiro,* ed. Baer-Werner. Rio de Janeiro: Editora Campus.

Jatene, Heliana da Silva (1938). *Reabertura da fronteira sob controle: a colonizacao particular dirigida na Amazonia.* Uberlandia, MG: UFB

Miranda, Mariana (1982). *Government colonization projects and the expansion of the agricultural frontier : a case study in Altamira.* Belo Horizonte, MG: IGU. Fundacao Joao Finheiro.

Oliveira, Joao Mariano (1983). *A esperanca vem na frente.* Tese de Mestrado. Sao Paulo : USP

Santos, Milton (1982). O espaco e seus elementos: questao de metodo *Revista Geografia e Ensino,* 1, 1: 19-30.

Turchi, Lenita Maria (1979). *Eolonizacao dirigida: estrategia de acumulacao e legitimacao de um estado autoritario.* Tese de Mestrado Brasilia : UNB.

Turchi, Lenita Maria (1981). Colonizacao dirigida no processo de expansao e ocupacao da fronteira agricola: Territorio Federal de Rondonia. In: *Anais do* 20 *Encontro Nacional de Estudos populacio nais.* Sao Paulo: Associacao Brasileira de Estudos Populacio nais : 298-334.

TWENTY

The Challenge of Urbanization in Contemporary Arab Gulf States

ISHAQ Y. QUTUB

INTRODUCTION

There has been a growing concern by social scientists in studying urbanization in Arab countries. Although this part of the world experienced urban growth for centuries after the advent of Islam, earlier studies have treated urbanization in a descriptive manner, pointing out general trends and characteristics and little attention was given to an analysis of urbanization until the past decade.

This paper will attempt to discuss the urbanization growth in the Gulf States located along the Arab Gulf waters, mainly: Kuwait, Bahrain, Qatar, United Arab Emirates and Oman. More specifically, the paper:

- gives a brief historical background of those events relevant to the urbanization process;
- provides theoretical treatment;
- projects the present demographic trends in the States concerned, since quantitative population composition is indicative of present and future urbanization in the area;
- discusses some urban characteristics and development trends indicating how the States in question experience a unique urban growth, unlike that of other Arab countries;
- singles out some socio-economic factors influencing urbanization with emphasis on the labour force structure;
- briefly discusses determinants of a future urban strategy relevant to the region in view of the current socio-economic and political developments taking place in this part of the world;

– points out the need for social research relevant to urbanization in the countries of the region.

Historical Perspective

Historical evidence of flourishing cities in the Arab countries is ample throughout the various phases before and after the spread of Islam. Their urban structure reflected the economic, political, social and spiritual value systems of the various historical eras. Writings on Arab civilization, most of all by the Arab sociologist Ibn Khaldoun, have described the nature of Islamic urban society and culture as compared to Bedouinism.

The Arab world today exhibits a great population concentration in towns and cities along four distinct and rapidly urbanizing corridors:

1. North Africa parallel to the Mediterranean coast.
2. Along the Nile from north to south.
3. Northwest parallel to the Mediterranean seashore.
4. The valley of the Tigris and Euphrates rivers including the oil-producing corridor.

These corridors comprise the bulk of Arab cities with a population of over 60 million inhabitants.[1] A focus of urban growth can also be discerned along the southwestern strip of the Arabian Peninsula.

The settlement patterns in Arab countries show a concentration of population either in major cities or in a great number of very small settlements. A striking characteristic of this pattern is the scarcity of medium sized settlements.[2]

The Gulf States are situated along a strip of land stretching nearly 1,000 kilometres in length and between 200 and 300 kilometres in width, covering an area of about 226,000 square kilometres. The environment is largely desert, with dry hot weather six to eight months of the year with temperatures reaching up to 50 degrees Centigrade and humidity reaching 80 per cent in cities close to the water. Easterly and westerly winds are constant and carry sand and dust in addition to high humidity, making living difficult, especially in summer months.

The States share a long and common history, full of wars and competition between the Eastern and Western nations. Each with its own special interest has attempted the domination of the Area.[3] Historically, the Gulf States have always maintained very mobile population: nomads on the move, trading and conquering Arabs, commercial stations between Southeast Asia and the Middle East, as well as conquering Europeans and the oil corporations. Politically, the region is closely affected by the instability prevailing in the countries around, e.g.: Palestine, Lebanon, Iraq and Iran.

The same instability applies to the indigenous population of the countries of the Gulf region themselves. Disputes among the tribes in Saudi Arabia, Kuwait, Bahrain, United Arab Emirates and Oman were dominant for hundreds of years before the discovery of oil and before independence. Even now, there are disputes on the borders of some of the countries.

When members of one tribe disagree with the Emir of their State, they just move across the borders to a neighbouring State and request refuge, instantly they are welcomed and given citizenship in addition rights and privileges. These concessions are granted for political and social reasons, such as increasing the population of the host State and intensifying the loyalty of the tribes.

International capitalism and Western technology have manipulated economic activities derived from crude oil, thus widening the gap between petroeconomic activity and the distribution of oil income.[4] This has adversely affected the role of the tribe as socio-political unit and has promoted cultural-political changes as well as changes in urban development and population structure.

Population changes were more significant in the Gulf States and, in spite of the naturalization process, the immigrant groups who came in to work outnumbered the local population: in 1985, the nationals in Kuwait represented only 42 per cent of the population, and in UAE only 27 per cent. Also internal migration from Bedouin settlements to cities, due to economic and political factors, has increased to the extent that Bedouinism is now diminishing.

In view of the lucrative returns from the employment and other benefits given by the governments, traditional economic sectors have disappeared and have shifted to modern commercial sectors and the public service sector. Local manpower has moved into non-productive sectors, which has caused an increasing dependency on a foreign labour force in the semi-skilled, skilled and non-skilled occupations.[5] Although oil was discovered in the countries of the region during the same period, the investment of revenues was delayed and varied from one State to another, thus affecting the rate of their socio-economic development.

The same traditional production pattern had prevailed in all the regions of semi-urban settlements scattered along the sea coasts of the countries, stretching from Kuwait to Oman: namely, simple agriculture in oases, sea fishing, simple commerce and trading, camel herding and pearl diving. These activities, in addition, to shipbuilding, and the handicrafts of tent-making, hunting equipment, carpets and other articles had affected their social relations and social structure for centuries.

The discovery of oil and the subsequent increasing revenues induced modern development linked with westernization. The region emerged into a transitory phase between traditional tribal societies and modernized systems of education, communication, hostpitalization, recreation and commercialization. Traditional value systems have been influencing modern social systems and social change is facing traditional forces in various aspects of urban life.

Theoretical Treatment

In theorizing urban processes in the Gulf States, consideration should be given to historical, political, economic and social development for each of the phases of development. Other factors include the cultural, spiritual, heritage and values, ideologies and demographic trends. Urban expansion in the present and in the future, development of specific conceptual framework, by which analysis and interpretation of various urban processes can be readily feasible, and a meaningful synthesis of interrelationships of the various elements inherent in the process.

In the Gulf States, the city is the State and the various States are but a concentration of the constituent population in one major habitation called "City". Reviewing various theoretical attempts during the past half century, especially those propagated by E. Burgess (1923), Homer Hoyt (1934), Pitrim Sorokin, Lewis Wirth (1958), Robert Redfield (1941), Zimmerman, Walter Christiler (1933), Ulman (1941), Thomilson (1969), and Hawley (1971), it is possible to deduce that the various theoretical attempts suppose that

(a) people and institutions make decisions and directives related to place and time, technology, growth, and expansion on rational basis;

(b) that such attempts should seek answers to queries such as where people live? Where offices, markets, houses, playgrounds, public utilities are located and the time-motion dimensions in relation to various activities of different classes of people.

Other theoretical attempts have been made by Duncan-Shnor (population, social organization, technology); Max Weber (Social values), Lewis Memford (environment issues), Phillip Hauzer-Kingsly Davis (Demographic-organization approach), and finally Alvin Boskoff (various historical, ecological, cultural, psychological approaches).

However, it is difficult to ascertain that any one of the mentioned theoretical formulations and approaches can be applied to the case of the Gulf States. The urban characteristics and the inherent factors which explain the urban processes during the past three decades could not readily be applicable.

The fact that Gulf States are different from other Arab States in total population and structure, proportion of urban population, size and location of cities, economic resources, available land and the level of industrialization would not permit a single approach to urban planning applicable to all of the States. The development of small and medium-sized towns should be seriously considered. The diversification and decentralization of industrial and commercial sectors and locate them away from large cities is imperative to urban planning.

Contemporary urban planning in Gulf States is biased in favour of Western models and is moving towards the tendency to denigrate traditional forms and special arrangements such as haras (urban quarters), souks (markets) bazzars, khans, pedestrian streets and alleways – as useless and nostalgic residues of the past. Attempts, and considerable attention are being directed towards the preservation of the prevailing traditional vis-a-vis Islamic architecture in the process of Western like urban planning.

However, future urban life in the Gulf States requires synthesis of the urban ethos of openness, vitality, rational and secular interests so vital to city growth together with the more intimate and communal social cohesion.[6]

In treating urbanization and Social Change in Arab States, Janet abu Lughud stated the salient facts and features of urban process in Gulf States. She pointed out that: Population increase is very rapid and is almost exclusively urban destination; a significant proportion of the new population is foreign, and the starting point of development/modernization during pre-oil days was quite low, as measured by levels of education, existence of trained manpower and national infrastructure (roads, transportation, schools, hospitals, etc.). She added that urbanization in Gulf States is an "unprecedented case of instant urbanization, propelled not only by the collection within the capital city (or few towns) or virtually all of the citizens of the States who had previously been scattered, but also by the importation of labourers to service both the productive economy and the local citizens".[7]

As for the implication of such conditions on the resulting special changes; Abu-Lughud added the: (1) cities in Gulf States serve as sites for consumption rather than as centres for production, (2) cities are the only way that the greatly increased population can be absorbed and housed, (3) because of the extremely rapid rates at which cities have been growing and radical shift from nomadism to urbanism, and incredibly high percentage of current urban residents are "migrants", in the sense that they moved to the city from somewhere else.

There has been an ample evidence in Third World countries, in general, and Gulf States in particular, concerning the positive relationship between urbanization and the process of development; and that the degree and extent of the inter-relationships depend to a large extent on a number of factors: cultural, social, economic and administrative.

International migration is a significant factor in the urbanization process and population distribution in the Gulf States. Migrants tend to prolong their stay (settle) in urban complexes.

H. Azzam in his article on "Urbanization and Economic Development in Arab States", hypothesized that States which achieve higher and rapid economic growth rates will experience more comprehensive changes in the population structure. He concluded that Urbanization processes and population distribution during the past two decades have continued to exceed the process of industrialization and economic growth, with growth rates higher than those of the productive sector in the countries of the region. He also found a positive relationship between the rates of growth, and that urban development will pave the way for an overgrowth in the services sector which is by and large an unorganized sector.[8]

Demographic Characteristics

The absence of a clear population policy in the Gulf countries has created a constant population mobility and instability. Political and economic considerations govern short or long-term population forecasts and the subsequent socio-economic development. Population policy is dictated not so much by national or local factors as by its strong attachment to Arab and international political-economic strategies such as oil prices, the Middle Crisis, the Arab-Israeli conflict, inter-Arab relations, as well as interreactions among the Gulf countries themselves.

The governments concerned are overburdened with problems of providing the necessary services for the inflow of the non-national labour force required for the massive development projects and new corporations, in addition to maintenance of the current social services, e.g. hospitalization, education, housing, traffic, recreational outlets, etc.[9] In other words, the prevailing problems and the necessity of meeting the needs of the growing population of non-nationals have prevented officials from formulating long-range policies. In addition, the political, economic and social variables interacting at the local, regional and international levels prevent the formulations of clear-cut policies.

The societies of the Gulf countries are among those with high fertility rates. In Kuwait annual birthrates were recorded at 48 births per 1,000 population, in Bahrain 48 and UAE 49.4. Similar figures apply to Qatar and Oman.[10]

At the same time mortality rates have noticeably decreased. For example, in Kuwait death rates decreased from 25 per thousand persons in 1954 to 14 in 1975; in Bahrain from 20 per 1,000 persons to 15; and in UAE from 17 to 15 in the same period.[11]

The growth of population in the Gulf states from 1940 up to the year 2000 is shown in Table 20.1. The data indicate that from the early 50's up to 1980, the population increased nearly four times,and it is expected to reach over 7 million by the year 2000. The annual rate of increase varied from one State to another, being highest at 7.11 per cent in the UAE and lowest in Oman and Bahrain at 3.02 and 3.9 per cent respectively.

TABLE 20.1: **Population of the Gulf States in various years (in thousands)**

Years	Kuwait	Bahrain	Qatar	UAE	Oman	Total
Forties						
1947	—	100	15	—	—	—
Fifties						
1954	201	124	30	55	435	845
1959	257	143	40	80	460	980
Sixties						
1961	321	156	55	86	500	1,118
1968	613	190	80	180	620	1,683
Seventies						
1970	750	220	85	190	660	1,245
1971	782	216	117	200	680	1,995
1975	953	275	144	251	765	2,428
Eighties						
1980	1,372	302	220	796	891	3,581
Nineties						
1990	2,194	406	326	1,215	1,218	5,359
2000	3,166	528	434	1,635	1,651	7,374
Ave. ann. rate of increase (%)	6.29	3.29	5.13	7.11	3.02	(3.2)
Urban pop. 1980 (%)	83.8	87.1	83.7	65.3	16.1	(46.2)

Source: *Demographic Year Book* (United Nations 1980). Rates for Arban Word.

As for the distribution of population according to indigenous and foreign population, Table 20.2 indicates the absolute numbers in various States.

The data reveals the following facts:

1. The rate of population increase of nationals is influenced mainly

by natural increase plus naturalization (restricted in members and categories). As for that of non-nationals, their growth is dependent on the prevailing need for labour force required for various economic sectors.

2. Non-nationals in the State of UAE and Qatar recorded fluctuation ending in decrease, while in other States a gradual increase was recorded.

TABLE 20.2: **Population in Gulf States: 1975-1985 (Nationals & Non-Nationals) in Thousands**

	UAE	Bahrain	Oman	Qatar	Kuwait
Total 1975	535,1	261,1	766,	146,7	1006,5
Nationals	194,3	201,6	666,	63,7	475,4
Non-Nationals	330,8	60,	100	84	531,1
(%) of Non-Nationals	(63)	(23.9)	(13.0)	(57.3)	(53.8)
Total 1980	977,4	336,6	984,	206,6	1,374.8
Nationals	280,1	233,3	805,	84,6	569,6
Non-Nationals	697,3	103,4	179,	132,	508,3
(%) of Non-Nationals	(71.3)	(30,7)	(18.2)	(59.1)	(58.6)
Total 1985	1116,8	434,7	1292	241	1625.5
Nationals	403,8	267,1	973	115	682.5
Non-Nationals	713	185,6	320	126	943.00
(%) of Non-Nationals	(63,8)	(36,5)	(24,7)	(52,3)	(58)

ECWA — Based on official sources and records.

TABLE 20.2A: **Rates of Population Increase 1975 - 1985**

(Percentage)

	1975/80			1980/85			1975/85		
State	Nat.	N.N.	Total	Nat.	N.N	Total	Nat.	N.N	Total
U.A.E.	7,31	14,91	13,43	7,32	,45	2,67	7,22	7,68	7,55
Bahrain	3,91	10,91	5,04	3,38	8,56	5,12	3,14	9,73	5,08
Oman	3,79	11,69	5,01	3,79	11,62	5,46	3,79	11,63	5,34
Qatar	5,79	7,46	6,85	6,14	,65	3,35	6,07	4,05	4,96
Kuwait	5,52	8,22	6,24	3,63	3,16	3,35	3,63	5,74	4,79

Source: ECWA — Estimates based on official records.
N = Nationals, N.N. = Non-Nationals.

The decrease is attributed, by and large, to economic situation related to the decline of income from oil revenues which had influenced expansion in production, services, and the infrastructures (labour-intensive) which require importation of manpower.

The ratio of non-nationals to nationals has increased from 20 per cent in 1975 to 31.8 per cent in 1980 to 35.4 per cent in 1985, as a result of increase in incoming migration of non-nationals with high dependency ratio. At the average, there are 5 dependents accompanying every middle income foreign employee.

In short the economic factor -- mainly oil income -- proportionately affects the rate of population growth among non-nationals.

The United Arab Emirates consists of seven Emirates which became united under one federation in December 1971. The Federation, however, did not replace private planning by each individual Emirate with independent budgets, etc. There are several federal ministries but internal developments are not coordinated.

The rate of increase of population in the different Emirates has varied. When oil production first began in a single place in the Gulf, it had a minimal effect on the others. Now all the UAE reflect a transformation of population, whether oil has been discovered within their territories or not.

TABLE 20.3: **Distribution of the Countries of the United Arab Emirates in various years**

(in thousands)

Emirates	1968	1974	1975	1976
Abu Dhabi	46.2	95	235	451.8
(1982) Dubai	59	100	206	276.3
(1969) Sharjah	31.5	55	88.2	159.3
(1974) Ras Al-Khaimah	24.5	45	57.3	73.9
(1968) Fujairah	9.7	15	26.5	32.2
(1968) Ajman	4.2	8	21.5	36
Um Al-Quiwain	3.8	7	16.8	12.4
Total	179.2	325	651.3	1041.9

Source: Enid Hill, "Modernization of Labor in the Arab Gulf States, Man and Society, Seminar at the University of Basrah (Iraq, 1979), pp.275-376.

The distribution of population among the constituent Emirates between 1968 and 1980 is shown in Table 20.3.

The transformation to wage labour has signified different things in different Emirates, and the population increases must be considered in relation to certain unique conditions occurring in each.

With respect to distribution of labour force by sectors, the nationals represent only 20 per cent of those employed in the public (governmental) sector, and the rate decreases to 15 per cent in the private sector.

It can be noted that the population increase in the smallest Emirate is fivefold in seven years, while in the next two, it only increased by about two and a half times in the same period. The reason, probably, lies in the characteristics of the population increase, which was most likely a mixture between Bedouin settlers and foreigners (Arabs and others). In Ajman and Um-Al-Qaiwan, there are small modern industries, such as a mineral water bottling plant, a machine and tile factory and a cement plant. Development is funded by the federal government, and visible local growth is in the form of housing, office blocks and a few hotels.[12]

The total population in 1977 reached 862,000 persons, 50 per cent of whom were between the ages of 15 and 34 with a higher ratio of males over females. Non-nationals accounted for 75 per cent of the total population. In terms of labour force engaged in economic activities the nationals represented 35 per cent although only 25 per cent of the total population.

TABLE 20.4: **Workers in 1976 According to Nationality (Total: 239, 555)**

Nationality	Per cent
Arab	20.2
Indian	41.6
Pakistani	24.2
Iranian	2.4
Oman	11.6
Total	100

Source: Annual Statistics Year Book (Ministry of Planning, Central Bureau of Statistics, 1978).

In the composition of the labour force in 1976, the non-nationals represented varied nationalities (Table 20.4), and with respect to the distribution of the migratory labour force, the Emirate of Dubai employs nearly 50 per cent Abu Dhabi 20 per cent, Sharjah 22 per cent and the remaining Emirates 4 per cent.

Population Density and Natural Resources

The population density reflects marked differences between the urban settlements and the rest in each country (Table 20.5).

The density of the urban areas also varies: for example, the density of the City of Kuwait is 25,000 persons per sq. km. In Bahrain urban density reaches over 12,000 persons per square kilometre. This heavy concentration of population in relatively limited areas of land presents several problems for planning comprehensive socio-economic development.

TABLE 20.5: **Population, Area and Density in the Gulf States in 1980**

State	Population (000)	Area sq. km.	Density
Kuwait	1,372	17,818	77
Bahrain	302	822	485
Qatar	220	11,000	20
UAE	796	329,556	2.4
Oman	891	212,457	4.1

Source: League of Arab States – Statistical Bureau.

Imbalanced Distribution of Population

Let us take Kuwait as an example. The 1985 census indicate that there are several small areas inhabited by tens of thousands of persons, while other similar areas are inhabited by a few hundred only. The densities in Kuwait reflect a high degree of uneven population distribution. The census shows that only 6 per cent of total land area is inhabited. In this small portion of land population density reached 1,664 persons per sq. km. The density varies from one area to another, e.g. Hawalli area encompasses 120,000 inhabitants pkm, Sabahiyya new community 60,000 pkm, and Abdellah Al-Salem 2,000 pkm (located 7 kilometres west of Hawalli). This condition creates a wide range of problems, e.g. overpressure on the infrastructures and services ranging from

TABLE 20.6: **Rates of Urban Growth in the Gulf States, 1960-1980**

Country	Total pop. (000)		Rate of growth %			Level urbanism %			Rate of increase %	Urban ave.
	1960	1980	Total pop.	Urb. pop.	Rur. pop.	60	70	80		
Bahrain	162	302	4.1	4.2	4.3	78.4	78.1	77.9	(-).5	-2.76
Kuwait	270	1,372	4.4	7.4	2.2	72.3	76.4	88.3	16	190
Oman	494	891	4.1	14.4	3.7	44.4	61.8	75.9	3.9	119.4
Qatar	59	220	8.0	15.0	-.3	72.9	79.8	86.1	13.2	130.7
UAE	119	796	33.0	17.5	-.2	40.3	57.4	72	31.5	278.8

Source: UNI Patterns of Urban and Rural Growth (New York, 1980), pp. 128-43.

schools, roads, security, health and the human as well as natural environment.

The Gulf States have high fertility rates, with birth rates of around 48 per thousand annually, in some, the death rate has dropped sharply – Kuwait has around five thousand – whereas it has remained relatively high in others – Oman has around 18 per thousand. These features lead to differences in the natural population growth rates among Gulf States.[13]

The number of males exceeds the number of females more especially in the age range of 15 years and above, where the ratio reached 290 males per 100 females in the UAE in 1975.

Over 60 per cent of the population in the Gulf States falls in the age bracket of 15 to 59 years. But for the indigenous population those below 14 years of age represent about 50 per cent, reflecting a youthful population.[14]

Over half of the population is illiterate, and among women the rate is well above 70 per cent. Large numbers of the foreign labour force engaged in non-skilled economic activity are illiterate.

Urban Characteristics and Growth

Urbanization in the Gulf States can be analysed with respect to the political, economic and social history of the region. Historical references indicate that traders on camel caravans between Najd (Saudi Arabia) and Syria, as well as sea traders from India, Pakistan, Iran and Africa, passed through the area. Markets, commercial centres, trading spaces and rest stations were the main establishments. The following table indicates urban growth in the Gulf States.

The table 20.6 indicates that the UAE has experienced the highest rate of growth (33%) of the total population. As for urban growth, Oman, Qatar and UAE experienced an annual rate of growth ranging from 14.4 per cent to 17.5 per cent. As for level of urbanism, practically all States are classified as highest level in Developing Countries and Arab States.. This is an artificial growth since the majority of non-nationals are temporary residents.

The modern history of the Gulf States has been characterized by instability and constant confrontations with colonists and corporations.

Phases of Urbanization

It is possible to delineate three phases of urbanization:

(i) Traditional Phase
(ii) Initial Phase
(iii) Rapid Urbanization Phase

Each will be briefly discussed:

Traditional Phase

This phase extends from the Islamic era until the discovery of oil in the 30's and 40's of the 20th century. Cities were small with populations ranging between 2,000 and 15,000 persons. They were surrounded by mud-built walls and defensive castles with narrow roads, and housing complexes accommodating extended families. The Emir's Palace was the focal point from which radiated roads and markets. Traditional and tribal social relations prevailed. The colonialists and foreigners resided in separate quarters usually at some distance from the national settlements. Traditional values prevailed, e.g. strong kinship relations, veiling of women, and gathering nightly in the Dewaneya. Specialized markets of weapons, gold, textile, garments, herbs, shoes, etc., were symbols of traditional city planning.

Initial Phase

This phase is marked by the discovery of oil and subsequent investments of revenue and political independence. The oil promoted socio-economic changes that effected the traditional tribal structure and economic institutions. A statement about the impact of the discovery of oil in Bahrain says "No Society or Government has been rescued so accidentally and at the right time as was Bahrain by the oil. It was about to face an economic catastrophe in 1932.[15]

In this phase, commercial institutions flourished, light industries were scattered about without previous planning. The oil companies started employment schemes for nationals. The abundant flow of income encouraged massive governmental construction schemes including housing, roads, hospitals, schools, markets and recreation facilities to accommodate the inflow of migrants. Types of industrial development included bricks and tiles, furniture, soft drinks, cold storage, cement and dairy products. All the industrial establishments were in or just outside the city suburb.

The major developments in this phase included the establishment of an infrastructure of the modern state. At first planning encountered many problems due to factors such as an open policy to the outside world, the ambitious projects of officials and the influx of Bedouins and rural residents into the cities to be close to the rulers. Development included the armed forces, the police (in order to safeguard the sovereign), communication, education, mass media financial institutions, airports, seaports and hotels to accommodate the foreign experts and labour force.

Aside from internal migration and the international migration (Arab, Asian, European and African) comprising over 60 nationalities, legal and illegal migration (internal and external) contributed to the growth of slum areas lacking basic services around the cities. In this stage, the primary objective of the States was to establish an adequate infrastructure to accommodate the development schemes. The lack of clear population policies made it difficult to formulate long-range plans. Walls and castles were torn down to allow for new construction and horizontal expansion. Never in their history were the Gulf societies as heterogeneous as in this interval. In some States the indigenous population became a minority. Ethnocentrism prevailed among the foreign and local groups.

Rapid Urbanization Phase

The initial phase lasted for about two decades (about half a decade in the case of Bahrain), and then the stage was set for rapid urbanization due to several contributory factors:

- Increasing oil revenues and the ensuing investment programmes at home and abroad, as demonstrated by doubling the budget for various sectors.
- Continuing high fertility rates and decreasing mortality rates because of social values and polygamy as well as health services.
- High wages which stimulated an increase of individual as well

as foreign labour (both males and females) who sought employment mainly in the service sector.

- Increased cooperation among the Gulf States in view of the political tensions in the area – case of Afghanistan. The Iranian Islam Revolution, threats of big power and the Arab-Israeli conflict.
- Cultural changes which included modernizing education: expanding mass communication via the media, arts, television, motion pictures, plays, museums, scientific conferences, seminars at various levels -- local, regional and international–and intensifying relations with the Islamic countries.

As a result of rapid urbanization, the countries have encountered a wide range of problems; maintaining; immorality; increased divorce rates, high ratio of crime; housing problems; pollution (sea, land and air); lack of technical manpower among the natives; and boundary and other long-standing problems among the Gulf countries themselves.

Modern economic sector covers the production as well as the services. The new organization structure of economic inter-relationships have replaced the traditional relations which prevailed for centuries. Included in this sector are the financial centres, monetary exchange services, light industries, construction, and related socio-economic services.

In addition to the light industries which comprised only 5 per cent of domestic National product in 1980, new heavy industries, e.g. Gas and Petro-chemical (Kuwait), Aluminium (Bahrain), Steel (Qatar), Cement and Chemical fertilizers in the Emirates. The per capita of industrial production in the Gulf States has reached 737 U.S. dollars in 1980, while the average in other Arab States reached 159 U.S. dollars. Agricultural sector's contribution was estimated at 1 per cent in the same year.[16]

Commerce and trading between the Gulf States and the rest of the Arab States is low compared with that of the rest of the world. Exports to Arab States represented 8.3 per cent (7,6 billion dollars), while imports from Arab States was 5,4 million U.S. dollars or 8.7 per cent of total imports.

As for consumption, Gulf States consume electricity as per capita nearly 4 times higher than by other Arab States. The States enjoy modern highways and transportation network, and are linked with the rest of the world with telestar and telecommunication channels.[17]

The health services also have improved considerably as indicted in Table 20.7.

TABLE 20.7: **Health Indicators in Gulf States**

Population ('000)

State	Physician per pop.		Hosp. Beds per pop.		Life Expectancy		Infant Mortality	
	1970	85	1972	85	1972	80-85	1960	85
Emirates	1,	1.0	1,	.,4	44	70,6	135	45
Bahrain	1,2	1.2	.,5	.,3	55	68,2	-	37
Oman	8.7	2.6	.,9	.,7	42	49,7	193	122
Qatar	1,4	,6	.,2	.,1	45	70,6	80	45
Kuwait	1,1	,7	.,2	.,3	66	71,2	89	30

Source: Arab Fund for Social and Economic Development — Kuwait, 1985.

The data indicated that the population/physician ratio has improved considerably in all States, due to increased awareness by the concerned Government and changes of attitudes towards accepting modern health practices.

Life expectancy has recorded an increase in the State, the highest being in Kuwait, and the lowest in Oman (least urbanized Gulf State). The rate of native medical staff does not exceed 5 to 10 per cent of total professional staff. The rest are non-nationals.

Socio-economic Indicators and Urbanization

The process of urbanization, which plays a major part in the theory of modernization, will be different in a "planned economy" than in the modernization model.[18] Land reform, equal distribution of wealth and all kinds of services in various parts of the country tend to control the pull-and-push factors.

The natural resources of the Gulf States would enable them to produce services such as education of welfare without really being industrialized. This applies only in short-term development and industrialization is necessary for the long term.

Socio-economic indicators in this region are not related to urbanization (Table 20.8). For example, Bahrain having the lowest income per capita scores high on literacy, while the UAE having the highest income per capita scores low on literacy.

TABLE 20.8: **Urbanization and some Socio-economic Indicators in the Gulf States, 1980**

State	Urban pop. %	Econ. act. pop. 15 years %	Per capitia US $	Illiteracy rate male	female
Kuwait	90	35.6	16,60C	30	48
Bahrain	79.5	30.7	1,750	40	45
Qatar	85	54.2	9,890	60	85
UAE	69	58.2	17,500	62	55
Oman	13	27.6	2,100	60	65

Source: United Nations, *Demographic Year Book*, 1980, *ECWA Bulletin.*

Urban Social Structure

Urban societies in the Gulf States comprise nationals and non-nationals. The national are subdivided into two main groups with an emerging new group–the rising middle class. One group consists of the original settlers affiliated to well-known tribes associated with the ruling ones; the other group comprises those who have become citizens through naturalization. Each has certain privileges and rights well known in the traditional social relations value systems. There are social boundaries which define the extent and nature of social interaction. These boundaries become apparent when situations like marriage and intimate relations are involved. Tribal status, as well as kinship affiliation, stands out with respect to issues relevant to sharaf (honour) of the family. Formal interaction in daily activities and in business between the two segments is normal, but beyond that the restrictions are carefully observed.

Among the non-nationals class differentiation is marked on different lines. Within each nationality, one can identify three levels of social differentiation, although all share a common element by being alien and temporary residents. The upper class consists of well-to-do families who have acquired wealth through long years of residence and have friendships with the Sheikhs and Emirs and consequently have become close to the national elite. They comprise mercantile capitalists who maintained this status before the discovery of oil and increased their wealth from various sources, such as construction and commercial activities. The middle class consists of educated technicians who are becoming an integral part of the economy: managers, bankers; engineers, lawyers, university professors, medical doctors, pharmacists, and so forth, this includes those who managed to acquire a position in the construction industry. In the stock market and in real estate and in certain production activities, this class is rather limited in numbers, influence, and role in the socio-economic-political structure. The lower class comprises the largely illiterate, unskilled labour force who cannot afford to have their families joining them due to the high costs of living. They include those who crossed the borders illegally over the past three decades and now aspire to acquire citizenship.[19]

The urbanization process in the Gulf States includes the transformation of the indigenous population into a wage–labour force or owners–partners of private economic establishments. A Bedouin or a peasant can become "modernized" in two ways: either by leaving the desert or the land and taking up city employment, or work in business; or through the transformation of agriculture into large estates, growing commercial crops and hiring landless peasants for a wage. The government encourages farming activities and offers services and easy loans as well as low cost houses to promote settlement. Bedouinism in an ecological sense is disapearing gradually, and every Bedouin family, which seeks houses, gardens and jobs, finds the facilities made available by the respective Municipality authorities. As one writer put it:

> On the average, every – formerly nomadic – family has by now at least one son in one of the local administrative organizations, another son usually joins the Defence Force or is a partner in some business, and one might run a taxi, while the father still leads a traditional life.[20]

Another case is indicative of the transformation process:

> A Bedouin woman who received a house free from the government subsequently divided it into flats, has twenty people working for her and she owns ten cars, but she still keeps camels in the desert.[21]

The transformation of former nomads into urban property owners and capitalist investors occurs mostly in Kuwait, Qatar, Dubai and Abu Dhabi. The Government purchases land from middle and low-income individuals or families for public projects, e.g. roads, public buildings, commercial centres, etc. This provided the initial capital for the recipients to open a business either as an agent for a foreign company or for themselves, or to invest in the stock market.[22] Housing projects initiated by the Government of the Gulf States start by grant of a piece of land, then loans to build, then supervising the construction. The installation of electricity, water, sewage, roads, markets, schools, infirmaries and other facilities for the various income groups has contributed effectively to the urbanization process.

Residence in the city by Bedouins and their families does not necessarily indicate that they become urbanized in the Western sense. Tribal values and customs are fully observed. For example during the mid-year school vacation (usually three weeks), most of the Gulf Kuwaiti families leave their homes and camp out in the desert (Al-Barr) taking with them a television, transistors and modern appliances. In contrast, for the summer vacation the majority go outside Kuwait to Europe, England or some Arab countries on the Mediterranean coast.

The original madina in the Gulf States has been largely demolished or become encircled by a metropolitan area constructed according to the usual Western pattern.

> The original town now represents a mere fraction of the built-up area. New and distinctly alien elements have been added to the townscape – villa development, flats, shops, government offices, mosques, schools and hospitals.... Stone and mud have been replaced by bricks and concrete and indigenous architectural forms have almost entirely disappeared.... The urban population is now living in a Western style of urban environment no longer distinctly Islamic, or Arabic.[23]

The rural and Bedouin migrants flocking to the cities face a double adjustment, not only to the urban ways of their countrymen but also to the urban ways of a foreign culture. Few studies have been made on the adaptation process or the relations between the built environment and human behaviour.

Socio-economic factors Influencing Urbanization

Oil stands out as the most important factor in influencing

urbanization in the Gulf States. The economy depends, by and large on oil revenues and very little on local production. The State is the only source for distributing income and in subsidizing various service sectors (e.g. foods, gasoline, education, health, etc.). This condition has created a gap between levels of production and levels of consumption.[24]

The main sources of national income for the countries of the region are given in Table 20.9. The great wealth of these countries has permitted the rapid establishment of adequate education and health services, which have assisted the modernization process. As a result, within one generation, more cities in the oil-rich Arab countries have moved from among the most primitive to a reasonably modern physical setting.

TABLLE 20.9: **Sources of National Income and the Gulf States, 1980**

State	Resources	%
Kuwait	Oil	60
Bahrain	Refined oil	70
Qatar	Oil & natural gas	90
UAE	Oil & liquified gas	90
Oman		95

Source: Nazir Hamada, *City and Environment in the Arab World* (1981).

The management of the oil resources, together with a rapid development process toward the tertiary sector; services related to banking and investment, trade and commerce, and tourism. Since these services tend to congregate in the major cities, where airports and activities of government are located, the economic boom has been concentrated in the capital cities. Even when manufacturing activities did develop, it was uneconomical to locate them further than the outskirts of these major cities, particularly in view of the general absence of effective population distribution and regional development policies. As a result, the major cities have dominated the urbanization process.[25]

The influence of industrialization and labour force characteristics and migration or urbanization are now examined.

Industrialization

Apart from oil, the industrial sector is insignificant in Kuwait, this sector represented 8.7 per cent in 1983-1984 and in the other Gulf States the situation was not much different.[26] The availability of oil and capital in abundance does not automatically imply the achievement of sound economic and industrial development. The Gulf States lack the basic infrastructures, required for such development, namely, markets, a technical labour force and know-how.[27]

The major industrial projects incorporated in the development plans of the States are mostly derived from oil and are very similar.[28]

The UAE is planning to establish steel mills; an aluminium smelter is being set up in Bahrain; and Dubai is developing a big industrial complex in the desert at Jabal-el-Ali (a foreign community). The Gulf States are also increasing their capacity to refine oil, up to 85 per cent, so that they will gradually become major suppliers of refined petroleum, fertilizers and other petrochemical products.[29]

More specifically, an indicative list of major projects includes:

- Kuwait – Petrochemicals, cement and pipes, building material, fertilizers; agriculture (vegetables);
- Bahrain – Aluminium;
- UAE – Aluminium, petrocnemicals, cement, steel;
- Qatar – Steel mill, petrochemicals, fertilizers;
- Oman – Natural gas, fertilizers.

TABLE 20.10: **Number of Petrochemical Projects in Gulf Region**

State	1963	1976	1983
Kuwait	2	13	35
Bahrain	6	—	10
Qatar	—	5	16
UAE	—	—	12
Oman	—	—	7

Source: A.B. Zahlan, "Science and Technology Syndrome in the Arab World", ECWA/UNESCO Seminar on Technology Policies in the Arab States, Paris, 1984.

This list indicated a duplication of investment and a lack of coordination among the States which will affect manpower recruitment and stability. If we consider the investment plans of the countries in the petrochemicals, we find the same trend, namely, duplication and lack of coordination. As Table 20.10 shows, all States are investing heavily in petrochemical industries.

The pace of industrial development is slow because of the acute scarcity of skilled human resources and low level of local technology.

Dairy products and poultry have started to flourish recently in the region; e.g. in 1981 the UAE established 127 poultry and seven dairy projects scattered in various Emirates to encourage Bedouin Settlement.

Governments also attempt to encourage promotion of the private sector, through joint ventures, or extending loans, subsidies, no taxation and permits to recruit a foreign labour force with supporting labour laws and regulations. However, the tendency of the private sectors is to concentrate on fast profit-making enterprises rather than long-term investment, leaving the latter to the government.

TABLE 20.11: **Loan Facilities for Private Sector According to the Type of Economic Activity in Arab Gulf States, 1981**

(million Arabic Dinars = 955 Kuwaiti Dinars)

Economic activity	UAE	Bahrain	Oman	Qatar	Kuwait	Total
Commerce	784	82	118	130	647	1,761
Industry	136	40	4	10	152	342
Agriculture	7.2	0.6	1	—	38	46.8
Housing & construction	657.2	113	41	33	393	1,237
Transport	46	13	4	8	—	71
Individual projects	148	35	28	36	—	247
Others	106	17	21	22	598	764
Total	1,885.2	304.6	219	242	1,330	4,468.8

Source Abdul Hamid Zakariya, "Role of Private Sector in Council of Cooperation among Gulf States," Seminar on Cooperation Requirements in Gulf States Local and International Framework, Kuwait, 1982.

Table 20.11 gives an indication of the economic interests of the private sector in their utilization of loan facilities. About 40 per cent of all loans are invested in commercial enterprises. New in importance is housing and construction with 27.6 per cent. Industry represents only 7.6 per cent. Reasons for the lack of private investment in industry include lack of experience, need for high capital investment, complexity of management and inadequate market feasibility. Investment in agriculture represents 1.5 per cent of total loans for various economic, technical reasons. However, in spite of continued efforts by the Government to subsidize this sector, progress is minimal. Out of the total area of the countries concerned (3,600,000 hectares) only 3.7 per cent is actually cultivated.[23] This important sector of the economy requires intensive development for various obvious reasons, including employment of the indigenous Bedouin tribes and settling them in villages. In turn, this would contribute to the redistribution of the high urban population.

Although, in most cases the Government provides land, loans, tractors, fertilizers and housing. Bedouin families within reclaimed areas hire foreign agricultural workers, and they themselves take up jobs in the city as well as collecting the profits from the farms. Consequently, sedentarization of Bedouins follows the pattern of immediately integrating them into urban life, rather than providing them with the opportunity to adapt gradually to urbanization through new generations. As a result, Bedouins take up lower status urban employment, live on various forms of public assistance and are mostly absorbed in the armed forces, the national guard and the police. They are also employed in non-productive jobs, e.g. as night guards, taxi drivers and so forth.

Labour Force Characteristics

During the past decade, the labour force has been a major concern of officials, planners and social scientists. The desire is to encourage increasing participation of national manpower in technical work, top management and policy-making; to strike a balance among the foreign nationalities (between Arabs and Asians and among various ethnic groups); to minimize the socio-political problems of migratory labour; to develop regional cooperation with regard to checks and controls of mobility of the foreign labour force; to maintain the Gulf Arab social and cultural identities; and to upgrade the quality of the infrastructures required for the high rates of population increases due to migration.

One cannot discuss or elaborate on each of the above issues within the limits of this paper. Intensive research studies are needed but it is imperative to say something about the total volume of migration and its implications.

The data show the following:

- Non-nationals represent over 70 per cent in Kuwait, Qatar, UAE, while in Bahrain and Oman about 50 per cent, in 1985;
- In 1975 non-nationals represented as high as 84 per cent in UAE, Qatar, and as low as 31 per cent in Oman;
- Non-nationals have decreased in UAE, Qatar and Kuwait in the eighties, due to a marked decline in petro-dollar revenues;
- Increase in the rate of nationals in the labour force is attributed mainly to deportation of expatriated or their voluntary return to homeland due to lack of job opportunities.

Table 20.12 reveals the rate of annual growth in manpower in the Gulf States.

TABLE 20.12: **Rate of Annual Growth in Manpower during 1975-1985**

(Percentages)

State	1975-80			1980-85			1975-85		
	Nat.	N.N.	Total	Nat.	N.N.	Total	Nat.	N.N.	Total
UAE	3,34	13,97	13,65	3,84	-.46	.,03	3,79	6,75	6,33
Bahrain	5,67	12,94	9,30	7,37	8,79	8,11	6,47	10,86	8,71
Oman	1,61	9,4	4,37	1,16	10,68	5,53	1,38	10,04	4,95
Qatar	7,55	6,52	6,61	7,37	-,25	1,30	7,18	3,14	3,95
Kuwait	3,21	18,82	9,60	1,80	6,73	-,68	3,54	5,75	5,14
Total	1.48	18,82	9,93	1,80	6,73	4,87	1,64	12,78	7,40

Source: ECWA — Estimates based on official records.
N = National; N.N. = Non-National.

The table indicates the following:

- During the 5-year period at late seventies UAE recorded the highest rate of annual increase in the labour force (13.65%) while Oman the lowest (4.37%);

- The rate of increase of national labour force was highest in Qatar (7.55%) followed by Bahrain (5.67%), while Kuwait was lowest (3.21%), which means the two States have a better policy for enlisting nationals in employment, replacing foreigners;
- As in the 5-year period of early eighties, the situation varied. The annual rate of increase has declined drastically in the case of UAE (.02%), Kuwait (.68%), Qatar (1.3%). In Oman only the rate has increased by about 1 per cent;
- The rate of non-national had minus score, e.g. Kuwait (1.3%), Qatar (-.25%), UAE (-46%) due to the fact that those were mostly affected by a decline in petro-dollar revenues;
- During the 10 year period (1975-1985) the rates of total labour force decreased by half in the UAE, Kuwait, Qatar, due to return of expatriates to their homeland;
- As for national, the rate of annual increase has changed slightly, due to more persons attending high schools, and higher education or unemployed.

Development of national manpower has not proven successful in the Gulf States. The majority of them prefer employment in the service sector, and in economic activities with assured high net profit.[31] University education is further evidence of prevailing orientations. One study has revealed that there were 24 faculties in Management, General Sciences, Engineering and Agriculture, but their enrolment of students (22,254 in 1979-1980) represented only 36.5 per cent of the total enrolment – 16.3 per cent Management, 7.7 per cent General Sciences, 10.6 per cent Engineering and 1.9 per cent Agriculture. The majority of the students (63.5%) were enrolled in colleges of Liberal Education and Law.[32]

The national manpower can be increased through naturalization. The countries of the region have been granting citizenship to other nationalities but rather conservatively. Kuwait gave citizenship to 4,662 persons in 1971 and to 8,760 persons in 1979.[33] There are over 90 nationalities represented in Kuwait, and Palestinians (Jordanians) have traditionally topped the list. Resident permits for non-Arabs, mostly Asians, comprised 45 per cent of total granted.

The Asians discovered the Arab region at the beginning of this century and several hundreds especially Iranians and Indians became citizens. However in the early 70s, the number of Asians increased at the rate of 24.2 per cent annually. Accordingly Asian representation increased from 17.7 per cent in 1970 to 33.6 per cent in 1975, while Arab representation from 35 per cent to 30 per cent in the same period (rates include Saudi Arabia).[34]

The Philippines presence in the Gulf region has increased especially rapidly. Filipinos registered as workers in 1979 numbered 136,557; 80 per cent of them were in Ssaudi Arabia and the rest in other Gulf States.

Under half of the non-nationals stay in Kuwait for less than four years, but only 12 per cent of them stay longer than 15 years. Duration of residency is influenced by economic, social and political considerations. Male residency is longer than female, because most female employment has increased due to the demand for domestic service in homes, hospitals and hotels, and also for semi-professional jobs such as secretarial work and teaching.[35]

Despite the presence of different ethnic groups for varied durations, the nationals and non-nationals seem wide apart, and it is difficult to expect that real integration will ever take place, even after naturalization. In a study of the assimilation of Palestinians in Kuwait society – those who stayed five years or more – it was found that the majority intend to return to Palestine when feasible, and social intercourse or marriage with Kuwait nationals was minimal, relationships being limited to working hours or when discussing business.[36]

Ethnic groups tend to cluster together in neighbourhoods in the cities. For example, the migratory population in Qatar consists of the following groups, who tend to live in separate communities in Doha and its suburbs:

- Foreigner (British, Dutch, American);
- Arabs from non-Gulf countries;
- Arabs from Gulf countries, mainly Saudi Arabia, Bahrain and Oman;
- Indians and Pakistanis;
- Iranians;
- Batan from the Pakistani mountains.[37]

The Iranians, Indians and Egyptians tend to start with male migration and to commute once a year, or more, to their home countries. In the lower professions, male migration is greater because of low wage and the high cost of living. Also new regulations prohibit family migration for those with low income.

About 40 per cent of the total migrants to the Gulf States in 1985 were illiterate with no significant differences between males and females. Those with education of high school level and above constituted only 15 per cent of the total migrants. Western nationalities are the most educated, followed by Arabs – (Palestinians and Jordanians) and are characterized by a high educational level – and then Asian nationalities.

The majority of non-national males and females (84 per cent and 78 per cent respectively) in 1985 were aged between 15 and 29 years. About 33 per cent males and 19 per cent of the working women were not married. Most of the married females working in Kuwait live with their husbands.[38]

Socio-economic Implication of Migration

The increasing flow of migrants in the Gulf countries increases the competition among the different nationalities not only in terms of work conditions, extent of participation in civil and social life, participation in the labour unions' political and cultural activities, and the impact of social intercourse between migrants and nationals.

There is a considerable and growing social resistance among nationals to further augmentation of the non-national population. However, expatriate labour is essential for the economic development of these countries, and it is difficult to limit the expansion of expatriate communities without taking drastic action to cut economic growth.

Concern about the volume of non-nationals is threefold: (1) Outnumbering of the indigenous population; (2) A growing responsibility to provide infrastructure utilities, such as power and water, and increasingly, education and health services; (3) Increasing social problems resulting from the lack of social cohesion among over 90 nationalities living in the region.

The importing countries find it imperative to their political and social stability to increase the rate of labour turnover among non-nationals so as to shorten their period of stay and prevent them form establishing roots in these countries. However, productivity is decreased because of this constant turnover and the recurring need for adaptation to the social as well as physical environment. The national budget incurs financial strains to meet the foreigners high wages and costs. Foreign labour is also unlikely to invest locally, since regulations give nationals preference to the rights of investments – stock market, cooperative societies, real estate, imports in case of joint ventures, nationals must hold 51 per cent of capital and a higher percentage of the net profits.

Administrative problems are often encountered due to the diversity of educational orientation backgrounds of the managerial class. This tends to create disorganization and waste of human energy. Loyalties are more towards ethnic identity rather than the enterprise.[39]

The work camps of Asian contracting corporations, which operate on self-sufficency basis – food, personnel and equipment – tend to form new communities, alien to the urban structure and to national authenticity. These turn-key contracts by Asian contractors contribute little to the improvement of local skills and technical know-how. There has been a growing concern about Asian migration, but the nature of economic structure and planning means that this trend will continue for decades, and the concern must be towards minimizing the social, economic and political impacts on the nationals' identity and social structure.

Future Urban Strategy

The present pattern of development is radically transforming the Gulf States from tribal societies to societies with a high level of urbanization comparable to that found in Europe, Canada and Australia. The transplantation of this alien urban culture is bound to create a hiatus between the urban and the folk and, a dichotomy in their social and economic development.

The affluent Gulf societies will continue to be confronted with many socio-economic problems, such as the transfer of technology, manpower availability and cut-throat competition in marketing industrial products of a similar type, e.g. petrochemical products and infrastructure facilities. Keen competition is now going on for the construction of shipping berths and dry docks, in addition to contrast competition for highly skilled and technical manpower.

Urbanization in the Gulf States exhibits poorly interrelated components, in terms of its social, economic and physical infrastructures. However, it took industrialized countries 150 years to reach level of urbanization that is being attained in 10 to 15 years by Gulf cities.

The absence of consistent population policies in view of the constant mobility of large segments of population and the diversity of nationalities makes it difficult to plan for urban development in the short or long terms. Yet land utilization, land ownership, and the cost of acquisition on inner city blocks are becoming obstacles to urban renovation and development. Legislation is needed to organize the real estate markets and to put a limit to utilization of urban areas.[40] Present urban development and expansion are based on the belief that immigration will continue "for ever", because the structural expansion is far beyond the needs of the indigenous populations.

The need for a greater measure of integration in the Arab Gulf is evident. Long-term development strategy must be toward creating an economic structure which can serve the long-term interests of the population. The oil is a wasting asset, and the markets provided by the existing States are not large enough to constitute coherent economic units once oil is depleted. They cannot benefit from the economies of scale which make major industrial development feasible.[37] Emphasis is on the physical fabric of settlements rather than on man himself, his activities and needs and what the building means to him.

Future urbanization should be linked with socio-economic development plans and creating urban centres around industrial schemes with modern urban life infrastructures. Urban centres with basic services should also be developed near rural settlements (or farms) with the objectives of the decentralization of services and redistribution of population.

The administrative organization of municipalities lacks sound coordination with socio-economic and political institutions as well as other functional governmental and non-governmental agencies. Urban residents are constantly annoyed by drilling, reconstruction, relocation, extension of underground pipes for water, electricity, sewage and the like, which are usually carried out without coordination.

Needs for Urban Research

The need for research in Gulf countries covers nearly all aspects of urbanization. The existing research depends largely on demographic analysis based on data which, in most cases, are neither accurate nor up-to-date.

Since all Gulf cities have experienced change in their social and economic structures – both demographically and spatially – it is of primary importance to focus research on the nature of the changes that have taken place: the scope and magnitude of the changes; the factors which contributed to the changes; the processes of change, and the impact of these changes in relation to the social and economic structure of urban societies. The study should identify both quantitative and qualitative changes. Such a study would help social scientists and administrators to develop models for the future growth of cities and be able to plan for such growth of cities in view of national socio-economic planning.[41]

Major cities and capitals in the Gulf countries have been playing an increasingly important role in economic development. Therefore, research should aim at an assessment of the economic bases of those cities. Under this heading several issues can be identified, namely:

- Relationships between industrialization and urbanization. What strategies can be developed to accommodate industrial growth in the urban process ?
- Linkages and clustering of economic activities in major cities. What are the advantages and disadvantages of clustered versus dispersed development ?
- Expenditure on water, transportation, housing, education, health, welfare, recreation, etc., on the basis of different assumptions: e.g. cost of capital drains on balance of payment.

Rapid urbanization growth, especially when it does not follow planned schemes, tends to produce a wide variety of socio-economic and political problems which require scientific investigation in order to identify the size of such problems. The main problems which are considered of priority in Gulf Eastern cities include the following:

- Housing Research should focus on identification of needs, at present and in the future, for all types of housing for different social classes, considering the space required for expansion.
- *Transportation.* This is a problem that should be viewed in terms of social-psychological as well as technical-physical dimensions. It is becoming one of the major ills of city life, and research should focus on such issues as time vs space, and protection of inhabitants from pollution.
- *Recreation.* Urban growth created the need for public recreational facilities and institutions for leisure time activities. What are the needs for future urban growth in terms of crime, e.g. suicide, murder, theft, drugs, and factors contributing to it, should be undertaken.
- The shanty towns, the slum suburbs, the tin-can house settlements around the cities. These settlements are uncontrolled, unplanned and lack basic services. They are occupied largely by migrants from Bedouin and rural areas as well as those who find their way illegally into the country. Investigation into the structure and function of such conglomerations is of primary importance. Often such settlements produce social problems (disease, prostitution, crime) and constitute a threat to the urban community structure.
- Acculturation of migrants to the city – or deculturation of migrants from the country.

To aid in the understanding of the whole urban phenomenon, some crucial questions require research at the regional level:

- What patterns of urban growth are more conducive to total economic growth in the light of rising population pressures ?
- What degree of urban concentration is actually a functional prerequisite of agrarian reorganization and of real modernization?
- Are the Gulf cities overurbanized ?

The foregoing are some remarks which include suggestions for topics of research which can be modified and adapted in view of some practical issues related to the actual administration of the research, such as the financial allocations, the countries covered, the time element, the composition of the team of scientists and the scope of subjects selected for research.

Collaboration of social scientists from different disciplines and from a variety of countries with similar problems, who are ready to participate in teamswork, can produce results which can help in planning future urbanization policies and developmental schemes, not only for the gulf regions, but also for other oil States and developing countries.

NOTES

1. Mustafa Tolba, "The holistic cóncept of the environment — natural and man-made," paper presented to Conference on Role of Municipality in Environment Protection of Arab Cities held in Kuwait, December, 1981.
2. Ibid.
3. Mahmoud Ali Al-Daoud, *Arab Gulf and International Relations* (in Arabic) League of Arab States, Institute of Higher Studies, Al-Makef Publishing House, Cairo.
4. M. Rumaihi, "Gulf States BC a study in development," paper presented to 2nd Conference on Women in the Gulf, March/April, 1981.
5. Ali K. Akuwari, "Nature of social and economic development," paper presented to the 2nd Conference on ideology Framework of Social Action in Arab World, Sept., 1981.
6. Samir Khalaf, "Some salient features of Urbanization in the Arab World" in *Ekistics,* Vol. 300, May 1983, p. 222.
7. Janet Abu Lughad "Urbanization and Social Change in the Arab World", *Ekistics*, Vol. 300, May 1983, p. 223.
8. Henry Azzam, "Urbanization and Economic Growth in Arab States — patterns and linkages" in *Al-Tammeya Al-Arabeya - Centre for Arab Unity Studies,* Beirut, 1984, p. 298.
9. A.F. Al-Nafeesi, "The Gulf Council - political strategy framework," lecture given in Kuwait, 20 April, 1982, Kuwait University and Economic Society Symposium.
10. *United Nations Demographic Yearbook* (1976).
11. Ibid.
12. For further details see: Amer Kubaisi, "Highlights on the manpower problem in UAE," paper presented in the Seminar on Man and Society in the Arab Gulf, organized by University of Basra, Iraq, 1979, pp. 286-90.
13. J.S. Birks and C.A. Sinclair, *International Migration and Development in the Arab Region,* (ILO, Geneva, 1980).
14. See I. Qutub et al., *Urban Growth and Development in Gulf States* (Arabic) (Al-Matbouat Press, 1980), p. 47.
15. M. Rumaihi, "The human capital — continued development in the Gulf States," (Arabic), paper presented to Conference on issues for Human Resource Development, Kuwait, 1975.
16. Qutub, op. cit.

17 Abdul Latif Al-Hamad, *Economic changes and Future Development in Gulf States* — Publication of Arab Fund for Economic and Social Development. Kuwait, 1986.

18. Emre Kongar, "Some theoretical observations on the development of the Arab World vs theory of modernization ", paper presented at the Seminar on Man and Society in the Arab Gulf, held at the University of Basra, Iraq 1979.

19. See M. Rumaihi, op. cit.

20. Frauke Heard-Bey, "Development anomalies in the Bedouin oases of Al-Alliwa," *Asian Affairs*, Vol. 61 (1974), p. 280.

21. Christine Osborne, *The Gulf States and Oman* (London, Croom Helm, 1977), p. 38.

22. John Duke Anthony, *Arab States of the Lower Gulf* (The Middle East Institute, 1975), p. 106.

23. P. Beaumont et al, *The Middle East: A Geographical Approach* (London, John Wiley, 1976).

24. Ali K. Al-Kuwari, *Role of Public Projects in Economic Development* (Arabaic) (Kuwait National Council for Arts, Series no. 42).

25. Riad Tabara, "Growing cities of the Arab World", *Arab Times*, Kuwait, 17th April, 1982.

26. Henry Azzam, "Patterns of urbanization and economic development in the Arab region" (Arabic), paper presented at Seminar on Population Distribution and Development in the Arab World, Univ. of Kuwait, ILO and Arab Planning Institute, Nov, 1981.

27. Jassem Al-Manai, *Industrial development in Bahrain,* Ph.D. thesis presented to Sorbonne University, 1980, France.

28. M. Wajih Badawi et al, "A study on methods of transfer of technology and its relation to the industrial development in Arab Gulf States" (Arabic), paper published in Afaq Iqtisadiya (UAE, Jan 1980), p. 67.

29. *The Economist,* 10 December, 1977.

30. Abdel Maqsoud Ali, "Food security in Arab Gulf States", paper delivered to the First Conference on Food Security held in Dubai, 1981.

31. Nader Ferjani, "The problem of manpower in the Arab Gulf and its horizon," paper presented at a Seminar on New Aspects of Cooperation in the Arab Gulf States—Local and International Framework, held in Kuwait, April, 1982 (in Arabic).

32. Osama El-Khoudi, "Towards establishment of a technological base in the Arab Gulf States," paper presented to the conference (see footnote no. 41) in Arabic.

33. Kuwait — Ministry of Interior Report published by *Arab Times,* May 4, 1982.

34. See Birks and Sinclair, op. cit.

35. Annual Reports of the BES, OEDS and NSB by M. Abdella on Export of Filipino Manpower (Institute of Labour and Manpower Studies, Manila, 1979).

36. See Study on "Assimilation of migrant Palestinian families in Kuwait society," by I. Qutub and Wajeeh Yasseen, *Social Science Journal* (University of Kuwait, 1981), Special Issue.

37. Juhain Sultan, "Oil and its impact on migration in Gulf societies", *Arab Gulf Journal* (University of Basra, Iraq), Vol. 11, no. 1 (1979).

38. I. Qutub, "Socio-economic impact of migration in Gulf societies", *Arab Gulf Journal* (University of Basra, Iraq), Vol. 11, no. 1 (1979).

39. Qays Al-Momen, "Asian migration to the Arab Gulf and its role and impact on Arabization of the Gulf," paper presented at conference held by University of Basra, Iraq, in Nov. 1979.
40. United Nations, *Fund for Population Activities – Populi,* Vol. 3, (1981).
41. Timothy G. Niblock, "Theory and the prospects for integration in the Arab Gulf," paper presented in the Seminar on Man and Society in the Arab Gulf held by the University of Basra, Iraq, 1979.

TWENTY-ONE

Regional Structural Change in International Perspective: A Project Report

VIJAI P. SINGH

I. THE REGIONAL ECONOMIC RESTRUCTURING

A Framework for Analysis

Industrial nations have been the major beneficiaries of global economic growth. These nations maintain a high standard of living due to their strong position in the international economy. This has led to the internationalization of the domestic economy. Many products and services are subject to foreign competition making it more difficult for national governments to protect less competitive industries even though these industries may employ a substantial proportion of the work force. The restructuring of industrial economies has implied growth of some sectors and decline of others, population redistribution (leaving many communities with a smaller population and tax base), allocation of capital to the most promising sectors and readjustment of businesses. These processes have had an uneven impact on regions.

Old industrial regions that once led economic growth have suffered massive unemployment, physical deterioration, population decline, fiscal hardships and have become less attractive for new businesses. The key industries that fuelled industrialization, economic growth and prosperity in these regions lost much of their special functions in the emerging national and international economies. Restructuring creates a new mix of industry and business. Its impact in some regions has been so severe that readjustments are not left to market forces. Explicit regional and local economic development initiatives are being considered and implemented through the participation of the private sector, public sector and major research universities. The mechanisms for developing such policies are varied and often fraught with a variety of impediments.

This paper is divided into three parts. The first part outlines the experiences of selected European and American regions with respect to the restructuring of their economies. Similarities and differences between them are identified and directions for economic development and job creation are presented. This section focuses on the factors that have contributed to slow policy responses in dealing with the problems associated with rapid employment losses in manufacturing industries and population decentralization at the community and regional levels. Since this section addresses only broader issues of regional policy it becomes necessary to seek a deeper understanding of the magnitude of the problems and describe specific actions for their amelioration. Therefore, the second section analyses population, labour force and employment in the Pittsburgh region over a period of ten years. The third and the last section presents the process of public-private and university partnerships and specific programmes that have been developed to respond to the economic and social distress caused by the restructuring of the Pittsburgh regional economy.

The Process of Regional Decline

The mature industrial regions in Western Europe and the United States had a greater concentration of coal, steel, textiles, aluminium and heavy industrial equipment manufacturing that contributed significantly to their industrialization and economic growth. These regions had a special economic role in their respective national economies. They enjoyed employment growth, prosperity and attracted potential workers from less developed areas, including immigrants from other countries.

Major technological breakthroughs, discovery of new sources of energy and raw materials, and the world-wide industrialization process created new challenges for the once economically powerful industrial regions (Caves, 1980: 501-544; Bluestone and Harrison, 1982: 140-190; Pfaller, 1983: 7-32; Commission of the European Communities, 1984: 17-119; Cyert and Mowery, 1987: 1-23). It became difficult for the coal industry to compete with the availability of relatively cheaper oil especially within the context of growing environmental regulations. Many steel producing regions suffered from product substitution, technological obsolescence, over-capacity and competition from efficient producers (Jones, 1981: 9-16; Lawrence and Dyer, 1983: 55-85; Borrus, 1983: 60-105). As Singh and Borzutzky (1986: 8) point out:

> Given the pre-eminent importance of the steel sector in the regions, the changes in the world market for steel and the appearance of new, more efficient producers such as Korea or Brazil had a traumatic and irreversible effect on these regions. High unemployment and declining production had been the two most serious consequences of this process.
>
> Two phenomenon converged to produce this crisis. First, the decreased demand for steel products in the world market and second, the competitive disadvantage of the old steel producers located in these regions which cannot compete with the modern, efficient producers located either in the Asia, Latin America or the United States' sun belt. However, the steel industry has not been the only one affected by this phenomenon, the old textile manufacturers, shipyards and others have also suffered from the same process.

The responses of the affected sectors were marginally incremental and often disjointed. Policy-makers in business and public sectors reacted in ways that alleviated the immediate problems but did not provide long-term solutions. Drawing on the experiences of Ruhr, Schlieper outlined four distinct historical phases (1986: 3-10). The first phase (1947-1959) which Schlieper calls "repression" was characterized by the private and public sectors' indifference towards impending restructuring of basic industries. Growing demand for steel, coal and other products during the post-war reconstruction period delayed any consideration for restructuring. Instead of modernization and rationalization, production capacities were expanded. This phase was followed by a period of "defence" (1958-1967) during which the pressure for restructuring was stultified through economic and political means. The consequences of the increase in energy supplies and foreign competition were understood. But the full-scale restructuring of the coal industry in Ruhr was deferred in favour of minor production cut-backs and import restrictions; by the end of the 1960s, mines began to be closed and unemployment grew rapidly.

It was during the third phase (1968-1978) called "preparation" that the magnitude of restructuring was recognized as an inescapable reality. The decaying industrial infrastructure and substantial employment losses in the manufacturing sector brought real nightmares for the regional leaders. The steel industry's decline in the 1970s and 1980s produced massive employment losses in Ruhr that could not be compensated by the modest employment gains in the non-manufacturing sectors. Foreign competition and reduction in world-wide demand for steel confirmed the benefit of steel plant modernization in Germany but these benefits did not accrue to the steel workers in Ruhr because the modernized plants were built in other regions of Germany.

Perhaps even more so than in Ruhr, a substantial proportion of Pittsburgh's economy was based on such durable goods industries as steel, stone, clay, glass, electrical and non-electrical machinery. The restructuring of Pittsburgh's economy also began in the 1950s but the severe employment losses due to plant closings began in the late 1970s and early 1980s.

The non-manufacturing sector has grown and between 1972 and 1986, the Pittsburgh region has made substantial employment gains. The regional economy has become more diversified and service oriented. But service employment growth in the region has lagged behind the U.S. For example, between 1983 and 1985, the region's non-manufacturing employment grew slightly less than one per cent per year as compared to more than two per cent for the United States.

In addition to Pittsburgh, other areas such as Chicago, St. Louis, Birmingham, Philadelphia, Cleveland and Detroit that have a large urban core also experienced substantial losses in their manufacturing employment. (Gurwitz and Kingsley, 1982: 87-122; Summers and Luce, 1985: 13-46). These regions had a concentration of recession-prone manufacturing industries in varying degrees and have lost not only manufacturing employment but also experienced substantial population decline especially in the central cities. Singh and Borzutzky (1986: 21-22) reported that:

Among the mature industrial regions, Pittsburgh has suffered greater population losses than Cleveland, Detroit, Boston, Philadelphia, St. Louis, Chicago and Birmingham, respectively. Denver, Tampa and Atlanta have shown impressive population gains since 1960, closely followed by Seattle and San Francisco. Clearly, the most important factor associated with population change is the state of the regional economy. Regions that showed economic stability and vitality were also more likely to attract young and educated workers seeking employment and entrepreneurial opportunities. However, other factors such as quality of environment, cultural amenities, quality of education and health care services also affect choice of a place for living and working.

A closer examination of the Pittsburgh region shows that the regional economy's restructuring that began in the 1950s was accompanied by changes in the population's size and composition as well. In the initial phase of the population decentralization, the migration was from the more urbanized areas to suburban areas in search for improved housing. But subsequent population losses were attributed to migration. Many young and educated moved out of region in search of better economic opportunities. Also, primarily due to lower fertility rates and selective migration of younger people, the region's population is aging faster than the nation's. Another consequence of these processes is reflected in the decline of the labour force growth.

Many other mature industrial regions in the USA have faced the problems associated with declining population, increase in the proportion of the population's elderly, and younger worker's migration to other regions that offer better economic opportunities. The decline of manufacturing industries and population has eroded the tax base of many communities in these regions and they are less and less able to provide basic public services and amenities to their citizens. The answer to industrial restructuring problems lies in a coordinated approach of public and private sectors for economic revitalization.

Giarratani (1986: 2) pointed out that –

. . .in a period of strong growth in the national economy, it is very

> convenient for local policy makers to neglect fundamental regional economic problems. This is a familiar theme in matters of economic policy generally; as long as the size of the "pie" is getting larger, it matters little that one's share of that pie is getting *relatively* smaller. It is when a region experiences absolute as well as relative decline that policy is forced to deal with the most difficult challenges, and this is more likely to occur when the national economy is weak. In this event, regional policy must come to rely less on "trying" the local economy to the nation and must seek to develop such autonomous strengths as may be feasible.

Each of these regions must undertake a careful analysis of their comparative advantage and initiate programmes for economic development and job creation.

Policy responses to regional structural change involve understanding of the causes of regional decline. But it has been a difficult process. The Federal Reserve Bank report (1987: 4) observed that "The sheer size of these industries and their dominance of the region significantly affected their local economies in ways that produced resistance to change. The industries' demand for labour drove up wages and employed the best and brightest workers and managers. . . . As these dominant industries matured, institutions and coalitions formed to preserve the industries that had brought employment and prosperity to the region. These forces created a barrier to the development of new economic activities and weakened the competitive advantage of doing business in these areas." The causes of regional decline are associated with regional, national and international factors (Cyert, 1985: 2-4). Kunzmann (1986: 11) provided a framework in comparing causes of decline in Ruhr and Merseyside. We added the Pittsburgh region in this comparison.

Institutional Imperatives

In industrial democracies, it is the private sector that has the prominent role of responding to changes in the domestic and international economy. However, the major concerns for businesses are to make profits and increase their market share. They prefer to operate from locations that help them promote these objectives. Historically, coal, steel, textile, automobile, and chemical industries have had greater concentrations only in certain regions. Therefore, when

Causes of Regional Decline: Merseyside, Ruhr and Pittsburgh

Economic Base	Merseyside	Ruhrgebiet	Pittsburgh
Loss of national and international importance of region's goods and services	Liverpool lost its importance as a leading world port and decline of ship-building industry	Decline of coal and steel	Substantial decline of durable goods industry, especially steel, stone, clay and glass, electrical and non-electrical machinery
Strong labour unions have resisted change	Militant dock workers union contributed to the spatial shift of labour related activities	Strong unions in steel and coal have lost membership and influence	A negative image for labour-management relations.
Centralized decision-making and intervention interfere with development consistent with regional policy strategy	Sectoral intervention by the central government has created tensions at the regional level	Decentralized government structure enables local and regional authorities to pursue this agenda	Excessive decentralized government and quasi-government structures intervene with coordinated policy strategies
Regional image	Considered a prototype declining industrial region in Western Europe	Fear of deterioration of environmental quality due to concentration of heavy industry and unused industrial sites	In spite of decline of basic industry and slow recovery the region is considered a prototype for Public-Private Partnership in the USA
Educational base	Limited role for the universities and technical institutions	Lack of universities until 1968. New universities are playing some role in the region's economic reintegration	The region's universities and other institutions have become a significant force in regional economic recovery

such industries, irrespective of their size, underwent restructuring the economic impact was much more deeply felt in these regions where they were concentrated than most elsewhere. The role of different levels of government in helping the affected regions in a country has neither been obvious nor the degree of their effectiveness clear. The intergovernmental structures sometimes facilitate economic readjustment strategies and other times are perceived as cumbersome and ineffective.

Wight, commenting on the role of the European economic community, suggested that the national government should pay more attention to regional policy and the administrative structure of the European economic community should facilitate effective coordination. However, he maintains that the regions should be granted incentives and support to develop their own strategies for economic development. Wight (1986: 6) observed that:

> There are important advantages to be gained from local knowledge and experience when it comes to developing policies. Leaving most of the responsibility with the states given greater scope to diversity and experimentation in developing specific policies to meet specific problems. The "parochial dimension' is important, and it is interesting to note that in the U.K., there is now considerable pressure for the Scottish Development Agency to be replicated in the regions of England. Principally, it must be said, that pressure arises from the lack of any organization with the Agency's range of powers, functions and budget in other parts of the U.K. but also in recognition of the value of an organization with local knowledge and local accountability. There would of course be dangers in replicating the approach taken in one region or state in another location but the argument for local responsibility remains strong.

This is quite consistent with what has happened in the USA. However, many feel that the U.S. economic policy should be sensitive to the interests of the regions.

Public policies for economic revitalization and job creation should be seen within the context of intergovernmental structures. Kunzmann (1986: 13-14) points out that in the U.K. it is the central government that plays a dominant role in regional policies. But in Germany, it is the state government that has the primary responsibility. In Britain the role of local governments is determined by the central government, but in Germany they have more autonomy in deciding the programmes of action that would alleviate economic and social consequences of regional restructuring. The western European countries have developed a variety of incentives to promote regional economic development (Yuill and Allen, 1986).

In the case of the United States, Peters and Reaves have provided a detailed analysis of intergovernmental structures as they are related to the economic realities of the 1980s. Historically, state and local governments have used a variety of incentives to attract new businesses but they have recently felt helpless in the context of growing international competition. Public pressure on the federal government has been growing as some of America's major industries have suffered a substantial decline. Since the promising sectors employ fewer workers, they have not yet built the kind of political base equivalent to the steel and automobile industries. Since the state and local governments determine incentives for attracting new firms and helping the existing ones, it is difficult to coordinate a response in the form of a national industrial policy (Peters, 1986: 9-14). In fact, Reaves (1986: 2) points out that at the regional level, there is so much political fragmentation that it is difficult to develop a region-wide policy within a reasonable period of time. Allegheny County, which is one of the four counties that comprise the Pittsburgh region, has 130 municipal governments each of which has the authority to develop its own strategy for economic development. In addition, there are a variety of other public and private organizations that have emerged to address economic development problems in the Pittsburgh region.

As the national level, Peters (1986: 19-27) argues that it is difficult to develop a highly-directed industrial policy. The reasons include, ideology, parochial imperatives, institutions, incrementalism and economic structure. Previously, government was not supposed to interfere in economic matters but now there are some who favour a limited role for it. Usually, the U.S. Congress has favoured a general rule that would provide assistance to all those affected by a particular problem. Therefore, policies that favour a particular region run counter to the American political tradition. It is difficult to develop special incentives or subsidies for a particular industry to protect them from foreign competition. American bureaucracy is ideological and fragmented and it is difficult to develop priorities at the national level that can be implemented in a coordinated fashion at local and regional levels. As a matter of fact, the business community itself is fragmented in various interest groups and associations and fails to present a demand that would address the fundamental problems it faces. The case is the same for labour unions in their dealings with industry.

Policy Structures

Schlieper, Hesse and Kunzmann have discussed economic development programmes for Ruhr. Hesse (1986: 3) points out that basic industries in Ruhr were protected by the sectoral and regional assistance until the mid-1960s. The decline of basic industries necessitated a more comprehensive economic development programmes. It included development of labour, capital innovations, technology transfer, environmental protection, urban development and cultural amenities. The new "Action Programme for Ruhr" launched in 1979 envisioned cooperation among government, industry and university. Federal and State Governments provided funds for university-based research in coal, steel and energy fields to promote development of the new technologies. Job training programmes in the area of high youth unemployment have been initiated. Greater involvement of the private sector in apprenticeships and local governments' aggressive efforts to create new service jobs in the local economy have had good beginnings. The state government encouraged educational institutions to invest in secondary and vocational educational programmes to train youth for the occupations that are likely to grow in the future (Kunzmann, 1986: 13-17; Schlieper, 1986: 12-13).

The 1984 "North Rhine Westphahia initiative for future technologies" has targeted certain fields in which the Ruhr has comparative advantage. These include environmental technology, energy, bio-technology and communication. Small and medium-size companies are considered appropriate targets for technology transfer. However, changes in the mix of the regional economy have important consequences to the labour force. It is hoped that there is a proper coordination between changes in the regional economy and vocational and technical education (Hennings, Kahnert and Kunzmann, 1987: 3-27). Hesse expressed concerns about the suitability of organizational structures to the long-term nature of regional restructuring. The organizations are rigid and the decision-making system is complex. These often interfere with the regional economy's speedy restructuring. It is important to re-examine the current governmental structure and make appropriate changes so that policies for restructuring can be implemented effectively. Also, it is important that regional industries should become more competitive–domestically as well as internationally (Hesse, 1986: 5-8).

Kunzmann argues that regional economic recovery of Ruhr is very much tied to its image. Important physical improvements were necessary to present a positive image of the region. A number of projects for urban renewal, neighbourhood improvements and rehabilitation of former industrial sites have already begun. Improvements in the region's infrastructure such as transportation and other public facilities are being upgraded. More attention is being paid to parks, recreational and cultural facilities to make Ruhr an attractive area to live and work. According to Kunzmann (1986: 19) cultural and environmental qualities are also important considerations for entrepreneurs, not just tax breaks and other subsidies. Infrastructure, land and qualified labour force are other locational factors for businesses.

In Merseyside, Kunzmann (1986: 15-17) discussed several initiatives that supported the regional industries. The Central Government created enterprise zones that have helped regional companies find physically and economically attractive sites. Small companies are able to secure funds and consulting services from a local public-private partnership organization. But the formation of a technology park in 1983 through the cooperation of the public and private sector and universities was a major economic development initiative. The Central Government has stepped in along with regional and local efforts to provide training and retraining programmes for the regional labour force. Several programmes were implemented in the 1970s to improve the area's physical appearance, including inner-city neighbourhoods. Local governments were given authority to improve existing industrial areas and provide financial assistance to businesses. Many of these programmes, however, lacked coordination and continuity. In Merseyside, the programmes for economic and social revitalization are not yet fully embedded into the regional economic restructuring which is a long-term process.

We would discuss in detail in the next section that the restructuring of Pittsburgh's regional economy produced massive unemployment among the workers in the durable goods industries and loss of population partly as a consequence of younger and educated worker's migration to other regions of the USA. Our analysis would reveal that the existing governmental structure did not permit a comprehensive and well-targeted economic development strategy. In spite of these impediments, as will be discussed in the third section, the Pittsburgh region has forged ahead by creating public-private-university partnerships in an effort to attract new business and industries and to create jobs. The key to this type of partnership is the sharing of common objectives by the major interest groups. For example, it is in the interest of the public sector to have a strong economic base and it is good for the businesses to be socially responsible. Universities get an opportunity to expand their research agenda in such areas as biotechnology, robotics and artificial intelligence among others. It is important to note that the Pittsburgh region has developed new institutional structures to respond to regional issues and avoid the cumbersome bureaucratic governmental structures.

The Pittsburgh region has had considerable success in developing civic organizations with the support of the private and public sector to address regional problems which did not fall exclusively within the domains of the existing institutions. Each of these organizations had their responsibilities clearly defined in such a way that some of them worked to build consensus on particular policy strategies at the regional level while others were mainly responsible to implement them. However, the top leadership in these organizations participated in the deliberation of each other's agenda. The mayors, county commissioners and other key public officials participated directly or indirectly in such discussions. Section three of this paper has dealt with the major programmes for economic development and job creation through public-private-university partnerships.

The preceding analysis suggests that each region that has experienced restructuring of its economy must assess its comparative advantage domestically as well as internationally. It is not to suggest that the industries that have failed to compete in the past cannot be revived. The critical issue is whether there are other sectors that may provide a stronger economic base in the long run (Appelbaum, 1984: 23-48; Clark, 1985: 1-30). For example, in the case of the Pittsburgh region, substantial levels of investments are being made in the high technology industries. But the region is attempting to develop those components of the steel industry that have a comparative advantage. But as Giarratani (1986: 3) has commented, it may not be such an easy decision for the region's policy-makers.

> In this respect it is, perhaps, most important for policy-makers to admit frankly that some regions may never attain the size, stature, and prosperity by which they had been traditionally characterized. While it is certainly true that regions are capable of restructuring and finding new prosperity, it is equally true that such adjustment may proceed over the course of generations, and also that the current and foreseeable economic conditions for the region may not be conducive to growth, even under the most optimistic circumstances. Facing the fact that an economy is now (perhaps, permanently) smaller than it had once been may mean new and warranted attention to the efficiency with which public revenues are spent, including in some instances, an admission that many financial inducements offered to industry in order to spur growth may simply represent a waste of scarce tax dollars. At yet another level, facing the reality of decline can force the rationalization of local municipal authorities, just as private firms may face reorganization in response to market conditions. The point is this: realism is an essential aspect of regional policy.

Therefore, the regional policy-makers must be prepared to make what may seem to be politically unpopular decisions even though they make economic sense. It is not suggested that the communities that have suffered population dislocation, high and persistent unemployment, and erosion in their tax base should be ignored. As a matter of fact, there ought to be explicit programmes to help communities to deal with this financial distress. The unemployed in addition to receiving benefits should be trained in such a way that they can find employment in the growing sectors of the regional economy. However, the region should be prepared to take bold actions to revive the regional economy by attracting new firms and providing financial and technical support to existing firms for their survival and expansion. Appropriate data and information on the regional economic and population trends should be analysed in the national and international contexts. The organization of data should be consistent with the administrative jurisdiction responsible for developing and implementing economic development policies. The next section provides a brief overview of the kinds of data that may be considered in developing a regional policy. The information should be relevant in helping understand underlying causes and providing important clues for developing effective policy responses.

II. POPULATION, LABOUR FORCE AND EMPLOYMENT TRENDS IN THE PITTSBURGH REGION

This section examines statistical trends in the changes in population, labour force and employment. Demographic trends are strongly associated with economic conditions. Usually, a region that boasts a robust economy is more likely than other regions to attract younger and more educated workers, as well as entrepreneurs. The restructuring of mature industrial regions contributed to population decline in the urban cores and to the virtual dissolution of many small communities which were closely tied to now declining industries. The selective out-migration of younger persons reduces family formation and increases the component of the older population in the region. This section provides an in-depth analysis of population, labour force and employment trends in the Pittsburgh region. Some of the issues identified in this section are addressed in the third section for their amelioration through policies designed to initiate economic development and job creation at the regional level.

Population Trends

Pennsylvania has been a net out-migration state and a substantial population loss has occurred in the urban core of the state's major metropolitan areas. The population decline in the 1950s and 1960s was partly related to long-term restructuring of manufacturing industries, especially the steel industry (Robertson *et al.*, 1986: 35-39; Summers and Luce, 1987: 37-50; Singh et al., 1987: 63-92). According to Table 21.1, the Pittsburgh Primary Metropolitan Statistical Area (PMSA)[1] lost less than one per cent of its population between 1960 and 1970, but declined further to 5.5 per cent between 1970 and 1980. Between 1980 and 1985 the rate of population decline had slowed. By contrast, during the 1960s and 1970s population of Pennsylvania grew 4.2 per cent, and 0.5 per cent, respectively, but population growth came to a virtual half between 1980 and 1985.

The corresponding percentages for the USA were 13.4, 11.4 and 5.4, respectively. It is clear that while the Pittsburgh PMSA has lost population over a period of 25 years, the State of Pennsylvania has made modest population gains. The urbanized areas and communities that had greater concentrations of heavy manufacturing and mining suffered severe population losses. Even at the national level, the rate of growth was cut to less than a half–from 13.4 per cent between 1960 and 1970 to 5.4 per cent between 1980 and 1985. The slower population growth at the national level is attributable to a dramatic decline in the fertility.

TABLE 21.1: **Population Change in the Counties of the Pittsburgh Primary Metropolitan Statistical Area, Pennsylvania and the United States**

(1960-1985)

	(in thousands)				Per cent Change		
SW PA Counties	1960	1970	1980	1985	60-70	70-80	80-85
Allegheny	1,628.6	1,605.0	1,450.0	1,385.6	-1.4	-9.7	-4.5
Fayette	169.3	154.7	159.4	156.7	-8.7	3.1	-1.7
Washington	217.3	210.9	217.1	213.4	-2.9	2.9	-1.7
Westmoreland	352.6	376.9	392.3	383.7	6.9	4.1	-2.2
PGH PMSA	2,367.8	2,347.5	2,218.8	2,143.4	-0.9	-5.5	-3.4
PA	11,319.0	11,800.8	11,864.7	11,863.7	4.2	0.5	0.0
USA	179,323.2	203,302.0	226,545.8	238,741.0	13.4	11.4	5.4

Sources: "Estimates of the Population of Pennsylvania Counties and Metropolitan Areas: July 1, 1981 to 1985," U.S. Bureau of the Census, August, 1987; *Census of Population*, U.S. Bureau of the Census, 1960, 1970 and 1980.

Allegheny County, which is the largest and most urbanized county in the Pittsburgh PMSA, lost 23,000 persons between 1960 and 1970, but it lost 155,000 persons, or 10 per cent of its population, between 1970 and 1980 (See Table 21.2). Between 1980 and 1985 it lost 75,100 persons or 5.2 per cent of its population. Other counties were relatively small but they too lost population, though the rate of decline was much less than that for Allegheny County. A partial explanation is that these counties were less urbanized and had slightly higher fertility rates and experienced far lower migration rates than

Allegheny Country. The City of Pittsburgh faced more dramatic declines in its population than Allegheny County or the entire PMSA. Between 1960 and 1970 it lost 84,000 persons or 14 per cent of its population. A substantial proportion of the people who left the city settled in the nearby suburbs or other parts of Allegheny County. Again, between 1970 and 1980, the city lost another 96,000 persons or 18.5 per cent of its population. These later trends suggested that many people who left the city in the 1970s did not move to the suburbs for better housing or different life style but moved long distances in search of new job opportunities.

TABLE 21.2: **Components of Population Change in the Counties of Pittsburgh Primary Metropolitan Statistical Area and Pennsylvania, 1980-85**

(Per cent of 1980 population in parentheses)

Area	Change in Population	Natural Increase	Net Migration
Allegheny County	-64,000	10,400	-75,100 (-5.2%)
Fayette County	-2,700	1,300	-4,000 (-2.5)
Washington County	-3,600	1,800	-5,400 (-2.5)
Westmoreland County	-8,500	4,100	-12,600 (-3.2)
PGH PMSA	-78,800	17,600	-96,400 (-3.3)
Pennsylvania	-1,000	201,000	-202,000 (-1.7)

Source: "Estimates of Population of Pennsylvania Counties and Metropolitan Areas: July 1, 1981 to 1985," *U.S. Bureau of the Census*, August, 1987.

Migration is usually selective where younger and educated persons are more likely to move than others. In addition, the lower fertility rate has raised the median age overall, but more so in the urbanized areas than most elsewhere. The preceding analysis showed that the decline in birth rate and migration affect both the composition and distribution of the population. The proportion of younger persons in the region continued to decline and, therefore, the size of the labour force will be smaller in the future and the ratio of dependent persons (below 15 years and above 65 years) to productive workers (16-64 years) will be larger, putting a tremendous burden on the society. Out-migration reduced the proportion of younger workers in the labour force and the only age group which increased consistently was the 65-years-and-above cohort. Population projections showed a continued decline in the region's population but at a somewhat slower pace. This was at least partly related to improvement in the regional economy. But the region, and especially Allegheny County and the City of Pittsburgh, is facing serious problems associated with a smaller population base and older, dislocated as well as chronically unemployed workers. Many of these are concentrated in the inner cities and small towns such as in the Mon Valley where many steel mills and other manufacturing facilities have been permanently closed.

Labour Force Trends

Figs. 21.1, 21.2 and 21.3 provide per cent change in the labour force, employment and unemployment for Pittsburgh PMSA, Pennsylvania and the United States. The labour force comprises all civilian persons who are above sixteen years of age and who are working or actively seeking work. Age structure of the population (which is related to fertility and migration patterns) determines changes in the labour force. Between 1977 and 1986, labour force change in the Pittsburgh PMSA has been volatile, reflecting the overall economic conditions of the region (Fig. 21.4). In the Pittsburgh PMSA, the labour force grew at modest rates until after 1982 and then declined dramatically, showing a three per cent loss between 1983 and 1984. This graph also shows that the Pittsburgh region had done better in terms of labour force growth compared to the state of Pennsylvania until 1982. The state could not avoid the impacts that the Pittsburgh region faced in the early 1980s when consequences of recession of 1980 began to be felt deeply.

At the national level, the rate of growth in the labour force diminished slightly between 1977 and 1986 but it picked up again. In fact, between 1983 and 1984, while the region had suffered its most severe decline, the U.S. labour force grew more than two per cent. The decline in the regional labour force occurred primarily due to out-migration of working age adults from the region and large numbers of discouraged workers who decided to drop out of the labour force, at least temporarily. But, as the general economic recovery began in 1983, the economic outlook in the Pittsburgh region brightened as well. Labour force growth after 1984 accelerated both in the region and in the state, reflecting the return of the workers who had left the labour force earlier.

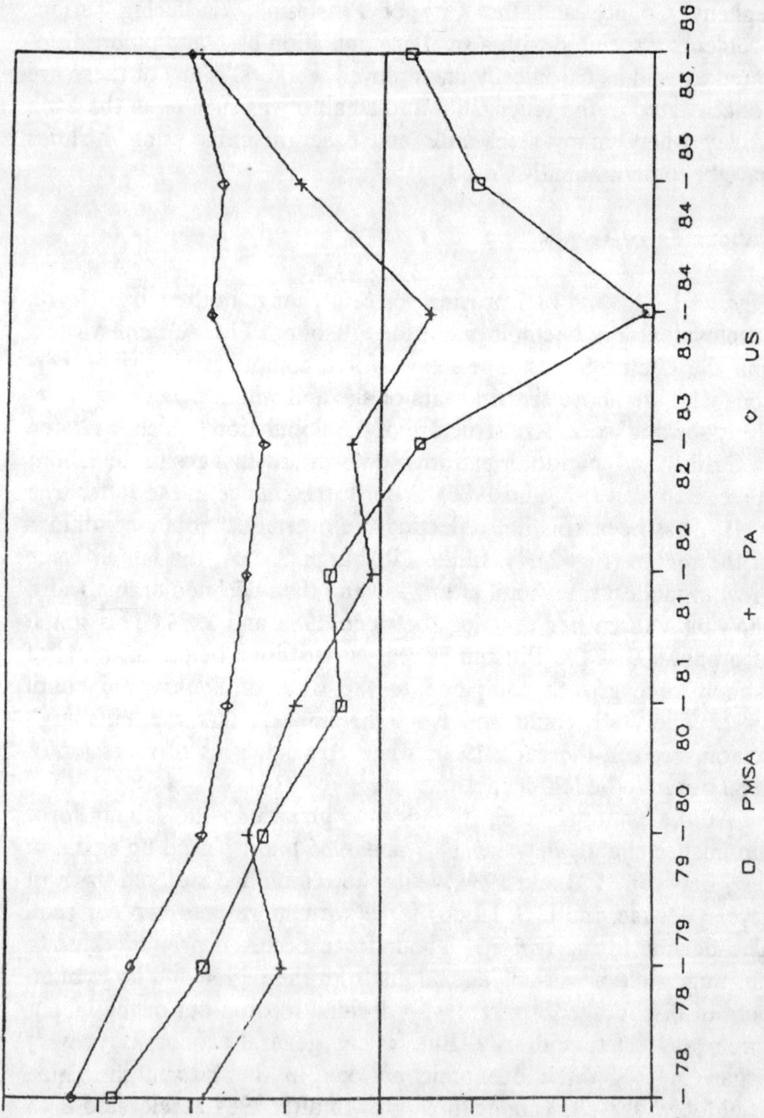

FIG. 21.1: Labour Force Change in the Pittsburgh PMSA, Pennsylvania and USA 1977-1986

Source: "Civilian Labour Force Data Series File 1977-1986," Pennsylvania Department of Labour and Industry, Harrisburg, PA, 1987.

Fig. 21.1 illustrates that the gap in labour force growth rates between the nation, the state and the region widened considerably between 1982 and 1984 but began to narrow somewhat in 1985. In 1986, there was a convergence of growth rates between the USA and the state of Pennsylvania. The regional labour force growth has begun to narrow the gap with the USA and the state but it has a long way to go. It is important for the region to stem further decline in its population which has resulted from selective out-migration of relatively younger and educated persons. The steady proportional growth of the 65-years-and-older group in the population can be reversed through aggressive economic growth strategies in areas in which the Pittsburgh region has comparative advantage. This should encourage labour force growth in the region which would be attractive to new industrial and business enterprises.

Employment Trends

The employment growth in the region is related to the mix of industry and business as well as to performance. Just like labour force trends, employment change between 1977 and 1986 has been dramatic. The Fig. 21.2 shows that the rate of employment growth continued until almost 1980 after which it began to decline rapidly, falling below four per cent in the Pittsburgh PMSA, below two per cent for the state and almost one per cent for the USA in 1982. Once the recession was over, there was a rapid growth in employment. However, as the figure shows, the employment growth in the Pittsburgh region was slower compared to the state or the USA. Still the gap between the region, state and the nation narrowed considerably.

Fig. 21.3 shows changes in unemployment between 1977 and 1986. It is clear that the Pittsburgh region had smaller rates of unemployment than the state until the recession of 1980. After that, the regional unemployment rate escalated and, despite the improvement in the regional economy, it remains substantially higher than the state's or the nation's. In the region itself, the number of jobless has been reduced from more than 140,000 people in 1983 to less than 80,000 in 1986. The improvement in the jobs has continued and further reduction in the rate and level of unemployment is expected. One clear indication of this trend is the narrowing of differences in the unemployment rates between the region, state and the USA as the U.S. economy has improved.

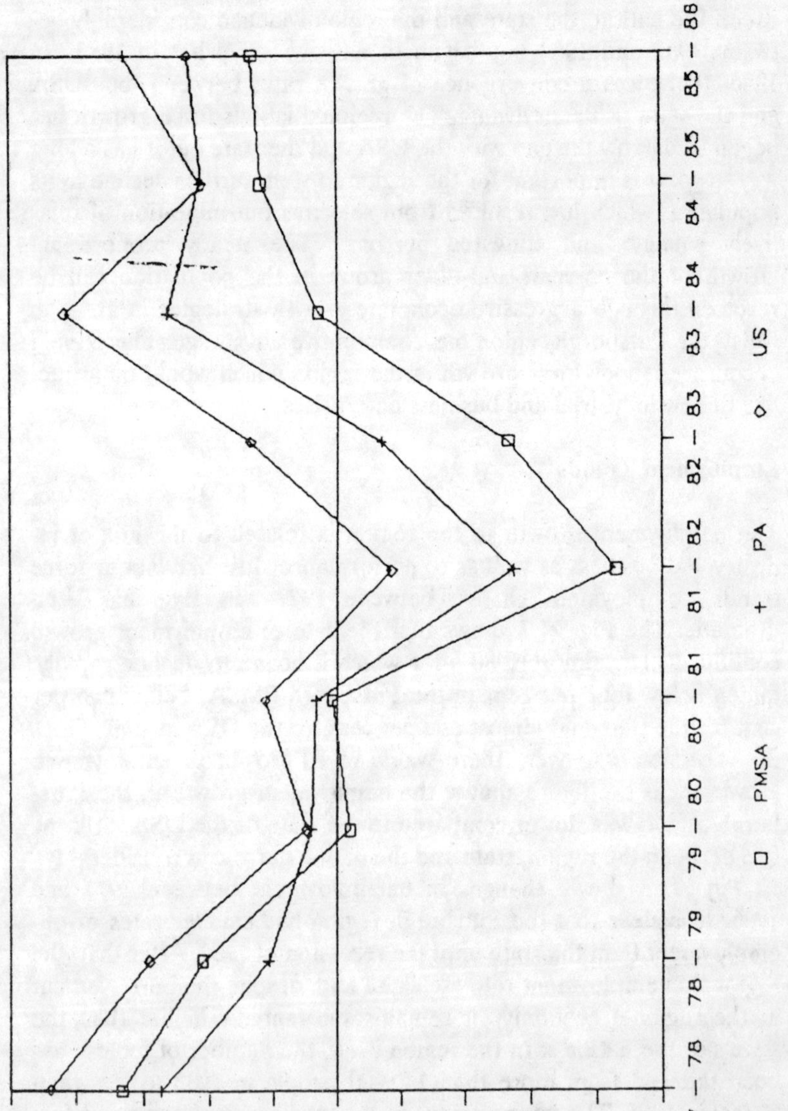

FIG. 21.2: Employment Change in the Pittsburgh PMSA, Pennsylvania and USA 1977-1986

Source: "Civilian Labour Force Data Series File 1977-1986," Pennsylvania Department of Labour and Industry, Harrisburg, PA, 1987.

Manufacturing Employment Trends

The Pittsburgh region has had a comparative advantage in steel and coal since the early part of this century. The area had a strong manufacturing base, supported by the availability of raw materials and access to waterways for transporting goods. The manufacturing industry brought prosperity to the region and provided stable and well-paying jobs. The people settled in small communities near the manufacturing facilities and their way of life was closely tied to their workplace. Strong unions emerged to protect and enhance the interests of workers. The region as a whole began to look upon these industries as the backbone of its economy. Substantial proportions of regional capital and labour went in support of these industries and their suppliers. But the mix of industries in the Pittsburgh region was sensitive to cyclical changes.

Historically, the region's economy has relied heavily on such durable goods industries as primary and fabricated metals; stone, clay and glass; and electrical and non-electrical machinery. The steel industry, which had been the anchor of Pittsburgh regional economy, lost its share steadily since the 1950s. ". . . As the steel industry came to dominate the economy of western Pennsylvania, labour, capital and public resources were all geared towards producing steel. During steel's heyday, workers, managers, and government officials positioned themselves to extract as much as possible from the industry. As the industry declined, resources were slow to move away from what had been a stable source of income and support." (Federal Reserve Bank, 1987: 11). According to the American Iron and Steel Institute (Giarratani and Houston, 1986: 25), the market share of the Pittsburgh region's steel production was 25 per cent in 1950, 20.2 per cent in 1960, 18.7 per cent in 1970, 17.5 per cent in 1980 and 12.4 per cent in 1983. It rebounded slightly in 1984 to 13.7 per cent but there is every indication that the role of the steel industry in the Pittsburgh regional economy will never be the same.

According to Table 21.3, in 1979 there were 72,100 workers in primary metals which dropped to 39,600 in 1983, and 27,300 in 1986. In other words, 45.1 per cent of jobs were lost between 1979 and 1983 and 31.1 per cent between 1983 and 1986. Fabricated metals, which employed 20,700 workers in 1979, lost 36.2 per cent jobs between 1979 and 1983 and 12.1 per cent between 1983 and 1986. Non-electrical machinery, electrical equipment, transportation

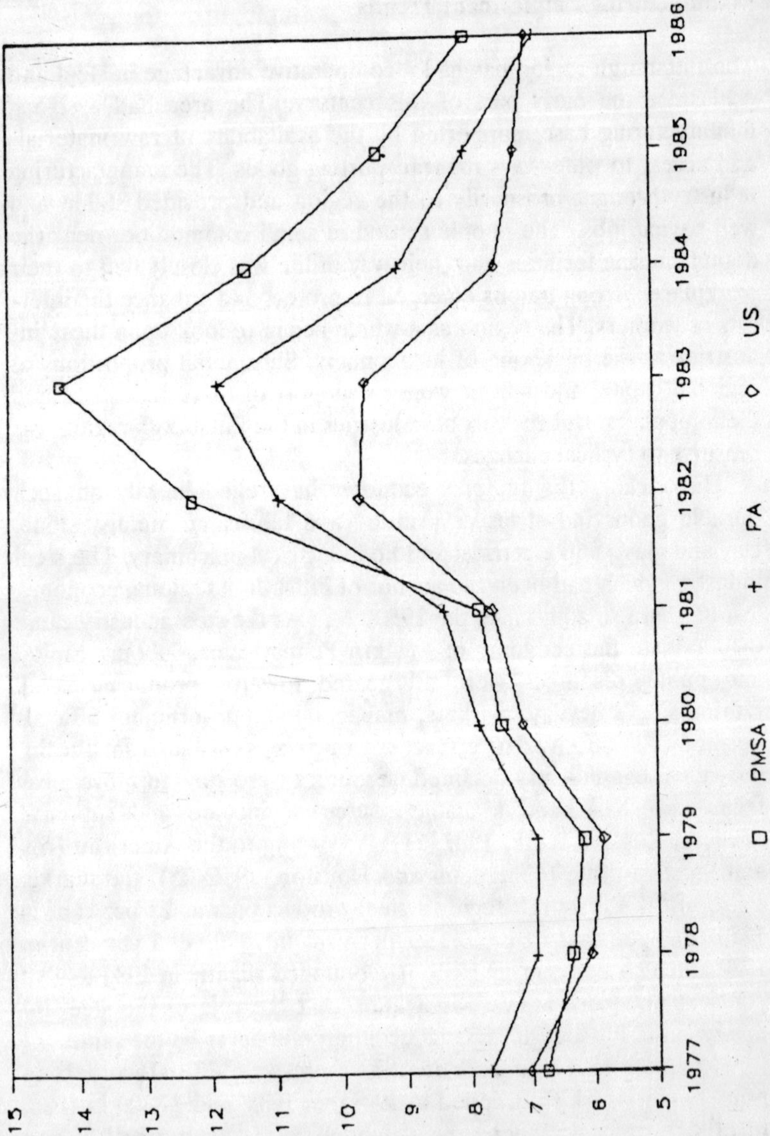

FIG. 21.3: Unemployment Rate in the Pittsburgh PMSA, Pennsylvania and USA 1977-1986

Source: "Civilian Labour Force Data Series File 1977-1986," Pennsylvania Department of Labour and Industry, Harrisburg, PA, 1987.

TABLE 21.3: **Industry Employment Change, Pittsburgh PMSA, 1979-1986**

(in thousands, except for per cent)

	1979	1983	1986	Change 79-83	83-86	79-83	Per cent Change 83-86
Non-Agricultural Employment*	916	835	843.7	-81	8.7	-8.8	1
Manufacturing	224.5	154.2	129.3	-70.3	-24.9	-31.3	-16.1
Durable Goods	180.7	115.6	93.7	-65.1	-21.9	-36	-18.9
Stone, Clay and Glass	16.5	11.8	10.3	-4.7	-1.5	-28.5	-12.7
Primary Metal Industries	72.1	39.6	27.3	-32.5	-12.3	-45.1	-31.1
Fabricated Metal Products	20.7	13.2	11.6	-7.5	-1.6	-36.2	-12.1
Machinery, Except Electric	23.3	18.4	16.5	-4.9	-1.9	-21	-10.3
Electric and Electronic Equipment	22.8	15.4	12.6	-7.4	-2.8	-32.5	-18.2
Transportation Equipment	13.6	7.9	5.8	-5.7	-2.1	-41.9	-26.6
Instruments and Related Products	7.3	6.3	6	-1	-0.3	-13.7	-4.8
Other Durable Goods	4.3	3	3.6	-1.3	0.6	-30.2	20
Non-Durable Goods	43.8	38.6	35.6	-5.2	-3	-11.9	-7.8
Food and Kindred Products	10.8	9.5	7.9	-1.3	-1.6	-12	-16.8
Apparel and other Textile Products	3.8	2.8	2.1	-1	-0.7	-26.3	-25
Paper and Allied Products	2.9	2	2	-0.9	0	-31	0
Printing and Publishing	8.9	8.9	8.9	0	0	0	0
Chemical and Allied Products	9.9	9	9.3	-0.9	0.3	-9.1	3.3
Petroleum and Coal Products	3.6	2.8	0.8	-0.8	-2	-22.2	-71.4
Rubber and Misc. Plastic Products	3.4	3.5	4.3	0.1	0.8	2.9	22.9
Other Non-Durable Goods	0.4	0.2	0.2	-0.2	0	-50	0
Non-Manufacturing	688.7	679.8	712.6	-8.9	32.8	-1.3	4.8
Mining	12.6	7.5	6.7	-5.1	-0.8	-40.5	-10.7
Contract Construction	46.4	37	40.2	-9.4	3.2	-20.3	8.6
Transportation and Public Utility	58.8	47.9	44.7	-10.9	-3.2	-18.5	-6.7
Wholesale and Retail Trade	203.5	203.2	213.3	-0.3	10.1	-0.1	5
Finance Insurance and Real Estate	44.7	48.1	51.5	3.4	3.4	7.6	7.1
Services	206.2	227.2	252.5	21	25.3	10.2	11.1
Government	116.5	108.9	103.7	-7.6	-5.2	-6.5	-4.8
Federal Government	18.4	17.4	18	-1	0.6	-5.4	3.4
State and Local Government	98.1	91.5	85.7	-6.6	-5.8	-6.7	-6.3

Source: "Pittsburgh PMSA Non-Agricultural Wage and Salary Employment 1979-1986", P.A. Department of Labour and Industry, 1987.

* The Total Non-Agricultural employment includes those workers who were involved in Labour-Management Disputes.

equipment and stone, clay and glass, all suffered staggering employment losses running into thousands of workers over a very short period of time. The instruments industry was doing well until 1979, but the recession reversed the trend. The durable goods industry lost 87 thousand jobs between 1979 and 1986. However, as the Table 21.3 shows, all of these industries rebounded and the level of decline was far less in 1986 than before. Overall, the per cent decline between 1983 and 1986 was only half of what it was between 1979 and 1983.

Within the manufacturing industry, the decline of employment in the non-durable goods sectors was far less than in the durable goods sectors. For example, non-durable goods sectors declined 11.9 per cent between 1979 and 1983 and 7.8 per cent between 1983 and 1986, which was about only one-third of the decline compared to durable goods sectors. Much of the employment loss in the non-durable goods sectors came from food and kindred products. The general economic recovery contributed to the improvement in the employment situation after 1983. The employment decline in paper products, printing and publishing levelled off and there was employment growth in chemical products and rubber and plastics.

In spite of some employment rebounds in the manufacturing industries, the region has not yet fully recovered from the massive decline of the steel industry. There were 90,500 fewer jobs in 1986 than in 1975. It is important to note that of these lost jobs, more than 55,000 were in the steel industry alone. The 1980 recession had devastating impact on the manufacturing industry. For example, in 1980 manufacturing jobs in the old Pittsburgh SMSA accounted for 28 per cent of all jobs dropping to 18 per cent in 1985. It meant that in 1985 there were 97,500 fewer jobs in manufacturing than in 1980. Manufacturing employment in the region has shown gradual improvement. The region has begun to initiate economic development strategies in the products and services in which it has comparative advantages. However, one should not expect that dominance of manufacturing industry in the regional economy which existed in the 1950s and 1960s. The regional employment recovery in this industry has lagged behind national growth trends.

Non-Manufacturing Employment Trends

The decline of employment in the manufacturing industries has had devastating impact on many communities that were dependent on them. The other areas of the region that were less dependent could not avoid the impact either. As the region struggled to revive some parts of the manufacturing sectors, it came to look upon the employment growth in the non-manufacturing sectors as an excellent opportunity for rebuilding a strong regional economy. As we will examine in the third section of this paper, the region has forged a coordinated strategy to accomplish this objective.

The number of jobs in the non-manufacturing sector increased during much of the 1970s. Between 1975 and 1983, the region gained almost 89,000 jobs in this industry. Within the non-manufacturing, services have grown faster than in any other sector. For example, wholesale and retail trade was once the largest employer, but not any more. Wholesale and retail trade created almost 26,000 new jobs between 1975 and 1986. However, the service sector added more than 81,000 jobs between the two time periods. Services continued to grow even during the worst recessionary period of the early 1980s.

The construction industry rebounded as did transportation and public utilities, fire and government services. Much of the employment gain in the government sector came from the federal government. Partly as a consequence of difficult economic conditions and reduction in federal subsidies state and local employment situations did not improve much. On the whole, non-manufacturing employment grew 4.8 per cent between 1983 and 1986, compared to a modest decline of 1.3 per cent between 1979 and 1983. Such services as finance, insurance and real estate, which are responsive to consumer and business needs, are likely to grow. The larger sectors, such as services and wholesale and retail trade would find it easier to expand employment provided the manufacturing sector also continues to grow. Such export-oriented services as health, research and development are likely to grow in the future.

It is important to note that both manufacturing and non-manufacturing employment did not grow as fast in the Pittsburgh region as in the USA. The region has realized that the industries that were once its specialities could not compete with other producers. Pittsburgh has not yet given up on steel and other manufacturing industries. Special projects have been developed to make certain parts of the steel industry competitive. Improvement in other manufacturing industries has begun. But the region has entered into the high technology business and health services to compensate for losses elsewhere. These would help attract new business firms as well as export services outside the region. The Federal Reserve Bank noted that "... the exporting of engineering services generated an estimated 13,000 jobs for the Pittsburgh economy in 1982" (1986: 15). Computers and Robotics, in which the region has comparative advantage, would lead the way for important innovations in the region's manufacturing industries.

This analysis has shown that population decline in Pittsburgh region can be addressed only in conjunction with regional economy. A lopsided and consistent increase in the older component of the region's population and out-migration of younger and skilled workers would produce labour shortages in the very industries on which the region has pegged its hopes for economic revitalization. Employment growth in the non-manufacturing sectors have compensated for job losses in the manufacturing sectors. The region has finally realized that it cannot survive by just brooding about the substantial decline of the steel industry. Even the region's public officials have become bold enough to talk about the good economic life for the Pittsburgh region beyond the steel industry. The region has begun to concentrate on particular products and services in which it has comparative advantage. Also, a significant proportion of dislocated workers are reluctant to leave the region. Therefore, economic development strategy attempts to create new employment opportunities by making certain parts of the manufacturing sector competitive in the region. These workers are encouraged and helped to acquire new skills that would enable them to find jobs in the growing sectors of the regional economy.

III. PUBLIC-PRIVATE-UNIVERSITY PARTNERSHIPS

Economic Development in the Pittsburgh Region

The major employment and population shifts in the Pittsburgh region presented in the preceding section suggested the need for vigorous attempts towards economic development and job creation. Job losses and population decline are concentrated more in some areas than others. The communities that once depended on the steel industry have been devastated on both counts. Other areas felt the impact only indirectly as their economic base consisted of high technology, research and development and health services, among others. Therefore, any regional economic development initiatives should be sensitive to the issues that affect the entire region as well as to the areas that have special needs and require immediate attention (Bergman, 1986: 1-14; Pennsylvania Business Roundtable, 1987: 13-15). For policies to be effective they must address the needs of workers, communities and businesses.

The multi-faceted nature of regional restructuring requires active involvement of governmental institutions, area businesses, research universities and the affected communities in determining economic development programmes and their implementation (Posvar, 1983; Posvar, 1984). In the Pittsburgh region, these stake holders understood that their own interests can be best served through cooperation with one another. For example, it is in the interest of the public sector to help build a strong economic base and it is good for the business to be socially responsible. Universities get opportunities to expand their research agenda with biotechnology, robotics, and artificial intelligence among others. It is important to note that the Pittsburgh region has developed new institutional structures to respond to regional issues and avoid jurisdictional disputes between bureaucratic governmental structures discussed earlier. The leaders in the public institutions have realized their limitations and have cooperated in developing partnership institutions so that important challenges facing the region can be addressed on a timely basis.

In this section, the roles of some partnership organizations will be discussed in the context of regional economic development. These organizations have distinct as well as overlapping functions and interlocking board memberships are common. Therefore, they do not compete with each other. In addition, economic and social conditions of the milltowns are presented and particular programmes that are targeted to bring jobs and revitalize the communities will be discussed.

Ahlbrandt (1986: 6-12) has described business-oriented civic organizations that have been active in regional economic development. Most important among them is the Allegheny Conference on Community Development (ACCD) which was established in 1943 mainly to attract new businesses for the city, and improve its infrastructure and environment. The ACCD was successful in pollution control, environmental improvements and new downtown construction. It focuses on broader community issues and avoids concentrating on the narrow concerns of a particular industry. It works closely with the city and county governments to develop consensus on major projects. ACCD's most recent accomplishments include construction of new high-rise buildings in downtown Pittsburgh, a convention centre and a light-rail rapid transit system. ACCD also helped establish another civic organization known as the Regional Industrial Development Corporation which develops industrial parks in the region, providing efficient and modern office space and financing for light manufacturing and service companies. The three industrial parks house some 180 companies and employ more than 15,000 workers.

In spite of its major successes, ACCD was considered an organization dedicated to downtown development. But the major economic and demographic shifts in the larger Pittsburgh region made this organization realize that the city's future was closely tied to the region and, therefore, an expanded role for ACCD was in order. In 1981, it created an Economic Development Committee to assess the region's problems and opportunities in the context of changes in the national and international economy. Task forces were established to evaluate the region's current conditions and future prospects in the areas of advanced technology, manufacturing, service, corporate headquarters, international trade, infrastructure, human resources, business climate, and quality of life. Initiatives for business and job creation included university-industry cooperation, high technology corporate executive network, corporate technical support programme, Pittsburgh seed fund, export trade development programme, federal procurement technical assistance programme, occupational forecasting and job training evaluation, public transportation and infrastructure (ACCD, 1983: 31-39). The ACCD did not recommend any special programmes for steel and heavy manufacturing that historically were the backbone of the regional economy although their recent decline had produced major economic and social dislocation in the region.

In the process of restructuring of the Pittsburgh regional economy, knowledge and technology have emerged as the pivotal components. The region's two major universities–the University of Pittsburgh and the Carnegie-Mellon University have become active partners with the public and private sectors to help the region move away from the reliance on the manufacturing sector to a more diversified economy (Posvar, 1983). As heavy manufacturing was undergoing massive decline in the early 1980s, new high technology firms were taking a foothold in the region. The two universities also saw a special role for themselves in developing products and services that had comparative advantage. The private sector welcomed such initiatives and the public sector began to push hard in this direction.

The State Government was also concerned about the decline of its manufacturing bases not just in the Pittsburgh region but in other parts of the state as well. It wanted to establish programmes that would help the state maintain its economic strength. Therefore, in 1983 the state began the Ben Franklin Partnership Program "charged with stimulating and supporting economic development through advanced technology . . . stimulate economic expansion by creating a critical mass of new advanced technology industries and by introducing advanced technologies in traditional industries in order to modernize and expand them" (WPATC 1986: 1). There are four regional partnership centres in the state under the Ben Franklin Partnership: the centre in the Pittsburgh Region is known as Western Pennsylvania Advanced Technology Center (WPATC).

The Center's structure reflects a partnership between the area's universities and colleges, the Commonwealth of Pennsylvania and the private sector. WPATC facilitates joint research for which funding has come from a variety of sources, including the state. The Center provides entrepreneurial assistance and supports and monitors education, training and research programmes. It promotes commercial and industrial development which are technology based and in which the region has comparative advantage. The Center helps new entrepreneurs who need help in business and financial planning as well as incubator facilities. The promotion of cooperative applied research between the educational institutions and the private sector brings new technology into the market place and provides the region a special nitch in the national economy. The Center works with educational and training institutions and the private sector employers to determine future training needs. Some of the WPATC sponsored projects include:

Robotics and Computers

Carnegie Mellon's Robotics Institute, related research in artificial intelligence at both CMU and Pitt, and the Software Engineering Institute combine to make robotics and computers one of our strongest R&D areas.

Projects focused on applications of robotics will increase the efficiency and cost-effectiveness of manufacturing. We also selected a number of software development projects that have strong commercial potential for local firms.

Camdex Colour Slide System

Camdex Corporation and Format 2 have begun testing prototypes of the Robotic Film Indexer (RFI) and the Computerized Spectrum Controller (CSC), companion devices designed to automate the production of 35mm slides. Development of the software controls that will integrate the operation of RFI and CSC continues, and the initial version of the CSC hardware has been completed. Project leaders are discussing manufacturing and distribution strategies with several Pittsburgh firms, and are seeking funding for commercialization.

REX: Robotic Pipeline Excavation

Carnegie Mellon University and Dravo Corporation have been developing a robotic excavation system (REX) for gas pipelines. This project is part of Dravo's effort to revitalize the firm's industrial base by redirecting corporate resources into product lines with commercial viability. The project group has developed a field-worthy system for mapping utility pipelines, three groups of algorithms to analyse electromagnetic fields without human intervention, excavation hardware and strategies, and a data base to describe pipe configuration. The REX project currently supports 78 jobs with an inhouse payroll of 24.

Factory of the Future for Smaller Manufacturers

This project illustrates the cooperative efforts in the region for technology transfer. Research faculty and graduate students at the Flexible Manufacturing Laboratory at Carnegie Mellon's Robotics Institute are working with a consortium of Western Pennsylvania companies to develop new product lines in robotics and computer-aided manufacturing. Each company in the group has initiated a project which has led directly to transfer of technology to that company. Some examples include software to generate robot "move-paths" in an automated gas-arc welding process, computer-aided design software to enhance die making facilities, a new design for a flexible mold for stainless steel building panels, and automation of a new welding operation.

Microprocessor-Based Predictive Maintenance Systems

The University of Pittsburgh and Industrial Maintenance Systems, Inc. (IMS) completed development work on a computerized, microprocessor-controlled prototype device that can accurately simulate various stress situations common to rotating machinery such as motors and turbines. The device is part of a system being designed to detect equipment malfunctions at an early stage so that repairs can be made during regularly scheduled maintenance shut-downs. This one-of-a-kind system promises great market potential and enormous financial savings to industry. In March of this year, IMS moved its major R&D efforts as well as its headquarters to the University of Pittsburgh Applied Research Center (UPARC) at Harmarville.

Biotechnology

This focus is natural for Western Pennsylvania because of the leading-edge research in biotechnology taking place in area hospitals and universities and the fast-growing number of companies evolving from this applied research. The recently opened UPARC is already giving further impetus since one of its primary functions is to serve as an incubator for biotechnology start-up companies.

Recognizing the enormously varied possibilities for biotechnological products, the Center has broadened its definition of biotechnology, now to include such diverse categories as optics, pharmaceuticals, laboratory equipment and diagnostic devices.

Advanced Materials, Processes and Devices

Here WPATC has been maximizing existing strengths in building upon historical interrelationships between traditional industries and the universities. We are assisting companies which are developing advanced products and new processes that can help revitalize the region's ailing but still important heavy industries. These innovative technologies will not only help our older companies to weather intense international competitive pressures but will also lead to the formation of new companies which will serve emerging markets.

University of Pittsburgh Applied Research Center facilities are contributing to this research category, just as they are to biotechnology. The Metals Casting Institute and the newly formed Center for Hazardous Materials Research, both located at UPARC, are performing multi-group research.

New Optical Devices for Scientific Instrumentation

The University of Pittsburgh and EG&G Princeton Applied Research have begun to commercialize a new optical filter for use in laser research and in creating scientific instruments. Market analysis indicates significant commercial potential. In addition, engineering was completed this year for a holder for the optical filter, and one patent has already been issued. A new division of Princeton Applied Research will result from commercialization and will create an estimated 20 new jobs in manufacturing, marketing, and R&D by the end of 1987. EG&G Princeton Applied Research has begun to investigate manufacturing sites in Pennsylvania.

Automated Manufacturing of Low-Cost CO_2 Lasers

Ben Franklin Partnership funding and generous support from the private sector are enabling participants to expand Aerotech's laser product line. The University of Pittsburgh and Aerotech, Inc. have nearly completed the design for a light-weight, low-cost CO_2 laser for the outpatient medical market. A work station has been designed for CO_2 laser work at Aerotech and components are being ordered and assembled. The firm has relocated its helium-neon laser production division from California, opening new manufacturing facilities in Pittsburgh and creating new jobs (WPATC, 1986: 5-7).

Between 1983 and 1986 WPATC helped start 96 new companies and 99 existing companies expanded their operations. Its projects created 1,233 new jobs and 384 jobs were saved. These and other accomplishments were realized by offering a variety of services to entrepreneurs and technology transfer in the new and existing companies. But the governmental organizations have special responsibilities for providing infrastructure and services to facilitate economic development.

Most of the milltowns which were economically dependent on the steel industry are located within Allegheny County. A substantial portion of economic activities and population are concentrated in Allegheny County which includes the city of Pittsburgh. The County leadership has taken a more pro-active stance in the area of economic development. It works with the state government, businesses and universities to promote economic development.

> Because of the fragmented approach to the economic development planning and the general bias toward a free market, plus the historic dependence on big steel and other major institutions to provide direction to the region's economy, we lack sufficiently sophisticated data access and analytic capabilities by which we can better understand economic trends affecting us and the progress being made in responding to them. The county has begun to address its problem in this area through a recent contract between the County Planning Department and the University of Pittsburgh Center for Social and Urban Research. (Reaves: 15)

The major priority for the county has been in developing land and other infrastructural facilities. New highways have been planned to link the Pittsburgh international airport with redevelopment sites where major factories are located. Another major function of the County is training and retraining of the labour force. Under the federally-funded Job Training Partnership Act, the County provides classroom and on-the-job training to new entrants and dislocated workers (Reaves: 7-11). The City of Pittsburgh's leadership is intimately involved in deliberations on economic development programmes. Its commitment is to support major economic development initiatives by providing high quality public services, recreational and cultural facilities. It works with private profit as well as non-profit organizations in neighbourhood revitalization programmes. Therefore, the state, the county and the city are working with private sector organizations and universities for regional economic development. Strategy 21 is one such initiative.

In 1985, the mayor of the City of Pittsburgh, the three commissioners of Allegheny County and the presidents of the University of Pittsburgh and Carnegie-Mellon University submitted a proposal known as Strategy 21 to the state of Pennsylvania. The proposal contained strategies for revitalizing the region's economy through selective diversification while at the same time retaining some of its traditional components. The concept was based on utilizing research strengths of the two universities and the positive climate for multifaceted partnership among public-private-educational institutions. The major goals were as follows:

1. Reinforce the region's traditional economic base as a centre for the metals industry and an international corporate headquarters;
2. Convert under-utilized land, facilities and labour force components to new uses, especially those involving advanced technology;
3. Enhance the region's quality of life, thereby attracting new residents and increasing tourism; and
4. Expand opportunities for women, minorities and the structurally unemployed.

In pursuance of these goals, the Mayor, the County Commissioners and the University Presidents propose to expand their regional partnership to include the Commonwealth of Pennsylvania by advocating that future state funding focus on five specific project areas:

1. *Greater Pittsburgh International Airport Area Redevelopment* – The modernization of the Greater Pittsburgh International Airport through the construction of a new midfield terminal complex and the development of the adjacent property in Findlay and Moon Townships made possible by the opening of the Southern Expressway would have a dramatic effect on the region's economy. It would strengthen the region's attraction as a corporate headquarters and convert seriously under-utilized land to diverse, new business purposes with heavy job creation potential.
2. *Allegheny Redevelopment* – The projects in this area – Three Rivers Stadium, with its Center of Science and Technology; the Strip District; and Herr's Island – would serve to transform under-utilized land into riverfront attractions enhancing the region's quality of life and serving as a magnet to increased

tourism. In addition, the Herr's Island project would include a corporate conference centre that would reinforce the region's existing strength as a centre for corporate activity, and an area for research and light manufacturing uses aimed at attracting advanced technology activities.

3. *Mon Valley Redevelopment* – The human toll of economic dislocation in the Mon and Ohio Valleys has made the proposed Metals Retention/Reuse Study critically important to the region's future. The study would make possible informed decisions by the public and private sectors that would provide needed support to those metals facilities with the greatest long-term potential and would assist in the conversion to new uses of those facilities which are no longer viable. This comprehensive analysis of not only Mon Valley facilities, but all those in the county and the region, would then become the basis for an action plan calling for further capital funding. Meanwhile, the immediate needs of the Mon Valley would be addressed by a series of site-specific improvement projects which would provide infrastructure essential to further development. The Pittsburgh/J&L redevelopment project would be an early and major effort in the transformation of the Pittsburgh economy through advanced technology.
4. *Transportation Improvements* – Essential to making the Greater Pittsburgh International Airport a regional transportation hub and to opening up the adjacent under-utilized land to economic development is the proposed 6.8 mile Southern Expressway linking the Parkway West to the Beaver Valley Expressway.

   Similarly, in order to convert underutilized Mon Valley facilities to new uses, it is essential to provide better highway linkage between these proposed new economic development areas and major inter-regional highways such as the Pennsylvania Turnpike, the Penn-Lincoln Parkway and Route 51.
5. *University Advanced Technology Research* – The advanced technology research projects being developed by the University of Pittsburgh and by Carnegie-Mellon University would have the multiple effect of (1) assisting in the revitalization of the metals industry through the introduction of new technology; (2) strengthening the region's attraction as a corporate headquarters by increasing the local availability of research and development expertise; and (3) capitalizing on the comparative advantage that

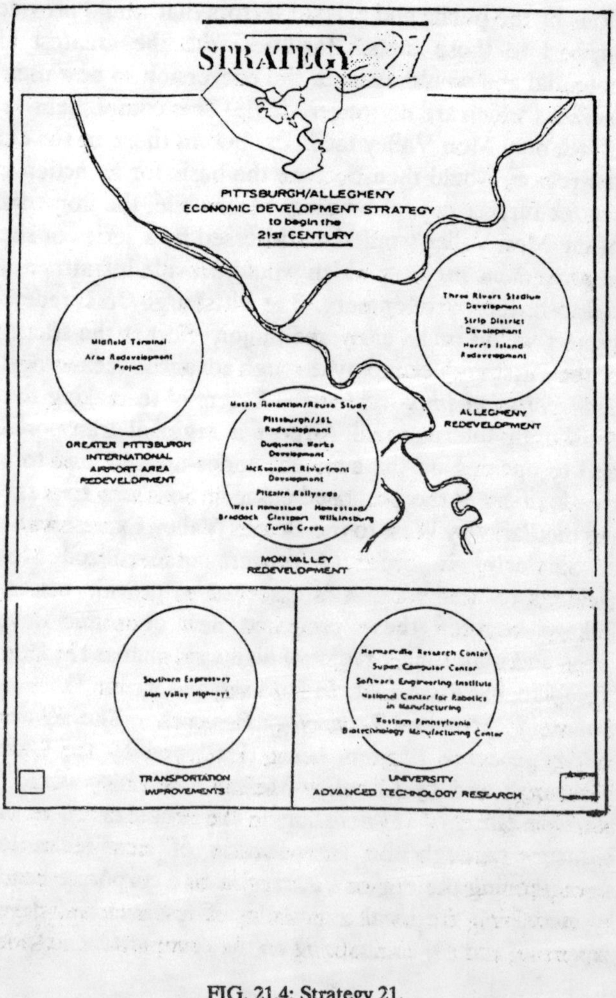

FIG. 21.4: Strategy 21.

> research efforts of the Pittsburgh university community have over those of other competing universities, as demonstrated by the awarding of the $ 103 million Software Engineering Institute contract to Carnegie-Mellon University. The synergistic effect of these research projects would advance the economic revitalization of the entire region (Strategy 21, 1985: 1-2).

These projects are presented in the form of a Fig. 21.4 that shows clusters of projects by geographic area and their importance in the overall economic development strategy for the region.

These projects utilize the research strengths of the University of Pittsburgh and the Carnegie-Mellon University in advanced technology as represented in their programmes in computers, biotechnology, engineering and robotics. Pittsburgh is still the third largest corporate headquarters in the USA which gives the region access to top businesses and its leadership. A substantial proportion of funds for these projects would come from the State of Pennsylvania. The state had played a pivotal role in important partnership initiatives in the past and the public-private and university partnership for these projects has become equally compelling.

The decline of milltowns in the Mon Valley of the Allegheny County presented a real challenge for the public officials. Rapid employment losses mainly due to closing of several steel mills and reduction in the workforce of the others posed a serious threat for the survival of many communities. The unprecedented population decline, tax base and deterioration of infrastructure in many of the Mon Valley communities required immediate action.

Mon Valley consists of communities along the Monongahela and Youghiogheny Rivers and Turtle Creek. These communities were developed almost one hundred years ago to provide a workforce for the steel mills and factories spread along the rivers. It has a population of 270,000 divided in 38 governmental units. The Mon Valley communities are spread over 140 square miles. The economy of the Mon Valley was closely tied to the steel industry and other manufacturing activities.

That decline of the steel industry has devastated the Mon Valley is reflected in the substantial decline of jobs, per capita income and the population. The Mon Valley also invokes a negative image where people do not find the area attractive to living, working or doing business. Most people in the area have limited opportunities outside, and therefore new policies were needed to create new employment opportunities in these communities. Since many steel mills are closed permanently new businesses must be attracted that can use the area's labour force. The job-training programmes should help make many former steel workers employable in other types of jobs. In 1986, the state of Pennsylvania proposed a multi-tierred revitalization strategy in which "the principal focus of economic and community development efforts clearly should be on the string of population centres adjacent to the river. This is where the greatest concentration of people and distress is located. Intensified community development efforts also make sense in the surrounding distressed towns and townships. Also, specific economic development opportunities throughout the area-at-large could be focal points of local efforts. In fact, both state and local participants in the revitalization process should be continuously alert to opportunities *outside* of the Valley which could benefit the area's businesses, communities, and people" (Pennsylvania Department of Commerce, 1986: 5).

A number of studies and deliberations were conducted to assess the erosion of the economic and population base and coping strategies that distressed communities and the unemployed used. (CMU, 1983; Posvar, 1984; Cunningham and Martz, 1986). It was agreed that strong public leadership was needed to harness resources in the region towards revitalization of the distressed communities.

A commission consisting of unemployed steel industry representatives, and members from labour, churches, chamber of commerce, local government, education, retraining and human resources was appointed to make recommendations for immediate action. The areas included manufacturing, non-manufacturing, transportation, education and labour, environmental systems, housing and human services and local government. The chairman of task forces are expected to meet periodically to monitor activities for economic revitalization and initiatives that help preserve some stability.

The commission felt that some steel making capacity should be retained while other types of manufacturing and non-manufacturing enterprises should be encouraged. For example, clearing the old factory sites and river front for use by small entrepreneurs as part of the valley-wide economic development effort has a great deal of support in the communities. The Mon Valley has had an inadequate transportation network and more recently, even the existing roads needed improvement. The commission favoured linking the area with an expressway so that goods and services can be moved with ease. Since most of the steel jobs are gone, it has become essential to improve education in the area. Training programmes for the unemployed as well as the new labour force entrants are coordinated in the context of emerging employment structure in the valley in particular, and the region in general.

A great deal of debate at the regional level has involved the future of manufacturing in the valley. It is clear that the valley cannot expect a reversal in the decline of manufacturing and, therefore, workers must find employment elsewhere. Small manufacturing has staged a modest comeback. For example a galvanizing facility closed previously has reopened, so has a glass-making plant. A specialty steel operation is doing well while future initiatives in steel are being examined in the global, national and regional contexts. There seems to be good prospects for plants that produce semi-finished steel and a continuous caster. There is a demand for such products in the region which are currently brought from outside the region. The small businesses, whether manufacturing or non-manufacturing, would receive both technical and financial assistance from the County and the region's business development organizations such as the Regional Industrial Development Corporation. One of the major recommendations of the commission is to establish a Business Technical Assistance Center to provide the following services to new and existing businesses:

- liaison with local government regarding sites, zoning and development regulations,
- business plan development,
- incubators,
- market definition and analysis,
- public relations and advertising,
- production process evaluations,
- technology assessment and transfer,
- engineering and design,
- applying for public and private financial assistance,
- financial planning, accounting and legal services,
- federal procurement,

administrative/business management support,

- bid preparation,
- sales and export assistance,
- training programmes,
- office services (Mon Valley Commission, 1987: 25).

The Center's staff would include experienced businessmen and other professionals in finance, marketing and engineering. The Center would be funded by state, county and private organizations.

The county government has taken bold steps in establishing business incubator facilities which enable small start-up companies to share support services. The Business Assistance Center might take the initiative in contacting Mon Valley businesses to identify their needs to help them.

As mentioned earlier, the Mon Valley has begun to diversify its economy. The land clearance and improvement in the physical infrastructure of communities and the active involvement of the Business Technical Assistance Center could attract hospitals, banks, real estate and other commercial services (Mon Valley Commission, 1987: 33-36).

It is not possible to summarize in this paper various actions that would be taken to rejuvenate social and economic life in the Mon Valley. It has been realized that many workers and families cannot move to other regions for a variety of reasons. Their future is closely tied to the economic conditions in the Pittsburgh region and both public and private sector leaders have taken steps to bring about a well-coordinated strategy for the Mon Valley's revitalization. The construction of the new expressway and other transportation improvements would facilitate commuting between the Mon Valley and the City of Pittsburgh, industrial parks, and other business and commercial centres throughout Allegheny County. The improvement in the physical appearance and public services would make the communities attractive for residential purposes. With its diversified economic base in place, the Mon Valley could begin to regain its economic and social stability.

Discussion

The restructuring of mature industrial regions has been a long term process. Many regions adjusted quickly by diversifying their economies and establishing new industries and businesses in which they had a comparative advantage. Timely response depended on two factors: (1) whether a region was historically dominated by a single industry and (2) the health of the national economy. Regions that were heavily dependent on a single industry such as coal, steel, textiles or automobiles, were more likely to delay any vigorous attempts towards diversification or modernization of their aging industries. Modernization involved introduction of new technology in the production process, assessment of production capacity in the context of demands and product modification. These initiatives threatened employment for workers and if labour-management relations were poor, it was almost impossible to introduce any significant change. However, when the national economy was robust, workers from potentially declining industries were less likely to resist change because they felt that they could find employment in the growing sectors or move to other regions where employment opportunities were better. Complacency on the part of industries in the old industrial regions in the USA delayed the introduction of new technology and the substitution of capital for labour to improve quality of product and reduce cost of production.

Therefore, the management, workers and labour unions contributed to the economic difficulties of old industrial regions. Any hope of significant protectionist intervention on the part of the national government was also dashed. Besides, it was not clear how such actions during the recession would bring a turn around in those industries that had been declining for some time and the management was not prepared to make substantial capital investments. It was a painful lesson for regions such as Pittsburgh that the federal government's own industrial policy was not sensitive to regional economic problems. This realization forced some regions to examine their comparative advantage and develop their own programmes for economic development and job creation.

Civic organizations and major research universities were compelled to respond to the continuing economic plight of their particular regions. These bodies expanded their own missions to include regional economic development as an important agenda. Universities are heavily involved with the region's private sectors in developing new technologies and products that can strengthen the area's economy. Social scientists are engaged in a variety of studies, including regional econometric modelling, that would demonstrate how a region's economy works as well as help to develop occupational forecasts that can be used in establishing appropriate training and retraining programmes. Since much of the job growth in the 1980s has come from small and medium size companies, it has become more critical now than ever to ensure the availability of a technically trained labour force in the region. In fact, the Pittsburgh region has made concerted efforts to accomplish these objectives.

As the economies of the old industrial regions began to disintegrate, the governmental institutions were also pushed to broaden their roles. The jurisdictional imperatives could not be used as an excuse for non-action. A great deal of pressure came from the people themselves. It was no longer sufficient for government to deal only with tax incentives, roads, and bridges in improving business climate. The state and county governments in the USA learned quickly about the conditions of the regional economy and its impact on particular communities and sub-population. They worked with the private sector, civic organizations and universities to develop regional economic development plans in which substantial public funds were required. Similar initiatives are underway in Germany and the U.K. as well. The county and local governments have developed programmes to improve the economic base of milltowns and strategies to stabilize population. Dislocated workers are participating in the specially tailored training programmes that would help them find jobs in the area itself.

The recession of 1980 brought a new era for public-private and university partnerships. The partners themselves enhanced their own interests by cooperating in regional economic development initiatives. A strong regional economy provides a strong tax base and helps retain highly trained manpower. It also directly and indirectly generates resources for the benefit of educational and other non-profit institutions. Even though the economies of old industrial regions are becoming more and more service oriented, some of them have begun to modernize certain components of their old manufacturing industries. The use of modern technology and mechanization along with a skilled labour force make such an initiative promising. It would introduce some economic stability, as the manufacturing employment is expected to decline even further in the next few years. The growth of non-manufacturing, especially in the sectors in which a region has a comparative advantage must be pursued relentlessly. The old industrial regions have to compete even harder to maintain their market share. Technological changes and product substitutions would inevitably create displaced workers in the future. As long as workers possess basic skills it would be easier for them to be absorbed in the growing sectors of the economy. The regional economic development policies of different regions in the USA and Western Europe are comparable in some respects and unique in others. There is, therefore, a great deal to be learned from each other's experiences as regions respond to structural changes in their respective economies.

REFERENCES

Ahlbrandt, Roger S., (1986). "New Partnerships for Regional Economic Development." (Paper presented in the Conference on the Regional Structural Change in International Perspective, Essen).

Allegheny Conference on Community Development (ACCD), (1984). *A Report of the Allegheny Conference on Community Development, Volume I* (Pittsburgh: Allegheny Conference on Community Development).

Appelbaum, Eileen, (1984). "High Tech and the Structural Employment Problems of the 1980s," in Eileen Collins and Lucretia D. Tanner (eds.), *American Jobs and Changing Industrial Base* (Cambridge: Ballinger Publishing Company).

Bergman, Edward M., (1986). "Introduction: Policy Realities and Development Potentials in Local Economies," in Edward M. Bergman (ed.), *Local Economies in Transition* (Durham: Duke University Press).

Bluestone, Barry and Bennett Harrison, (1982). *The Deindustrialization of America* (New York: Basic Books, Inc.).

Borrus, Michael, (1983). "The Politics of Competitive Erosion in the U.S. Steel Industry," in John Zysman and Laura Tyson (eds.), *American Industry in International Competition* (Ithaca: Cornell University Press).

Carnegie-Mellon University, (1983). *Milltowns in the Pittsburgh Region: Conditions and Prospects* (Pittsburgh: Carnegie-Mellon University).

Caves, Richard E., (1980). "The Structure of Industry," in Martin Feldstein (ed.), *The American Economy in Transition* (Chicago: The University of Chicago Press).

Clark, David, (1985). *Post-Industrial America* (New York: Methuen).

Commission of the European Communities, (1984). *The Regions of Europe* (Luxembourg: Publications of European Communities).

Cunningham, James and Pamela Martz (eds.), (1986). *Trouble in Electric Valley: Local Leaders Assess the Difficult Future of Their Community* (Pittsburgh: University of Pittsburgh).

Cyert, Richard M., (1985). "The Plight of Manufacturing: What Can Be Done," *Issues in Science and Technology* 1: 87-100.

Cyert, Richard M. and David C. Mowery (eds.), (1987). *Technology and Employment: Innovation and Growth in the U.S. Economy* (Washington, D.C.: National Academy Press).

Federal Reserve Bank of Cleveland, (1987). *Annual Report: 1986* (Cleveland: Federal Reserve Bank).

Giarratani, Frank, (1986). Comment on "Regional Economic Responses to Structural Change," (Presented in the Conference on Regional Structural Change in International Perspective, Essen).

Giarratani, Frank and David Houston, "Economic Change in the Pittsburgh Region," in J. J. Hesse (ed.), *Regional Structural Change and Industrial Policy in International Perspective* (London: Oxford University Press, Forthcoming).

Gurwitz, Aaron S. and G. Thomas Kingsley, (1982). *The Cleveland Metropolitan Economy* (Santa Monica, CA: The Rand Corporation).

Hennings, Gerd, Rainer Kahnert and Klaus R. Kunzmann, (1987). "Restructuring An Industrial City in Germany: The case of Dortmund," (Dortmund: Institute Fur Raumplanung).

Hesse, J. J., (1986). "The Political Responses of Regional Governments to the Problems of Regional Structural Change," (Paper presented in the Conference on Regional Structural Change in International Perspective, Essen).

Jones, Reginald H., (1983). "Toward a New Industrial Policy," in Michael L. Watcher and Susan M. Watcher (eds.), *Toward A New U.S. Industrial Policy?* (Philadelphia: University of Pennsylvania Press).

Kunzmann, Klaus R., (1986). "Policy Strategies to Overcome Regional Structural Change: A Comparison of Merseyside and the Ruhrgebiet," (Paper presented in the Conference on Regional Structural Change in International Perspective, Essen).

Lawrence, Paul R. and David Dyer, (1983). *Renewing American Industry* (New York: The Free Press).

Mon Valley commission, (1987). *Report to the Allegheny County Board of Commissioners for the Economic Revitalization of the Monongahela, Youghiogheny, and Turtle Creek Valleys* (Pittsburgh: Allegheny County).

Pennsylvania Business Roundtable, (1987). *Partnership for Pennsylvania's Development: A 10-Year Economic Strategy* (Harrisburg: Pennsylvania Roundtable).

Pennsylvania Department of Commerce, (1986). *Forging Revival and Renaissance* (Harrisburgh: Department of Commerce).

Peters, B. Guy, (1986). "The Politics of Industrial and Regional Policy in the United States," (Paper presented in the Conference on Regional Structural Change in International Perspective, Essen).

Pfaller, Alfred, (1983). *Trade Restrictions Against Low Cost Imports. What is at Stake?* (Bonn: Friedrich Ebert Stiftung).

Posvar, Wesley W. (convener), (1983). *Recommendations for Southwestern Pennsylvania's Regional Development Strategy for the 1980s and 1990s* (Pittsburgh: University of Pittsburgh).

Posvar, Wesley W. (convener), (1984). *Municipal Financial Distress and Emergencies: Issues and Intervention Strategies* (Pittsburgh: University of Pittsburgh).

Reaves, Raymond L., (1986). "Regional Economic Planning Response to Structural Change: The American Approach Via Allegheny County, Pennsylvania," (Paper presented in the Conference on Regional Structural Change in International Perspective, Essen).

Robertson, Norman, et al., (1986). "Long-term Regional and Industry Trends In Pennsylvania Economy," (unpublished working paper), (Harrisburg: Business Council of Pennsylvania).

Schlieper, Andreas, (1986). "Regional Economic Responses to Structural Change," (Paper presented in the Conference on Regional Structural Change in International Perspective, Essen).

Singh, Vijai P. and Silvia Borzutzky, (1986). "The State of the Regions," (Paper presented in the Conference on Regional Structural Change in International Perspective, Essen).

Singh, Vijai P., Oto Okugawa and Kiyofumi Kawaguchi, (1987). "Regional Structural Change and Restructuring Strategies," (in Japanese), *Ritsumeikan Review of Industrial Society* 23 (September): 63-92.

Strategy 21: Pittsburgh/Allegheny Economic Development Strategy (1985). (Pittsburgh: Office of the Mayor).

Summers, Anita A. and Thomas F. Luce, (1985). *Economic Report on the Philadelphia Metropolitan Area 1985* (Philadelphia: University of Pennsylvania Press).

Summers, Anita A. and Thomas F. Luce, (1987). *Economic Development Within the Philadelphia Metropolitan Area* (Philadelphia: University of Pennsylvania Press).

TWENTY-TWO

Third World Peasantry: An Overview

P. B. DESAI

This paper constitutes an overview* .[1] of the two volumes on *Third World Peasantry* edited by R. P. Misra and Nguyen Tri Dung. The volumes have 21 essays by 23 scholars on the state of peasantry in some 14 countries of the African, Asian and Latin American parts of the so-called Third World. There is here a formidable fare that should help the reader to realize the plight of the peasant form of farming which only a few decades ago had dominated these predominantely agricultural economies. The editors have done a commendable job in bringing together so much material on the impact of varied approaches to development, particularly agricultural development, on the patterns of living and livelihood of those who, by force of circumstances, continue to cling to their peasant ways. The contributions provide perspectives, reflections and empirical evidence on the subject. They unavoidably differ in content, style and scholarship. The editors have tried hard to impart a thematic unity in the presentation of the collection of the essays.

This unity lies in placing the discussion in the common context of development. Some of the essays are theorical or conceptual; many others report analysis of empirical data on the changing conditions of peasantry in given geographical settings. If they are so inclined, planners, policy-makers and students of development have a great deal to learn from these contributions. They may, thereby realize that development is not an unmixed blessing or that it may strongly tend to bypass some sections of the people and harm their interests.

---

1. * R.P. Misra and Nguyen Tri Dugn, *Third World Peasantary: A Continuing Saga of Deprivation*, New Delhi: Sterling Publishers, 1985.

It may, in any case, fail to take into account the adverse impact it may exercise particularly on the economically weaker, socially disadvantaged and politically unorganized groups in society.

Even so, for a student of peasantry as a class, the "saga" may be seen as limited to the deploration of the travail of peasantry subjected to newer forms of oppression, exploitation and deprivation by the interplay of forces of economic growth, euphemistically called development. Peasantry's passive and helpless endurance of deepening deprivation depicted time and again in these essays is heart-rending. It leaves one wondering whether there is anything more to it than meets the eye. Is there no silver lining to the darkening cloud of deprivation? It seems obvious that the so-called saga has virtually bypassed the heroic historical role the peasantry has played during the same post-Second World War period in the revolutionary movements of China, Cuba and Vietnam. The fare provided by the two volumes would have been richer had it thrown light also on many heroic resistance movements of peasantry that were localized and were crushed down by the entrenched forces of reaction.

We will, for the present purpose, set this crucial gap aside and concentrate on what is on the plate. The concern of the editors has been with the increasing demobilization and deprivation of those whom they call peasants. They plead "that the social relations which made or marred the future of peasantry have not undergone any substantial change for the better. . . . The average peasant in almost all the Third World countries is in a pitiable condition . . . much of the peasantry is fragmented and pauperized and living in a hopeless future partly in isolated rural settlements and partly in the slums and shanty towns of ever growing cities (Vol. I, Preface). Yet, they proceed to contend, "Planned efforts at rural development, their weaknesses and pitfalls notwithstanding, have not gone in vain. There are visible achievements and gains." (Vol. I, Preface). It is difficult to reconcile these observations, we can only suggest that the latter achievements and gains have been obtained at the cost of the mere survival interest of the peasantry. This renders it much too optimistic to hope "that a strong peasantry, given the political and institutional backing even in the capitalistic mode of production, can become a great asset for national development." (Vol. II, Preface)

Without sharing this hope with the editors, we may look upon this rich fare as serving to arouse intellectual curiosity in the search for the peasantry that invariably tends to get lost in the maze of facts and figures on macrolevel agricultural growth as well as on microlevel rural development programmes. One thing that emerges from the mystifying proliferation of writings on agricultural and rural development is that the plight of the peasants at the grassroots level is traceable to the continuing march of capitalistic transformation of national economies that have not been freed from the dependence historically imposed on them by their colonial past. That past continues to cast its shadow and transform only the form and not the substance of development. Under the circumstances, we can only try to probe into these contributions for any indication of hope that the dependence may yet be liquidated. Plight of the peasantry is one of the surest symptoms of the deepening of that continuing dependence. Our probe will consider the theoretical or conceptual contributions first. This will be followed by the impressions from the totality of empirical evidence about the position and role of "peasantry" in development. Finally, we reflect upon the concerns about the future of the peasants and their mode of production.

I. THE STATE OF THE DEBATE

Let us begin with the lessons an anthropologist (George Dalton 2, Vol. II) wishes us to learn from the "Modern Transformation of European Peasantries". The piece is persuasive but rather long-winding. It is the story of what happened to the peasantry in western Europe in the course of the insolent march of world capitalism whose origin can be traced to the 15th century. It is argued that the preponderant but variegated peasantry hibernating at the bottom of the socio-economic structures under feudalism emerged at long last as a small homogeneous class of modern "gentleman farmers" in the post-industrial era. It speaks of the many dimensions of progressive change that transformed Western societies and also changed the position of the peasantry as a part of that long-drawn-out process. The peasantry, it is said, had retained much of its character through the succession of revolutions in the world economy, which western Europe has dominated all through. Changes began with revolutionary progress in world transportation that helped the emergence of an international economy. This was accompanied by agrarian revolution which in turn was followed by the industrial and then by the sway of imperialism which retains its inequitous hold on the prevailing international economic order.

The author chooses to elaborate the impact of this fundamental economic transformation on peasantry by calling attention to the political, legal, social and cultural correlates and consequences that accompanied the evolution of capitalism buttressed by scientific and technological progress. In the process, the fundamental transformation of the mode of production from the feudal to the capitalist loses its centrality and emphasis comes to be misplaced on the rise of national states which succeeded the firm establishment of capitalism. It also overplays welfarism of the National State which can be seen as a palliative for the ills perpetrated on society by capitalism. In the course of this long process of peasantry's attrition, the untold misery they suffered in the rural areas where some of them stayed back and in the new urban areas where most of them had to move in is missed in this historical narration. It fails also to refer to an important outlet that the European peasantry had enjoyed in the emigration to the New World in order to escape the rigours of the ascending capitalist class. To applaud the emergence of democracy in the states ruled by canons of capitalist market economy is of little avail, for the democracies have still to outgrow their captive states.

Apologetic Conclusion

The conclusion drawn from the European experience is rather apologetic. It pleads for explicitly taking into account the complexities inherent in all peasant societies. We admit the complexities arising from the fragmentation of peasantries in the developing countries but we must not at the same time forget the common exploitation they are subjected to by the remnants of feudalism and the emerging class of "ungentlemanly" capitalist farmers in league with the new non-agricultural urban capitalist classes. It argues also that the transformation of peasantry is necessarily a long-drawn-out process. It did take centuries for European peasants to emerge as modern gentleman farmers but that had occurred during the phase of world's history that was sharply different from the contemporary post-Second World War history. The past phase of history need not repeat itself, if for no other reason than that in most developing countries political systems have assumed the command of socio-economic transformation. That this may not avoid the pains of perturition for those who are peasants today is quite a different matter.

There is indeed no easy way out of their agonizing plight for the Third World peasantry on account of the stranglehold on the world economy of Western capitalist imperialist economic and political regimes. This is the main thrust of Pausewang's consideration of "A New International Economic Order for the Peasant in the Third World" (1, Vol. I) commenting on the progress of the Third world's movement for a fundamental reshaping of international economic relations in their favour. Pausewang asserts, "The 'New International Economic Order' is a vision based on a growing dissatisfaction with established economic relations and comprises rather diffused, inconsistent and non-operational ideas about an alternative order." Widely shared is his pessimism about the outcome of the moves of thc Third World for the reform of international economic relations for the reason, among others, that "virtually all the participants in these negotiations have substantial interests directly or indirectly tied to the very economic system they are expected to reform". Sadly, it must be admitted that the deep penetration of the imperialist hegemony of the West into the power bases of many, if not most, developing countries renders them impotent to attack the predation of the West from the core of the World economy.

The inroads of the West-dominated world market into developing national economies have perpetrated ruin on the Third World peasant, rendering him utterly helpless against the odds he cannot easily perceive. Illustrating his cogent argument by drawing upon the working of revolutionary reform of agrarian relations in Ethiopia during mid-seventies, Pausewang identifies the complex of four inter-related forces that thwart the progress of peasantry. These four elements are price fluctuations, trade and transport costs, the pricing system and direct privileges over resources and/or work of others; they are but different aspects of the basic inequality built into the power structure of society. The accentuation of this basic inequality is uncannily traced to the proliferation of colonialism fed by the conversion of economic into political power and vice versa. The Ethiopian peasant acquired control over land resources through reforms but could benefit only marginally therefrom in the face of an unhelpful power structure and the inexorable intrusion into their economy of world market forces. So long as power relations at all levels from the grassroots upwards to the international exchange do not change in his favour, there is little hope of the peasant coming out from under the dead weight of the predatory privileges buttressed within national economies by the international power structures.

In the context of the gloomy prospects of the present economic system, the author speculates about a possible way out. In this he draws some inspiration from the experience of Vietnam which "seems to have achieved a degree of equality which few other countries in the World can measure up against". The recipe is to somehow achieve a feasible level of equality in the distribution of economic and political power. This equality will not be a gift of the present power bases. This can be achieved only through the political process of peasant mobilization. What is important in his regard is to achieve at the local level as much self-sufficiency as possible and as little exchange as necessary. From the local level upwards self-sufficiency must ascend to the regional and national level. Hopefully, the author contends, "Within given structures, or changing them where possible measures which give the poor as much as possible local self-determination, and resources to help them mobilize their own strength, can hardly go wrong." The logic of the proposition cannot be questioned. Its operational feasibility can be. The author is aware of this and, therefore, adds a proviso that in the process the peasants should not provoke the political authorities to crush such movements in the beginning and put the peasants into new and stronger bonds. Yet, we must unequivocally admit that "equality of distribution, new models of decentralized authority, a reorientation of production and not just of aid to basic human needs, and new measuring instruments of exchange of use values and work, will not be developed at all, unless they are developed from below". The fight against inequities of international relations must start at the lowest grassroots level of the peasant or village community.

The transformation of the preponderant peasantry into a miniscule class of gentleman farmers in Europe was admittedly an integral part of the crystallization of the present predatory world economic order subserving the interests of the "North Allantic" imperialist capitalism. Pausewang has shown how unshakeable still are the foundations of that order. The course of its proliferation has involved a progressive accentuation of the deprivation of the Third World peasantry which retains its preponderance within the economies of the so-called developing countries of that world. Their continuing preponderance is not their strength but a weakness for the reason, among others, that the proliferation of the capitalist order has resulted in their fragmentation. Against the odds that this history created for them, the peasantry everywhere in the Third World has offered some resistance and tried at times even to fight back. Sadly, however, their fights have met with little success, except in cases where they became the vanguard of successful revolutionary struggles in countries like China, Cuba and Vietnam. In most cases, where they were not so placed in the liberation of the oppressed and exploited masses, they were subjected to repression by the entrenched power structures. This story is told with a telling effect by Gerrit Huizer in his essay on "Peasant Movements Reacting to Pauperisation: the Dialectics of Liberation" (2 Vol. II). This is perhaps the only contribution in the "Saga" that addresses its theme squarely and directly. The story is quite disturbing; even more disquieting is its reference to the insensitivity of social science approaches to problems of peasantry, that smack of servility to academies held captive by the world imperialism.

Third World Peasantry at Receiving End

Huizer's survey is not, and is not meant to be, exhaustive. It concentrates on the peasant movements that had failed to achieve their purposes and were more or less ruthlessly crushed. Drawing upon the considerable literature that has grown around the strife of peasantry through recent history, he provides ample evidence to support the conviction that peasantry in the Third World has almost always been at the receiving end, a fact easily traced to the predation of the power base at the core of the international order. He begins his survey by rejecting the notion gripping the academics, who have been concerned with peasantry, that the peasant is a passive, apathetic and distrustful being, who is bereft of achievement, motivation and resistant to change. This "holier than thou" attitude is traced to the failure of the concerned scholars, planners and policy-makers to closely identify themselves with the poor peasants and their cause. They entertain the notion that the benevolence can be conferred on the peasantry from above. They do not, therefore, interpret peasantry's growing frustration and unrest as a positive sign of their vast potential that can be channelled constructively. Those few social scientists who have gone below to identify themselves with the poorest of the peasants in order to politically participate in their struggle have done better and left insights into the stark realities of peasantry's deprivation. His exploration of the peasant movements leads him to believe that "social science research could and should be practised in an emancipatory perspective" in recognition of the largely ignored potential of the peasantry for mobilization and organization. Asserting that "peasants have one important thing in common with practically all other human beings they (can and do) change", he raises the big question about "how the peasantry's potential for resistance (to undesired change) can be transformed into active mobilization challenging the overall system in a revolutionary way".

The two major factors introduced by colonialism to the detriment of the masses of peasantry were the privatization of land ownership, which made land a marketable commodity and the introduction of cash crops like sugar, tobacco, coffee, tea, cocoa, bananas, cotton, rubber, sisal and palm oil. These served to integrate agriculture into the modern economy, the world market or the North Atlantic capitalism. This meant a drastic change that penetrated deep into the rural society to drastically alter agrarian relations to virtually decimate the poorer sections of the peasantry. This generated an undercurrent of resentment and resistance which at times burst into revolts. These peasant movements were ruthlessly repressed by the might of imperial power often through its local compradors. The conclusion that the author draws from the varied experience of such movements is appealing. "The heavy toll in human lives with which overwhelming military power generally crushed the movements of unarmed or badly armed peasants testifies to the potential power of poor peasants to stand up for their interests and refute some scholarly suggestions as to their political incompetence." The scholarly suggestions failed to perceive peasants' distrust as a part of "the subsistence ethic", a rational safety first approach. "Generally poor peasants have a rather clear and not a mystified view of their deplorable situation. It is mostly repression which keeps the peasants from acting collectively on their own behalf than a lack of consciousness or some inherent political competence." In their utter helplessness against economic forces released by modernizing development, their apathy assumes the form of a mild civil disobedience and give expression to their latent resentment in folk and folk humour recalling better times of the past. Often, the resentment finds open expression in popular religious movements like Taoism, Islamic Revival, Black Theology and Theology of Liberation. These movements tie in with latent resistance and make it possible for them to endure and keep alive a sense of dignity under exploitative and humiliating conditions.

Commenting on the odds faced in organized mobilization of the peasantry, the author notes the need of peasants for help from outsiders. But peasants have, from experience, learnt to accept outside leadership with due reservation. They do not trust even well-meaning intellectuals unless they are convinced of the latter's firm, unequivocal and long-term commitment to their cause as in the case of the Chinese Revolution. They fear oppression of their moves by the landed vested interests buttressed by the state apparatus including police and armed forces and often supported by strong international power base. The scale and intensity of oppression peasantry faces is illustrated by the killing of 15,000 to 30,000 peasants in their 1932 uprising in E1 Salvador and the 1965 Indonesian massacre of half a million peasants by the army and the Islamic Young League given arms for the purpose. "In view of such tremendous risks of state and international intervention, it is only natural and testifies to an earthy kind of intelligence, that peasant distrust as allies certain self-styled revolutionary leaders . . . perhaps as much as they distrust other urban agents such as merchants and development workers". The very real fear of repression compels them to use only peaceful means to demonstrate their power of organization. They used, as a rule, a non-violent civil disobedience strategy, much before it was dramatically popularized by Gandhi during India's freedom struggle. But even these peaceful assertions of their power have been met with disproportionately violent repression by landed interests, generally with the support of the state apparatus. The peasants were, therefore, left to realize the need for radical change in the overall power structure in favour of the oppressed and exploited masses. Peasant violence has, in any case, been a means of the last resort.

The merit of this contribution is enhanced by its pointed reference to the role of female peasants. Peasant women are generally doubly exploited but poor women, it is contended, have "even a greater arsenal of ways to survive under completely adverse conditions than poor men . . . and have greater potential for resistance, when there is a possibility to express it". In support are cited, among other examples, the ages-old Chinese women-oriented or even feminist counter-culture which facilitated their participation in Taiping Rebellion and the Communist Revolution, the leading historical role that women played in Vietnam, the traditional women's organization in Nigeria, the 1958 Kom Women's uprising in Cameroon and Women's participation leading to radicalization of peasant women in several parts of South India. To illustrate women's potential for active participation in radical peasant movements, the author quotes Sundarayya's account of the ruthlessly suppressed violent struggle of Telengana in India which asserted, "Their awakening to new social equality (and) to a moral and cultural life, their stubborn fighting quality gave a glimpse of that tremendous revolutionary spirit and energy smouldering in our economically and socially oppressed womenfolk. If we only take a little trouble to enable it to emerge from the old tradition-bound shell and try to channel it in the proper revolutionary direction, what a mighty upheaval it will lead to." Women have made or are making similar contributions to liberation movements in several other countries including Russia, Cuba, Algeria, Mozambique, Guinea-Bissau, Nigeria, Namibia, Mexico and Bolivia. The ignored and de-emphasized women's participation is given credit for preventing liberation movements from slipping into reactionary reformism. To emphasize women's potential to give movements a radical and revolutionary perspective, the author draws attention to Eleanor Leacock's observation, "Precisely because women's oppression is so deeply embedded in the entire economic, political and social structure of capitalist society, to the extent that women organize around the problems they face, they can unify diverse struggles for class, race and national liberation. . . . The very totality of their oppression means that when they move to change their situation, they move against the entire structure of exploitation".

Dialectics of Struggle the Main Base

Dealing with the question of "reform versus revolution", the author points out that whether or not mobilization of peasantry takes a revolutionary course depends mainly on the dialectics of the struggle, which is subject influence from the nature of reaction it provokes from the exploitative power bases buttressed by the international lobbies of imperialism. The potential of the reformist becoming a revolutionary as well as of the revolutionary turning into a reformist movement is ever present, the relative probability of the two depending on the strength and solidarity of peasant mobilization and the reaction it encounters. Peasantry is not homogeneous and the middle, comparatively better-off peasants remain vulunerable to the pressures from the power base which is adept in creating Trojan horses within the peasantry. The power elite are sophisticated enough to use smoother means. Political flexibility of the old and newly emerging power elites or of pressures from important foreign interests influence the dialectics of the struggle. Peasant radicalization faces the danger of being transformed into support of the power base through corruption and cooption, especially when its leadership is usurped by the middle peasants. That the outside interests succeed in getting the national power elite to launch upon reformist measures to squash peasant mobilization in its incipient stages is illustrated by several instances that followed the success of the peasantry-based Chinese and Cuban Revolutions. Those of them that followed the Chinese Revolution included India's Community Development Projects inspired and supported by the Ford Foundation and the Indo-American Technical Mission, Village Aid in Pakistan, Rural Reconstruction in Taiwan and the Philippines where it was supplemented by police action under Magsaysay. A similar role was played by the Alliance for Progress, USAID and the Rockefeller Foundation in Latin America after the Cuban Revolution.

That these reformist interventions do not result in any lasting improvement in agrarian relations is clear enough. They do not resolve the fundamental contractions and fail to stem peasant deprivation and unrest. In India, for example, the CDPs benefited the well-to-do section of the rural society and the subsequent Green Revolution led to further polarization within the peasantry. In some areas in India, it is said, the polarization seems to be so sharp that "religious barriers which formerly kept the middle and also certain categories of the poor peasants separated from the landless and low-caste workers are breaking down." In many areas, this enhanced the organisability and revolutionary potential of the masses considerably. The more or less radically reformist policies have been able to neutralise the militancy of peasant movements in several countries like Mexico, Japan, Bolivia, Venezuela and Peru. But in many such instances, new contradictions have emerged to heap new frustrations on the bulk of the peasantry, on account of the failure of industrialization to syphon off peasant discontent and the failure of implementing the reforms fully to the general benefit of the peasantry as a class. The lesson of experience that "half-hearted reforms . . . are counterproductive from the political point of view" has not sunk either into the national or into the international power elite. Among the latter, the World Bank has been increasing its stake in rural development in the Third World in the hope of containing resistance to the hegemony of world capitalism. The author quotes an informed opinion in this regard which maintains that "on the whole the programmes of this agency are purposely designed to avoid solutions which would challenge the dominant capitalist entrepreneural system prevailing in most Third World countries. In view of the alarming rural pauperization of peasants in many Third World countries, it is not surprising that the World Bank and similar development agencies, in addition to their traditional betting-on-the-strong model, are now designing programmes mostly for the individual advancement of the middle peasants". This course could be self-defeating in a pervasive state of relative and even absolute deprivation. "It is not unlikely that the middle peasants will, in due course, discover that the common resistance together with pauperizing poor peasants to the prevailing free market and betting-on-the-strong development model, is more profitable in the long run than aspiring individual advancement under great risks". If this happens, the peasants may find comrades among small merchants, entrepreneurs and artisans facing overwhelming competition from multi-nationals in all fields. Inconclusive though the prospect appears to be, it seems to the author that "in the long run pauperization which accompanies such dependent development, together with a growing awareness among the masses that foreign international interests are behind this, will lead to a combination of anti-imperialist sentiment with frustration. This combination could transform (potential) mobilization against national elite (and their police forces and army) into an anti-imperialist or revolutionary struggle. It is tempting to share, with the author, Alexandrov's view that "the future direction of the peasant movement will . . . most probably be towards the growing militancy of the rural proletariat and semi-proletariat in opposition not only of traditional inequalities but to modern capitalist exploitation as well".

Machinations of the Power Elite

The author concludes with a reflection on the role of social scientists and the power elite. That the machinations of the latter at the international level are counterproductive to the interests of the poor in the Third World countries are not perceived by most Third World scholars, including those whom power elite do not coopt to work as comparadors. The author directs pointed attention in this regard to academic offensives launched by the 1969 Rockefeller Report on the Americas and the Triangle Papers issued by Trilateral Commission sponsored in 1973 by David Rockfeller, the Chairman of the Chase Manhattan Bank. The Rockfeller Report was the response of the corporate power elite to the strong emergence of emancipatory protest movements all over the Third World. It pronounced, "The need to give more attention to the potentially subversive role of universities, the Church, the military and also women, as part of nationalist movements in some Latin American countries" and propagated the concept of Western Hemisphere security under U.S. hegemony. "A strong trust in "security" strategies to safeguard orderly, i.e. Western development became increasing by predominant among the Western economic power elite the next few years, as a reaction to signs of dissidence in the Third World countries." The other Trilateral Commission was meant to squash the tendencies towards self-reliance on the part of the Third World countries which had begun to advance the imperative of a New International Economic Order. The Triangle papers issued by this Commission propagated guidelines for policies to strengthen the dominant Western economic system and note that "the present policies of such international agencies as the World Bank and the International Monetary Fund (IMF) seem to be large in line with the broad outlines of the Trilateral Commission". To counter the Third World support to strategies of "self-reliance" and even "dissociation" from the Western economic influences, these papers strongly advocate proper management of interdependence between the Trilateral economies and those of the Third World. In the light of these subversive inroads of the Western power elite into social sciences of Third World countries, the author calls upon the rural social research establishment "to dedicate some of its attention to the intentions of its funding agencies, and in general the broader political context in which research is functioning or may be used", and to resist the "colonization" of the social sciences anywhere.

Regretting the abundant display of naivety by the Western scholars and the native scholars under the spell of Western frames-of-reference and research methodologies in their approach to Third World peasantry, the author pleads with them to overcome "the view from above and from outside bias" which is generally practised by social science establishments. This basically patrician view must be replaced by a "from within and from below perspective" that facilitates participatory action research making field experience a political experience that requires the scholar to expose the forces that imprison him and the forces that imprison the native". In view of the subversive inroads of the power elite into social science research the author proceeds to maintain that "it is time that Western scholars operating in and from the metropolitan centres also begin with a more careful look at where they precisely stand. For example: rather than simply continuing snooping in other countries at people of the lower classes who have been systematically underdeveloped by these scholar compatriots, a reasonable justification for continuing research in Third World countries could be a careful look at what those compatriots . . . have been and are doing there and why". In respect of all scholars, native as well as foreign, the author finds two weaknesses they must overcome. "At present", he contends, "social scientists are amply trained in tabulating, drafting questionnaires, observation and interviewing but there is hardly any systematic training to become sensitive to the needs and values of fellow human beings, individually or in groups. Even less attention is given to oneself, as a human being grown up with all the biases one's society imposes. The second weakness is the lack of development of the capacities to bring into the objective sphere experiences, impressions and biases through introspection and discussion in small groups. It is easy enough to agree with the author that "such sensitivity training is probably a good way to overcome the alienating dehumanizing effects of current social research methodology which is basically manipulative and not emancipatory"

That the approach to the question of peasant mobilization fails to achieve the level of sensitivity based on the view from outside and from above is evident in one of the contributions in this saga, which deals rather perfunctorily with the comparative experience of peasant mobilization in China and India. The author detests the romantisized evaluation of Mao, the architect of peasant mobilization in China and condescends to give Gandhi his due for successfully enlisting the participation of peasant masses in the struggle for India's independence. We do not wish to add to the voluminous writings on the goals, methodologies and results of the struggles that these two eminent Asians had led. But we may concede that Mao made peasantry the vanguard of the Chinese revolution, while Gandhi coopted undifferentiated peasantry as one of the identifiable sections whom he helped to mobilize from both rural and urban areas for assault on the British rule. The piece touches upon the Chinese experience in the margin; its main purpose seems to be to narrate briefly a selection of some of the unceasing succession of peasant movements in India since 1920. Its conclusion advances the contention that "in the study of peasant society and peasant mobilization, one should always guard against the emergence of 'Peasantism' based on a very narrow perspective of social and political development of societies". The lesson the author draws from Gandhi's success in peasant mobilization is, "A peasant per se is narrow in his outlook and goals. A peasant has never made history; he can be mobilized to make history under proper leadership and with alliances." Nobody can deny the need of proper leadership and of alliances but many would wonder whether the charge of narrowness of outlook lies at the door of peasants or the author's.

II. THE STATE OF PEASANTRY

Reform, Reconstruction Development

Asia

The rest of the saga contains a varied fare of concepts, constructs and conclusions based on the generalized experience of peasants under colonial rule and development regimes of several countries spread east to west across the Third World from the Philippines to Fiji. It is perhaps because the saga is confined to "continuing deprivation" that it leaves out, as noted earlier, the peasantry-based successful revolutions in China, Vietnam and Cuba, even though they offer many precious lessons for the rest of the Third world. A more serious limitation of the saga, however, is its sidetracking of the series of more or less radical peasant movements in the Indian subcontinent that were ploughed under by the might of the British rule and thwarted by the development approaches of the native inheritors of that rule. What we have in place is a substantive account of these movements and their outcomes, "Perspectives of Agrarian Reconstruction: India in the Asian Context" (Vol. 1, 2). Drawing upon the more recent developments and changes in the agrarian scene in India, this paper seeks to provide a broad typology of emerging agrarian patterns in South and South-East Asia and to suggest some hypotheses regarding the implications of each of these types for economic and social development (and then attempts) to review and evaluate the current thinking of social scientists on the relative merits of each type of agrarian structure in terms of achieving the twin objectives of economic growth and social equity.

The author's identification of the wide gulf between the "book view" and the "field view" as a factor vitiating development in many Third World countries raises high expectations about his subsequent analysis. The expectations are not however, realized. This could be because of the conceptual constraint exercised on the analysis by its rather uncritical acceptance of "growth with social justice" as the goal of development. This catchy but unrealistic definition of development's goal, it may be recalled, had emanated from the World Bank sources to divert the Third World's attention when it was faltering on the path of GNP growth. It is no doubt difficult to quarrel with relevance of justice for growth but it must also be admitted that its profession has proved difficult to be translated into practice. The power bases dispensing development are yet incompetent in most developing countries to integrate into growth the liquidation of pervasive inequality particularly ruinous to peasantries. The typology is left, therefore, only to facilitate conceptualization of the possible course that agrarian relations may take within development regimes professing egalitarian ideals but failing to prevent continuing accentuation of inequalities. In essence, the typology helps to envisage whether in the course of development the liquidation of semi-feudal relations implanted by colonialism on the communitarian peasant economies of the Third World countries will result in the rise of capitalist farming or in the rise of self-employed peasant economy or an admixture of the two. The author provides on interesting classification of the national or sub-national regional economies on the basis of the available data and information on their development experiences. He then proceeds to advance three conceptions of the economic growth, together with their attributes. The first conception relates to development essentially capitalist in nature, in which the landlord or the rich peasant acts as the main agent of growth, which is clearly not conducive to attainment of equity. The second posits co-existence of curbed and contained landlords or rich peasants and specially protected small peasant cultivators; the characteristic feature of mixed economies that have so far failed to deal with inequalities. The Third envisages peasant agriculture within a cooperative framework: egalitarian in nature in the long run but as yet in the realm of aspiration in much of the Third World. The author's predilection appears to favour the third course in the interest of imparting social justice to growth.

The third egalitarian conception being so rare and the first inequitons one being hazardous, the second seems to have become modal among the developing countries. It is, therefore, on this conception of the mixture of the regulated capitalist farming and pampered peasant cultivation that the author mainly focuses his survey of the relevant literature. This brief survey presents a cross-section of scholarship that has been invested on the assessment of trends in agricultural development that have operated since the Second World War. The survey is instructive enough to reveal the persisting groping for a modal of development that effectively combines growth with equity. This rather speculative literature considers a wide range of issues including the socio-structural and the technological aspects of agricultural growth as well as the interaction between the two in the course of that growth. That the growth process is fraught with political consequences and that political considerations inevitably exercise considerable influence on social action determining the path of that growth process are duly recognized by the scholars the author has drawn upon for his survey. He rightly concludes his discussion of this modal conception by pointing out that "there have been no significant attempts in India or other countries to work out on both a theoretical and empirical base an alternative strategy of equity-oriented economic growth".

The author finally turns to the third peasant-oriented perspective of development pioneered by Ladejinsky and Thorner. In essence, this conception holds out a promise of combining productivity raising advanced technology with structural relations so transformed as to minimize the incidence of inequality in the pursuit of agricultural development. "In the process", Thorner contends, "the older concentration of power in the hands of the village minority can be reduced and the nexus of forces constituting the 'depression' broken up. In the long run what holds out the best hope is any programme that will get rural mass into motion, make them into a self-propelling force generating their own energy . . . whatever demerits our proposals may have, at least no one can say that they do not begin at the bottom." The alternative is attractive and is, in principle, supported by server scholars the author quotes. Its feasibility remains severely constrained by the politics of horse-trading dominated by an entrenched alliance of the political, business and landed interests. As the author concludes, "the blending of the community with the market principle is (its) quintessence. The realization of such a perspective, however, is not just a techno-economic question. It is primary a politico-economic question and, more fundamentally a cultural and moral question. This will constitute the basic challenge in the coming decades not only in the narrow rural context but in the broad national context. This conclusion is not apparently meant to be conclusive; it adequately demonstrates how very easy it is for scholars to descend from the book-view to a hypothetical field-view and how difficult it is for them to ascend from a realistic field-view to a concrete book-view. The formulation of the typology and the conceptions remain a priori. Their translation into social policy and action calls for much deeper appreciation of the ground level realities of deepening deprivation generated by the grip of power politics on the economy, that stifles democratization of the development process.

Five of the remaining contributions deal with the evolving situations in Asian countries. They obviously differ in focus, content and style of presentation; some are empirical studies while others debate conceptual issue. Each reflect upon the obtaining political, economic, social and cultural conditions in the given historical context. Common among them is the source of influences that constitute the root of the transformation of national economies, inescapably impinging on the survival of the peasant form of life and living. That source is the penetration of world capitalism deep into agrarian production structures. We do not propose to go here into the details of each contribution. Our purpose is to draw attention to the varied forms that the processes pushing peasantries into hopeless plight seem to take.

Let us begin this exercise with the eastern part of the Third World spectrum. Here, we have a historical account of how the peasantry had fared in the face of a powerful collusion of the landed interests and the economic, social, political, bureaucratic and even military forces, that served to transplant on to the traditional self-sustaining peasant economy are agro-industry based capitalist farming oriented to the world market under the title "poverty, peasantry, patrons, proletarianization; Piat, Philippines" (Vol. I, 4). The author focuses pointed attention on the marginality of changes in the traditional patron-client relationships caused by the integration of the local economy into the national and international market first by the introduction of cultivation of tobacco as a cash crop and then by industrial growth based on cane sugar. Patronclientage is used to designate "a personalized, face-to-face, informal and enduring contractual relations between persons of unequal status and power, imposing reciprocal obligations, differing in kind, on each of the parties. In a situation dominated by monopsony of land-ownership and preponderated by servile, tributary, rent-paying, family-labour-based tenant cultivator, this system remained viable in the long-lasting expansion of labour-intensive tobacco cultivation within an expending frontier. The far-reaching political and economic events initiated not the displacement but a redefinition of the patron-client relations. These events included the imposition of martial law, land reforms designed to secure land to the tiller, and the establishment of the large scale capital-intensive sugar industry. The redefined patron-client relations weakened the position of tenants leading to the emergence of landless labour class and the land reforms failed to greatly benefit the actual tiller because they were evaded by, among other means, switching over to cane cultivation. The small land-owning class thanks to their access to power, emerged as the new elite class who without relinquishing rural residence adopted the Western style consumerist way of life. These changes could not prevent further pauperization of the peasantry and seem to have so far prevented the crystallization of even wage labour into a proletarian class. It is not denied that these changes emanating from the macro level may yet change the situation to ease the plight of the peasantry. As the author concludes, "in a sense, the economic logic of capitalist development is promoting class consciousness in Piat more rapidly than language or behaviour would indicate".

Peasant Statism is a Myth

Then we have two expositions on Javanese farming: "The Economic History of Javanese Farmer" (Vol. II, 9) and "Modernization without Development in Rural Java" (Vol. I, 5). The content of the two is partly overlapping and partly complementary. The former reflects upon the drastic and ruinous disorganization of the peasant farming perpetrated by the colonial rule in order to profit from the cooption of the Indonesian agriculture into the world market by implanting on to it first the *Culture System* (1830-70) and then the Corporate Plantation System (1870-1900). Refuting the apologetic positions, advanced by some Western writers, that posited static character or involution to the Javanese peasants, the author asserts that peasant statism is a myth and gives adequate evidence to show that "rice farmers in Java are among the most diligent in Asia with high productivity rates". What had severely compromised their performance was their back-breaking exploitation by the colonial rule and its the Dutch planters. The preying of colonialism had, when it ended, left the peasantry fragmented, with a highly skewed distribution of land ownership and related resources so that food production had begun to prove insufficient for the country's population. The food situation, mainly the availability of rice, was further compounded by rapid growth of population.

The new regime of the newly independent nation was required, therefore, to desperately promote rice production as a part of its development planning. A series of rice intensification programmes were launched, some of them with the active involvement and financial support of foreign aid giving agencies. These programmes attempted to increase productivity by vigorous expansion of the use of modern farm inputs, including fertilizers, high yielding varieties of seeds, irrigation, pesticides and insecticides, improved farming, processing and marketing techniques and extension education and training. They met with varying degrees of success, none of which has been claimed as quite satisfactory. The structure of land ownership tended to be skewed further; the replacement of the traditional rice-cutting knife by the sickle reduced the input of labour time; the commercialization of the harvesting operation by the introduction of a system of contracting out and of piece-rate payment too reduced the numerical requirement of labour at harvest times; the milling of rice replacing hand-pounding drastically reduced employment of female workers and the use of mini-buses for transporting rice from farms to market centres reduced the demand for labour and draft animals. The intensification of rice cultivation led to the increase not of new employment but of underemployment within agriculture. Large land-owning farmers benefited disproportionately while many marginal farmers lost their stake in rice cultivation. The dispossessed marginal farmers and landless labourers streamed into cities in search of work thereby intensifying congestion in urban informal sectors. As a result of this kind of modernization of the rice economy, new contradictions emerged to handicap the process of developing the national economy. This experience, on the whole, shows "how difficult it is for governments of the developing countries . . . to formulate rural and agricultural policies and programmes which are capable of combining the aims of rapid economic growth with equal distribution so that social justice for all people is attained".

The Sri Lankan Experience of "Development and Peasantry" (Vol. II, 8) relates essentially the same story of adversity imposed on peasantry by the colonial rule and the continuation of their economic plight in the course of the subsequent period of independence despite the apparent concern for them of a comparatively softer state. In their determined pursuit of self-interest in making the peasant economy a part of the world commodity market, the colonial rulers pauperized much of the peasantry. Their policies successfully transformed land into a marketable commodity; brought it under the plantations of coffee, tea, rubber and coconut; created a variety of predatory classes like absentee landlords, trading middlemen and money-lenders; and subjected peasantry to an interplay of bureaucratic and local level political interests. The rice economy, the mainstay of the population, was ruined and the eco-system was damaged beyond repair; this inflicted a grievous loss on the peasantry's livelihood. The attitude of the colonial administration was "unimaginative and misguided, when (on rare occasions) it was not hard-hearted. The final outcome was the underdevelopment and impoverishment of the peasantry; the peasant economy settled at a lower equilibrium with a more impoverished peasantry". In the last phase of the colonial rule beginning with 1920s, there was a semblance of change in the attitude of colonial rule towards peasant agriculture. This change is traced to such factors as food supply problems that had surfaced during the preceding period of the world war; the concern of the nationalist movement for the alleviation of impoverishment of the peasantry; the avowed desire of the rule to preserve the peasantry as a social group; and the introduction of universe at franchise together with the introduction of internal or local self-government. Several enactments were passed and schemes were introduced to buttress peasant proprietriship as a means to maintain the *status quo*. The main thrust of the policy was to exploit the development potential of the dry zône through reiteration of irrigation works. But in practice little progress was made since the authorities had not taken into account the problems of land tenure, primitive technology and inequalities in distribution.

When, in 1948, the country became independent, the peasantry was faced with the acute problem of landlessness, greatly differentiated structures and extremely poor living conditions. Soon, therefore, Sri Lanka embarked upon planned development. A number of formal development plans have been attempted since then. The author refers to them as "paper plans", as they have brought only little structural change in the country's economy. The basic pattern of underdevelopment has remained untouched; this pattern is characterized by the vulnerability of the economy to external market forces; increased penetration by transnational aid and financial interests; high levels of unemployment and underemployment; and the deepening poverty of the masses.

World Bank Main Source of Inspiration

In the field of agricultural and rural development, directly impinging on the status of peasantry, the World Bank is said to have been the main source of inspiration. This has meant a "bimodal strategy of development", which emphasized the need to rehabilitate and sustain the large plantation sector along with the development of the peasant sector. The focus of development has been "peasant agriculture rather than the peasantry"; its strategy is to expand dry land colonization, to promote rapid modernization of technology including tractorization, chemical fertilizers and HYV seeds, and to introduce only moderate institutional reforms. The modernization drive has been a very partial success; it helped the rich and middle peasants, accentuated interdistrict and interzonal differences; was often misapplied to result in "overadoption"; and contributed to the marginalization of small cultivators. Similar results flowed from the village expansion and colonization schemes associated with major irrigation projects. The land reform and credit expansion did not make much of a difference; often they turned sharecropping tenants into agrarian proletariat whose conditions so deteriorated as to cause political tensions and unrest. There was increased polarization between the rich landlords and the mass of poor peasantry but no peasant organization or movement has emerged therefrom. When attempts were made to organize peasants for a decentralized and participatory development, they were thwarted by excessive interference by local politicians. The author, therefore, concludes, "There was no major agrarian transformation over the period. The basic structure of the peasantry with a preponderance of poor peasants remained and there was increasing impoverishment among those at the bottom . . . the benefits of many government 'pro-peasant' programmes have failed to reach the marginal groups. . . . Increasing penetration of transnational interests represents another challenge to the peasantry in the coming years. This makes the development of effective peasant organization an imperative need."

That "land reforms" could be reactionary and ruinous to the peasantry is sharply brought out by the piece on "Peasants in Iran: Will they survive? (Vol. II, 6). The author of this crisp piece narrates how during 1962-74, through a series of legislative measures avowedly designed to promote agriculture, the despotic regime of the Shah broke up viable communitarian institutions of peasant agriculture that regulated land and water rights. This facilitated the dispossession of the mass of peasantry pushing them to urban centres to become proletariat serving the labour needs of the simulated construction boom and the insatiable demands of the Western-style consumerism of the elite classes. Foreign capitalist interests not only appropriated the urban industry (based particularly on oil) but penetrated deep into the rural and tribal areas to take over much of the land for the so-called agri-business farm corporations. In being so co-opted into the international economy, the country lost its self-sufficiency in food and became subject to an enormous drain of wealth by Western capitalism. "The final outcome was that within a short period, Iran became a big importer of food items . . . its agricultural base was systematically weakened and fundamentally disorganized. Foreign cultural, social and economic demands . . . were placed over and above national priorities as the centre of gravity of policy decision-making decidedly shifted outside the country to imperialist centres." This is indeed a sad story of economic modernization grievously compromising national independence and of a "monarch" bargaining away his own sovereignty to world imperialism for an access to Western consumerist affluence.

But the despot did not survive. He only pushed the mass of peasantry into the fold of the emergent revolutionary people's movement led by Ayatulla Khomeini, who had invoked religious fundamentalism to mobilize the Iranian people for the overthrow of the Shah. In the immediate aftermath of the revolution the peasants took over the lands they had lost to the royal family, landlords and corporations and started to reorganize agricultural production. But this revolutionary fervour did not last long. The new regime stepped in to prevent the resulting disruption of law and order. This led to a bureaucratization of much needed agrarian reconstruction. The new bureaucrats and technocrats who exercised executive power were themselves strong advocates of capitalist mode of production and they did not appreciate the revolutionary fervour displayed by the peasantry. The functions of land distribution and agricultural development were taken over by the government, with the Ministry of Agriculture heading a host of departments looking after different aspects of that process. A series of land reform Acts were passed to undo the damage the Shah had inflicted on Iranian peasantry. But their direction has been uncertain and their implementation tardy. As a result, the fate of the Iranian peasantry hangs in balance. Policy advice from within the country is forthcoming in plenty but so far no viable set of integrated measures for a peasantry-based programme of agricultural development has been formulated.

Turning from Asia to Africa, we have four contributions dealing with the theme in respect of Kenya, Sudan, Ethiopia and Nigeria, all with a colonial history of varying durations. Colonial penetration into the peasant economies of these countries displayed similar ruthlessness in its self-serving bid to incorporate peasant production into the world commodity markets in order to maximise generation of surpluses which could be drained away to the "home" countries. There are differences among them in the interplay of colonial and of succeeding nationalist interests which have continued to push the peasantry as a class in each deep into the state of deprivation and abject poverty. The Ethiopian case bears some similarity with that of

Iran in the ruthlessness with which native despotism had trampled peasantry under its heavy feet. While in Iran despotism had used successfully the so-called "land reforms" for dispossessing and pauperizing the bulk of the peasantry, the Ethiopian despotism was liquidated while it was beginning to contemplate rudimentary land reforms. In Iran, peasantry could play only a supplementary note in proping up revolutionary fundamentalism, but in Ethiopia it took the lead by attaining a high level of mobilization for the nationalist struggle against despotism. The final outcome for the peasantry does not, however, seem to have been more than marginally better in Ethiopia than that in Iran. The situation has remained in a flux and the fate of peasantry bristles with great uncertainties.

This eloquent contribution on "Agrarian Reform and Class Struggle in Ethiopia" (Vol. I, 7) provide evidence on the kind of plight into which the peasantry and pastorals were pushed by the unleashing of agrarian capitalism by imperialist interests without uprooting oppressive feudalism; on how frustrating the attempts of land reforms prompted by international agencies could be in the situation of unchanged exploitative production relations and on how successful peasant mobilization against oppression leads to transformation of social relations beneficial to organized peasantry in the short run. The 1974 revolution led by peasantry liquidated despotic feudal relations and introduced radical reorganization of agriculture into cooperative farms without disruption and created conditions for economic progress based on the stabilization of the new non-exploitative community-based cooperative relations of production. However, reactionary forces soon emerged within and outside the government to frustrate orderly development of the collectivist agrarian economy. Divisive forces of varied kind emerged to thwart the consolidation of peasant organization and thereby to disrupt agricultural production and economic progress of the nation. The political situation remained in constant turmoil to the disadvantage of peasantry which had begun to wield power at the local level.

A Succession of Famines

Under the circumstances power concentrated in the hands of a small group of military elite and proliferating bureaucracy, who swore by land reforms favouring tillers of soil but in practice thwarted the process of operationalizing them in all manner of ingenuous means. The military ruling elite and the bureaucracy, constituting the new bourgeoisie, facilitated the continuing inroads of world capitalism into the agrarian economy. The uncertainties, political and economic, continue to plague Ethiopian peasantry and agriculture rendering prospects of increased food production uncertain. In fact, the agrarian situation has worsened to cause a succession of famines in more recent years. The situation today in the middle 1980s appears to be more desperate than ever. "A revolutionary agrarian reconstruction is essential", the author concludes, for building an independent national economy geared to the basic needs and interests of the masses. But the present regime cannot carry out such a programme and is limited by its very nature. The land reform (of 1974-77 had) paved the way for this and removed some of the constraints. The removal of these constraints, however, can also help the bureaucratic bourgeoisie and imperialism to develop a neo-colonial peripheral type of bureaucratic capitalist society." It would appear that the present plight of the Ethiopian peasantry and agriculture provides convincing evidence that such a society has already emerged and is getting well-entrenched.

The impact of the colonial policies, including implantation of new forms of tenures, introduction of cash crops and creation of large plantation estates for European settlers was similarly adverse on the indigenous economies in both Kenya and Nigeria. The worst sufferers were the peasants whose subsistence economy was shattered, producing a non-viable admixture of the marginal farmers and semi-proletariat; while "estates" depleted their land resources, they were increasingly pauperized by the surpluses extracted from their meager production to feed the drain of wealth flowing out of the home countries. Post-independence development affecting peasantries was essentially different in nature between these two African countries. In Kenya, political subjugation, cultural subordination and economic exploitation unleashed by the Apartheid capitalism of the colonial rule led ultimately to the Mau Mau revolutionary movement which resulted in the withdrawal of colonialism. By that time, the indigenous economy was in a shambles and the peasantry was well on the downfall to emerge as a sweated semi-proletariat hanging on to small bits of land, each grossly inadequate to feed an average family. The peasantry as a class gained little from the planned development that followed the independence. The author concluding his review of the entire colonial and the subsequent development periods speculates on the future of the peasantry (Vol. II, 6). Candidly he asserts that "one thing we seem to know about the peasantry is that we know little, if not actually anything". He proceeds, however, to note several alternative outcomes advanced by others.

The first of these alternatives asserts that a capitalist social structure envisaged to emerge from the land reforms of the 1950s has not materialized and will not materialize. The reasons are: the farm sizes are too small; the existing large farms are "subject to the peasant cyclical order", whereby accumulated assets in a household are dispersed as a result of inheritance; and the larger settler estates have been occupied, as a result of settlement schemes and land sales, by numerous land-holders signifying the expansion of the peasantry. It is further argued that the development of foreign capital in industry and commerce militates against the evolution of capitalist class, "caught as it were between an expanding peasantry on the one hand, and equally expanding foreign capital on the other hand". The second position argues that increased commodity production comes not from the capitalist farms on the large farm sector but from the emergence of a middle peasantry; there seems the relocation of production from the capitalist state to the middle peasantry. The capitalist strata dissolve into the middle peasantry, as the peasantry as a whole gets differentiated under the impact of foreign merchant and foreign state finance capital; middle peasants may equally emerge from among the mass of peasantry. The third position contends that the peasants get replaced in the course of agricultural growth by "a working class with patches of land", that is, the peasants get proletarianized. The author concludes that the future of peasantry remains uncertain; theoretical speculations and empirical evidence remain inconclusive; peasants have made great contribution to the Kenyan economy and there is no doubt that they will still be around for tomorrow's research based on today's controversies.

On "the demobilization of the Nigerian peasantry" (Vol. I, 8), we need not repeat the consequences of their colonial exploitation. What is interesting here is the plight perpetrated on the peasantry by the way-wardness of the post-independence development induced by the oil boom of the seventies. The new development process that was inspired by foreign economists and donors not only bypassed the peasantry but also uprooted from their state of colonial "mobilization" as the lowest rung of sweated rural producers of commodity exports. This process began in early 1960s; it placed undue emphasis on capital injection as against the mobilization of population. The government, instead of becoming a partner with farmers to help them improve their performance, saw itself as their direct competitor in production activities. Violating all norms of accountability and efficiency, the government agencies established large plantations that became an "insatiable drain on public revenue with workers agitating for higher and higher wages against lower and lower output". Similar was the fate of the so-called farm settlement schemes that were meant to relieve urban problems. Instead of increasing agricultural production, it turned the country dependent on food imports on an increasing scale. This bureaucratic intervention into rural areas proved to be very expensive in terms of resources. Indeed, it served to increasingly push peasants into urban centres as it strengthened their belief "that agricultural and rural existence was a tragedy from which they must save their own children".

Rural Masses Uprooted and Impoverished

With the oil boom of the early 1970s, the national plans became shopping lists of construction projects. Under the plea of bringing about a Green Revolution, River Basin Authorities and the Food Production companies were set up to fritter away enormous sums of money on the import of machinery and fertilizers. There followed "the National Accelerated Food Production Programme" and "Operation Feed the Nation"; the haste with which they were pursued led to gross abuses of a great variety and circumvented the need to extend services to the farmers. The urban-centred nature of these activities widened the gap between the urban and rural areas depriving the latter of hired labour so very necessary especially at harvest time. In the subsequent period of growing food crisis and drying up of oil surpluses, appeared "the new gospel of integrated rural development programme as preached by the World Bank". A series of expensive IRD schemes were implemented with the active participation of the World Bank but they all suffered from several crippling limitations; indeed, "they made no effort to organize the farmers to look after their own interests and to strive to defend them when they were threatened. The peasants were left as passive beneficiaries of a bonanza of services from a benevolent government". As the author concludes the government's effort "has succeeded in uprooting, impoverishing and disorienting the rural masses. It is still to induct them into some relatively stable new patterns of group membership, organization and commitment. To achieve the latter type of peasantry's social mobilization requires, above all, an abiding vision of a goal, a goal which involves not only transforming a people but re-creating for the better the physical and human environment within which they have to live and earn their living".

In respect of Africa, the remaining piece relates to Sudan (Vol. II, 8). It is a general survey of what happened to peasants and pastorals drawn from a variety of traditional economic and socio-cultural settings during and after the colonial period spanning from 1899 to 1956. The author seems to be a little sanguine about the development of the national economy during the colonially wrought cooption of Sudanese agriculture into the world market particularly with the rapid spread of cotton as the principal cash crop. Railways, irrigation and urban growth changed the production base and production relations to the disadvantage of peasants and pastorals. Accompanying the growth of modern mechanized agriculture in irrigated areas in the vicinity of the white-and-blue Nile, were the processes of social disorganization of peasantry, their marginalization and proletarianization. The seasonal migration streams were stabilized between peasant areas and newly-irrigated areas of capitalist farming. After a spell of unstable employment in the latter areas, most peasants felt it unavoidable to migrate into the fast growing urban centres to hibernate there in sub-human conditions in slums and shanty towns. These processes that meant grievous demobilization of the peasantry and the accompanying more ruinous spread of desertification have continued during the succeeding era of independence. The author sums up, "In recent years Sudanese peasants have experienced some major changes in various aspects of their social life. Although they continue to practice subsistence cultivation, many of them are more and more drawn into the modern sector of the economy, into areas of modern farming and urban centres. In the development schemes, the dislocated peasants are reduced to an agrarian proletariat for they are chiefly employed as hired farm workers who receive low wages and work under harsh conditions. In several ways, the peasants who found their way to towns are worse off than their fellow hired workers on the (agricultural) schemes". The author admits the preliminary nature of his impressions and suggests more detailed and more intensive studies of the changing status of peasantry in the context of the modernization of the national economy.

The Latin American situation differs rather sharply from that of both Asia and Africa. Agricultural or rural densities are considerably higher in Asia than in Latin America and peasants overcrowd agriculture in Asia, while in Latin America they coexist with large capitalist farms. The difference between Africa and Latin America is not so much in agricultural or rural densities but in the preponderance of native peasantry in agriculture in Africa and their relative insignificance in Latin America. Even more significant is the fact that penetration of industrial capital had begun much earlier but it has been faster in most Latin American countries than in the countries of the Asia and Africa. The contributions from Latin America all concentrate on the post-Second World War developments, marked by acceleration of the invasion of international financial capital. None of them refer to the decimation of the native peasantry by settlers from Southern European countries in the course of their appropriation of the land resources of Latin America over a period stretching back to the 15th century. It is true that Latin America was sparsely populated but there were indeed settlements of 'Red Indians' all over the continent, most of which were destroyed by the European settlers. By the time of the first world war, the available land was divided into large estates of latifundia and dispersed peasantry or minifundia, scraping livelihood from small bits of land; both were of European origin. The few pockets of "Indian" habitations that had survived in parts of the continent that were not easily accessible had survived by sufferance or by chance to form the lowest rung of the historically crystallized social orders everywhere predominated by European settlers who through sheer passage of time became the new natives of the respective Latin American countries. As the new settlements grew in population through natural increase and immigration, social differentiations appeared in which the new peasantry came to form one of the lower social strata. It is with the problems of these peasantries, that the contributions deal with. In some of them, the scope of discussion is limited to one country while in others it deals with geographic regions each comprising several countries. We refer below first to the former country-specific studies and then to those dealing with larger regions.

We have here four country studies. Of these two relate to Brazil, one to Columbia and one to Peru. We begin our review with the two contributions on Brazil. Of the two, the first by Sorj (Vol. II, 5) reflects on the role of agro-industry and the state of class formation in agriculture. In the period up to 1960, the author finds no drastic change in production relations in the course of increasing monetization, commercialization and specialization of agricultural production oriented toward internal consumption and the transfer of surpluses from agriculture to industry. The period witnessed the rise of industrial bourgeoisie without elimination of large rural landowners. It is the second contemporary period beginning with 1960 that it is of particular interest in the present context. In this phase, agriculture came directly under the command of industry which appropriated both its forward and backward linkages within the rapid foreign finance dominated capitalist growth of the macro-economy. In this period, Brazil witnessed rapid increase in the complexity of its social structure, in its geographical dimension and regional densities as well as in the repression of the organized forms of resistance and struggle of the rural working masses. Indeed, a highly developed and sophisticated industrial structure has developed without modifying the country's dependency on technology and capital goods; in the process, the military regime has, from 1964, allied with large monopolistic national and foreign capital, relegating even the large landowners in agriculture to a position of subservience. However, the very creation of sophisticated ultra-modern capitalist industrial structure warranted modernization of agricultural production which in turn called for drastic modification of production relations within agriculture. This was sought to be achieved by diversification of cropping patterns, horizontal expansion of land under cultivation particularly along the Amazon frontier, liberal credit policies, mechanization and subsidized supply of new inputs, establishment of large agro-industrial complexes and of integrated capitalist agro-industrial enterprises, and the emergence of highly capitalized small producers specializing in certain crops.

But this many-sided modernizing inroads into agriculture did not quite eliminate the small traditional producers, the peasants. Their position has been re-defined in a process of marginalization; indeed pauperization has occurred involving a large majority of these producers. As the author notes, "they are increasingly transformed into large pockets of unemployed labour, barely capable of guaranteeing their own basic subsistence . . . (and, therefore) they find themselves within a permanent process of urban proletarianization in which non-agriculture income accounts for an increasingly important part of total household income". The peasant class coexists with other classes of the capitalist society but only to be subjected in their penury to a process of semi-proletarianization; socially occupying the lowest rung of that society, they have no political power and when they try to assert by unionization, they are ruthlessly repressed and suppressed. To squash the rural tensions that even so surface from time to time, the government is considering a new policy whose central thrust is to support the product and not the producer. In all probability, the ruling bourgeoisie may devise a sort of agrarian reform that may include expansion of social services, cooperativization, diffusion of unions and associations, and buttressing the position of middle-size proprietors. However, the outcome for the small producers of this type of reform by the present political dispensation is uncertain. In dispensing social services, the rural population may be manipulated through a series of control mechanisms and processes of ideological integration; cooperatives may be used by the state to discipline the small producers and may constitute a relatively easy organization to manipulate them especially in a situation of low social mobilization; the unions may be transformed into simple instruments for the provision of services, thereby deactivating them as a force for social and political mobilization; and similarly buttressing the position of middle peasants as capitalized producers may too deactivate potential rebellion by the large mass of household producers. In the ultimate analysis the success of this kind of "reform" will depend not only in the state's coercive force but also on the capacity for organizing political struggle on the part of the rural labour. The latter capacity remains dormant.

The second piece on Brazil (Vol. I, 10) takes up the case of the Amazonian Frontier to explore the impact of Brazilian path of agricultural development on peasant social differentiation. Against the historical background of penetration of the most modern international financial and industrial monopoly capitalism supported by the state, the author draws particular attention to the last two decades, "in which capital accumulation in the international industrial and financial sectors has created the conditions for the capitalization of agricultural activities. The state . . . has stimulated the capitalization of agriculture by making possible its link-up with industry in two ways: by vertical integration through subsidies for modernization and productivity and by the horizontal expansion via the directed occupation of the Amazon Frontier". In the process, labour market became unified, with large masses of population mobilized to meet the requirements of the various spatial poles of development – the cities and the frontier; monopoly appropriation of land speeded up; the cooption of large estates by capital lent bitterness to land disputes and resulted in limiting the spatial mobility of peasant units, intensifying at the same time their labour mobility. Peasantry entered a phase of its dissolution/differentiation. Associated with the increasing sway of industrial and finance capital was the absolute increase of wage-earners, leading to change of permanent into temporary workers within urban nuclei and an intensification of the process of urbanization. The author contends, "Thus the importance of the peasantry is tending to decline, though it subsists and is adapting itself to expropriation. . . . In Brazil, the recent transformation of class structure has been in the direction of: (1) crystallizing capitalist relations in the large agricultural enterprises which use modern technology; (2) strengthening an important sector of capitalised family units; and (3) proletarianizing and partially reproducing the peasantry".

Focusing pointed attention on the spatial dimension of the peasantry's dissolution/differentiation process, the author notes that on the Amazonian frontier, where the labour market is not completely formed, the peasants predominate. There, an estimated one million of them constitute the most fully organized rural social group, offering resistance to expropriation. The rapid incursion of a variety of capitalist interests into this vast virgin Amazonian half of the country is tending partly to a dissolution of the peasantry (into an unorganized proletarian mass) and partly to sustain the small peasant producers. Their continued existence serves to reduce labour cost, to an extent, in two ways: "(1) by producing cheap food stuff to supply local rural and urban labour force and ensuring part of their reproduction of their own lands; and (2) by farming enclaves of backward capital formation which makes it possible for them to sell their labour when necessary and so pressing wages down. From the peasants point of view, this ability to exercise more than one class of economic activity is a survival strategy which allows him to maintain his ties with the land". The state facilitates these processes by a series of interlinked policies – regional development, land policy, credit polity, urban policy etc. The author, while indicating labour mobility as a necessary structural condition for capitalist development of the Amazonian frontier, suggests the possible emergence of social mobilization under certain conditions. He then proceeds to highlight the problems that may arise in the application of a strategic solution for peasants' mobilization. These problems arise from several features of the development of the Brazilian economy. These include: (1) the attempt to integrate peasants into the national economy by means of top-down policies; (2) social-spatial labour mobility conditioning the functioning of the economic structure and (3) the high social and political cost of socio-spatial mobility. On the other hand, economic contradictions, the state's need for legitimation and the impediments to such a large scale spatial organization may all serve to strengthen the small agricultural producers. On balance, the author asserts that the fate of the peasantry rests on the solution to the crucial political problem of how to induce the participation of the people in the development or growth process. "To go back to a proposition of strengthening a non-capitalized peasantry", the author concluded, "seems not only utopian but also anachronistic. Social mobility that brings about peasant differentiation means opportunities for change and originates different forms of capital, which constitute concrete social forces. They open new spaces for manoeuvre inside the regime, that may bring real benefits to small producers. . . . "

Peasants the Political Powers

In respect of Columbia (Vol. I, 12) the authors of "Agrarian Policies and Peasant Organization" narrate an interesting story of the rise of officially supported peasant organization and its helplessness when that support came to be withdrawn when political power passed on from the liberals, their supporters, to the conservatives who embarked upon a programme of rapid capitalist development enveloping the industrial as well as agricultural sectors and rural as well as urban populations. They cover the period from 1960 onwards. The agrarian reform had sought during the 1960s to correct without much success the grossly unequal distribution of landownership; it was held out not only as an instrument of social change but also as a means of economic development. It was comprehensive enough to cover legal matters relating to land ownership and occupation; engineering aspect of infrastructure as of roads, irrigation and technological inputs; and developmental requirements of credit, colonization and land augmentation. But by 1970, it was clear that the reform had been of little help in improving the peasants' lot; it remained confined to a mere colonization programme that "did not touch the real problems of high concentration of landownership and the distribution of the peasant income". On the contrary, during the decade the characteristic capitalistic development was forfeited at a faster rate and the concentration off the ownership of land (including land taken under lease) increased more rapidly than before.

But the reform did promote the peasants organization; indeed on the initiative of the government (of the Liberal Party) a peasants' organization called the ANUC was formed and was provided with ample financial resources. This political alliance between the government in power and peasants is said to have been initially successful. Its success did not last long; with the change in party in power at the centre, the financial help and backing the ANUC had been accustomed to receive dried up almost totally. The ANUC then embarked upon the path of confrontation and became a rebellious autonomous organization. The government responded by creating a rival parallel organization. Faced with the hostilities from outside, the internal weaknesses of the ANUC surfaced to push it into a crisis from which it has failed to recover. Apart from the lack of financial support from the government, the crisis within ANUC is traced to several other crucial organizational factors such as its lack of concrete programme; a clear contradiction between its ideological rhetoric and the specific grievances of the various peasant groups; the schism that developed between its leadership and the ranks; internal power struggle between several of its groups; the confusion about its political role causing the disillusionment among peasants; the damage to its morale caused by its poor performance at the polls; lack of accountability on the part of those who handled financial aid from non-governmental sources; and the combination of resistance organized by vested interests, intransigence of bureaucracy, apathy of the Church and repressive measures of the government. Thus after 10 years of existence, the ANUC ended in a languid condition.

In the 1970s, a new policy, Integrated Rural Development (IRD), was launched to promote agrarian capitalism by granting financial help to the large landowners. The basic idea was held to be "to intensify the reproduction of capital in the rural areas by redirecting credit and investments". The new policy, the IRD, was launched in 1976 with the support of the international credit agencies; its defined objectives were: "In economics, an increase in production, the stabilization of prices and eventually a reduction in the real costs of production of the foodstuffs of popular consumption .... In the social field, an increase and betterment of public services to satisfy the basic need of peasants, opening of new economic opportunities and an improvement of their incomes". A phased programme was launched with credit, technology, marketing, organization, training and conservation as its production components; with rural electrification as its infrastructure component and waterworks, education and health as its social components. The success that has attended this IRD programme has been very partial; a large number of peasants attended the organizational courses; water ponds were installed but mainly for rearing fish and credit flowed but only marginally No significant progress has been achieved in the fields of marketing, technical assistance and actual reorganization of the peasantry. The IRD remained a programme of credits and promotion of the traditional agriculture favouring the consolidation of the landowners' economy. On the whole, the results were very modest and very uneven. Where IRD succeeded in a few regional pockets, it led to a process of differentiation of the peasantry, aggravating thereby the already existing social inequalities. The overall conclusions that the author reached from his review of developments since 1960 is that the countryside slowly became depopulated by outmigration of people to the cities where large concentrations of peasants were formed; there was no significant change in the structure of land tenancy which was very unfairly distributed, there was an expansion of the agrarian frontier which offered new settlement opportunities to satisfy their basic needs; even so, the Columbian countryside remains convulsed in the grip of acute crisis which the Integrated Rural Development has failed to alleviate.

On Peru, the contribution (Vol. II, 4) offers reflections on the impact of regional constellation of political and economic power on the peasantry that forms a numerically preponderant group within the population, comprising natives whose roots go back to ancient Inca civilization. In the course of more than four centuries old appropriation of their country by the white (Spanish) settlers, these peasants have been relegated to a position of most deprived and exploited lowest unintegrated stratum of the present Peruvian society. They continue to occupy the long stretch of Andes highlands and the surrounding vast expanse of the jungle country, scratching their meagre livelihood from land, suffering exploitation heaped on them by the whites who have striven to incorporate the national economy into the mainstream of western capitalism. In more recent years, their presence has been viewed as constituting a peasant problem which is inseparable from the search for Peru's national integration and identify. The author candidly canvasses only an approach to the understanding of this long standing problem and refrains from offering a solution. He rightly asserts that the peasantry has to be "one of the central bases of nationality as its historical roots are the most ancient" and that the solution to the peasant problem from "an essential part in resolving the national problem and that of national identity".

After examining the varied stages of development in different regions, the author concentrates his attention on the forms of power dominating the indigenous peasantry. He deplores that "most agricultural and peasant development projects do not take into account the broad complexities of the political dimension or, in any case, assume that it is some kind of an appendix which can be ignored". His potent argument is that politics consists not only in its institutional manifestations but is also a means to organize power in the society that takes into account the political, productive, economic and social conditions in which its different sectors and classes are found. Political power is used to generate surpluses through the exploitation of the peasant masses located in their diverse regional settings. The ascendant capitalism, the author contends, in its attempt to create new economic space for itself, has rendered, in the Andean countryside, obsolete the antiquated forms of domination based on regional oligarchies and on gamonalismo (local chieftainship system) and has hegemonized by a new type of subordinate ruling class. Under this dispensation, "social spaces hegemonized by local power group, accompanied and backed up by state officials, organize and bring together small surpluses from different units, the (peasant) communities". Their existence is explained by the fact that the main dominating classes, the industrial and financial bourgeoisie have little interest in exercising direct political and economic domination in the Andean zone. Denied entry into the mainstream of the nation's economic and social life, the surviving original Inca natives find themselves subject to devious forms of exploitation devised by the local power groups for their own interest of the national bourgeoisie.

One of the two remaining contributions on Latin America focuses attention on the new context in the evolution of small peasant enterprises in Central America and Andean countries (Vol. I, 11). The new context is characterized by comprehensive government strategies of agricultural reconstruction adopted in response to world crisis in which these countries found themselves burdened with external debt leading them to place an overriding emphasis on export promotion. The strategies were aimed at rapid all round increase in agricultural productivity. As a result, in the Andean countries the traditional *hacienda* (large landed estates) diminished in importance and middle ranking capitalist enterprises benefited; while in Central America there has been a rapid modernization of farming techniques in the big estates. "This general policy has worked against the small peasant farms, whose staple products are more vulnerable to market forces. It appears that the state has renounced its role as a protector of the small peasantry in crisis. All measures aimed at benefiting the small cultivators have been piecemeal. . . ." The new dynamics of agricultural capitalism have increased the instability of peasant economies; in this process of capitalistic rationalization of production structure, the traditional forms of marginal tenancy farming have been eliminated, all permanent employees have been displaced by the new technology and the use of labour has been strictly limited to seasonal needs. Mounting labour surpluses as a result of this process led to far-reaching migratory movements towards towns and cities in search of part-time work and towards the frontier in search of land to settle the family on. Even with all the modernization of agriculture, peasant production has managed to occupy a prescribed place in the market. Peasants, while continuing to cultivate traditional food products, are forced to commercialize a part of their production despite increased risks of losing their self-sufficiency.

Global Economic System's Inability to Provide full Employment

The painful outcome of the penetration of capital into agriculture under the guise of agrarian reforms has been the creation of a cheap labour force in a constant frustrating search for employment. In Central America the great increase in the number of self-employed merely camouflages two problems: "a proletariat which has to exist by cultivating small farm plots, and an impoverished peasantry that has to find other jobs during a part of the year". In the densely populated areas of the pacific coast of Nicaragua, it is said, "a rural lumpen proletariat bides its time in cities, waiting for the harvesting season". Similar is the overall situation in most of other countries of the region; everywhere temporary work has occurred on a massive scale as a result of general unemployment, most peasants are sellers of both their own labour and their goods. "The increased time spent by the peasant family in temporary work", the author notes, "is the most striking indication of the inability of the global economic system to find a solution to the general problem of unemployment through industrialization and urbanization. The indefinite and painful perpetuation of the process of fragmentation of the peasantry has generated in a permanent state of flux: everyday, the peasant is less peasant than the day before". Only a small minority of them has managed to accumulate the capital necessary for its farms in this era of agricultural modernization.

In his search for a framework for rural development, the author expresses his disappointment on the failure of the peasant cooperatives which became popular in 1960s to resolve the problems of agricultural intensification and commercialization. The organization of peasant cooperatives has been diverse; some are managed by the state as no more than groups of wage earners. While others are small, communitarian, and self-managing groups. By and large, they are the creation of the state bureaucracy; their initial efficiency rests on bureaucratic support but left to themselves they deteriorate and stagnate, with their activities centring around a store distributing manufactured goods. More recently, while the state has lost interest in the cooperatives, agricultural cooperatives controlled by capitalist farmers have increasingly absorbed the peasant cooperatives. This trend of absorption of weak and smaller cooperatives by capitalist farmers is often aided by the state particularly when it operates such diffused and less production-oriented measures such as the Integrated Rural Development (IRD) programmes. The IRDs are in force in almost all the countries under consideration for quite some time now. They "are aimed primarily at the utilization of underemployed workers in rural areas, and of disposable resources within the traditional peasant sector. In practice, the IRD model breaks down as programmes or projects aim at standardization and incorporation, and mindlessly implements both goals". Under the circumstances, the author places some hope on community-oriented self-management projects. In support he cites the Kanar project in the Southern Sierra, which has demonstrated that "it is not as important to give priority to profitable agricultural enterprises as it is to seek a balance between economic efficiency, equitable redistribution, and preservation of social values". The project had tried out this approach and it is claimed to have resulted in a modest process of modernization. It has been viewed by the author as "a type of survival model where improvement in quality of life is paramount". The author concludes that IRDs as well as the community-oriented projects may attract primary importance in the opening up of new perspectives in regional policy. It is at once conceded, however, that "the possibility of a different type of regional development which would lead to important transformations in structures of production and systems of redistribution, and which would be better able to define the status of the peasant as a wage-earner depends on the increased vitality of regionally based social movements in which the peasantry will play a principal role".

Finally, we refer to an empirical study of situations and trends in "Peasant Agriculture in Latin America" (Vol. I, 9). Deploring the relative neglect of peasantry in the abundant analysis of agricultural modernization in Latin America, the author draws attention to the positive adaptive responses of peasant agriculture which continues to play quite a significant role in the national agrarian economic structure. Peasant agriculture is defined to be one where the family is the essential nucleus of both production and consumption. It is taken to include small landowners, tenant farmers, sharecroppers, settlers occupying frontier lands, squatters and persons holding family-size units under the agrarian reform process. Internally, there are a host of differences within the so defined peasant agriculture, relating to the size of agricultural units, its capacity to provide occupation to family labour force, reproductive potential, technological pattern, the degree of its integration with the market, its agro-ecological setting, economic resource base and its development potential. These internal differentiations not-withstanding, the author finds it eminently worthwhile to examine the status, trends and prospects of peasant agriculture comprising those units where the work of cultivation is done by the family. His analysis shows that somewhat over a half of the rural population or approximately one-fifth of the total population of Latin America is directly linked to peasant agriculture comprising around 13.5 million productive units occupying a little less than a fifth of the total land area devoted to agriculture. These facts highlight the social significance of peasantry as regards both the rural and the total population of Latin America.

On the economic significance of peasant agriculture, the author compiles data from varied sources to show that its contribution to both internal consumption and exports is sizable. "Family-based peasant agriculture mainly produces food . . . and has played an important role in supplying Latin America with food." Citing statistics on market supplies originating in peasant agriculture, the author maintains that in Brazil, Mexico, Columbia, Peru, Central America and in most of the other Latin American countries, a large part of the production that goes to feed their populations is produced on farms using family labour. The peasant share in the production of export crops, including coffee, cocoa and cotton is large, rising to over 70 per cent in respect of coffee in Equador and Bolivia and to over 65 per cent in respect of cocoa in Equador, Peru and Venezuela. It is true, however, that their share in export is not the same as that in production, for, when there is a drop is demand in the international market for any of these commodities, the exporters reduce their purchases from the small producers; when the conditions are favourable, the exporters expand their purchases from this stratum. In effect, the peasant production for export acts as a sort of cushion which allows the medium-size and large producers to regulate the volumes marketed in their own favour. With regard to livestock production the peasant share is much lower. This is true, however, mainly of cattle rearing requiring goats, pigs and poultry, the peasants contribute in most of these countries much more than a half of total production.

In order to show that peasant agriculture is not any stagnant pool, the author cites several examples of it having recorded significant rates of growth. In Equador, it has been demonstrated that peasant agriculture typically grew at least as fast as the sector taken as a whole; in fact between 1954 and 1974 the share of the peasant units in the sector's overall production had increased from 57 to 63 per cent. In Chile, production of legumes (beans, lentils and chick-peas) in which the peasants specialized doubled during 1975-79 in response to rise in their prices. The similar peasant responses to market price changes have been recorded in respect of cold and temperate climate crops in the Andean region of Bolivia, of soyabean in Brazil, of fresh vegetables, tubers and roots in most other countries. This evidence indicates that there is an effective capacity for expansion of production through the peasant economy. Of even more crucial importance is the fact that the bulk of the rural labour force is retained within peasant agriculture; labour on family farms accounted for 85 per cent of the agricultural work force in Brazil in 1970, 82 per cent in El Salvador in 1974, nearly 70 per cent in Mexico in 1970 and over 65 per cent in Equadoe in 1974. According to the author's estimate, workers permanently linked to peasant units represent more than 70 per cent of the total agricultural work force. Hired workers play a nominal role in peasant agriculture; their share in the total increases with the increase in size of farm beyond the one that is commonly accepted as the family size unit.

Capitalist Penetration Causes Rural-to-Urban Migration

Several structural changes are occurring within agriculture in Latin America which are not conducive to progress within its peasant subsector. While peasantry is expanding in absolute numbers sharing high population growth rates at the national level, capitalist penetration into the agricultural sector is preventing any increase in opportunities for permanent employment. This is forcing a part of the peasantry to swell migration streams to towns and cities. Meanwhile, the same modernizing forces of change in production technology are leaving the peasant sub-sector to be fragmented. This is reflected in increase in the number of small family holdings. With a shrinkage of their average, a partial depeasantization at the family level, and proletarianization of significant proportions of peasantries. Decreases in the size of family holding leading to decreasing family incomes in the face of grossly inadequate absorption of the labour force both within and outside agriculture has created a situation of semi-proletarianization of peasantry which for sheer survival combines self-employment in shrinking size of family farms and part-time wage employment in rural as well as urban areas. "This makes peasant agriculture a shelter for the labour force which enters and leaves the labour market according to the conditions of that market." In some parts, this process has advanced to a stage where in the survival strategies of peasant families non-agricultural activities predominate as a source of income; this has been suggested as a road to depeasantization. What has been notable about this process is that the link of those who obtain employment outside agriculture away from home does not snap. Their non-agricultural income surpluses flow back into their places of origin, which are used in diverse non-agricultural pursuits. The family (then) becomes a key element in the articulation of the different tertiary, peasant and mining activities."

The author views peasant agriculture as dynamic and capable of change. Empirically, this dynamism is reflected in peasants' participation in produce markets, in their changing needs and aspirations and in their response to mounting demographic pressures. Noting that peasant agriculture has become increasingly articulated through the market, the author emphasizes its functional character within the overall economic system as an important source of staple foods at low prices. Their market participation contain an element of compulsion; their needs for cash often force them to sell what is not strictly speaking a family surplus. The peasant's role is passive. The author remarks, "The influence of the market does not extend to peasant agriculture, the merchantile part of the peasant economy is not independent of the non-merchantile part". As a part of the on-going process of economic and social development, peasants cannot escape the market or evade the diverse impact of the macro processes of change. They are led in consequence to modify traditional customs, habits and forms of behaviour under the impact of such developments as the extension of educational programmes, the increasing outreach to communication media, the expansion of transport infrastructure and the multiplication of rural-urban contacts. The principal effect of demographic pressures on peasant agriculture is intensification of land use, with a shortening of periods in which land is kept as fallow. It is within the capacity of peasant agriculture, it is argued to generate the necessary investment for intensification of cultivation as well as for new colonization of lands on the frontier where such a scope existed. Indeed, Latin America experience provides many examples of the investment of labour in activities meant to intensify agriculture and to make it possible where none existed before. Only, the nature of this investment is different; it is based on the peasant's familiarity with the environment and it makes use, fundamentally, of an abundant resource such as labour, which is applied to modify the physical environment, to provide drainage, to irrigate and to improve land.

Attention is then turned to the reluctance of peasants to use new technology. The evidence here suggests that the response of peasantry to technological advances is entirely rational and that they are not averse to make use of technologies that are viable in their circumstances. They reject mechanization because it is unsuitable on account of physical factors, the smallness of their farms and their cropping pattern and because it tends to destabilize them requiring them to unduly monetize their economy and increasing their dependence on the market. But the peasants do adopt technologies (improved seeds, chemical fertilizers, etc.) not to improve their family incomes but mainly to compensate for a scarce resource – land. The peasant cannot afford to use any cost-accounting calculus to operate his farm; for example, to compensate for a fall in prices of his produce, he responds by increasing his market supplies in the hope of maintaining the amount of cash he must have. His technological choices are thus limited to those that help him to improve yields with the maximum possible utilization of his land and labour resources. He readily accepts the use of improved seeds, viable changes in his cropping pattern involving the raising of new crops, and the use of chemical fertilizers. The author cites an analysis of peasant practices, which reveals that "most of them have a real technical rationale" and insists that "technology should not be the application from outside of a substitute practice which will subsequently be rejected, but should rather be something which is grafted into the heart of a reality and a rational practice". It is, therefore, deplored that the technology offered on the market, or the one favoured by official programmes, is a negation of the technological needs of peasant economies. "This lack of correspondence between demand and supply reflects" it is asserted, "a direct relationship between the type of technology offered and the state action promoted by the power structure of classes within society, while at the same time, it provides one more argument for the view that technology is an endogenous factor of the economic system".

In the light of the increasing agrarian heterogeneity brought about by the functioning of the world economic system of which Latin America, along with Asia and Africa, form the vast periphery, the author admits the need to allow within the structural framework for the coexistence of different forms of agriculture. His plea is not to look upon the social and economic fact of peasant agriculture as something left over from the past, that is stagnant, deteriorating, impervious to technology and undergoing a process of decomposition. Instead, "we must accept the plurality of experiences that each agrarian system represents and try to make a more objective analysis and a more balanced formulation of strategies and policies. We must recognize agrarian heterogeneity in order to understand each of its elements and become familiar with its particular dynamics and contributions, as well as with its inefficient aspects, its pressures, and sometimes its environmentally unsound actions without neglecting the conflicts inside and outside the sector.

Finally, a world about the peasant problem in Fiji, beyond Latin America, in the Pacific. Both the ethnic groups. the Fijians and the Indians–the descendants of indentured labour brought in for plantations mainly of sugarcane are predominated by peasants. The latter cannot own land under the law but lease in plots of 4-04 ha per family. They specialize in cane production for the formerly Australian and now the government sugar factory which being the only buyer of cane enjoys a position of monopsony. These Indian peasants combine to some extent cane production with subsistence crops for their own use. They are socially advanced but face insecurity of their tenancies which are for a fixed term of 30 years. In course of their historical development they had often fought with the management of the sugar factory for reasonable cane prices. They did not have much conflict with the Fijians, from whom they obtained the leases, until recently. For want of any other rural outlet, the expanding Indian population managed to get jobs in urban areas but there they progressively faced a shrinking outlet which is increasingly attracting competition from the Fijians. The problems of the Fijian peasantry stem from the determined attempt of the British rulers to preserve their community-based traditional structure and the associated cultural traditions, norms and customs. In their case, there is no private or individual ownership of land; all lands are communally owned in a way that maintains a hierarchy of rights of cultivation and the sharing of produce. Social life is dominated by the status of the Chief who occupies that position on the basis of partriarchal lineage. In this static structure, Fijians live a life of social and economic security but with the passage of time, thanks to advances in education and health and the penetration of the Christian church, the tendency on the part of individuals to break away from the tradition-bound society is on the increase. This break is often achieved by migration to urban areas. Development of agriculture and indeed of the whole national economy is constrained by the dependence of the Indians on monoculture of cane which is rendered uncertain and insecure by the denial to them of the ownership of the land they cultivate and by the cultural constraint on the Fijians that blocks the transition, in their case, "from a communal, sharing and caring mode of production to an individualistic, profit-maximizing, and capital accumulating mode of production". Modernizing influences encouraged by the government's economic planning are flowing in but the full development of the country's more than adequate resources will be contigent on the resolution of the conflicting interests of the two ethnic groups, the Fijians and the Indians. The arena for that resolution is primarily political.

III. A PARADOX OF PALLIATIVES

The moral that emerges from the above exploration of reflections, conceptions and conceptualizations and of facts and figures on the state of peasantry in greatly diverse settings is essentially the same. Everywhere from the Philippines to Fiji, that state is one of unrelieved pight of peasantries that have been rendered much too helpless to withstand the inroads of capitalism buttressed by imperialism during the era that ended with the Second World War and entertained thereafter by economic development in a harried and hurried pursuit of the mirage of modernization. The mass of upright "rustics" with robust common sense constituting the backbone of society, has been progressively fractionalized, proletarianized and pauperized. Their abiding common sense enables them to improvise a variety of survival strategies as groups and families, if not as a class, but bereft of political power they are, left to hibernate in their helplessness. At times and on occasions when they gained access to power, they have shown their mantle, courage and political foresight but the odds have remained against them and even their well-organized struggle have been relentlessly suppressed. Where they gained not merely an access to power but were also able to lead revolutionary struggles, they have established social orders free from inequities of the kind they had themselves suffered within their displaced unequal society. It is the success of the latter peasantry-led struggles, that raises the hope that peasantry's potential for mobilization is not and empty dream only, it will take a long and bitter struggle to turn that dream into a reality.

What may make that struggle harder to win are the current approaches convassed by the votaries of free market economies, like that of the IBRD's Integrated Rural Development. For an idea of the nature of these recipes we refer to the last of the contributions to the saga on "Modernization and Development Potential by Traditional Grass-Roots Peasant Organizations" by Michael Cernea. The problem with this persuasive piece is that the mystic of modernization casts a spell but without clarity about the posited relationship of that mystic with the so-called traditional organizations. Whatever organizations that peasantries in developing countries had inherited from the hoary past are in a shambles because of the very process of "modernization". The piece begins with an allegorical reference to the formation of a colony of bees. The allegory is misplaced because bees enjoy an instinctive autonomy while the peasants' options remain severely constrained by the development–induced marginalization of their position within the agrarian economy of which they must continue to form a part. There is no Queen Bee to decide for them and they would certainly prefer to keep their conscience, however, low they may descend on the social scale. This is not to deny that organization is so very important for alleviating the pauperization of peasant masses. To look for a Queen Bee or an Orwellian Big Brother is, indeed, a denial of their right to exercise human volition. Both the Queen and the Big Brother will bring about an order to the present state of disorganization but at a tremendous cost of freedom that humans have learnt to cherish.

But we may set aside the mischievous allegory and examine the substantive intent underlying it. In this regard, the author reflects upon "modernization of the social organization of agricultural productive activities" more in terms of "the dialectics of the development process itself than in terms of the end-model the process will produce". This rather curious statement may indeed mean that we may specify for the peasants the role they must play in development without sharing with them the notion of their relative position within the structure of agrarian relations that may emerge from development. In effect, this exploration of the common development style and its divergent organizational patterns forecloses, at its very start, the overriding issue of the peasants' future status in a given developing society. It is the same tragedy, we witness often enough, of devising means without reference to the end. Shall we assume that the peasant is dumb enough to enter even the so lighted a tunnel without being enthused on what is in store for him at its other end? Or shall we let the peasant determine for himself his own feasible niche in the developed society of the future and limit ourselves to placing before him the strategic options he may have for moving towards that position in the new development dispensation? The latter course is easy to take, for it can be said of the peasant in his present plight that he is not looking up to grab the moon in the sky; his ardent desire is for a small enough space on the earth where he can live his materially modest life of dignity and self-respect. His long enough experience has taught him that political freedom has not alleviated his penury and that within evolving situation he can expect no more than two square *meals* a day and an entirely need-based shelter.

This they fail to secure because of the impact of technological innovations which they cannot absorb, as the author contends, for want of requisite "social organization". The author terms this deficiency "organizational underdevelopment" and draws attention to the adverse consequences on technology, productivity and output, flowing from the peasantry's traditional dependence on networks of social relations performing mainly non-economic functions. The small and discrete production units characterising peasant economies are, it is said, "limited in their capacity to grow and to develop economic activities". In the course of development, other sectors have experienced relatively accelerated organizational development further aggravating the said organizational underdevelopment of the peasantry. "Rural Poverty", it is argued, "is a direct consequence of . . . the opportunities afforded for surplus extraction by the better organized (non-agricultural) sectors from the vulnerable, isolated, weak and unorganized productive units in agriculture". This conclusion of the author needs a significant modification in the light of the fact that agriculture as a whole has not remained static anywhere in the developing Third World. There has indeed been considerable growth and diversification of agricultural production in several developing countries thanks to the introduction of technological packages that go under the rubric of "Green Revolution". A modern sub-sector has in the result emerged within agriculture to represent a small section of agricultural producers who have been able to adopt new technologies because of their comparatively more substantial land holdings and access to subsidized credit for the requisite investment. This has led to further fragmentation of the peasantry into large land-owners, medium size farmers, small or marginal farmers and agricultural labourers, with the latter two constituting the bulk of peasantry. Small peasants have been forced in this process to join the ranks of agricultural labour to to move out to cities and towns in order to scratch their livelihood in informal sectors of those cities and towns. It must also be noted that the green revolution being contigent on irrigation potential has exhibited a very uneven spread giving rise to new regional imbalances which have in the context of expanding agricultural produce market adversely affected also the peasantry in areas benefiting little from the technological progress. The numerically small better-off farmers easily find new ways to organize themselves into powerful lobbies to protect their newly gained prosperity, while the bulk of the peasantry find their traditional organizational arrangements of little avail in the face of these trends of modernizing agricultural production. This is what has led to the deepening of "organizational underdevelopment" the author speaks of.

Whether the author's invocation of traditional informal organizations that had emerged in the distant past to specifically carry out certain productive agricultural activities would be a viable proposition in the new context is, to say the least, uncertain. Those organizations served such purposes as the sharing of peak time work load, water management and the meeting of short term credit needs.

The author himself deplores the failure on the part of policy-makers and development practitioners to ignore and underestimate "the development, function and potential of (these) grassroots, production-oriented peasant organizations." He proceeds then to advance a plea that the traditional organizations should be utilized as a resource for development provided "they are amenable to developmental activities". That they may not be so amenable is recognized in the author's insertion of the corollary that "the need to strengthen, change and develop these organizations should not be overlooked". This apparently well-meaning argument seems to dismiss the probability that policy-makers and development practitioners may indeed have found that these grass rootslevel organizations are not after all amenable to developmental activities of the kind that meet the urgent need of a rapid increase in, say, food production. The planners might have thought it wiser in the particular situation they faced not to wait for the time consuming process of organizational transformation for increased food production. That in their effort to generate the green revolution for speedy increase in the volume of production, they could not prevent marginalization of the peasantry is altogether a different matter. They probably considered it strategically unavoidable to postpone the day of reckoning for a "higher" purpose of achieving macro level self-sufficiency in domestic food supply in as short a time as possible.

Underemployment Compounded by Increased Unemployment

This is not to deny that the need to reorganize production relations within agriculture has grown more and more acute with the passage of time. This is borne out, for example, by Indian agricultural progress toward near self-sufficiency in the course of the last two decades. Since the famine years of middle sixties, Indian Planning has concentrated on generating the green revolution in the most promising areas with proven irrigational potentials. The strategy has been quite successful but this success has involved considerable cost in terms of the accentuation of interpersonal inequities and of interregional imbalances. Plight of the peasantry all over the country, including the areas so favoured, has increased and rural poverty has tended only to deepen in the course of this pursuit of self-sufficiency in food. Polarization between the rich and the poor has been greatly accentuated within the rural areas almost everywhere, there has been an enormous increase in the supply of agricultural labour in absolute terms; the age-old curse of underemployment has been compounded by a substantial increase in unemployment. In the result, the social tensions and political unrest have manifested to cause grave concern to the established order. There is widespread disenchantment with the development's orientation to macro-level goals and the search for a viable strategy of decentralization is on. But there is no guarantee that the strategy that may yet emerge will adequately take care of the need for organizational transformation that accords a central role to the pauperized peasantry. They constitute the rural poor for whose benefit planning has mounted a series of beneficiary-oriented poverty alleviation programmes which have failed so far to enable peasants to stand on their own feet. The experience of this planning strategy is rather disheartening. In any case, it holds out no promise of success for any endeavour to regenerate traditional organizations that had been devised to sustain peasant poverty without any compromise of their individual self-respect and dignity.

The author seems to concede this position when he finally turns to consider "issues in organization building". He rightly concludes, "Informal peasant organizations are not, of course, the only answer, nor are they the only concern with respect to improving the effectiveness of the rural development policies." He stresses, therefore, the need for developing strong formal operations, various forms of peasant unions and other action-oriented organizations. Because of his limited and exclusive concern with the securing of definite production goals, he overstresses the degree of complexity as a major point of difference between informal and formal peasant organizations and is led to illustrate the success of organizational development by drawing attention to agricultural cooperatives of East European countries and the communes of China. These are not novel examples of the organizational transformation of agriculture for the planners and policy-makers of most developing countries. These transformations have been achieved not within free market economies but by people's democracies. The two social systems are poles apart. So, the question remains as to the viability of communes and cooperatives of the Chinese and East European variety within the development strategies of the "softer" states which most developing countries have. This is clear from the data cited by the author in respect of the Romanian experience. Neither of the two types of complex cooperatives tried out in Romanian may work in developing counties where planning is operated within the so-called mixed economies. Interestingly, the term "cooperatives" in the case of Romania is an international misnomer; they form a part of the process of the agricultural collectivization. The collectivization, were it feasible in the free market economies, could be a solution for agricultural reorganization. But collectivization, apart from it being contingent on the suspension of democratic rights, has been noted to involve considerable costs, both human and material. Collectivization takes a long time to mature and has to be tempered in the long term by allowing some scope for private or individual initiative on small plots of individual ownership combined with a free market outlet. More serious consequence of collectivization or the cooperativization of the East European variety is the liquidation of peasantry itself, that is, of the family as a basic production unit. This can be attempted only through revolutionary changes and not by any development process that concerns itself with economics alone. The prerequisite is fundamental political change which is nowhere occurring at present in the vastness of the Third World. The hope for the economic betterment of peasantry lies thus not in any reorganization of their economy but in their organization as a class for the assertion of their political rights. If peasant masses are to survive for achieving the feasible progress of their production potential, they will have to organize for access to political power which is fashioning economic development everywhere in the Third World. Integrated rural development, poverty alleviation and employment guarantee schemes and a host of other such beneficiary-oriented gimmicks are no substitute for decentralized, self-reliant self-development for peasants as well as other exploited sections of society in any developing country. For this, democracy must inform not only the political life but equally also the economic and social life of a people; it must also percolate from the macro national to the micro grassroots levels. Peasants have led and fully participated in, the struggles for political freedom; their energies remain to be invoked for the attainment of economic and social freedoms within politically free and independent developing societies of the Third World.

Index